COLLECTED WORKS OF ERASMUS

VOLUME 70

Albrecht Dürer (1471–1528) *Christ on the Mount of Olives*. Etching.
By permission of the Metropolitan Museum of Art,
gift of Mrs George Khuner, 1968 (68.793.1)

COLLECTED WORKS OF
ERASMUS

SPIRITUALIA and PASTORALIA

DISPUTATIUNCULA DE TAEDIO, PAVORE,
TRISTICIA IESU

CONCIO DE IMMENSA DEI MISERICORDIA

MODUS ORANDI DEUM

EXPLANATIO SYMBOLI APOSTOLORUM

DE PRAEPARATIONE AD MORTEM

edited by John W. O'Malley

University of Toronto Press

Toronto / Buffalo / London

The research and publication costs of the
Collected Works of Erasmus are supported by
University of Toronto Press.

© University of Toronto Press 1998
Toronto / Buffalo / London
Printed in Canada

ISBN 0-8020-4309-7

∞

Printed on acid-free paper

Canadian Cataloguing in Publication Data

Erasmus, Desiderius, d. 1536
[Works]
Collected works of Erasmus

Partial contents: v. 70. Spiritualia and Pastoralia.
Includes bibliographical references and index.
ISBN 0-8020-4309-7 (v. 70)

1. Erasmus, Desiderius, d. 1536. I. Title.

PA8500 1974   876'.04   C74-006326-X rev

University of Toronto Press acknowledges the financial assistance
to its publishing programme of the Canada Council and the Ontario Arts Council.

Collected Works of Erasmus

The aim of the Collected Works of Erasmus
is to make available an accurate, readable English text
of Erasmus' correspondence and his
other principal writings. The edition is planned
and directed by an Editorial Board, an Executive Committee,
and an Advisory Committee.

Contents

Introduction

The five pieces contained in this volume are among the twenty that the editors of CWE have selected for inclusion in the series of spiritual and pastoral works, *spiritualia and pastoralia*. The basis for this category is Erasmus' famous enclosure with his letter to Hector Boece of 15 March 1530, in which he listed his writings and divided them into nine *ordines*.[1] The fifth *ordo* contained the works pertaining to *pietas*, the starting-point for our designation. For further discussion of the issues raised by the category, I refer the reader to the pertinent pages of my general introduction to this series, CWE 66 ix–xii.

That introduction is presupposed as background for what I have to say here, and I urge the reader to consult it. By editorial decision it was meant to serve for all the volumes of the series and to deal in a general way with the wide variety of questions connected with these twenty pieces and with Erasmian *pietas*. Its arguments will not be repeated for the present volume.

Towards the end of that introduction, I dealt briefly but in somewhat more detail with the three works contained in volume 66. I indicated that similar treatments would introduce the works in the subsequent volumes of the series, and such a treatment is what I will undertake for the five in this volume. These five works, except for their pertaining to the *spiritualia and pastoralia*, have no special reason for being grouped together here and appear in CWE 70 simply for reasons of editorial convenience. They are arranged in chronological order according to the year of the *editio princeps*. With the exception of the 'Sermon on Mercy,' they appear here in English for the first time in modern translations.

A few general observations may be made about them. As do so many of the other works in this series, they represent the 'Erasmus nobody knows.' Despite the huge surge of interest in Erasmus in the past thirty years, since the observance of the five hundredth anniversary of his birth in 1969, they

* * * * *

1 Allen Ep 2283. See also CWE 24 694–702.

have been studied by only a few scholars. In their treatment of *pietas* they assume an intrinsic relationship among three realities that Erasmus believed his contemporaries often insulated from one another – spirituality, theology, and ministry.[2] A propensity for developing the implications of this relationship is characteristic of Erasmus' approach to *pietas* and distinguishes everything he wrote concerning it, especially by the 1520s.

We know that his works 'pertaining to *pietas*' were widely read in the sixteenth century, dealt with issues then lively, and, presumably, had great impact. Yet they are missing today in any significant way from most studies that deal with sixteenth-century spirituality, theology, and ministry. The Erasmus that dominates our imagination is still the Erasmus of *The Praise of Folly*, of the *Colloquies*, of the debate with Luther – and, perhaps, of *The Handbook of the Christian Soldier*. In other words, the Erasmus of this volume has received little consideration by scholars outside a narrow group of Erasmus specialists. The works of this Erasmus deserve attention because of their merit and also because they are as typical of him as anything he wrote. Moreover, they are, except for the 'Short Debate,' all works of his maturity.

I

The 'Short Debate Concerning the Distress of Jesus' originated with a discussion at Oxford in October 1499 between Erasmus and John Colet about the nature of the fear and dread Christ experienced in the garden of Gethsemane shortly before his capture by the Roman soldiers and his execution. Did Christ fear the loss of his own life, or was he afraid for some other, more altruistic reason? Since the two friends disagreed profoundly and even heatedly over the answer, they later exchanged letters on the subject. From this exchange, as Michael J. Heath explains below, Erasmus constructed the 'Short Debate.' In Erasmus' catalogue of his writings to Hector Boece, 1530, he failed to mention the piece, almost certainly because of its originally epistolary form. It is none the less appropriate for inclusion among the *spiritualia*, as even a cursory reading of it will confirm, and it is in fact found along with the other writings *ad pietatem pertinentia* in the fifth volume of the Leiden edition of his writings.

* * * * *

2 See my introduction to cwe 66, as well as Manfred Hoffmann 'Erasmus on Church and Ministry' ersy 6 (1986) 1–30, and Hilmar M. Pabel 'Promoting the Business of the Gospel: Erasmus' Contribution to Pastoral Ministry' ersy 15 (1995) 53–70.

Although the 'Short Debate' has been neglected by scholars, our understanding of it has been greatly enhanced by two studies. G.J. Fokke has reconstructed how Erasmus developed the text, and also made keen observations about the 'balanced Christology, incarnate and transcendental at the same time' that Erasmus here early espouses.[3] James D. Tracy has analysed the patristic and medieval sources on the question at issue and compared Erasmus' treatment of the question with his contemporaries' – Jacques Lefèvre d'Etaples and Thomas More.[4]

A number of features related to the piece are worth noting. First of all, as Heath indicates, the 'Short Debate' is Erasmus' first published work of scriptural exegesis, a genre in which within a decade he would establish himself as one of the most proficient masters of all time – a mastery clearly adumbrated at this early date. It is ironic that here he turns his skill against Colet, the person generally credited with successfully urging him to give his talents a more theological direction.

Perhaps more impressive, here Erasmus addresses a properly theological issue. Indeed, he enters a maze of Christological issues, where so many have lost their way. He moves with sure foot – with surer foot, most theologians today would probably conclude, than did Colet. Not one to underestimate his accomplishments, Erasmus takes special delight in them towards the very end of the 'Debate' with the point that he has done quite well against Colet 'on a topic so thoroughly theological, or, in other words, a subject not my own!'[5] The 'Debate' establishes that Erasmus had acquired by this early date a command of traditional doctrine and theology that was profound. On many issues controverted in the sixteenth century, he would prove to be more dependably orthodox in the long run than most of the enemies who attacked him.

Erasmus' propensity for landing on his feet doctrinally is due to the incomparable depth and breadth of his knowledge of Christian sources, especially the Bible and the Fathers. What the 'Debate' shows, however, is that, contrary to what is often assumed, he also had a decent grasp of some 'modern' theologians, that is, the scholastics, and was willing in some instances to

* * * * *

3 Fokke 161–87, especially 185
4 Tracy. See also Santinello; Daniel T. Lochman 'Colet and Erasmus: The *Disputatiuncula* and the Controversy of Letter and Spirit' *The Sixteenth Century Journal* 20 (1989) 77–87; Maria Grazia Mara 'Colet et Erasme au sujet de l'exégèse de Mt. 26, 39' in *Théorie et pratique de l'exégèse* ed Irena Backus and Francis Higman (Geneva 1990) 259–72.
5 See 66 below.

accept their conclusions, even though this might mean disagreeing with his beloved Jerome. He explicitly cites Bonaventure in a favourable light and in other places seems unmistakably to be alluding to scholastic teaching. The 'Debate' thus serves to qualify most generalizations that have been made about Erasmus' relationship to the scholastics. It is of paramount importance to realize that he opposed them not so much on account of their doctrines or teachings, their conclusions, as on account of their method, which was wrong and harmful.

Thus, it is significant that this 'disputed question' is not cast by Erasmus in the form of a scholastic disputation. He attributes to Colet a dislike for that form that he certainly shared. He therefore adopts 'the free and easy form of discussion the ancients used.'[6] This was no minor issue. The disputation was eschewed because it was part of the scholastic system that almost forced one to resort to proof-texting as the method of exegesis, and precluded an understanding of statements in the sources as determined by their context – the method Erasmus advocates and here pursues. He must intend some irony with his choice of title – 'little disputation' (*disputatiuncula*).

If Erasmus here characteristically rejects a medieval mode of arguing, he deals with a subject related to a devotional subject immensely popular in the late Middle Ages, the passion of Christ.[7] Its popularity was a result of the turn towards the humanity of Christ dating from the twelfth century, with an ever increasing focus, especially in northern Europe, on Christ's death on the cross. In the fifteenth century this focus widened to encompass the entire sequence of events related to Christ's suffering, including those before the crucifixion such as the so-called agony in the garden. The most famous text dealing with Christ's agony in the garden was written some thirty years after Erasmus' 'Debate' by his other friend, Thomas More; More wrote it in the Tower of London on the eve of his execution, a situation that gave it a poignancy and emotional force not present in Erasmus' more theoretical treatment.[8]

The devotional practices related to the passion of Christ often took bizarre forms and displayed emotional excess. In any case, this burgeoning focus on the agony in the late Middle Ages must be taken into account when speculating on why this particular subject arose for discussion, then

*****

6 See 66 below.

7 See Richard Kieckhefer 'Major Currents in Late Medieval Devotion' in *Christian Spirituality: High Middle Ages and Reformation* ed Jill Raitt with Bernard McGinn and John Meyendorff (New York 1988) 75–108, especially 83–9.

8 Thomas More *De tristitia Christi* ed and trans Clarence H. Miller *The Complete Works of St Thomas More* 14 (New Haven and London 1976)

debate, between the two friends. Erasmus makes no allusion to any popular abuses or aberrations when treating the subject. He does not condemn
or satirize devotion to the agony as he would do later with certain medieval
practices. He would find it unthinkable to condemn or satirize something
so evidently based on the biblical text. What he does is characteristic. He
gives recollection of Christ's suffering a firm theological base, and then indicates the heartfelt yet dignified emotions and actions appropriate to such
recollection. This is a good example of how he connects piety and theology.

The 'Debate' deals directly with fear, but in doing so it must deal more
broadly with a range of human emotions, and these become one of the major
subjects of the work. In his discussion of the emotions, Erasmus of course employs the classic categories, which he has fitted into his already almost fully
developed anthropology, deriving from classic sources. We might therefore easily miss how psychologically perceptive he shows himself, as in his
awareness that in times of stress competing, almost contradictory emotions
swirl within the same person at the same moment.

In most late-medieval devotion to the sufferings of Christ, the emotions that dominate are sadness and grief, originating in an intense sense of
identification with Christ or 'compassion' with him. Compassion with Christ
suffering sometimes utterly eclipsed other aspects of the life of Christ and
almost obliterated any attention to the resurrection, towards which Christ's
passion supposedly pointed.[9] While Erasmus does not repudiate compassion with the suffering Christ, he does not take the compassion itself as the
centre of what he wants to say about the meaning of what Christ under-
goes. He emphasizes again and again that the suffering is an expression of
love. He returns to the point persistently, and insists that he and Colet are
in agreement on it. Notably muted in this approach is an understanding of
Christ's suffering as atonement to an angry God.

This rather bright interpretation is consistent with the patristic and
liturgical tradition upon which Erasmus based his reflections, not a novelty
he manufactured out of some purportedly humanistic optimism. In this regard the 'Debate' served as a silent criticism of the darker aspects of popular
piety in his day and as a potential instrument to reform it.

II

The 'Sermon on Mercy' sparkles with a similar but more notable brightness.
Like the 'Debate,' the 'Sermon' takes God's love as its central theme, for as

* * * * *

9 See Richard Kieckhefer *Unquiet Souls: Fourteenth-Century Saints and Their Religious Milieu* (Chicago 1984) 89–121.

he several times informs us Erasmus equates mercy with love and also with grace. These are three terms meaning the same thing. The piece is, then, a 'Sermon on Love' or a 'Sermon on Grace' – a 'Sermon on Mercy.'

In his dedicatory letter Erasmus accurately describes the piece as a 'panegyric,' and he employs all the rhetorical devices at his command to produce a work that, while long and repetitious, moves along with lyrical beat and joyous heart. Hardly had the Latin version appeared in 1524 than it was translated into several vernaculars.[10] For decades, until mid-century, when Erasmus had been repudiated and his works suppressed by almost all the contestants in Europe's religious struggles, it remained among his most popular works.

The work is striking in how Erasmus strings together passages from the Bible, especially the Psalms, so that he himself seems almost lost behind the word of God. When he emerges he moralizes a bit, as is his wont, but for the most part he speaks in a language that does little more than paraphrase the sacred text, sometimes with expressions of surpassing beauty, as when he says of God, 'He welcomes us to his household and takes us into the bedchamber of his love.'[11]

The positive content and tone of the 'Sermon' owe much to the genre of the panegyric in which Erasmus professedly casts it. The piece represents, therefore, the revival of classical rhetoric and the application of it to sacred discourse that had begun in Italy in the early fifteenth century and that gradually had spread to northern Europe by the beginning of the next century. These new literary forms, especially the deliberative and demonstrative genres of classical rhetoric, effected a dazzling revolution in how preaching was conceived and executed. The demonstrative genre, or panegyric, which Erasmus here adopts, had as its intent to stir emotions of wonder, joy, gratitude, and admiration, precisely the emotions to which he consistently has recourse in the 'Sermon.'[12] It was the 'art of praise and blame' – *ars laudandi et vituperandi*. As early as 1504, Erasmus had had success in a secular form of the genre, his 'Panegyric for Archduke Philip of Austria,' even though he found the subject and the exercise difficult;[13] and he employed it

* * * * *

10 See eg John Arthur Gee 'Hervet's English Translation, with Its Appended Glossary of Erasmus' *De immensa Dei misericordia' Philological Quarterly* 15 (1936) 136–52, and James Devereux 'An English Glossary by Gentian Hervet' *Moreana* 14 (May 1967) 5–10.
11 See 89 below.
12 See John W. O'Malley *Praise and Blame in Renaissance Rome: Rhetoric, Doctrine, and Reform in the Sacred Orators of the Papal Court, c.1450–1521* (Durham 1979).
13 CWE 27 1–75

in other works such as 'The Education of the Christian Prince' and even *The Praise of Folly*.

Although the new forms of preaching were widely known and utilized in elite circles by 1524, they were still new enough to impress the hearer (or reader) by the contrast with their medieval counterparts, especially the cerebral 'university sermons' or moralizing 'penitential' sermons of the scholastic tradition, which even at this date were more generally practised than their humanistic counterparts. In 1524 Erasmus was already at work on his *Ecclesiastes*, his great treatise on how to preach according to classical and patristic models.[14] The 'Sermon' is an example from the master of how the new genres might be applied. It is important, therefore, as much for its form as for its content.

In 1530 Erasmus listed this work as among those pertaining to *pietas*, and in a letter to Alonso Ruiz de Virués in 1528 he grouped it with a few other writings as among those 'that do not deal with controversial matters' – *quae non tractant contentiosa*.[15] Readers today without hesitation would agree with this description. The sixteenth century was more cantankerous, and with the passing of years the 'Sermon,' while faring better than some of Erasmus' other works, was viewed with suspicion merely because he had written it.[16] None the less, it seems to rise above the doctrinal storms.

But is that really true? Is the 'Sermon' innocent of issues controversial in the sixteenth century? We can perhaps take it as axiomatic that the sermon is as sophisticated as its author and that its surface simplicity conceals theological art. We can take it as axiomatic that whenever Erasmus deals with *pietas* he does so out of a doctrinal base.

Silvana Seidel Menchi claims credit for being the first to note that in the same month in 1524 Erasmus published both the 'Sermon' and his more famous 'On Free Will,' his attack on Luther's teaching, and to suggest that the 'Sermon' can be considered a statement by Erasmus on justification.[17] Her position has merit. While Erasmus was composing this work, we must assume, the other lay heavy on his mind.

There is no mystery as to why Erasmus designated the work as concerning mercy, for seemingly it had been commissioned to honour a chapel recently dedicated to the Mercies of God, as Michael J. Heath indicates in his

* * * * *

14 See John W. O'Malley 'Erasmus and the History of Sacred Rhetoric: The *Ecclesiastes* of 1535' ERSY 5 (1985) 1–29.
15 Allen Ep 1968:61–4
16 See Bataillon *Erasme et l'Espagne* I 304–6, 468, 766–7, and Silvana Seidel Menchi *Erasmo in Italia, 1520–1580* (Turin 1987) 155–67.
17 See Silvana Seidel Menchi *Erasmo in Italia, 1520–1580* (Turin 1987) 155.

introductory note. But in the sermon Erasmus equates mercy with grace and uses the two words interchangeably, even applying to mercy such qualifiers as 'prevenient' and 'elevating' usually reserved to grace. Our conclusion must be that when he talks about mercy he is talking about grace.

If one were to change the title to 'On the Immense Grace of God,' or, more literally, 'On the Boundless – or Infinite – Grace of God,' it would sound less innocent. With such a title in the sixteenth century one would be entering treacherous waters indeed. There is no doubt that in the sermon one hears at least faint echoes of the controversy over justification, as when Erasmus warns about selling one's good works. But even in its totality it cannot be read divorced from that controversy, as though it were created in a vacuum, or as though it were a devotional work above, below, or beyond doctrine.

The work is irenic in tone, and we can take Erasmus at his word that he had no intention of using it as a decoy behind which to speak again on something as incendiary as justification. It is, as Heath says, a work of pastoral piety. But it perforce has doctrinal implications, highlighted in that Erasmus chose, almost provocatively, to use the word grace.

The pervasively bright view of creation and human capabilities in the 'Sermon' gives the topics a configuration quite different from that in Luther's dourer treatment. The piece is a testament as much to Erasmus' theological and cultural distance from Luther as to his sharpened awareness by 1524, following the Lutheran crisis, of the profound implications for *pietas* of the primacy of grace over human effort.

III

Within about a year of the 'Sermon,' Erasmus produced his treatise on prayer, *Modus orandi Deum*. In a letter to Maximilian of Burgundy the Elder, 30 March 1525, he described it as a devotional work – *ad pietatem* – composed in his old age.[18] (He was in his fifties.) But like the 'Sermon,' this treatise on a seemingly neutral topic responded to controversies of the day. In this case, however, Erasmus explicitly acknowledged the fact in a letter to Jean, cardinal of Lorraine, when he declared he wrote it against Luther in defence of prayers to the saints.[19] The treatise therefore helps mark Erasmus' definitive repudiation of Luther's movement and his willingness to broaden his criticism beyond the central issue of justification.

* * * * *

18 Allen Ep 1563:5–6 / CWE Ep 1563:8–9
19 Ep 1559:136–8

Although less than a fifth of the treatise deals with invocation of the saints, that might be enough to surprise people who know Erasmus only from his colloquies and *The Praise of Folly*. A defence of prayer to the saints is the last thing they would expect from Erasmus, who so often satirized the practice and pleaded for a Christocentric godliness. Without doubt, Erasmus' position here indicates a tempering of his tongue in the light of the new religious situation, as he himself admits, but it also clarifies the limits of his earlier criticism. There is no reason, once again, not to take him at his word when he says he meant no more than to oppose superstitious excesses. He invokes the old canonical principle *abusus non tollit usum* – abuses do not mean that the institution itself must be abolished. His defence of prayer to the saints is measured, however, careful not to claim too much, just as it also manifests his incredibly broad grasp of the Christian tradition on the issue.

That issue constitutes, however, only a relatively small part of the treatise, which deals for the most part with more basic questions about prayer, such as its importance, its function in our lives, and to whom and for what we should pray. Erasmus has recourse to the patristic tradition for his fundamental answers to the questions but, as John N. Grant indicates below, also seems dependent on scholastics such as Aquinas, a reliance that again defies received wisdom about Erasmus' relationship to the 'modern theologians.'

Erasmus had, in any case, plenty of literature to draw upon in constructing the *Modus orandi Deum*, beginning with Tertullian's treatise on prayer. There is hardly a major medieval author who did not have something to say on the matter. We must not allow that fact to obscure the originality of the treatise for Erasmus' own and subsequent times. Although from the High Middle Ages onward many authors wrote about prayer, none composed a treatise like this one that stood on its own and did not form part of a larger work, that was of a certain length and comprehensiveness, that with critical self-awareness based itself on the great classics of Christian antiquity, and that was written in a style and form to appeal beyond cloister and academe. In fact, for all that was written on prayer, it would be difficult to find anything in the Middle Ages or in Erasmus' own day quite like this treatise.

One might cite works such as Hugh of St Victor's *De modo orandi* or his *De meditando seu meditandi artificio*, but these are very short and are constructed on quite different principles.[20] Closer to Erasmus' day is Savonarola's *Sermone della orazione*, first published in 1492. It is one of the

* * * * *

20 PL 176 977–88, 995–8

very few works explicitly and solely devoted to the subject in Erasmus' era that precedes the *Modus*. Savonarola deals with some of the same topics Erasmus undertook, but the similarity pretty well ends there.[21] The *Sermone* enjoyed popularity in certain devout circles, but unlike Erasmus' *Modus* it never achieved wide circulation in Europe. Erasmus, with his new form and style, in effect created for his age a new genre. He may not himself have been fully aware of his accomplishment, for he seemingly forgot to mention the work in his inventory of 1530.

The *Modus* has another quality that sets it off from the mainstream of writing on the subject in the late Middle Ages and early modern era. Unlike those in the mainstream, Erasmus' work has nothing to say about meditation, methodical contemplation, or, as it was often designated, 'mental prayer.'[22] Savonarola published in the late fifteenth century his *Trattato in defensione e commendazione dell'orazione mentale*.[23] This was simply the tip of the iceberg of a polymorphous tradition that received great impetus from medieval mystics such as Bernard of Clairvaux and Gertrude the Great, that developed along different lines from the Franciscan *Meditationes vitae Christi*, that in the early sixteenth century manifested itself in the *alumbrados* in Spain, and that reached classic expression in the *Spiritual Exercises* of Ignatius Loyola and the mystical writings of Teresa of Avila.

Neither in the *Modus* nor elsewhere does Erasmus manifest the slightest interest in this tradition – or, better, these traditions. When he writes about prayer he always means prayer from the heart, but such prayer will be expressed in well-known formulas or composed by the individual largely from the words of Scripture. He draws his inspiration especially from the Psalms, from the Fathers, and from the liturgy, not from the radical turn inward that manifested itself so clearly beginning in the twelfth and thirteenth centuries and gained such force in the sixteenth.

Like so many of Erasmus' achievements 'pertaining to piety,' this one goes practically unnoticed outside an extremely limited circle of scholars. It is typical that in the long and important article on prayer in the *Dictionnaire de spiritualité*, perhaps the most authoritative instrument for research in the

* * * * *

21 Girolamo Savonarola *Operette spirituali* ed Mario Ferrara 2 vols (Rome 1976) I 189–224
22 See Massimo Marcocchi 'Spirituality in the Sixteenth and Seventeenth Centuries' in *Catholicism in Early Modern History: A Guide to Research* ed John W. O'Malley (St Louis 1988) 163–92.
23 Girolamo Savonarola *Operette spirituali* ed Mario Ferrara 2 vols (Rome 1976) I 157–85

field, Erasmus' treatise is not even mentioned. The subject has been ignored. This neglect makes Hilmar M. Pabel's new and major study of Erasmus and prayer especially helpful and welcome.[24]

Largely responsible for the neglect is the persistent image of Erasmus as at best only superficially concerned with the devout life – and that image itself is a consequence of his being rejected by the major players in the religious polemics of the sixteenth century. Even the *Modus* did not escape criticism. Although a significant section of the work was obviously directed against Luther, the myopic rage for orthodoxy that seized many Catholic authorities discovered heretical or dangerously ambiguous lines in it. For some theologians and censors the defence of prayers to the saints was not vigorous enough, but more specifically troublesome were lines like 'Perhaps it is a good principle of Christian doctrine to revere everything pertaining to divinity but to affirm nothing except what is explicitly stated in the Scriptures.'[25] This sounded dangerously like Luther's 'Scripture alone.' For these and other reasons the Republic of Venice placed the *Modus* on its Index of Prohibited Books in 1554, and in 1559 it appeared *nominatim* on the Index of the Spanish Inquisition.[26] It fell under the infamous papal Index of 1559 simply by being part of Erasmus' *opera*, all of which were banned.

Erasmus supported another Lutheran-sounding proposition that for different reasons we would hardly expect from such a great classicist. In straightforward terms he advocated using the vernacular languages in the sacred liturgy.[27] He advocated, moreover, an active participation of the congregation in the liturgy that sounds strikingly modern. This is a good example of how the pastoral instincts in Erasmus overcame the conservative mentality of the scholar and classicist.

His pastoral instincts and his emotional sensitivity combined with his exquisite sense of language to produce lovely prayers, which he scattered throughout his writings; the few he proffers here are good examples – for instance, the judge's prayer, 'O Lord, may your wisdom that controls all things be present so that while I am judge no one may suffer unjustly or be wronged.'[28] Most students of Erasmus have not noted how many prayers he

* * * * *

24 Hilmar M. Pabel *Conversing with God: Prayer in Erasmus' Pastoral Writings* (Toronto 1997)
25 See 186 below. See also Bataillon *Erasme et l'Espagne* I 154–5, 268, 272–3.
26 Bataillon *Erasme et l'Espagne* I 759, 762
27 See 211–12, 218 below.
28 See 219 below.

composed and inserted into his writings, to say nothing of the collections he put together and published, which appear in CWE 69.[29]

IV

In 1533 Erasmus published his catechism, or, to give the full and proper title of the *editio princeps*, 'A Plain and Devout Explanation of the Apostles' Creed, the Precepts of the Decalogue, and the Lord's Prayer' – *Dilucida et pia explanatio symboli quod apostolorum dicitur, decalogi praeceptorum, & dominicae precationis*. He wrote it at the behest of Sir Thomas Boleyn, the father of Henry VIII's second wife, who requested from Erasmus also his *Enarratio* of Psalm 23 (Vulg 22), 'The Lord is my shepherd,' 1530, and his 'Preparing for Death,' 1534, the last piece in this volume. Boleyn received Erasmus' catechism gratefully and submitted it for consideration to the newly appointed archbishop of Canterbury, Thomas Cranmer. The ironies and complex loyalties of the age are amply illustrated by this relationship of Erasmus to Sir Thomas at the precise moment when Henry VIII resolved the crisis of the royal divorce by taking Anne Boleyn as his wife, an action that led to the execution of Erasmus' friend More in 1535.[30]

At the time of publication the catechism was received enthusiastically, and Erasmus related with satisfaction that Froben's *editio princeps* sold out in three hours at the spring fair in Frankfurt.[31] It had some eight printings within two years, and was translated into English almost immediately as 'A Playne and godly exposition or declaration of the commune Credo.'[32] Its subsequent history has yet to be written. It seems to have had at least some modest circulation in England, where in 1547 Edward VI's commissioners ordered it to be used in Winchester College.[33] It was used by some missionaries

* * * * *

29 See also Margaret Mann Phillips trans 'Prayers: Some New Prayers, with the addition of more new ones, by which young people may accustom themselves to speak to God by Desiderius Erasmus of Rotterdam' ERSY 8 (1988) 12–34; Alice Tobriner 'The "Private Prayers" of Erasmus and Vives: A View of Lay Piety in the Northern Renaissance' ERSY 11 (1991) 27–52; J. Trapman 'Erasmus' *Precationes*' in *Acta Conventus neo-Latini Torontonensis* ed Alexander Dalzell et al (Binghamton 1991) 769–79.
30 On Boleyn, see CEBR I 161–2.
31 Allen Ep 2845:14–17
32 See ASD V-1 200. See also E.J. Devereux 'The English Editions of Erasmus's *Catechismus*' *The Library* series 5, 17 (1962) 154–5.
33 See CEBR I 162. See also Ian Green *The Christian's ABC: Catechisms and Catechizing in England, c.1530–1740* (Oxford 1996).

to Portuguese India and Spanish Mexico.[34] It never achieved, however, anything like the diffusion and status of Luther's, Peter Canisius', or Robert Bellarmine's catechisms, or even the wide circulation of such lesser-known works as the catechism of Juan de Avila.[35] In fact, after an initial burst of interest, Erasmus' catechism began to sink almost into oblivion.[36] Among the probable reasons for this sharp decline, one is obvious – the market was about to be flooded with such works, and the best chance of success lay with those supported by ardent partisans in the religious controversies. Modern scholars have paid little attention to the work.[37]

A year after Erasmus' catechism was published, Luther in a letter to Nikolaus von Amsdorf denounced it, along with other writings by Erasmus, in scathing terms.[38] J.N. Bakhuizen van den Brink describes Luther's attack as 'the most severe that ever touched the person and works of Erasmus.'[39] Luther railed against Erasmus as a liar, a viper, the very mouth and organ of Satan. He castigated the catechism, put together with diabolical artifice, for sowing doubts in the believer about the dogmas of faith by telling about all ancient heresies against the articles of the creed. Who has ever dared talk this way, Luther asked, about the Symbol of faith?

Erasmus responded in print within a month with his *Purgatio adversus epistolam non sobriam Lutheri*.[40] This was the final bout in the hostilities between these giants of their age, for within two years Erasmus was dead.

* * * * *

34 See Aldolfo Etchegaray Cruz 'Présence de saint Augustin dans l'*Enchiridion* et le *Symbolum* d'Erasme' *Recherches Augustiniennes* 4 (1966) 182.
35 See Carlos Maria Nannei La '*Doctrina cristiana' de San Juan de Avila (Contribución al estudio de su doctrina catequética)* (Pamplona 1977), and John W. O'Malley *The First Jesuits* (Cambridge, Mass 1993) 116, 120, 126.
36 It is not even mentioned, eg, in Jean-Claude Dhotel *Les origines du Catéchisme moderne d'après les premiers manuels imprimés en France* (Paris 1967).
37 See, however, Adolfo Etchegaray Cruz 'Présence de saint Augustin dans l'*Enchiridion* et le *Symbolum* d'Erasme' *Recherches Augustiniennes* 4 (1966) 181–97; Rudolf Padberg *Erasmus als Katechet* (Freiburg im Breisgau 1956); Karin Bornkamm 'Das Verständnis christlichen Unterweisung in den Katechismen von Erasmus und Luther' *Zeitschrift für Theologie und Kirche* 68 (1968) 204–30; Jean-Pierre Belche 'Die Bekehrung zum Christentum nach Augustins Büchlein de Catechizandis Rudibus' *Augustinana* 27 (1977) 26–69, especially 41–8.
38 WA *Briefwechsel* 7 no 2093 29–31; see also 2086. For further discussion of this exchange between Luther and Erasmus, see C. Augustijn 'Einleitung' to Erasmus' *Purgatio adversus epistolam non sobriam Lutheri* ASD IX-1 429–40, and Irena Backus 'Erasmus and the Spirituality of the Early Church' in Pabel *Erasmus' Vision* 95–114, especially 111–14.
39 See 'Introduction' ASD V-1 182.
40 ASD IX-1 427–83

The catechism was not the primary reason for Luther's rage and vitriol but an occasion to vent long-standing antagonisms and a symptom of the profound chasm separating the two men. The outburst indicates, none the less, how resistance to Erasmus was increasing in important quarters and how sensitive and polemical the ancient genre of the catechism would become by the third quarter of the century. Erasmus' catechism was prohibited by name by the Spanish Index of 1559.[41]

The early sixteenth century marked one of the great turning-points in the history of catechesis, and it is impossible to understand Erasmus' work and its reception without fitting it into the radical shifts that began to take place during that time, shifts that were well codified by century's end and that have remained more or less operative until today. Although in recent years a number of important studies of this phenomenon have appeared, we need more works that are comprehensive and broadly comparative in their approach.[42]

The general nature of the changes that took place are, however, clear. By the thirteenth century but with mightier energy in the late fifteenth, a new concern about organized instruction of the faithful in the 'art of Christian living and dying' emerged in some parts of Europe. The subject-matter of this instruction, often known simply as 'Christian Doctrine' or 'Christianity' (*Christianitas*), consisted essentially of three almost invariable elements – the Apostles' Creed, the Ten Commandments (or Seven Capital Sins), and the Lord's Prayer – but these were usually accompanied by some combination of other elements such as the eight Beatitudes, the seven spiritual and corporal works of mercy, the five senses of the body, the five commandments of the church.

Erasmus' catechism is special, but certainly not unique, in that it is made up of only Creed, Commandments, and Lord's Prayer. It tacks on the Commandments, however, as a weak epilogue and the Lord's Prayer as an even weaker one, referring the reader in the last instance to commentaries on it by 'learned and pious men,' and making explicit mention of Erasmus' own *Precatio dominica* of 1523. Froben in fact published the *Precatio* in one of his printings of the catechism, 1533. The catechism thus consists almost entirely in an explanation of the creed. The result is a lucid and straightforward but also a lengthy, detailed, and immensely learned commentary.

* * * * *

41 See Bataillon *Erasme et l'Espagne* I 762.
42 See Berard L. Marthaler *The Catechism of Yesterday and Today: The Evolution of a Genre* (Collegeville 1995). For further bibliography, see the notes to John W. O'Malley *The First Jesuits* (Cambridge, Mass 1993) 115–26.

Luther's Large Catechism of 1529, in contrast, opens with a long treatment of the Decalogue, followed by one of relatively few pages on the creed, which is in turn followed by an ample commentary on the Lord's Prayer; in the fourth and final part his catechism concludes with a section on baptism, Eucharist, and confession – subjects often not accorded separate and explicit teaching until Luther singled them out.[43] Juan de Valdés' catechism, published in 1529 a few months before Luther's and entitled 'A Dialogue on Christian Doctrine,' to take another example, in effect begins with relatively few pages on the creed, continues with twice as many on the Decalogue, and continues further with many other subjects such as the Lord's Prayer, the Sermon on the Mount, the four cardinal virtues, the seven gifts of the Holy Spirit, contemplation, devotion to the Virgin, chapters 5 to 7 of the Gospel according to Matthew.[44]

Erasmus' heavy concentration on the creed was unusual for the age, and it should put to rest forever the old shibboleth that he was uninterested in dogma. For Erasmus catechetical instruction consisted almost entirely in learning the dogmas hammered out by the church especially in the Trinitarian and Christological controversies of the patristic age, which make up the content of the creed in his treatment. Although this emphasis was special to him, it was symptomatic of several other developments in sixteenth-century catechesis. First, the creed came to be explained ever more as a summary of abstract doctrines and ever less as a summary of biblical history from Adam to the Acts of the Apostles, which is probably how it more often was explained in earlier times.[45] Erasmus typically describes what he is about to examine as a 'philosophy' of which the matter is 'a holy life,'[46] but it is a *philosophy*, not an account of God's great deeds, not a sacred narrative.[47]

Second, catechetical instruction evinced a tendency to assume a life of its own, independent of the liturgical and sacramental life of the church, whereas late medieval practice had tied it to that life by making it preparation for confession and communion. That is to say, at least in certain quarters

* * * * *

43 Luther WA 30/1 125–238
44 Juan de Valdés *Valdés' Two Catechisms: The Dialogue on Christian Doctrine and the Christian Instruction for Children* ed José C. Nieto (np 1981) 83–165
45 See eg Francis Xavier *The Letters and Instructions of Francis Xavier* trans and ed M. Joseph Costelloe (St Louis 1992) 150–60. See also Juan de Valdés *Valdes' Two Catechisms: The Dialogue on Christian Doctrine and the Christian Instruction for Children* ed José C. Nieto (np 1981) 142–9.
46 See 240–1, 245–6, 277–9, 352, 357–9 below.
47 See John W. O'Malley 'Grammar and Rhetoric in the *pietas* of Erasmus' *Journal of Medieval and Renaissance Studies* 18 (1988) 81–98.

catechism began to lose its almost mystagogical character as a learning of one's religion in order to practise it, especially by participating in the liturgy and partaking of the sacraments, and assumed the ever more intellectual character of a learning *about* one's religion in order to defend it, argue it, or just understand it.

By the early sixteenth century the invention of movable type had helped further this shift in orientation, and also had radically changed such instruction from its originally oral form into learning from the printed page. Well before Luther's famous catechisms of 1529 a number of other catechisms were in print. By 1529, and especially thereafter as a result of Luther's example, the question-answer format began to prevail, and Erasmus utilizes it here. Moreover, by the time Erasmus produced his catechism what earlier had been the preoccupation of relatively few individuals and of elite circles had exploded into widespread agitation and action that eventually touched every stratum of society. Both Catholics and Protestants began to wage a relentless war against 'ignorance and superstition,' a war to which the catechisms that rolled off the presses eloquently testified. The catechisms thus became catalysts for reducing illiteracy among the lower classes, who needed to be taught reading in order to make use of them.[48]

Two further changes are crucially important for our subject. First of all, with the outbreak of the Reformation, catechisms, while generally keeping the traditional elements, gave them an explanation or configuration that made them implicit or explicit vehicles for confessional viewpoints and polemics, as is patent, for instance, as early as 1526 in the catechism by the Anabaptist Balthasar Hubmaier.[49] Erasmus in his catechism wanted to do nothing more, as Bakhuizen van den Brink has pointed out, than explain the fundamentals of the Christian religion as contained in the creed accepted by all Christians.[50] But neutrality was impossible by 1533. Not to address certain issues, for example, was already a decision concerning them that zealots could not abide. Or, to say something as innocent to our ears as 'The whole of the Law agrees with our gospel' was, in an age when the words Law and gospel were already battle cries, to open fire.[51]

* * * * *

48 See Paul F. Grendler *Schooling in Renaissance Italy: Literacy and Learning, 1300–1600* (Baltimore 1989) 333–62.
49 In English translation in Denis Janz *Three Reformation Catechisms: Catholic, Anabaptist, Lutheran* (New York 1982) 131–78
50 See 'Introduction' ASD V-1 183.
51 363 below

Second, when in 1529 Luther published both a Large Catechism, as a kind of resource for pastors and other teachers, and a Small Catechism of only a few pages to be given to children under instruction, he set a pattern that many authors, both Protestant and Catholic, would henceforth follow. This pattern was not without some precedent, but Luther's example gave it currency and urgency. As early as 1514 Erasmus in effect had tried his hand at a small catechism when he rendered into Latin such a composition written in English by John Colet for use in St Paul's school for boys in London, which Colet founded.[52] It begins with the Apostles' Creed and contains other traditional elements. In 1524 Erasmus published his brief, intriguing colloquy 'An Examination Concerning the Faith' – *Inquisitio de fide* – which as a presentation of the creed adumbrates in a minuscule way the incomparably longer commentary that is this catechism.[53] The 'Examination,' even given its obvious relationship to Luther's excommunication, can be considered a catechetical work in its own right.

In his catechism of 1533 Erasmus constructs a dialogue in which a youth who has just reached the age of discretion asks for instruction; at a certain point the catechist describes his pupil as an 'immature child,' whom he has taught the bare 'basics' of his faith. As Louis A. Perraud points out below, the dialogic form is strikingly artificial here, not least of all in the supposed capacity of the child to absorb the hardly 'basic' ideas the catechist teaches. The child may be immature, but at the same time he must be precocious and extraordinarily curious to be able and to want to master what the catechist provides! Erasmus' indications to the contrary notwithstanding, this is a Large Catechism, in the technical sense of the term. Under the guise of the catechetical form, Erasmus has devised what today might pass for an advanced textbook, suitable for university students. The weight of its erudition doubtless contributed to its early sinking from view.

None the less the catechism contains many features of interest to students of sixteenth-century culture and religion. Among these, once again, is Erasmus' recourse to Aquinas, a recourse substantiated by the Amsterdam critical edition. Not too much, surely, should be made of this, for Erasmus constructs his work in a humanistic style and bases it on humanistic learning. Still, the abstract character of his exposition and the attention given to heretics, which Luther so bitterly castigated, bears some

* * * * *

52 ASD I-7 179–89 / CWE 85 92–107
53 LB I 728–32. See Thompson *Inquisitio* / CWE 39 419–47.

resemblance to features of Aquinas' procedure in his catechetical sermons on the creed.[54]

Erasmus takes up issues that already were being agitated but that soon would become even more prominent in the Catholic church and the Council of Trent. He seems to accept, for instance, an unwritten source of revelation along with Scripture.[55] His discussion of the canon of the Old Testament makes distinctions Trent would not.[56] He defends, briefly and cautiously, the need sometimes to keep Christians from access to the sacred text – which prima facie we would not expect from the author of the fervent *Paraclesis*.[57] He adroitly deflects the question of the apostolic origins of the creed.[58] He stands firmly on the side of seven, no fewer, sacraments.[59] And he says provocatively of the Ten Commandments, 'They need no interpretation.'[60]

V

On 19 June 1533 Thomas Boleyn asked Erasmus to write a little book on preparing for death,[61] and by early 1534 Froben had published the *editio princeps* of Erasmus' work on the subject. Like the catechism, 'Preparing for Death' entered English history bristling with ironies. Though dedicated to Anne Boleyn's father, it was read and appreciated by Catherine of Aragon the summer before she died.[62] It was enthusiastically received in England as well as elsewhere in Europe, and was probably read by Thomas More in the Tower of London before his execution.

This turned out to be one of Erasmus' most popular works. It ran through some twenty Latin editions in six years. During that same period it had a number of vernacular printings – four in French, two in Dutch and Spanish, and one in each of German and English.[63] Even as Erasmus'

* * * * *

54 See Thomas Aquinas *The Sermon-Conferences of St. Thomas Aquinas on the Apostles' Creed* trans and ed Nicholas Ayo (Notre Dame 1988).
55 See 348 below.
56 See 332–4 below.
57 See 334–5 below.
58 See 253 below.
59 See 340 below.
60 See 364 below.
61 Allen Ep 2824
62 See Allen Ep 3090:29–53.
63 See ASD v-1 334–5, and Carlos M.N. Eire *From Madrid to Purgatory: The Art and Craft of Dying in Sixteenth-Century Spain* (Cambridge 1995) 26–7, where two Spanish translations in 1535 are indicated.

reputation declined, this treatise continued to be popular, achieving possibly as many printings as any single work he produced.

Only in Spain did enthusiasm for it soon evaporate, since it arrived there just when anti-Erasmianism was in full swing. It also had almost immediately to compete with a work on the same theme by Alejo de Venegas, *The Agony of Crossing Over at Death*, 1537, that for several decades fairly dominated the Spanish market.[64] Although Venegas' work was in important ways different from Erasmus', it was inspired by it and transmitted aspects of the Erasmian heritage even as Erasmus' name became anathema. This is just one example of how Erasmus continued to exert immense influence long after his writings had been banned or vilified.

Erasmus' 'Preparing for Death' fits, generally speaking, into the literature of the *ars moriendi* tradition, which originated in the early fifteenth century, gained momentum in various forms in the first half of the sixteenth century, and reached a climax in the next hundred years in Catholic and some Protestant cultures.[65] Concern about death and dying was a trait of late-medieval sentiment; Luther, for instance, preached a sermon on the subject in 1519 which ran through twenty-two editions in three years.[66] The concern sometimes devolved into exotic forms, as in the *danse macabre* and fascination with the decaying corpse. The theme of the *ars moriendi* tradition, in contrast, was for the most part consolation and comfort.[67] This theme was consonant with certain strains in Italian humanistic literature, which, however, represents a different devotional tradition.[68]

* * * * *

64 See Carlos M.N. Eire *From Madrid to Purgatory: The Art and Craft of Dying in Sixteenth-Century Spain* (Cambridge 1995) 25–7, and Bataillon *Erasme et l'Espagne* I 598–613.

65 See eg Bettie Anne Doebler *'Rooted in Sorrow': Dying in Early Modern England* (Cranbury, NJ 1994), and John Patrick Donnelly 'Introduction' in *Robert Bellarmine: Spiritual Writings* ed and trans John Patrick Donnelly and Roland J. Teske (New York 1989) 13–46. See also Robert N. Watson *The Rest Is Silence: Death as Annihilation in the English Renaissance* (Berkeley and Los Angeles 1994).

66 Martin Luther 'Eyn Sermon von der bereytung zum sterben' WA 2 685–97

67 See Carlos M.N. Eire 'Ars moriendi' in *The Westminster Dictionary of Christian Spirituality* ed Gordon S. Wakefield (Philadelphia 1983) 21–2, with bibliography; *The English Ars moriendi* ed David William Atkinson (New York 1992), with bibliography; and the seminal work on the subject, Mary Catharine O'Connor *The Art of Dying Well: The Development of the Ars moriendi* (New York 1942). For somewhat different aspects of the subject, see John W. O'Malley *The First Jesuits* (Cambridge, Mass 1993) 174–8.

68 See A. Tenenti *Il senso della morte e l'amore della vita nel Rinascimento (Francia e Italia)* (Turin 1957); Remo L. Guidi *La morte nell'età umanistica* (Vicenza 1983); George W. McClure *Sorrow and Consolation in Italian Humanism* (Princeton 1991).

None the less, there was no strong precedent for the form Erasmus' treatise assumed, that is, a continuous discourse that was more than a collection of disparate pieces, which is what the two versions of the original *Ars moriendi* had been. Savonarola's 'Predica dell'arte del bene morire,' 1496, and Josse Clichtove's considerably longer *Doctrina moriendi*, 1520, probably most closely anticipated what Erasmus accomplished, but neither of these works achieved wide circulation and each was based on different principles of development. At this point we have no evidence that Erasmus utilized either of them in writing his own. It seems safe to say that Erasmus' treatise created for the genre its 'modern' or humanistic form.[69]

The treatise was, moreover, original in its content. It gave powerful impetus to a shift in the literature on the art of dying from a focus on the moment of death to a focus on how to live one's entire life so as to be ready for death. The *ars moriendi* thus became an *ars vivendi*. True, this new orientation was already perceptible in Savonarola and Clichtove, but it was pervasive in Erasmus' treatise, just as it was the leitmotif of the life of Cornelius, one of the interlocutors in Erasmus' well-known colloquy 'The Funeral,' 1526.[70] Erasmus' portrait of George in that same colloquy satirizes those who postpone preparation for death until they are dying, and on their deathbeds must therefore put their trust in some quick and noisy fix from routinized rites and talismans.

Not in such things nor in the individual's own righteousness are Christians to place their trust, but in the righteousness of Christ. This is the dominant theme of 'Preparing for Death.' This is what it means to live well in order to die well. The treatise is nowhere more original than here. Erasmus takes the pieces of the tradition of *ars moriendi* and gives them a theological base and centre. Although his development of the subject is somewhat meandering and repetitious, he makes this weakness

* * * * *

On a related issue, see John M. McManamon *Funeral Oratory and the Cultural Ideas of Italian Humanism* (Chapel Hill 1989).

69 The importance of Erasmus' work is recognized in a general way in studies dealing with death and dying in the sixteenth century, and a few studies deal more directly with it. See Thomas N. Tentler 'Forgiveness and Consolation in the Religious Thought of Erasmus' *Studies in the Renaissance* 12 (1965) 110–33; Ernst-Wilhelm Kohls 'Meditatio mortis chez Pétrarch et Erasme' in *Colloquia Erasmiana Turonensis* ed J.-C. Margolin 2 vols (Toronto 1972) I 303–11; Peter G. Bietenholz 'Ludwig Baer, Erasmus, and the Tradition of the "Ars bene moriendi"' *Revue de littérature comparée* 52 (1978) 155–70; David W. Atkinson 'Erasmus on Preparing to Die' *Wascana Review* 15/2 (1980) 10–21; and, especially, Léon-E. Halkin 'Erasme et la mort' *Revue d'histoire des religions* 200 (1983) 269–91.

70 ASD I-3 537–51

almost a strength by returning again and again to his theme, 'Christ is my righteousness.'

Erasmus thus redefines the genre. He takes what had been essentially a loose concatenation of warnings and moral maxims, of bits of sage advice and lists of instructions about how to perform certain traditional deathbed observances, and he centres these pieces around a Pauline interpretation of the death and resurrection of Christ. He centres them in the paschal mystery, thus imbuing the genre with a profoundly theological orientation. Even while making use of the late-medieval emphasis on the 'imitation of Christ,' on Christ as the pre-eminent exemplar of courage in the face of suffering and death, he subordinates that essentially moralistic idea to a doctrine that is not only radically anti-Pelagian but also the axis and culmination of Christological belief.

Erasmus insists several times in the treatise on the importance of confession and the Eucharist in Christian life and death, but he fits them into his larger theological scheme. He encourages the use of images of Christ and the saints, and similarly traditional practices, but he makes clear that their role is subordinate and supportive in godliness, not determining of it. He takes the Platonic theme of *meditatio mortis*, beloved in the Renaissance, and configures it in Pauline terms.

He not only offers a devout reflection on the meaning of Christian life and death but suggests the need for changes in attitudes and practice on the part of those who minister to the dying. The treatise is another example of how Erasmus in his maturity consistently weaves together the three threads of spirituality, theology, and reform of ministry.

The ultimate impact of the treatise on western attitudes towards death is of course impossible to measure, and after the middle of the century Erasmus' work had many competitors, some of which took a darker view of the subject. But in this treatise, one of the most widely read works of his age, he eloquently articulated a description of death as transformative in the Pauline and Johannine sense, as being an entrance into life and beatitude.[71] It is difficult to believe this powerful statement left no trace.

The Pauline resonances of 'Preparing for Death,' similar to those in so many of Erasmus' later works, intimate that his encounters with Luther helped move him to an ever deeper appreciation of the significance for godliness of Paul's teaching on grace.[72] From a certain perspective, he moves closer to Luther's position than he was in 1524, but their personalities and

* * * * *

71 See 411–12 below.
72 See eg James D. Tracy *Erasmus of the Low Countries* (Berkeley and Los Angeles 1996) 154–6.

cultural differences still drew an impassable line of demarcation between them.[73] Even in this treatise he takes aim at what he understands as Lutheran confidence in salvation.[74]

Yet we cannot lose sight of what has happened to Erasmus' *pietas*. The present treatise and even the other works in this volume allow us to see with new clarity how Erasmus over the course of the years ever more profoundly grounds *pietas* in the mystery of Christ's death and resurrection, especially as that mystery is interpreted by Paul. True, Erasmus is remarkable in the continuity of his teaching on *pietas* from the early days of the *Enchiridion* until the end of his life. From the first he found for it a firm doctrinal and theological foundation in the sacrament of baptism, in the mystery of the body of Christ, in the spiritual power of the word of God in the Scriptures, and in other Christian doctrines. But especially from 1524 onwards the Pauline doctrine of justification, located in the force of Christ's death and resurrection as the paschal mystery, moved towards the centre of his teaching and took on deeper and deeper spiritual significance for him. He thereby achieved a synthesis of doctrine and spirituality almost unparalleled for its depth, coherence, and eloquence of expression.

Erasmus produced 'Preparing for Death' in a remarkably short time after he received Boleyn's request. Despite his haste, he wrote a unified and moving piece, made more poignant by his awareness of his own physical frailty. Ten years earlier in a consolatory letter to Joost Vroye he had reflected at length on the many friends he had lost to death.[75] Even earlier he had composed a consolatory declamation on loss suffered as a result of the death of a loved one.[76] In the present treatise he wrote easily on the subject because he had written on it before and because the occasion allowed him to speak directly about what he considered most important in life. Among the prayers he published the next year, 1535, the year before he died, was one entitled 'In Grave Illness.'[77] That prayer concisely and gracefully summarizes 'Preparing for Death' and in doing so goes to the heart of Erasmian *pietas* in its most mature expression.

JWO'M

* * * * *

73 See John W. O'Malley 'Erasmus and Luther: Continuity and Discontinuity as Key to Their Conflict' *Sixteenth Century Journal* 5/2 (1974) 47–65.

74 See 428–9 below.

75 Ep 1347

76 Composed in 1509, the *Declamatio de morte* was first published in 1517 and later incorporated into *De conscribendis epistolis*; see CWE 5 25–7, and 25 156–64.

77 LB V 1203

ACKNOWLEDGMENTS
The individuals and institutions who assisted in the preparation of the various pieces in this volume are acknowledged in the introductions to those items. Once again we are indebted to Mary Baldwin, Lynn Burdon, Penny Cole, Theresa Griffin, and Philippa Matheson for their indispensable contribution of preparing the text for publication and bringing it into print.

A SHORT DEBATE CONCERNING THE
DISTRESS, ALARM, AND SORROW OF JESUS

Disputatiuncula de taedio, pavore, tristicia Iesu

translated and annotated by
MICHAEL J. HEATH

De taedio Iesu originated in a discussion at Oxford between Erasmus and John Colet in October 1499. Erasmus had been due to return to the Continent after a brief stay with his pupil and patron, William Blount, Baron Mountjoy, but, following the treason of the Earl of Suffolk, a royal proclamation was issued on 20 August forbidding anyone to leave England. Erasmus made his way to Oxford, preferring, he wrote to Colet, 'to spend a month or two in the company of men like yourself rather than of those decorated men at court.'[1] He was lodged, naturally enough, at St Mary's College, a house of the Augustinian canons regular, and his discussion with Colet probably took place there, in the presence of the prior, Richard Charnock. The debate seems to have become fairly heated: it was followed by an exchange of letters in which each man clarified his views but yielded very little to the other. Eventually Erasmus expanded the letters into the present treatise; the development of the text has been studied by G.J. Fokke, on the evidence of the letters preserved in the Gouda MS 1324.[2] The completed work was published among the *Lucubratiunculae* in February 1503.[3]

Whether or not Erasmus heard any of Colet's controversial Oxford lectures on the Pauline Epistles, it is obvious from the postscript to *De taedio* that he knew of the uproar they had caused. But rather than commit to paper his thoughts on so dangerous a topic, Erasmus devoted his first published essay in scriptural exegesis to what James D. Tracy describes as one of the most familiar topoi of late-medieval devotional literature.[4] The discussion with Colet concerned the implications of Christ's agony in the garden of Gethsemane. It was an episode which, by raising fundamental questions about the mystery of the Incarnation, had troubled Christianity from the very start. The gospel accounts of Christ's physical suffering fuelled

* * * * *

1 Ep 108:120–2, the prefatory letter here. See also Epp 106–7, an opening exchange of compliments between the two.
2 The Latin texts are being published by André Godin as an appendix to his edition of *De taedio Iesu* in ASD. Fokke 164–71 shows that Allen was mistaken in the order he assigned to Epp 109 and 111, drawn from the Gouda MS; if Allen's order is reversed the structure of *De taedio* is restored. Some of the parallels between these letters and *De taedio* are indicated in my notes.
3 Antwerp: Dirk Martens (NK 835); there was a second edition from the same press in 1509 (NK 836). I have found no trace of a separate first edition listed in F. vander Haeghen's *Bibliotheca Erasmiana* 3 vols in 1 (repr Nieuwkoop 1961) I 77. Erasmus sent Colet a copy of the *Lucubratiunculae* in 1504 (Ep 181:49–50).
4 Tracy 31; Tracy's article gives the most comprehensive account of the background and implications of Erasmus' treatise, which, as the author says, has seldom been the object of any special study.

the incredulity of potential converts among the Jews and pagans.[5] Erasmus refers several times to the storms the episode caused in the early church and to the lack of agreement among the Fathers. The central issue was whether Christ in his human nature truly feared his own death, as Erasmus maintained, or whether he was afraid and saddened because he could foresee the grim fate of the others involved: the apostles, the Jews, or even the city of Jerusalem.

This question overlaps with several others concerning the human nature of Christ and the characteristics of his will. The early church was rocked by the 'docetist' controversy, when many Gnostic sects asserted that Christ did not assume a real body but an imaginary one (δόκησις = apparition or phantom); they maintained, therefore, that the whole physical life of Christ, including the resurrection, was appearance only. It was a doctrinal dispute almost as old as Christianity itself, and indeed some thought that the Gospel according to John was in part written to confute docetism.[6] The problem was not resolved until the Council of Chalcedon in 451 produced its definitive statement on Christ's human nature.[7] Similarly, the agony in the garden played a major role in the debate over monothelitism. This belief that Christ had a single will, identical with the Father's, apparently conflicted with Matthew 26:39: 'None the less, not as I will, Father, but as you will.' The alternative thesis that Christ possessed a separate human will (itself divided by some, including Erasmus, into two parts)[8] eventually prevailed, and monothelitism was condemned by the Council of Constantinople in 681.[9]

These early controversies influence the arguments and the authorities used by Erasmus and Colet. Unexpectedly, Erasmus generally sides with scholastic theologians against the early Fathers.[10] Augustine, Ambrose, and Jerome, writing before the church's position became entirely clear, leaned towards the conclusion that Christ was not truly afraid for himself. Later commentators quoted by Erasmus, such as Bede and Bonaventure, could make unequivocal statements, based on the recently established orthodoxy,

* * * * *

5 On the repugnance felt by sophisticated contemporaries for the doctrine of the Incarnation, see eg Kasper 179 and Screech 19.
6 Cf Kasper 118 and 113–23 for a succinct historical survey of attitudes to Christ's suffering and death.
7 See 32 and n78 below.
8 See 58 below.
9 See nn30 and 129 to the text.
10 Normally Erasmus had little but scorn for the schoolmen and their style; see Santinello 81–2 and, for a contemporary example, the *Antibarbari* CWE 23 26 and 67.

about Christ's human nature and dual will. Erasmus makes what use he can of the early Fathers' eclecticism, but his suggestion (19–20) that they could be cited in support of either side is disingenuous and corroborates Colet's accusation that in the debate Erasmus sometimes resorted to mere rhetorical tricks.[11] However, Erasmus' views were certainly more in tune with recent thinking, and in addition his analysis of Christ's kenosis, his deliberate and exemplary self-abasement in his human nature, echoed the *vita Christi* tradition in which Erasmus had been brought up. The Christology of *De taedio*, with its distinctive insistence on Christ's love, humility, and gentleness,[12] anticipates the *Enchiridion* (also published in the *Lucubratiunculae* of 1503), where the psychological theories outlined in *De taedio* are also fully developed.

Erasmus may have put *De taedio* into its final form while working on the early Fathers at Courtebourne in the winter of 1501–2.[13] He was able then to verify and expand his patristic references, having complained of a shortage of books in Oxford. He now made selective use of Origen's commentary on Matthew, which had in fact inspired Jerome to play down the intensity of Christ's suffering.[14] To produce a semblance of true debate, Erasmus was also willing to quote the Fathers against himself in lengthy passages ascribed to Colet. That these represented something of Colet's thoughts is shown by the text of one of his replies, unavailable to Erasmus when he published *De taedio* in 1503; the letter turned up later and was published at the end of *De taedio* in the Froben edition of 1518. It appears to be merely a preliminary and general reply to Erasmus' arguments and is thus rather disappointingly laconic. Colet argues that the Scriptures are less open to multiple interpretations than Erasmus supposes, and that Jerome's reading was divinely inspired and thus unassailable.[15]

Apparently, in the debate Colet made no use of his humanist learning. He had returned from Italy with a reputation for rare erudition but had supposedly been persuaded to abandon rhetoric by Erasmus' arguments in the unpublished second part of the *Antibarbari*. Colet eventually repaid the debt by showing Erasmus how to bridge the gap between scholarship and

* * * * *

11 Cf Santinello 101–4.
12 See in particular 65–6.
13 See Epp 165–9 and Godin *Erasme lecteur* 13–26.
14 66 and n168; see also n142.
15 The text is in LB V 1291–4 and the brief preface is Ep 110. On its place in the debate, see Fokke 173, who demonstrates that other replies by Colet have been lost.

religion.[16] But this is more apparent in Erasmus' later exegetical works than in *De taedio*, where Erasmus the poet and collector of classical adages and exempla sometimes takes over the discussion. In a richly illustrated passage on the psychology of courage (27–35), Erasmus extracts half a dozen maxims or anecdotes from one short chapter of Aulus Gellius (12.5) on 'the decrees of the Stoics concerning ways and means of enduring pain,' and embellishes his case with examples from Roman history and with the subtle portrayals of fortitude in Virgil and Homer. He finds stylistic inspiration in Gellius' description of a storm at sea and in evocations of warfare by several ancient poets. Throughout the debate Erasmus makes self-conscious use of rhetorical devices recommended by Quintilian, and alludes more than once to the methodology of the Platonic dialogue, implying that this discussion between humanists ought to proceed in that loose and amiable form. But in fact some of Erasmus' arguments more closely resemble the syllogistic methods of the schoolmen.[17] *De taedio* contains a remarkable mixture of classical learning and theology.

A few weeks after their original discussion in Oxford the two men were involved, with several others, in another theological argument. Erasmus describes in awed terms Colet's passionate commitment to his cause, 'a sort of holy frenzy ... something of superhuman exaltation and frenzy.' On this occasion Erasmus played the role of conciliator when the debate threatened to get out of hand.[18] But it is generally agreed that Colet's example steered Erasmus towards theology,[19] and their steadfast friendship until Colet's death in 1519 suggests that these early disagreements cast no lasting shadow between them, even though at times the tone of *De taedio* seems far from amicable. It is not so much the use of martial imagery, which, to judge from Colet's extant replies, became a kind of jocular leitmotif in the debate. But the linking passages often have an abrasiveness, enhanced by the apostrophic form, that suggests a certain asperity. There is one curious piece of evidence that Erasmus had qualms, much later, about the tone and even the content of *De taedio*. In the *Ciceronianus* of 1528 Bulephorus

* * * * *

16 On all this, see CWE 23 8–10; Erasmus describes Colet's 'conversion' in the 1520 preface to the *Antibarbari*, Ep 1110 (text also in CWE 23 16).

17 Good examples are the discussions of *alacritas* (46–7) and of the two parts of the soul (63–4). Fokke 182 points out other examples.

18 See Ep 116 CWE 2 229–33 for the details (the quotation is lines 33–4). Erasmus calmed things down by telling a sort of biblical shaggy-dog story.

19 See Santinello 86–94; A.G. Dickens and Whitney R.D. Jones *Erasmus the Reformer* (London 1994) 35–40; and G. Marc'hadour 'Erasme et John Colet' in *Colloquia Erasmiana Turonensia* ed J.-C. Margolin 2 vols (Toronto 1972) II 761–70.

describes mockingly a speech he had heard at Rome, on the subject of Christ's passion, unedifyingly stuffed with rhetorical tricks and 'pagan' allusions.[20] Interestingly, *De taedio*, on much the same topic, contains a number of these allusions, for example to the deaths of Phocion and Socrates and to the self-sacrifice of the Decii and Marcus Curtius. It is an indication of the way in which Erasmus' formal scriptural exegesis became markedly less syncretic after *De taedio* and the *Enchiridion*.

Despite Erasmus' misgivings, *De taedio* does not seem to have aroused much controversy, presumably because its conclusions on Christ's nature and will, maintained in *De libero arbitrio*,[21] coincided with orthodox thinking. The treatise apparently escaped ecclesiastical censorship entirely. The theory that Christ in his human nature showed true fear to comfort his less robust followers had become commonplace and found favour also with the many sixteenth-century exegetes, including most Reformers, who preferred to accept the literal meaning of an awkward gospel text rather than seek the convoluted explanations of their predecessors.[22] Erasmus' treatise also illustrates the way in which Christ's agony entered humanist controversy, being cited in attacks upon Stoicism. Mistrust of Stoic apathy crossed confessional boundaries, and Christ's display of emotion was used in evidence against the Stoics by such different thinkers as Coluccio Salutati, Josse Clichtove, Calvin, and Pietro Martire Vermigli.[23]

But the most relevant – and poignant – contemporary commentary on Christ's agony was made by Thomas More, as he faced his own martyrdom in the Tower. The last substantial work from his pen was the meditation *De tristitia, tedio, pavore, et oratione Christi ante captionem eius*,[24] a title strikingly close to Erasmus'. More took much the same line as his old friend, maintaining that the episode provided an example and comfort for those who were not blessed with the holy zeal of the early martyrs. For that purpose Christ's divine nature, exceptionally, allowed his human nature to predominate for a time; by this kenosis Christ showed that in times of crisis it is

* * * * *

20 CWE 28 384–7; Erasmus is generally to be identified with Bulephorus, and the speech may in fact be one he had heard in Rome in 1509.
21 See Fokke 176–7.
22 See Tracy 48–51 on Lefèvre d'Etaples and Bucer as representative of this trend.
23 For references, see Jill Kraye 'Moral Philosophy' in *The Cambridge History of Renaissance Philosophy* ed C.B. Schmitt and Q. Skinner (Cambridge 1988) 368–9.
24 Translated by Clarence H. Miller as *The Sadness, the Weariness, the Fear, and the Prayer of Christ before He Was Taken Prisoner, The Complete Works of St Thomas More* 14 (New Haven and London 1976). The treatise was first published in 1565. See also Santinello 116–28 and Tracy 46–9 for a comparison of More's work with those of Erasmus and Lefèvre d'Etaples.

not essential to violate nature and that there is nothing dishonourable in the struggle between reason and fear. More too considered that the episode provided weapons against the errors of docetism and monothelitism. There are several possible echoes of Erasmus' treatise, such as the discussion of the martyrs' eagerness and Christ's reluctance, and the example of the deserving but frightened soldier.[25] It is also possible that a faulty recollection of Erasmus' work (More had very few books in his cell) led More to confuse the 'phantasy' of the Stoics with the 'propassion' of the theologians.[26]

The text here translated is LB v 1265–92, checked against a draft of the ASD text generously supplied by its editor, André Godin. His apparatus includes variants from the early draft of part of the treatise in Gouda MS 1324; comparison with the completed work shows that Erasmus worked hard to clarify his thought and to polish his style, often abridging the earlier effusions. The other variants are taken from the *Lucubratiunculae* published at Antwerp in February 1503, Strasbourg in September 1515, and Basel in July 1518 and October 1519,[27] and from the Basel *Opera omnia* of 1540. But the printed texts are virtually identical: in the later editions some misprints are corrected, a few small stylistic improvements are made, and marginal summaries and headings are added, especially in the 1518 Basel edition.

In translating, I have tried to preserve the nuances of the psychological terms. At one point (53) Erasmus aligns *reformidatio, timor,* and *pavor,* which I normally translate as 'dread,' 'fear,' and 'alarm.' The first belongs to the family of words used most often by Erasmus to describe Christ's emotion as his death approached; it has overtones of reluctance brought about by reflection on the future. The others represent more spontaneous reactions to immediate threats. Sometimes *pavescere,* 'to be alarmed,' is strengthened to *expavescere,* translated as 'to be terrified.'[28] Another difficult term is the opposite emotion, *alacritas.* Usually translated here as 'eagerness,' it has overtones of 'joy' which it is sometimes useful to introduce.[29] Translations

* * * * *

25 *Complete Works* 14 (see the preceding note) 55–9 and 85; the second case is particularly close to the passage below, 30.
26 Ibidem 243; for the terms, see 26 and 35 below.
27 The treatise was not published separately but appeared in editions of the *Lucubratiunculae,* including Antwerp (Martens) 1503, 1509, and 1520; Strasbourg (Schürer) 1515, 1516, 1517, and 1519; and Basel (Froben) 1518, 1519, and 1535.
28 As Tracy 44 points out, Erasmus actually used this intensification to strengthen the Vulgate translation of Mark 14:33 (LB vi 206E).
29 On the difficulty of translating *alacritas,* see Tracy 40–1; Screech 87; and especially G. Marc'hadour 'Thomas More on the Agony of Christ' in *Concordia discors: studi su Niccolò Cusano e l'umanesimo europeo offerti a Giovanni Santinello* (Padua 1993) 495–500.

of Scripture are my own, as no English version exactly matches Erasmus' text.

I am grateful to the Leverhulme Trust for the award of a Senior Research Fellowship which enabled me to undertake this work.

MJH

DESIDERIUS ERASMUS TO THE LEARNED AND ELOQUENT DIVINE,
JOHN COLET

Most learned Colet: I no more deserve the reproof in your last, than the praise you bestowed on me in your earlier letter.[1] All the same, I can tolerate your undeserved reproaches with a good deal more equanimity than your previous compliments, the justice of which I was unable to recognize. For if one is accused, then not only may one clear oneself with no disgrace attached, but one is blamed for failing to do so; whereas the studious rebuttal of compliments, on the other hand, appears to betoken a nature starved of praise, hungry for it, and not sincerely endeavouring to avoid it but really seeking more frequent or more lavish praises. What I suppose you were seeking to do was to try me out in both kinds: to see whether I was complacent when a testimonial from such a great man reflected glory on me, and again whether the provocation of a petty jibe showed that I had a sting to use. Surely you must be the most dependable of friends, when you are so very cautious, thorough, hesitant, and experimental in forming new friendships. But I have indulged a fancy to jest with you over this. In fact, I am as glad to accept reproof from a true friend now as I was earlier to be praised, even falsely, by the most highly praised of men. So in future you may praise or scold your friend Erasmus as you wish, so long as a letter from you flies to me here every day, which is the pleasantest thing that could happen to me.

Now let me briefly turn to your letter, in order to make sure that the boy who brought it shall not return to you empty-handed. When you tell me that you dislike the modern class of theologians, who spend their lives in sheer hair-splitting and sophistical quibbling, you have my emphatic agreement, dear Colet. It is not that I condemn their learned studies, I who have nothing but praise for learning of any sort, but these studies are isolated, and not seasoned with references to any well-written works of an older age, and so they seem to me likely to give a man a smattering of knowledge or a taste for arguing. But whether they can make him wise, others may judge; for they exhaust the intelligence by a kind of sterile and thorny subtlety, in no way quickening it with vital sap or breathing into it the breath of life; and, worst of all, by their stammering, foul, and squalid style of writing, they render unattractive that great queen of all sciences, theology, enriched and adorned as she has been by the eloquence of antiquity. In this way they choke up, as it were with brambles, the way of a science that early thinkers had cleared and, attempting to settle all questions, so they claim, merely

* * * * *

1 Ep 106

envelop all in darkness. Thus you can see her, once supremely revered and full of majesty, today all but silent, impoverished, and in rags; while we are seduced by the attractions of a perverted and insatiable passion for quibbling. One quarrel leads to another, and with extraordinary arrogance we quarrel over insignificant trifles.[2]

Moreover, lest we seem to have made no progress beyond the discoveries of the early Fathers, we have had the effrontery to lay down a number of fixed procedures that God used, we claim, in working out his hidden purposes, though it would sometimes be more pious to believe in the fact while conceding to the omnipotence of God alone the knowledge of how it comes to be. Further, in our eagerness to show off our knowledge, we sometimes debate questions of a sort intolerable to truly religious men, as when we ask whether God could have taken the form of the devil or an ass. Perhaps one ought to put up with such things when a youth dabbles in them slightly for the sake, as it were, of whetting his mind's edge; but these are the things over which we grow old – even die – as upon the rocks of the Sirens,[3] relegating all literature to an inferior place in comparison with them. And moreover, nowadays practically no one devotes himself to the study of theology, the highest branch of learning, except such as, having sluggish or disordered wits, are scarcely fit for letters at all.

Now, I would wish to say these things not of good and scholarly professors of divinity, for whom I have an especially warm regard and respect, but only of the squalid mob of carping theologues, who hold all men's culture worthless save their own. Inasmuch as you, Colet, have undertaken to do battle with this invincible tribe, for the sake of restoring to as much of its early splendour and dignity as you can that ancient true theology, overgrown as it is with the entanglements introduced by the modern school, as God loves me, you have assumed a responsibility of the most creditable sort, one that is a true labour of love towards theology herself, and will enormously benefit every studious person, and this most flourishing university of Oxford in particular, yet nevertheless is, to be quite honest, an extremely difficult and unpopular undertaking. Your difficulties, indeed, will be surmounted by a combination of scholarship and hard work; as for unpopularity, your generous nature will manage without trouble to overlook that. Even among divines themselves there are, too, not a few who could and would offer assistance to endeavours as honourable as yours; or rather, everyone will lend a hand, since there is not a soul, even among the doctors,

* * * * *

2 Erasmus uses the proverbial 'goat's wool' (non-existent, and would be worthless if it did exist); *Adagia* I iii 53.
3 Virgil *Aeneid* 5.864

in this famous university who has not listened with the greatest attention to the lectures you have given on the Pauline Epistles for the past three years.[4] In regard to this, which should one praise more: the modesty of the professors, who are not abashed to appear merely as audience at the lectures of a man who is young in years and unprovided with the authority of the doctorate, as it is called, or your own unequalled combination of learning, eloquence, and moral integrity, which they judge to be worthy of this honour?

What surprises me, however, is not that you have taken so heavy a burden upon your shoulders – your strength is fit to match it – but that you are inviting my insignificant self to share in this grand undertaking. For you urge, or rather almost demand with threats, that, just as you are doing by your lectures on Paul, so I should try this winter to set alight the enthusiasms of this university, which you say are cooling down, by lecturing either on old Moses or on that eloquent stylist, Isaiah. However, I have learned to live with myself,[5] and am well aware how scanty my equipment is; and I can neither lay claim to scholarship enough for the prosecution of such high aims, nor suppose myself to possess strength of character enough to be able to endure the ill will of all those determined defenders of their own. This no assignment for a recruit, but for a highly experienced general. Please, however, do not call me shameless for declining the tasks you suggest; I should be utterly shameless did I not do so. It is you, dear Colet, who are less than wise in demanding water from a stone, as Plautus puts it.[6] How could I ever be so brazen as to teach what I myself have not learned? How can I fire the cool hearts of others, when I myself am trembling and shivering all over? I should think myself more irresponsible than irresponsibility itself if in a matter of such importance I plunged in wholeheartedly at a venture and, as the Greek proverb has it, began to learn pottery on the largest size of jar.[7] But, you will say, I had relied on you; and you will complain that I have

* * * * *

4 Colet's lectures on the Pauline Epistles, which interpreted them in their historical setting, rather than as a treasury of proof texts to be taken out of context and used in dialectical construction of dogma, were revolutionary and attracted large audiences despite his youth and lack of a doctorate. E.H. Harbison has called them a milestone in the history of Christian scholarship; *The Christian Scholar in the Age of the Reformation* (New York 1956) 58. Cf P.A. Duhamel 'The Oxford Lectures of John Colet' *Journal of the History of Ideas* 14 (1953) 493–510, and *Erasmus and Cambridge: The Cambridge Letters of Erasmus* ed H.C. Porter and trans D.F.S. Thomson (Toronto 1963) 16ff.
5 Persius 4.52; *Adagia* I iv 87
6 *Persa* 41; *Adagia* I iv 75
7 *Adagia* I iv 15

disappointed your hopes. If so, you should reproach yourself and not me; for I have not deceived you, inasmuch as I never promised, or even held out a prospect of, anything of the kind; it is you who have deceived yourself, in refusing to believe me when I told you the truth about myself. And I have not come to these shores to teach literature, in verse or in prose. Literature ceased to have charms for me as soon as it ceased to be necessary to me. As I reject this task because it falls below my purpose, so I reject your proposal because it is too great for my powers. In the one case, dear Colet, I do not deserve your reproaches, because I never intended to become a professor of what is called secular learning; in the other case your exhortations are wasted on me, since I am only too well aware of my inadequacy.

But even were I fully adequate to the task, I should still be in no position to undertake it, for I am shortly returning to Paris, whence I came. As I am kept here for the present, partly by the winter season and partly because the recent flight of a certain duke[8] prevents my leaving safely, I have betaken myself to this celebrated university in order to spend a month or two in the company of men like yourself rather than of those decorated gentlemen at court. And so far am I from wishing to oppose your honourable and pious endeavours, that I promise I shall diligently encourage and support them, since I am not yet qualified to work with you. For the rest, as soon as I feel myself to possess the necessary stamina and strength, I shall come personally to join your party, and will give devoted, if not distinguished, service in the defence of theology. Meanwhile, nothing could afford me greater pleasure than daily debates between us on the subject of Holy Writ, continued as we have begun either face to face or by means of letters. Farewell, dear Colet.

PS My host and our common friend Richard Charnock, that kind and reverend gentleman, has asked me to add warm greetings on his own behalf.

Oxford, at the college of the Augustinian canons, commonly called St Mary's

* * * * *

8 Edmund de la Pole, Earl of Suffolk, was the eldest son of Elizabeth, sister of Edward IV. Guilty of treason, he fled to Calais in the summer of 1499, and on 20 August a royal proclamation forbade anyone to leave the kingdom. He was, however, soon allowed to return; cf *Letters and Papers Illustrative of the Reigns of Richard III and Henry VII* ed James Gairdner 2 vols, Rerum Britannicarum medii aevi scriptores (Rolls Series) 24 (London 1861–3) II 377, and J.D. Mackie *The Earlier Tudors, 1485–1538* (Oxford 1952) 167ff.

A SHORT DEBATE CONCERNING THE DISTRESS, ALARM, AND SORROW OF JESUS AS THE CRUCIFIXION DREW NIGH; AND CONCERNING THE WORDS IN WHICH HE SEEMED TO PRAY FOR DELIVERANCE FROM DEATH: 'FATHER, IF IT BE POSSIBLE, LET THIS CUP PASS FROM ME'

DESIDERIUS ERASMUS OF ROTTERDAM TO HIS FRIEND JOHN COLET[1]
In the course of our sparring match yesterday afternoon, Colet, while you made a great many observations characterized by weight as well as wit, I was not fully convinced of the soundness of your position, yet found it easier to record my dissent from it than to refute it, my own impression being that my weakness lay not in the view I espoused but in my presentation of it. As for you, in your modest way you put aside argument for the time being, but as I took my leave you begged me to think the matter over privately with closer attention and greater precision, and said you had no doubt that if I did so I should forthwith proceed to vote for your point of view. Here you did rightly, in my opinion; for you were aware that, as the famous writer of mimes so wisely remarked, the truth is sometimes lost to sight when arguments go on too long,[2] especially when the whole discussion is conducted in the presence of those whose opinion of our own scholarship we consider crucially important. Now, on this occasion Prior Richard Charnock[3] was present; to you he is a very old friend, while he has only recently been host to me, but he has virtually the same love and admiration for each of us. Again, there are times when the passion for debate which nature implants in us, and the eagerness to maintain one's own position, seize hold even of gentler temperaments; you may find someone who will give up his ancestral domains, but 'no man alive his brain-child e'er would quit.'[4] So I was happy, dear Colet, to follow your instructions: I went over the whole discussion again

* * * * *

1 For the opening of the work I follow the CWE translation of Ep 109:1–41. On the relationship of Epp 109 and 111 to the complete *De taedio Iesu*, see my introductory note.
2 Publilius Syrus 416, quoted by Aulus Gellius *Noctes Atticae* 17.14.4
3 Charnock (CEBR I 300–1) was prior of St Mary's College, Oxford, where the debate probably took place.
4 Martial 8.18.10

privately and looked at it in a harder and more concentrated way, freeing myself from every shred of prejudice while I put together and weighed the arguments on both sides; indeed I altered things round so as to adopt your arguments exactly as if they were my own and to criticize my own no less severely than if they had been yours. Nevertheless, in spite of these measures I was visited by no new considerations, and repented of nothing I had said. Accordingly I shall attempt if possible to record the entire controversy in writing and, so to speak, repeat the performance – not because I am better equipped than I then was, but with a view to expressing in a slightly more orderly and systematic form the thoughts I then voiced haphazard, not being prepared. For even if your resources are adequate, it still makes a great deal of difference how skilfully you fight, once battle is joined. Let us, however, proceed chiefly by the method of proof, since under present conditions I lack the help of texts to fall back on. You are, of course, luckier than I am in this respect; but why should I mind? In a literary battle the wise soldier would rather be defeated than win; that is, he prefers learning to teaching. If I am overthrown I come away better instructed, while if I prevail over you I shall not lose any of your affection.[5] But now I am ready for battle.

If memory serves, you made the following points in our debate concerning the distress, alarm, and sorrow of our redeemer Jesus and the words in which he seems to pray for deliverance from death: 'If it be possible, let this cup pass from me.'[6] You declared yourself dissatisfied with the interpretation generally accepted and disseminated by modern theologians, who conclude that Christ as a true man was at that moment temporarily deprived of the protection of his divinity, and that, because of the frailty of our natural condition, which he had assumed together with many of our woes, he shuddered at the cruel and terrible ordeal that drew ever closer and threatened to crush him. It was this emotion, they say, that wrenched from him the cry of a man filled with dread: 'My Father, if it be possible, let this cup pass from me'; the cry was our own, by which they mean that it is a testimony to human frailty. However, apparently mastering his emotion, he added at once, as befits a good and dutiful son, 'Nevertheless, not as I will, Father, but as you will.'[7]

You argued that nothing could be less consistent with Christ's charity (warmer, indisputably, than any other) than for him to shudder at the

* * * * *

5 From this point the text of Ep 109 is different, being that of the original letter preserved in the Gouda MS 1324, as published by Allen.
6 Matt 26:39; cf Mark 14:36; Luke 22:42.
7 Matt 26:39

imminence of the death which, for the love of us, he so fervently desired, and to pray for deliverance from it. You added that, since many of the martyrs suffered the most inhuman tortures that the executioners could devise with hearts that were not only dauntless and unafraid, but even joyfully eager,[8] as if exulting in their fate, and since some even took satisfaction from their torments because, clearly, their love was strong enough to absorb the pain, you found it patently absurd to claim that Christ shuddered at either the infamy or the pain of the cross, since he is true love, true charity, and had come for no other purpose than to release us from the power of death and give us life by his own unmerited death. Again, the fact that from every pore he sweated drops of blood,[9] that in his heart he was sorrowful unto death and had to be uplifted by the comfort of angels,[10] and that he tried, as it were, to cajole his Father, and prayed for deliverance from the cup of death: you preferred to attribute all this to anything but a dread of death. You asserted that charity has a particular power and duty to banish all terror, to replace sorrow with joyfulness, to take no thought for itself but to pour out all it has for the benefit of others.[11] You found it both inappropriate and inconsistent to suppose that he, who loved the human race with such passion, could have approached death not merely with reluctance but with great trepidation. And to prove your point, you voiced strong disagreement with those who, in establishing the hierarchy of charity, invented stages in the development of love that are quite incompatible with the very essence of charity, saying for example that, after God, each of us holds himself most dear, and that, when the stakes are equal, we always put our own interests before our neighbours'.[12] You maintained that this theory would destroy one of love's unique and fundamental qualities, which is that it neglects its own concerns and takes thought for others: love of oneself is no love at all. Moses would rather be blotted out from the book of life than let his people die.[13] Christ, the very pattern of charity, destroyed himself to

* * * * *

8 *Alacres*: on the range of meaning of this term, see my introductory note.
9 Cf Luke 22:44.
10 A conflation of Matt 26:38 and Luke 22:43
11 Cf 1 Cor 13:4–7.
12 An allusion to Thomas Aquinas *De ordine caritatis* (*Summa theologica* II–II q 26 art 4). The corresponding classical theory that nature planted in us an instinctive self-love and desire for self-preservation is attributed to 'an ailing Stoic' by Aulus Gellius *Noctes Atticae* 12.5.7; see also n54 below. Condemnation of *philautia* or self-love is an enduring theme of Erasmus' ethics; see eg *Adagia* I iii 92 and *Moria* CWE 27 98–9 and 116–17.
13 Exod 32:32

ensure our survival. Paul, that other mirror of perfect love, wished to be an outcast from Christ[14] to help his brothers according to the flesh. There you have it, Colet: a summary of your arguments against me, which I have set down as briefly as I could, yet without misrepresenting you, and without intentionally omitting or trivializing any of your points (something Quintilian recommends in refuting an opponent's case).[15] Indeed, you will not deny that I have made some points rather more forcefully than you did originally.

But now we shall pass on to discuss the topic itself, having first invoked that deity who to some extent, certainly, was distressed for us, not himself; was alarmed for us, not himself; sorrowed for us, not himself; sweated for us, not himself. He alone knows in what frame of mind he prayed to his Father: may he keep us from pursuing merely our own ideas and may he deign to share his thoughts with us. You supported your view by quoting Jerome, the only one, according to you, to have glimpsed the truth of this matter when he altered the reason given for Christ's alarm and distress and wrote, as you claimed, that the Saviour Jesus was merely praying that his death, by which he wished to bring salvation to all the world, should not prove fatal to the Jews. This explains his anguish of alarm and dismay, bitter to the point of death; hence the bloody drops of sweat that dripped from his whole body to the ground. You said that this was proved conclusively by the fact that as he made the eternal sacrifice on the cross, Christ prayed again for his murderers, saying to the Father: 'Forgive them, for they know not what they do.'[16] For you the meaning of both texts is practically the same. 'Let this cup pass from me' means 'Let the Jews not kill me to their own perdition,' and so does 'Forgive them, for they know not what they do.'

Now if, Colet, you put forward this view of yours (or of Jerome's) without necessarily rejecting all others, then I too shall go along with it, for I am always happy to agree with our Jerome, and no less unhappy to disagree with Colet. Nothing prevents us from extracting different meanings from Holy Writ, which is a miracle of fertility, and from reading a single text in more than a single way. I have learned from that holy man Job that the word of the Lord is manifold;[17] I know that manna did not taste the same to every palate.[18] But if your adherence to that single interpretation

* * * * *

14 *Anathema* in Latin; Rom 9:3
15 Quintilian *Institutiones oratoriae* 5.13.27
16 Luke 23:34
17 Cf Job 11:6; but not so much a quotation as a comment on Job's experiences.
18 Erasmus allegorizes manna in the same way in the *Enchiridion* cwe 66 32 and especially 69. The story of the manna that nourished the Israelites is told in Exod 16, but the miraculous variety of its taste belongs to the Jewish historical

leads you to condemn and reject a widely accepted view found in a number of authorities, then I protest, and feel free to disagree – and shall disagree, until you order me to think like you. And I know that, honest as you are, you will issue no such order unless you can back your case with sufficient proof. I agree that Jerome said that people should be ashamed if they thought that the Saviour feared death and said, 'Let this cup pass from me,' because he was afraid to suffer.[19] I do not agree that practically no one has said that Jesus, having assumed human form, in his human frailty dreaded death, which is by its nature painful. You press me with quotations, but what if Jerome held both views? What if he put forward mine more often than yours? What if he alluded to both in the same passage? And what if he did not really agree with your view, or even with what he had written, since, as he states openly in his letter against Rufinus, he thinks that the maximum of freedom is permitted in writing commentaries?[20] For in them it is important not merely to trumpet one's own opinions, at all costs, but to say what others have thought. This is common practice among all writers of commentaries, but Ambrose and Jerome had a particular penchant for wandering through the various authors and, without risk to themselves, setting down the thoughts of others. In expounding Holy Writ, both of them set out to match Origen, who was accustomed, as we know, to give a range of conflicting views on the same topic and thus to provide the reader with ample scope for reflection. Reread the passage on which you base your argument: unless I am much mistaken Jerome also records the view that you are attacking. But for the moment, given our shortage of books, the battle will be by logic against logic, theory against theory, argument against argument.

A first point: was Christ anguished only because he foresaw that his death would bring destruction on a few Jews or perhaps because, as Hilary suggests, he foreknew that the apostles, shocked and perplexed by it, would abandon him?[21] But if he foresaw all these events just as clearly at the moment of his conception as he did at this moment, then he must have known such anguish right from the beginning. If you assume a continuing cause, you cannot but assume a continuing effect. Why, then, should he pray to

* * * * *

tradition of the Aggadah, which records that it tasted like milk to children, like bread to adolescents, like honey to the old – and like ashes to the heathen.

19 Jerome *Commentarius in Matheum* 4.26.37 PL 26 197
20 Jerome *Epistula adversus Rufinum* 3.11 PL 23 465. It is true that Jerome adopts an eclectic approach to exegesis, but Erasmus' is not among the four possible causes of Christ's sorrow mentioned by Jerome: concern for Judas, for the apostles, for the Jews, and for the fate of Jerusalem.
21 Hilary *Commentarius in Matthaeum* 31.5 PL 9 1068

avert the Jews' destruction only at this late stage? Why at this time and no other? Why not in different terms? In fact he had earlier lamented the destruction of Jerusalem, but in the clearest terms possible.[22] On the cross he prayed for his murderers, for the blasphemers, but in quite unmistakable terms; the circumstances were then appropriate for such sentiments. Here no small leap of the imagination, as it were, is required to make the facts and the words apply to the destruction of the Jews, unless you distort them quite outrageously.

'Is it not obvious,' you ask, 'that he is praying to save the Jews from self-destruction, when he says, "Let this cup pass from me"? He means the cup they are about to offer him.' Not at all: if you insist on the words, they seem to me more appropriate to the Father, who did offer him a cup, than to the Jews. This becomes as clear as day from a similar passage where Christ alludes to his death, 'Shall I not drink the cup that my Father has given me?'[23] Thus the Father gives the Son a cup to drink, and the Son, as a man, a man weak with the woes of humanity, is filled with genuine dread of imminent death and begs his Father to take the cup from him. The pronoun *iste* helps my case, too; you know only too well whether it should apply to the Father, to whom Christ is speaking, or to the Jews.[24] Mark's words imply the same: 'And he prayed that, if it were possible, the hour might pass from him.'[25] What hour could that be, but the hour of his execution, now close at hand? Mark then adds the actual words he used: 'Abba, Father, all things are possible to you; take away this cup from me.' Thus if you scrutinize Christ's language, not one syllable can be found to support your opinion.

Now, if you are looking for circumstantial evidence, you will find exactly the same amount, by which I mean none at all that supports your case. Take the rhetoricians' advice and summarize what happened earlier, what took place at the time, and what followed. He had said to Judas, 'What you do, do quickly.'[26] The servants of sin draw nigh. The traitor arrives with his hapless troop. Jesus wishes by his example to teach the thousands of

* * * * *

22 Matt 23:37–8, Christ's prophecy of the destruction of Jerusalem; Erasmus discusses these interpretations more thoroughly in Ep 111 CWE 1 214–16.
23 John 18:11
24 *Iste*, meaning 'that of yours'; cf Ep 111 CWE 1 216 n134. Santinello 107 cites this as an example of Erasmus' use of Lorenzo Valla's grammatical method of exegesis.
25 Mark 14:35, followed by the next verse
26 John 13:27. The following account of the agony in the garden is mainly a conflation of John's story with that of Matthew (26).

martyrs, destined to emulate his death, how they must behave when the executioner stands grimly by, his barbarous instruments at the ready. Jesus
seeks a secluded place, suitable for prayer; he lets his distress show, to spare
the martyrs humiliation when they suffer like him; he throws himself to the
ground, to show the martyrs that they need not meet their fate trusting only
in their own strength or merits; on the contrary, distrusting themselves completely, they should look for succour only to their head. Beset by sorrow, he
begs the Father to take death from him, if it be possible. But he overcomes
this feeling of weakness and submits totally to his Father's will. He enjoins
the sleepy apostles to watch and pray. The spirit indeed is willing, but the
flesh is weak. Then he goes to meet his pursuers. They are bewildered, so
he reassures them; they hang back, so he calls out to them. He even bestows
a kiss on the traitor and calls him friend. I hope you can see, Colet, that
all the circumstances, before, during, and after the incident, show conclusively that Christ Jesus, through the frailty of the condition he had assumed,
shrank from approaching death, but that, given divine aid and the strength
of his obedience, he went on to face it with all steadfastness.

It is true that nowhere do the theologians seem to me to have spoken
more confusedly than on this gospel text. Some deny that Christ was ever
filled with dread, as your Jerome does. Augustine, in his exposition of Psalm
21, does not disagree: 'For he was garbed in his body,' he says, 'that is, the
church; unless perhaps you think, my brothers, that when the Lord said,
"Father, if it be possible, let this cup pass from me," he was afraid to die.'[27]
Ambrose seems sometimes to accept that Christ was distressed by death and
sometimes to deny it. He accepts it when he says, 'as a man, unwilling to
die, but as God, keeping his promise.' Then he denies it when he writes,
'For you suffer, Lord Jesus, not for your wounds but for mine; not for your
death but for my frailty; when we thought you were in pain, it was not for
yourself but for me that you suffered.' Again, a little later: 'He appeared
sorrowful, and was indeed saddened, not by his own passion, but by our
dispersion.' And a little later: 'He was sorrowful because he was leaving
us, his children.' And in the same passage: 'He says, "Take this cup from
me," not because God the Son of God feared death, but because he did not
want the evil ones to perish on his account.'[28] What is more, Hilary even
calls it impious folly to maintain that it was for himself that Christ dreaded

* * * * *

27 Augustine *Enarratio in psalmum* 21 4 PL 36 172
28 The quotations are selected from Ambrose's *Expositio in Lucam* 56–62 PL 15
   1818–19. To combat docetism, Ambrose maintained that Christ's agony was
   real, but attributed it to anything but self-pity.

his death.[29] Any diligent researcher will find among the other commentators the same diversity of opinion on this text.

But it is perhaps surprising that they so dread to ascribe to Christ a dread of death when they have no qualms about ascribing to him, more or less unanimously, two different wills, the one divine and the other human, and not merely different by nature, but actually in conflict: what the one wants the other rejects. Similarly they give Christ two sets of passions, of the mind and of the flesh; the one yearns for death and the other rejects it. The church has stamped its authority so firmly on this theory of the two wills that anyone who thinks differently is branded a heretic.[30] Some commentaries suggest that he shunned death because of the condition he had assumed, others that it was not natural but an exception to what was ordained.[31]

They have even greater problems with these words of Christ: 'My Father, if it be possible, let this cup pass from me; nevertheless, not as I will, but as you will.' And 'Father, if you will, take this cup from me.'[32] First, why did Christ need to pray at all, since he was not only omniscient, even as a man, but also omnipotent? Second, why did he pray, when he knew his prayer would not be answered? If he was praying not to be killed by the Jews, he could foresee that he must be killed; if he was praying for the Jews not to be killed, he knew that they would be killed. If it was that they should not perish for causing his death, he knew that great numbers would perish along with Judas. Finally, why pray for something that his Father opposed? This is the most perplexing thing: why, as if unsure of his Father's will, or of his power, does he say, 'If you wish,' and 'If it be possible,' as if there were something he did not know?

Augustine, troubled by this and many similar questions, changed his mind over Christ's dismay and alarm and decided that all these passages

* * * * *

29 Hilary De Trinitate 10.29 PL 10 368. Erasmus returns to Hilary's commentary in his annotation on Luke 22:44; according to Hilary, some Greek manuscripts of Luke omitted the drops of bloody sweat and the comforting angel in order to conceal Christ's human weakness. Erasmus implies that Hilary disapproved of this manipulation, though the text does not support him.

30 Doubtless a reference to the Council of Constantinople in 681, where the monothelitist heresy was finally condemned; cf n129 below on Bede.

31 Dispensatio in Latin, in the sense of a special divine provision (cf Eph 3:2) rather than in the more familiar ecclesiastical sense of the relaxation of a law in a particular case. Erasmus has in mind Ambrose Expositio in Lucam 57–8 PL 15 1818; he discusses the question more fully later (53).

32 Matt 26:39; Luke 22:42

referred only to his body.[33] Jerome and Ambrose,[34] on the other hand, give several different explanations for his sorrow, either because they leave us free to choose any one of them, or because they do not think it unreasonable to suggest several causes for a single effect. The head and the body are one; Christ took his members' frailty upon himself, and it was for them that he was filled with distress, dismay, sorrow, alarm, and agony; for them he sweated blood (all these expressions are in the Gospels). It was for them that he prayed to the Father that the cup of bitter death should pass from him, that is, from his body, from Peter, from Paul, from the martyrs. Similarly, hanging on the cross, he prayed to his Father in the words of the psalm I quoted earlier, some of which are quite inappropriate to the Virgin's son, such as 'God, my God, why have you forsaken me? The confession of my sins is far from saving me.'[35] What can he mean by 'my sins,' when the Scriptures testify that 'he did no sin and no guile was found in his mouth'?[36] Augustine has a neat answer: 'He made our sins his own, in order to make his righteousness our righteousness. On the cross he made our sins his own, and similarly, as his ordeal drew nigh, he made our trepidation his own and prayed for our deliverance from death, not his own.'[37] Now this is a reading full of piety and thus especially likely to stir love for the Saviour in our hearts. And it extricates us with ease from all the problems caused by the wording of his prayer. But we are still, apparently, stuck in the same mud[38] on the question of the alarm he felt.

In fact you gave a different reason for his alarm, even though it conflicts with the circumstantial evidence available to us. He did not dread death for himself, he was not distressed for himself, and yet, you said, his emotions were real. 'For he did not,' as Ambrose says, 'take on the appearance of incarnation, but the reality. He must therefore have taken on pain, in order to conquer sorrow, not to shut it out.'[39] If you are also arguing here

* * * * *

33 That is, to the church; cf n27 above.
34 Cf nn19 and 28 above.
35 A quotation from Ps 22 (Vulg 21):1; only the first part appears in Matt 27:46 and Mark 15:34. This utterance of Christ was always problematical and is omitted by Luke and John from their later accounts (cf Kasper 118); but to quote the first verse of a psalm often implied the whole psalm, and Ps 22 (Vulg 21) does end as a song of thanksgiving.
36 1 Pet 2:22
37 Augustine *Enarratio in psalmum* 21 3 PL 36 172. The preceding passage summarizes Augustine's reading of the episode.
38 *Adagia* I iv 99
39 Ambrose *Expositio in Lucam* 56 PL 15 1818

that Christ was truly alarmed, but by the danger to his body not to himself,
I must ask, along with the modern theologians, why do you refuse to allow
that death filled Christ with dread, even if it were only an emotion Jesus
assumed temporarily and not an essential part of the nature he assumed?
I know that you are generally quite happy to disagree with the new breed of
theologians, but let us carry out the test recommended by Plato in the *Parmenides*[40] and see whether the view I share with them is in any way unreasonable. If it is not, why should we be distracted by some other, more con-
trived reading; why abandon a simple, satisfying, and well-tried solution
and go looking for one that is nowhere to be found in the Scriptures?

'But,' you will say, 'there is much in your view that is unreasonable.
It detracts from the perfect charity and the perfect obedience of Jesus. It is
hardly evidence of an all-consuming love to pray for deliverance from death,
when the martyrs, in their love for him, went to their death filled with eager
joy, when Paul wished for it, Andrew thirsted for it, Martin longed for it;[41]
and it is more consistent with unquestioning and absolute obedience to accept willingly whatever your father desires than to say something like, "I do
not want to die if, with your consent, I can escape; but if you want me to
die, I shall disregard my wishes and obey yours." If Christ loved to perfection both humankind and his Father, why does he reject the opportunity to
redeem us? Why does he dread obeying his Father's wishes, even though
one of love's qualities is to accept the unacceptable? Why does he pray to be
spared the cup that God offers him? Any rebellion on his part must detract
from his love for us; any refusal, for whatever reason, must undermine his
absolute obedience to his Father. Neither befits him, who was the peerless
paragon of perfect love and perfect obedience.'

You went on to argue that the same person could not have said, 'Get behind me, Satan; shall I not drink the cup my Father gave me?'[42] and 'If it be
possible, take this cup from me,' unless the latter applies to the death of the
Jews, the destruction of Jerusalem, the desertion of the shocked disciples,
and the sufferings of the martyrs. Look how many reasons you have to invent because you dread to admit the only one that is both uncomplicated and
true. I suppose, Colet, that it was like a foaming reef in the distance, which

* * * * *

40 In the Platonic dialogue that bears his name, the Eleatic philosopher Parmenides uses the method of division by contradictories or opposites to cast
doubt on his own theories; on the method, see *Parmenides* 136C.

41 On Paul see eg Acts 20:24, 21:13. Erasmus takes Andrew as an exemplary
martyr below, 45. St Martin of Tours was a fourth-century bishop particularly
venerated for his charity; cf *De vidua christiana* CWE 66 200 and n41.

42 Mark 8:33 conflated with John 18:11

frightened you, as it did Jerome,[43] into trimming your sails and changing course.[44] You would rather make a long and tortuous detour to avoid it than steer a straight course. But scan it more carefully, and you may find that what looks so fearsome and dangerous from a distance is in fact a wraith, not a reef.[45] Beware: while busily avoiding imaginary rocks you may run aground on real ones.

However, my present purpose is not to refute the view that you accept, but to support my view, which you reject. So let me try to show you, by that traditional method of argument used in the Academy,[46] that Jesus, as a complete and real human being by the nature he received from the Virgin Mother, dreaded and shrank from his own death; that human emotion made him pray for deliverance, and human will made him refuse; that it was for this that he knew distress, became sorrowful unto death, sweated drops of blood, and felt agony. And that all this in no way detracts from his obedience, which was, I believe, entire and perfect in him, nor from his love for us, which was greater than any love could be. Indeed, far from diminishing his love for humankind, these emotions greatly enhance it. Finally, though we deny him the outward signs of eager joy, which are in your view inseparable from charity, yet we must allow to him, and to him alone, an inward joy unmatched by all the martyrs.

What more could you ask, Colet? 'Fine promises,' you will say, 'but now you must fulfil them.' I shall try. But while you are considering the quality of my arguments, you must temporarily put from your mind your own views, of which you are so very fond that you tried to impose them on me less by argument than by entreaty. First of all, I think you will agree with me that our redeemer Jesus took on the complete nature of a man, with all the feelings that would have existed in Adam had he continued in his original state: a sensible body and a sensible soul subject to the natural passions. Nor will you deny something that Augustine and many others confirm, and that Bonaventure skilfully explains in his commentary on the *Sentences*, book three, distinction fifteen:[47] Jesus deigned to take on not only a human nature, but even one that was subject to many of our

* * * * *

43 The explanations attributed to Colet here tally almost exactly with those given by Jerome in his commentary on Matthew (n19 above).
44 Cf *Adagia* I ix 60.
45 Erasmus plays on *nubes*, 'cloud,' and *rupes*, 'rock.'
46 That is, using Socrates' method of proceeding by question and answer
47 In his commentary on the seminal *Liber sententiarum* of Peter Lombard 3.15.1.b–d; *Opera omnia* 10 vols (Florence 1882–1902) III 327–42. For a discussion of Bonaventure as a representative scholastic theologian on this question see Tracy 34–6.

afflictions. Read his self-portrait in the psalm, 'My soul is full of afflictions,'[48] and Paul's confirmation of it, 'It behoved him to be like his brothers in all things.'[49]

He took these afflictions upon himself, of course, in order to cure us of them. Yet he did not take them all. For every affliction is either a sin, or the result of sin, what the theologians call chastisement.[50] He was untouched by our sinful afflictions, and of course it would be quite inappropriate that he, who was to intercede for the sins of all, should himself harbour a sin for which he must intercede. As for the 'chastisements,' he took on only as many as would be of service to us without compromising his dignity, or, as Bonaventure puts it, only those that are in general attendant upon the universal condition of fallen humanity; he dispensed with those that befall us as individuals. Among the latter are diseases, physical disabilities, mental defects arising from physical defects, deformity, monstrosity, and similar things. He was immune to all these, both as an affront to his dignity and as immaterial to our salvation. Among our universal afflictions are numbered the helplessness of childhood and the frailty of old age, thirst, hunger, weariness, sorrow, pain, drowsiness,[51] and the thousand trials of our earthly life. Although these arise from sin, they are not in themselves sins and can be found alongside blameless virtue, and so Christ took them to himself when he took our nature, as a penalty by which to atone for our impiety. He took on many, but not all: not, for example, our inclination towards sinfulness, born of Adam's sin though not in itself a sin; nor yet our lack of knowledge, a penalty of original sin and something we all share.

But although I attribute to Christ a child's helplessness and inability to speak, I do not thereby take away the perfect wisdom that entered his soul at birth and from that moment, without ceasing, enlightened him. The same is true of our reluctance to do good, something that afflicts almost all of us, but which is caused by personal failings; it comes later in life, an affliction not of the whole race but of the individual. Finally, since Christ took on the kind of existence enjoyed by Adam before his sin, then (according to some) he did not take on the necessity of dying, which binds the rest of us together. However, I will leave that undecided. But why should we so dread

* * * * *

48 Ps 88 (Vulg 87):3, quoted by Bonaventure
49 Heb 2:17
50 *Malum poenae*, literally, 'an affliction as punishment' (for original sin)
51 *Dormituritio*, a word apparently coined by Erasmus; later (39) he uses the equally rare verb *dormiturire*.

to ascribe to Christ this dread of death, often a more painful affliction than death itself, and so much a part of the human condition that it carries no hint of sin – especially since he was both a perfect man and, as far as was possible, a party to our afflictions?

In fact, if you will allow me to address you a little more philosophically, I shall venture to say – possibly with the approval of some theologians, and leaving to one side the question of sin – that it is only human nature to dread death, and that, such is the human condition, there would have been a place for it even in the state of innocence. Sin is indeed contrary to nature, and we are driven to it only by a corruption of nature. Piety is something completely natural, and it is only because our original nature was corrupted that we ever deviate from it. Since death is truly the offspring of sin[52] and the enemy of nature, which yearns to live for ever, then it is by nature so terrifying to every creature that even the brute beasts and, I might almost say, the very plants (to which some attribute a dormant soul)[53] recoil at nature's urging from anything hostile or dangerous. Nothing is more hostile to nature than death, whose role is to bring extinction, from which every living being shrinks. And the more precious something vulnerable is, the more terrifying is the agent of its destruction. But nothing vulnerable is more precious than life, and above all human life. Therefore the Stoics, who generally expect rather more of their wise man than human frailty can bear, not only will allow him this dread of death, but even give it the leading place among the 'first principles of nature.'[54] For the earliest lesson that nature teaches us is to avoid, at first instinctively but later by reasoning too, anything that threatens her gentle rule, and still more anything that may destroy it entirely, and in every way to protect and cherish our existence.

If our fear were the result of guilt or corruption, then I agree that Christ could not be assumed to share it with us. But it is highly illogical to ascribe to him a complete human nature and yet to deny him something so totally inseparable from nature. If it is equally natural for the soul to be pained by present troubles and to be afflicted by those that are to come, why do we not attribute both feelings to Christ, as a man, or else deny him both? In fact I shall give you clear proof that he had reason to fear death not only as other mortals do, but even more keenly than anyone else.

* * * * *

52 Cf Rom 5:12; James 1:15.
53 Aristotle *Historia animalium* 7.1 588b and *De anima* 2.2–4 413–16
54 The phrase is in Greek and is found in Aulus Gellius *Noctes Atticae* 12.5.7, attributed to 'the philosophers of old.'

I know of three things, at least, that can intensify dread: the value of whatever is under threat, the magnitude of the threat – and the knowledge of both. Should we mere mortals, who deserve to die, be somehow threatened with death, how we tremble, how we blench! Yet the worth of our existence is infinitely lower than Christ's: how little we understand the value of our existence! We may dread extinction, but our fears are never so overwhelming that we do not hope for something better. If there is no hope at all to buoy us up, then our lack of knowledge comes to the rescue: the less we know about death's bitterness, the less we dread it.

Moreover, the impact of this affront to nature is all the keener and sharper on those who are by nature worthier and nobler than the rest. No human body was ever nobler than Christ's, no soul more worthy. Thus the impact on him was more painful by far than on anyone else, whether of the wounds that hurt his body and through it his soul, or of those that directly struck at his soul's essence. Thus we cannot compare the lowliness of our clay to the excellence of his, the pain of our death to the torment of his, the uncertainty of our fears to the absolute clarity and certainty of his foresight, nor our ignorance to his foreknowledge. Is it any wonder that such a man, a man so self-aware, should have been terrified by the kind of death that he could not merely foresee with his mind's eye, but actually behold spread out, as it were, before his eyes, since he had complete foreknowledge of every detail of his torments? For this reason Jerome calls this the 'propassion' (the Greek is προπάθεια), meaning the beginning of passion.[55] But the first onslaughts of dreadful experiences are the most painful.

At this point, Colet, I can easily guess what you are murmuring in reply as you read on. 'Although it may be human,' you say, 'to shudder at death, surely no one would claim that it is characteristic of someone so very brave as Christ to dread a death that was to be both glorious and salutary, and to show his dread in so remarkable a manner. When I contemplate the human nature that he assumed and the horrors of his death, when I think of his sensitivity of body and soul, keener by far than any other, and his total

* * * * *

55 Jerome *Commentarius in Matheum* 4.26.37 PL 26 197, following Origen's *Commentarii in psalmos* 4.5 PG 12 1141 and 1144. As Erasmus recognizes later (57), Jerome intended the term to suggest something less than the full suffering of the passion; Christ's higher powers were not overthrown by the lower, as that would be inappropriate in the model of human perfection. Jerome also uses the term to distinguish between an innocent impulse (*propassio*) and a culpable desire (*passio*), in his commentary on Matt 5:28 PL 26 38; Erasmus dismisses this in relation to Christ below, 57.

foreknowledge, I do indeed see many reasons why he should have been more paralysed by terror than any mortal; but conversely, when I turn my gaze upon his charity, his obedience, and his bravery, I expect to see eager joy and readiness to suffer. Of course I admit that someone paralysed by the fear of death is human, but clearly I cannot call him a brave man when his shaking limbs ooze bloody drops of sweat, when I see his sorrow, continuing unto death, or as bitter as death, when I hear his prayer for deliverance from death. And it is the mark of charity to be overwhelmed by other people's afflictions, not one's own.'

I shall answer you on charity and obedience shortly. But for the moment I shall merely ask whether or not you call brave someone who is paralysed when a terrible danger bears down on him. What do you think makes for bravery? To be insensible to things that are dangerous and hostile to nature? But that is so far from what I think of as brave, that I would call such a person inhuman, rather, or stupid and lacking self-awareness. Nature implanted in us an affection for the essentials of life, teaching us to pursue whatever is conducive to survival and to recoil from whatever harms us. It is no sign of bravery to take arms against nature, like the Giants.[56] For 'bravery is the knowledge of what is endurable or unendurable,' according to Socrates' definition.[57] Or, if you prefer, 'the steadfast performance of honest endeavours.' And shameless shirking is called cowardice or idleness.[58]

Thus bravery is not insensitivity to these threats to nature, but rather the ability to endure and overcome them with a steadfast heart. It follows that someone is not lacking in bravery if, when danger approaches, he shudders inwardly, his face turns pale, his heart beats faster, his blood ebbs away, and his suffering wrings from him a groan; but rather it is someone whose fear of danger leads him to refuse some noble undertaking – indeed the brave are all the braver since they have had to overcome a natural desire to flee. It is honourable to plunge, unbidden, into danger and hardship, but it is natural to be afraid and natural, also, to feel pain. For the effect of feeling pain in the present or fearing it in the future is the same, though in the one case the pain begins in the body and spreads to the mind, while in the

* * * * *

56 A reference to the myth of the Titans, first related in Hesiod's *Theogony*, and frequently used by Erasmus to illustrate arrogance and unnatural ambition; eg *Adagia* III x 93 and *Ciceronianus* CWE 28 376 and 397
57 Cf Plato *Protagoras* 360D, but probably quoted from Aulus Gellius *Noctes Atticae* 12.5.13. The second definition is akin to Erasmus' own in *De conscribendis epistolis* CWE 25 109.
58 The Latin *ignavia* has the sense of both 'idleness' and 'cowardice.'

other suffering starts in the mind and overflows into the body. Thus anyone unmoved by the imminent threat of some terrible danger is either unaware of his peril or simply brutish and stupid; anyone insensible to pain when it starts is like a block of wood,[59] less than human, in fact barely alive. Certainly neither is wise. No fool can be called brave. Infants, drunks, and madmen will take a sword-thrust with a laugh. Why? Because they do not understand the danger. And that is why we think of them as pitiable, not brave.

By contrast Virgil, in depicting the extraordinary bravery of his character Aeneas, is not afraid to give him all the outward signs of alarm, shuddering, trembling, groaning, and so on. For example, when a storm suddenly breaks at sea, he writes, 'At once Aeneas' limbs give way in a chill of terror / And he groans.' Again, hearing Polydorus' voice, the hero says, 'I was struck dumb; my hair stood on end and my voice stuck in my throat.' He often ascribes similar reactions to the Trojans, who were renowned for their bravery, for example when they heard the Harpies: 'At this my comrades' blood was chilled and froze / In sudden dread.' Again, Virgil will not conceal the painful struggle in the hero's heart when he must leave people and places that are naturally dear to us all. He writes, 'He buries his anguish deep in his heart, / And feels deep sorrow in his mighty breast.'[60] Scholars observe the same device in Homer's poetry; he will depict terror in cowards and heroes alike, but not in the same way. Although these writers will allow a brave character to groan, turn pale, or shiver, they draw the line at unseemly wailing, girlish lamentations, or cries of impotent rage. But, you may say, is it not foolish when constructing an ideal model of bravery to give him reactions so different from approved notions of bravery? I should reply, to those who accuse Homer and Virgil of being foolish here, that they have little sense themselves. I call that the kind of foolishness that Quintilian lists among the faults of the orator.[61]

Our authors did not eliminate fear from their heroes, but used it discriminatingly, aware that there is a kind of terror that is steadfast and heroic, arising not from cowardice but from nature, and found, of necessity, even

* * * * *

59 A familiar image used by Terence; cf CWE 28 501 n101.
60 The quotations are from the *Aeneid* 1.92–3, 3.48, 3.259–60, and 1.209 coupled with 4.448 to convey Aeneas' similar reaction to leaving his home in Troy and, later, his mistress Dido.
61 Probably a reference to Quintilian *Institutiones oratoriae* 1.1.8, also noted in the *Antibarbari* CWE 23 28:20; Quintilian is condemning the semi-educated who seek arrogantly to impose their half-baked views on others.

in the very bravest of us. Aristippus once turned white.[62] So, in another storm, did a certain Stoic, commended but not named by Gellius,[63] when ceaseless gales were hammering the ship, the ink-black sky was lowering, smoking fireballs were raining down and typhoons threatening to send the ship under at any moment. However, one man was quite unmoved by the danger, some nameless rogue, a rich Asiatic, says the author, and a worthless, abandoned libertine; soon after, as the storm abated, he reproached the philosopher for being afraid. Which of these would you call brave? Perhaps neither; but if we must choose one, it would have to be the philosopher.

'But he turned pale,' you say. Of course: he was human. Wise, certainly, learned, brave, a philosopher – a Stoic, no less – who had learned and taught that death is neither bad, nor wrong, nor fearsome to the wise. Yes, he was all these things, but he could not, even so, cease to be human. He bowed to nature's command and gave way to terror; the other, heedless, careless, did not even blink, so sluggish was his torpor. It is a strange phenomenon that he alone, so spineless when pleasure beckoned, should appear fearless when danger arose – but it was an illusion. Do you suppose that, when the two Decii made that glorious decision to sacrifice themselves to save their country and flung themselves on the enemies' swords, their blood did not run cold and their hearts beat faster? That Mutius Scaevola was no whit terrified as he entered the enemy camp alone? That Marcus Curtius felt nothing as he spurred his horse and galloped into the yawning chasm? And Marcus Attilius Regulus, as he returned to the Punic camp? And Codrus, king of Attica? And Menoeceus the Theban?[64] Did they all feel nothing?

* * * * *

62 Aristippus of Cyrene, a disciple of Socrates; the allusion is to Aulus Gellius *Noctes Atticae* 19.1.10, though a more common version of this story is that Aristippus was moved from his calm not by a storm but by the discovery that he had boarded a pirate ship.
63 Erasmus borrows much of his descriptive language from the story told by Aulus Gellius *Noctes Atticae* 19.1.1–9.
64 All famous examples of self-sacrifice; cf *Ciceronianus* CWE 28 385. Publius Decius Mus, father and son, restored the Romans' fortunes in battle by this means (Livy 8.9 and 10.28); Mutius Scaevola entered the besieging Etruscans' camp to assassinate their chief Porsenna and, captured, convinced him of his danger by thrusting his right hand into a brazier (Livy 2.12); Marcus Curtius sacrificed himself to fulfil an oracle (Livy 7.6). Regulus, a Roman consul released by the Carthaginians to make peace, returned to their camp to face torture after failing deliberately in his mission; his case is discussed at length by Cicero *De officiis* 3.26–31 and by St Augustine *De civitate Dei* 1.15 PL 41 28–9 (see also 5.18 PL 41 162–5 on the other Romans here). Codrus was the legendary last king of Athens, who allowed himself to be killed in battle to fulfil an oracle

The history books are full of virtuous heroes who volunteered for glorious death; do you imagine that they were completely unmoved as they stared danger in the face, and merely charged in like wild beasts to meet their fate? If so, far from singing the praises of bravery, you would be denying its very essence. For they were either less than brave, or never brave at all, if they did not know or feel the danger they faced. But on the contrary, these men were sufficiently intelligent to know that the risks were great, and sufficiently human to feel, as they set forth, their hearts lurch, their blood ebb away, their pulse beat faster; but they were brave, and none of this could make them swerve from steadily fulfilling the obligations of the brave.

If you were watching a man fighting bravely in the line, would you immediately brand him a coward if he changed colour, if his hair stood on end, if he let out a groan? You would do him an injustice. But if he deserted his post, threw down his shield, and turned tail to run, then of course you would be right to accuse him of cowardice. The law prescribes a reward for bravery.[65] Will you put the case against him, alleging at once that the law does not apply to him, that he is no brave man, merely because his colour and his voice faded away just before the fight – and, you might add, because he failed even to control what cannot decently be mentioned? Even a moderately skilled defence lawyer will find it easy to destroy your case with a 'definition,'[66] explaining that to be brave does not mean to be unafraid as danger draws near, but to face it bravely, endure it steadfastly, and win through to the end. 'My physical and mental agitation,' he will say, 'was not the result of any vice or virtue, but of nature and necessity. What makes me brave is that my country's safety is more important to me than my own well-being and that I did not shirk the combat, and on those grounds I demand the reward decreed by the law. Shall I be cheated of my prize, though I overcame nature herself as well as the enemy?' I would go further; he should be deemed twice brave, because for love of his countrymen he dismissed his own feelings along with the danger and, braver yet, mastered himself before routing the enemy.

* * * * *

(Valerius Maximus 5.6), while Menoeceus ('Menicaeus' in the early editions), son of Creon, killed himself to atone to the gods for the slaying of the dragon by Cadmus, a story dramatized by Euripides in the *Phoenissae.*
65 Perhaps a reference to Roman law, which, for instance, specified the reward for those who rescued their comrades in battle or threw down besieging enemies from the walls: cf *Institutio principis christiani* CWE 27 265–6 and n14.
66 *Finitio*, a rhetorical term explained by Quintilian *Institutiones oratoriae* 7.3.2 as a brief, pertinent, and lucid exposition of a matter

Will you riposte with the barbarian slave in Livy, who suddenly attacked and slew the Carthaginian Hasdrubal for having killed his master? Though seized at once by the guards, he wore the look of a man who has escaped, and even under the most appalling torture his expression was such that he seemed to be laughing.[67] Or that fierce gladiator from the imperial school who used to laugh, they say, as the surgeons cut into his wounds?[68] But by the same token you can throw in the whole regiment of gladiators, who will dash into combat like wild beasts.[69] And alongside them, all those desperate people who take their own lives, and finally those pitiful felons whom we have often seen going to the scaffold with a smile, joking with the bystanders, cursing their judges, and generally behaving, on the point of death, as if they were merely drunk.[70] Shall we call them brave, since nothing can terrify them and no ordeal upset them? Or shall we call them mindless, brutish, and stupid?

Will you say that someone is not brave because his expression changes when he suddenly treads on a snake, or sees a ghost, or hears a sudden clap of thunder? The person you are imagining is not brave, but ἀνάλγητος, ἀναίσθητος, ἀπαθής, that is, insensible, insensate, and unfeeling. Panaetius, the most learned of the Stoics, does not insist that his wise man should practise ἀναλγησία, insensibility, and ἀπάθεια, lack of feeling, and indeed considers them incompatible with being human.[71] Ambrose exempts Christ from both, as follows: 'Nor should people be praised for their bravery, if they are more stunned than hurt when they take a wound.'[72]

Ἀναλγησία and ἀπάθεια seem to apply more to pain in the mind, ἀναισθησία to physical pain. Scotus calls the first of these tristitia, sorrow, and says that only physical pain should, strictly speaking, be called dolor, pain.[73]

* * * * *

67 Livy 21.2; Erasmus quotes the passage almost word for word.

68 Quoted from Aulus Gellius Noctes Atticae 12.5.13

69 By this Erasmus probably means hired soldiers in general, a target of his reproaches in Querela pacis, Dulce bellum inexpertis, and similar pieces; cf J.D. Tracy The Politics of Erasmus (Toronto 1978) 88–90 and passim.

70 Erasmus uses the same example in De contemptu mundi CWE 66 143.

71 Panaetius was a Rhodian Stoic much praised by Cicero in De officiis, though the source for this remark is Aulus Gellius Noctes Atticae 12.5.10. The Greek terms can be used in the positive sense of 'indifference to the world' or in the negative senses that Erasmus prefers here.

72 Ambrose Expositio in Lucam 10.56 PL 15 1818

73 John Duns Scotus (d 1308) is often cited by Erasmus as the archetypal scholastic quibbler. Here he is quoting Scotus' commentary on the Sententiae of Peter Lombard 3.15 Ad solutionem; eg Tertius liber super sententias (Paris: J. Granjon, 1513) fol 30r.

That man had all the subtlety of a Chrysippus;[74] his view is based, he claims, on something Augustine wrote: 'Fleshly pain [*dolor*] is merely a hurt given to the soul by the flesh. Similarly, pain [*dolor*] in the mind, which is called sorrow [*tristitia*], is the mind's distaste for things that happen to us against our will.'[75] As if it were not obvious from this text that, on the contrary, pain [*dolor*] is an affliction found in both mind and body, while sorrow exists only in the mind. In fact those who use words carefully very often use 'sorrow' to describe a facial expression, and use 'pain' more often of the mind than of the body. Astonishingly sharp, those eyes – sharper even than Lynceus'[76] – which enabled Scotus to see things that are not there!

But I digress: when it comes to those passions with which nature has endowed us, the philosophers expect even the wisest to practise μετριότης, moderation, and not δέρησις, abstinence.[77] And the theologians are so reluctant to attribute insensibility and insensitivity to Christ that they will not even allow him complete ἀοργησία, the inability to be angered. Moreover, the church condemned as heretics those who sought to ascribe to Christ an impassive nature completely incapable of feeling pain.[78] But, as I said earlier, it is more natural to dread some evil that is yet to come than to be troubled by one that is already here. Nature planted this principle all the more firmly in us because, in her judgment, it is vital for survival to avoid anything that might harm us. If that should fail, then we must be brave and suffer what cannot be avoided. Do we not often see people endure with great

* * * * *

74 Chrysippus was a prolific Stoic philosopher of Tarsus, renowned for his exploitation of the ambiguities of language; see Aulus Gellius *Noctes Atticae* 11.12.1. Erasmus used him as a byword for tortuous reasoning in the *Antibarbari* CWE 23 56 and 77, and again in the *Moria* CWE 27 128.

75 Augustine *De civitate Dei* 14.15 PL 41 424; in an earlier chapter (9.4 PL 41 258–60) on the perturbations of the mind, Augustine had discussed several of the themes and examples here.

76 *Adagia* II i 54; Lynceus was the proverbially sharp-eyed Argonaut.

77 Μετριότης is a familiar term in Greek philosophy (eg Plato *Republic* 560D, Aristotle *Politics* 1315b2); δέρησις is an unfamiliar term which gave trouble to Erasmus' compositors. It presumably represents τήρησις ('vigilance'); the form here may be compared with the contemporary pronunciation of *synteresis*, meaning literally 'preservation, careful guarding or watching' and a scholastic term for conscience: see *Oxford English Dictionary* (1971 edition) under 'synderesis' and 'synteresis.'

78 Probably a reference to the Council of Chalcedon in 451, where the monophysite position was finally condemned and the dogma of Christ's two natures explicitly defined. On heterodoxy in the early church, see my introductory note.

bravery afflictions whose approach filled them with helpless terror? Why is that? Because anticipation makes for a harder and more difficult struggle with nature. Apparently even the most rudimentary creatures can sense very quickly the approach of danger and, as if filled with dread, draw themselves in. Aristotle writes that even sponges can sense the sounds made by the fishermen; they contract and cling on more tightly, and can be pulled off only with difficulty.[79] If nature implanted a dread of extinction in sponges, will you deny it to a human?

However, the books tell us that a number of outstanding individuals did have sufficient strength of character to face death with a calm and resolute countenance. For example, the Athenian general Phocion was so unafraid at the point of death that he made sport of his wife and of the poison too. When she let out a womanish wail and cried, 'Husband, must you die an innocent?' he replied with a smile, 'What do you mean, wife? Would you rather I died guilty?'[80] Then the supply of poison ran out because so many victims had drunk it before him, and the executioner was reluctant to make any more himself; Phocion told his friends to pay the man, adding ironically that in Athens you were not even allowed to die for free. When Socrates was condemned by the judges' ballot, his habitual expression changed not at all. Later, when the day of execution was very near, Crito came upon him sleeping peacefully. Then, when told that the ship from Delos would soon arrive, he was still completely unmoved. On the final day he behaved no differently than in the rest of his life, debating merrily with his friends and interspersing serious topics with those sudden jokes of his. When he drained the hemlock he looked as if he were drinking wine. Finally, as he breathed out his soul, his last words were a joke to his friend Phaedo, more distressed than he by his death, telling him to pay for the cock that he had promised to sacrifice to Aesculapius.[81]

Now, since it is beyond dispute that Phocion was the most principled of all commanders and Socrates the most saintly and blameless of philosophers,

* * * * *

79 Aristotle *Historia animalium* 5.16 548b
80 This jest is attributed to Socrates, rather than to Phocion, by Diogenes Laertius 2.35; the following story of the poison is in Plutarch's *Life of Phocion* 36. Erasmus brings Socrates and Phocion together again in a similar list of heroes in the *Ciceronianus* CWE 28 385.
81 The details concerning Socrates' death are found in Plato *Crito* 43A–D and *Phaedo* 117–18. His execution was postponed until the return of the state galley from its annual mission to Delos for the religious ceremony commemorating Theseus' exploit against the Minotaur. Socrates' final remark refers ironically to Aesculapius, the god of healing.

there can be no reason to doubt their bravery and accuse them of torpor, insensibility, or dull-wittedness. I shall not take you to court, Colet, to determine whether many of these had such strength of character that when facing danger they did not experience the same emotions as ordinary mortals. Their example does prove that, especially among the wise and the good, the human spirit may remain unconquered. But I will not allow you to measure bravery by these examples, which owe more to their natural inclinations than to moral principles, to their physical and not their intellectual make-up. Socrates was not necessarily brave because his expression did not change as he took the hemlock; nor would he have been a coward if in the same circumstances he had happened to turn pale.

The signs of fear and fearlessness are found alike in the brave and the coward, the wise man and the senseless half-wit. If nature has endowed me with more hot blood or thicker spirits than others, does that make me braver? Conversely, if she has given me colder blood, and less of it, together with thinner spirits, does that necessarily make me less bold?[82] I cannot change nature and stop myself blenching if I suddenly come upon some horrifying sight; but I can exercise self-control and stop even death deflecting me from the straight path. Thus fearlessness, since it depends on one's physical constitution or some other natural cause, should not be required of the wise, nor mistaken for bravery in those who are merely ἀνάλγητος or ἀναίσθητος, insensible or insensate.

Those who have known war's tumults at first hand tell us that, as soon as the mail-clad lines are drawn up on either side, with the horns blaring out their harsh anthems, the trumpets sounding their deadly taratantara,[83] the terrible war-cries rising to heaven from each side, then usually the braver the soldier, the paler he becomes, and the brasher the noise a man made as the battle began, the quicker he is to flee the field.

Quintilian has no objection if an orator, as he rises to speak, is pale and mildly apprehensive; it is the mark, he declares, of an intelligent speaker aware of the risks he runs. He even says that it had become the stock-in-

* * * * *

82 References to contemporary physiology, based ultimately on Aristotle (eg *De partibus animalium* 2.25–30 647–9). According to the theory of the four humours, someone in whom the sanguine humour predominated ('more hot blood') was considered naturally brave. Similarly, the thicker the vital spirits running through the arteries, the greater the vitality of the subject. Clearly Erasmus was not convinced of the connections made between physical and moral attributes.

83 There is a series of allusions here to famous descriptions of war in Horace *Odes* 4.14.29–30; Virgil *Aeneid* 8.2; and Ennius *Annales* 140 (143).

trade of all the most esteemed orators.[84] Demosthenes, the founder of Greek eloquence, was reluctant to rise and speak unless his features betrayed signs of nervousness.[85] Cicero will not deny that he was more nervous than anyone at the beginning of a speech,[86] and yet no one handled a greater number of more serious cases than he did – or with greater bravery. If on these grounds you charge Cicero with cowardice, he will instantly (being a ready speech-maker) countercharge you with ignorance and say you know nothing of the nature and meaning of bravery. The greater his natural dread, he will say, the more his bravery is to be honoured and applauded, since natural disabilities which come about through no fault of our own increase our opportunities to cultivate virtue.

Anything you cannot attribute to natural gifts may be added to the total of your virtuous deeds. Take a pair of brave men; if one of them was born with less and colder blood but simply ignores this natural disability, he deserves greater credit for bravery than the other, who is well provided with the hottest of hot blood, when in a similar crisis he too makes light of some dreadful danger. In the latter nature claims some of the credit for his conduct, while in the former everything results from his own virtue. Despite your efforts, you will diminish the glory attaching to bravery, not increase it, if you allow bravery itself fewer chances to shine.

I can see, Colet, that you have been shaking your head for some time and that so far you remain unconvinced. But patience: I shall not rest until I have answered every point. 'What are the Stoics to me,' you say, 'when I am discussing Christ?' And yet when we talk about Christ, who is the truth,[87] if the Stoics have said something that is not too far from the truth, it does not seem incongruous to be able to cite it. 'I do not care,' you say, 'however truly they spoke. But you have not even dealt fully with their views on the ideal wise man. Not one of the Stoics would allow the wise man συγκατάθεσις, or assent;[88] nor do all of them allow φαντασία, meaning

* * * * *

84 Quintilian *Institutiones oratoriae* 12.5.4
85 This trait is not apparently recorded of Demosthenes: in a similar passage in the *Moria* CWE 27 100, he is replaced by Plato, Theophrastus, and Isocrates.
86 Quintilian *Institutiones oratoriae* 11.1.44, and eg Cicero *Pro Milone* 1.1, repeated by Plutarch *Life of Cicero* 35.3
87 Cf John 14:6.
88 *Assensio*, assent to the reality of sensible appearances, which is voluntary, unlike our instinctive reactions to the sudden visions described next. In this passage Erasmus (or Colet) is following Epictetus as expounded by Aulus Gellius *Noctes Atticae* 19.1.15–20. On the Stoics' theories see also *Enchiridion* 5 CWE 66 44, and Cicero *Academicae quaestiones* 2.12.37 and *De fato* 17.

terror brought about by a sudden vision of evil. As Flaccus wrote of the Stoic sage, "If the world should collapse and fall about him, its ruins would find him unalarmed."[89] Moreover, even those who admit this kind of terror do not allow that it is an opportunity to act well, but merely a pardonable fault, to be ignored not commended, because such mental visions usurp rational thought and are thus beyond human control. Moreover, they do not allow their sage excessive or lasting terror, and allow it at all only when some sudden vision of great evil assaults the senses and stirs up disorder in the mind before its ruler, reason, can pass judgment on it. But as soon as reason perceives that this false vision of evil, which has terrorized the senses, is not in fact evil, then at once, wielding its sceptre, it soothes the feelings and calms the mind. Finally, did any Stoic ever allow his wise man to do what you say Christ did, to refuse to face death and to fear death? They will not allow him συγκατάθεσις, "assent," but you foist it on Christ; are not refusal and fear of death "assents to reality"?

'Terror and fear are not the same thing. The wise man may sometimes be terrified, but he fears nothing, since he believes that nothing need be feared except evil, and considers nothing evil except moral turpitude;[90] that therefore is the one thing he fears, but it does not terrify him. Why should it terrify him, when it lies in his own power to avoid it? Death, they say, is as natural as birth; it carries no moral taint and is thus to be feared only by fools. For what could be more foolish than to dread, as though it were the worst of all evils, an event that is by no means evil and is even a natural necessity? They also believe that the wise man will never fear the rest of nature's enemies, such as disease, hunger, thirst, and pain. If they are inevitable, say the Stoics, and if they really are evils, then why double the evil? If they are not evils, then fear of them is an evil in itself. If what you fear is not inevitable, then why draw down evil on yourself with your vain fears? In every one of these cases it is wrong to be afraid. Either one mistakenly takes for an evil something that is not, or one knows that something is not evil but none the less fears it, which is both foolish and illogical. But the Stoics' wise man is never mistaken or illogical.

'Now, let me list how many things that are unworthy of him you attribute to Christ, who is not merely wise, but the very fount of wisdom. First of all, how could he be terrified, when nothing unexpected could assail his senses, as he had complete foreknowledge of everything? How truly wicked to allege that some terrifying visions of evil could have seized

* * * * *

89 Horace *Odes* 3.3.7
90 A Stoic maxim cited eg by Cicero *De officiis* 3.29.106, and Aulus Gellius *Noctes Atticae* 12.5.7

Christ's reason and stunned or overthrown it, so that vain terrors and phantoms overwhelmed the composure of his senses, and overwhelmed him so completely that he oozed bloody drops from every pore, and so long that his distress persisted unto death! For I think that that is Jerome's reading of "My soul is sorrowful unto death": he suggests that death was not the cause of Christ's sorrow, but its end.[91] "But surely," you will say, "for a while Christ's reason was benumbed?" Not at all. Why then did he take so long to shake off his dread, painful as it was, of a non-existent evil? Why did he fear something that was not only not an evil, but the source of everything that is good for us? Why did he refuse something so desirable? What produced that state of mind in him, which could not be allowed to persist? And finally, even though a while ago you yourself removed from Christ any propensity to sin, you now give him the sort of emotions that most persistently tempt us to sin. Although you have just distanced him from any reluctance to act aright, you now foist on him a dread of death, even though that death was a work more pleasing to God and more meritorious than any other.'

You overwhelm me, Colet, with a heavy shower of weapons, as it were, which I could parry all at once by saying that the same feelings did indeed exist in Christ as in us, but in a different way and to a different effect. But I prefer to deal separately with the host of questions you have mustered.

First, I would ask you to concede that it is permissible, at need, to deviate from the Stoics' teachings; it is almost traditional to argue about the precise terms they use. Nothing, they say, is to be feared which is not evil, and nothing is evil except moral turpitude. Death is not morally wrong, and thus is not to be feared. It may suit the Stoics to agree that nothing may be called evil except moral turpitude, but how does that affect my case? Scripture teaches me that death is evil, in the verse 'God did not make death, and takes no pleasure in the destruction of the living.'[92] If God is the creator of all that is good, and is not the creator of death, then death is evil. 'It was the devil's spite that brought death into the world.'[93] If death is evil, why should it not also be feared? As a real man, Christ shrank from death as from something evil in itself, and born of evil. Unless I am mistaken, Ambrose is clearly saying the same in his commentary on Luke: 'And he was pained by it because he did not make it himself.'[94]

* * * * *

91 Jerome *Commentarius in Matheum* 4.26.38 PL 26 197; Jerome's view is that Christ remained sorrowful until he was able to deliver the apostles by his passion.
92 Wisd of Sol 1:13
93 Wisd of Sol 2:24
94 Ambrose *Expositio in Lucam* 10.58 PL 15 1818

Wait a moment; I know what you are going to say. 'He was pained,' you will claim, 'not by his own death, but by the death of all of us, as is made clear by the passage in Ambrose, which, with your rhetorician's trickery, you have omitted. "And perhaps," says Ambrose, "he is sorrowful because since Adam's fall we are all compelled to depart this life, and to begin the journey we have to die." Do you not understand that this refers not to Christ's death, but to ours?'

I agree, Colet, that the words are no help, but their theme supports my case. For if God was pained by our death because he did not make it, he must have been still more pained by his own, which he did not make either. And of course it caused him pain, not as a profitable work that was pleasing to God, but simply as death. Death is in itself evil, a necessary evil, at least, if not a moral evil, even though for our sake Christ turned this evil into good. As the means of our restoration, he longed for it passionately; as the offspring of sin,[95] it caused him grievous pain.

Next, you claim on similar grounds that I would foist on the Saviour reluctance to do good because he shrank from death, but I am depicting the whole nature of the man, complete with all his emotions, fear, sorrow, hope, joy, desire, anger, hatred, and any others that may be considered morally indifferent. 'But,' you will say, 'that is to endow him with those troublesome urges that impel the rest of us towards wickedness. It would seem worse than wicked to ascribe to Christ any trait that would encourage him to do wrong, since you admit yourself that he was entirely free not only from all sin, but from any kind of propensity to sin.'

On the contrary, Colet, I do not consider it wicked at all to give Christ these emotions, which certainly do lead to sin – but in us, not in him. As I say, he possessed the same emotions, but not in the same way or with the same effects. What Maro wrote in Platonic vein is true of us: 'Hence they fear, desire, sorrow, rejoice, nor see again / The free air, enclosed in darkness and a gloomy cell.'[96] Our passions always distract our reason, spurning right and pursuing wrong. Why should that be? Obviously through no fault of nature, but through our original sin, the vestiges of which are so deeply imbedded within us that, though our passions can indeed be curbed and restrained, they cannot be entirely eradicated. In us, therefore, through a corruption of nature, our passions in their blindness gravitate towards what

* * * * *

95 Cf James 1:15.
96 Virgil *Aeneid* 6.733–4; 'hence' refers to the imposition of the body upon the soul. Augustine quotes these famous lines in the same context in *De civitate Dei* 21.3 PL 41 711.

should be shunned and spurn what should be pursued; they enwrap our minds in shadows, dictate to our reason when they should obey it, and stir up endless disorder, either by pursuing or evading all the wrong things, or by pursuing or rejecting even the right things with too much ardour. Consequently most of them are transformed from mere misfortunes into excuses and opportunities for sin. But since Christ put on a human nature that was subject to many of the ills arising from original sin but free from any taint of sin itself, he could not in fact be lured towards evil by the passions natural to us. Rather, any that dwelt in him added to the total of his virtue and merit.

Nor must he be saddled with the defects that some authors claim are natural to us, such as ignorance, foolishness, an inclination towards evil, a reluctance to do good, because death is supposedly the debt we owe to nature; for they are alluding to fallen nature, not the nature that God created. I know that in common parlance any characteristic that has been with us since birth and is not produced by our experiences in life is called 'natural.' But by this we do not mean nature as created in the beginning, but nature corrupted by sin. Since Christ took nothing from fallen nature except the handicaps imposed on us as chastisement,[97] and there was in him no capacity for sin, I shall boldly ascribe to him the natural passions appropriate to mind and body respectively: grief, joy, hatred, fear, and anger in the mind; in the body, hunger, thirst, drowsiness,[98] weariness, suffering, death.

What am I subtracting from Christ's perfect goodness when I say that he knew hatred, if in him hatred was no more than the rejection of true evil? Why should I not affirm that he knew anger, if his anger was no more than a detestation of evil that in no way challenged or disturbed his use of reason, nor hindered his unbroken and serene contemplation of heaven? If ever we are pushed by our passions into a fall from grace, it is still entirely our own fault. The fact that we are tempted, far from being a sin in itself, becomes for pious souls a chance to earn great merit. Thus it is no surprise that his natural passions did not impel Christ towards sin, given that they offer so many of us the chance to do good; they did not plague him, because he had no share in original sin and was thus not constrained as we are by its vestiges within us. But more of this later.

* * * * *

97 Reading *poenae*, as in some early editions, and not *pene* (LB); on the sense, see n50 above.

98 *Dormiturire*, a verb absent from almost all dictionaries and perhaps coined by Erasmus; it did not appear until 1537 according to R.E. Latham *Revised Medieval Latin Word-List* (London 1965) 156.

Now, you said that my Stoics allow their sage only a moment of terror, such as may disturb the mind briefly until reason reasserts itself, and
that they will permit him such fleeting alarm only if a φαντασία, a terrible
vision, has suddenly burst upon his senses. Be that as it may, what exactly
do you mean by 'terror'? Is it a massive shock, an attack of panic, as it were,
which completely unhinges my reason and drives me out of my mind? Far
be it from me to attribute anything so monstrous to Christ. Or do you mean
by 'terror' a vexing, painful dread of impending evil, which certainly deals
a hard blow to the emotions, but does not unbalance the mind, and is not
necessarily produced by one of those terrible visions we spoke of, but instead is transmitted from the mind to the body? In fact, far from cutting
reason off, it is actually produced by our reason as it weighs the gravity of
the approaching evil.

I can see nothing to prevent either of these lasting for some time. For
the first kind (which Christ does not share with us) often damages people's
mental faculties so badly that they never return to their senses. The second
must necessarily last for as long as the impending evil hangs over us. The
Stoic in Gellius' story, which I told earlier,[99] was alarmed for as long as
the storm raged, and never regained his accustomed composure until the
sea subsided and the skies cleared. All that time his mind was far from
untroubled, and yet reason was not inactive within him. The philosopher
was battling against his thoughts, and could hardly be called brave had he
not done so. Our struggle is not with nature but with our own shortcomings.
Our dread of death is unnatural, and it would be wrong to ascribe to Christ
a struggle like ours. But there is no need to do so. He was not alarmed, as
the philosopher was, by an inescapable consequence of his humanity, and
he possessed a mind that could not be unhinged, as the Stoic's was.

Temptation lies in wait for us in the most ordinary and natural things;
almost everything that happens presents us with a challenge. Illness strikes
and must be fought, or it may crush the spirit and strip its victim of the
strength to resist. You recover, but here comes another battle: now you must
not succumb to some squalid pleasure. If disaster strikes, you must fight to
prevent it breaking your heart; if success comes, you must fight to stop it
going to your head. Thus the members experience the same feelings as the
head, but in a different way and for different reasons.

All this would be more than enough, Colet, if you were not so thoroughly enamoured of your own opinion. Even now, shaking your head,

* * * * *

99 See 29 above.

you declare yourself unconvinced and prepare to tighten the knots on me. 'This is a pretty speech,' you say, 'and you make the best of a bad case. But that is precisely why it cannot but seem to be a slight on Jesus' perfect charity if you suggest for any reason that he dreaded his own death. I grant you that it is natural to dread death, more natural even than to desire food. I grant you that it is unconnected with original sin. But the role of charity is to surmount nature and bring it to perfection. Hunger is one of nature's sternest tests, but exceptional love can shrug off its pangs. Death is a powerful opponent, but love is stronger[100] and can make death itself desirable and even pleasant. Epicurus believes that a clear conscience has immense power; he claims that, even inside Phalaris' bull, the wise man will cry, "I feel no pain; it's very pleasant."[101] If the mere semblance of virtue has such effect in a philosopher, will true and perfect charity have less effect in Christ? Granted, it is not a dereliction of duty to accept death with sorrow instead of willingly, eagerly, and joyfully, but it argues a lesser love.'

It seems to me that I cut through that knot earlier in the discussion, but let me clarify the point and speak, as the saying goes, a little more bluntly.[102] You say, Colet, that the most ardent lover will consider light, and even pleasant, what should be the heaviest burdens. 'If it is true,' you say, 'that to a lover nothing is difficult, and if passionate lovers take delight in any trial they must endure for the one who has fired their love; if we agree too that the Redeemer's love is so warm and so immense that all the loves of the whole human race fused into one could not compare with his affection, then why does he sweat with the dread of death? Why is he anguished? Why distressed? Why does he pray to be spared the cross? If he fears for the disciples, I can see that this is the lover's role; but if it is for his own death, for himself, then however ably you deploy the arts of persuasion, not even Pitho[103] herself could convince me that this is not a slight on the Redeemer's charity. Even allowing that nature played her allotted role, why did love fail to play its role? It may be natural to dread death, yet to be filled with

* * * * *

100 Cf Song of Sol 8:6.

101 Cf Ep 109:102–3, though the anecdote is attributed there merely to 'a philosopher.' See *Adagia* I x 86 on the brazen bull in which the tyrant Phalaris roasted his victims.

102 Latin *Minerva paulo pinguiore, Adagia* I i 37; see CWE 31 85–6 on this untranslatable image. The opening of the sentence alludes to the proverbial method of dealing with apparently insoluble problems; cf *Adagia* I i 6.

103 Pitho or Peitho, the goddess of persuasion, daughter of Mercury and Venus; cf *Ciceronianus* CWE 28 343 on her powers.

such abject terror is not the effect of nature pure and simple, but of nature corrupted and damned.

'Again, it is the role of charity to eliminate natural frailties. Peter panicked at the maidservant's words, lost all control, and denied Christ, having vowed only hours before to die for him.[104] Why? Because his love was still weak. He did indeed love Jesus, but not yet in the spirit. Fleshly love, human love, is frail and unequal to such storms. But once emboldened by the fire of the Holy Spirit, what did Peter do? He, who had so recently been paralysed by a maidservant's words, faced without fear both the elders and the judges and "went rejoicing from the sight of the council, because he was counted worthy to suffer reproach for Christ."[105] Obviously nothing could be more different than to be paralysed by fear and to go off rejoicing under threat of execution. As his love had grown, his fears had decreased; it is clear that God's love was working in him to perfect nature.

'So, to sum up rapidly, though it is natural to dread evil, such painful dread as this belongs not to our original nature, but to our fallen state. Though Christ took the latter upon himself (which I will grant you for the moment, to give me the right of reply), yet the power of his love drove out all its frailty and produced for him a quite different kind of existence. But the Christ you have invented for me is a sort of chimera; you mix together, like fire and water,[106] perfect charity and craven fear. And you persist in dressing up your impertinent case in all the fine colours of rhetoric.'

If only, Colet, your condemnation of my skill in rhetoric were as well founded as my praise of yours. For during our debate you kept on making that very point, protesting that a good case was being wrested from you by mere verbal ingenuity, and that truth was being suppressed by eloquence. But that is a charge I could truly repay with interest.[107] You will see how plainly I shall deal with you, how I shall hide nothing. I will contradict none of the points you have just made. I admit the possibility, the natural possibility, that one strong emotion can cast out another, or even override the physical senses, and that it is the nature of love to make things appear sweet that are intrinsically bitter. I will even add that the more intense the love, the greater its effect. What more could you ask? I agree that divine and spiritual love is infinitely more efficacious than fleshly or human love; I agree

* * * * *

104 See Matt 26:35, 69–75.
105 Acts 5:41
106 *Adagia* IV iii 94. The original Chimera was a monstrous creature, part dragon, part goat, and part lion.
107 Erasmus uses a Greek verb meaning to repay or retaliate.

that Christ's charity was so much more complete than ours that they cannot even be compared.

Yet, though it is generally true that anything human love does for us divine love does more effectively, I cannot entirely agree that Christ's divine and measureless charity did for him what a more limited love did for the martyrs; I disagree, though only on its power to ward off feelings of dread (I shall be dealing later with the joy it produced in them). The reason for this phenomenon is that in humans any strong emotion is in competition with others, and as each one is more or less powerful, it either overwhelms or succumbs to the others. In Christ, however, it was by no means the same: in him every movement, of the mind or the body, found nothing to oppose it, whether different or similar, and continued to fulfil its natural function. In him intense joy could not cast out milder feelings of pleasure, nor intense pain suppress some milder hurt; sublime pleasure could not block extreme pain, nor agonizing pain stifle sublime pleasure.

Besides, Colet, if you choose to measure Christ's charity only according to that effect which you say is peculiar to love (and rightly, as far as we humans are concerned), then you must see how you are belittling his love by your diligent but ill-advised efforts to extol it. For you imply that his charity could not achieve something that blind love can do for guilty lovers, that human love can do between friends, that love – a similar love, but infinitely less than the Redeemer's – could achieve for many thousands of martyrs. The first of these have scarcely the haziest notion of true love, and yet apparently, far from exhausting them, their insane exertions seem to lend them strength: amid the darkening gloom and biting winds of a freezing night, they burn with passion; sleepless nights cannot weary them, hunger cannot touch them, and trysts with ghosts and goblins hold no terrors for them. In a word, they consider mere bagatelles things that anyone not in love would find quite unbearable. How boldly they march into manifest danger! How avid they are for wounds and even death! But then, could anything make them flinch, when even death seems sweet? No need to seek examples in the history books: every day we see for ourselves things far harder to credit than anything we have read. Was not that slave I mentioned earlier[108] so overwhelmed by joy that neither mind nor body could feel the torments inflicted on him? If you measure Christ's charity by its effectiveness in blotting out painful sensations, small wonder that it could do what love could do in a slave and a barbarian.

* * * * *

108 31 above

In his *Letters*[109] Plinius Caecilius, nephew by his mother of the Pliny who wrote *The History of the World*, recounts a memorable deed performed in his time by a noblewoman called (I think) Arria. Her husband was suffering from a foul and incurable ulcer. As soon as she learned from the doctors that there was no hope left for him, she went to her husband's bedside and plunged a sword into her breast. She turned towards him as she struck and said: 'I feel nothing; it does not hurt. I am glad to be dying with you.' You could overrun my position with a whole army of similar examples.

That being so, such heroism is less surprising among the martyrs, in whom the flames of a powerful love burned so much brighter. I shall not bother to argue about the extent to which each one of them faced death, for the sake of Christ alone, with more joyful eagerness than Christ did for the love of all. But I shall ask whether anyone, even the greatest coward, ever showed terror in quite the way he did. Someone filled with utter dread will break out in a cold sweat. Christ sweated blood, not just from his face but from every pore, and so freely that the drops trickled to the ground. Someone very timid will turn pale and tremble. But Jesus agonized, which is what happens when someone gives up the ghost. So, did the martyrs love more passionately than Christ, the members than the head? Did the slave love more fervently than he? Or the woman? Last of all, does a foolish youth love his girl more than Christ loves his bride? 'Of course not,' you say. Right, but that is the implication of your argument. 'And I maintain it,' you say, 'if all those things are interpreted to mean that Christ dreaded his own death. I say that his love for us would have been diminished if it was for his own sake that he was filled with such dread of death, the death that he was to undergo for our sake.'

But, Colet, that argument too is irrelevant to the matter in hand. I shall grant you for the moment that Christ was perturbed by the danger to his members, not to himself, that he sweated for their sake, and agonized for them. Since you measure charity by the eager joy the victim shows, let us assume for the sake of argument that Christ's own death did not fill him with dread. Now, how was it that so many martyrs were filled with eagerness? There are two stages, and each requires an immense effort of love: they must first shake off their dread and then replace it with a spirit of eagerness. Why do you expect to find one of these, the absence of dread, in Christ, but not the other, the spirit of eagerness? Especially since love drives out fear,[110]

* * * * *

109 Pliny the Younger *Epistles* 3.16
110 Cf 1 John 4:18.

precisely, by flooding it with joy. And I do not imagine you will claim that Jesus' affection was strong enough to make him die for our sake, but not strong enough to let him face death with eager joy.

Now, if you will admit that the Redeemer's love cannot properly be measured by this sort of thing, why can you not accept the dread he felt? If, however, you do judge it by these standards, why do you expect to see eagerness as well? Did Peter, then, show more fervent love than Christ? Peter says, 'I lay down my life for you.'[111] Christ says, 'Take this cup from me.' Did Paul show more complete love when he desired to be loosed and to be with Christ, or again when he cried, 'O wretched man that I am, who shall deliver me from the body of this death?'[112] The head prays to be spared death, and the member welcomes it? Was Andrew's love so much more intense because he approached the cross so much more eagerly?[113] Compare them: the crosses are alike, but their victims very different. As soon as Andrew glimpsed the cross from afar, he was filled with delight, transported by joy, and poured out his thanks in a torrent of jubilant words. Did anyone ever go to a banquet more eagerly than he went to the place of suffering? This was the disciple. But in the same circumstances the master was grieved, weighed down by distress, sorrowful unto death, and dripping with bloody sweat.

You will interject, 'Yes, but not because of his own death.' What does it matter, since he certainly provided no such example of eagerness as Andrew did? Agatha,[114] a mere girl, skipped happily into her dungeon, for all the world as though she were invited to a party. How many beardless youths and unwed maids dauntlessly defied the tyrants' savage threats! Amid fire and the sword their eyes never lost their sparkle. What brave and spirited speeches they made amid their torments! None of this applies to Christ. He was taken as a sheep to the slaughter,[115] meekly acquiescent; no attempt to escape, no resistance.

* * * * *

111 John 13:37
112 Rom 7:24, preceded by an adaptation of Phil 1:23; see Screech 139 and 182 on Erasmus' use of these texts in discussions of ecstasy.
113 According to tradition, after a ministry in northern Greece and Scythia, St Andrew was martyred on an X-shaped cross at Patras c 70 AD. A number of early hagiographies recount his sufferings; see Corpus christianorum, series apocrypha 6 521–6 and 650 n2.
114 St Agatha was a third-century Sicilian martyr, sent to a brothel to induce her to repudiate her faith. Subsequently her breasts were removed, but St Peter appeared and restored her. She died next day under renewed torture.
115 Acts 8:32, quoting Isa 53:7

But is there really nothing here to compare with all the tales told of the martyrs? Not in the Gospels; they tell of grief, distress, sweat. He allowed himself to be accused on trumped-up charges and to be condemned; he kept silence, made no riposte to the blasphemers' taunts, prayed for his murderers. I am happy with the evidence that for salvation no more is required than to endure the ordeal with patience. But I cannot for a moment see where I am to find evidence of inestimable charity according to your system of values. No transports of joy, like Andrew's, no eager or exultant speeches. The books tell us that the dearest wish of not a few pious souls was to seek out martyrdom; they were convinced that those found worthy of the martyr's crown would find themselves among the blessed. Christ prayed that the hour should pass from him. The martyrs prayed for the very thing that the Saviour prayed to escape.

'But,' you will say, 'he was praying not to avert his own death, but that of his followers.' That also I will grant you; and yet you are still floundering in the water,[116] as they say. Very well, he did not pray for deliverance from death; but he did not welcome it either. He did not flee the executioner, but he did not volunteer, he did not seek out and demand death, as many martyrs habitually did. He endured the ordeal with constancy, but found no pleasure in it. Finally, he endured it but also felt the pain; charity deadened the martyrs' senses. And so one of the following must be true: either their love was greater than his, or we cannot use the same criteria to judge of our head's love. You will reply that the martyrs were made strong by another's power, not their own; that Christ was bereft of his divinity. You have almost, as Plautus said, hit the nail on the head.[117] But more of that shortly.

For the moment I shall try again to wrest from you the weapon with which you expected to make a quick end of me. You say that the members were made strong by the weakness of the head; that by Christ's dread the martyrs were made fearless. But this gets you nowhere: you pay by borrowing, as the saying goes,[118] and in loosening one knot, you tighten another. Out with it: how did Christ fortify his martyrs so well against the rack that either they felt nothing, or at least what they felt seemed as nothing beside the joy they knew? The only possible way, I believe, was by increasing their charity; the more generously God imparted the gift of his love, the more eager each of them became. See how, willy-nilly, you fall into the same trap every time. I ask if any of the martyrs loved more ardently than Christ. You

* * * * *

116 *Adagia* I iv 100
117 *Rem acu tetigisti, Adagia* II iv 93, derived from Plautus *Rudens* 5.2.19
118 *Adagia* I x 23: *Versuram solvere,* 'To pay by a switching-loan'

deny it. But many suffered more eagerly. You cannot deny it. Therefore, either Christ's love was not as great as the martyrs', or it did not produce the same effect in him that it did in the others. No doubt you would prefer to concede the latter point; you cannot completely deny either.

But now, what is implied by saying, as you do, that the martyrs were made strong by another's power, not their own? Of course they were made strong by charity, yet no one can deny that the greatest charity of all, no matter where it came from, dwelt in Christ. Let us suppose that his divine nature withdrew and did not at that moment impinge on the sensible part of his soul; this seems to be your conclusion, based on Ambrose.[119] But assuredly it did not deprive him of charity as well. If charity always does what you claim, and is cold and lifeless if it ever fails to produce that effect, then Christ's charity cannot have been all that we believe it was. Incidentally, we must note your expression 'by another's power,' which implies that Christ was made strong by his own power and not another's. Unless one understands this properly, it will not square with the truth. For Jesus' charity too came from elsewhere, not from himself. Everything in him belongs to another and was bestowed freely upon him. The charity that God freely bestows on the human martyr is also bestowed on himself as a man by Christ as God, and bestowed freely. The difference is that not only are all good things gratuitously given us, but also our sins are forgiven us. In him there was nothing to be forgiven.

Listen now; let me make it clearer why Christ's incomparable charity cannot properly be judged by the criteria you suggest. By a similar reckoning, will not the sensation as well as the fear of evil be driven out by the immense power of love? Does not nature provide that exceptional pain or pleasure should prevail over other, less intense feelings? Now I think you will allow that Christ's ordeal, even judged against the punishment of second death,[120] was more painful than any other, judged by its effect on every lineament of the soul and every nerve in the body. But it is logical to suppose that if his death was more painful physically than any other, then his dread of it must have been more excruciating mentally than any other. And as his boundless charity made the pain of his death no whit more bearable, so nothing lessened the intensity of his dread. Why will you admit the one

* * * * *

119 Quoted 51 below. On the 'sensible' and 'rational' parts of the soul, see 63 and n162 below.
120 Cf Rev 20:14 and 21:8 on the hideous 'second death' awaiting the wicked after the Last Judgment, interpreted by St Augustine as the death of the soul in *De civitate Dei* 13.1–8 PL 41 377–82.

but reject the other? By your own reckoning an acute feeling of pain will compete with strong feelings of love no less than fear or dread, since in us another strong emotion can eliminate either of these.

It is possible to prevaricate up to a point over his dread of death, but when it comes to his physical suffering you have nowhere left to hide. If sublime love can coexist with extreme pain, why should it not also coexist with extreme dread, especially since Christ's dread arose from the simple fact that his mind felt in advance, as it were, the pain of such an affront to nature? I could thus make a countercharge[121] against your contention that I am diminishing the Redeemer's love by insisting that his death filled him with dread. But I shall prove that point later. For the moment, Colet, I shall merely say in self-defence, before counter-attacking, that it is not I who belittle Christ's charity; it was so great, I agree, that all the martyrs' charity put together cannot be compared to it; but I think that it must be judged by somewhat more reliable criteria than yours.

Love can make people go eagerly to their death and ignore pain, but, equally, it may not have this effect, not only in Christ, but in us. For example, some modern commentators argue that all the love felt by the Virgin Mother of God, second only to Jesus' own love, could not alleviate the sword of sorrow which, we read, pierced her entire soul.[122] Eagerness goes with love only in the same way that pallor goes with anger, blushing with shame, laughter with joy, tears with sorrow. These things are outward signs, not causes, and are extrinsic to the emotions they betoken. For example, not everyone who turns pale is necessarily angry, and anger does not turn everyone pale; it does not follow that the paler someone is the more upset he is, nor that someone will get angry because he turns pale. Pallor is extrinsic to anger: if you take away the pallor the underlying anger remains unchanged. You may take it for granted that the same is true for all the other signs and emotions.

* * * * *

121 Erasmus uses the rhetorical term ἀντικατηγορία, explained by Quintilian *Institutiones oratoriae* 3.10.4 as 'mutual accusation'; Erasmus' belongs to the first category of ἀντικατηγορία, wherein both parties bring the same charge against one another (Quintilian 7.2.9).

122 Cf Luke 2:35, traditionally interpreted as a prophecy of the Virgin's reaction to the crucifixion, the subject of many a *pietà*. Later, Erasmus protested against over-sentimental interpretations and took the view that the Virgin was consoled in her suffering by the prospect of humanity's redemption; see the sermon attached to the *Liturgia Virginis Matris* ASD V-1 99–107, and Léon-E. Halkin 'La Mariologie d'Erasme' *Archiv für Reformationsgeschichte* 68 (1977) 51.

Outward signs of this kind were more conspicuous in some of the martyrs than in Christ, but the underlying cause was beyond compare and beyond price in the Redeemer, and that is a better criterion than those outward and commonplace signs. Shall I give some examples? Andrew, who may represent them all, did indeed love fervently, but he loved him whose supreme goodness had already inspired him. Nor did Andrew love any one person as much as Christ loved every one of us. Christ was the first to love: he loved in the face of insults and abuse, he loved the turncoat, he loved his enemy. Andrew bought nothing with his death, but repaid two debts, the one to nature and the other to Christ. Christ was the first to pay, freely, with his death, a death far more valuable than the debt he owed either to nature or to sin, and he paid not for himself but for us, as it was for us that he was born and lived and suffered. Finally, Andrew suffered through necessity, Christ through choice.

When I see so much persuasive evidence of Christ's charity, I am not in the least concerned by his lack of eagerness. Will you insist that someone who bestows such gifts must be reluctant to do so unless it is done with a careless laugh? In fact I find this the clearest proof of his love, in that he did not grant himself the same eager joy he bestowed on his members. Though free from all guilt, he chose to take on our chastisements in the manner not only of the more robust members, by undergoing death, but also in that of the weaker members, by apprehending death in his mind before it was inflicted on his body.

'But if he dreaded his own death,' you will say, 'it suggests a man who was self-centred.' Not at all, but rather a complete man subject to the ills of the human condition. He dreaded his death, but not for himself. He experienced death, not through us but in his own person, though it was for our sake, not his own; and similarly he recoiled from his own death, but for our sake, not his own. 'Come now,' someone might argue, 'when Jesus was hungry, surely he was thinking of himself more than of us? A desire for food cannot be anything but self-interested.' But in fact no one pursues that line and concludes that he loved us less because he went hungry; on the contrary, his love was all the greater because he chose to go hungry for our sake. His hunger was part of the nature he assumed. Did he not assume it willingly for our sake – and also for love? Therefore he went hungry for our sake, willingly and for love. Ask why he went hungry, and everyone will say it was because he was a man. Why did he become a man? Because, of course, he loved the human race more than words can say.

Similarly, his dread, his distress, his bloody sweat, all were part of the condition he had put on. The more woes you assign to him (though not those tainted with sin or shame), the more you increase and glorify the Saviour's love. Even if some of them were the inevitable consequence of the nature he assumed, yet since he assumed that nature voluntarily, whatever disabilities came with it cannot but be attributed to his free will and to his spontaneous love. The fact that he went hungry and the fact that he recoiled from death both spring from the same source. Why do you revere the one, as evidence of Jesus' love, but take offence at the other?

Is it not true that the more he took on the disabilities of our condition, the more he loved us? And is not the worst of all humanity's woes our dread of death? Which one of us, then, is diminishing his love? You, who deny that he took on that particular affliction, which may be more painful, almost, than death itself, or I, who maintain that, for love of us, he did not refuse even that? Can you subtract such a large amount from the total, and yet accuse me of belittling the Redeemer's love? Did not those who ascribed to him a body and a soul insensible to all pain do the most harm to his love? And do not those who would deprive him of the thing that is most like death, and closest to it, seem to do him almost as much harm?

'But,' you may say, 'it would do greater justice to his love to say that he was exceedingly glad of his death, but grieved for the destruction of the Jews and the desertion of the disciples.' I do not dispute that, Colet, but I would go further. I agree that Jesus' mind was less deeply troubled by the pain that racked his body than he was by our sins and by the ingratitude of those to whom his death was to bring final damnation instead of salvation. I agree, too, that he was more profoundly grieved by the loss of a single soul than by the scourges, the nails, the cross. I should not greatly object to the hypothesis that this unwonted sorrow was provoked by several different causes which entered the Redeemer's soul at the same time. None of these need be discarded if we put this natural cause alongside them. But it adds not a little to the sum total of his love. All of them flow from the same source, namely, charity. His grief over the death of other people was, as anyone can see, an act of love. But so were his alarm and distress when, as a vulnerable human being, he saw death draw nigh to him; the greater his vulnerability, his despair, his acceptance of our common frailty, the greater the love he showed in assuming it of his own free will. The apostles were scandalized by his death,[123] but they were still in the flesh; you are scandalized by his dread of death. In both cases it would be better to take comfort from these events.

* * * * *

123 Matt 26:31–3

I think I can prove that it was his own death that filled him with dread by quoting the exact words of some of those who deny it. In his commentary on Luke, Ambrose set out to tone down the scandal which he thought this passage would cause: 'A good many seize upon this passage to prove that the Saviour's sorrow was a weakness implanted in him from the beginning, and not one that was taken on only for a time; they try to distort the natural meaning of the words. For my part, I do not think that it needs to be explained away, and indeed it is here that I find the most wonderful evidence of his holiness and his majesty; for he would have brought less benefit to me had he not taken on my own feelings.'[124]

Now, what does 'implanted from the beginning' mean? From the time of human innocence, I suppose.[125] But that cannot be: there was then no death, which is the punishment of sin, and thus no awful fear of death. What about 'a weakness taken on only for a time'? This refers, of course, to his human nature, which shrank from death because the flesh is weak. Now, to be upset by someone else's afflictions is not a sign of weakness but of perfection, the work of virtue rather than nature. All is made clearer when Ambrose says, 'He had taken on my own feelings.' My feelings tell me not to approach death with eagerness and joy, but to recoil from it. How else can Christ be said to have taken on this feeling, born of weakness? Just as I, in my human frailty, am paralysed by fear at the approach of death, so he was filled with dread by his death, which was to be far more painful than mine.

A little later, Ambrose writes: 'For "God did not make death, and takes no pleasure in the destruction of the living." And he was pained by it because he did not make it himself.'[126] If he was pained by death because he did not make it, and did not even make his own, then he was also pained by his own death. Moreover, Ambrose had written earlier, 'For this reason too Christ recoils from death, showing his true humanity';[127] is he not showing clearly that Christ dreaded his own death? He took death upon himself to convince us that he was human like us, and he dispelled any further

* * * * *

124 Ambrose *Expositio in Lucam* 10.56 PL 15 1818

125 As Tracy 33 n11 suggests, it is more likely that this meant 'from the beginning of Christ's earthly life.' But Erasmus' essential point is that Ambrose attributed a 'weakness' to Christ, which Erasmus sets out to define in terms of his own line of argument.

126 Ambrose *Expositio in Lucam* 10.58 PL 15 1818, already used 37 above. The scriptural quotation is Wisd of Sol 1:13.

127 Cf Ambrose *Expositio in Lucam* 4.12 PL 15 1616; the sense is repeated in Ambrose's commentary on the agony in the garden (ibidem 10.59 PL 15 1818).

doubt by being filled with dread of death. Does not Athanasius make this point very clear when he writes, 'For his humanity recoils from the passion through the frailty of the flesh'?[128] Now, perhaps you are worried because 'frailty' suggests to you some defect, rather than the penalty of sin. If, when death draws near, you are filled with joy but worry about your friends' deaths, which may be many years off, it suggests perfection of the spirit, not weakness of the flesh. Bede's words are equally relevant: 'For Christ reveals two wills, to wit, a human will that recoils from suffering because the flesh is weak, and a divine will, which is ready and eager for it.'[129] All these writers, Colet, specifically mention weakness of the flesh, and yet you will consider only readiness of the spirit.

'But then,' you say, 'what of the fact that – if you are quoting them correctly – they all deny that Christ was afraid of death and maintain that he was grieved by our woes, not his own, and distressed by our sins, not his own suffering?' Listen to what I shall say, friend Colet. All the woes that Christ took on were our woes, not his. All our blessings are his blessings, not ours. He suffered a death that was his and not his. It was his because he suffered it in reality, and it was ours because it was on our behalf that he paid the price of death, which originated with us. The feeling of dread was ours, not his, and yet it was also his. It was ours because it was for our sake that he took on our mortal condition; it was his because he really experienced it, in his own mind and body, not in ours.

I will go further. He feared death, and did not fear it. He dreaded it, and did not. He desired it, and did not. 'You are setting me a Platonic riddle,' you reply. No, I am offering you a lifeline to help you escape from the labyrinth,[130] so to speak, of these confusing and conflicting ideas. He feared death, not as we do, out of necessity, but voluntarily, and yet he was truly afraid. He feared our afflictions, not his own, and for our sake, not his own. He was afraid, not because his passions seized and overwhelmed

* * * * *

128 Athanasius *De incarnatione contra Arianos*, probably quoted via Aquinas *Catena aurea in Lucae evangelium* 22.11; *Opera omnia* 25 vols (Parma 1852–73; repr New York 1949) XII 233. Athanasius does indeed use the episode to demonstrate the duality of Christ's nature.

129 Bede *In Matthaei evangelium expositio* 4 PL 92 115, but probably found by Erasmus in the same passage of Aquinas' *Catena aurea* (see the preceding note). Bede qualifies as one of the 'modern' theologians, writing after the Council of Constantinople, which in 681 outlawed monothelitism (the belief that Christ had only a single, divine will); hence the clarity of Bede's statement.

130 See *Adagia* II x 51, where Erasmus points out that such allusions to the story of Theseus and Ariadne were often applied to convoluted rhetoric.

his reason, as ours do, but in untroubled serenity of mind. And death filled him with dread in exactly the same way. He was unwilling to die because death is in itself evil and inimical to the nature he had assumed. He was willing to die because it would procure salvation for those he loved.

Now you must bear in mind that Christ's fear, dread, and alarm belong to the category of human woes that the Redeemer took to himself without guilt, and that all these emotions dwelt within him quite separately from his divine nature and in no way impeded the readiness of his spirit. They did not dictate to his reason or in any way disturb his composure. They did not dim the joy his soul found in endless contemplation of the divine, nor diminish the pleasure his soul felt at the prospect of humanity's salvation. Bear all this in mind and you need not be afraid to combine in him complete dread and perfect eagerness, sublime joy and intense pain, supreme bliss and extreme suffering.

In fact I do not think it matters much whether one says that his sufferings were a necessary product of the particular nature he took on, or else that his sorrow was not a necessary concomitant of the Redeemer's humanity, but something he took on, exceptionally, for a limited time. In either case it was equally spontaneous, since in the first case his assumption of a human destiny was itself spontaneous. However, it is more likely that he assumed it as an exception; just as in raising Lazarus a little earlier he had 'groaned and been troubled,'[131] so now he deliberately summoned up sorrow and alarm.

For I believe that there were many ways in which Christ could have avoided any such burden of fear. First of all, his soul already contained something that can make our own souls, and bodies too, impervious to death and to all pain: the perfect knowledge, contemplation, and enjoyment of the Godhead, as Christ himself testifies in the Gospel, saying that he knew the Father as the Father knew him.[132] These delights might easily have lifted all such burdens from both body and mind, throughout his life, had he not chosen to make an exception, in his pity for us, and to spare himself nothing to relieve the misery of our human condition. What is more, the fiery flames of love so filled his mind that, even without his contemplation of the Godhead, they alone would have sufficed to banish from him not only fear but any feeling of pain. A powerful joy filled his mind, because humankind was to be restored, and that could easily have driven out all

* * * * *

131 John 11:33; Ambrose makes the same parallel, and Erasmus' whole argument here draws on his *Expositio in Lucam* 57–8 PL 15 1818. On the theory of 'exception' (*dispensatio*), see n31 above.
132 John 10:15

troublesome thoughts, being infinitely more abundant and more powerful. Here I am setting against his apprehension of death not only his delight in our salvation, but also his sorrow for the slaughter of the wicked, in many ways more painful to him than death itself.

Finally, with a measure of human constancy and strength of mind, he might have banished, or eased considerably, the dejection and perhaps even the pain he felt. Why could he not do what all those pagans did? We find various ways to soften the blows of everyday misfortune: we find reasons or precedents that encourage us to bear them more bravely, we divert our thoughts from our troubles towards something more pleasant, or we contemplate the rewards of suffering, or the merits of the one for whose love we are suffering. Jesus allowed himself none of these to help alleviate the miseries that he took on with our nature. He assumed a body that was less tolerant of cold, heat, fatigue, hunger, and pain than any body has ever been. He assumed a soul that was endowed with the most acute sensitivity in every one of its faculties. Anyone else subjected to an ordeal of equal severity would have felt much less pain than he did. He allowed himself none of the things that ease the pain of our afflictions: the happiness, when we are restored to health, that drives out all care, the love that lightens the burdens even of fools in love, the indomitable strength of character that made even pagans brave; not even that natural, commonplace 'redundance,'[133] as it is called, through which pain yields to pleasure, or one pain blots out another. For example, you do not notice the loss of a penny if you have just made ten pounds,[134] and you do not feel a pinprick if simultaneously your arm is broken with a cudgel.

Ultimately, if the pain is too great to bear, nature will obligingly rob us of practically all feeling; for example, when a ship is wrecked, a building collapses, or a deadly disease strikes. But the Redeemer's soul was fully conscious of all his sufferings until the very moment it departed. His body took the full impact of every single blow; a thousand fell on him and he felt each one, every single one, as though it were the only one. He felt every conceivable bodily ailment as keenly as if his mind were suffering nothing; likewise, he felt every kind of mental anguish as keenly as if his

* * * * *

133 This term, whose meaning Erasmus illustrates here, was applied to Christ's suffering by Thomas Aquinas *Summa theologica* III q 46 art 6; Aquinas maintains that during this episode Christ's 'superior powers' did not overflow (*redundare*) into his lower being.

134 *Triobolus*, a coin worth three obols, used to denote a trifling sum by Plautus (eg *Poenulus* 1.2.168), and *talentum*, a large sum of money in the ancient world

body were not in pain. He felt every kind of pain, of both mind and body, singly, collectively, and in equal measure, in such a way that his sublime charity could do nothing to ease his burden of suffering, but rather added greatly to it. For the more tenderly he loved the human race, the more he was tormented by the thought that his own painful death, which was more than sufficient to save us all, would prove profitless, even harmful, to so many of us. He was grieved by the coming destruction of the Jews, but that did nothing to lessen his natural feelings of dread. The thought of death made him shudder, but in no way lessened his distress over the fate of the Jews.

In short, to help him cope with the human afflictions he took on with his new existence, he refused absolutely to avail himself of the blessings with which, as we read, he was richly endowed. They fall into three categories, corresponding to three stages of human life: spotless innocence, when freedom from guilt must have meant freedom from punishment; the plenitude of grace, which takes away natural frailties; finally, the enjoyment of divinity, which will banish from us the very capacity to suffer hurt.

'But what is the point,' you say (and it is a question you kept asking, somewhat testily, during our debate), 'of heaping upon Christ this pile of heart-rending woes? It was his charity that did the most good, and I would rather we developed that theme instead of all this bloodshed.' Yes, 'bloodshed' was the very word you used. Colet, practically the same thing has happened to us as Socrates says happened when he debated with Protagoras;[135] you set out, when our debate began, to add something to the Redeemer's love, but have diminished it, whereas I have enlarged and not decreased it, contrary to your expectations. I have thrown into the scale a weighty argument that you wished to see removed. Perhaps you think that virtue does not increase when there are more opportunities to do good? Will you really call me cruel and bloodthirsty because I insist on the Redeemer's many sufferings? On the contrary, I should consider myself foolishly sentimental, and profoundly ungrateful, if I did not acknowledge this great affliction which, along with so many others, he deigned to take upon himself for my sake, and if I should conceal, or even deny, his extraordinary generosity.

It was appropriate, for so many reasons, that Christ's[136] death should be more painful than any other, since it alone was to atone for so many other

* * * * *

135 Plato *Protagoras* 361A–B; the protagonists ended up defending the positions they had begun by attacking.
136 The possessive is omitted in LB.

deaths and to wash away the sins of the whole world. His sacred death not only provided enough to pay the bill for original sin, but also left a remainder, so to speak, which would be more than enough to wash away our everyday sins. The great well from which all our spiritual gifts are drawn had to be filled. A powerful example was being given, which would inspire even the coldest of hearts towards love, and encourage the most sluggish to emulate it for the health of their souls. The inexhaustible treasury of merit through which we were to receive heaven was being built. I am well aware that in the laying up of merit Jesus' charity played by far the biggest part. As Gregory puts it: 'The true proof of his love lies in the result of its operation. Through his physical and mental sufferings, his charity redeemed us; the more painful and the more numerous his sufferings, the more we realize how precious our salvation was to him and how high was the price he paid. As his sorrows were heaped up like a pile of kindling, the inextinguishable flame of his love burned ever brighter.'[137] That is why learned theologians[138] have been led to lay great stress on the bitterness of Christ's passion, bluntly ascribing to him such depths of suffering that nothing in this life is or could be worse. And the theologians' view is in line with the words of Holy Scripture. Christ alone knows the measureless measure and numberless number of his sufferings. Here he speaks in a prophetic book: 'Look and see if there be any pain like mine.' Similarly, in a psalm: 'My soul is full of troubles.'[139]

That is why Jerome's interpretation holds no great attraction for me. He calls the Redeemer's suffering 'propassion'[140] rather than passion, something that, to use St Bernard's distinction, overtook but did not overwhelm him.[141] If they define 'passion' as something that dethrones reason, and 'overwhelm' as being driven out of one's mind, I do not object. But I should not hesitate also to call 'passion' these feelings which not only overtook Jesus' mind (or at least the lower part of it), but most violently overwhelmed it.

* * * * *

137 Gregory the Great *Homilia in evangelia* 30.1 PL 76 1226
138 The question is discussed at length by Thomas Aquinas *Summa theologica* III q 46 art 6 and also by Bonaventure (n47 above) 3.16.1.
139 Lam 1:12 followed by Ps 88 (Vulg 87):3; both texts are quoted by Aquinas in his discussion (see the preceding note).
140 Jerome *Commentarius in Matheum* 4.26.37 PL 26 197; see n55 above. 'Propassion' for Jerome means a mere beginning of passion or suffering.
141 *Turbare/perturbare*; Bernard of Clairvaux used this distinction several times, though not in this context: see CCL *Thesaurus Bernardi Clarevallensis concordantiae* under *perturbare*. According to St Bonaventure this distinction had been applied by Seneca to sorrow in the philosopher (cf Santinello 108).

Similarly, when the evangelist says, 'He began to be distressed and dismayed,' does this really mean that distress and dismay merely touched his mind and did not take it over?[142] Even though he cries out that his soul is brimming with troubles, and that he is sorrowful unto death?[143] And while I believe that his death was more painful than any other, I also think that his sorrow, the first stage, as it were, of his death, was as deep as could be and left him only along with life itself. It will not do, either, to suggest that the word 'began' implies that he felt the beginnings of an emotion that could not be allowed to develop fully within him; compare the theory that our first impulses, as they are called, cannot be considered culpable so long as we reject them at once.[144] Or perhaps the idea is that he took to himself feelings that could not be allowed to develop in his members, feelings of sorrow and distress. I prefer to think that the phrase 'He began to be distressed' applies to his feeling of dread, which he took on just for a limited time, whereas his grief over the death of the wicked was always with him. It is nature's way, too: everyone knows for certain that they will die some day, but they do not worry about it until death seems to be imminent.

I think, Colet, that I have already proved my case. But in order to convince you more fully, and because you are so very keen on eager joy as an expression of love (in fact our whole debate arises from that point), I declare that even among the whole army of martyrs there never was so much eagerness of spirit and holy rejoicing as there was in the mind of Jesus in the very hour when he felt distress and dismay and sweated drops of blood. In that very hour, I repeat, he rejoiced inwardly with inexpressible gladness because at last the time ordained by his Father was coming, when by his death he would reconcile humankind to himself as God. No one was ever so fond of life that he wanted to live more than Christ wanted to die. None of us has ever yearned so ardently for immortality as he thirsted for his death. What more do you need? You can add something more, if you will, to this mass of evidence. As for me, I cannot find words adequate to express the thoughts that occur to me. 'But,' you ask, 'how can you reconcile an eager thirst for death with this supposed dread of death that paralyses him?' Given the qualities that we ascribed to Christ just now, there is no reason why the same person at the same time should not have dreaded

* * * * *

142 This is Origen's interpretation of Matt 26:37, developed at some length in his *Commentarii in Matthaeum* 23.90 PG 13 1741.
143 Cf Matt 26:38.
144 This theory is applied by Jerome to his distinction between *passio* and *propassio* in his commentary on Matt 5:28 PL 26 38.

and desired, welcomed and rejected, the same thing, and experienced the extremes of both joy and suffering during his ordeal.[145]

First of all, as there were three natures in Jesus' person, it would not be illogical to ascribe three wills to him. Although commentators usually give him only two, divine and human,[146] some divide the human will in two, making three in all: one belongs to his divine nature, one to his reason, and the third to his frailty, or flesh. Of course, all three could be called a single will in so far as they are all directed to the same end, just as in common parlance, when people agree or disagree about the same thing, we say that they are 'of one mind' or 'of one will.' Thus, were it not for the other poison it concealed, one might usefully cite the Eutychians' opinion[147] concerning the agreement between Christ's divinity and humanity, which remained unimpaired by his dread of death. However, I suspect that the Eutychians would have denied Christ a human will, since they refused to give him a human soul, a doctrine that smacks of manifest heresy.

But to return to the point. If we give the Redeemer three wills, it is not a natural impossibility that one of them should be filled with dread, and another with longing. But let us examine whether this tallies with reason, and determine which was the will in Christ that was different from the Father's and made him unwilling to die. In our own minds we often feel conflicting impulses and are apparently equally willing and unwilling to do something. We behave badly of our own accord and yet feel annoyed with ourselves, as if it were against our will. Sometimes, too, we do the right thing of our own accord, but none the less feel our mind tugging in a different direction, as if it were doing good against its will.

These impulses reflect the two parts of our soul.[148] The one, dwelling down amid the grosser bodily organs and anchored in the flesh, is brutish and inclined towards evil; the other shines like a beacon amid the smoky

* * * * *

145 This paragraph is very close to a passage in Ep 109 CWE 1 208–9.
146 The orthodox doctrine promulgated at the Council of Constantinople in 681 and propagated eg by Bede; see n129 above. Among later theologians to discuss the plurality of Christ's will are Bonaventure (n47 above) 3.17.2 and Thomas Aquinas *Summa theologica* III q 18 art 1–3.
147 The Eutychians were a monophysite sect named after Eutyches, a fifth-century abbot of Constantinople. They held that in Christ after the hypostatic union there was only one nature, thus denying him a concrete and individual human nature. Their doctrine was condemned by the Council of Chalcedon in 451, which concluded that Christ was perfect God and man, consubstantial with the Father and consubstantial with man, one sole being in two natures.
148 Cf the development on the outer and inner man in the *Enchiridion* CWE 66 41–3.

fogs of instinct, and always strives towards good. It is pure and simple, and is called 'reason' by the philosophers. The other, since it deviates from the supreme good, which is one and pure, is called by many different names after the various false objectives it sets itself. However, they come under the general heading of πάθη, that is, passions, or disorders, or appetites. Paul calls the one 'the law of the mind,' and the other, variously, 'the law of sin,' 'the law of the members,' 'the flesh,' and 'the body.'[149]

However, I myself see no reason why this should compel us to conclude that human beings possess two wills. For in our primordial state, the soul was an entity endowed with a single will that strove of itself towards good; but it was so fashioned that, at the whim of its director, it could be depraved and directed elsewhere. But although it was depraved by original sin, it did not immediately begin to be a separate will, unless perhaps a change in the objective of a power also changes its character.[150] No, the will, like an iron bar between two magnets, is attracted towards both sides at once: towards good by the power of our original state of innocence, which, though corrupted by sin, was not destroyed by it; towards evil by vice, or rather by the vestiges of original sin. It is like bending down a branch of a palm tree, which is naturally springy; it is still the same branch, and keeps its natural resilience, which is merely in abeyance. As soon as you let go, the branch will spring back into place.

However, leaving these questions undecided, let me hasten to the point at issue. No one is so irreverent as to attribute to Christ this dissension and endless strife between reason and passion, spirit and flesh. It can exist in us without sin, if our minds do not consent to it, yet because it originated in sin and entices us to sin, it is incompatible with the Redeemer's dignity. When Augustine remarks that there is some degree of sin whenever the flesh desires something against the spirit,[151] either he means by 'sin' the corruption of the will that attracts it to evil, or else he is discussing not mere instincts but desires that involve some measure of approval and pleasure. For though even Paul cries out that he feels in his limbs a law that rebels

* * * * *

149 See in particular Rom 7:23–5.
150 Erasmus resorts to scholastic jargon here: the 'power' is one of the three powers of the soul (will, intellect, and memory). The suggestion is that when, at the fall, the human will took as its object evil rather than good, its nature was changed sufficiently for it to be considered a different entity. The two similes that follow are inspired by Pliny and feature in Erasmus' *Parabolae* CWE 23 221 and 263; the first is also applied there to moral hesitation.
151 Cf Augustine *Sermones* 128.5–6 PL 38 716–17 and *De natura et gratia* 54.63 PL 44 278.

against the law of his mind,[152] it is unthinkable that so irreproachable an apostle should have deferred in any way to these baser instincts.

However, to pass rapidly on, it seems to me that three different kinds of impulse can be detected in the human mind. The first belongs to the spirit and impels us purely towards the invisible, the good, and the eternal; the second belongs to the flesh and does the opposite, tempting us towards evil simply because it is evil. For a certain inclination towards wickedness has been left in our flesh, and it means that, even when the effort and the rewards involved are equal, we find more pleasure in doing evil than good. The third kind of impulse is midway between these two, attracted neither towards good for its own sake, nor towards evil for its own sake, but instead towards anything that is favourable to nature; and it recoils from anything that threatens our survival, or even our peace of mind. The first of these impulses derives from judgment and grace, the second from corruption, the third from natural instinct. We may exclude the second altogether from Christ, and indeed almost entirely from those excellent persons who, by intense spiritual exercise, have so thoroughly chastised their body and reduced it to obedience that it will follow the dictates of reason with little or no resistance, like an animal that used to run wild but has been broken by long training. The best among us are inherently averse to wrongdoing simply because it is wrong. But occasionally even they will refuse or hesitate to do something that provokes mixed feelings, a worthy act, given the circumstances, but one repugnant to our natural instincts; for example, suffering death, when it is for Christ, or hunger, when the church decrees a fast, or hardship, when brotherly love imposes it.

Now, just as any inclination towards something is to some extent an act of the will, so aversion and dread seem to be acts of refusal. In this sense hunger and thirst are partly acts of will, the will of nature, not of the spirit or the flesh. But if such feelings of inclination or dread, being natural and not intrinsically connected with the spirit or the flesh, are simply natural, there is nothing to prevent them existing even in the best of us, and ultimately even in Christ. It is in this sense, I think, that Christ's words to Peter must be interpreted: 'When you were young, you girded yourself and walked where you wished; but when you are old, you will hold out your hands, and another will gird you, and will take you where you do not wish to go.'[153] I should not blame you for scorning this as some mere fancy of

* * * * *

152 Rom 7:23
153 John 21:18; a prophecy of Peter's martyrdom

mine, were it not that St Augustine supports me. Expounding the gospel text
I have just cited, he says: 'Peter was brought, all unwilling, to face his ordeal;
unwillingly he came to it, but willingly he conquered it. And he put away all
feelings of frailty that make us unwilling to die, feelings so natural that not
even old age had set Peter free of them.'[154] You will notice that the feeling is
called frailty, not an inclination towards evil; it is a dread, deeply implanted
in us by natural instinct, of anything that is inimical to nature. No one can
doubt that, because it was holy, Peter went to his death with great joy in
his heart; nor that, because it was a means to salvation, he was unwilling
only in as much as it was death, the one thing in the world most inimical to
nature. Now if you ask me what kind of will it was in Christ that made him
unwilling to die, I shall reply that it was the same as that he foresaw in Peter,
simply a natural dread of death, which in the best of us, and especially in
Christ, is not opposed to the spirit, nor connected with the flesh.

   Do not protest, my dear Colet, that I have invented this division of humanity into three parts, spirit, flesh, and soul; I am following Jerome's lead.
Jerome followed Origen, and Origen Paul.[155] Paul, of course, followed the
Holy Spirit. But in using this division I am giving Christ only spirit and
soul, with no part that is flesh. Some theologians[156] call flesh what I here
call soul, the part in which we must assume Christ feared death, as did Peter, the closest and thus the most similar to the head; I shall not take issue
with them over the words, since we are agreed on the facts. This natural
weakness, so deeply implanted in human nature that it can be conquered
but never eradicated, is the surest evidence of humanity, and the Redeemer
not only took it upon himself, but did so in a remarkable way. I would in
fact venture to say of Christ what Augustine said of Peter, 'Unwillingly
he came to death, but willingly he conquered it.'[157] That he shrank from
death was a sign of weakness, natural but not sinful. His love for us conquered his weakness but did not eliminate it altogether. How did Christ
conquer death? Was it not by suffering death himself? In the same way he
conquered fear by yielding to it, deliberately and willingly, for love of us.
But it was imperative that the three disciples who had earlier seen him in his

* * * * *

154 Augustine *In Ioannis evangelium tractatus* 123.5 PL 35 1969
155 On this topic, see the chapter of the *Enchiridion* 'On the Three Parts of Man:
    Spirit, Soul, and Flesh' CWE 66 51–4.
156 Eg Origen *Commentarius in epistolam ad Romanos* 1.5 PG 14 850–6, and Tertullian
    De carne Christi 10–13 PL 2 817–22
157 See n154 above.

majesty[158] should now witness his frailty; therefore, speaking as a man to men for the sake of humankind, he exposed his human frailty in human terms by saying, 'Father, if it be possible, let this cup pass from me.'[159]

The fact that he said, 'If you will,' and 'If it be possible,' does not imply hesitation, but shows his subordination of natural instinct to the divine will. It is as if he were saying: 'My Father, I am conscious within myself of an instinct belonging to the nature I took not from you but from my mother, which violently dreads and recoils from that most bitter cup of death; but this is my will, not yours. For the one thing we do not share is that I have been made into the likeness of sinful flesh and have been revealed as a man in my condition of mind and body. But the promptings of nature can in no way affect my readiness to drain the cup that you offer me. In the flesh, which is weak, I am frightened, but in the spirit, which is ready and willing, I eagerly thirst for it. It will indeed be exceedingly bitter for me, but it will bring salvation to those whom I love with you and in you. My human senses make me reluctant to die, because death is inimical to nature. My spirit thirsts for death because it thirsts for the salvation of the human race. But your will be done, not mine. For the first is truly my own, and not shared with you; the second is not mine, but yours, you who bestow all holy desires that we humans feel, and who have made me everything that I am. I claim nothing for myself; everything that I desire in the spirit is yours, since you are the Father of spirits.'

There, Colet, you have a will in Christ that is not the Father's. Now let me show you some ways in which he was also at one with his Father in being both willing and unwilling to die. For even in the higher part of his soul, which was always in perfect harmony with the Godhead, Christ seems to have been, to some extent, reluctant to die. He was displeased by death because it was the penalty for sin, since of course sin displeased him, as did the author of sin, the devil. By this reckoning his divine nature did not wish for death any more than it wished sin to be committed. It is now not a man, but God, who says, 'I do not want the sinner to die.'[160] Still less, of course, does he want the righteous to die. He is no less averse to death than to sin, which begets death.

Again, the nature he had adopted made him both willing and unwilling to die. If the human part of his nature had been allowed to determine

* * * * *

158 At the transfiguration, Matt 17:1–8; Erasmus expands on this traditional interpretation of the choice of disciples in his Paraphrase on Mark (CWE 49 162).
159 Matt 26:39; Erasmus elucidates this verse very similarly in Ep 109 CWE 1 208.
160 Ezek 33:11

his wishes, taking nothing else into account, then he would be unwilling to die; on the other hand, since the fall, which could not be wished away, death had become necessary for the restoration of humanity; so he was willing to die. In theory, he was willing to die because his death would bestow immortality on the holy and the deserving; in practice, he was unwilling because he knew that his death would give many others a pretext for sinfulness, though they themselves, and not his death, would be responsible for it. You can already see, I hope, that it is idle for Hilary[161] and some others to interpret the words 'Take this cup from me' as a prayer by the head that the hour of suffering should pass not from himself but from his members, since all these arguments, except possibly the first, prove that Christ both willed and did not will the bodily death of his followers as much as his own.

Now you demand that I keep my promise to show how in Christ a spirit of supreme eagerness could coexist with the most intense suffering. But unless I am mistaken, I have already done so, more or less. I have shown that, given the division of the soul into two parts, the rational and the sensible (as the moderns[162] call them), there is no reason why Christ could not at one and the same time be willing and unwilling to die. I have also shown that he could have done the same in just one part of his soul. If you will agree that one man, in the two parts of his soul and even, indeed, in the same part, could be both willing and unwilling, could both dread and desire the same thing, in equal measure and at one and the same time; then you cannot but concede that in exactly the same way he could be filled with both sublime joy and abject misery, especially as my case is supported by the suggestion that his divine nature was temporarily suspended and its redundance[163] withdrawn.

I am not trying to persuade you of this merely by entreaty. Either you must allow Christ these feelings, or else you must argue that throughout his life he suffered none of the handicaps of our human condition. It was in the lower part of his soul, where the nails and the crown of thorns also pricked him, that he felt distress and dismay, all the more miserable as death drew nearer. To the extent that Jesus' soul was in touch with bodily sensation, he was afflicted by horrible suffering; to the extent that it was in touch with his divine nature, he was filled with triumph and boundless joy by

* * * * *

161 Hilary *Commentarius in Matthaeum* 31.4 PL 9 1067
162 Eg Thomas Aquinas *Summa theologica* III q 18 (n146 above). This psychological theory is discussed more fully in the *Enchiridion* CWE 66 41–54.
163 For this term see 54 and n133 above.

precisely the same thing, his death. That intense feeling of dismay did not restrain his eagerness for death, but neither did his eagerness diminish his feeling of dread, because, in this exceptional case, the feeling in his rational part did not overflow into the sensible part of his soul. And within that same rational part, though filled with matchless joy by his death, which, to his delight, was destined to ensure our salvation, he was simultaneously much tormented by the knowledge that many people would, through their own fault, transform this powerful, salutary, and life-saving medicine into a death-dealing poison.

There is nothing here to shock anyone of ordinary sensitivity. I accept that Jesus was as much moved by the death of the wicked as he was glad for the salvation of the faithful, and I revere his inestimable charity. I accept that he thirsted for death as the wellspring of life for us, and I honour his boundless love. But I also accept that he was unwilling to die, that he shrank from death, and I respect all the more his charity towards us, whose miserable frailty he deigned to assume, he whose power sustains the universe. I accept that he rejected death because he rejected sin, and I wonder at his charity. I accept that he was reluctant because for many his death would prove to be an obstacle to faith, and I cannot but reflect on the magnitude of his charity. He was at once willing and unwilling, afraid and unafraid, happy and sad. All these things inspire me to love him in return, since they all flow down together from the same source, love.

I cannot now see what more you could ask, Colet, unless perhaps you are still troubled by a small doubt as to why Christ Jesus should have preferred, on the eve of his death, to show outward signs of dread rather than eager joy, though I admit that in his mind eagerness for our salvation far outweighed any feeling of dread for his own death. It was because, in my view, he was setting us an example of gentleness, patience, and obedience, not fearlessness. On display were the lineaments of humanity, not the trappings of divinity. He was setting an example for us to love and to emulate, not merely to admire. In fact, if you retrace Christ's whole life from the cradle onwards, you will find much evidence of gentleness and patience, but none of this eager joy. It was more than enough to face death for us with love, not exultation, and he wished us to admire nothing in the manner of his death so much as his charity towards us.

Could anyone have faced death more lovingly? He did not banish from the feast the disciple who betrayed him, nor refuse him the communion of his body; he did not repulse him as he bestowed the unholy kiss, and even called him friend to revive his spirits. What could be more lovable than his last conversation with his followers? What does it convey but his unique love for us? He did not bemoan his own fate, but comforted his fainthearted friends. A show of eagerness would have done us little service, but his dismay brought us gain. It was essential that he, who paid the penalty of death for our sake, should be considered a true man subject to the woes of our condition. If he had gone through the ordeal with eager joy on his face and in his words, like a man practically devoid of feeling, how much wider might the Manichees' madness have spread? They claimed falsely that the body he assumed was unreal, even during this episode, when he showed such obvious signs of a human nature.[164] It might have been hard to believe that his death was real, had not his obvious dread of it been set before our eyes as proof. Ambrose agrees when he writes: 'How were we to imitate you, Lord Jesus, unless we followed you as a man, unless we believed that you had died and had seen your wounds? Again, how could the disciples believe you were to die, unless they witnessed your sorrow as death drew near?'[165] This patient endurance of his ordeal – nothing bold and fearless – was more conducive to proving the truth of his human nature. In the same way it was better suited to our feelings, since he wished to win our love rather than our admiration.[166]

Finally, it was more in accordance with the oracles of the prophets, who preferred to represent Christ in such a guise that they compared him to a gentle lamb, or else depicted him bruised by blows, disfigured, abandoned, and an outcast,[167] but never as eager, proud, and bold. They represent him as quiet, not boastful. It is for the proud and haughty to face torture with a dauntless heart and to make some fine, brave speech upon the very rack. But Christ wanted his death to be of the most humiliating kind. He reserved the glory, the joyful eagerness, for his martyrs; it was for them, to make them strong, that the head became weak. The Lord became deeply distressed so that his servants would be less distressed. Perhaps it was because he does not expect us to go against nature and show eager joy amid great torments that he did not choose to exhibit it in himself. Instead, he set us an example of charity and gentleness, the gentleness he had earlier told us to learn from

* * * * *

164 The 'docetist' belief that Christ could not have assumed a real body, but only an apparent one, was not confined to the dualist Manichees, but was widespread among the Gnostic sects in the early centuries of Christianity; it arose from their view that matter is inherently evil.
165 Ambrose *Expositio in Lucam* 10.57 PL 15 1818
166 This is clarified in Ep 109, which continues, 'for whereas we admire bravery, we love and affectionately embrace that which is gentle and weak' (CWE 1 210:128–9).
167 Probably inspired by the depiction of the Man of Sorrows in Isa 53, celebrated as a prophecy of Christ's passion

him, saying, 'Learn from me, for I am gentle and humble in heart.'[168] And even in the hour of his death he continued to commend love to us.[169]

But that is enough, I think, on this topic, and probably far too much for a man of your learning. In other circumstances all these arguments could be developed rather more fully, defended rather more carefully, and set out rather more precisely. But I know to whom I am writing. Whether I have persuaded you, I do not know, though I believe that in one way or another I have shown that my view, which I share with modern theologians, is more in keeping with the words of the evangelists, more consonant with the words of the prophets, and not incompatible with the writings of the earlier theologians; and that my argument chimes sweetly with reason and leaves nature unscathed. So far from detracting from the Redeemer's courage, charity, and obedience, it greatly enhances them. Your argument, by contrast, leads to the selfsame conclusion that you found so shocking in mine. But alas! how reckless it is for me, the newest of new recruits, to try conclusions with such a mighty general, and especially for a mere rhetorician, as you call me, to take on a topic so thoroughly theological or, in other words, a subject not my own!

But I felt that I might risk all before you, who so skilfully deploy all the choice learning of the ancients and have brought home from Italy so many treasures in both languages[170] that on these grounds alone the theologians can scarcely do Colet justice. That is why I have chosen for our discussion the free and easy form of discussion the ancients used, both because I prefer it myself and because I knew that the newfangled modern method of disputation[171] greatly displeases you; precise and practical, as it seems to its devotees, but to you niggling, nit-picking, threadbare, and thoroughly sophistical. And it may be that you are right. But if, as the Greek adage puts it, not even Hercules can take on two,[172] be sure that you cannot stand alone against such a multitude. Let us not begrudge them their well-honed platitudes, but content ourselves with the rough-hewn

* * * * *

168 Matt 11:29, quoted by Origen in his *Commentarii in Matthaeum* 23.92 PG 13 1742, which Erasmus seems to be following here
169 Cf John 15:9–17. The preceding three paragraphs are closely paralleled towards the end of Ep 109 CWE 1 209–10.
170 The two languages are Latin and Greek. On Colet's visit to Italy, from which he had returned in about 1496, see CEBR I 324 and Ep 1211.
171 A reference to scholastic disputation, a favourite target of Erasmus' own satire over many years; see eg the prefatory letter here; the *Moria* CWE 27 126–9; and the preface to the *Enchiridion* CWE 66 8–10.
172 *Adagia* I v 39 CWE 31 419; quoted here in Greek

style[173] of such as Origen, Ambrose, Jerome, Augustine, Chrysostom, and other veterans like them. Beauty is in the eye of the beholder; let Darby marry Joan.[174] It is foolish to perform a play, however brilliantly, if no one is watching. Besides, I should not want to run any risk if what I have written happens to go astray and falls into other hands; it was my intention not to expound my own ideas but to elicit your views. Perhaps I really agree with you, but am pretending to differ (like Glaucon, in Plato, who rails against justice to provoke Socrates into praising it)[175] so that, equipped with your defence, I can subsequently protect my position against others. But now I await your mail-clad column, deployed with all the skill of Nestor.[176] I await your mighty war-trumpet. I await your Coletic missiles, flying straighter than Hercules'. In the meantime I shall deploy the forces of my intellect, concentrate my strength, call up my reserves – of books – to help me survive your initial onslaught. As for your other propositions, based on Paul's Epistles, since they are dangerous to debate,[177] I prefer to discuss them face to face on our evening walks,[178] and in conversation not in writing.

Farewell, excellent Colet, glory of this university and my joy.

From Oxford.

* * * * *

173 *Pingui Minerva*; cf n102 above.
174 Literally, 'let Cascus marry Casca'; *Adagia* I ii 62 CWE 31 201–2: 'An old man takes an old bride'
175 Glaucon undertakes an ironic defence of injustice in Plato's *Republic* 357–62. Cf Ep 1110, the preface to the *Antibarbari* CWE 23 16.
176 Nestor, king of Pylos, was renowned as the most eloquent and wisest of the Greek generals before Troy; cf *Adagia* I ii 56: *Nestorea eloquentia*.
177 On Colet's 'revolutionary' lectures in Oxford on the Pauline Epistles, see the prefatory letter, 11 and n4 above.
178 The phrase is in Greek, the word περίπατος, 'walk,' having the secondary sense of 'philosophical discussion.'

A SERMON ON THE IMMENSE MERCY OF GOD

Concio de immensa Dei misericordia

translated and annotated by
MICHAEL J. HEATH

The *Concio de immensa Dei misericordia*[1] was first published by Froben at Basel in September 1524, together with an enlarged version of the *Virginis et martyris comparatio*. It had apparently been commissioned by Christoph von Utenheim, bishop of Basel, who had recently founded a chapel dedicated to the Mercies of God. Although described as a sermon, the work is far too long to have been actually delivered at the consecration of the chapel. On 20 June 1524 Erasmus had sent a draft for comment to Bishop Christoph, who replied three weeks later, approving of the work but urging Erasmus to be cautious: 'No further matter should be added beyond what I suggested,' and in particular nothing that might excite the Lutherans or those who observe the genuine old-fashioned faith.'[2]

We do not know what Utenheim's suggestions had been, though he goes on in this letter to recommend that some potentially controversial additions at the end of the work be removed. But it appears that Erasmus took heed, since there is little polemical material in the book. In later correspondence Erasmus several times cited *De immensa Dei misericordia* as a work whose pious aims could give offence to no one. He considered it very suitable, along with the *Virginis et martyris comparatio*, the *Modus orandi Deum*, and his commentaries on the Psalms, for the widest possible diffusion through new editions and translations.[3] Though published in the same month as *De libero arbitrio* and soon after the *Exomologesis*, *De immensa Dei misericordia* seems to have aroused little controversy, no doubt because here Erasmus' concerns are pastoral rather than doctrinal.

As an example of ideal Erasmian preaching, grounded in Scripture and designed to uplift the hearts of the faithful, *De immensa Dei misericordia* could hardly be bettered. Erasmus describes his sermon as an encomium of that mercy of God through which eternal salvation is prepared for all. Gently but insistently he urges the necessity of humility and hope, worship and repentance. While his strictures on human pride awake echoes of the satirical past, the exhortations against despair that dominate the second part of the sermon show Erasmus at his humane best. No doubt the book owed

* * * * *

1 This is the title generally used. However, LB entitles the work *De magnitudine misericordiarum Domini concio* ('A Sermon on the Magnitude of the Lord's Mercies').

2 Ep 1464:14–16; Erasmus' letter of 20 June is Ep 1456. See also Ep 1341A: 782–4.

3 See Ep 1581:116, Allen Epp 1746:17, 1968:62, and 3049:40. However, in a letter of 1529 (Allen Ep 2165:39) he puts this *Concio* in the more dubious company of the *Institutio christiani matrimonii* and the *Paraphrases* as a candidate for vernacular translation.

much of its popularity to this inspiring litany of consolation. Erasmus addresses his imaginary audience in an invigoratingly direct style, avoiding both the arid intellectualism of the scholastic sermon and the otiose rambling of the monastic preachers. His discourse mingles the free homiletic style of the Fathers, based on copious scriptural quotation and exegesis, with elements of the classical demonstrative and deliberative rhetoric that he was to recommend in the *Ecclesiastes*.[4]

As Erasmus points out, *misericordia* (mercy, pity, compassion) is an elastic term in Holy Writ.[5] God's mercy can encompass generosity, punishment, clemency, forgiveness, reward, and finally redemption; Christ is mercy incarnate. Divine mercy is given the contrasting functions of elevating humanity towards God in a properly humble spirit and of consoling and healing the desperate. Erasmus' pastoral advice is directed against the twin evils of pride and despair, the Scylla and Charybdis of the fallen world. He seeks to humble pride through examples of punishment and forgiveness, such as the contrasting fates of Pharaoh and David, and through an analysis of human frailty, both physical and spiritual. Despair, exemplified by the exile of Cain and the suicide of Judas, is countered by evocations of the multitude as well as the magnitude of God's mercies.

Erasmus thus assembles abundant scriptural evidence of God's compassion and of his encouragement of the human aspiration towards salvation. Interestingly, the most detailed passages of exegesis draw on the 'minor prophets' Joel, Habakkuk, and Micah. Erasmus expounds not only their evocations of divine mercy but also their prophecies of the Incarnation, its most sublime expression. Erasmus' copious quotation, throughout this work, of the Old Testament tradition of mercy[6] suggests a desire to redress an imbalance that he himself had perhaps helped to perpetuate. Against the persistent Christian perception that the God of the Israelites was more just than

* * * * *

4 On Erasmus and preaching, see Jacques Chomarat *Grammaire et rhétorique chez Erasme* 2 vols (Paris 1981) II 1053–1153; John W. O'Malley 'Erasmus and the History of Sacred Rhetoric: The Ecclesiastes of 1535' ERSY 5 (1985) 1–29; and Manfred Hoffmann *Rhetoric and Theology: The Hermeneutic of Erasmus* (Toronto 1994) 28–60. Some editions of *De immensa Dei misericordia* identify in the margin the rhetorical techniques being used.

5 On the complex matrix of Hebrew and Greek terms used in the Scriptures to convey the concept most often translated *misericordia*, see C.R. Smith *The Bible Doctrine of Grace and Related Doctrines* (London 1956).

6 Shimon Markish counted 102 references in *De immensa Dei misericordia* to the Old Testament, against a mere 60 to the New: *Erasmus and the Jews* trans A. Olcott (Chicago and London 1986) 46.

merciful, he argues that the Old Testament is as much a testament of mercy as the New, especially since mercy is justice in a higher form; how often in early times was God's power tempered by mercy! Indeed, the two may most fruitfully be combined: 'Let us worship his merciful power and delight in his powerful mercy' (101).

However, the sermon does not deal only with the mercy of God. In the final part Erasmus moves on to discuss human mercy, defined by Augustine and the schoolmen as the compassionate will to alleviate another's misfortune, and one of the essential forms of Christian charity.[7] Indeed, for Erasmus charity and mercy are virtually interchangeable: 'What is charity towards one's neighbour, if not mercy?' (135). In this last section the underlying premise is the Beatitude, 'Blessed are the merciful, for they shall obtain mercy' (Matt 5:7). The act of bestowing mercy on one's neighbour is a means not of earning merit but of calling God's mercy to our assistance in a manner preferable, Erasmus hints, to more formal spiritual exercises. Again the Old and the New Testaments are reconciled in Matthew's quotation of Hosea: 'I desire mercy and not sacrifice' (Matt 9:13; Hos 6:6). In a sense our charitable works must be as gratuitous as God's bestowal of gifts upon us, as we obey Matthew's injunction to be perfect, as our Father in heaven is perfect (Matt 5:45). It is not merit but faith that obtains mercy.

There are already traces here of contemporary doctrinal disputes, and it is in fact possible to read parts of De immensa Dei misericordia as an oblique contribution to the debate over free will, and more specifically as a commentary on the role and operation of divine grace in justification. The conventional Thomist view was to see grace as the action of God's mercy,[8] but Erasmus makes the two virtually synonymous. 'What is the grace of God, if not the mercy of God?' (102). Again, in reviewing the different categories of divine mercy on display in the Old Testament, he refers explicitly to terms applied by scholastic theologians to grace rather than mercy: prevenient, consoling, elevating, and medicinal, among others. However, he does not enter into the old controversies over created and uncreated grace or the related contemporary debate over inherent and infused grace that preoccupied Luther and his opponents.[9]

In general terms Erasmus, aware of the dangers of Pelagianism, held the view that 'the Christian was saved in and through the grace that Christ

* * * * *

7 Cf Thomas Aquinas Summa theologica II–II q 30 art 1 obj 3 citing Augustine's definition in De civitate Dei 9.5 PL 41 261.

8 Thomas Aquinas Summa theologica I q 2 art 112 obj 1

9 For a succinct discussion of these points, see the articles 'Grace' by E.M. Burke in the NCE VI 658–72 and by J. vander Meersch in DTC VI-2 1654.

brought to earth and in no other way,'[10] and that God's grace is thus the first cause of salvation. It is a position that Luther could have approved. But in *De immensa Dei misericordia* Erasmus' identification of mercy with grace and his discussion of mercy in the human sphere reflect the traditional teaching that the human will enjoys a certain freedom. Humanity must choose to co-operate with grace, as David did; the invitation can be rejected, as it was by Pharaoh. As in the formal debate with Luther, Erasmus seems to accept a certain efficacy of the human will, while acknowledging that the effect of divine grace is far greater. Man is weak, according to Erasmus, rather than evil, as Luther held. Erasmus cherished the free human response, through faith, hope, and especially charity, to the divine motion involved in the bestowing of grace on humanity. In *De servo arbitrio* Luther had taken the extreme position: 'Here we must bow down in reverence for the God who is full of compassion for those whom he justifies and saves without their being in any way worthy of it.' Erasmus accused Luther of praising God's mercy towards some so excessively that God was made to appear more cruel than just towards others.[11]

It may be that Erasmus' insistence in *De immensa Dei misericordia* on the mercy of the God of Israel is also a covert reproach to Luther. Although in this sermon (117) Erasmus explicitly condemns only the ancient heretics, the Manichees, for making the God of the Old Testament capricious and ultimately evil, Erasmus had revealed elsewhere his suspicion that Luther's view was similar.[12] But if there are echoes here of the controversy with Luther, Erasmus did not entirely avoid the wrath of his own church. Two passages were later singled out for censure by the Roman Inquisition, the one (104–5) a restrained and partly veiled attack on the trade in indulgences, the other a phrase (115) that the Roman authorities presumably understood to hint at the superfluousness of auricular confession, though Erasmus had been far more outspoken on this in his detailed treatise on confession, *Exomologesis* (March 1524).

In such a work of pastoral piety it would be idle to expect a display of Erasmian wit or classical scholarship, but there is room, early on, for the occasional humanist aside. The ancient Giants and the sacrilegious Salmoneus are enlisted to illustrate worldly pride, though Erasmus half apologizes for appealing to mythology. Ancient history supplies exemplary

* * * * *

10 John W. O'Malley in CWE 66 xxiii; he points out, however, that the problem is made complex because of Erasmus' reluctance to use technical language.
11 For references and a concise recent discussion of these issues, see C. Augustijn *Erasmus: His Life, Works, and Influence* trans J.C. Grayson (Toronto 1991) 141–4.
12 *De libero arbitrio* LB IX 1242F; see also Ep 1881.

tyrants, from Alexander to Trajan, but Erasmus fears that his audience may find the evidence of secular history unconvincing and reinforces the lesson with scriptural counterparts such as Pharaoh and Ahab. An anecdote concerning Socrates' self-restraint is topped by a similar story of St Francis of Assisi. In each case Erasmus distances himself from the 'foolish philosophers' who prefer Plato and Aristotle to Christ. Greek fatalism has no place in the voluntarist system evolved by the Fathers, and no doubt contemporary enthusiasm for ancient Stoicism is being reproved when Erasmus asserts that God's compassion knows no bounds, being 'excessive and immoderate, the sort of thing that passes for a fault among humans.'[13] The literal meaning of the adjective in Erasmus' title, 'unmeasured,' is a constant reminder that when it comes to divine mercy the Golden Mean of the ancients is irrelevant.

De immensa Dei misericordia was reprinted in October 1524 by Froben, and further printings were issued that year at Antwerp, Strasbourg, and Cologne. The book was soon translated into German, Dutch, English, Spanish, and Italian.[14] It was first translated into English by Gentian Hervet 'at the request of Margaret Countess of Salisbury,' and this reasonably full and accurate version was published in London by T. Berthelet, probably in 1526. Two modern versions are in fact less reliable.[15]

My translation is based on the text in LB, checked against the first edition and the *Opera omnia* of 1540. The text in the latter has been lightly edited[16] and the concluding prayers are omitted, as they are from LB, but otherwise the text remained virtually unchanged. Translations of Scripture are my own, as no English version exactly matches Erasmus' text.

* * * * *

13 89 below. Erasmus was perhaps inspired by Augustine's chapters on the passions in *De civitate Dei* 9.4–5 PL 41 258–61.

14 See Allen v 509 and F. vander Haeghen *Bibliotheca Erasmiana* 3 vols in 1 (repr Nieuwkoop 1961) I 72–3, which also lists later translations into Czech and French. On the Spanish translation of 1528 and the popularity of the work in Spain, see Bataillon *Erasme et l'Espagne* I 304–6 and 542n, and on the three different Italian translations, see Silvana Seidel Menchi *Erasmo in Italia, 1520–1580* (Turin 1987) 95–9, 142, and 155.

15 *The Immense Mercy of God* trans E.M. Hulme (San Francisco 1940) and *Concerning the Immense Mercy of God* trans John P. Dolan in *The Essential Erasmus* (New York 1964) 222–70

16 This was perhaps done in the October 1524 Froben edition 'reviewed by the author' (Allen v 509), which I have not seen; improvements in spelling and punctuation and the correction of two scriptural quotations (130 and 138) suggest a fairly vigilant reader.

I am grateful to the Leverhulme Trust for the award of a Senior Research Fellowship which enabled me to undertake this work.

MJH

TO THE RIGHT REVEREND FATHER IN CHRIST AND DOCTOR OF
DIVINITY CHRISTOPH, BISHOP OF BASEL, FROM ERASMUS OF
ROTTERDAM, GREETING.[1]

Your lordship having established, with that piety which we all revere, a
most elegant chapel dedicated to the Lord's Mercies, I have prepared an offering for it, a panegyric in praise of mercy; nor have I ever complied more
readily with your wishes, most honourable of prelates, though it is always
a great pleasure to fulfil your commands. No subject could be more appropriate, either to that pious charity which makes you passionately desire that
all mortals, through God's mercy, should achieve salvation, or to the very
wicked age in which we live. Surely in such a deluge of misfortunes it was
meet and right to exhort all to take refuge in the divine mercy. This task I
undertook all the more readily from the thought that I should at the same
moment fulfil a most holy desire of yours and also do something not un-
pleasing to God. I only wish that this passion we both share may be so ef-
fectual among our fellows that as many as possible, moved by our pleading,
may cast away their wickedness and seek the Lord's mercy. And may that
mercy ever deign to watch over you in your honourable old age!

Basel, 29 July 1524

* * * * *

1 The prefatory letter is Ep 1474, to Christoph von Utenheim. On the circumstances, see Epp 1341A and 1456.

A SERMON ON
THE IMMENSE MERCY OF GOD

Dearly beloved brothers and sisters in the Lord:[1] since it has been agreed that today we should speak about the magnitude of the mercies of the Lord, without whose protection human frailty can achieve nothing whatsoever, let us join in prayer and beg the Lord of us all for mercy. May he so govern the instrument of my tongue and so touch your hearts that, just as we shall depart, through the Lord's mercy, the more enriched by heavenly grace, so each one of us shall bestow on our neighbour, more generously than before, the offices of mercy. For some it is the custom at this point to salute the Virgin Mother, and we shall not deny that she is ever worthy of the highest honour.[2] But it will seem more appropriate to our present subject if you will repeat the following prayer after me:

Jesus Christ, almighty Word of the eternal Father, you have promised that, wherever two or three are gathered together in your name, you will be with them.[3] You see how many are gathered here in your name; deign therefore, according to your promise, to be present at this gathering, that through your Holy Spirit entering our hearts we may all understand more fully the magnitude of your mercy; that we may also give more ready thanks for the mercy we have so often known, and make more earnest supplication for your mercy in all our necessities; finally that we, your servants, may strive to show towards our fellow servants[4] the same mercy that our Lord has so amply shown to us. Amen.

* * * * *

1 As suggested in my introductory note, it seems unlikely that this 'sermon' was actually delivered before a congregation.
2 Cf Ep 1581:526–36 to Noël Béda, where Erasmus defends Louis de Berquin's recommendation that preachers invoke the Holy Spirit rather than the Virgin at the beginning of a sermon. He returned to the point in the *Ecclesiastes* LB V 873C–D.
3 Matt 18:20
4 Probably a reference to the parable of the unjust servant in Matt 18:21–35

If, as the rhetoricians teach, people will always listen carefully and attentively when they know that the subject particularly concerns them,[5] then none of you must doze off during this address, since the salvation of every one of us equally depends upon the mercy of the Lord. There are none, be they young or old, commoner or king, poor or rich, slave or free, scholar or simpleton, sinner or saint, who have not known for themselves the Lord's mercy, and who do not need the Lord's mercy whenever they seek to do good. But what could be more agreeable than to hear it argued that through God's mercy eternal salvation is prepared for all? It is therefore right and proper that all of you who have come to hear this sermon should prove yourselves not merely attentive, but willing and eager. For whoever makes the most of this address will be making the most of himself or herself.

Among the many evils that drag the human race towards eternal perdition, there are two particular diseases – deadly diseases – that must above all be avoided by anyone who holds piety dear and who aspires to the fellowship of eternal bliss. They are self-confidence and despair. The one is born in a proud heart which, blinded by self-love, rebels against God; the other arises from weighing on the one hand the magnitude of the sins committed and on the other the severity of God's judgment, without taking his mercy into account. Both these evils are so contagious, so execrable that few can decide which is the more detestable.

For what could be more insane or more desperate than that mere mortals, creatures of earth and ashes who owe their whole being and all their powers to God's goodness, should turn their horns[6] against God, by whom they were created, by whom they are redeemed, by whom they are in so many ways summoned to partake of eternal life? It is an act of ingratitude to spurn one from whom you receive such gifts. It is an act of madness to attempt revolt against one who can destroy you with a nod. It is an act of impiety not to acknowledge your Creator, not to respect your Father, not to love your Saviour.

Unhappy Lucifer was the first who dared it. Claiming for himself what God had freely given him, he spoke these words in his heart: 'I shall ascend into heaven, I shall raise my throne above the stars of God, I shall sit upon the mount of the congregation, in the regions of the north, I shall soar above the level of the clouds; I shall be like the Most High.'[7] How I wish that at least his unhappy fate, if not his impiety itself, would deter mortals from

* * * * *

5 Cf Quintilian *Institutiones oratoriae* 4.1.47.
6 *Adagia* I viii 68: *Tollere cornua*, meaning to be carried away by pride or anger. 'Earth and ashes' alludes to Ecclus 10:9.
7 Isa 14:13–14

following his unholy example. For 'if God did not spare the angels who rebelled, but cast them into Tartarus and bound them with eternal chains to await the Day of Judgment,'[8] what fate awaits a mere human, a mere worm who has no sooner crawled from the earth than he must be returned to it, if he lifts up his head[9] against God? The lowlier a person's status, the more odious his arrogance in aiming to equal God.

An ancient myth relates that a rebellion once arose among the gods, which compelled Jupiter himself to abandon heaven and flee to Egypt, there to hide disguised as an animal; but more wicked were the plots of the earth-born Giants, who conspired against Jupiter and piled mountain upon mountain to storm heaven and drive Jupiter from his citadel.[10] You are right to laugh: these are mere pagan myths. But the ancient scholars none the less intended to wrap a meaning in the cloak of such myths, something that would depict human behaviour. Salmoneus was hurled into Tartarus because he imitated the lightning and thunder of Jupiter.[11] Agreed, it is a myth: but how many puny mortals have there been who have in reality and in earnest demanded divine honours for themselves? Was not Nebuchadnezzar, who had deemed himself a god, turned into a brute beast by God, that he might change back from a beast to a man?[12] Alexander the Great wished to be thought the son of Jupiter, and let himself be worshipped at feasts.[13] The emperor Domitian wished to be styled 'God and Lord' in all his letters and documents, and even in speeches.[14] Hadrian decreed divine honours for his favourite Antinous.[15] But why do I mention these cases, when it was traditional with the Romans to make their emperors gods when they had ceased

* * * * *

8 2 Pet 2:4

9 *Erigat cristas*, 'raises his crest'; *Adagia* I viii 69

10 Erasmus seems to confuse two myths. The war between the Olympian gods and their predecessors resulted in the flight of Saturn to Italy. It was the later revolt of the Giants that caused the Olympians to flee in disguise to Egypt, until Jupiter called in Hercules to overthrow the insurgents. They were a byword for pride; cf *Adagia* III x 93: *Gigantum arrogantia*.

11 Salmoneus was a king of Elis whose punishment is strikingly described in Virgil *Aeneid* 6.585–94.

12 Dan 4:31–7

13 Alexander exploited the rumour, fostered by his mother, that he was the offspring of Zeus Ammon; see Plutarch *Life of Alexander* 3.1–2.

14 Suetonius *Domitian* 13; cited as an example of tyrannical behaviour in *Institutio principis christiani* CWE 27 223

15 The young and handsome Antinous was drowned in the Nile in 130 AD; he was deified by the Greeks at Hadrian's request, despite rumours that the oracles attributed to Antinous had been composed by the emperor himself. See *Historiae Augustae scriptores Hadrian* 14.4–7.

to be men? Some were even paid divine honours during their lifetime: what
unholy madness to accept them when offered, and what hopeless blindness
to seize them for themselves!

If the evidence of history is unconvincing, let us hear what the apostle
Paul wrote to the Thessalonians – about Nero, according to some commentators: 'And the man of sin shall be revealed,' he says, 'the son of perdition,
who opposes and exalts himself above all that is called God and that is worshipped; so that he sits in the temple of God, displaying himself as if he
were God.'[16] But perhaps it will not seem too strange that men who used to
worship as gods cattle, apes, dogs, and still more worthless things, such as
silent stones and blocks of wood,[17] should themselves wish to be considered
gods: they were, at least, far superior to some of the things to which the
people awarded divine honours. In the Acts of the Apostles Herod, knowing full well that there is but one God, whose worship cannot be shared, let
himself be acclaimed by the assembly: 'It is the voice of a god, not a man.'
Immediately he was struck by an avenging angel, and that pitiful 'god' died,
consumed by worms: there is no disease more foul or more painful.[18]

How I wish that there were not among Christians some who imitate,
not to say surpass, Lucifer's wickedness! What? Are you now waiting for
me to reveal some secret of the confessional?[19] What would be the point,
since in some places we hear the hallowed name of God being taken in vain
everywhere – in the marketplace, in the churches, at banquets, at play? But
that is nothing: we hear God's name abjured and the holy name of Christ
openly reviled; we see people bite their forefinger and utter threats against
God, or thrust their thumb between the index and middle fingers[20] and direct against God, the fount of all glory, a gesture that is commonly used
to insult and humiliate our fellows. Are there not found among Christians
– if they can be called Christians – people who, to obtain riches, soon to
be forfeited, or else some disgusting physical pleasure or some ephemeral
honour, have deserted their true prince and made an unholy pact with the
enemy, Satan? They recite a spell by which they abjure, now and for ever,

* * * * *

16 2 Thess 2:3–4
17 Cf Rev 9:20. Erasmus develops this mockery of ancient paganism in his 1525
    In psalmum quartum concio ASD V-2 198.
18 Acts 12:20–3
19 As was apparently done in sermons by the foolish or wicked confessors whom
    Erasmus castigates in the contemporary *Exomologesis* LB V 153E–F
20 The gesture known as the fig. Rabelais (*Le Quart Livre* chapters 45–7) constructs
    an episode around the *Papefigues*, a people who insulted the pope with this
    gesture.

whatever covenant they had made with Christ, and sacrifice the first-fruits of their body to the lower world, to whose prince they have pledged their entire soul. Whenever such things are discovered we see them punished by public execution.

Did even Lucifer go so far? The Son of God had not died for him, and yet he dared not utter blasphemy against God, but merely claimed equality of honour. That unhappy land, where once five cities flourished, is now a noxious and baleful lake that yields foul pitch instead of the sweet waters of Jordan; to keep alive for posterity the memory of its fearsome fate, its inhabitants were sunk in lust and debauchery. Even so, we do not find that any of them took impiety so far as to pursue God with insults, to curse him, or to threaten him. And yet they all perished, buried beneath a storm of fire and brimstone.[21] And now, to our horror, we find people confessing the name of Christ who will dare what Lucifer did not, what Gomorrah did not, who will dare, I say, to add to their other abominable crimes the crime of blasphemy.

I see, my dearest brothers, that you shudder at the very mention of these things, and no wonder; I myself tremble in every limb, and in my heart, as I speak of them. However, it is not the sole purpose of my speech to demonstrate how great an evil is despair of forgiveness, but also how immense is God's mercy, whose praise I have undertaken today, in that it will even tolerate such people as these and guide them towards repentance. Now perhaps we flatter ourselves that among us examples of the crimes I have just mentioned are rare; but what does it matter if our tongues do not speak blasphemy when the entire lives of many people speak nothing else but blasphemies against God? Some are slaves to gluttony and worship the belly as God,[22] while others aim relentlessly to accumulate wealth by fair means or foul. Some pursue high office by means of murder, treachery, poison, and sorcery, others oppress the poor with their tyranny, while others, to satisfy a whim, will set the world ablaze with war. And as they pursue their evil designs they never blush or falter, but with a harlot's audacity they glory in the worst of deeds while mocking the lives of the devout. Do they not proclaim by their very deeds that there is no God, that God's promises are vain, that God's threats are empty, that the gospel message is false when it

* * * * *

21 See Gen 19:24–5 on the fate of the cities of the plain, Sodom and Gomorrah, which had earlier (Gen 14:2–10) been allied with three neighbouring cities and had fought a battle in the valley of Siddim, 'full of bitumen pits,' which became the Dead Sea.
22 Cf Phil 3:19.

promises the blessings of heaven to those on earth who mourn, who hunger
and thirst after righteousness, who are meek, who suffer persecution and
endure insult for righteousness' sake?[23] What could be more detestable than
such blasphemy as this?

And yet, if there can be anything worse than the very worst, then despair is worse even than this whole Lerna[24] of crimes. Sinners, when apparently allowed to do, unpunished, whatever they want, are elated by success
and say in their hearts: 'How does God know? And is there knowledge in
the most high?[25] He takes no thought for the affairs of humanity.' Moreover, just as it is less unrighteous for someone to believe that God does not
exist than to believe that he is cruel or vain, so it is less impious to deny
flatly that God exists than to believe that he is merciless and thus rob him
of that virtue without which kings are not kings but tyrants.

But all those who abandon hope of forgiveness and cast themselves
into the abyss of despair are not only denying God's omnipotence by believing that there is some sin he cannot wash away: they also make him a
liar. He has promised through the prophet that he will straightaway forget
all sins as soon as the sinner is grieved for them.[26] By contrast, the heirs of
Cain say, 'My sin is too great for me to deserve forgiveness.'[27] What are you
saying, wicked one? If God, overcome by the magnitude of your sin, cannot
forgive, then you take away his omnipotence; if he will not do what lies in
his power, he is false and vain, unwilling to fulfil the promise he so often
gave through the mouths of the prophets.

Everything in God is infinite. But he has three particular attributes:
supreme power, supreme wisdom, supreme goodness. Now although power
is usually ascribed as a special quality to the Father, wisdom to the Son, and
goodness to the Holy Spirit, yet each one of them is enjoyed equally by
all three Persons. He revealed his supreme power in creating by his will
alone this wonderful universe, filled in every corner with marvels, so that
the very gnats and spiders proclaim the boundless power of the creator.
Again, he showed himself the lord of nature when he divided the waters
of the Red Sea, when he stopped the flow of Jordan and let the people
walk across its dry bed, when he halted the sun and moon while Joshua
fought, when he cured the lepers with a touch and called the dead back to

* * * * *

23 Cf Matt 5:4–11.
24 A reference to the many-headed hydra of Lerna; see *Adagia* I iii 27.
25 Ps 73 (Vulg 72):11
26 Cf Isa 43:25.
27 Gen 4:13

life.[28] And while he built his creation with ineffable power, he preserves and governs it with equal wisdom, proving that he is no less wise than omnipotent.

Moreover, his goodness is evident in all things: it was an act of supreme goodness to create the angels and this world, since he himself could desire nothing to complete the supreme happiness that he takes from his own existence; yet he created the human race with the express intention of unfolding for our benefit the full magnitude of his goodness and mercy. In this way God wished to provoke not only our love but our admiration. A king's power and majesty are often admired even by those who hate or envy him. But clemency and generosity are loved even by those who have no need of them, perhaps because they have considered the lot of humanity and know that any one of us may some day have need of them. But there is no mortal, never has been and never will be, who does not need the mercy of God. As the Old Testament reminds us, 'Not even the stars are pure in the sight of God, and in his angels he discovers iniquity.'[29] And Paul cries to the Romans, 'There is no distinction: all have sinned and fallen short of the glory of God, that every mouth may be stopped and all the world be subject to God's judgment.'[30] Let us also hear how the mystic musician chimes in, when with great eagerness of spirit he urges all the righteous to hymn the glory of God on a spiritual lyre, a ten-stringed psaltery, with a new song and a loud cry of triumph. 'The Lord,' he says, 'loves mercy and judgment; the earth is full of the mercy of God.'[31] Judgment is mentioned only once, but mercy appears twice and is given this eulogy: the earth is filled with it. I would venture to add, on the authority of holy Job and of the Apostle, that not only is the earth full of God's mercy, but so too are heaven and hell. What are the lines in Psalm 35? 'Your mercy, O Lord, is in the heavens, and your truth reaches to the clouds.'[32] The lower regions felt the effect of the Lord's mercy when he broke down the shadowy gates and led the prisoners to the heavenly kingdom.[33]

* * * * *

28 See respectively Exod 14; Jos 3 and 10:12–13; Matt 8; John 11.
29 Job 25:5, 4:18
30 Rom 3:22–3, 19
31 Ps 33 (Vulg 32):2–5
32 Ps 36 (Vulg 35):6
33 After his crucifixion Christ descended into hell and freed the righteous, to whom heaven had been closed since Adam's sin. The language here echoes Ps 107 (Vulg 106):14–16.

Those who contemplate the works of God, which according to Moses' mystic narrative he completed in the first six days, cannot but be enraptured and astonished by his ineffable power and wisdom, and must cry out, with the whole church, 'The heavens and earth are full of your glory.'[34] They cannot help but burst into the song of the three children: 'Let all the works of the Lord bless the Lord; praise and exalt him for ever.'[35] Let the whole creation, all that is in the heavens, beyond the heavens, upon the earth, below the earth, in the waters, and in the air: let all proclaim in words everlasting the glory of the Lord.

But what does Psalm 144 tell us? 'The Lord is compassionate and merciful, slow to anger and full of mercy. The Lord is gentle to all, and his tender mercies are above all his works.'[36] Is there something, then, more wonderful than God's creation of the heavens and the countless shining stars, than his creation of the earth, with its great diversity of animals, trees, and other creatures, than his creation of so many legions of angelic intelligences? Would anyone dare to say so, were it not that the prophet clearly proclaims that the Lord's tender mercies surpass the glory of all his other works? And yet no one will doubt the truth of this, if they will consider, in a spirit of pious enquiry, how his redemption of humanity was still more wonderful than his creation of us.[37] Is it not more wonderful for God to become man, than for the angels to be created by God? Is it not more wonderful that God, wrapped in swathing bands, lies crying in a manger, than that he reigns in the heavens he built? It is now, indeed, that the angels sing, 'Glory to God in the highest,' as though witnessing the most stunning work of all.[38] They see the lowest depths of humility but they discern the highest peaks of exaltation.

Is not the whole design for the redemption of humanity – Christ's life, Christ's teaching, Christ's miracles; his suffering, cross, resurrection, reappearance, ascension; the descent of the Spirit and the transformation of the world by a few humble, simple souls; is not this whole design, I say, replete with miracles that are impenetrable even to the angelic intelligences themselves? The wicked demons see and understand his plan for the world's

* * * * *

34 Cf Isa 6:3; Hab 3:3.
35 Song of Three Children 35 (Dan 3:57 in the Vulgate)
36 Ps 145 (Vulg 144):8–9
37 An echo of the prayer said by the priest during mass when adding a drop of water to the wine in the chalice: 'Deus, qui humanae substantiae dignitatem mirabiliter condidisti, et mirabilius reformasti ...'
38 Cf Luke 2:14.

creation, but his plan for the world's restoration was hidden from them, and here one art outwitted another: the art of mercy outwitted the art of malice. The world's creation was a work of power; the world's redemption was a work of mercy. 'He has horns coming from his hands,' says Habakkuk, 'and it is there that his strength is hidden.'[39] What more contemptible than a cross? What weaker than its victim? But beneath that weakness lay hidden the immense power of divine mercy, which broke, subdued, and destroyed all Satan's tyranny.

The same prophet, since he had ears to hear and eyes enlightened by faith, heard the whole creation, from every part of the world, tell of God's greatness, and was afraid. He considered the works of God, and was stunned by amazement. And yet, as though God's greatness were still not sufficiently manifest in all these things, he added something that he felt surpassed all these works: 'You shall be made known between two animals.'[40]

At the intersection of the Old and the New Testaments God became a man and produced that uniquely astounding miracle of his mercy. That, no doubt, is why the prophet adds, 'When you grow angry, be mindful of mercy.'[41] Of those who have done something extraordinary, we are accustomed to say, 'Elsewhere he has surpassed the rest of us, but in this he has surpassed himself.'[42] It will be no crime to say something similar of God: 'In all his deeds God is incomparable and inimitable; in his mercy he surpasses himself.'

There is no virtue that the Holy Scriptures extol in God as much as mercy, which they sometimes call great, sometimes exceeding great; sometimes they exalt its brimming abundance by evoking its multitude. The prophet-king combines in a single text the magnitude and the multitude of God's mercy: 'Have pity on me, O God, according to your great mercy, and according to the multitude of your mercies blot out my iniquity.'[43] Where there is great misery there is need of great mercy. If you consider how grievous was David's sin,[44] you realize the magnitude of God's mercy; if you remember how many different sins were contained in his single crime,

* * * * *

39 Hab 3:4, interpreted as a prophecy of the crucifixion
40 This paragraph is based on the Septuagint version of Hab 3:2. The Hebrew, followed in English versions, is rather different. The 'animals' were read as a reference to Christ's birth in a stable.
41 Hab 3:2
42 Cf *Adagia* I ii 58, where Erasmus quotes Plato *Laws* 1.626E.
43 Ps 51 (Vulg 50):1
44 The murder of Uriah; see 2 Sam 11.

you see the multitude of God's tender mercies. A terrible sin is never committed alone: guilt is joined to guilt like the links in a chain.

First, David committed both murder and adultery, two capital crimes, and both more serious in a king whose duty was to punish such crimes when committed by others. For the more princes sin, unpunished, on earth, the more they offend God. David bore the sword that avenges murder and yet committed murder himself. On his orders adulteresses were taken to be stoned, but he himself forced a woman into adultery. Moreover, his adultery was made especially grave by the fact that he had whole flocks of wives and concubines at home; it was not need but caprice that made him covet another man's wife, so that he seemed to get more pleasure from stealing her than from defiling her. For if someone is driven by poverty to steal from the rich, the crime is not comparable to robbing a beggar of his only coat when you have plenty of your own. Nathan the prophet exposed the horror of David's crime with his parable of the rich robber and the penniless victim.[45]

Now there is no murder more cruel than one that is committed not on an impulse or in a moment of madness, but with premeditation and after waiting for a favourable moment. Uriah was guilty of no crime; the king knew that he was faithful, and indeed abused his loyalty to engineer his doom. Uriah could not bear to enter his house and sleep with his wife while the ark of God lay under canvas and the general, Joab, and his people slept on the ground, but this display of honour did not deflect the king from his wicked plan. The next day David invited him to dine and got him drunk, looking, we must suppose,[46] for a chance to destroy him if in his cups he should blurt out something compromising. But Uriah, even when drunk, refused to enter his house and enjoy his wife. Another trick was then employed to ensure the death of this brave and loyal warrior. Suspecting nothing, he was given the fatal letter; the king, relying on his transparent honesty, had no fear that he would break the seal and read it.

The guilt for the murder was shared with General Joab, in the same way that David shared his adultery with Bathsheba. Nor was Uriah the only one to die. To cover up the plot, a great many more were put in danger; a whole company of soldiers was sent beneath the enemy's spears to ensure the death of one innocent man and to serve the king's lust. So you see how many crimes are involved in a single crime. Had it been a single grievous sin, great mercy would be called for. But in this case David, realizing that his sin was manifold and complex, begs for a multitude of tender mercies.

* * * * *

45 2 Sam 12:1–4
46 This parenthesis was added after the first edition.

Psalm 35 truly reveals the wide extent of God's mercy: 'You shall save, O Lord, both man and beast, as you have multiplied your mercy.'[47] God not only preserves the human race, but also deigns to preserve the beasts for our benefit. Again, how joyful is the prophet's spirit in another psalm, when he says, 'I shall hymn the Lord's mercies for ever more.'[48] Thus in heaven too the Lord's mercy is praised in song, as another psalm also tells us: 'Give thanks to the Lord, for he is good and his mercy is everlasting.'[49] Now it might appear that the ending of all misery, when it comes, will put an end to the hymning of his mercy, were it not that the very bliss that the righteous enjoy in heaven will be a gift of mercy, and that the torments of the damned, too, will be greatly eased by much mercy from God.

But what can one say when an entire life is corrupted by a thousand evils and a whole Lerna[50] of sins? No doubt one must cry, with Asaph, 'O Lord, do not remember our former iniquities, but hasten to bring us your mercies, for we are brought very low.'[51] Again, in another psalm: 'Revive me, O Lord, with your many mercies, according to your decree.'[52] Once more, in another passage David seems to reproach God, saying, 'Where are your former mercies, O Lord?'[53] Again, in Psalm 106: 'Let them give thanks to the Lord for his mercies and his wondrous works for the children of mankind.' This verse reappears several times in the psalm like a refrain.[54] Similarly, in the preceding psalm: 'And he bestowed on them his mercies in the sight of all who had carried them captive.'[55] The psalmist uses 'mercies,' because he has been recalling the many impious deeds by which they had provoked God's anger. And when David was surrounded by woes, he said, 'It is better that I fall into the Lord's hands, for his mercies are many, than into the hands of men.'[56]

As one crime very often involves a number of crimes, so one mercy involves a number of mercies. He redeemed the human race once and for all, but how manifold was his mercy here! Foreseeing this with the eye of

* * * * *

47 Ps 36 (Vulg 35):6–7
48 Ps 89 (Vulg 88):1
49 Ps 107 (Vulg 106):1
50 Cf n24 above. In the development that follows, Erasmus is showing the aptness of the plural *misericordiae* in such cases.
51 Ps 79 (Vulg 78):8
52 Ps 119 (Vulg 118):156
53 Ps 89 (Vulg 88):49
54 Ps 107 (Vulg 106):8, 15, 21, and 31
55 Ps 106 (Vulg 105):46
56 2 Sam 24:14

faith, Isaiah says, in the guise of God promising the Saviour Jesus, 'And I shall make with you an everlasting covenant, the sure mercies of David.'[57] When appeased, God uses a similar figure[58] in Jeremiah, saying, 'And I shall show you mercies and take pity on you.'[59] When many ills are threatened, many mercies are promised. Similarly, when after sending many afflictions God is reconciled to his people, he speaks as follows in Zechariah: 'I shall return to Jerusalem with mercies and my house shall be built there.'[60]

But why rehearse these examples from the Old Testament, in which the term 'mercies' is so often encountered? Yet it is believed by some heretics that that Law comes from a just but not a good God, even though it expounds the mercies of the Lord more fully than anything else. It is therefore no surprise that the apostle Paul, in tune with the prophets' words, writes as follows in his second letter to the Corinthians: 'Blessed be God, the Father of our Lord Jesus Christ, the Father of mercies and the God of all consolation, who comforts us in all our tribulation.'[61] But the Apostle adds something to the idea of mercy. For the role of mercy is to pardon wrongdoing. Here there is something greater: God the avenger becomes God the comforter. That is why I cited those passages from the prophetic books: we must understand that by this figure of speech is meant the immense and ineffable mercy that God shows towards all of us in every kind of trouble.

The same thing is signified by another figure, which is either *anadiplosis* (which in Latin you might call *conduplicatio*) or else something very like *anadiplosis*.[62] For just as the Hebrews call 'good good' something they wish to seem outstandingly good, and 'bad bad' something notably bad, so in the prophetic books God is frequently called 'merciful' and 'the merciful one'[63] because of the surpassing magnitude of his mercy. Thus one reads in Psalm 144: 'O merciful one and merciful Lord' – and as if this were not enough, it goes on: 'Patient and rich in mercy.'[64] Again, in another psalm: 'The merciful one, the merciful Lord made remembrance of his wondrous

* * * * *

57 Isa 55:3
58 That is, the use of the plural
59 Jer 42:12
60 Zec 1:16
61 2 Cor 1:3–4. On the 'heretics,' see n209 below.
62 The Greek term is found in Demetrius *On Style* 140 and the Latin in the anonymous *Rhetorica ad Herennium* 4.38, where it is defined simply as a repetition of the same word.
63 *Misericors* and *miserator*, adjective and noun; besides its many appearances in the Psalms and the prophetic books, the phrase recurs in James 5:11.
64 Ps 145 (Vulg 144):8

deeds.'[65] Likewise in Joel: 'Rend your hearts and not your garments, for
the Lord, the merciful one, is merciful and ready to repent of the evil he
has threatened.'[66] And in Jeremiah: '"And so my heart has been moved for
him," says the Lord, "and being merciful I shall show him mercy."'[67] What
is 'merciful mercy' if not mercy that knows no bounds?

It is for the selfsame reason that, since everything that belongs to God
is boundless, Holy Writ appears to ascribe to him mercy that is excessive
and immoderate, the sort of thing that passes for a fault among humans.
Be persuaded that nothing in God can be construed as a fault, and let your
faithful hearts accept this turn of phrase, realizing that the Scriptures, to
make allowance for mere human understanding, use this figure to convey
the wondrous, unparalleled abundance of God's mercy.

To make things clearer and to help you understand more fully, ponder the following example. If a king had enacted strict laws against murder and then pardoned one particular murderer, this might perhaps be put
down to clemency. But if the same person went on to commit murder again,
ten times or more, and the king forgave him each time, would not everyone
protest that the king's clemency was excessive, that he was undermining the
rule of law and encouraging wickedness and sin by failing to punish him?
In the same way a father who forgave his son once or twice for squander-
ing his money would perhaps be called lenient and kind. But if he trusted
the wrongdoer with money more often than that, would not everyone say,
'He is far too lenient and is ruining his son by his indulgence'? The same
could be said, with still more justification, if he did the same with a servant.
Again, if a husband caught his wife in the act of adultery but took her back
and forgave her, no doubt everyone would be surprised that so tolerant a
husband was to be found, a man ready to share his bed with such a woman.
But if the woman went on betraying her husband's trust, coupling with one
lover after another, and he still took her back, would not the whole town
say that he was an arrant fool – or else his wife's pimp?

But God, who is our king, our father, our master, our bridegroom, excludes no kind of sin, sets no limit to the number of our sins; as soon as we
change our ways, he will remit the penalty that his eternal law has threatened. He welcomes us to his household and takes us into the bedchamber
of his love; he not only welcomes us, but even forgets all our misdeeds. On
his shoulders he brings the lost sheep back to the sheepfold and invites the

* * * * *

65 Ps 111 (Vulg 110):4
66 Joel 2:13
67 Jer 31:20

congregation of saints to share his joy. He goes to meet the prodigal son returning home from his far journey; he offers him the robe and the ring and orders that the fatted calf be killed.[68]

What do these examples reflect but God's unbounded and, so to speak, excessive mercy? It should certainly seem less remarkable if one of us more than once forgives a sinner, when we have ourselves committed the same sin in the past, or may do so in the future, or if a king pardons someone whose services he has found useful in the past; or again, if a father forgives his son because he values his company in his old age, if a master pardons a servant whose work is useful, or a husband an adulterous wife whose company he has found agreeable in the past. Among us, those who pardon others are often afraid of the person they forgive, or cannot take revenge even if they want to. But God, who wants for nothing and can, if he wills it, destroy us with a nod, tolerates us, calls us, welcomes and embraces us, even though we have so often spurned, abandoned, and denied him.

There is no stronger love nor closer bond than between a husband and wife, and thus no anger is more implacable than when marital fidelity is betrayed. And yet, hear what our lenient Lord says in Jeremiah to his adulterous spouse, defiled by her many adulteries: 'It is commonly asked: "If a man puts away his wife, and she leaves him and takes another man, may he return to her later? Will that woman not be polluted and defiled?" Now you have fornicated with many lovers; yet return again to me, says the Lord, and I shall receive you.'[69] A husband will not take back a wife whom he has put away, perhaps for some minor fault or reason, if after the separation she has joined herself to another man, for a husband's love cannot survive such a relationship with another man. But God does not reject his bride, for whom he died and whom he cleansed with his own blood, when she returns after deserting him so often and whoring with unclean spirits. It is no wonder that his mercy is exceedingly great, since his love for us is exceedingly great. Paul did not hesitate to write to the Ephesians, 'We were by nature the children of wrath, as others were, but God, who is rich in mercy, for the exceeding love he bore us, quickened us in Christ when we were dead through sin.'[70] In his Gospel John expresses more clearly our Father's exceeding love for us: 'God so loved the world that he gave his only-begotten Son, that all who believed in him should not perish, but have

*****

68 Allusions to two famous parables in Luke 15
69 Jer 3:1; attributed to Isaiah in both the first edition and the 1540 *Opera*, but corrected in LB
70 Eph 2:3–5

eternal life.'[71] Paul concurs absolutely in his letter to the Romans: 'He did not spare even his own Son, but delivered him up for all our sakes; how shall he not also, with him, give us all other gifts?'[72]

When set against all human love and mercy, and against our deserts, do not God's great love and great mercy indeed seem unbounded? And the truth of this will be still more apparent if we weigh the nature of God, who so loved and attended us with his mercy, against the nature of humanity, on which God deigns to bestow such honour. Let all examine their own hearts and see how often, after receiving a name at baptism and abjuring Satan and all his pomp, they have betrayed the sacrament and defected to their bridegroom's foe; how often, after receiving absolution for their sins from the priest, they have relapsed into worse sin, and indeed how often they fall back that very day into the sin they have repudiated. Let no one be deceived, my dear friends; all who steal or commit adultery, who hate or slander their brother, or who pursue the honours of this world have betrayed their bridegroom Christ, abandoned their father, deserted their king, and fled their master.

But perhaps there will be a better opportunity later on to discuss these things more fully. For the moment, to help you understand the full breadth of the Lord's immense mercy, you should know that in Holy Writ the word 'mercy' sometimes implies munificence, sometimes prevenient grace, or elevating grace, and quite often consoling grace; elsewhere it implies medicinal grace, but very often pardoning grace, or even punishing grace.[73]

In my opinion the Lord's words in Luke, 'Be merciful as your Father is merciful,'[74] refer particularly to beneficence, since ideal beneficence means doing good to your enemies. Matthew made it clearer in a similar form of words used by the Lord: 'Be perfect,' he says, 'as your heavenly Father is perfect, who makes the sun rise upon the good and the bad, and the rain fall upon the just and the unjust.'[75] Since we possess nothing that we have not received freely from God, then everything we do, everything we are,

* * * * *

71 John 3:16
72 Rom 8:32
73 Although some of these categories of grace were the subject of theological debate (see nn81 and 104 below), Erasmus does not enter into the controversies over sufficient and efficacious grace, created and uncreated grace, and inherent and infused grace that preoccupied his predecessors and contemporaries; see my introductory note. Erasmus bases his categories upon the *functions* of divine mercy depicted in the Scriptures.
74 Luke 6:36
75 Matt 5:48, 45

everything we possess is God's mercy. Indeed the whole creation, the angels and the world, is God's mercy. Had he created them for himself, his power or wisdom could be praised; but since he created all things for us, must we not acknowledge in them God's immense mercy? For whom do the heavenly bodies turn, for whom does the sun shine by day, and the moon and stars by night, if not for humankind? For whose benefit was all this created, where before there was nothing? For whom do the floating clouds provide shade and moisten the fields? For whom do the winds blow, the rivers run, the springs bubble, the seas ebb and flow, the lakes lie still? For whom does the earth bring forth so many creatures and so many treasures, if not for humankind?

God subjected all these things to humankind, and wished that humanity alone should be subject to him, as Paul also testifies when he writes to the Corinthians, 'All things are yours, but you are Christ's, and Christ is God's.'[76] The Eighth Psalm echoes Moses' account in Genesis, wondering at God's goodness in providing, of his mercy, so many useful things for us: 'What is man, that you should be mindful of him? And the son of man, that you should care for him? You have made him a little lower than the angels, and crowned him with glory and honour; you have set him above all the works of your hands. You have set everything beneath his feet, all sheep and cattle, indeed all the beasts of the field, the birds of the air, and the fish of the sea.'[77]

I would add the thought, still more sublime, that we owe even the heavenly angels to the Lord's mercy. My words would carry little weight, were it not that Paul clearly teaches this in his letter to the Hebrews (for he is speaking of the angels): 'Are they not all ministering spirits,' he asks, 'sent forth to minister for those who shall be the heirs of salvation?'[78] In both the Old and the New Testament we often read about ministering angels who revive the starving, free prisoners, defend territory, drive out evil, and refresh the faithful with good news. As the Lord himself says in the Gospel, 'Their angels ever behold the face of the Father who is in heaven.'[79] What more wonderful honour than that mere mortals should have angels as their guardians?

Therefore whatever you possess, mortals – and while you remain with Christ, you possess all things – you owe it all to his mercy. If you think

* * * * *

76 1 Cor 3:21, 23
77 Ps 8:4–8
78 Heb 1:14
79 Matt 18:10

otherwise, Paul will rebuke you: 'What do you possess that you did not receive? And if you received it, why do you boast, as if you had not received it?'[80]

Now, whenever you see evil in others, you must acknowledge God's prevenient mercy. David spoke of this more than once: 'And his mercy shall go ahead of me.'[81] You were not born a bastard, a cripple, blind, poor, or dull-witted, as so many are born; give thanks for his prevenient mercy. Any one of the evils that befall human beings could befall you, did not God give you the protection of his mercy. Again, you are not guilty of adultery, perjury, murder, or sacrilege as, alas! so very many are. Acknowledge the mercy of God: you would be guilty of them, had not God's mercy kept you safe. When a certain physiognomist declared that Socrates was a man of immoderate appetites and eager for pleasure, his pupils, knowing their tutor's incredible moderation, were torn between scorn for and indignation towards the man; but Socrates rebuked them and championed him, saying that he had divined the truth: 'I would be all those things, had not philosophy taught me moderation.'[82]

What Socrates ascribed to philosophy, that excellent man Francis ascribed, more correctly, to God's mercy. For one day a companion, at his request, hurled at him all the insults that could be aimed at a wicked man, accusing him of sacrilege, parricide, slander, debauchery, and sorcery; Francis bore it all very patiently and lamented his own sins. Later on his companion asked why he had been made to utter such lies against an innocent, since none of it truly applied to him. 'You told no lie,' replied Francis, 'I would have been all those things, and many more, had not the mercy of God preserved his servant from those evils.'[83]

God's mercy does not protect us merely by urging us to be good; it also assists us in our efforts, accompanies us on the journey, and finally enables us to complete a task that it is beyond human power to achieve.

* * * * *

80 1 Cor 4:7

81 Ps 59 (Vulg 58):10. Erasmus uses 'prevenient' in the non-technical sense of 'preventive' or 'protective.' As defined by the Council of Trent, prevenient *grace* ensures the commencement of justification as, through Christ's vocation, God summons us from our sins without any anterior merit on our part (Denzinger 1525).

82 The story is told by Cicero *Tusculan Disputations* 4.37.80, and by Erasmus in the *Apophthegmata* 3.80 LB IV 163D.

83 This story is told in the life of St Francis in the thirteenth-century *Legenda aurea* compiled by Jacobus de Voragine; see *The Golden Legend: Readings on the Saints* trans W.G. Ryan 2 vols (Princeton 1993) II 226.

The apostle Paul seems to me to have this kind of mercy in mind when he very often, but especially in his salutations, prays for grace and peace; in his letters to Timothy he actually adds 'mercy.'[84] For without prejudice to a better interpretation, if anyone has one, it seems to me that 'grace' here refers to our calling: we are called by faith, that is, willingness to believe. That faith is a gratuitous gift of God, and for that reason those to whom it is given owe it to God's mercy. 'Mercy' here refers to the divine gifts that are distributed to each of us according to the measure of our faith.[85] 'Peace' refers to that complete innocence of life without which there can be no friendship with God or true harmony with our brothers.

But whenever we are rescued from the evils that afflict us, we must not attribute it to the stars, to fortune, or to our own wisdom; we must ascribe the whole to God's mercy. Nobody snared in the toils of sin can be freed unless divine mercy intervenes. Psalm 129 teaches us this: 'For with the Lord there is mercy; with him there is plentiful redemption, and he shall redeem Israel from all her iniquities.'[86] Moreover, God's mercy also rescues us from physical ills, as Paul shows in his letter to the Philippians. Epaphroditus was sick unto death, 'but God had mercy on him,' he writes, 'and not only on him, but also on me, that I should not have sorrow upon sorrow.'[87]

There is no difference between elevating mercy and consoling mercy, except that we are elevated when the ills that pressed upon us are removed, whereas consolatory mercy is present whenever, in the midst of affliction, it lightens the burden of adversity with an admixture of good fortune, 'in the time of trial,' as Paul says, 'providing relief that enables us to endure.'[88]

These ills themselves are often sent by a merciful God, either to cleanse us of our past misdeeds, or to deter us from those we might commit, or to give us an opportunity to demonstrate our virtue. That is how Abraham was tempted, and Job tested by various ills; it is how all who have ever lived faithfully in Christ Jesus have been tried in this world, like gold tried in the fire,[89] by various afflictions. What of those who murmur against God whenever they fall ill, or their wife or child dies, whenever they suffer some loss of property or the harvest fails: do they not know that these are sure signs of God's mercy towards us? Let us listen instead to Solomon's advice:

* * * * *

84 1 Tim 1:2; 2 Tim 1:2
85 Cf Rom 12:3.
86 Ps 130 (Vulg 129):7–8
87 Phil 2:27
88 1 Cor 10:13; on elevating grace, see n104 below.
89 Cf 2 Tim 3:12; Zec 13:9.

'My son, do not reject the chastening of the Lord, nor be weary of his correction; for the Lord corrects those he loves, like a father who delights in
his son.'[90] Paul echoes this idea, in somewhat different words, for the Hebrews: 'For the Lord chastises those he loves, and scourges every child he
takes in.'[91] Therefore, my beloved brothers, whenever a storm of adversity
blows up, take Paul's advice and 'endure the chastisement, knowing that
God is dealing with you as his children.'[92] Listen to the Father's voice as
he mercifully corrects his children in Psalm 88: 'If they have profaned my
statutes and have not kept my commandments, I shall visit their iniquities
with the rod. Nevertheless I shall not deprive him of my mercy nor do violence to the truth I have spoken.'[93] Similarly Paul threatens his children,
whom he loved, saying, 'Which do you wish: that I come to you with a rod,
or in a spirit of gentleness and kindness?' He continues: 'What interest have
I in judging those who are outside?'[94] Nothing is more bitter than for children to hear their father say, 'Do what you like, it is nothing to me.' His
words suggest that he is giving up on them. Such indifference in a parent
is undoubtedly harsher than any reproach.

If therefore indulgence is cruel, punishment is merciful. 'The righteous
one shall punish me,' says the psalm, 'and it will be a mercy; he shall rebuke
me, but the oil of the sinner shall not anoint my head.'[95] The Roman general
Paullus Aemilius, having achieved the remarkable success he planned, had
a premonition of some approaching disaster.[96] And Polycrates, the tyrant
of Samos, tried to buy off envy of his perpetual good fortune by losing a
valuable ring.[97] How much more should we, who live such godless lives, be
afraid that God's vengeance is looming over us whenever worldly fortune
smiles upon us for a while? For when, in the prophetic books, God wishes to
express implacable anger, he threatens to withdraw his rod from them and
halt the afflictions by which their sins are cured. May we, my dear friends,
be spared such 'happiness' as this. Instead, if our Father's mercy allows us

* * * * *

90 Prov 3:11–12
91 Heb 12:6; Paul has quoted the passage from Proverbs in the preceding verse.
92 Heb 12:7
93 Ps 89 (Vulg 88):31–3
94 1 Cor 4:21, 5:12
95 Ps 141 (Vulg 140):5
96 Aemilius conquered Macedonia in a single battle, but saw his premonitions
   realized when his two sons died within days of his formal triumph in Rome;
   see Plutarch *Life of Aemilius Paullus* 36.
97 He threw the signet-ring into the sea, but it was returned to him in the belly
   of a fish. The story is told by Herodotus 3.40–3.

some respite, let us give him thanks and take care not to abuse his kindness; but if adversity closes in, we must none the less give him thanks and submit ourselves entirely to his will.

To keep your body in health, you will go to a doctor, and you will entrust yourself to a surgeon to be bandaged, cut open, or cauterized. To win eternal salvation for your soul, will you not entrust yourself to your Creator, Master, Father, and Saviour? You would not dare tell a doctor what particular cure to prescribe for you; shall we then prescribe for God the ways in which he must look to our salvation? The apostle Paul put up with the angel of Satan threatening and buffeting him, because it helped to safeguard the gifts he had received: 'When I am weakened,' he says, 'then I am strong.' And he cheerfully boasts of his infirmities, which enable him to possess the power of Christ that dwells in him.[98] Who are we to beg to be spared this aspect of God's mercy, when he procures our salvation with a range of afflictions, like bitter medicines? Ordinary people, when they see some nobleman who is wealthy, handsome, and loaded with honours, tend to say, 'What a lot he owes to God!' That is the way we mortals judge things, gauging happiness merely by external appearances. But if you apply God's judgment to the case, you will generally find that the obscure, impoverished, unhealthy outcast owes more to God's mercy than those lucky ones whom the foolish crowd treats like gods. Pile up as many of the world's misfortunes as you wish, you are still exceedingly fortunate if you win eternal bliss at the price of these fleeting woes.

Now all of us are familiar with pardoning mercy, which we also call clemency – unless we think ourselves immune from any sin. But what does the apostle John tell us? 'If we say that we are without sin, we are liars, and there is no truth in us.'[99] If even the stars are not pure in the sight of God, if he found iniquity even in his angels,[100] if no one is innocent in the sight of God, not even a newborn babe, which of us can boast that our heart is pure? Among mortals, many appear to be righteous; with God no one is righteous, but 'all our righteousness is like a rag that is stained with a woman's monthly flow.'[101] Paul feels the law of the flesh in his limbs struggling against the law of the mind, and cries, 'Unhappy man that I am, who will free me from the body of this death?'[102] Job is rightly held in high

* * * * *

98 See 2 Cor 12:7–10.
99 1 John 1:8
100 Cf n29 above.
101 Isa 64:6
102 Rom 7:24

esteem, and yet we can deduce from his dealings with God that he was not entirely free from sin. The prophet David himself also shrinks from God's judgment, unless it be tempered by much mercy: 'Do not enter into judgment with your servant,' he says, ' because no living creature will be justified in your sight.'[103]

Now let each one of us go down into the secret chamber of the conscience and consider how often, how deeply, and in how many ways we have offended God, how everything, even our good deeds, is blemished by our different faults; we shall then understand how much we owe to the immense mercy of God, who so patiently bears with our frailty, who so often invites us to repent, who so quietly remits every offence to those who change their ways.

Let me add to all this one more thing which will perhaps seem unlikely to some: when God destroys the wicked who have plumbed the depths of iniquity, and casts them into hell, even then his mercy is not forgotten. He rescues the Hebrews by parting the sea waves, but drowns Pharaoh and his host. He showed mercy to both sides: elevating mercy to his people, punishing mercy to the king, already hopelessly abandoned to evil; he prevented him from adding to his sins and suffering still worse torments in hell. It was medicinal mercy[104] that sent the plagues to invite him to repent. Broken by misfortune, he had for a moment begun to change his ways, but then, struck by wicked remorse for his wholesome remorse, he said, 'I do not know the Lord, neither shall I let the people go.' He was not even moved by the final miracle to leave off the pursuit but, blinded by anger, recklessly entered the sea. God in his mercy put an end to Pharaoh's hopeless wickedness; if he could not be healed, at least he could perish less painfully.[105]

The same conclusion must be drawn from the other Old Testament examples of God's severity, such as those burned in the fire, swallowed by the earth, cut down by the sword, or killed by serpents. For in the gospel writings all is mercy, and there are very few examples of vengeance. It was a light punishment when Elymas was suddenly blinded and learned not to oppose the gospel message.[106] Paul consigned to Satan a few who were

* * * * *

103 Ps 143 (Vulg 142):2
104 Elevating grace enables the believer to rise above sin, whereas medicinal grace deals with its consequences. The distinction was made by Thomas Aquinas *Summa theologica* 1 q 2 art 109 obj 2–8 and by the Council of Trent (Denzinger 1541 and 1572).
105 The story is told in Exod 14.
106 Acts 13:8–11

afflicted in the flesh, that their souls might be saved in the Day of Judgment and that they might be shamed into producing better fruits.[107] None was more serious than the sudden collapse of Ananias and Sapphira when Peter rebuked them, and yet it is unclear whether their souls were saved by the death of their bodies.[108]

Finally there is the idea that the damned souls of the wicked suffer less than they deserve in the underworld. Some attributed so much to God's mercy that they believed that even the evil demons and the damned must one day, after long aeons, be restored to grace. Although this view was supported by a great author,[109] it was condemned by the orthodox Fathers. I only mention it here to show how magnificent an opinion of God's mercy was held by those great scholars who spent their days and nights immersed in the holy books and who proclaim, celebrate, and sing in praise of almost nothing but the mercy of God.

I have now demonstrated clearly enough, I hope, that it is God's mercy alone that gives us every good thing that we are or that we possess, that protects us from the evils that haunt us, that rescues us from the oppressors, that revives us in the midst of our woes with heavenly comfort and keeps us strong and eager, that amid these fleeting afflictions either teaches us the ways of repentance or trains us to perfect virtue, and that will not lay to our charge the sins into which so often we relapse. But to help you see more clearly its immense height, breadth, and depth, I would ask you to examine with me, for a short while, your own selves: first, the part that makes you the most worthless of creatures, and then the part in which you surpass other creatures; finally you must survey the evils that surround and threaten you from outside, and then the blessings you have been taught to expect. Contemplating all these will prove to us the fullness of God's mercy, to which truly there is no limit or measure.

If we examine this puny body, the instrument or habitation of our soul, you will find hardly any creature so weak, worthless, and indeed wretched as ourselves. Inquire into its origin: the foundation of our race was clay. Then consider, each one of you, how little grandeur there is in those fluids from whose coagulation the rudiments of a human foetus are first formed while still in the depths of the female womb. Then how far removed from

* * * * *

107 See 1 Cor 5:5; 1 Tim 1:20.
108 Acts 5:1–10
109 Origen: see eg his *Commentarii in Matthaeum* 10.3 PG 13 841 and n30 and *Commentarius in Iohannem* 13.58 PG 14 512 and n64. On the controversy over this, see Godin *Erasme lecteur* 419.

nectar and ambrosia are the fluids by which the unborn child is nourished. I shall not now go into the sordid details of human birth; simply call to mind what you have often seen. What is more wretched than human childbirth? How protracted and how dangerous are the struggles of women in labour, how piteous their cries! At last the child itself creeps forth and instantly greets life with tears and wails. Whereas nature provides the rest of her creatures, straight from birth, with some kind of defence or protection – shells, bark, hide, thorns, hair, bristles, down, feathers, scales, fleece – and even protects some tree-trunks from heat and cold with two kinds of bark, only the human infant is naked, cast at birth upon the bare ground to weep and wail.[110] Who would not consider even the hen's chick emerging from its broken shell more fortunate than the human child?

Then think of the swathing bands, the toothless mouth, the speechless tongue, the eyes that cannot bear this new light and seem to long for the dark womb they have left, and the fontanelle still pulsating (a sure sign of feebleness in any animal). In short, an altogether weak and feeble body in which none of the parts yet knows its function. Most other creatures display their natural abilities right from birth. Some are swift, like the horse. The butterfly emerges from its chrysalis and at once takes wing. It is not safe to wrestle with a lion cub. Fish swim straight from the egg and tadpoles wriggle at great speed before they have acquired the name or the shape of frogs. Only the human child has no natural talent – except for wailing. How long does it take to learn to walk, to change from quadruped to biped, how long before it can talk? It cannot even feed itself unless shown the way. Add to this so many different kinds of disease that it is impossible to count them, many of them new and thus difficult to treat, although many of the old familiar ones are equally incurable. The new-born are vulnerable to them all, and indeed some children are born with diseases, such as leprosy and epilepsy, from which many die before they have begun to live; not to mention defective or even monstrous births.

Now consider with me how childhood is notoriously exposed to many ills; how fleeting is youth, how careworn are the years of maturity, how wretched is old age, and, finally, how brief is a whole life's span before we reach old age, which in fact very few of us attain. Let any of you who have reached maturity reflect upon the course of your past life, calculate

* * * * *

110 A similar passage on human frailty at the beginning of the adage *Dulce bellum inexpertis* (IV i 1; LB II 952A–C) demonstrates the illogicality of war between humans. The classical archetype is the prologue to Book 7 of Pliny's *Naturalis historia*.

how many diseases and perils you have escaped, and give thanks for God's mercy. I would even count among our major physical ills the fact that the seeds of all vices are deeply implanted in us. How great a proclivity towards anger, lust, extravagance, envy, ambition, and greed do we carry with us from our mother's very womb, whereas other creatures live happily within the bounds of desire that nature has set! How wearisome for us all is the struggle against these remnants of the old Adam! And how few succeed in it! Our spirit is weighed down by the earthy mass of the body and is dragged down, willy-nilly, towards things of which it disapproves.

Next, consider the host of dangers that besets us in the world outside, and you will discover that many more die by accident than from disease. How many are carried off by lightning, earthquake, landslide, flooding of lake, river, and sea, polluted air, poison, dangerous beasts, collapsing buildings – and bad doctors? But nothing brings greater disaster than war. However, these evils threaten only the body with extinction. So many dangers hang over the spirit, from the flesh, its familiar enemy, from the world, which uses soft words to smother it or violence to oppress it, from the evil spirits who sometimes transform themselves into angels of light.[111] Who would not be frightened by their numbers, their power, their cunning, their malice, and their insatiable thirst for destruction? Amid all these woes, who would not be paralysed by the thought of death, which is certain for us all but whose hour is unknown, of the rigour of the Last Judgment and of the endless torments of hell?

I can see you shudder at the mere mention of such great woes, and not unreasonably; but the more you see woes and dangers here, the more you owe to God's mercy, which not only protects those who trust in it, amid all these troubles, but also turns them all into an opportunity to achieve greater happiness. We owe every calamity to the sin of the old Adam, but we owe the happiness that emerges, with interest, from calamity to the new Adam of mercy, who is Christ Jesus, to be praised by all for ever more. Satan expelled us from paradise, but Christ has opened the gates, not to the earthly paradise but to the kingdom of heaven. The serpent imposed on us the manifold sorrows of this life, Christ restored to us the eternal joys of the life everlasting. Satan, through his wiles, brought us the body's death; Christ, through his mercy, gives us eternal life; all who entrust themselves wholeheartedly to him need fear no sort of enemy. He has conquered the world,[112] he has broken all Satan's tyranny and turned the flesh into spirit.

* * * * *

111 Cf 2 Cor 11:14.
112 Cf John 16:33.

To conquer the world showed his power; to do it for us showed his mercy. Let us worship his merciful power and delight in his powerful mercy.

We can do all things through him, since he gives us power as long as we abide with him. We possess all things through him, for in him is the sum of all good things, while his mercy protects us on every side, elevates, consoles, and enriches us, as the prophetic psalm says: 'The Lord will surround with mercy those who trust in him.'[113] How many woes lie in wait for those who have put their trust in their physical assets, in wealth, chariots, horses,[114] worldly wisdom, and their own deeds and merits! But what gives the righteous sure protection? 'But I am,' says the psalmist, 'in the multitude of your mercy.' And a little later: 'O Lord, you have surrounded us with your good will as with a shield.'[115] When you hear the words 'good will' you know that trust in your own merits is excluded. When natural strength deserts us and merits fail, mercy will come to the rescue. The warrior's shield covers but one part of the body, the shield of divine mercy protects our entire being against every attack: from above, against the fiery darts[116] of the wicked spirits that rain down from the heavens; from below, against the wiles of the serpent gliding beneath our heels; from the front, against the dangers to come; from the rear, against renewed attack from the past; from the right, against arrogance brought on by worldly success; from the left, against the disappointment of failure.

Relying on this shield, the psalmist cries, 'The Lord is on my side; I shall not fear what men may do to me.'[117] And elsewhere, 'I shall not fear the peoples that surround me in their thousands.'[118] More spirited still, Paul wrote to the Romans, 'If God is for us, who is against us?'[119] That outstanding warrior had put on the panoply[120] of faith, which protects us, a confidence not in works but in the mercy of God. Equipped with that armour, he scorned not only hardship, hunger, nakedness, danger, and persecution, but even the tyrant's sword that threatened instant death.[121] Human cruelty can do nothing when the protective mercy of God is present; indeed, what was bolder still, Paul scorned not only life and death, but angels, principalities,

* * * * *

113 Ps 32 (Vulg 31):10
114 Cf Ps 20 (Vulg 19):7; Isa 31:1 etc.
115 Ps 5:7, 12
116 Cf Eph 6:17, in a favourite passage of military imagery.
117 Ps 118 (Vulg 117):7
118 Ps 3:6
119 Rom 8:31
120 *Panoplia*, rare in Latin and an allusion to the Greek of Eph 6:11, 13
121 Cf 2 Cor 11:23–7.

powers, things present and things to come, force, height, depth, and finally any other creature, whether in heaven, on the earth, or under the earth.[122] And this is the man who, conscious of his frailty, calls himself a vessel of clay: 'We keep this treasure,' he says, 'in vessels of clay.'[123] Where then does this fragile pot find so much strength? 'By the grace of God,' he says, 'I am what I am.'[124] What is the grace of God, if not the mercy of God? Let us join Paul in boasting of our infirmities, that the power of Christ may dwell in us.[125] For it is more fitting that we glorify the mercies of God by contemplating our miseries.

However, it is also useful, my fellow mortals, to contemplate that part of yourselves in which you surpass all other creatures. For if you judge by physical qualities, you will see that you are inferior to many species of animal. Camels are taller, tigers are swifter, bulls are stronger, swans are whiter, peacocks are fairer, and fishes, if we believe the proverb,[126] are healthier. In fact, they nearly all surpass us: lynxes and eagles have better eyesight, vultures a better sense of smell, and deer and ravens live longer. And yet if one considers the endowments of the human body, one will find in them cause to praise God's mercy. How sharp are our senses, how symmetrical our limbs, how well designed our organs for their various functions! Indeed Lactantius, a man of singular eloquence, published a book on this subject entitled *On the Workmanship of God*.[127] It can be read with profit, if we remember to ascribe to God's generosity any good things in the body, since they all proceed from God's mercy. Otherwise, anyone inclined to boast of the body's endowments should take heed of this: 'All flesh is grass, and all its glory is like the flower of the field.'[128] And this: 'Why are you proud, earth and ashes?'[129]

Nor have we any reason to claim credit for the endowments of the spirit, which make us more remarkable than other creatures. He who created

* * * * *

122 Cf Rom 8:38–9.
123 2 Cor 4:7
124 1 Cor 15:10
125 Cf 2 Cor 12:9.
126 *Adagia* IV iv 93, based on the belief that fish are insensible to pain. The animals' attributes here represent a series of commonplaces, no doubt originally based on Aristotle and Pliny.
127 *De opificio Dei*, written in 303–4 AD, a famous demonstration of divine providence based on the wonders of human anatomy
128 Isa 40:6
129 Ecclus 10:9

the body also created the spirit. He fashioned the body from mud and imparted the spirit by the breath of his mouth. That is why in the other animals the soul perishes with the body, while our soul survives its body until it receives it again in the promised resurrection. The power of the soul is demonstrated by death itself; once the soul has left, all that remains is a useless corpse: where are its heat, its colour, its movement, the activity of all the senses? And yet, even while the soul is held in thrall by this weak and unhappy body and can act only through bodily organs, which frequently impede its natural powers, how remarkable, none the less, is the swiftness and perspicacity of the human mind! How vast the treasure-house of the memory! Is any of nature's secrets so deeply hidden, in the heavens or on earth, that human intelligence has not observed, analysed, and understood it? It is a great thing that many predict from the position and movement of the stars something of what will happen in years to come; but it is a greater thing that from the created world can be deduced the eternal power and divinity of its architect, as Paul testifies.[130] How rapid is human thought; in a short space of time the human intellect can consider so many things simultaneously! How immense is the power of memory, which faithfully retains the forms and the names of so many things presented to it by the senses!

I shall not even mention here those who have studied so many arcane subjects, and languages not their own, and who remember what they have learned. Each one of you should just think how many people's faces and names you can remember, how many animals, trees, plants, places, and countless other things you can recognize by their shape and can name from memory. Unthinking people call these natural gifts, but in truth they are the gifts of God's mercy, which are allotted to each of us not according to our deserts, but according to his loving-kindness. Although the prodigal son, in the capriciousness of his human will, abused all these gifts, not only was he not deprived of his existing gifts, but through grace he was given a more generous endowment of divine gifts. Through the Law God instructed us, through the Son, whom he sacrificed entirely for us, he taught us the secrets of his wisdom,[131] through his Spirit he enriches our souls with various gifts that transcend human powers. He gives us understanding of the mystic Scriptures, which light the way and comfort us in all troubles; he gives us knowledge of the future, the power to speak in tongues, to scorn witchcraft, to banish disease, to raise the dead, to cast out evil spirits, to overthrow the

* * * * *

130 Cf Rom 1:20.
131 The first edition has 'of God' rather than 'of his wisdom.'

gates of hell; he gives us the right to be members of Christ, children of God, joint heirs to the heavenly kingdom to which there shall be no end.[132]

At this point, remember how you were created partly, at least, from mud; then remember how sin brought you lower than the beasts of the field. Remember, again, to what honour, to what bliss you are called, and you will see that the Lord's mercies are without number and without measure. What more vile than the dung-beetle? Yet the dung-beetle is clean compared to the sinner in his squalor. What more sublime than the angels? Would it not be beyond all reason to make an angel from a dung-beetle? But now he has made humans, who were lower than the beetle, greater than the angels and has changed them, I would dare to say, into God. For why should I not dare to say what Holy Writ dares: 'I have said, "You are gods, and all children of the most high"'?[133] Whatever is born of God is to some extent God. Whatever is joined to the body and spirit of Christ acquires the right to share his holy names. If there is nothing here that you can ascribe to your own merits, glorify God's mercy, worship God's mercy, extol God's mercy.

Should people try to claim some part of the credit for themselves, the apostle Paul will instantly refute them, attributing it all to God's grace. The word 'grace' resounds throughout his letters, and whenever you hear it you must realize that God's mercy is being commended to you. It is by grace that we are cleansed of our sins, by grace that we believe, by grace that through the Spirit his love, through which we perform the works of piety, is poured into our hearts.[134] 'For we are not sufficient to think anything by ourselves, as if it were our own, but all our sufficiency is from God.'[135] If Paul spoke the truth, what becomes of those shameless people who will sell their good works to anyone, as if they still possessed so much themselves that they could enrich others? Wretched are those who hawk their good deeds in this way, and cursed are those who trust in the works of mortals! Anyone suffering from the first disease must listen to what the Laodicean church was told in the Apocalypse: 'You say, "I am rich and well endowed

* * * * *

132 Erasmus lists a number of the divine gifts promised or delivered in the Gospels, the Acts, and Paul's letters.

133 Ps 82 (Vulg 81):6; cf John 10:34. The patristic tradition, echoed by medieval theologians, held that people are beatified through participation and may in this sense be called gods; see eg Thomas Aquinas *Summa theologica* 1 q 2 art 3 obj 1 ad 1.

134 Cf Rom 5:5.

135 2 Cor 3:5. The passage following, down to 'the more wretchedly naked they are,' was recommended for deletion in the *Index expurgatorius* LB X 1821, presumably because it appears to attack the trade in indulgences.

and I want for nothing"; you do not know that you are wretched, miserable and poor, blind and naked.'[136] But it is a still graver sin to promise riches to others from the abundance of your own good works. What, in fact, does the Holy Spirit advise in this case? 'I advise you,' it says, 'to buy from me gold that has been tried in the fire, that you may become truly rich.'[137] And you, who know your own poverty, why beg from the beggars? 'If anyone lacks wisdom,' says James, 'let him ask it of God, who gives to all liberally and without reproaches. All good giving and every perfect gift comes from above, from the Father of light.'[138] Will you seek from humankind the cloak of good works? The more magnificently clothed people think they are, the more wretchedly naked they are. Admit your misery and mercy is at hand. Among mortals, some will charge for a favour, others expect a service to be returned with interest; nothing costs more than something bought by entreaty. With God, nothing is so freely given as what is bought with the two mites[139] of prayer and trust, since in this case the seller of mercy has himself supplied the money to pay for it.

I have already said a great deal, my good brothers, about God's mercy, but there would still be far more to say if I wished to quote all the passages in the mystic Scriptures where the magnitude of God's mercy is commended to us. It remains to urge you briefly not to show yourselves unworthy, through arrogance, of the manifest mercy of God, or to despair of God's mercy through unwarranted despondency. After that I shall indicate briefly some ways in which God's mercy may be called to our assistance. This will be the culmination of my sermon, if as I speak the Lord's mercy honours us with its presence.

Nothing repels God as much as persistent stiff-necked pride: 'For he resists the proud but bestows grace on the humble.'[140] This blind madness and mad blindness are induced in many by worldly success; as though oblivious of their creator, they live as their whims dictate, giving so little thought to amending their lives that they even 'glory in their wickedness, powerful in iniquity.'[141] And, as we read elsewhere, 'They rejoice to do evil and delight in wickedness.'[142] Solomon wrote of them, 'When the wicked have

* * * * *

136 Rev 3:17
137 Rev 3:18
138 James 1:5, 17
139 Cf Luke 21:2, the widow's 'small coins.'
140 1 Pet 5:5
141 Ps 52 (Vulg 51):1
142 Prov 2:14

come into the depths of evil, they show contempt.'[143] Paul also wrote of such people, 'God has given them over to their depraved desires so that they do the things that are unseemly.'[144] Some of these promise themselves permanent immunity from punishment for their misdeeds; they scorn salutary advice and will not accept anything that might encourage them to repent, saying, 'God can keep his heaven if he will leave us the earth.' Moses speaks of them in his song; having recalled God's many great favours to the people of Israel, he adds, 'The beloved grew fat, and unruly; he grew fat, sleek, and bloated; he abandoned God his maker and deserted God his salvation.'[145] Psalm 72 depicts their kind: 'They are not in trouble as others are, and they shall not be scourged with their fellows. That is why pride has seized them; they have been overcome by their own impiety and iniquity; they have yielded to their hearts' desires. They have conceived and spoken wickedness; they have spoken iniquity in high places. They have set their mouths against heaven and their tongues have walked through the earth.'[146]

But now hear the outcome of such unblest bliss: 'Nevertheless, you have punished them for their deceits and cast them down when they were exalted. How are they brought into desolation and ruined in a moment! They have perished for their iniquity. In your city, O Lord, you shall bring them to nothing, like a dream that vanishes upon waking.'[147] All who follow Lucifer and rise up against God shall suffer the fate threatened by the Lord in the Gospel: 'I beheld Satan falling like lightning from heaven.'[148] And Chorazin, swelling with godless pride in her fleeting worldly wealth, is told, 'Woe to you, Chorazin; though your arrogance now lifts you to heaven, the Lord's vengeance shall cast you down to hell.'[149] Paul too was once swollen with pride, clinging fiercely to the law of his fathers and 'breathing threats and slaughter against the Lord's disciples'; that is why, when the Lord's right hand struck him suddenly to the ground, he heard these words: 'It is hard for you to kick against the pricks.'[150] But since in his case it was

* * * * *

143 Prov 18:3
144 Rom 1:28
145 Deut 32:15
146 Ps 73 (Vulg 72):5–9, omitting part of verse 7. The Vulgate version, following the Septuagint (cf PL 29 263A), is rather different from English versions, which follow the Hebrew text.
147 Ps 73 (Vulg 72):18–20
148 Luke 10:18
149 Allusions to Matt 11:21–3; Isa 14:11
150 Acts 9:1–5

error and not perversity, he obtained mercy. Soon, as he perceived, the Lord forgave the sinner; not only forgave him, but even transformed the wolf into a sheep, the tyrant into an apostle.

But the curse remains on those who persevere in their sins and finally become too thick-skinned[151] to take any interest in doing good, saying to God, 'Leave us alone; we do not wish to know your ways.'[152] They talk like the people in Isaiah who, summoned by the Lord to weep and wail, to shave their heads and put on sackcloth, instead make merry and exult, slaughtering cattle and sacrificing sheep to eat the meat, drinking wine and saying, 'Let us eat and drink, for tomorrow we die.'[153] The same prophet tells of those who mock the Lord's threats, when he calls them to repent: 'Precept upon precept, precept upon precept; warning after warning, warning after warning; a little more here, a little more there!'[154] Similarly, people elsewhere say, 'We shall not listen to the Lord, but shall die in our sinfulness.'[155] For them, as the old proverb puts it, patience, too often abused, turns into fury,[156] for when the Lord's mercy is scorned it makes his condemnation all the harsher. So in Isaiah the Lord they have mocked adds, 'And the word of the Lord shall come to them: precept upon precept, precept upon precept; warning after warning, warning after warning; a little more here, a little more there; saying that they shall go forth and fall back, and be bruised, and snared, and taken.'[157] Unblest, they set out and, leaving their first foul desires behind, go on to things that are worse and worse. They plunge into the abyss of impiety, they are enmeshed in the bonds of sin, they are trapped in the toils of eternal damnation; spending their days amid pleasures, in an instant they plunge down to hell. How truly wretched they are, condemned to perdition! They are like bloated victims fattened for the slaughter: the enormity of their sin cannot puncture their arrogance, nor God's great gentleness soften them to repentance.

God in his clemency will tolerate your sinfulness time and again, to allow you to change your ways. He will grant you time to repent, and will not in the meantime withdraw his blessing from you. He will give you health, wealth, and the other good things of life, heaping (as it were) coals of fire

* * * * *

151 *Callo ducto*; cf *Adagia* III i 35.
152 Job 21:14
153 Isa 22:12–13
154 Isa 28:10, spoken ironically
155 Cf Ezek 3:20, 18:24; John 8:24.
156 Publilius Syrus F13 (178)
157 Isa 28:13

upon your head,[158] so that even if you cannot hate your sin because it is intrinsically vile, you may at least begin to hate it because it displeases so kind a Father. Aeschinus, a young man in a play, is so moved to discover his father's indulgence towards his erring son that he obeys him scrupulously from that moment on. This is what he says: 'What is happening here? Is this what it means to be a father or to be a son? Had he been my brother or my comrade, could he have been more kind? Is he not a man to be loved, to be taken to one's heart? Well! his forbearance has filled me with a great desire to do nothing thoughtless to offend him; forewarned is forearmed!'[159]

If parental indulgence can teach decent children to hate sin, why should you, a miserable sinner, harden your heart more and more against your Father's great goodness, and also ignore Paul as he tries to recall you to your senses? 'Do you scorn the riches of his goodness, tolerance, and patience? Do you not know that God's kindness is there to lead you to repentance? But by the hardness of your impenitent heart you are storing up wrath for yourself in the day of wrath and revelation of the just judgment of God.'[160] No beast is so wild that it cannot be tamed by human kindness; and yet when God, with unparalleled generosity, calls you to him, you grow more rebellious. No material is so hard that it cannot be softened by human art: copper melts in the furnace, iron softens in the fire, horn becomes pliable when filled with wax, and the unrivalled hardness of a diamond can be overcome by goat's blood.[161] And yet your heart, harder than horn, harder than iron, harder than a diamond, is not softened by the fires of hell, the gentle indulgence of the Father, nor the blood of the spotless Lamb shed for you, nor indeed by anything sterner than all these. Take up your trophies and enjoy the triumph of impiety! You are the victor, poor wretch, you have triumphed over God's arts and have won a hapless victory. 'Unhappy the land,' as Paul says, 'and close to accursed, which, though it has often drunk the rain from heaven, brings forth nothing but thorns and thistles.'[162] How much unhappier is the land which, though watered so often by the rain of God's mercy, solidifies into a stone so hard that it can receive no impress of the Holy Spirit. God's finger wrote the law of Moses upon stone tablets; your heart is thus harder than those stones, since the Spirit of God can write no part of the gospel law upon it. Who can sunder

*　*　*　*　*

158 Cf Rom 12:20.
159 Terence *Adelphi* 707–11
160 Rom 2:4–5
161 According to Pliny *Naturalis historia* 20.1.2
162 Heb 6:7–8

for us the rocks that are our hearts, if not the one whose death split the
stones asunder, that the dead might arise from their tombs?[163] What can
give us hearts of flesh, if not the Word of God, which was made flesh for
our sake?[164]

But more hopeless still are those who make excuses for their sins and
hold blasphemous and godless opinions. They say that there is no God in
heaven or that, if there is, he holds aloof from human affairs; that there is
no life after the body's death, and no immortality awaiting those who have
lived godly lives in Christ Jesus; that there is no torment awaiting those who
have served Satan, that the threats of Scripture are vain and the Gospel's
promises empty. Others pervert the Scriptures to present their crimes as
good deeds; they constrain the word of God, whose rule should be used to
restrain our depraved appetites, to endorse their wickedness, and add to all
their other crimes, like a terrible epilogue,[165] the sin of heresy.

Quite rightly, when you hear of such impiety, your faces turn pale,
you begin to tremble in every limb, and it is clear how much you abominate
the things you are hearing. If only we did not hear of such things happening even among those who profess the name of Christ! I have shown you
Scylla, by whom a great many are seized and destroyed. I shall also show
you Charybdis,[166] a danger graver than grave and more dreadful even than
the other. I refer to people who, following Cain and the traitor Judas, are
plunged into eternal perdition because they despair of forgiveness. They
are destroyed, just the same, but the manner of their ruin is not the same.
Pharaoh, whose heart is hardened, may say, 'I do not know the Lord, neither shall I let the people go.' But what of Cain? 'My sin is too great for me
to deserve forgiveness.' And then Judas: 'I have sinned; I have spilled innocent blood.'[167] Both of them realize the enormity of their sin, both confess
it, both are ashamed, but both of them recoil from the face of the Lord, with
whom alone are to be found 'mercy and the abundant redemption of sin.'[168]
For the following is written concerning Cain: 'Cain departed from the sight
of the Lord and dwelt in exile in the land to the east of Eden, etc.'[169] And

* * * * *

163 See Matt 27:51–3.
164 John 1:14. The expression 'hearts of flesh' is found in Ezek 11:19 and Ecclus
17:16.
165 *Colophonem imponere*; cf *Adagia* II iii 45.
166 On the proverbial uses of Scylla and Charybdis (Homer *Odyssey* 12.235–46),
see *Adagia* I v 4 CWE 31 387–9.
167 Exod 5:2; Gen 4:13; Matt 27:4
168 Ps 130 (Vulg 129):7
169 Gen 4:16

Judas departed from the holy supper and did not return. Unhappy are those who so depart from the sight of God's mercy that they cannot return!

I believe that this was Jeremiah's meaning, when he wrote, 'Do not weep for the dead, nor grieve over him; weep and wail for the one who departs, for he shall return no more.'[170] He wants no tears for the dead, because some day they may live again. All our tears should be reserved for those who turn away from the fountain of eternal life and never return, through repentance, whence they have gone. That spendthrift the prodigal son had left his home and his loving father to go into a far country, but he did return.[171] Peter had completely abandoned the Lord when he denied him three times; but he soon returned, when he recalled what Jesus had said, and began bitterly to weep. He had lost his senses, but returned to his right mind and returned to Jesus.[172] As Isaiah cries, 'Remember this, and be confounded; let your hearts be restored, you transgressors.'[173] Peter remembered, and his heart was restored; the heart of stone, the heart of pumice, from which no tear-drop could be squeezed, was taken from him. He was given a heart of flesh,[174] from which at once there sprang a fountain of tears, made bitter by the pain of repentance, but made wholesome by the return of his innocence. Judas, however, did not return to Jesus, but went to the priests and Pharisees, took the fatal coins, and then turned to the wretched noose and hanged himself.

It was for our instruction that the Lord allowed such things to happen to his own disciples. You can see how very different was the outcome for the two apostles who sinned. Although the Lord in his kindness repeatedly urged Judas to mend his ways, he persisted with his wicked plan. But when Jesus looked at him, Peter remembered the Lord's words, came to himself in a moment, and, as if unworthy of the Lord's presence, betook himself, not to a noose, but to tears; in other words, not to despair, but to a remedy. Judas imitated Cain, the first to commit his crime; he did indeed acknowledge the magnitude of his sin, but he did not remember God's messages. Throughout the sacred books they invite us to return, call us to repent, and promise us mercy. Is there a single page in the sacred books that does not resound with God's mercy?

* * * * *

170 Jer 22:10
171 See Luke 15:11–32.
172 Matt 26:69–75
173 Isa 46:8
174 See n164 above.

I include not only the books of the New Testament, which is the law of grace, but also those of the Old Testament, which is supposed to be more severe. Let us hear how gently the Lord, in Jeremiah, calls his people to repentance, portraying them as a bride who has deserted her husband and prostituted herself to all comers: ' "Turn again, you rebellious children," says the Lord, "for I am your husband." '[175] Again, in Job: 'The Lord opens the ears of the sinners to his rebuke, and tells them to turn back from their iniquity.'[176] But the poor wretches who stop up their ears against the Lord's voice are like the deaf asp, which deliberately blocks its ears against the voice of the wily snake-charmer.[177] 'This day,' says the psalm, 'if you have heard his voice, do not harden your hearts.'[178] 'This day' means our own times, as long as we live this life, and while life lasts the Lord speaks to us constantly, calling us to repentance, offering us ready forgiveness.

Did I say forgiveness? God's mercy is greater than that: it promises rich rewards to those who return to him. For as we read in the book of Job: 'If you return to the Almighty, you shall be restored and shall put iniquity far from your tabernacle; he shall give you flints for your dust, and streams of gold for your flints.'[179] Hark to the Lord's mercy, in Isaiah, as it summons us to repent: 'If you seek,' it says, 'seek; turn again and come.'[180] If you seek an end to your woes, do not seek it from the children of earth, in whom there is no salvation, nor from sorcerers, nor from the noose, but seek it from me; I alone am able and ready to forgive. Only turn away from the shameful things you have loved and, having turned back, come to me.

Again, through the same prophet, he summons the whole race of mortals to him, saying: 'Am I not the Lord? And there is no God beside me. There is no just and holy God except me. Turn again to me and you shall be saved, all the ends of the earth, because I am God and there is no other.'[181]

The Lord says these things to nations sunk in idolatry, murder, sacrilege, parricide, incest, and blasphemy; so why should you, poor wretch, turn from the Lord in despair? In days of old, when sin reigned unpunished among the gentiles, it seemed that God's mercy was confined within

* * * * *

175 Jer 3:14
176 Job 36:10
177 Cf Ps 58:4–5 (Vulg 57:5–6).
178 Ps 95:7–8 (Vulg 94:8)
179 Job 22:23–4
180 Isa 21:12
181 Isa 45:21–2

the narrow bounds of Judaea. However, through the gospel his mercy has been extended to all the ends of the earth.

Once again, in Jeremiah, he threatens punishment to the obstinate, but offers ready forgiveness to those who mend their ways: 'If that nation,' he says, 'against which I have spoken shall repent of its evil, I too shall repent of the evil that I had thought to inflict on them.' And although a little earlier he was threatening to overthrow, uproot, and scatter them, he quickly promises the opposite, saying, 'I shall speak of a nation and of a kingdom that I shall build and plant.'[182] Similarly in Ezekiel he promises to those who return not only forgiveness, but even the 'amnesty' celebrated in the Greeks' proverb,[183] that is, oblivion for all their previous crimes. For although he had just enumerated all kinds of misdeeds and wickedness, he added: 'But if the wicked repent for all the sins they have committed, keep all my statutes, and do that which is lawful and right, they shall live and not die. I shall not recall all the iniquities they have committed. Why should I take pleasure in the death of the wicked, says the Lord God, rather than in seeing them turn back from their ways and live?'[184] And a little later: 'Turn back and repent of all your sins, and your iniquity shall not be your ruin. Cast aside all the transgressions by which you have transgressed and make yourselves a new heart and a new spirit. Why should you die, house of Israel? Since I do not desire the death of those who die, says the Lord God, turn again and come to me.'[185]

Why do you despair, poor wretch, since God sent his Son to earth to bring you good hope? He is, of course, the mercy of God of whom the psalmist sings, 'We have taken up your mercy, O God, in the midst of your temple.'[186] Take your place in the temple and embrace mercy. He rises again, crying, 'I do not desire the death of the sinner, but rather that he be converted and live.'[187] Hearken to his voice, unhappy sinner, shake off your dreams of death and rise again with Christ, that you may live in him. He returned to life for you, lest the death due to sinners overwhelm you forever.

* * * * *

182 Jer 18:8–9
183 *Adagia* II i 94 (also mentioned in I vii 1); in some of the original editions, 'amnesty' is in Greek; it is rarely used in Latin.
184 Ezek 18:21–3
185 Ezek 18:30–2; in the Vulgate the last word is *vivite,* 'live,' rather than *venite,* 'come.'
186 Ps 48:9 (Vulg 47:10)
187 Ezek 33:11

And let no one think that this divine clemency is not readily available, or is available only to those who have committed a few trifling sins. Hark to the Lord's clear promise: 'If at any time the sinner bewails his sins, I shall not recall all his iniquities.'[188] God has not excluded any kind of crime, he does not weigh up the magnitude or the multitude of your misdeeds.[189] Simply bewail your sins, and he will readily cast all your past crimes into oblivion. In our human frailty we cannot live without committing lighter sins, and for them we must invoke God's mercy every day, saying, 'Forgive us our debts, as we forgive our debtors.'[190] Our prayers will be heard, provided that we have heard our neighbour's plea for forgiveness.

Now there is also a certain hierarchy of mortal sins. Some people are light sleepers and can be woken by the merest whisper; others sleep more soundly and it will take a shout to wake them, while some sleep so deeply that a hard shaking will scarcely rouse them. Similarly, in the sight of God some sinners are barely dead at all, some are more obviously dead, while others are the most completely dead of all. But no kind of death is so doleful and hopeless that he cannot banish it with a word; at the sound of his voice even those lying in the tomb rise again. No one is so profoundly gripped by the sleep of death that he cannot be roused through him.

Some faithful interpreters of Scripture consider that this threefold distinction between sins is symbolized for us in the three corpses who, as we read, were restored to life by the Lord Jesus. He raised the ruler of the synagogue's twelve-year-old daughter at home, before very few witnesses, and forbade them to reveal what had happened.[191] This represents people who first lapsed into some sin not through malice aforethought, but through youthful indiscretion or human frailty; they are not yet hardened[192] to evil and have not yet contracted a foul cancer from their crime. Stretching out

* * * * *

188 Cf Ezek 18:22.
189 Confessional practice drew distinctions between various 'kinds' and 'species' of sins; see Tentler 134–40.
190 Matt 6:12. This passage may be compared with Erasmus' discussion in the *Exomologesis* LB V 157B–F of medieval 'contritionist' theory, which suggested that true contrition ensured the forgiveness of sins, even before formal confession was undertaken; cf Tentler 281–94. It was, however, generally agreed, following St Augustine's ruling in *De symbolo ad catechumenos* 7.15 PL 40 635–6, that venial ('lighter') sins could be washed away by prayer, whereas mortal sins must be formally confessed and expiated.
191 Mark 5:22–43
192 Cf *Adagia* III i 35: *Callum ducere.*

his hand, the Lord Jesus finds it easy to raise them, even concealing their sinfulness and protecting their modesty.

However, it cost him a greater effort to raise the widow's son. Already the body was being carried to burial. The Lord encounters them just in time and is moved by the woman's tears; he has them set down the bier and he raises the young man. First he sits up, then he speaks, and finally he jumps from the bier and is returned to his mother.[193] No doubt he represents those who are so far gone in vice that they cannot be recalled from sinfulness merely through feelings of guilt; they must be more gradually recalled to life through more visible repentance. People 'sit up' when they abandon sin and rise to the challenge of leading a better life; they 'speak' when they confess their sinfulness and acknowledge God's mercy; they are 'returned to their mother,' alive, when they complete the treatment and are restored to the fellowship of the church.

Lazarus, however, was already rotting in the tomb. His despairing sisters and friends could only weep for him. In this case Jesus asks to be shown the grave; he weeps, he groans and is troubled in spirit. He has the stone removed and in a loud voice commands Lazarus to come forth. He comes forth, but he is bound; he is loosed, and thus finally returned to his sisters.[194] It was no great feat for the Lord to revive a four-day corpse; it is a greater feat to restore a sinner who has been rotting, not living, for forty years amid every kind of sinfulness. 'The child,' says the prophet, 'who is a hundred years old shall die, but the sinner who is a hundred shall be cursed.'[195] But the Lord Jesus will deign to revive him too, if only he will at last heed the summons. Each day Jesus cries out, 'Arise, girl; arise, young man; Lazarus, come forth!' But alas! all too many of us are too far gone in death to heed his summons to new life. To heed him is simply to believe him. Unbelief stops up the ears of the wicked and prevents the voice of Holy Scripture reaching their minds. Let us beg the Lord that, in his mercy, he will deign to direct his almighty voice towards these desperate wretches and cry to them, 'You deaf and dumb spirit, I command you to come out of him and never enter him again.'[196]

Now, to help you understand how readily available is the Lord's mercy to those who would change their ways, listen to David: 'I have said, "I shall confess my own unrighteousness to the Lord," and you have forgiven the

* * * * *

193 Luke 7:12–15
194 John 11
195 Isa 65:20
196 Mark 9:25

impiety of my sin.'[197] Mercy is shown to a man who has not yet confessed, but is merely contemplating confession. Bewail your sins, confess them, but before the Lord.[198] Many bewail their sins before men, weep before men, confess before men, rend their garments, but before men; they put on the hair shirt and sprinkle their head with ashes, but before men. If all this is done before God, that is, wholeheartedly and from the purest of intentions, then the Lord's mercy will not be found wanting. 'Rend your hearts,' he says, 'and not your garments. For God will not despise a humble and a contrite heart.'[199] 'Let us weep,' says the psalmist, 'before the Lord who made us.'[200]

Many undertake a fast, but not the kind of fast that the Lord desires; many change their clothing but do nothing to change their inclinations. And yet it turns out that these things must also be done before men, so that those whom our wickedness has incited to sin may be summoned by repentance to change their ways. But it is useless to do these things before men unless they have first been done in the sight of God. Judas confessed his sin, but only to the Pharisees;[201] had he confessed to the Lord, he would at once have been enfolded by the Lord's most tender mercy.

To make our confession more acceptable to the Lord, the prophet Hosea even prescribes the form of confession for us when he says: 'Come with your words ready and return to the Lord. Say to him: "Take away all our iniquity and accept our gift, and we shall offer the calves of our lips."'[202] Let us too return to him; we have strayed in so many ways from him who alone takes away the sins of the world and who poured out his precious blood for our sins. Let us say to him, 'Take away from us all the evil we have done.' Without payment? 'And accept our gift.' What gift? 'The calves of our lips.[203] We shall give thanks for your mercy, to which we shall owe any good that we do after our fall from grace. You will take from us what is ours and receive from us what is your own.'

Now see how well the prophet Joel agrees with Hosea, making the same point in different language. Through him God has made dire threats

* * * * *

197 Ps 32 (Vulg 31):5
198 The phrase 'but before the Lord' was recommended for deletion in the *Index expurgatorius* LB X 1821, no doubt because it reflects the 'contritionist' theory that was perceived as a threat to the practice of auricular confession to a priest: see n190 above.
199 Joel 2:13; Ps 51:17 (Vulg 50:19)
200 Ps 95 (Vulg 94):6
201 Matt 27:3–4
202 Hos 14:2
203 That is, the sacrifice of praise; cf Heb 13:15.

against those who ignored the mercy he offered them, but then he adds,
'Turn again to your God, for he is gracious and merciful, patient and many-
mercied, and powerful against evil' (or, as the Greek texts have it, μετανοῶν,
meaning 'repents of the evil').[204] The magnitude of your crimes has cast
you down, but the magnitude of God's mercy shall lift you up; see how
many ways the prophet finds to extol it. 'He is gracious,' which the Seventy
translated ἐλεήμων, 'merciful.' And although that should be sufficient to prevent us despairing of forgiveness, he adds 'and merciful,' which the Seventy
translate οἰκτίρμων, 'compassionate,' to let us know that, as well as offering
comfort, he is grieved by our ills. Not content with this, he adds 'patient,'
which in the Greek is more meaningfully translated μακρόθυμοσ, that is, 'gentle in spirit, and very slow to anger'; we know how human mercy is very easily changed into indignation. And yet, sinner, you still despair? Then hear
what follows: 'many-mercied,' which is in Greek πολυέλεος. Though your
sins be many, have no fear, his mercies are many. What now remains but
for you to turn again and answer his summons? But the threat of punishment deters you. Listen, and breathe again: 'He is powerful against evil.' It
is not clear why the word that the Seventy translated as μετανοῶν, 'repents,'
was rendered by St Jerome as praestabilis, 'powerful'; for in Latin praestabilis comes from praestari, 'to be capable of performing.' But the prophet
refers to 'evils,' the afflictions that beset us because of our sins. He takes
away our sins and remits the everlasting punishment that we thoroughly
deserve.

What, then, is left to do? Nothing, except to acknowledge God's mercy.
No doubt that is the meaning of the next passage in Joel: 'And he will leave
a blessing behind him, an offering of meat and drink to the Lord our God.'
Doubtless this was what Hosea meant by 'the calves of our lips,' that is, the
sacrifice of praise and thanksgiving.[205]

When someone has frequently and grievously offended someone else,
how difficult it is to reconcile them, how long the insults linger in the memory, how slow anger is to cool, how easily the old animosity is rekindled for
the most trifling reason, how peevishly compensation for the offence is ex-
acted! And yet if harmony is restored between them, even like this, they are

* * * * *

204 Joel 2:13; in the following development, Erasmus compares the readings of the
Septuagint with St Jerome's translation of the Hebrew text PL 28 1086B and
nn. For a useful commentary on the range of the Hebrew and Greek words,
see C.R. Smith The Bible Doctrine of Grace and Related Doctrines (London 1956)
35–46; see also 64–6 on 'mercy' in New Testament Greek.
205 Joel 2:14; Hos 14:3; cf Heb 13:15.

described as 'forbearing.' God, offended so often, of his own accord summons us to repent, invites us to seek forgiveness, revokes his threats, rescinds the punishments of hell, offers kindness instead of chastisement, and, so far from turning away from the reformed sinner, of his own accord goes to meet him as he returns and welcomes the convert, as the saying goes, with open arms.[206]

No doubt this is the meaning of his promise in Zechariah: ' "Turn back to me," says the Lord of hosts, "and I shall turn back to you," says the Lord of hosts.'[207] What does he mean by 'turn back to me'? Acknowledge your misery and seek out my mercy. What does he mean by 'and I shall turn back to you'? Instantly, I shall change from avenger to patron, and assist your efforts; with my good will you will achieve whatever you cannot do by yourself.

None of us can usefully hate our sins unless God intervenes to replace our hearts of stone with hearts of flesh,[208] unless he creates in us hearts that are pure and unpolluted, unless he instils in our innermost being a spirit that is true and undefiled.

But why am I spending so much time listing a few Old Testament passages that reveal the Lord's wondrous mercy? Every single book of the old covenant proclaims, hymns, and insists upon the mercy of God. And what becomes of those, more delirious than heretical, who make two Gods out of the One: one in the Old Testament, who was merely just and not also good; and another in the New, who was merely good, and not equally just?[209] Clearly, they have not heard the refrain that returns so often in the Psalms: 'Confess to the Lord, for he is good, for his mercy is everlasting.'[210] What of the insane Manichees, who taught that the one who addressed us so lovingly through the prophets, and who made Moses' law, was not the true God, but one of the noxious demons?[211] He is the same God, the God of both laws, the same truth, the same mercy, through Jesus Christ our Lord, except

* * * * *

206 *Adagia* II ix 54: *Obviis ulnis*
207 Zec 1:3
208 See n164 above.
209 Probably a reference to Gnosticism; see n211 below. In his commentary on Ps 38 LB V 427C, Erasmus cites similar contempt for the Old Testament as an example of the 'ill-tuned harp' played by some modern commentators.
210 Ps 118 (Vulg 117):1
211 Erasmus attributes this doctrine to the Gnostics as well as to the dualistic Manichees in the *Explanatio symboli* 274 below. The doctrine was frequently attacked by St Augustine, eg in *De moribus ecclesiae catholicae* 1.10.16 PL 32 1317–18.

that what is mere shadow in Moses' law becomes truth in the gospel; in the one it is promised and in the other fulfilled. In the one many great mercies were shown to the Jews, in the other a veritable fountain of mercy – a sea of mercy, rather – flowed over all the nations of the world, and its flood washed away and destroyed the woes of every mortal. This, of course, was the blessed flood of mercy. The ancient flood drowned the sinners, sparing only a tiny band, whereas this healing flood destroys the sins but spares all those who believe in the Son of God.

The one who, in the Old Testament, promises forgiveness to the Hebrews if they will change their ways is present in the Gospels and cries out to everyone: 'Come to me, all you who labour and are burdened, and I shall refresh you. Take my yoke upon you, and you shall find rest for your souls. For my yoke is easy and my burden is light.'[212] Reread the whole story of Christ's life: what do you find if not an endless display of mercy to all? Freely he healed the sick, fed the hungry, rescued those in peril, cleansed the lepers, gave sight to the blind, restored the weak and infirm, cast out devils, restored the dead, and absolved the penitent. Similarly, look at all his teaching: what pervades it all if not the immense mercy of God? How many parables does he use to fix that very idea unshakeably in our minds? What else is conveyed by the parables of the sheep brought back on the shepherd's shoulders, the piece of silver that was lost and found, the healthy who need no doctor, and the servant whose debts were forgiven him? Or, again, by the parables of the creditor who forgave both the debtors, the publican and the Pharisee, the injured traveller whom the Samaritan tended, the steward who was generous to the debtors, the steward who cheated his master, and the prodigal son who was taken back?[213]

Indeed, does not the very word 'gospel' hold an immediate promise of mercy?[214] For what does it promise? 'Sight to the blind, release to the prisoners, healing to the broken-hearted; in short, the year of the Lord's favour,'[215] since he desires nothing more than the salvation of humankind. And what does the very name of Jesus, that is, 'Saviour,' promise to the sinner, if not salvation and mercy? If he had come proclaiming himself a judge, we should all have reason to be afraid; but since he is called saviour, how can you now despair of salvation?

* * * * *

212 Matt 11:28–30
213 These parables are found in Luke 7, 10, and 15–18.
214 *Evangelium*, 'gospel,' comes from the Greek meaning the reward for good tidings.
215 Cf Luke 4:18–19.

Finally, to buttress our confidence in salvation (since it seemed impossible that the great Lerna[216] of crimes that tainted the entire human race could be expiated by the blood of goats and calves), the Son of God himself mounted the altar of the cross and sacrificed himself for our sins, a victim sufficient to atone for each and every sin of us all. Even while hanging on the cross he prays for those who have crucified him and for those who insult and mock him; and yet you think that he will deny you forgiveness if you admit your sin and beg for mercy? Trust in the merciful one, and you shall know mercy.

There is nothing that faith cannot obtain from Christ. If you distrust the doctor you will hinder your own recovery. So far from ignoring the prayers of the poor wretches who cry out to him, God will bestow mercy on someone even if it is someone else who prays for him, provided that it is done with trust and faith. The Canaanite appeals to him, and her daughter is healed; the centurion shows his faith, and his servant is cured; the ruler of the synagogue asks, and his daughter is restored to life; the father begs, and his son is rid of a wicked devil.[217] The apostles cry out, 'Save us, Lord, we perish,' and they are all saved.[218]

On many occasions he did not even wait for their prayers to be spoken. He perceives the faith of the bearers, and says to the paralysed man, 'Be of good cheer, my son; your sins are forgiven you.'[219] The mother and her companions do no more than lament, and the dead youth arises; Martha and Mary do no more than weep, and Lazarus lives again; Mary the sinner laments, then anoints and kisses him, and hears these words: 'Your sins are forgiven you.'[220] An admission of error is sufficient prayer; lamentation and faith are more than sufficient. The woman troubled by an issue of blood secretly touched Jesus' garment and immediately felt the power of mercy flowing from him.[221] We read that many others were also cured by touching Jesus' garments.

In fact there is nowhere that his mercy is not available; on every occasion he will console the afflicted. If you dare not approach Jesus, if you cannot touch Jesus, then at least secretly touch the hem of his garment; approach

* * * * *

216 Another reference to the many-headed hydra of Lerna; see *Adagia* I iii 27. The rest of the parenthesis refers to Jewish expiatory sacrifices.
217 These miracles are related in Matt 15, 8, 9, and 17 respectively.
218 Matt 8:25
219 Matt 9:2
220 Luke 7:12–25; John 11:1–46; Luke 7:44–50
221 Matt 9:20–2

some holy person, in whom the light of piety shines, and ask him to commend you in his prayers to our merciful Lord. For it is often through such
people that he reveals his power, ever ready to procure salvation for each
and every one. It was for this that he had come; this was the food he must
eat to bring sinners to repentance.[222]

In Genesis, again, the ungodly had provoked the Lord's anger by their
sins, yet at Abraham's prayer he would have pardoned all the cities marked
for destruction, had it been possible to find ten righteous men there.[223] The
people of Israel fully deserved death and destruction, yet at the prayer of
Moses alone the Lord withheld his sword of vengeance.[224] Blind, ungrateful
people, who spurn the Lord's mercy when it is always and everywhere so
close at hand!

But still more wretched are those who despair of something that is
there for the asking, without charge. God is easily appeased and slow to
avenge. What else could these words mean: 'And why should you die, house
of Israel?'[225] Elsewhere, again, he bemoans the fact that he has stretched
out his hands all day to an unbelieving and rebellious people.[226] Again, in
Micah: 'My people, what have I done to you, and how have I wearied you?
Answer me this.'[227] Similarly, in Isaiah: 'What more should I have done to
my vineyard that I have not done?'[228]

The Lord does all that he can to save us; why, then, do we wilfully
abandon hope of salvation? In the Gospel he even sheds tears for Jerusalem,
who was bringing ruin upon herself by persisting in her sin. 'How often,'
he says, 'have I wished to gather you to me, as a hen gathers her chicks
under her wings, but you would not.'[229] Our most merciful Lord laments
that he is not allowed to save those wretched creatures; how can we distrust
him and pretend he would not save us? In the Gospel the whole house resounds with joy because the son who was dead lives again; he that was lost
is found.[230] Our good Father summons the whole company of angels and

* * * * *

222 This sentence refers once more to the crucifixion. Payne 324 n60 cites this
    passage to illustrate Erasmus' characteristic desire to make divine mercy more
    vivid by citing concrete examples, particularly those concerning Christ.
223 Gen 18:32
224 See Exod 32:1–14.
225 Ezek 18:31
226 Isa 65:2
227 Mic 6:3
228 Isa 5:4
229 Matt 23:37
230 Cf Luke 15:32.

saints to rejoice with him over one sinner brought to repentance;[231] why then do you despair, poor wretch, and hinder your own salvation while denying the Lord so much joy? Are we to believe that he will refuse forgiveness to the penitent, when he feels such pain for the death of sinners and takes such pleasure in the conversion of the wicked? He invites us all to the wedding feast, he wants his house to be filled, he compels even the blind and the lame to come in.[232] Why do you resist, poor wretch? Why can you not be torn from the husks given to the pigs?[233] Why do you fight against the Lord's mercy? Christ is the wisdom of God.[234] As Solomon tells us, wisdom left her father's house and came into the world: 'She cries aloud in the open air and raises her voice in the streets; she calls out where the crowds meet and makes her speech by the open gates of the city, saying: "How long, you simpletons, will you indulge your simplicity? Fools desire the things that will harm them and the unwise hate knowledge. Turn back at my rebuke. Look, I will lay my spirit before you and show you my words." '[235]

What is more foolish than to be deprived of eternal blessings for the sake of things that are frail and fleeting? What is more wise than to gain immortality at the price of a little suffering? Thus all who persist in their sins prove themselves fools and those who change their lives for the better prove themselves wise. What pains we take to acquire worthless chunks of metal while spurning or – more foolish still – despairing of the great treasure that is on offer, and is offered free of charge. God is rich in mercy.[236] A human treasury becomes exhausted as the money is given away; the treasury of mercy can never be exhausted.

Let me add something else to help alleviate any despair of forgiveness. God has pledged his word to humanity and, as Paul says, he cannot forswear himself.[237] He does not refuse to argue it out, if he seems not to have fulfilled his promise. These are his words in Isaiah to the people when they were thoroughly defiled: 'Wash yourselves, be clean; remove the evil of your thoughts from my sight; cease to do evil, learn to do good; pursue justice, succour the oppressed, give the orphan his rights, defend the widow:

* * * * *

231 Cf Luke 15:10.
232 See Luke 14:16–24.
233 Cf Luke 15:16.
234 1 Cor 1:24
235 Prov 1:20–3
236 Eph 2:4
237 2 Tim 2:13

come, let us argue it out, says the Lord.'[238] Do you hear that, you sinner? What more does our merciful Lord require of you, but that you mend your ways? Do not be downcast by the enormity of your sins, but hear how forgiveness is available to all: 'Though your sins be like scarlet,' he says, 'they shall be as white as snow; though they be red like crimson, they shall be as white as wool. If you are willing and obedient to me, you shall eat all the good things the earth provides.'[239]

Is anyone so mad as to refuse to be saved? What could be easier than to hearken to our most loving Father, who would make us do only what will help to ensure bliss for us? 'If you are willing and obedient,' he says. No one can save someone else unless the latter wants to be saved. But salvation is through faith, and faith comes through hearing his word.[240] The word that brings salvation is nigh; it is in your heart and on your lips.[241] Simply keep your heart's ears open for it. Suppose that a certain king said to a group guilty of treason or lese-majesty, 'I forgive you entirely for all that you have attempted or done so far, and there is forgiveness for you all, so long as you refrain from such crimes in the future.' Would not everyone agree that the prince was showing extraordinary mercy in refusing either to punish the criminals physically or to confiscate their property? But God even offers a reward to those who mend their ways: 'You shall eat all the good things the earth provides.' For those whose crimes offend the giver of all things are quite unworthy to enjoy the good things of this world.

But are not the gifts promised by the Gospel still more generous? 'I shall give you a new heart, I shall give you a new spirit, through which you shall be changed from slaves of the devil into the children of God, through which you shall be made members of my only-begotten Son, through which you shall succeed to the inheritance of the heavenly kingdom. This is,' he says, 'my beloved Son: hear him.'[242] You Jews, why do you avert your ears from the truth and turn to the tales of the Talmudists and the Deuterotists?[243]

* * * * *

238 Isa 1:16–18
239 Isa 1:18–19
240 Cf Rom 10:17.
241 Cf Rom 10:8.
242 The last sentence is part of Matt 17:5; the rest of the speech contains reminiscences of a number of New Testament passages, such as Rom 8:17 and 1 Cor 6:15.
243 The Talmud is the body of Jewish civil and ceremonial law with its associated commentaries, a byword among contemporary Christians for obscurity. Erasmus uses the rare word *Deuterotae* for those who study the Deuterosy, the tradition of the Elders among the Jews.

You philosophers (or rather, morosophers),[244] why do you close your ears to this teacher but give attentive ear to your Platos and Aristotles? You, unhappy spawn of Eve, why do you listen to the serpent, whose vain promises will lure you to your doom, and not to the Son of God, who invites you to share eternal bliss with him? 'Repent,' he says, 'for the kingdom of heaven is at hand.'[245] The Son makes a promise, the Father gives his word, and in the meantime we are given the Spirit as a pledge: how can you hesitate to embrace all the bliss that is offered you?

The message of the apostles is no different from the Lord's: 'Repent, and be baptized, every one of you, in the name of Jesus Christ, for the remission of your sins, and you shall receive the gift of the Holy Spirit.' And then: 'Keep yourselves from this corrupt generation, that you may be saved.'[246] Abandon your unclean, foul, and wretched lives and receive eternal life. All hasten to him: soldiers, publicans, harlots, idolaters, parricides, magicians, pimps, the incestuous. No one is excluded; the portals of mercy are opened equally wide for all. Your past life will not count against you, so long as you are penitent.

Do not imagine that the Lord's mercy does not extend beyond baptism, although Montanus shut the church doors against those who had relapsed since baptism;[247] the Lord never closes the gates to the kingdom of heaven. We are granted entry to the church, once and for all, through baptism, which was prefigured by the ark of Noah; but if we are shipwrecked there remains for us all, through the mercy of God, a 'second plank,'[248] or rather a way back into the ark, through repentance. For baptism is not repeated, just as Christ's death was not, but there remains the water of tears, by which the

* * * * *

244 Literally, 'foolish-wise,' a term coined by Lucian *Alexander* 40 and used in a pejorative way by Erasmus in the *Moria* CWE 27 88, though Rabelais (*Le Tiers Livre* chapter 46) used it in a more positive context.
245 Matt 4:17
246 Acts 2:38, 40
247 Montanus was the founder of a second-century sectarian movement famous for its severe asceticism. Erasmus argues in the *Explanatio symboli* 345 below that this proscription was made not so much to remove hope from the sinners as to deter others from following them. He also suggests there that the practice was upheld by the third-century heresiarch Novatian, and compares it with the ancient church's rule that penance could be performed only once in a lifetime (see n252 below).
248 This expression, designating ecclesiastical penance after baptism, dates back to Tertullian *De poenitentia* 12 PL 1 1330; Erasmus probably found it in Jerome *Epistolae* 84.6 PL 22 748.

stains of sin can be washed away; there remain 'the soda and the soap'[249] of salutary contrition.

Those whose sins had been freely forgiven once and for all and who, being buried with Christ, through baptism, were raised with him into newness of life[250] ought to have continued to live according to the gift they had received. But the merciful one, our merciful Lord,[251] aware of the frailty of human nature, wished to make available to all, until the end of our lives, the remedy of repentance.[252] In truth, since none can be sure when their last day will dawn, we must all take care not to trifle with God's goodness; but if we do relapse, we must hasten at once to apply the remedy, before the illness becomes established and harder to cure.

Long ago, certain people ran great risks by postponing baptism until their last day; some called them 'the bedridden,'[253] others 'the sprinkled,' as if they were not legitimate[254] Christians. But a greater risk is run by the sinner who puts off using the remedy of repentance, which is everywhere available. There is not always someone on hand to baptize you, but even if you are prostrate in bed you can confess your wrongdoing to the Lord and resolve to amend your life. There is not always someone on hand to wash your body, but there are always tears with which to wash the stain from your soul. It was not unreasonable to doubt whether baptism would be effective when people whose lives were despaired of, and who were barely alive, were sprinkled with water rather than bathed in it. For they made it plain that, had they been allowed to live for ever, they would have

* * * * *

249 Cf Jer 2:22.
250 Cf Rom 6:4.
251 On this repetitive figure, see 88 above.
252 Payne 318 n1 compares this passage with others on the principle of the 'second chance,' eg in the *Explanatio symboli* 340, 343 below; *De praeparatione ad mortem* 431–3 below; and the *Ecclesiastes* LB V 882E. The fact that absolution through the sacrament of penance was constantly available reflects the contemporary church's abandonment of the ancient form of penance, which could be performed only once, as Erasmus explains in *Exomologesis* LB V 159E.
253 *Clinici*, from κλίνη, 'bed,' described by Erasmus as a jocular nickname in the *Ecclesiastes* LB V 933E. According to St Cyprian, such people postponed baptism in order to avoid the penalties of subsequent sin (*Epistola ad Magnum* 13 PL 3 1196–7).
254 The adjective is in Greek in the text; literally it means 'of or belonging to the race' and thus 'lawfully begotten.' The implication is that such people had not been properly reborn through baptism, because they could be only sprinkled with water rather than immersed. For the background to this question, see Payne 157 and 305 n15.

gone on sinning for ever. But it was still more justifiable for great men to doubt whether repentance can bear fruit when it is deliberately postponed, when people resort to it only when the end is near, and will not do so until death is imminent. For just as a field that is frequently watered by rain from heaven but produces nothing for the farmer but thistles and thorns is cursed and consigned to the fire,[255] so sometimes God, when his goodness has been persistently ignored, will give people up to their own depraved desires.[256]

Therefore, my dear brothers, it is most advisable not to postpone for long the amendment of your lives, but to respond at once to the Lord's summons and to root out the old Adam with all his deeds and desires; otherwise the Lord, too often unheeded, will in his turn refuse to heed us when we cry to him. Terrible is the voice in which he threatens those who will not hear when he calls in mercy: 'Because,' he says, 'I called and you refused to listen, because I stretched out my hand and no one heeded it, and because you spurned all my counsel and ignored all my rebukes, I in my turn shall laugh at your doom. I shall make mock of you because your fears have been realized, because sudden calamity has descended on you and doom has rushed upon you like a whirlwind, and because tribulation and anguish have come upon you. In that day they shall call my name and I shall not heed them. They shall rise early, but they shall not find me, because they hated knowledge and entertained no fear of the Lord; nor did they accept my counsel, and they despised all my reproof.'[257]

God tries many different kinds of reproach to help us reform. When finally our obstinacy has thwarted every remedy, he gives us up as hopeless and abandons us to our own will. In the same way a doctor will try every method known to his art to cure an illness, but when he has seen the patient vomit out every kind of medicine, he finally abandons the patient to the illness, as someone who has lost the will to live.

'I will sing to you, Lord, of mercy and judgment,' says the psalm.[258] A day of judgment awaits us all when we have departed this life. As long as this life lasts, there is hope of mercy. Therefore, while you live, beg the Lord for mercy. But those who are at their last gasp, or burdened with extreme old age, have already, to some extent, ceased to live. If you are one of those who pull their 'cord of iniquity'[259] from one day to the next, and make no

* * * * *

255 Cf Heb 6:7–8.
256 Cf Rom 1:28.
257 Prov 1:24–30
258 Ps 101 (Vulg 100):1
259 Cf Isa 5:18.

end of sinning, then listen to the advice of the Hebrew sage: 'Turn again to the Lord,' he says, 'and abandon your sins. Make your prayer before his face and lessen your offences. Return to the Lord, turn from your unrighteousness, and thoroughly hate all that he abhors. Learn the just ways and the judgments of God, and stand before the most high God in his holy place of prayer. Go into the realms of holy eternity with the living and those who confess to God; do not die in the error of the godless but confess before you die. Confession by the dead will perish as though it were nothing. Confess while you live, confess while alive and well; praise God and boast of his tender mercies, for great are the Lord's mercy and pardon for those who return to him.'[260]

As you have heard, God's great mercy awaits you, so long as you confess to the Lord while you are 'alive and well.' But what shall we say of those whose bodies have become too enfeebled for sin, but whose thoughts still run on the attractions of sin? And of those who, their bodies being decayed with age, cannot perform vile deeds, but continue to say foul things? How will people 'confess to the Lord while alive' if they stop living before they stop sinning? What about you, who are in the flower of your youth? Why put off mending your ways until tomorrow, next month, next year? If you were afflicted with dropsy, and a certain cure for the disease were readily available, would you say, 'I'll get my illness treated next year'? I am sure you would not be so foolish, but would be quick and eager to get yourself cured. Yet in diseases of the mind, which are so much more dangerous, will you hesitate, procrastinate, adjourn your case,[261] and indeed postpone your salvation until the day you die? Yet who can guarantee that you will live even until tomorrow?

Now none of this is intended to implant in anyone despair of forgiveness, but to remove from everyone their unconcern about their endless capacity for sin. There are sins that are not forgiven in this life or in the life to come, though God forbid that any of us should be brought to those! And therefore it is safest to avoid sin altogether. The next best thing is to wipe out at once, by repentance, any sin we have thoughtlessly committed. 'The righteous fall seven times in a day, but rise again.'[262] This, however, was said of the lighter sins, and in the Holy Scriptures the Lord frequently threatens terrible punishments to prevent us from wallowing constantly in the mire of

* * * * *

260 Ecclus 17:25–9 (Vulg 17:21–8); the Vulgate version, following the Septuagint, is rather different from English versions, which follow the Hebrew text.
261 *Comperendinare*, a legal term meaning to defer a trial for at least three days
262 Prov 24:16

sin, secure in the knowledge that forgiveness is easily available. We were not given the healing draught of repentance to allow us to continue willingly in our sickness, but rather to prevent anyone who happened to relapse from dying for all eternity. In Amos the Lord thunders out the same words many times: 'For three or four transgressions, shall I not turn away from them?'[263]

It is a 'transgression' even to think of doing evil. It should produce instant remorse. But it is a greater transgression to intend to put your thoughts into practice, and you must at least direct your feet from that path to a better. However, the most serious offence is to put your shameful plans into infamous action. And even here we feel no remorse, but instead add a fourth transgression to the list by becoming accustomed to wrongdoing and piling one crime upon another. Would not the Lord be justified at this point in turning away from us? Justified indeed, did not his mercy outweigh his justice. Look what comes after those dire threats, in the same prophet: 'Thus says the Lord to the house of Israel, "Seek me and you will find." Seek the Lord and come.'[264] Let us heed the Lord's threats, and sin no more; let us heed his summons, and despair no more. Otherwise it will go hard with us, if he carries out the threat he makes through the prophet, and after the third or fourth transgression turns his mercy from us and abandons us to our own will. In fact things would still go badly for a great many of us if the Lord turned away his face only after the thousandth transgression. But as soon as his righteous anger bursts forth, mercy intervenes: 'Lord God, be gracious, I beseech you; who shall raise up Jacob, for he is weak?' And again: 'Lord God, be still, I beseech you; who shall raise up Jacob, for he is weak?'[265] That is how our excellent advocate mercy pleads our frailty. Now hear how easily available is forgiveness to those who repent: 'The Lord is moved to mercy over this. The Lord has said, "It shall not be."'[266] You see how quickly he is sorry for his threats of vengeance, if we are truly sorry for our sins. 'It shall not be,' says the Lord. Tell me, what mother could so easily be mollified by her child?

Thus, since our Lord is so receptive and our advocate so effective, is there any reason why anyone should despair, and either persist in his sinfulness or, like Judas, have recourse to the noose? This is why the Lord, taking every care over our salvation, has allowed the most eminent and virtuous

* * * * *

263 Amos 1:3; a 'refrain' in the first two chapters of the book
264 Amos 5:4, with a reminiscence of Matt 7:7; the standard texts read *vivetis*, 'you shall live,' rather than *venite*, 'come.'
265 Amos 7:2, 5
266 Amos 7:3

men to fall into grave sin: their example consoles us and raises our hopes of forgiveness. Who is more often lauded in the holy books than King David? He was a king, he was a prophet, he was 'a man after God's own heart,'[267] and Christ was promised from his line. And yet how foul and how frequent were the offences this great man committed! Through Nathan he was given a rebuke and a dire warning by the Lord. But David changed all God's anger into mercy with just a few words: 'I have sinned against the Lord,' he said. And Nathan replied at once, 'The Lord also has put away your sin; you shall not die.'[268] The threats were very wordy, to get him to change, but mercy's speech was very brief: 'You shall not die.'

Similarly, Hezekiah heard Isaiah say, 'You shall die and not live.' Hezekiah 'wept with a great weeping.' The prophet who had announced his doom had not yet left the middle court, and the Lord's mercy called him back. 'Turn again,' it said, 'and say to Hezekiah, the leader of my people: "Thus says the Lord, the God of your father David: 'I have heard your prayers, I have seen your tears, and I have brought you healing. On the third day you shall go up to the Lord's temple.'"'[269]

The third book of Kings has this to say about Ahab: 'But there was no other like Ahab, who sold himself to do evil in the sight of the Lord.' This is what he was told: 'You have killed, and in addition you have stolen.'[270] For he had killed Naboth and seized his vineyard. The king, at last truly terrified by the Lord's dire threats, rent his garments, put on a hair shirt next to his flesh, fasted, slept on sackcloth, and went about with his head bowed. Ahab was a hardened sinner; he had often scorned the Lord's reproaches, he had piled crime upon crime, and in the end he was less repentant than terrified by the fear of imminent retribution. Yet the Lord in his immense mercy spoke to Elijah: 'Have you not seen that Ahab humbles himself before me? Since he has become humble for my sake, I shall not inflict the punishment in his time.'[271] If false repentance has sufficient power to wrest the avenging sword from God's hand, what will be achieved by those who undergo a sincere change of heart, and not through fear of punishment, but through love of God, hating what they have done?[272]

* * * * *

267 1 Sam 13:14; cf Acts 13:22.
268 2 Sam 12:13
269 2 Kings 20:1–5
270 1 Kings 21:25, 19
271 1 Kings 21:29
272 These two attitudes reflect the medieval distinction between 'attrition,' a preliminary to true repentance brought about by less laudable motives, and true contrition; see Tentler 250–301 and *Exomologesis* LB V 152A–E.

To make the same point the Lord allowed Peter, whom he had designated head of his church, to fall spectacularly from grace. He merely had
to weep to obtain mercy. But since the Lord entrusted to Peter the feeding
of the sheep for whom he was to die, surely he should have rebuked him
for the sin of denying him three times? Not at all: the offence was so thoroughly diluted by his tears that no trace of it remained in the memory of
our compassionate Lord. Paul was struck down, as persecutor of the Lord's
church, and became the 'teacher of the gentiles.'[273]

We have before us great examples of sinners, and also of penitents; we
must not try the Lord's patience by following their example of sinfulness,
but, if some are beset by sin, they have the examples of repentance to save
them from despair. It is truly perverse to follow the sinners but refuse to
follow them when they repent. How many princes use David's example
to excuse their adulteries and murders? However, in other respects David
possessed so many outstanding virtues that when they were weighed in
the balance his sin could be forgiven; if only the others would imitate his
repentance as closely as they do his mistakes! He published his sin among
all the nations of earth; he spurned the court's pleasures, put on a hair shirt
instead of purple, ate ashes for his bread and filled his cup with weeping,
drowned his bed with tears every single night and watered his couch with
weeping.[274]

Nor was he ashamed to compose and to sing aloud a song of repentance for all sinners: 'Have mercy on me, O God, according to your great
mercy. And according to the multitude of your mercies blot out my iniquity.'[275] He was a judge, and passed a death sentence upon himself. For
he was exceedingly angry, and cried, 'As the Lord lives, whoever has done
this thing deserves to die!'[276] He could not be more clearly condemned than
by his own words. God was his judge and yet, as if reversing the roles,
allowed the accused to judge himself. The judge was convicted, and God,
who delegated the judgment to him, triumphed. David was glad to be defeated and God was merciful in victory, assuring the sinner that his sin was
forgotten. Previously David had lived triumphant, drunk with calamitous
prosperity, delighting in the woman he loved and delighting in the sweet-
est of children. But after turning to the Lord he at last saw the true position and 'the difference between the righteous and the wicked, between
those who serve God and those who serve him not,' as another prophet

* * * * *

273 1 Tim 2:7; Peter's story is told in all the Gospels.
274 Allusions to Pss 102:9 (Vulg 101:10), 6:6 (Vulg 6:7)
275 Ps 51:1 (Vulg 50:2), perhaps the most familiar of the penitential psalms
276 2 Sam 12:5

puts it.[277] When sinners confess their wickedness from the heart and accept
that they deserve punishment, then the Lord is justified and triumphs by
being judged, that is, by handing over the decision to human beings, as if
he were himself to be judged.

In another sense, those who decide their own guilt almost make God
appear unjust and false; he would have his mercy acknowledged by all,
and is glad that our unrighteousness redounds to his glory, since wherever
sin flourishes his gratuitous goodness will also flourish.[278] This was not the
case with old Adam who, when summoned to confess, put the blame on
his wife. Again, when she was called to confess, she laid the crime on the
serpent. If they had known David's song 'Have mercy on me, O God,' they
would not have been banished from the Garden. What did Cain, a true son
of his parents, say when invited by the Lord to repent? 'Am I my brother's
keeper?'[279] If he had said, 'I have sinned; have mercy on me,' and if he had
meant it, God's mercy was ready and waiting for him.

There are two kinds of sorrow: sorrow according to the flesh, like Judas', which brings death, and sorrow in the eyes of God, which brings salvation and lasting joy. Paul loves all his people dearly, yet he is glad to have
brought the second kind of sorrow to the Corinthians by condemning the
man who had seduced his father's wife, since this kind of sorrow, like bitter
medicine, leads to perpetual joy.[280] And in the meantime the certain hope of
salvation, mingled with repentance, tempers the bitterness of their sorrow.

Similarly, when David had frankly confessed his sin and exposed himself to God's vengeance, this is how he found hope in God's mercy: 'Sprinkle me, Lord, with hyssop and I shall be clean; wash me and I shall be
whiter than snow.'[281] It is not his own good deeds that promise him purification, but the sprinkled blood of the spotless Lamb; though he admits that
from his mother's womb he was stained with filth, yet he hopes that this
washing will restore his innocence, purer than the driven snow. Not only
does he hope that his innocence will be restored, but also that the pain of
repentance will be turned into spiritual joy. 'Bring to my ears joy and gladness,' he says, 'and my humbled bones shall dance for joy. Restore to me
the joys of your salvation and establish a princely spirit within me.' Wonder
with me at the sinner's confidence, as he promises himself yet more: 'And

* * * * *

277 Mal 3:18. The first edition has *injustum,* 'unrighteous,' rather than *impium,*
    'wicked'; the latter is the standard reading.
278 Cf Rom 5:20.
279 Gen 4:9
280 See 1 Cor 5; 2 Cor 7.
281 Ps 51:7 (Vulg 50:9)

my tongue,' he says, 'shall exalt your righteousness. O Lord, open my lips, and my mouth shall proclaim your praises.'[282] Having received such mercy from the Lord, he will exhort others to mend their ways. Similarly, the Lord said to Peter, 'And once you are recovered, you must lend strength to your brothers.'[283]

David would have perished, had he relied on God's justice alone, but being unequal to his opponent he appealed to God's mercy and as a result he hymns the Lord's mercies for ever more. On earth some litigants, when their case seems lost, will appeal to another court, if they can, even though they are not sure to find a new judge better disposed to them; it often happens that an appeal makes things worse. But for us, my dear friends, by far the safest course is not to pit ourselves against God's justice, not to 'kick boldly against the pricks,'[284] but to appeal at once to the court of mercy. Now in an earthly court they say that there is no safer course than to deny the charge completely, if there are the slightest grounds for doing so; the rhetoricians teach that the least effective defence is what they call *deprecatio*,[285] when the accused says, 'I have done wrong; forgive me.' In the heavenly court, on the contrary, nothing is safer than to confess voluntarily to all your misdeeds and to implore the judge's mercy. And since in all the Holy Scriptures God's goodness so lovingly invites us to do so, and there are so many notable examples to encourage us, why should anyone despair for himself or herself and prefer to grow old in evil?

In God, whose nature is perfect unity, there is nothing that conflicts with anything else; yet if we reflect on the things that happen to us, there appears to be a conflict between God's justice and his mercy. Justice summons us to punishment, but mercy, as James puts it, κατακαυχᾶται τῆς κρίσεως, that is, 'triumphs over judgment'[286] like a conqueror. Has anyone ever cried, 'Jesus, have mercy on me!' and not at once obtained mercy? The woman of Canaan cries, 'Have mercy, Lord,' and her daughter is healed;[287] let each and every sinner cry, 'Have mercy, Lord,' and the soul of each will be healed. The blind beggar cries, 'Have mercy on me, son of David,' and, throwing off his cloak, he receives his sight.[288]

* * * * *

282 Ps 51:8, 12, 14–15 (Vulg 50:10, 14, 16–17)
283 Luke 22:32
284 Cf Acts 9:5.
285 *Deprecatio*, a plea for mercy; this passage is based on Quintilian *Institutiones oratoriae* 5.13.5–7 (see also 7.4.17 for Cicero's rejection of this strategy).
286 James 2:13
287 Matt 15:22–8
288 Mark 10:46–50

We too must cry out, 'Have mercy on us, Jesus, Son of God'; let us cry it loud and long amid the clamorous crowds of evil thoughts, and he shall change us from beggars in this world into heirs of the kingdom of heaven. Anyone seeking the rewards of this life is like a blind beggar, dressed in a filthy cloak, asking passers-by for coins. Those seeking power, though it seems that their search is for something important, do no more than beg the crowd for a few wretched coins. Those who pursue office and the highest honours are really crying to the passers-by, 'Have mercy, spare a coin.' But if any cry to Jesus, 'Lord, have mercy,' he is ready and willing to give us himself.

The Lord is always with us and calls us to him; why not run to him, unhappy wretch? Why remain in your miserable rags? You may go up to the altar of mercy; why turn aside to the dungeon of madness? You may enter the refuge of divine compassion; why hasten to the pit of hapless despair? The Saviour offers his hand; why avert your eyes? A place in heaven is reserved for you; why rush headlong to the precipice? God's goodness seeks to enfold you; why take refuge in the noose of despair? The thief on the cross was told, 'This day you shall be with me in paradise';[289] why consign yourself to hell?

But now it is time to fulfil my promise and discuss, finally, the ways in which we may best obtain God's mercy. For prayer, tears, fasting, sackcloth and ashes – in other words, a contrite heart – have already been mentioned from time to time in my discourse, and these do of course obtain God's mercy; however, kindness to one's neighbour will also extract it, so to speak.[290] All of us should treat our neighbour as we wish God to treat us. The Greeks had a proverb, One favour begets another;[291] among us, however, one act of mercy begets another. 'Give and it shall be given to you; forgive and you shall be forgiven, and whatever measure you have dealt your neighbour, the same will be dealt to you by God.'[292]

Now I call it an act of mercy or alms-giving not only when you forego revenge or relieve someone in need, but also when you perform any service for your brother out of the goodness of your heart. Those who counsel the wayward, rebuke the delinquent, or even, sometimes, chastise the

* * * * *

289 Luke 23:43
290 Erasmus uses the strong verb *extorquere*. As Payne 194–5 points out, for Erasmus there are two indispensable presuppositions for receiving God's forgiveness, contrition and charity; cf *Exomologesis* LB V 160D and 161D.
291 *Adagia* I i 34
292 Luke 6:38

sinner, if it is done in a Christian spirit, are bestowing mercy on their neighbour. Those who spur on the idle, comfort the afflicted, or give hope to the
desperate are being merciful to their neighbour, and are either requiting or
inviting God's mercy.

Now Christian mercy should not be merely of the commonplace kind.
Even a pagan will give money to a beggar, anyone will help a friend in trouble, and even the gentiles sometimes forgive mistakes. The Gospel tells us
what our mercy should be like: 'Be merciful, that you may be true children
of your Father who is in heaven.'[293] If God's mercy towards us were nothing
out of the ordinary, then ordinary mercy would suffice towards our neighbour. But God commands his sun to rise on the good and the bad, and allows the world's rich harvest to be shared by the godly and ungodly alike;[294]
if we wish to be considered true children of God, we too must be generous not only to our friends, relations, and supporters, but also to strangers,
and even to our enemies and rivals. If God delivered up his only Son for
us when we were idolaters and the offspring of hell, does it seem too much
for us in our turn to perform some service for an enemy who, being human, is also our brother? And if the righteous Lord sacrificed himself for
our sins on the altar of the cross, does it seem too much for us to forgive
the neighbour who has done us wrong?

How insolent it is for sinners to cry, 'O God, have mercy on me!' when
they have refused mercy to their brother! They will deserve to hear these
words from the Gospel: 'You worthless servant! I have forgiven you all
your debts; should you not have shown mercy to your fellow servant?'[295]
Although he lacks for nothing, the Lord allows any kindness we have shown
our neighbour to be credited to him. Although any kindness we show our
brothers has already been shown abundantly to us by God, yet as if our
good deeds to our neighbour laid him under an obligation, he promises that
he will repay with interest 'the full amount, pressed down and shaken together.'[296] Is it not a full reward if, in return for taking in a pauper, the Lord
receives you into the kingdom of heaven? The best way to grow rich is to be
impoverished by this sort of outlay. The wise of this world do not let their
money lie idle in its chests, but deposit it with the bankers to earn interest.
Those who wish to grow rich in the things of heaven must open an account
with this most generous of trustees. We call the rich 'blessed,' and in the

* * * * *

293 A combination of Luke 6:36 and Matt 5:45
294 Cf Matt 5:45.
295 Matt 18:32–3
296 Luke 6:38

Gospel the merciful are called blessed, 'for they shall receive mercy.' 'Whoever shows mercy to the poor,' says the Hebrew sage, 'is lending money to the Lord, and their outlay will be returned to them.' And the prophet says, 'Redeem your sins by alms-giving,' since, as the chief of the apostles said, 'charity covers a multitude of sins.'[297] It sounds like a mere exchange, but the profits are enormous.

Similarly, the mystic musician says, 'Blessed are they who show mercy and kindness.'[298] Thus those who do good to their neighbour are lending to God. You have heard the terms of the loan, the rate of interest, the terms of redemption. Those who harm their neighbour are vulnerable to their victim; those who help their neighbour put the latter under an obligation. Do not seek revenge on someone who has harmed you, but place a deposit with God; forgive your neighbour a few trivial offences, and God in return will forgive all yours. Do not seek a reward from the neighbour you have helped, but ask God to return your outlay, and he will replace the ephemeral with the eternal.

There are various kinds of sacrifice by which God is placated: hymns, music, prayer, vigils, fasting, rough clothes. But no kind of sacrifice is more effective than showing mercy to your brother. 'Go,' says the Lord, 'and learn what this means: "I will have mercy, and not a sacrifice." '[299] He does not condemn other sacrifices,[300] but he sets mercy above them all. The Lord Jesus deigned to tell us with his own lips in the Gospel something he had said many years before through the prophet Micah. For when the Lord had rebuked his people for their invincible determination to do evil, the people were anxious to know how they might appease God, who was justly angered by their many sins, and asked: 'What may I fittingly offer to the Lord? Shall I bend the knee to the most high God? Shall I bring him burnt offerings and year-old calves? Can he be appeased by thousands of rams, or by many thousands of sleek goats? Shall I give my first-born for my transgression, the fruit of my body for the sin of my soul?'[301] So much for the people, who knew that humans can never make sufficient sacrifice to atone for all their sins, even if they were to sacrifice, above and beyond the many thousands of rams, their first-born child, dearest of all to them. But the prophet

* * * * *

297 The quotations are, respectively, Matt 5:7; Prov 19:17; Dan 24:27 (Vulg 24:24); 1 Pet 4:8.
298 Ps 112 (Vulg 111):5
299 Matt 9:13, quoting Hos 6:6
300 The first edition omits *reliqua*, 'other.'
301 Mic 6:6–7

indicates a more effective sacrifice by which God's anger may at once be appeased: 'I will show you, humans, what is good and what the Lord requires of you: that you act with justice, love mercy, and walk humbly with your God.'[302] To act with justice means to harm no one. To act with mercy means to do good even to those who do not deserve it.

The apostle Paul adds another element to the praise of mercy: 'If I give my body to be burned,' he says, 'but have not charity, it profits me nothing.'[303] It was a great thing that Abraham was prepared to sacrifice his only son, whom he loved; but it is a greater thing if people will give their own bodies to be burned for the love of God. But charity is more welcome to God even than this sacrifice. Now, what is charity towards one's neighbour, if not mercy? Therefore, although we are all perpetually in need of God's mercy in everything we do, it must be our constant concern to uplift one another by practising mercy and, by bearing one another's burdens,[304] to obey Christ's law, which requires mercy rather than a sacrifice[305] and would have us win his mercy by showing mercy to our neighbour.

Now, although my heart leaps for joy when I consider the Lord's great mercy towards us and how easily he would have us obtain it, yet a great sadness is born in my heart whenever I think how rare among Christians is an inclination to mercy. If we were truly merciful, our beneficence would extend even to the Turks, and we should heap coals of fire on their heads[306] so that, won over by our goodness, they would at last enter the fellowship of true religion. At the moment we Christians assault and harass our fellow Christians with war, brigandage, looting, and pillaging more cruelly than any wild beasts attacking their natural enemies. When it comes to money, we live exactly like those fish who are always ripping one another to shreds. Who is not prepared, for the sake of a tiny profit, to cheat his brother, though we ought to relieve his poverty for nothing? These days we seek a profit from our brother's helplessness. The greater the danger of my brother dying of starvation, the higher the price I will charge to supply his needs. How cruel and arrogant people are to the lower orders, how rebellious the lower orders are towards their superiors, and how rare is true

* * * * *

302 Mic 6:8
303 1 Cor 13:3
304 Cf Gal 6:2.
305 Cf Hos 6:6.
306 That is, make them ashamed: cf Rom 12:20. Erasmus often suggested that it would make more sense to show the Turks the value of Christianity than to make war on them; this is the burden of his *De bello Turcico* of 1530.

charity! The world is full of brawling, slander, and deceit. Not only do we exact violent retribution for the slightest offence, but we are quite happy to injure the innocent. And all the while it never occurs to us to consider how great is the mercy God has poured out for us, and that he will certainly take back what he has given unless we pass on to our neighbour what we have received.

'If you seek,' says the prophet, 'seek.' If we seek God's mercy, let us seek it truly and sincerely. 'Turn again and come.'[307] Mercy will turn to us, if we are turned towards her. The mercy of God came to us when the Son of God came down to earth; let us in our turn come to him. Our most compassionate Lord bends low to absolve the woman taken in adultery,[308] but we in our turn must lift up our hearts to him as he bends towards us. The first step is to reject evil. Doctors purge the body before introducing more healthy fluids. You too, sinner, must discharge from your heart the depraved desires that war against God, such as lust, avarice, extravagance, arrogance, anger. When those who persist in their sins implore God's mercy, are they not behaving just like a soldier who sues for peace with his sword and shield still in his hand? 'Ask, and it shall be given; seek, and you shall find; knock, and it shall be opened.'[309] If you ask for mercy, ask sincerely; if you seek it, seek it sincerely; if you knock at mercy's door, knock sincerely.

An example of someone who sincerely sought mercy? The prodigal son went about it in the right way, but had already left his pigs and returned to his father: 'Father, I have sinned against heaven and before you; make me like one of your hired servants.'[310] Now listen to the publican, who was conscious of his sins and dared not turn his eyes heavenward or approach the mercy-seat, but stood at a distance, beating his breast and saying, 'God be merciful to me, a sinner.'[311] To 'seek' is to undergo a complete change of character, to become sober instead of drunken, chaste instead of debauched, careful instead of spendthrift, generous instead of grasping, truthful instead of lying, kind instead of derogatory, open instead of devious, gentle instead of vengeful, merciful instead of cruel.

By contrast, to 'knock' is to commit a holy sin and do violence, so to speak, to God's mercy, by never ceasing to show mercy to your neighbour. You may cry to the Lord, 'Have mercy!' But if you wish to be heeded, be

* * * * *

307 Isa 21:12
308 John 8:1–11
309 Matt 7:7
310 Luke 15:18–19
311 Luke 18:13

sure that you in turn heed his call. He calls to you through his members who are needy and infirm. If you close your ears to them, he in turn will not heed your cries to him. He is revived through his weaker members, but he also thirsts, hungers, falls sick, and suffers through them, and through them he is neglected and offended. But it is still more insolent for people to say to the Lord, 'Have mercy on me,' when they have not only refused heartfelt sympathy to their brother, but also persecuted the innocent, oppressed the weak, denounced the blameless, robbed the poor, and cheated the naïve. Anyone who persists in such deeds will cry in vain for the Lord's mercy. If people who fail to revive Christ through his members will be told, 'Go, accursed ones, into the eternal fire,'[312] then what will be said to those who have, through his members, insulted and spat upon Christ, who have mocked, beaten, injured, denounced, and murdered him?

There is a famous line (in Publilius, I think), a maxim worthy of a Christian: 'To give to a worthy cause is to receive a favour.'[313] Why do you hesitate, grimly weighing up what the other person is worth? Any gift to a member of Christ is made in a worthy cause; likewise, any gift to a brother. In the end, any gift you make to another human being for the love of Jesus is made in a worthy cause. If you seek a profit, lend to him; if you fear a loss, you will find compensation here. After a stern rebuke, what does the Lord say in the Gospel? 'But rather give alms, and behold, all things are clean to you.'[314] When a storm rages at sea, you will not hesitate to exchange the cargo, however valuable, for your life; will you then be reluctant, when God's vengeance hangs over you, to give money to your neighbour? Do you stand idle when fire breaks out? But is any fire more fearsome than God's anger, since 'his anger flares up in a moment'?[315] Will you not use the instrument provided to put it out? What instrument, you ask? Who provides it? That fine man the son of Sirach: 'Water will put out a burning fire,' he says, 'and alms-giving will atone for sins.'[316]

There must be no ostentation in alms-giving, or it will not be worth the name. Those who hand out largesse with a fanfare of trumpets[317] are not giving alms but bidding for fame. For God, true alms-giving means that

* * * * *

312 Cf Matt 25:41.
313 Publilius Syrus B12 (55)
314 Luke 11:41
315 Ps 2:12 (Vulg 2:13)
316 Ecclus 3:30 (Vulg 3:33)
317 Cf Matt 6:2; for 'largesse' Erasmus uses *sportulae*, associated with the dole distributed to hangers-on in pagan Rome; cf Juvenal *Satires* 1.95 and 3.249.

your left hand does not know what your right hand is doing.[318] 'Lay up your treasure,' says the sage, 'according to the commandments of the most high, and it shall bring you more profit than gold. Lock your alms in the heart of the poor, and they shall protect you from all evil.'[319] A treasure is never more safely hidden than in the heart of the poor; it is far better locked away there than in an iron safe. You must forget what you have deposited and, if possible, the poor should not know the identity of their benefactor. When you have need of an intercessor, your alms will not be silent, but will plead with the Lord to deliver you from all evil[320] since you rescued your neighbour from some evil. He will gladly hear[321] what your alms have to say: 'Come, you blessed of my Father; for when I was hungry you gave me food, when I was thirsty you gave me drink, when I was naked you clothed me, when I had no roof you took me in, when I was sick you visited me, and when I was in prison you came to me.'[322] The righteous cannot recall these good deeds, and say, 'Lord, when did we see you in need of all these, and come to your aid?' But the others trumpet their own virtues – and are told, 'Go into the eternal fire.' Shall not our alms-giving be a timely intercessor for us, and free us from hell, that is, from all evil; and join us to the Lord, who is the fount of all good things?

Thus it only remains, my dear friends, to beg the Lord for mercy, that he may grant us the means to bestow mercy on our neighbour. For if we make no use of his mercy here and now, it will be in vain that we seek it hereafter; the greater his efforts to inspire us to mercy here below, the harsher shall be his judgment upon us. May our human passions be overcome by mercy towards our brothers, that God's judgment of us be overcome by his mercy. May it come to pass that with one heart and mind we shall together hymn the mercies of the Lord for all eternity, proclaiming that 'his tender mercies surpass all his works.'[323] To whom be praise and glory in all the ends of the earth and for all times. Amen.

Let us close our gathering with a prayer.[324]

* * * * *

318 Matt 6:3
319 Ecclus 29:11–12 (Vulg 29:14–15)
320 Perhaps an echo of the petition in the Litany of the Saints: 'Ab omni malo libera nos, Domine.'
321 *Vult audire*; the original edition reads *vultis audire*, 'do you want to hear ...'
322 Matt 25:34–6; the first edition reads *lecto*, 'bed,' instead of *tecto*, 'roof.'
323 Ps 145 (Vulg 144):9
324 This concluding passage, inspired by a number of the scriptural passages cited earlier, is omitted from the 1540 *Opera* and from LB.

Antiphon. Lord God our ruler, merciful and compassionate, long-suffering, rich in mercy and truth, keeping mercy for thousands, forgiving iniquity and transgression and sin, none being in themselves innocent in your eyes:[325]

Verse. Let your mercy be upon us, O Lord, as we have placed our hopes in you.[326]

Collect. O God, who manifest your mighty power above all through forbearance and mercy, so multiply your favour towards us that, hastening to receive the things you have promised, we may be made partakers of the blessings of heaven. Through our Lord, etc.

* * * * *

325 Exod 34:6–7
326 Ps 33 (Vulg 32):22

ON PRAYING TO GOD

Modus orandi Deum

translated and annotated by

JOHN N. GRANT

Erasmus' *Modus orandi Deum* (literally, 'The Method of Praying to God,' but translated here as 'On Praying to God')[1] was first published in Basel by the Froben press in October 1524. It was dedicated to the Polish diplomat Hieronim Łaski, who first met Erasmus in 1520 in Brussels and Cologne and whose meeting with him in Basel in May 1524 may have provided the impetus for this essay on prayer if, as Erasmus writes in the final paragraph, it actually was undertaken for Łaski's sake. On that occasion Łaski, accompanied by his two younger brothers Jan and Stanisław, visited Erasmus to find out his views on Luther (see Ep 1341A:1224–69), and one of Erasmus' stated aims in writing the *Modus orandi Deum* was to defend, against Luther, the validity and efficacy of invoking the saints (see Ep 1159:135–8). This he does by appealing, in the absence of explicit scriptural authority, to the consensus of the church on the matter from early times and by pointing to an inconsistency in the Lutherans' beliefs: they rejected the invocation of the saints but accepted the perpetual virginity of Mary, although this too lacked biblical support. Erasmus, however, had a more general treatment of prayer in mind since only about one-seventh of the work addresses the topic of the saints.

In the introduction (147–56) Erasmus discusses how praying, giving thanks, and singing hymns of praise are related to one another, and defines and differentiates the Greek and Latin words for prayer. Only then does he announce and list in a more formal way the topics to be addressed (157). First he will show how and why Christ and the apostles, by their teaching and example, stressed the importance of our praying constantly and fervently (157–79). This will be followed by four topics: to whom prayers should be directed (184–97); the proper disposition and attitude of those engaged in prayer (179–84); what we should pray for (202–5); how we should pray (205–29). This last subject embraces many questions. What words should we use? Should we pray silently or aloud? What is the place of prayer in public worship? When should we pray?

This brief description suggests a tighter structure for the treatise than it actually has. The same topic sometimes occurs in more than one section. In the introduction, for example, the question of where our prayers are to be directed arises, as does that of the appropriate style of life of those who pray. Moreover, Erasmus sometimes digresses. In his discussion of the giving of thanks he attacks at some length the wicked lives of priests who bring

* * * * *

1 A literal translation sounds cumbersome and does not fully reflect the broad scope of the work, which had many predecessors in antiquity and the Middle Ages, often given a general title such as 'On Prayer.'

the church into disrepute (150–2); after his defence of the invocation of the saints in prayer he turns to criticize the superstitious adoration of relics, the pagan elements in civic festivals, improper representations in art of the Virgin Mary or of saints, and the ostentatious adornment of the church by the noble and wealthy (197–202). Elsewhere he touches on the length of church services and on the language in which public worship should be conducted (212, 217–18), and he deviates from his topic to berate princes and bishops for inappropriate behaviour (219–21). Such digressions, however, usually bring relief from the many lengthy lists of examples and quotations that illustrate much the same point.

The essay would have profited from a final revision. To give but one example, a brief discussion of the difference in meaning between *oratio* and *precatio* in ancient usage is followed by a paragraph that claims to 'put aside concern with words ... and to proceed with matters of substance' (154), but there immediately follow four paragraphs devoted to similar lexicographical concerns! Occasionally the subject of sentences is not expressed where it is needed. Erasmus is also not averse to inserting asides which interrupt the sequence of thought (see, for example, 212, where he refers to a 'petitory' branch of rhetoric). Such interruptions may add a touch of informality, but they create difficulties for a translator, and parentheses have been used in this translation to aid the modern reader. This raises the question of paragraphing, which, it should be remembered, was almost non-existent in the early printed editions. In this translation very long sections which do cohere are broken into several paragraphs in accordance with modern usage (for instance, the long catalogue of examples of the use of prayer in the Old Testament at 169–73). Sometimes it is more difficult to decide where a paragraph break should occur, and readers may disagree with some of the divisions that have been made in this translation.

Erasmus had many predecessors who wrote on prayer. Surviving treatises devoted solely to this topic by Tertullian, Origen, and Cyprian go back to the first half of the third century, and these were followed by many more in antiquity and the Middle Ages. Whether Erasmus drew extensively on any specific earlier treatments of the topic is not easily determined; he certainly gives no explicit indication of such sources in the work itself. There are, however, some similarities between the *Modus orandi Deum* and the much shorter treatments of the topic by St Augustine in his letter to the widow Proba (*Epistolae* 130) and by Thomas Aquinas (*Summa theologica* II–II *quaestio* 83). Aquinas deals with such questions as whether God alone should be prayed to, whether the saints who are in heaven pray for the living, whether prayer should be spoken aloud, whether prayer should be long, and whether prayer should be subdivided into *obsecrationes, orationes, postulationes,* and *gratiarum actiones.* These and other topics are common to Aquinas and Erasmus. Some biblical quotations appear in both St Augustine's letter and the *Modus orandi Deum,* but this in itself is hardly surprising, even if the two works share another feature in devoting a section to showing how prayers in the Psalms express the same idea as the parts of the Lord's Prayer, and have several quotations in common (see 206 and nn 374, 380, 382, 386).

How difficult it is to show direct dependence may be illustrated from a comparison of the essay with Origen's Περὶ εὐχῆς. Origen deals with many of the same topics as Erasmus: the disposition of the mind in prayer, the distinction between the different Greek words for prayer, the role of the saints in prayer, how the Scriptures can supply examples of effective prayer, the need to avoid vain repetition, exegesis of the Lord's Prayer, the argument that prayer is unnecessary because of God's foreknowledge, the appropriate posture and place for prayer, the idea that righteous living is a form of prayer. Some similarities are referred to in the annotations. It is doubtful, however, whether Erasmus actually knew this work of Origen when he composed the *Modus orandi Deum,* although the editor of the work in the Amsterdam edition, J.N. Bakhuizen van den Brink, assumes so (see ASD V-1 117). Erasmus produced an edition of the works of Origen in 1536 near the end of his life, published posthumously, and the treatise on prayer does not appear in it. In fact, the date of the *editio princeps* of the Περὶ εὐχῆς is 1686.

While admitting that Erasmus never mentions Origen's Περὶ εὐχῆς, André Godin thinks it inconceivable that the humanist had not read the work.[2] The major evidence is as follows. In Allen Ep 1827:1–3 Erasmus reports that he was engaged in translating part of Origen's commentary on Matthew. His source was a manuscript from Ladenburg supplied to him by Wolfgang of Affenstein (Allen Ep 1844:91–3). That manuscript, now Cambridge, Trinity College 194 (B.8.10), also contains the Περὶ εὐχῆς and is the prime witness for its text.[3] But the date of Allen Ep 1827 is 23 May 1527, more than two years after the appearance in print of the *Modus orandi Deum,* and there is no evidence that Erasmus had seen this manuscript prior to the beginning of 1527.[4] Since the surviving manuscripts of Origen's treatise

* * * * *

2 Godin *Erasme lecteur* 626 n131
3 For an account of the history of the manuscript see *Origenes Werke* I ed P. Koetschau (Leipzig 1899) lxxxiii–iv.
4 See Allen Epp 1767 and 1774, which relate to the library at Ladenburg and were written in December 1526. Erasmus' translation of Origen's commentary

are very few,[5] it is extremely unlikely that Erasmus had access to another manuscript, now lost, containing the work before seeing the Ladenburg witness.[6] The similarities, then, between Erasmus' *Modus orandi Deum* and Origen's Περὶ εὐχῆς probably spring from their common subject-matter, with its inevitable questions, and from the common pool of relevant biblical quotations.[7]

All but one of the editions and translations of the *Modus orandi deum* have been based on the *editio princeps* of 1524. In March 1525, however, the Froben press published a second and expanded edition of the essay, described as *nunc per ipsum autorem diligenter et recognitum et locupletatum*, 'now carefully revised and enlarged by the author himself.' The editor of the work in the Amsterdam edition, who has used the second edition as his base text, has calculated that the expansion amounts to approximately one-sixth. The translation that follows is also based on the 1525 edition. The additions and changes to the *editio princeps* of 1524, except for a few very minor instances, have been recorded in the annotation. The Amsterdam edition will be the most accessible source for readers interested in the Latin text of the 1525 edition. Such readers will encounter a number of typographical and other errors in the Latin text. The most important of these have been pointed out in the footnotes.

While the notes in this translation in a number of instances add to those in the Amsterdam edition, they are heavily indebted to it, particularly for the identification of biblical quotations. An attempt has been made in the annotation to differentiate between 'cf' and 'see.' The latter usually refers

* * * * *

on Matthew was published in 1527 (Ep 1844 is in fact the dedicatory letter to the work).

5 For a brief account of the manuscripts and editions see E.G. Jay *Origen's Treatise on Prayer* (London 1954) 73–5. Jay reports that the Cambridge manuscript is the only surviving one to contain the whole of Origen's tract.

6 In light of the paucity of manuscripts of Origen's Περὶ εὐχῆς and of Erasmus' interest in the subject of prayer, it is very strange that Erasmus says nothing about Origen's essay if in fact it was in the Ladenburg manuscript when he was working on the commentary on Matthew. Dr David McKitterick, Librarian of Trinity College, Cambridge, has informed me that physical traces show the two works were together in one volume prior to their being bound in the eighteenth century, the date of their present binding. I am grateful for his assistance on this matter.

7 For chronological reasons the same argument must apply to similarities between Origen's Περὶ εὐχῆς and Erasmus' *Precatio dominica* (1523). These are adduced by Godin *Erasme lecteur* 626 n131 as further support for his belief that Erasmus knew Origen's treatise.

the reader to the biblical passages where events mentioned by Erasmus are recounted; the former usually suggests that Erasmus' phraseology is similar to but not exactly the same as a biblical passage. When Erasmus is directly quoting from the Vulgate only the reference is given. The Revised Standard Version has been followed for most of the translations of biblical quotations.

Thanks are owed to the Centre for Reformation and Renaissance Studies at Victoria University, University of Toronto, whose Erasmus collection includes a copy of the rare 1525 edition.

JNG

ON PRAYING TO GOD

TO THE HONOURABLE HIERONIM ŁASKI, BARON OF POLAND AND
PALATINE OF SIERADZ IN RYTWIANY, FROM DESIDERIUS ERASMUS
OF ROTTERDAM, GREETINGS.[1]

This is how gifts that spring from grateful friendship[2] are reciprocated, dear
Hieronim, my distinguished lord. You left with me a pledge of your love
for me; in return there comes to you a pledge of my same feelings for you,
as you required of me when you left here.[3]

Although all the sacred acts of Mosaic law have been put out of date
by the gospel, there is no sacred office that our Prince Jesus more diligently
handed down to us or that his disciples embraced with more devoutness
than 'the calves of our lips,' to use the words of Hosea.[4] This sacred act is
manifested in three ways: in prayers, in giving thanks (to which praise is
close), or in hymns (a hymn is when the mind thinks of the sublimity of
God and is inspired to praise him to whom all glory is owed).

In the third chapter of the Epistle to the Colossians the apostle Paul
links three terms of a similar nature when he says, 'Teaching and admonish-
ing one another in psalms, hymns, and spiritual songs, singing with thank-
fulness in your hearts to God.'[5] 'Psalm' means 'song' in Greek and seems to

* * * * *

1 Hieronim Łaski, a diplomat in the service of Sigismund I, first met Erasmus
  in 1520 and visited him in Basel in 1524. One of the purposes of his visit was
  to find out Erasmus' attitude to Luther. See CEBR II 194–6. Ep 1502, written
  to Łaski c October 1524, consists of the opening and closing passages of the
  Modus orandi Deum.
2 In Allen Ep 1502 *gratiarum* in the phrase *gratiarum munera* is printed as *Gratiarum,* 'of the Graces.'
3 See Ep 1341A:1263–5. Hieronim left Erasmus a silver cup when visiting him,
  and all that he requested in return was that Erasmus be his friend.
4 Hos 14:2 (Vulg 14:3)
5 Col 3:16

be a term common to everything that pertains to the praise of God or even
of a human being. Accordingly some psalms have the heading 'to David
himself' as if they were composed to praise him. A hymn in its proper
meaning seems to refer to the praise of a deity: 'A hymn is due to you,
O God, in Sion.'⁶ Consequently, even pagan poets call the poems in which
they exalt their gods 'hymns,' such as those still surviving poems that are
ascribed to Orpheus and Homer.⁷ In turn the spiritual song, which is ᾠδή
in Greek, seems to be something more sublime than either of these, indeed
to be that song of praise sung to God by the angels and the souls of the
devout that have already cast off their mortality. For in Revelation the virgins have a new song that no one can learn except those 'who follow the
Lamb wherever he goes,'⁸ and this is the point of the complaint in the psalm,
'How shall we sing the Lord's song in a foreign land?'⁹ Paul too says he
desires 'to depart and to be with Christ,'¹⁰ so that he can sing this song of
the Lord.

Paul also links these three terms in the same order in the Epistle to
the Ephesians. He says, 'But be filled with the Holy Spirit, addressing one
another in psalms, hymns, and spiritual songs, singing and making music
in your hearts to the Lord.'¹¹ All three of these are called spiritual,¹² because all praise of this kind may be referred to the glory of God even if
sometimes some part is given to a human. For the world also has its own
psalms, hymns, and songs in which we praise sinful demons or human beings as if they are gods or in which humans fawn upon humans, sometimes
praising even what is base not only in mortals but even in those whom they
worship as gods. Those who have drunk in the spirit of Christ, however,
know how to praise only the Father, Son, and Holy Spirit. To these alone
is owed whatever true praise there is, whether in heaven or on earth. Paul
adds, 'making music in your hearts to the Lord.' What is the point of 'to
the Lord'? Those who think their own virtues make them righteous are not

* * * * *

6 Ps 65:1 (Vulg 64:2)
7 Hymns to gods, among other works, were ascribed to the mythical Orpheus;
   see *Orphica* ed E. Abel (Leipzig 1885). For the so-called Homeric hymns, see
   Hesiod, Homeric Hymns, and Homerica ed E.G. Evelyn-White (Cambridge, Mass
   1954).
8 Rev 14:4
9 Ps 137 (Vulg 136):4
10 Phil 1:23
11 Eph 5:18–19
12 Erasmus seems to take the adjective *spiritualibus*, 'spiritual,' in Eph 5:18 to refer
    not only to *canticis* but also to psalms and hymns.

making music to the Lord, but 'are singing to themselves within,' as we say. In a similar fashion those who place their faith and glory in Moses, Francis, Benedict, Dominic, or Augustine are not singing to the Lord but to human beings.[13] Only when we mortals recognize how worthless we are in ourselves is God especially glorified. What is the point of 'in your hearts'? So that no one may think that God takes delight in the empty bellowing of voices or the modulated whinnying of musical instruments or in the organs that now noisily resound in churches everywhere. I say this not because I condemn the music of instruments if it is used in moderation, in sobriety, and if it is worthy of being part of divine worship, but so that I may show that worshipping in this way is worthless if the silent and reverent love for God is not present; this is the song that is most pleasing to God even if no sound of words accompanies it. Since God is always and everywhere worthy of wonder, a Christian ought never to cease from psalms, hymns, and spiritual songs.

Similar to these is the expression of thanks, which relates more to the goodness of God than to his greatness. A psalm is when we sing to him, 'Praise the Lord, O my soul, I will praise the Lord as long as I live, I will sing praises to my God while I have being.'[14] A hymn is when we sing to him, 'Let all the works of the Lord praise the Lord';[15] for here the mind is stunned at the might and incomprehensible sublimity of the Creator in all that he has created. It will be a song when the mind, inspired with longing for the celestial life and eagerly desiring to fly away from the body, sings to him, 'How lovely is your dwelling-place, O Lord of hosts. My soul longs, yea, faints for the courts of the Lord. My heart and my flesh sing for joy to the living God.'[16]The expression of thanks will be when we sing to him, 'Confess to the Lord, for he is good, his steadfast love endures for ever,'[17] and 'I will sing of the compassion of the Lord for ever.'[18]

* * * * *

13 St Francis of Assisi (1186–1226) was founder of the the Order of Friars Minor, who placed importance on complete poverty. The Rule of St Benedict (c 480–550) provided the basis for a monastic life in which the days were spent in prayer, spiritual reading, and toil. The Order of Preachers, founded by St Dominic (1170–1221), placed emphasis on teaching and preaching. St Augustine of Hippo (354–430) was one of the four traditional Latin 'Doctors of the church.'
14 Ps 146 (Vulg 145):1
15 Cf Ps 145 (Vulg 144):10.
16 Ps 84 (Vulg 83):1–3
17 Ps 118 (Vulg 117):1. In the RSV the verse begins 'Give thanks to the Lord.'
18 Ps 89 (Vulg 88):1

Just as blasphemy is the opposite of a hymn, so ingratitude is the opposite of expressing thanks. Those who credit to human strength what is owed to God and search out human praise for the kindnesses owed to him detract from his glory. Paul wrote to the Colossians, 'Whatever you do, in word or deed, do everything in the name of the Lord Jesus Christ,'[19] so that they would always have in their hearts what is on the lips of all Christians, 'Hallowed be your name.'[20] In the same way, not only do those who rant wildly against God with evil words blaspheme against him, but so too do those who live wicked lives even though they have professed his name. Christ says, 'so that they may see your good deeds and give glory to your Father who is in heaven.'[21] The martyrs sang the most pleasing song to God when they surrendered their bodies to the base desires of tyrants to be tortured by dreadful instruments even when their tongues had been cut out and they could not utter any words of praise. Are not now the lives of some Christians nothing but unceasing blasphemy against the Lord if they love only what is of this world? This is especially true of the lives of those who profess by their rank and title to be the leaders of the Christian faith. If, according to the view of Paul,[22] the name of God is blasphemed among gentiles because of the Jews who do not observe the Law, with how much more justification will the same be said against those who hold the highest offices of the Christian church and yet fight all their lives against the precepts of the Gospel?

Such persons bring the venerable name of Jesus Christ into bad repute not only among pagans but even among Christians. I[23] have no pleasure in relating what Turkish diplomats who have spent even a few days at Rome or at the court of other Christian princes are accustomed to say when they have returned to their own people.[24] It is also not difficult to divine what is said about us by peoples who were unknown to us till recently and whose lands and wealth we now assail by force – not so that we may win them for Christ (for that must be tried in other ways), but so that we may extend our own dominion and sovereignty and so that we may increase our wealth, which

* * * * *

19 Col 3:17
20 Matt 6:9
21 Matt 5:16
22 See Rom 2:24.
23 A substantial addition to the text of the *editio princeps* begins here, ending with '... the glory of Christ, their Prince' (152); see n31 below.
24 For a similar denunciation of the vices of Christians and how they might be viewed by the Turks, see Ep 858:108–11.

we place above God.[25] For they have seen so much greed, lust, and cruelty in the actions of those who profess the cross of Christ that those whom we attack as if they are wild beasts seem human, while we, compared with them, seem to be the beasts and not human beings, far less Christians.

With what great mental anguish are we compelled every day to listen to profane men – if it is right, despite the circumstances, for any Christian to be called profane – assailing the holy name of Jesus Christ because of the wicked lives that some priests are living. 'Are these the men,' they say, 'whom Christ has left to us as representatives of his power and teaching? Are these the men who handle God in their consecrated hands, are these the men who "bind and loose on earth"[26] in such a way that God will approve in heaven what they have decided?' Would that we could deny or at least take pleasure in correcting what they do not fear to add to such blasphemies. They are perhaps heretics, more harmful than pagans and semi-Christian Turks. There is justifiable outcry against those who abet the irreligious madness of such people. Yet who abets them more than priests who openly fight against the teaching of Christ during their whole life? Theologians and monks arraign such priests one after another on the grounds that they are everywhere held in disrepute and that, consequently, so is Christ.

Why do we prefer to imitate Adam and Cain rather than to listen to Paul? Adam cast the blame on his wife,[27] Cain preferred to vilify God rather than to recognize his crime;[28] neither wished either to confess or to correct his fault. Paul gives us loving and useful advice in the Second Epistle to the Corinthians: 'As servants of God let us commend ourselves in all things, to no one giving any offence so that no fault may be found with our ministry.'[29] What does he mean by 'in all things'? Surely not in fowling, in having many servants, in material resources, riches, sovereignty, in bishops' staffs, priests' caps, processions, threats, wars, wealth, or the alliances of princes. No, not at all. What, then, does he mean? I would not dare to give an answer if Paul had not specifically named all of them. He says, 'in great endurance, afflictions, hardships, calamities, beatings, imprisonments, tumults, labours, in wakefulness, in purity and knowledge,'[30] and everything else that is listed by that great but staffless bishop in these verses.

* * * * *

25 A rare reference in Erasmus' work to the discoveries in the New World
26 Cf Matt 16:19, 18:18.
27 See Gen 3:12.
28 See Gen 4:9.
29 2 Cor 6:3–4
30 2 Cor 6:4–6

These we turn away from, these we abhor, but it was through these that Paul glorified the name of Jesus Christ.

The Dominicans and Franciscans are angry that certain persons heap abuse on the names of their founders; they defend themselves in many ways, and refuse to do anything instead of recognizing the faults of their members who bring the names of Francis and Dominic into ill repute. It is the glory of Christ to which we must especially devote ourselves. Yet if we think we should devote ourselves to the glory of holy men, let us do what they did to earn rather than to court glory among mortals, let us put right these actions that provide material for those who revile us. I say this not because I excuse the abusive words of such men (for not only must we condemn those who denounce all members because of a few miscreants or who condemn the priesthood because of the vices of those who hold the office, but we must also not tolerate those who forget Christian moderation and call loudly for revolt against the vices of priests as if they themselves are free of guilt). Rather, I say this because I wish us to be completely blameless, following the advice of Paul, who wrote, 'to no one giving any offence.' By saying 'no one,' he makes no exception for anyone. When he adds 'any offence,' he removes every kind of offence, no matter how small.

For those who truly love the glory of Christ, their Prince,[31] there is always reason, then, to give thanks; just as there is never any occasion not to praise God, since he is glorious and wonderful in all things and wherever you turn your eyes, so his kindness to us is ever active. Thanks should be given not only in times of good fortune but also in the afflictions that he sends upon us. Often he sends them so that he may correct and save us, sometimes so that he may provide the material for us to exercise our virtue.[32] Paul gave thanks for saving Epaphroditus from a very serious illness.[33] He gave thanks when, after praying to the Lord three times that the desire of the flesh be taken away and that Satan, who was raining blows upon him, be driven off, he heard the words 'My grace is sufficient for you; for my power is made perfect in weakness.'[34] Paul was aware of this when he wrote in the passage we recalled a little while ago, 'always and for everything giving thanks in the name of our Lord Jesus Christ to God the

* * * * *

31 The end of the addition to the text of the *editio princeps* that began 'I have no pleasure ...' (150); see n23 above.
32 A sentiment common in Stoicism. Cf Seneca *De providentia* 5–8 and, in particular, 6: 'calamitas virtutis occasio est' / 'disaster is virtue's opportunity.'
33 See Phil 2:26–7.
34 2 Cor 12:9

Father.'[35] It is proper always to give thanks to him who always gives blessings to us, but who above all in his inscrutable plan transforms all things to our advantage, even those that seem harmful. Giving praise and thanks is, therefore, an everlasting sacred duty of all Christians, but especially so when we represent by the consecration of sacred bread and holy chalice the death by which he redeemed us and the union of his mystical body. Because of this the act is appropriately called the Eucharist,[36] although the same act is called *synaxis*[37] by the Greeks, that is, the process of being brought together, because at the same time the bonds of love among all members of the body of Christ are therein represented. Consequently, it is also called *communio*, 'communion,' in Latin.

Each of these actions, praising and giving thanks, so far from ceasing after this life, is actually brought to completion then. In this life our soul is weighed down by our mortal body, and both our praises and our thanks are incomplete, as is our knowledge of the Lord's greatness and goodness. In the life to come the more clearly we shall see, the better will be our praise, as we call out with the angelic spirits, 'Holy, Holy, Holy is the Lord of hosts, the whole earth is full of his glory.'[38] When we have obtained what we previously sighed for and have actually acquired what we previously sought after in hope, we shall sing with David, 'As we have heard, so have we seen in the city of the Lord of hosts, in the city of our God.'[39]

The giving of thanks is in a way the same as the giving of praise; sometimes, however, it is also a request, to which we now turn. Even in our own relations with each other those who give thanks to the rich in return for a kindness are silently appealing to them to be more generous and to bestow greater largesse. Yet who is richer or more generous than God? As it is, we sometimes rejoice when we give thanks for the gifts of God, but we do so with trembling, uncertain whether what has been given to us will always be with us. For 'those who are standing must take care that they do not fall.'[40] Sometimes because of our negligence the grace of God removes itself, as if from those who are unworthy of it, and sometimes God himself turns his face from us, although he has not been offended by us, and leaves us to

* * * * *

35 Eph 5:20. Eph 5:18–19 are cited above (148; see n11).
36 In Greek the word εὐχαριστία means 'thanksgiving.'
37 Cf *Explanatio symboli* 337 below / ASD V-1 281 and 1237n.
38 Isa 6:3. This is probably also an allusion to the Sanctus ('Holy, Holy, Holy . . .') at the end of the Preface at mass: see *Missale Romanum* I 745.
39 Ps 48:8 (Vulg 47:9)
40 Cf 1 Cor 10:12.

ourselves for a time, so that we do not come into greater danger through wicked self-confidence in our own strength. In the heavenly city the giving of thanks will be full of joys. The memory of past blessings will be free of all worry, and no fear of losing what we have will darken the joy of our hearts. Nothing will be missing from our prayers to make our happiness incomplete, especially when the whole body of Christ will be gathered together to share in eternal happiness and will be joined with its head. Moreover, as long as we are in this exile, everything is full of evils and the possession of blessings is either incomplete or uncertain. It follows, therefore, that we must always pray to God to snatch us from the evils that press hard upon us, to increase his gifts in us, to wish that what he has deigned to bestow on us be ours for ever, and to complete in the future life what he began with us in this life.[41]

First, then, if it seems right, let us distinguish what is a *precatio,* 'prayer,' and what is an *oratio,* 'prayer,' although to use the latter in the sense of 'prayer' is not at all approved of by those who more scrupulously respect the elegance of the Latin language. For while in Latin a person who asks is said *orare,* 'to ask for,' the word *oratio* is not appropriately used in Latin in the sense of prayer, nor is a person who asks properly called an *orator.* It is Christian usage that accepted *oratio* in the sense of prayer. As far as I know, none of the ancients dared to say *orator,* 'orator,' for *deprecator,* 'a person who prays,' as is now the current usage.

To put aside concern with words, however, and to proceed with matters of substance, for instructional purposes we shall distinguish these three terms: praise, the giving of thanks, and prayer, although they differ more in theory than in fact and are generally close in meaning. Prayer is a raising of the mind to God with the desire to gain some request from him. This definition itself already makes it clear how far from praying are those who mull over all their trivial and meaningless worries as they bellow out noisily and pointlessly psalms that they could not understand even if they were paying attention to them.

Paul sometimes joins the two words *oratio,* 'prayer,' and *obsecratio,* 'supplication,' as if they mean the same thing,[42] *oratio*[43] corresponding to προσευχή, 'prayer,' and *obsecratio* corresponding to δέησις, 'request.' For this is what he writes: 'Have no anxiety about anything, but in everything by

* * * * *

41 Cf Phil 1:6.
42 In this section Erasmus, rather unclearly, sometimes writes as if Paul himself were responsible for the Latin translation of the Greek New Testament.
43 Erasmus' text actually reads *precatio* and not *oratio,* an apparent slip.

prayer [*oratio*] and supplication [*obsecratio*] with thanksgiving let your requests be made known to God.'[44] Again in Ephesians 6: 'with all prayer and supplication,'[45] where the Latin *oratio*, 'prayer,' translates the Greek προσευχή, and *obsecratio*, 'supplication,' translates δέησις. (Instead of *obsecratio*, 'supplication,' Ambrose translates the Greek as *prex*, 'plea.')[46] In the First Epistle to Timothy Paul also joins together three words, προσευχή, δέησις, and ἔντευξις. 'First of all, then,' he says, 'I urge that supplications [*obsecrationes* = δεήσεις], prayers [*orationes* = προσευχαί], intercessions [*postulationes* = ἐντεύξεις], and thanksgivings be made for all men.'[47] (Ambrose translates δεήσεις as *deprecationes* and προσευχαί as *orationes*.)[48] But ἐντεύξεις could be translated by *interpellationes*. For in the Epistle to the Romans chapter 8, what is in the Greek, ὃς καὶ ἐντυγχάνει ὑπὲρ ἡμῶν, obviously with the verb from which ἔντευξις is derived, has been rendered by the translator as *qui etiam interpellat pro nobis*, 'who even intercedes for us.'[49] There are those, however, who think that the three words have the same meaning and that their being used together in this way only reflects the passion and urgency of the prayer.

   Those who try to demonstrate differences among them are in little agreement. Augustine in a letter to Paulinus thinks that by δεήσεις, *deprecationes*, are meant those prayers which are offered before what is on the altar is blessed; that by προσευχαί, *orationes*, are meant the prayers that are offered when it is blessed or, as Augustine said, 'is sanctified and prepared for distribution';[50] and that ἐντεύξεις are the prayers that are offered after the sacrament has been received and the priest blesses the people, like an

* * * * *

44 Phil 4:6, where *oratio* and *obsecratio* translate προσευχή and δέησις of the Greek New Testament respectively
45 Eph 6:18
46 Ambrose *Commentarium in epistolam ad Ephesios* PL 17 424C ('per omnem orationem et precem')
47 1 Tim 2:1. The Greek equivalents in the square brackets do not appear in Erasmus' text and have been added by the translator for clarity's sake. The order in which they appear in the Greek New Testament in 1 Tim 2:1 is δεήσεις, προσευχαί, ἐντεύξεις and not as Erasmus lists them in the preceding sentence. Origen takes 1 Tim 2:1 as his starting-point for distinguishing the meaning of the Greek words for prayer (Περὶ εὐχῆς 14.2–5). Thomas Aquinas also discusses these different kinds of prayer at *Summa theologica* II-II q 83 art 17.
48 Like Erasmus, Ambrose translates ἐντεύξεις by *postulationes* (*Commentarium in epistolam 1 ad Timotheum* PL 17 491D).
49 Rom 8:34
50 Augustine *Epistolae* 149.13–16 PL 33 635–7. The quotation, literally 'is sanctified and broken up for distribution,' is in col 637.

intercessor offering his people to the most compassionate power. Then at the end of mass prayers of thanks are also said.

In the Greek scholia[51] the following distinctions are made: δέησις is whenever we pray to be freed from troubles that press upon us or are threatening us, προσευχή whenever we ask for blessings in our prayers, ἔντευξις whenever we complain about those who afflict us, in the way that the widow appealed to the judge,[52] or, as Theophylact interprets the word, when we intercede on behalf of those who afflict us that they come to their senses.[53] The etymology of the actual words and the circumstances in which they are spoken support this differentiation. For the Greek δέομαι has the same meaning as both *egeo*, 'I need,' and *rogo*, 'I ask.' What is more, *rogo* is the word used by a suppliant. And those who need [*egent*] help because they are hard pressed by difficulties are suppliants. Similarly the Greek εὔχομαι means the same as *opto*, while εὐχή is the same as *votum*. Finally, ἔντευξις means the same as *intercessio* or *interpellatio*, and it is by means of intercession that a person who has great authority in the eyes of those who have been struck down comes to their aid when they are in danger. The first task is to be freed from evils, which is why even today we begin mass with confession and absolution of sins. The next task is to pray for blessings for ourselves and our brethren. The most perfect action, however, is to intercede with God on behalf of those who persecute Christ in his members; we should ask not that they pay the penalty for their wickedness but that they come to their senses and turn to God.

Ambrose talks about *deprecationes* as being prayers of intercession offered for kings, and *orationes* as being formal prayers for all the others who hold magistracies or other public positions. He applied the term *postulationes* to pleas offered for those who are overwhelmed by various evils; the priests pray that they may be rescued and that, when freed, they may praise the Lord as the source of their delivery.[54]

I myself, for what it is worth, think that the Greek tradition of interpretation is nearer the truth.

* * * * *

51 Notes, marginal or interlinear, found in some manuscripts of the New Testament; see P.R. Ackroyd and C.F. Evans *The Cambridge History of the Bible* 1 (Cambridge 1970) 325–6.
52 See Luke 18:3.
53 Theophylact (eleventh century) *Expositio in epistolam 1 ad Timotheum* PG 125 29B–C
54 Ambrose *Commentarium in epistolam 1 ad Timotheum* on 2:1 PL 17 492A–B

So far I have been discussing the relationship among the words we use and how they are appropriate to different circumstances. Now we must briefly show how assiduously the Lord Jesus and his friends commended to us the zeal for and constant use of prayer, not just by their precepts but also by their example. Then we must show why this teaching was handed down to us with such insistence. After that we shall show that there are four things in particular that should be considered in prayer: who it is whom you pray to, what should be your frame of mind when praying, what you pray for, and how you should pray.

To deal with the first topic, in the eighteenth chapter of Luke, when the Lord had shown in earlier words by what dangers human life is beset, he thought it right also to indicate a remedy. The most steadfast support in misfortune is the help of God, which he promised would always be available to us if we ask for it in impassioned and urgent prayers. To fix this precept more deeply in the minds of the listeners, he adduced the parable of the wicked and irreligious judge;[55] although the judge did not fear God and had no respect for his fellow human beings, he was worn out by the tireless intercessions of a widow and finally did what he was asked. Yet if such a poor woman pressed with such bothersome insistence to exact punishment from her adversary, how much more insistently ought we to ask for what concerns eternal happiness. If a wicked and shameless judge was worn out by the intercessions of a woman and did what was requested, how much more will God, who is kind by nature, hear the prayers 'of those calling to him.'[56] In chapter 11 of the same book the Lord commends the same thing by a different parable, of the nocturnal visitor who by shouting and persistently knocking at his friend's door succeeded in prevailing over his excuses; his friend rises from his bed in the middle of the night and, having given him all the bread that he needed, gets rid of the troublesome dunner, more overcome by weariness than motivated by good will.[57] Compare now that unfeeling friend with God, compare the three loaves with eternal life, and you will understand how much more urgently and how much more confidently we should pray to the Heavenly Father.

Although we do not read of the Lord's making any prescriptions to his disciples about their clothes, about food or drink, or about fasting,

* * * * *

55 See Luke 18:2–8. The parable is adduced in Augustine *Epistolae* 130.15 PL 33 500 and in Origen Περὶ εὐχῆς 10.2.
56 Luke 18:7
57 See Luke 11:5–8. This parable also occurs in Augustine and Origen (see n55 above).

nevertheless he carefully prescribed a form of prayer. He did not bid us seek this from Moses or the prophets, or from John, who handed down some fixed forms of prayer in his Gospel;[58] rather he proposed one of his own. He would not have shown[59] such diligence in this matter if prayer were not an important part of an upright life. Similarly, in Matthew chapter 6 how carefully he urges his disciples to pray![60] For although he had removed from them all concern for clothes, for food, for reputation, for safety, for life itself, he taught that all these things should be asked for from their Father with great confidence. He says: 'Ask and it will be given to you, seek and you will find, knock and it will be opened to you. For everyone who asks receives, and he who seeks finds, and to him who knocks it will be opened.'[61] So that they would not have any doubts about receiving what they asked for or something more useful for salvation than that, he adduced an example from the natural love of fathers for their sons. No father is so cruel or wicked that 'if his son asks him for bread, he will give him a stone, or if he asks for a fish, he will give him a scorpion.'[62] If human parents who are wicked and sometimes even idolaters are driven by natural feelings of love and duty not to deny their children when they ask for the necessities of life, how much less will the Heavenly Father, who is by nature generous and helpful and who looks after his children with ineffable love, deny his children when they ask for what he would actually bestow on them of his own accord without their asking?

He repeats this promise in the same Gospel at chapter 18: 'Again I say to you: if two of you agree on earth about anything they ask, it will be done for them by my Father in heaven.'[63] Similarly, in Mark chapter 11 he binds himself to us by an oath, as it were, saying, 'Therefore I tell you, whatever you ask in prayer, believe that you will receive it and you will.'[64] When the day of crucifixion was already close at hand, he consoled his disciples, whom he was to leave at the appointed time, with no greater source of help than prayer. He said, 'Whatever you ask of the Father in my name I will do it, that the Father may be glorified in the Son; if you ask anything in my name, I will do it.'[65] In chapter 15 he repeats and stresses what he had

* * * * *

58 See John 17.
59 The ASD text wrongly reads *rursus* here for *usurus*.
60 See Matt 6:5–15.
61 Matt 7:7–8. Cf Luke 11:9–10.
62 Matt 7:9
63 Matt 18:19
64 Mark 11:24
65 John 14:13–14

said so that it does not escape us: 'If you abide in me, and my words abide
in you, ask whatever you will, and it shall be done for you.'[66] A little later
he says, 'Whatever you seek from my Father, he will give it to you.'[67] In
chapter 16 he rebukes them for not having asked for anything up till that
time, declaring and almost swearing that they would ask for nothing in vain:
'Truly, truly, I say to you, if you ask anything of the Father in my name, he
will give it to you. Hitherto, you have asked nothing in my name; ask, and
you will receive, that your joy may be full.'[68] Similarly, in Matthew 24 he
directs us to prayer alone when the total destruction of the world is actually
taking place. 'Pray,' he says, 'that your flight may not be in winter or on
a sabbath.'[69] Lest anyone think that it is sufficient to pray without feeling
or as if half awake, he says this in Mark: 'Watch, be wakeful, and pray.'[70]
Likewise, he protects his disciples against the onset of temptation: 'Be awake
and pray that you may not enter into temptation.'[71] In Luke 10 he says, 'Ask
the Lord of the harvest to send out labourers into his harvest.'[72]

The teaching of the apostles does not differ from that of the Lord. Paul
in the Second Epistle to the Thessalonians chapter 5 says, 'Rejoice always,
pray constantly, give thanks in all circumstances,'[73] and in the First Epistle
to Timothy chapter 2, 'I desire that men should pray in every place, lifting
holy hands without anger or quarrelling.'[74] The same applies also to women.
Paul wishes unmarried girls and bachelors to remain free so that they not be
estranged from prayer,[75] and for the same reason he wishes that for a time
married couples should abstain by agreement from intercourse.[76] Especially,
however, he wants widows to devote themselves to prayer, day and night.[77]

* * * * *

66 John 15:7
67 John 15:16 (Vulg 15:17). Erasmus omits *in nomine meo*, 'in my name,' of the
Vulgate.
68 John 16:23–4. The RSV translation of verse 23 ('if you ask anything of the Father, he will give it to you in my name') reflects a different punctuation from
what is found in Erasmus.
69 Matt 24:20
70 Mark 13:33
71 Matt 26:41
72 Luke 10:2
73 Actually Erasmus quotes from the *First* Epistle to the Thessalonians, not the
Second (1 Thess 5:16–18).
74 1 Tim 2:8
75 See 1 Cor 7:8.
76 See 1 Cor 7:5.
77 A paraphrase on 1 Tim 5:5. Augustine cites the verse at the beginning of his
letter to the widow Proba (*Epistolae* 130.1 PL 33 494).

Peter sings the same song to us. 'Be sober,' he says, 'and be watchful'[78] in prayers. James also tells those who need wisdom to ask for it from God.[79] He bids whoever is afflicted and is sorrowful to pray. He sets great store by prayer: those who pray have granted not only requests for themselves but also requests for others on whose behalf they pray to God. He tells those who are sick to summon the elders so that by their prayers they may be freed from bodily and spiritual sickness.[80] In short, he wants all Christians to help each other by praying for each other before God. 'Pray,' he says, 'for one another, that you may be healed. The constant prayers of the righteous have great power in their effects.'[81]

Now we must consider with what zeal the Lord Jesus tried to fix in the minds of his disciples what he so diligently handed down, frequently urging them by his own example to pray, like a bird spurring on its young to fly. The Gospels often recall that the Lord withdrew into a solitary place[82] or climbed a mountain[83] in order to pray, sometimes even alone. There is no doubt that he prayed with his disciples every day, for we read that before eating he gave the blessing and gave thanks[84] and after eating sang hymns in praise of God.[85] Whenever he left the crowds and withdrew to pray, he taught his ministers to pray to the Lord for those whom they undertook to guide, knowing that the work of a teacher and a guide bears no fruit unless heavenly favour breathes upon them. There is no loss to the good work of teaching if it is sometimes interrupted by withdrawing to pray, since anyone who has withdrawn to do this returns to the task with all the more eagerness and strength, and the listener's desire to learn is more keenly felt after a short break.

Whenever the Lord was about to face a great task, he is said to have begun with prayer.[86] We read in Luke chapter 3 that when he had been baptized and left the water he prayed.[87] The dove descended and the voice of his Father was heard: 'This is my beloved Son. Listen to him.'[88] This was

* * * * *

78 1 Pet 5:8
79 See James 1:5.
80 See James 5:14.
81 James 5:16
82 See Mark 1:35; Luke 5:16.
83 See Matt 14:23.
84 See Matt 26:26–7; Mark 14:22–3.
85 See Mark 14:26.
86 See John 11:41–2; Matt 26:39.
87 See Luke 3:21.
88 There is slight confusion here on the part of Erasmus. He quotes loosely here from Matt 17:5, when Jesus had taken Peter, James, and John up the mountain

clearly an auspicious beginning to the task of spreading the gospel. In the same way too he began his call to the gentiles, as we read in John 12.[89] When some of them had come to Jerusalem to worship and sought through Philip and Andrew to see Jesus, our Lord prayed in this way: 'Father, glorify your name.' Then he heard a voice from heaven: 'I have glorified it, and I will glorify it again.'[90] He prayed when he was about to raise Lazarus from the dead, as is clear even from what John writes: 'Father, I thank you that you have heard me.'[91] For it is quite obvious that anyone who says that he has been heard has been praying. In addition, in the ninth chapter of Luke it was with prayer that he wished to begin the profession of his name, through which salvation would be available for all. This is what we read: 'As he was praying, the disciples were with him; and he asked them, "Who do the people say I am?" and "Who do you say I am?" '[92] Then he heard from the mouth of Peter the heavenly inspired profession of all Christians, 'You are the Christ, the Son of the living God.'[93] It is in Peter's name, then, that all who profess sincerely the name of Christ hear the words 'Blessed are you, Simon Bar-Jona.'[94] A little later in the same Gospel, when he was about to show some proof of his immortality, he was not transfigured until after he had prayed. Luke says, 'And as he was praying, the appearance of his countenance was altered and his raiment became dazzling white.'[95]

Nor does he dedicate his church to anything other than prayer. The church's type[96] was the temple of Jerusalem, from which he drove out the foul throng of sellers and buyers, and of which he said, 'My house shall be called a house of prayer.'[97] The house of God is a church in which all who are present (and indeed all who are truly Christian are present in it) ought to do nothing other than pray, since the everlasting zeal to live righteously is the same as never-ending prayer.

* * * * *

(the scene of the transfiguration). On the occasion of his baptism, the verse (Luke 3:22) reads 'You are my beloved Son. In you I am well pleased.'
89 See John 12:20–3.
90 John 12:28
91 John 11:41
92 Luke 9:18, 20
93 Here Erasmus quotes the words of Peter as given in Matt 16:16, not as given in Luke 9:20.
94 Matt 16:17
95 Luke 9:29
96 'Type' is used here in the technical sense of a prefiguration or foreshadowing of something that will later come to pass. See *The New International Dictionary of New Testament Theology* ed Colin Brown 3 vols (Exeter 1975–8) III 903–7.
97 Matt 21:13. Cf Isa 56:7.

The Lord prayed for Peter that his faith should not fail,[98] and he asked his Father to send another Advocate[99] to his disciples so that they would not fail in times of affliction. After the completion of the final supper that he took with his disciples before his death, 'he lifted his eyes to heaven'[100] and prayed at length that his Father's glory be illuminated through the gospel, and that not only the apostles be saved by professing it, but also all those from every nation of the earth who would believe in it in the future, right up to the end of the world. We read that when the power of darkness was already assailing him he prayed in the garden three times[101] and at great length. Not only did he pray on bended knee,[102] but he also prostrated himself.[103] When he kept finding the leading disciples asleep, he told them to keep awake and to pray that they would not come into temptation.[104] Finally, when that High Priest 'after the order of Melchizedek'[105] was performing on the altar of the cross that unique and powerful sacrifice foreshadowed in time past by the types of the law of Moses[106] and re-enacted now every day by the consecration of the sacred bread and wine, he called out in a loud voice and prayed to the Father for his members: 'My God, my God, why have you forsaken me?'[107] He finally showed that most absolute love of all when he prayed to his Father on behalf of those who were crucifying, abusing, and reviling him.[108] It was by these many examples that our Lord wished to stimulate us to pray.

Now let us see how the apostles did not abandon what was laid down by their teacher. After the ascension of our Lord, they entered an upper room and, of one mind, were constantly in prayer. 'All these with one accord devoted themselves to prayer,' says Luke, 'with the women and Mary, the mother of Jesus, and with his brothers.'[109] Similarly, when they were

* * * * *

98 See Luke 22:32.
99 The Holy Spirit; see John 14:16.
100 A close echo of John 17:1
101 See Matt 26:36–44.
102 See Luke 22:41.
103 See Matt 26:39.
104 See Matt 26:40–1.
105 Heb 5:6, 7:17. Cf Ps 110 (Vulg 109):4.
106 Cf Heb 9:18–28. The First Covenant was ratified by sacrifice (see Exod 24:6–8). In establishing the New Covenant Christ's sacrifice of his own blood transcended the sacrifices enjoined by Jewish law, being offered once and for all and not requiring repetition. For the technical sense of 'type,' see n96 above.
107 Matt 27:46; Mark 15:34
108 See Luke 23:34.
109 Acts 1:14

about to appoint Matthias in place of Judas, who had perished, they prayed, saying, 'Lord, who know all hearts.'[110] With such a beginning the Holy Spirit was given, which is when the kingdom of the gospel began. With such a beginning the number of the apostolic senate was restored. With such a beginning the first harvest of the gospel was consecrated, the first offerings, so to speak. For when three thousand had been added to the number of the disciples in one day,[111] what does Luke add? He says, 'They devoted themselves to the apostles' teaching and fellowship, to the breaking of the bread, and to prayers.'[112] Later Peter and John went to the temple about the ninth hour to pray, at that period the customary time for the Jews to pray, and in front of the doors they healed a lame man in the name of Jesus.[113] Similarly, when the priests and the Pharisees were trying by their threats to crush the glory of the gospel, which was growing stronger daily, that paltry flock of Christ sought refuge only in prayers. Luke says, 'They lifted their voices together and said, "Lord, who did make the heaven and earth,"' and so on.[114] 'And when they had prayed, the place in which they were gathered together was shaken; and they were all filled with the Holy Spirit.'[115] Later, when the numbers of believers continued to grow and grow – to such an extent that the apostles in looking after them all were weighed down by having to deal with more mundane matters – the apostles searched for deacons to be in charge of meals for no other reason than that they might have time to devote themselves to teaching and prayer. 'We,' they said, 'will devote ourselves to prayer and to the ministry of the word.'[116] We perceive that the apostles do nothing but teach[117] and pray, whether they are at work or at leisure. To the seven deacons that were chosen the authority of the ministry was given, by prayer as well as by other means. 'These they set before the apostles,' he says, 'and they prayed and laid their hands upon them.'[118] While the stones were being hurled at Stephen by the riotous mob, he knelt down and prayed, 'Lord Jesus, receive my spirit; do not hold this sin against them.'[119] The last sound that he made as he died was not a groan but a prayer.

* * * * *

110 Acts 1:24
111 See Acts 2:41.
112 Acts 2:42
113 See Acts 3:1–8.
114 Acts 4:24
115 Acts 4:31
116 Acts 6:4
117 The ASD text wrongly reads *dicere* here for *docere*.
118 Acts 6:6
119 Acts 7:59–60

The apostles were granted a special power to transmit by the laying on of hands the Holy Spirit to those who believed. They did not do this, however, without first praying. Peter and John set out for Samaria because they were aware that as a result of the preaching of Philip the Samaritans too had accepted the faith of the gospel and had been baptized, but that the Holy Spirit had not yet come to any of them. First of all, we read, they prayed for the Samaritans that they should receive it, then they bestowed upon them what was lacking by placing their hands upon them.[120] What of Paul, that wonderful champion of the gospel? What was the starting-point of his new way of life? Prayer, of course; for the Lord spoke these words to Ananias: 'And inquire in the house of Judas for a man of Tarsus named Saul; for behold, he is praying.'[121] What does 'he is praying' mean? It means he is seeking to become a Christian.

Although we read that the Lord did not always pray while he was performing miracles (because he had the power of raising the dead from his own nature, as he himself attests in John),[122] nevertheless the apostles are said to have prayed whenever they did this. For when Peter made Aeneas, who was paralysed, rise from his bed at Lidda, saying, 'Aeneas, the Lord Jesus heals you,'[123] what else is he doing but praying? Similarly, at Joppa, when he was about to raise Dorcas, he asked to be left alone, he knelt and prayed.[124] What of the centurion Cornelius, who had such devout faith that he was worthy of receiving the Holy Spirit before he had been baptized? What did he hear from the angel? 'Your prayers and your alms have ascended to heaven as a memorial before God.'[125] It was while he was praying that the angel brought the joyful news. It was while Peter was praying that he saw a vision about the conversion of the gentiles. 'Peter went up on the housetop to pray, about the sixth hour,' Luke says.[126] When the cruelty of Herod had increased to such an extent that after killing James he threw Peter, the leader of the apostles, into prison,[127] what did the Christians, already quite numerous, now do? They did not attack the king, they did not storm the prison, they did not stir up any riots in the city, they did

* * * * *

120 See Acts 8:14–17.
121 Acts 9:11
122 See John 5:26.
123 Acts 9:34
124 See Acts 9:40.
125 Acts 10:4
126 Acts 10:9
127 See Acts 12:1–3. The James referred to is James, the son of Zebedee. He was executed by Herod Agrippa I, king of Palestine, in 41–4 AD.

not have recourse to magic.[128] What, then, did they do? We read, of course, that 'earnest prayer for him was made to God by the church.'[129] Immediately he was freed by an angel and then made for 'the house of Mary, the mother of John, where many were gathered together and were praying.'[130]

At Antioch too, when Paul and Barnabas were fitted out with apostolic authority, nothing was done without prayer. 'Then,' Luke says, 'after fasting and praying, they laid their hands on them and sent them off.'[131] At Lystra, Iconium, and Antioch they fasted and prayed when they were ordaining presbyters for each church.[132] At Philippi Paul actually went out of the city, looking for a place of prayer, and there gained for Christ Lydia, a dealer in purple fabric.[133] Later, as Paul and his companions were on their way again to pray, a girl screamed at them. She was possessed by a python, from which Paul freed her.[134] Furthermore, whenever Christians gathered to break bread, they also gathered to pray, as the first disciples did almost every day. This custom came down also to later generations, so that whenever bishops or other distinguished men gathered, they began their meetings with each other with prayer, then there was communion, then conversation. When Paul was about to sail from Miletus, before he went to the ship he knelt and prayed with all his brothers,[135] some of whom he had summoned from Ephesus.[136] Similarly, when he was setting out from Tyre, he consecrated the sterile sands of the shore with a prayer. For this is what we read: 'And kneeling down on the beach we prayed.'[137] Of course this was what he had taught: 'In every place lifting holy hands.'[138] A prison was his temple at Thessalonica.[139] Indeed, even on trial before Agrippa and Festus he prayed while pleading his case in chains; he asked God that all who were

* * * * *

128 The second and third clauses of this sentence are omitted, erroneously, in ASD.
129 Acts 12:5
130 Acts 12:12
131 Acts 13:3
132 See Acts 14:6, 13:51, 13:14.
133 See Acts 16:13–14.
134 See Acts 16:16. The term 'python' is used in the Vulgate in the sense of an evil spirit that possessed the mind; cf Deut 18:11. It derives from Python, the serpent at Delphi slain by Apollo.
135 See Acts 20:36.
136 See Acts 20:17.
137 Acts 21:5
138 1 Tim 2:8. Cf Origen Περὶ εὐχῆς 9.1; Tertullian De oratione 13–14, 17 PL 1 1271–3, 1278.
139 See Acts 16:25. But this was at Philippi, where Paul and Silas prayed when imprisoned.

listening to him praying in the assembly should be rendered like him, not just to a small but to a great degree, with the exception only of the chains.[140] He also prayed on the ship when everyone else was distraught with fear, and the lives of all that were on the ship were entrusted to him by God.[141]

Paul also begins all his Epistles with prayer. For such conventional words as 'Grace to you and peace,' and so on,[142] are simply a form of prayer. All the Epistles begin in the same way except one, the Epistle to the Hebrews, which, even on these grounds, does not seem to be the work of Paul.[143] He ends most of them with prayer. The Epistle to the Romans has this closing: 'The grace of our Lord Jesus Christ be with you all. Amen.'[144] The First Epistle to the Corinthians has this: 'The grace of our Lord Jesus Christ be with you. My love be with you all in Jesus Christ. Amen,'[145] while the Second Epistle has 'The grace of our Lord Jesus Christ and the love of God and the fellowship of the Holy Spirit be with you all. Amen.'[146] The Epistle to the Galatians ends with 'The grace of our Lord Jesus Christ be with your spirit, brethren. Amen.'[147] The Epistle to the Ephesians has 'Grace be with all who love our Lord Jesus Christ with love undying.'[148] The Epistle to the Philippians has 'The grace of our Lord Jesus Christ be with your spirit. Amen.'[149] The endings of all the others are quite similar, even the one entitled 'To the Hebrews.'[150] He seems to have added these endings in his own hand as a signature, even in the Epistles that he dictated. For this is what he writes in the Second Epistle to the Thessalonians: 'I, Paul, write this greeting with my own hand. This is the mark in every letter of mine. The grace of our Lord Jesus Christ be with you all. Amen.'[151] Often in the middle of his Epistles he breaks forth into a hymn or an expression of thanks or into prayer, as if he has forgotten the topic that he is dealing with. In the

* * * * *

140 See Acts 26:29. Agrippa is Agrippa II, part of whose kingdom included Galilee. Porcius Festus was procurator of Judaea in 60–2 AD.
141 See Acts 27:24.
142 See eg Rom 1:7; 1 Cor 1:3; 2 Cor 1:2; Gal 1:3.
143 Cf Origen: 'Who wrote the Epistle to the Hebrews God only knows' (Eusebius *Historia ecclesiastica* 6.25.14 PG 20 585–6). The scholarly consensus now is that Paul is not the author of the Epistle to the Hebrews.
144 Rom 16:24. This verse is omitted in some versions.
145 1 Cor 16:23–4
146 2 Cor 13:13–14
147 Gal 6:18
148 Eph 6:24
149 Phil 4:23
150 Cf Heb 13:25: 'Grace be with you all. Amen.'
151 2 Thess 3:17–18. Erasmus omits the words *ita scribo*, 'it is the way I write.'

Epistle to the Philippians he says, 'And the peace of God, which passes all understanding, will keep your hearts and minds in Jesus Christ.'[152] Similarly, in Ephesians chapter 3, he says, 'For this reason I bow my knees before the Father of our Lord Jesus Christ,'[153] and then soon afterwards he bursts into a hymn: 'To him who can do all,' and so on.[154] When writing to the Romans, he prays, 'I could wish that I myself were accursed and cut off from Christ for the sake of my brethren,' and so on.[155] Shortly afterwards he bursts into praise: 'God who is over all, be blessed forever. Amen.'[156] His prayer in chapter 7 is similar: 'Wretched man that I am! Who will deliver me from this body of death?'[157] Again, in chapter 11 praise interrupts the argument: 'O the depth of the riches,' and so on.[158]

In many places Paul attests that in his daily prayers he remembered all who believed in Christ. We[159] can understand, then, that for good cause he writes, 'Be imitators of me, as I am of Christ.'[160] For here too, as in all other things, he recalled the example of his Lord. Writing to the Ephesians, he says this: 'For this reason I bow my knees before the Father of our Lord Jesus Christ, from whom every family in heaven and on earth is named so that according to the riches of his glory he may grant you to be strengthened with might through his Spirit,' and so on.[161] It was not enough for the teacher of the gentiles to undertake for the sake of the gospel such toil and so many dangers and to preach with untiring zeal its power, to visit all the churches, to strengthen by his writings those whom he could not visit. He did not think it enough to heal the sick, to drive out evil spirits, to raise the dead. He sought a surer means of support. What was that? On bended knees he prays for the salvation of those whom he had already won for Christ. With what solicitude he asks for their prayers in return, in the Epistle to the Romans chapter 15,[162] as well as in other places: 'I appeal to you, brethren,' he says, 'that you help me in your prayers to God on my behalf,' and so

* * * * *

152 Phil 4:7
153 Eph 3:14
154 Eph 3:20
155 Rom 9:3
156 Rom 9:5
157 Rom 7:24
158 Rom 11:33
159 A short addition to the text of the *editio princeps* begins here, ending at '. . . won for Christ' later in the paragraph.
160 1 Cor 11:1
161 Eph 3:14–16
162 The ASD text wrongly reads '4' here for '15.'

on.[163] He[164] talks about both things when writing to the Colossians: 'Continue steadfastly in prayer, being watchful, and praying also for us, that God may open to us a door for the word, to declare the mystery of Christ, on account of which I am in prison, that I may make it clear, in the way that I should.'[165]

From these examples the value of frequent prayer came down to our ancestors – to such an extent that whatever they did was prayer itself or was consecrated by prayer. First, as I have said, they began their meetings with prayer, their conversation and feasts were interrupted by prayer, they prayed when they dispersed, they prayed just before they went to sleep, and sleep itself was frequently interrupted for prayers. Matins began with a prayer, and traces of the old custom survive today in the church.[166] There are night prayers and morning prayers, prayers said at the first hour, and prayers said at the third, sixth, and ninth hours. There are evening prayers and there are prayers that follow dinner and precede sleep called 'Compline.'[167] Everything was consecrated by prayer: departures, arrivals, or any new venture – to such an extent that Philo entitled a book about the practices of Christians *On the Contemplative Life of Suppliants*.[168] I could gather here very many examples from ancient history that show us the great zeal for praying that our fathers possessed; for example, James, whose knees we read had skin that was as hard as that of camels because of the frequency with which he prayed.[169]

* * * * *

163 Rom 15:30

164 The final sentence of this paragraph is an addition to the text of the *editio princeps*.

165 Col 4:2–4. Erasmus omits 'in it with thanksgiving' after 'watchful.'

166 Erasmus is possibly alluding to the petition peculiar to the opening of Matins, 'Domine, labia mea aperies, et os meum annuntiabit laudem tuam' / 'O Lord, open my lips, and my mouth shall show forth your praise' (Ps 51 [Vulg 50]:17).

167 The hours of prayer in the *Breviarium Romanum*, listed in the order given here by Erasmus: Matins, Vespers, Lauds, Prime, Terce, Sext, None, Vespers (again), and Compline. Cf Tertullian *De oratione* 25 PL 1 1300 and Origen Περὶ εὐχῆς 12.2; and see E.G. Jay *Origen's Treatise on Prayer* (London 1954) 36–41.

168 Philo of Alexandria (c 20 BC–c 50 AD) was a Jewish thinker and exegete who combined Greek and Judaic thought. The work to which Erasmus here refers focuses on the Therapeutae, a pre-Christian monastic community of Egyptian Jewish ascetics. In thinking that Philo was talking about Christians Erasmus may have been misled by Eusebius (*Historia ecclesiastica* 2.17.3–24 PG 20 175–84), who thinks that the Therapeutae were Christian monks.

169 The James referred to here is 'the Lord's brother' (cf Mark 6:3), who was leader or 'first bishop' of the church of Jerusalem. He is sometimes known as 'James the Less' to distinguish him from 'James the Greater,' one of the

It is not my intention, however, to find exhortation to prayer from any-where other than the sacred books. Even books of the Old Testament pro-vide ample material for discussion of this topic. All the words of the saints there are nothing but a conversation with God. For[170] if they are not com-plaining, they are asking for something, or they are making vows or consult-ing about what is to happen, or they deplore their sins, or they commend the friends for whom they are fearful, or they give thanks for the kind-nesses they have received, or they burst forth into praise of God. The book of Psalms is nothing but a never-ending conversation with God. The Old Testament will continually supply you with very many examples of how powerful and effective it is to pray to God with a pure mind.

In the book of Genesis I do not think that Abel offered sacrifice with-out praying.[171] Certainly Enosh, the son of Seth, was the first to win praise for praying. About him it is written in chapter 4, 'He began to call upon the name of the Lord.'[172] The inventors of human skills are given only passing mention, Enosh alone is honoured with this praise, that he succeeded Abel by the will of God.[173] When Noah left the ark after the flood, his first con-cern was to build an altar to the Lord and to sacrifice with burnt offerings.[174] As soon as Abraham heard that land was promised to him, he built an al-tar and called upon the name of the Lord.[175] We read that he did the same thing every time he changed where he lived.[176] All the other patriarchs fol-lowed this example; I will not bore the reader by going through every exam-ple. In chapter 20 of the same book Abraham prays and Abimelech is freed from death, and his wife and throng of maidservants are cured of the steril-ity that the Lord had inflicted upon them in his anger.[177] In Exodus Moses prays to the Lord, and the frogs that had taken over the whole of Egypt

* * * * *

twelve apostles. For his piety see Eusebius *Historia ecclesiastica* 2.23.6–7 PG 20 197, reporting Hegesippus.

170 The sentence 'For ... praise of God' is an addition to the text of the *editio princeps*.

171 See Gen 4:4.

172 Gen 4:26. Erasmus follows the Vulgate. The RSV translation is 'men began to call upon the name of the Lord.'

173 Enosh succeeded Abel indirectly in that he was the son of Seth, the third son of Adam and Eve, of whom Eve says, 'God has appointed for me another child instead of Abel' (Gen 4:25). With the praise accorded to Enosh (Gen 4:26, see the preceding note) contrast Gen 4:2, where Abel is described as 'a keeper of sheep' and Cain as 'a tiller of the ground.'

174 See Gen 8:20.

175 See Gen 12:7.

176 See eg Gen 12:8, 13:18.

177 See Gen 20:17.

perish.[178] Again he prays to the Lord, and the thunder and the hail cease
to devastate the region of Egypt.[179] Similarly, when God was offended by
the golden calf that the Israelites had worshipped as a god, following the
custom of the Egyptians, and was preparing to destroy the whole people,[180]
Moses prayed for his people and 'the Lord repented of the evil which he had
said he would do to his people.'[181] It[182] would have been all over with Aaron
too, because he had yielded to the wicked wishes of the multitude and had
given the molten calf to be worshipped, had not Moses extinguished the
wrath of God by his prayers. He attests to this in Deuteronomy chapter 9.[183]
Previously, however, the outcome of the war with Amalek depended on the
hands of Moses while he was praying on the mountain.[184]

It was with prayer that the ark of the covenant was moved. For Moses
said, 'Arise, O Lord, and let your enemies be scattered and let them that
hate you flee before you.'[185] It was with prayer that the ark was set down:
'Return, O Lord, to the great numbers of the army of Israel.'[186] Prayer gave
the signal for battle, prayer sounded the retreat. Again, when the fire of
the Lord was engulfing outlying parts of the camp of Israel, the people
called to Moses, Moses called to the Lord, and immediately the avenging
fire was quenched.[187] He called again to the Lord, and as a result Miriam,
who had spoken against Moses, was freed of leprosy.[188] On another occasion
the people murmured against the Lord, who prepared to exact vengeance.
Moses, however, assuaged the fiery wrath of God with persuasive prayer,
and heard, 'I have pardoned, in accordance with your words.'[189]

When God was offended by the rebellion of Korah and was preparing
to destroy the whole people, Moses and Aaron fell to the ground on their

* * * * *

178 See Exod 8:12–13.
179 See Exod 9:33.
180 See Exod 32:7–10.
181 Exod 32:14
182 This and the next sentence are additions to the text of the *editio princeps*.
183 See Deut 9:20. Erasmus does not necessarily imply by this sentence his belief
     in the Mosaic authorship of Deuteronomy. He may mean simply that in this
     chapter it is Moses himself who speaks of the incident. For a brief account of
     the history of the question of Mosaic authorship of the Pentateuch see F.C.
     Eiselen in *The Abingdon Bible Commentary* (New York 1929) 134–9.
184 See Exod 17:11.
185 Num 10:35
186 Num 10:36
187 See Num 11:1–2.
188 See Num 12:13–16.
189 Num 14:20

faces and persuaded the Lord by their prayers to punish only the few in-
stigators of the revolt. The earth opened up and swallowed them alive.[190]
Later, when the hostility of the people towards Moses and Aaron had broken out again, and the Lord was once more preparing to destroy the rebellious people, Moses and Aaron fell prostrate on the ground and prayed. On
the orders of Moses Aaron stood among the dead whom the fire of the Lord
had destroyed and among the living who were already close to death. He
burned incense and won over the Lord by his prayers. The plague, which
had already destroyed more than fourteen thousand seven hundred people,
came to an end.[191] When the people were weak with thirst in the desert, and
it looked as if there were going to be a rebellion, Moses and Aaron fell prone
upon the ground and prayed, and a supply of water was drawn from the
rock.[192] Again, when murmuring arose because of the tedium of the long
journey, God in his anger sent fiery serpents on the people.[193] Terrified by
the many serpents that fell from the sky, the people called to Moses, who
called to the Lord. A bronze serpent was raised so that the sight of it would
free them from the danger of death.[194]

Joshua, the successor of Moses, prayed to the Lord and stopped the
course of the sun and the moon until he had punished his enemies. For
this is what you read in the tenth chapter of Joshua: 'Then spoke Joshua
to the Lord,' clearly begging for the help of the Lord. Then he spoke to
the sun and the moon: 'Sun, stand still upon Gibeon, and you, moon, in
the valley of Ajalon.'[195] In the book of Kings Hannah, the wife of Elkanah,
prays silently and instead of being sterile becomes the fruitful mother of
her renowned offspring Samuel.[196] When the people of Israel were in great
fear because of the rumour that the Philistines were attacking them, Samuel
called to the Lord and the Lord heard him.[197] Israel prevailed, since the
Lord turned all Israel's fear against the enemy.[198] Samuel also called to the

* * * * *

190 See Num 16:32.
191 See Num 16:48–9.
192 See Exod 17:1–6.
193 See Num 21:6.
194 See Num 21:9.
195 See Josh 10:12.
196 See 1 Sam 1:13–20. Erasmus gives the reference as the book of Kings, since
      the two books of Samuel were known as the first two books of Kings in the
      Vulgate.
197 See 1 Sam 7:9.
198 'The Lord thundered with a mighty voice that day against the Philistines and
      threw them into confusion' (1 Sam 7:10).

Lord and a great storm suddenly arose at harvest time with thunder and rain.[199]

I do not think I should pass over how David washed away a terrible and treacherous crime and appeased the anger of the Lord with suppliant prayer.[200] In chapter 24 he diminished by prayer the force of the plague that was sent by the Lord and was raging among the people, offering a sacrifice on the threshing floor of Araunah.[201] Solomon was granted all that he in his wisdom prayed for from the Lord – and much more.[202] Similarly, when the temple had been constructed and adorned, he dedicated it with a long prayer, as we read in the third book of Kings chapter 8.[203] Elijah called to the Lord and brought back to life the son of the woman of Zarephath.[204] As a result of a prayer that was by no means long, Elijah was granted fire from heaven to burn the whole sacrificial victim, even though it had been soaked many times with water.[205] He also prayed when lying on the ground at the top of mount Carmel, and a great rainstorm suddenly arose after a long drought.[206] Elijah's successor, Elisha, after praying to the Lord, restored the son of the woman who often took him in.[207] By prayers King Hezekiah delayed for fifteen years the death with which the Lord threatened him.[208] On the return to renew the temple of the Lord, soldiers for protection were not sought from the king, but the journey turned out well through prayers and fasting.[209] Nehemiah asked nothing of the king without first praying to the Lord of heaven.[210] Tobit prayed, as did Sarah, the daughter of Raguel, and for both their misfortune gave way to happiness.[211] For three nights Tobias, the son of Tobit,

* * * * *

199 See 1 Sam 12:17–18. Samuel prays for thunder and lightning from God in order to quell dissent with the choice of Saul as king.
200 Probably a reference to the sin David committed against Uriah and Bathsheba; see 2 Sam 11 and 12.
201 See 2 Sam 24:15–25.
202 See 1 Kings 3:5–14, especially 13.
203 See 1 Kings 8:22–53. See n196 above for why Erasmus gives the reference as 3 Kings.
204 See 1 Kings 17:17–24.
205 See 1 Kings 18:36–8.
206 See 1 Kings 18:42–5.
207 See 2 Kings 4:32–7.
208 See 2 Kings 20:2–6; Isa 38:1–6.
209 See Ezra 8:21–32.
210 See Neh 2:4–5.
211 See Tob 3. In response to their prayers Tobit was cured of his blindness and Sarah was given in marriage to Tobit's son, Tobias.

prayed with his wife, Sarah; when the demon had been killed,[212] they had
a happy marriage instead of a deadly one.[213] Was it not through prayer that
the brave heroine Judith overcame the enemy Holofernes?[214] Nor did Esther attempt her noble deed until she had begged for the favour of God by
three days of fasting and by prayer.[215] Although Daniel was enslaved to a
wicked king, he prayed to the Lord on bended knees three times a day.[216]
Jonah prayed from the belly of the whale, calling to the Lord, and he was
restored alive.[217]

It would be excessively scrupulous for me to gather precepts or examples about praying from each of the prophets, when almost all they talk
about is prayer. Those that I have already given should more than suffice
to show how concerned the ancients were with praying and how carefully
our Lord Jesus and his disciples commended the frequency and urgency of
prayer, by both their teaching and their example. When the pagans wanted
to drive off evils, to begin enterprises, to give thanks, or to guess the outcome of things, in their superstition they had their own rites of atonement,
their own expiatory sacrifices, auspices, auguries, omens, oracles, rings, incantations, triumphs, ovations,[218] and special prayers. Without them they
would not go into battle, take up magistracies or take possession of inher-
itances, marry, begin a sea voyage, mark out the boundaries for building
a city, consider state business, hold informal assemblies before the people,
or expiate lightning or portents. Instead of these many activities we have a
unique and simple means of help but one that is more powerful than them
all, namely, a simple prayer to God. Instead of the pointless procession of
triumphs, ovations, and supplications,[219] we have hymns and the giving of
thanks.

* * * * *

212 According to the account in Tob 8, the demon is not killed, but put to flight and
     bound by Raphael. Erasmus may be confusing the demon with Tobit's coun-
     tryman who had been murdered (*iugulatus*) and whose body Tobit concealed
     in his home before burying it at night (Tob 2:3–5); see n225 below.
213 Sarah's previous husbands had been killed by a demon before the marriage
     was consummated: see Tob 3:8.
214 Judith decapitated him; see Jth 13:6–10.
215 See Esther 4:16. Esther brought about the death of Haman, who was plotting
     the extermination of the Jews.
216 See Dan 6:10.
217 See Jon 2:2.
218 In the technical sense of *ovationes*, minor triumphs granted to Roman generals
219 Again in the technical sense of *supplicationes*, even less honorific triumphs than
     ovationes given to Roman generals

At this point someone may pose us a question. Since the Lord forbade his apostles to say much in prayer,[220] and attests that our Father knows what we need even before we ask, why does he also teach in Luke the need for constant prayer and the importance of never ceasing to pray?[221] Paul also bids us pray unceasingly.[222] These injunctions do not seem to be consistent. A second question is why there is a need for constant cries to God, when he is fully aware of what we require in our need. If there is something that by its nature is conducive to our well-being, he will give it of his own accord; if it is not, he will not give it even if asked. Finally, how is it consistent for him to condemn verbosity in prayers when we read that he himself in the garden prayed at great length and repeated three times the same words while he was praying?[223]

Let me respond briefly to each of these points. Hymns and the giving of thanks are not required of us so that God may receive any benefit from them, but so that we in our weakness may learn, by frequently contemplating his majesty and recalling his kindnesses to us, to fear and honour more and more the greatness of God and to love more and more his goodness. Accordingly, we profit from praying frequently, but not because God may thereby learn from us what we need. Rather, we will become accustomed to hope that we will receive from him what we need, and the longing for eternal life will be more and more kindled in us as we focus our minds frequently on passionately petitioning him who alone can give. Frequently singing hymns teaches us that all glory is owed to God alone, frequently giving thanks that whatever good is in us ought to be credited in its entirety to the kindness of God. If we constantly pray, the love of heavenly blessings continues to grow within us; unless this love is continually fanned, like the flames of a fire, by fervent prayers, at first it grows cool, then it is gradually extinguished. For just as somebody who does not give thanks for what has been received does not deserve it (in other words, somebody who does not acknowledge the generosity of God), so the person who does not long for happiness or longs for it half-heartedly does not deserve to receive it. Moreover, anyone who loves and hopes for something passionately

* * * * *

220 See Matt 6:7.
221 See Luke 18:1: 'And he told them a parable, to the effect that they ought always to pray and not lose heart' (RSV). Erasmus understands *deficere* in the Vulgate (ἐγκακεῖν in the Greek New Testament) to mean 'cease [from prayer]' rather than 'be disheartened.'
222 See 1 Thess 5:17.
223 See Matt 26:36–44.

must pray frequently to obtain the beloved object. What does it mean, then, never to cease from prayer? It means to long during the whole of one's life for that greatest blessing of all, promised to us in the next world.[224] When righteous persons direct all that they do in this life to that goal, whether eating or drinking or sleeping, their whole life is certainly like a never-ending prayer. For this is what Raphael says to Tobit: 'While you prayed tearfully and buried the dead, when you abandoned your meal and concealed a corpse during the day in your home, it was I who brought your prayers before the Lord.'[225] Clearly, each of Tobit's actions was a form of prayer.

The mind is frequently torn by many cares because of the needs of our weak bodies. To stir up the flame of this longing for heavenly blessings it is good often to distract the mind from the cares of this earthly life so that by private prayers it may become impassioned to love the heavenly life. Urgent prayer also results in our receiving more bountifully what is asked for, since to have prayed fervently for what God has promised us is in some way to have earned it. Finally,[226] God, who in his great goodness looks after our well-being in all ways, sees to it that the outstanding holiness, faith, and love of the saints become known to all. For example, although he knew how Abraham trusted the promises of God with all his heart, he nevertheless ordered the old man to sacrifice his only son, whom he loved as no other, in order that the patriarch's wonderful faith in God, which hardly anyone could believe, would be revealed to all.[227] He also knew what Hannah, the wife of Elkanah, longed for, and yet he allowed the poor woman to be worn out for a long time with grief, weeping, and fasting; he seemed to be deaf to her anxious prayers, to her daily sighs and groans, until Samuel, by rebuking her, also brought to light the endurance of the woman for us to admire. For when she is called a drunkard, she is not angered, she does not throw back an insult as most women are wont to do, but she satisfied the prophet with a very moderate response.[228] If this had not happened, the world would not have known of the piety of Hannah.

Furthermore, we read of the prayers of the saints being carried to God through the angels as intermediaries, just as Raphael says to Tobit that he

* * * * *

224 The greatest blessing of all (the *summum bonum*) is to be with God.
225 Tob 12:12. Raphael is referring to Tobit's actions described in Tob 1:18 (Vulg 20) and 2:3–5. Cf Origen Περὶ εὐχῆς 11.1, 31.5.
226 From here to the end of the paragraph is an addition to the text of the *editio princeps*.
227 See Gen 22:1–14.
228 See 1 Sam 1:14–15, but it was Eli who rebuked Hannah.

carried his prayers to the Lord,[229] and as in Revelation the angel stands by the altar holding the golden censer from which the most pleasing smoke of the incense ascends and is carried right to the sight of God.[230] Similarly, we read in Acts that Cornelius' 'prayers and offerings ascended to speak for him in the sight of God.'[231] Paul too, writing to the Philippians, advises them to make their petitions known to God.[232] My view is that whenever we come across these and similar examples in the Scriptures we should not interpret them to mean that it is through the angels as intermediaries that God learns what we pray for or that he is reminded of what we have done or that he learns through our cries what we long for. He knows our hearts better than we ourselves or even the minds of angels know them. He is not like some king who learns through his messengers what has happened elsewhere or who is reminded by an aide of what he has forgotten. This is the characteristic of the Scriptures, that they speak to human beings in a human way. God wishes us to ask him for what will be to our benefit, and it is not he who learns from our prayers what we need, but we ourselves. Finally, if ever he uses the services of angels, he does not use them because he has any need at all of these servants. Rather, we realize in this way more clearly how we are cared for by God since he has given us his angels as guardians and protectors.[233] The angels delight in their own love for us in bearing our prayers to God and in bringing to us in turn his gifts.

Moreover, the Scriptures say, in their own particular way, that the Lord does not know what he does not approve. He does not hear, therefore, the prayers of those who do not petition in the way that they should, while the petitions of those who pray in such a way that they deserve to be heard are known to him. That is why Paul sent his instructions, 'Have no anxiety about anything, but in everything by prayer and supplication with thanksgiving let your requests be made known to God.'[234] Those who are anxious and trust not in heavenly protection but in human resources and abilities are not heard. Those who do not pray earnestly are not praying and petitioning at all. Those who do not assign glory to God are not praying with

* * * * *

229 See Tob 12:12 (quoted above in the text).
230 See Rev 8:3–4.
231 Acts 10:4
232 See Phil 4:6.
233 On guardian angels cf *Declarationes ad censuras Lutetiae vulgatas* LB IX 850A; Augustine *De civitate Dei* 20.14 PL 41 680; Thomas Aquinas *Summa theologica* I q 113 art 1, 2, 4, 5.
234 Phil 4:6

thanksgiving, since they ascribe what they receive to their own merits rather than to the kindness of God. The prayers of those who stand with the Pharisees in street corners and 'who devour the estates of widows, while saying long prayers for appearance' sake,'[235] are not known to God.

Now those who think it impossible for anyone never to cease from prayer, as the Lord teaches in Luke,[236] or to pray without any remission, as the Apostle teaches,[237] should realize that the whole life of the righteous is a never-ending and everlasting prayer until the greatest blessing of all befalls them.[238] As soon as we have obtained this, we will cease from being tortured with longing, as has been said.[239] Alternatively, such sceptics should think that we are dealing with the figure of hyperbole; let them understand Paul's teaching to mean that whoever prays frequently and earnestly and does not cease from praying until what is asked for is granted is praying unceasingly. Thus it was said, 'Cry aloud, do not stop, lift up your voice like a trumpet.'[240] Even if we relax the concentration of the mind, prayer is not interrupted unless the desire for what we ask for is cast aside.

It remains to show how teachings apparently contradictory are consistent; for 'Do not say much'[241] and 'Pray without any remission'[242] appear to be in conflict. Perhaps someone may cut the knot in this way by responding that we are forbidden to be garrulous but not forbidden to display in our prayers our feelings at greater length. The immediate response to this, however, will be that Christ not only prayed for a long time, but also said the same words three times.[243] In Luke chapter 6 Christ spends the night praying to God, and if the prayer was spoken aloud, as it probably was, it could

* * * * *

235 A close paraphrase on Mark 12:40
236 See Luke 18:1 and n221 above.
237 See 1 Thess 5:17.
238 Cf Origen Περὶ εὐχῆς 12.2: 'The man who links together his prayer with deeds of duty and fits seemly actions with his prayer is the man who prays without ceasing, for his virtuous deeds or the commandments he has fulfilled are taken up as a part of his prayer' (Jay's translation).
239 Erasmus has referred above (175, and see n224) to the 'greatest blessing of all.' He did not, however, say there exactly what he states here. The words 'as has been said' may allude, therefore, to the theological axiom that the attainment of the summum bonum will satisfy all desire. Cf Augustine Confessions 1.1: 'You have made us for yourself, and our hearts will not rest until they rest in you.'
240 Isa 58:1
241 Matt 6:7
242 1 Thess 5:17
243 See Luke 6:12. Cf Augustine Epistolae 130.19 PL 33 501–2; Thomas Aquinas Summa theologica II-II q 83 art 14: 'Whether Prayer Ought to Be Long.'

not have been short. Accordingly, when the Lord instructs his disciples in Matthew chapter 6 not to speak at great length, he is simply telling them not to believe that God is swayed by the foolish babbling of those who continually ask for the same thing. For in Greek the word is βαττολογήσατε, 'chatter,' and for the Greeks anybody who frequently repeats the same words for no reason, whether through the vice of garrulousness, or because of his nature or out of habit, is said βαττολογεῖν, 'to chatter.'[244] Yet according to the teachings of the rhetoricians it is sometimes praiseworthy to repeat words, as Christ himself cried out on the cross, 'My God, my God.'[245] That was not *battologia*, 'chattering,' but an expression of the passionate and powerful emotions of the speaker. A prayer is not verbose as long as it matches the emotions. It is not *battologia* whenever deep feelings, like flames continually glowing more bright, express the same meaning in different words.[246] If this is not so, you will find a holy and almost ubiquitous *battologia* in all the Psalms: 'O Lord, rebuke me not in your anger.' Having said it once, the psalmist drives the point home: 'nor chasten me in your wrath.'[247] 'Have mercy on me, O God, according to your steadfast love.' He repeats this: 'According to your abundant mercy blot out my transgressions.'[248] He repeats the end of this verse in the next one: 'Wash me thoroughly from my iniquity and cleanse me from my sin.'[249] This, however, does not satisfy the king's emotions: 'Hide your face from my sins and blot out all my iniquities. Create in me a clean heart, O God, and put a new and right spirit within me.'[250]

The same *battologia* can be seen in the precepts of the Old Testament and indeed in the teachings of Christ, especially in the Gospel according to John. How often there does the Lord repeat the same things, in his zeal to impress upon his listeners the importance of mutual love, faith in him, and the urgency of prayer! This is not the *battologia* of the gentiles, but comes from his deep love or from his zeal to fix in our minds what, if forgotten, would destroy us. The Lord did not simply say, 'Do not go on at great

* * * * *

244 Erasmus is referring to Matt 6:7. Cf *Adagia* II i 92: *Battologia*, 'Vain repetition.'

245 Matt 27:4, 6. Erasmus is referring to the figure of *anadiplosis* or *conduplicatio*; see *Rhetorica ad Herennium* 4.28.38.

246 A figure of speech called *interpretatio* by the Roman rhetoricians; see *Rhetorica ad Herennium* 4.28.38. It is often a feature of elevated style.

247 Ps 6:1 (Vulg 6:2)

248 Ps 51:1 (Vulg 50:3)

249 Ps 51:2 (Vulg 50:4)

250 Ps 51:9–10 (Vulg 50:11–12). Erasmus writes as if the psalm was composed by David ('the king's emotions'). On the Davidic authorship of the Psalms see *The Abingdon Bible Commentary* ed F.C. Eiselen (New York 1929) 512–13.

length,' but added, 'like the gentiles; for they think that they will be heard
if they say much. Do not be like them.'[251] Moreover, this *battologia* is present
in the ancient hymns that poets composed to praise their gods. In them a god
is sometimes invoked by forty different names so that he may acknowledge
one at least from this great number. Such were the prayers of the prophets
who we read called out the name 'Baal,' and said nothing but 'Baal, answer
us,'[252] from morning to night. These same prophets importuned their god
at noon with even louder cries.[253] There were also heretics (who are called
Psalliani or Euchites)[254] who wrongly interpreted the Lord's word, that one
should never cease from prayer, and Paul's command, to pray without any
remission. The whole day they did nothing but repeat psalms and prayers,
vying with each other in the belief that whoever uttered as much as possible of the Psalms would be thought holier than the others. Yet not even then
did they satisfy the literal sense of 'never ceasing from prayer' and 'pray
without any remission.' They certainly interrupted their prayers with eating, drinking, sleeping, coughing, snoring, or yawning. Perhaps I shall say
more about this at the appropriate point when discussing how we should
pray.[255]

To do briefly, then, what we promised, we must first consider who
it is to whom we pray, and who it is doing the praying. If anyone has to
speak with the emperor, how carefully he gets himself ready in case there
is something in his dress, in his physical appearance, or in his words that
may offend an emperor's eyes![256] Yet this is a case of a human meeting fellow human, mortal meeting mortal, and often the suppliant is better than
the one who is being supplicated. What, then, about somebody preparing to
approach the throne of divine majesty, before which even the mightiest of
angels tremble? How carefully he should make himself ready so that nothing may offend the eyes of God. You do not speak to a king unless you
kneel on the ground. Do you draw yourself to your full height when you
speak to God? (I do not mean this physically, but in terms of your arrogance
and self-confidence.) You do not dare to address a king unless your clothes

* * * * *

251 Matt 6:7–8
252 1 Kings 18:26
253 See 1 Kings 18:27.
254 The Psalliani sang continuously, the Euchites prayed continuously. See Augustine *De haeresibus* 57 PL 42 40; Erasmus *Declarationes ad censuras Lutetiae
vulgatas* LB IX 897C–D, 898F, 899A; *Explanatio symboli* 331 below.
255 See 223–5 below.
256 More logically Erasmus might have written 'the eyes and ears.'

are spotless, your hair combed, your body washed and perhaps even per-
fumed lest odour give some offence. Do you address God when your conscience is defiled in so many ways? Many who are about to speak before the
princes of the world lose both voice and mind through a sense of unworthiness and reverence for exalted rank, even though this rank is a human one.
Do you speak to your God while yawning and doing other such things? You
call to God, 'Hear my prayer, give ear to the words of my mouth,'[257] and
you yourself do not comprehend what you say. I pass over those who ogle
and have obscene thoughts in their minds while their tongues utter sacred
prayers.

So that none of us may be deterred from prayer by considering the
majesty of God, let us realize that God's greatest attribute is his compassion
for and love of the human race. You approach the Creator, but he is also the
Redeemer. You go to the Lord of all, but he is also the Father of those who
trust in him. You approach the Judge, but you are also approaching him who
surrendered his only Son to death so that he might save all and condemn no
one. You approach the Judge, but time has been granted for compassion, and
since he is just, he cannot deceive by his promises. He promised through
his Son that he would refuse nothing to those who ask in faith and in the
name of the Son.

You who are praying should look at yourself too. You are a poor mortal approaching the throne of God. Nothing more exalted than God can be
thought of. What is more abject than mankind?[258] Even if we are upright
and guiltless in the eyes of our fellow humans, the purity of all humans
is still impurity when compared with divine purity. What, then, will mortals do in these circumstances? We should raise ourselves aloft so that we
can speak with him who lives in heaven – no, rather with him who lives
beyond all heaven and, to be more accurate, transcends all sublimity that
can be described in words or imagined in the mind. By some strange process it happens that the more we cast ourselves down, the nearer to God we
become.

Far from God was that Pharisee who stood very close to the high altar, talking about his good deeds and scorning all others when compared
to himself.[259] The publican, who prayed standing far from the altar, came
closer to God. 'For though the Lord is high, he regards the lowly, but the

* * * * *

257 Ps 54:2 (Vulg 53:4)
258 The ASD text erroneously has *homo quid abiectius?* instead of *homine vero quid
      abiectius?*
259 See Luke 18:10–14.

haughty he knows from afar.'[260] He treats the contemptuous with contempt and respects the pleadings of the humble and does not spurn their prayers. Do you want to know how sublime are those who abase themselves? The wise Sirach teaches this: 'The prayer of the humble,' he says, 'will pierce the clouds, but he will not be consoled until it comes near to God, and he will not descend[261] until the Most High looks upon him?'[262] Even today one can see some arrogant men praying. Though they are laymen, they are nevertheless puffed up because of their wealth or lineage; they burst into the priests' choir and sometimes drive them from their stalls. Neither in their gestures nor in their faces do they present the appearance of someone who is praying; you would say that they were flaunting themselves in a theatre. Princes are granted the golden stall closest to the altar, sometimes even more. If[263] you were to observe the arrogance in their eyes, the brazenness of their gestures, you would perceive that, so far from asking for anything, they think that God has a tremendous debt to them because they have adorned his worship with their magnificent presence. Their prayers are less pleasing to God than dead birds. We have seen even men of lowly birth pushing others aside and rushing to the altar so that they might touch the priest and even breathe their stinking breath on him, as if they were nearer to God than the others who withdraw further from the altar and will be more quickly heard by him. What is more, some persons, when dying, actually request that they be buried in the holy of holies very close to the high altar, as if prayers that are offered for the dead will reach them more quickly than others.

Someone will say, 'How can I raise myself to him who is highest of all by casting myself down, or how can I cast myself down by raising myself?' If you wish to fly up to God (for certainly prayer is a kind of flight of the soul), you must cast aside the burden of the flesh and put on wings. How will a soul crushed by the leaden burden of sins fly up to heaven? How can anyone raise himself up so as to reach the sublime when he is weighed down by much silver and gold, when he has nothing in his heart except earth, when he is completely of the flesh? The Father wants to be prayed to by those who pray to him in spirit.[264] Therefore you should become spirit, so that you may address the Spirit as spirit. If you are a sinner, cast aside the

* * * * *

260 Ps 138 (Vulg 137):6
261 Erasmus' text offers *descendet*; the Vulgate reads *discedet*, 'leave.'
262 Ecclus 35:17 (Vulg 35:21)
263 The next two sentences ('. . . dead birds') are an addition to the text of the *editio princeps*.
264 Cf John 4:23.

burden of your sins, strip off the desire to sin, abase yourself in sackcloth and ashes. Move yourself away from the altar along with the publican;[265] lie prostrate on the ground and beat your breast. With Mary Magdalene lower yourself to the feet of Jesus and weep.[266] Leave with Peter, as if you are unworthy of the sight of the Lord, and weep bitterly.[267] Above all, be your own accuser, call on nothing but the pity of God. By withdrawing from God you will in this way become near to him. What[268] can be lower than a seed of the cypress that is thrown into the ground? There, however, it finds moisture, with which it becomes strong and raises itself upwards. It is not enough to pray with your body prostrate on the ground. Cast down your whole soul. If you water it with many tears, like showers of rain, it will grow in wondrous fashion, reaching into the heights right to the very throne of divine majesty, and, even though you despise yourself, you will become great and precious to God. If you are not weighed down by a heavy burden of crimes, cast away for a while your paltry, trifling worries before you pray and speak with him who is the Highest. Cleanse away whatever has settled in your soul to make you seethe with animosity against your neighbour and wash away even slight faults, which are inevitably part of our life here. This is why the custom grew among Christians of cleansing themselves with a sprinkling of holy water when they were about to enter a church to pray.[269]

The very bodies that we carry around are exposed to many infirmities, and weigh down our souls; our earthly dwelling preoccupies and crushes our minds. 'The body laden with external vices weighs down the soul too, and fixes the particle of divine aura to the ground,' if it is right here to use the words of Horace.[270] Those who are rich in this life are compelled

* * * * *

265 See Luke 18:10–14.
266 Erasmus seems to add to the account of Mary Magdalene's meeting with the angels and the risen Christ (John 20:11–16) a detail from Christ's encounter with the sinful woman (Luke 7:38). The Gospels say nothing about Mary lowering herself at Jesus' feet when she sees him.
267 See Matt 26:75.
268 The next five sentences ('. . . precious to God') are an addition to the text of the *editio princeps.*
269 A person sprinkling himself with holy water when entering a church was thought to be renewed in the spirit of his baptism and thus to be purifying himself before approaching the presence of God. The use of holy water is ascribed to Pope Alexander I (d c 116) in the *Liber pontificalis* 1.127 Duchesne, but this is probably an anachronism and the practice a much later one.
270 Horace *Satires* 2.2.77–9. Erasmus reads *externis,* 'external,' for *hesternis,* 'yesterday's,' and *degravat* for *praegravat.*

to crawl frequently on the ground, whether they wish to or not, while the poor have to cope with a dowryless wife or abandoned children. Some not only are crushed by having to care for a wife, children, and relatives, but are also burdened by wealth, worldly honours, and magistracies and are engulfed by the stormy turmoil of business – these, to be sure, are like fish, immersed in an element too dense for them, moving this way and that along with the ebb and flow of the waves. (There are actually fish of the world, however, that have wings, which they often use to spring forth with a leap into the purer air; some indeed try to fly.) What advice shall we give to people like these? What else but that they should pray to the Lord that he deign to capture them in the net of the gospel and drag them to the shore of a more tranquil life?

Whatever kind of living thing we humans are, we should accept the possibility of metamorphosis so that instead of being, so to speak, a reptile, a quadruped, or a fish we may be transformed into a bird. This will happen if we take the wings of a dove that are desired by that mystic psalmist who, weighed down by many burdens, says: 'O that I had wings like a dove. I would fly away and be at rest.'[271] Doves are certainly harmless birds, but they are capable of the swiftest flight. The bridegroom in the Song of Songs is delighted by such doves.[272] You will be a dove if you plan evil against no one, if you judge no one, if you harbour false suspicions against no one. You will say, 'Where am I to get wings?' I shall point out two that will carry you easily to heaven: one is contempt for worldly things, the other is the desire for heavenly things. One will move you away from things of the flesh, as the holy psalmist says when he received the wings he asked for: 'I wandered afar, I lodged in the wilderness.'[273] The other will bring you close to the throne of God.

Happy is the solitude that draws our mind away from all association with vices or evil desires and even, as much as it can, from all the turmoil that arises from the cares of the flesh. Sometimes, however, we are called back to these by necessity, sometimes by love for our fellow human beings. Do you want to hear the first wing speaking? Listen. 'Wretched man that I am. Who will deliver me from this body of death?'[274] This is the prayer of someone who is eager to fly away completely from visible things. Do you wish to hear the other wing? 'How lovely is your dwelling-place,

* * * * *

271 Ps 55:6 (Vulg 54:7)
272 See Song of Sol 6:9 (Vulg 6:8).
273 Ps 55:7 (Vulg 54:8)
274 Rom 7:24

O Lord of hosts! My soul longs and faints for the courts of the Lord.'[275] 'As a hart longs for the flowing streams, so longs my soul for you, O God.'[276] This is the desire to dwell with immortality. Paul showed us both wings in the Epistle to the Colossians chapter 3: 'If you have been raised with Christ, seek the things that are above, where Christ is, seated at the right hand of God; set your minds on things that are above.'[277] Here you have the wing that carries you to heaven. Paul adds 'not on things that are on earth.' Here you have the wing that flees from earth. He indicates this one more clearly a little later, saying, 'Put to death, therefore, those parts that are earthly in you.'[278] He means by 'parts' the desires of the flesh. Then he says, 'seeing that you have put off the old self with its practices and have put on the new self.'[279] The old self is of the earth and therefore does not know how to fly upwards, but with eyes on the ground loves and seeks nothing except what is of the earth. Whoever is transformed into the new self now regards as worthless what he used to value most highly; what he used to think brought great profit he now judges brings great loss. Instead of being an earthbound beast he has become a bird of the sky.[280] He has become a dove and has two wings to raise him to the throne of God.

So far we have considered who it is who is asked and who does the asking. The current situation suggests that we should discuss briefly in passing to whom prayer should be directed.[281] We have the established prayers of the church handed down to us from very early days. Of those we call 'Collects' I am aware that most are directed to the Father, some to the Son, none to the Holy Spirit (though there is mention of the three Persons in all of them). We see that this practice was scrupulously observed by the ancients. For not even in the many prayers that are used at the feast of Pentecost is there one calling upon the Holy Spirit. This is true at least for those prayers that the priest pronounced on behalf of the whole people. Yet in the songs that the people chanted, an invocation of the Holy Spirit is not avoided,

* * * * *

275 Ps 84:1–2 (Vulg 83:2–3)
276 Ps 42:1 (Vulg 41:2)
277 Col 3:1–2
278 Col 3:5
279 Col 3:9–10
280 The ASD text omits the Latin for 'he has become a bird of the sky.'
281 By 'the current situation' Erasmus means the controversy stirred up by Luther and his followers. One issue of dispute focused on the invocation of the saints and their intercessory power, which Erasmus addresses in this section. He begins, however, with the nature of the Father, the Son, and the Holy Spirit.

for example, in sequences, hymns, and antiphons.[282] The ancients were very punctilious in not daring to say anything not found in Scripture. For that reason the prayers of all of them are generally directed to the Father, because it is written explicitly and frequently that the apostles were admonished to pray to their Heavenly Father, but in the name of the Son.[283] Moreover, in the Gospels the Son addresses the Father in his frequent prayers. He promises the Holy Spirit, but does not pray to it. Although the apostles are often told to petition the Father in the name of the Son, in John alone do we read, though only once, 'If you ask me for anything in my name, I will do it.'[284] The pronoun 'me,' however, is not found in most Greek manuscripts and is not in any of the Latin manuscripts either. Theophylact certainly does not have 'me' in his text and does not explain it in his commentary. Without doubt he would have done so if it had been, since he takes issue on that verse with the Arians.[285] He argues from the words 'If you ask anything, I will do it' that the power of the Son equals that of the Father. He would have had a stronger argument if the text had read, 'If you ask anything of me.' Yet such a reading raises troubling doubts. Is it consistent for anyone to ask for something from Christ in the name of Christ, unless perhaps we are asking for something from Christ as a man in the name of the Son of God? Stephen in Acts, however, was not afraid to say, 'Lord Jesus, receive my spirit.'[286]

The purpose of this discussion is not to cast doubt on whether the Holy Spirit should be invoked. I want to show, before talking about the invocation of the saints, how anxious and strict our predecessors were about doing anything that had not been handed down by the clear authority of Holy Scripture, especially on matters surpassing human understanding. St Hilary had the same scruples; only after a long silence did he vigorously strive in twelve books to show that the Son was true God, although the Father alone was said to be true God in the Gospels.[287] To my knowledge, he nowhere

* * * * *

282 The *Veni, sancte Spiritus* is the Sequence for the mass on the feast of Pentecost; see *Missale Romanum* II 596. Hymns to the Holy Spirit may be found in *Lateinische Hymnen des Mittelalters* ed F.J. Mone 3 vols (Freiburg im Breisgau 1853–5) I nos 179–95.
283 See John 15:16, 16:23–4.
284 John 14:14
285 Theophylact *Enarratio in evangelium Ioannis* (on John 14:14) PG 124 177–8. The Arians disputed the true divinity of Christ.
286 Acts 7:59
287 Hilary of Poitiers (c 315–67) wrote against the Arian heresy denying the true divinity of Jesus Christ in *De Trinitate* PL 10 9–472; see *De Trinitate* 1.13 PL 10

dares pronounce the Holy Spirit to be God,[288] and all he claims is that the Spirit be served; he never says it should be worshipped. He shrinks from saying that the Holy Spirit is something created, although Jerome is not afraid to pronounce the Son of God a creature.[289] Later generations, after very carefully examining the Scriptures and relying on the authority of their predecessors, are not afraid to call the Son of God true God and to direct their prayers to him, not in the belief that the Son can give anything that the Father will not give, but because they are convinced that the will and power of the Son is the same as the Father's, although the Father is the author and fount of all things. Perhaps it is a good principle of Christian doctrine to revere everything pertaining to divinity but to affirm nothing except what is explicitly stated in the Scriptures.

There is general consensus that the invocation of saints, especially martyrs, is accepted in the early orthodox writers. Most people, however, also agree on this, that it cannot be shown from the Scriptures that the invocation of saints is necessary (I am talking about those that have passed from this life).[290] In prayers hallowed by tradition there is no plea directed to a saint, but, rather, petition is made to the Father or to the Son that the intercession and merits of the saints may be of help for those who worship in piety their memory and strive to walk in their footsteps. None of the saints can say, 'Whatever you seek from the Father in my name,' or 'Whatever you seek from me I will do.' The apostles healed the sick and raised the dead, but in the name of Jesus and invoking the Father; for even if the Father's name is not expressed, nevertheless he is invoked in the Son, just as the Father is made manifest in the Son.

Two questions now arise: first, whether the invocation of the saints is devout practice, and second, whether it should tolerated. Admittedly, some claim that invoking the saints ought not to be tolerated because scriptural authority does not clearly hand down this practice to us. We could answer that it is better to infer that if Scripture neither enjoins nor forbids this

* * * * *

35B–C, 1.38 PL 10 49B–C. Erasmus' edition of St Hilary appeared in Basel in 1523. His preface to the edition may be found in Ep 1334; see lines 146–71 on the question of the relations between the Father, Son, and Holy Spirit.

288 Cf *Purgatio adversus epistolam Lutheri* ASD IX-1 461:531–462:539.

289 But Jerome *Dialogus contra Luciferianos* 9 PL 23 172C criticizes the Arians for believing that only the Father is true God and that Christ is a creature (*creatura*).

290 The parenthesis at the end of this sentence is an addition to the text of the *editio princeps*.

practice, we should neither require it as necessary nor, since by its very
nature it does not involve impiety, prohibit it as irreligious. For the sake
of argument, let us concede what these persons claim, that nothing not expressed in the Scriptures can be required by human ordinances. They overlook this principle, however, with respect to the perpetual virginity of Mary,
the mother of Jesus.[291] Although this is not a teaching based on clear scriptural testimony, it has been handed down to us by the consensus of early
orthodox writers.[292] No one, therefore, would think that we should tolerate
anyone who claimed that Mary had intercourse with her husband after the
birth of Christ, or even perhaps anyone who had doubts about this. Suppose the response of those who oppose the invocation of the saints is that
persons disputing or doubting Mary's perpetual virginity are not to be tolerated because they are trying to eradicate a probable belief, long approved
by overwhelming agreement throughout the world – something that cannot
be done without disturbing public tranquillity and without giving grievous
offence to the Christian flock.[293] We can object to them that the invocation of
the saints has also been handed down to us by early orthodoxy with a similar consensus, and that, therefore, this practice cannot be suppressed without as much scandal.[294] Yet[295] however much they shift their position on the
basis of chronology, 'as they have recourse to ancient records and evalu-
ate religious practices in terms of their antiquity,' as that man says,[296] they

* * * * *

291 The Lutherans accepted the perpetual virginity of Mary, while rejecting the
     invocation of the saints.
292 For defence of Mary's perpetual virginity see Jerome *De Mariae virginitate per-
     petua adversus Helvidium* PL 23 194–216; Ambrose *De institutione Virginis et Sanc-
     tae Mariae virginitate perpetua* PL 16 321–48; Hilary *Commentarius in Matthaeum*
     PL 9 921–2; Augustine *Sermones* 190 PL 38 1008. Erasmus addresses this ques-
     tion elsewhere: *Apologia adversus monachos* LB IX 1084A–E, with reference to the
     Modus orandi Deum; *Annotationes in Matthaeum* LB VI 5C–D.
293 The avoidance of strife in the church was a preoccupation of Erasmus, and he
     refers to it later at several places; see 199, 201, 223. See Hilmar M. Pabel 'The
     Peaceful People of Christ: The Irenic Ecclesiology of Erasmus of Rotterdam'
     in Pabel *Erasmus' Vision* 57–93, especially 72–6.
294 The consensus of the church played an important role in Erasmus' thinking;
     see McConica 77–99 and Hilmar M. Pabel 'The Peaceful People of Christ: The
     Irenic Ecclesiology of Erasmus of Rotterdam' in Pabel *Erasmus' Vision* 77–81.
295 The remainder of this paragraph and the next two ('. . . times of the church')
     are an addition to the text of the *editio princeps*.
296 Erasmus is here closely paraphrasing Horace *Epistles* 2.1.48, where the Latin
     poet is criticizing those who give greater esteem to poets long dead than to re-
     cent or contemporary poets. Erasmus substitutes *pietatem*, 'religious practices,'

certainly admit all the same that we must believe in some things that are not stated either in Scripture (and cannot be deduced from it by persuasive arguments) or even in the Apostles' Creed and in the Athanasian Creed, which is the one chanted at mass.[297] If, therefore, we must believe in the perpetual virginity of Mary because this teaching, without scriptural basis, has been handed down to us by more ancient sources than those concerning the invocation of the saints, the latter are, nevertheless, very old indeed. If votes are counted up, Mary's perpetual virginity has been challenged as often as the invocation of the saints.

There are many other such issues. The early Fathers had scruples about saying that the Son was consubstantial with the Father.[298] Not even those who claimed with all their strength this attribute of consubstantiality for the Son dared to declare the same for the Holy Spirit. They did not dare to say that the Son was true God, since they had found that this name is given to the Father alone in the Scriptures. Nowadays, no one would tolerate anybody denying that the Holy Spirit is true God or that the Spirit is consubstantial with the Father and Son.[299] How, then, do those who press[300] new dogma upon us justify their stance on a matter of lesser import when on such an important matter they admit that Christians must accept what is only deduced from the Scriptures and not stated there? They do not tolerate anyone doubting the consubstantiality of the Holy Spirit with those from whom it proceeds, although that is not stated, as I have said, in the Scriptures.[301] Yet on the question of the invocation of saints they demand clear scriptural evidence and cannot be appeased by any arguments. The Fathers

* * * * *

for *virtutem*, 'quality [of the poets].' The reference to Horace (simply *ille*) is surprising in its vagueness.

297 There is no invocation of the saints in either the Apostles' or the Athanasian Creed.

298 Erasmus must be thinking in this paragraph of the period before the Nicene Creed (325 AD), in which Christ is described as 'true God from true God ... of one substance with the Father.' See Kelly *Doctrines* chapter 5 'Third-Century Trinitarianism' 109–37.

299 The consubstantiality of the Trinity was affirmed at the Synod of Alexandria in 362 and the Council of Constantinople in 381. Cf Athanasius *Tomus ad Antiochenos* 5 PG 26 801B and *Epistola ad Serapionem* 1.27 PG 26 593C. On the Trinity see also *Purgatio adversus epistolam Lutheri* ASD IX-1 462:540–5 and note ad loc.

300 The ASD text wrongly reads *vigent* for *urgent*.

301 Cf the Athanasian Creed: 'The Holy Spirit is from the Father and the Son, not made nor created nor begotten, but proceeding.' Cf J.N.D. Kelly *The Athanasian Creed* (London 1964) 87.

went beyond scriptural authority and dared to say that there were three *hypostases* or *substantiae;*[302] we profess belief in the single *substantia* of three Persons. Where, however, has the actual word for 'persons' been transmitted in the Scriptures? About the properties and distinctions of the Persons much has been handed down to us that is not stated in the Bible, but we do not spurn it.

Those who press disputable dogma on us often concede that in other practices of ours, such as the eating of meat or fish, each of us is free to observe or not to observe what is neither approved nor disapproved of in the Scriptures. Let them at least make this same concession for invoking the saints. All the same, I grant that it cannot be shown clearly from sacred writings that the prayers of saints who have left this life carry any weight before God. Yet in Revelation the souls of the saints who had shed their blood for Christ demand in a loud voice that with the conquering of Satan's tyranny the kingdom of God should be brought to pass.[303] They accept, however, the temperate divine response, that they should await the time for the affirmation of the kingdom of God as predefined by him, and that meanwhile they should each accept in consolation white gowns, in other words, the glory of miracles that they did not have in the early times of the church.[304]

On this point I shall not listen to those who cast up the invocation of the saints as an example of a very old mistake. It is quite different for some practice to have developed in some way or another and for a practice that is by nature holy to have been handed down by those who were close to the time of the apostles and to have been approved for a long time by a large majority of the whole Christian world. Age[305] does not make right what is not right in itself, just as it is not proper to condemn anything just because it is old. To something that has credibility, however, the consensus of antiquity adds a considerable amount of weight, especially when the ancients are held in esteem.

* * * * *

302 See eg Origen *Commentarius in Ioannem* 2.75 PG 14 128–9, and cf Kelly *Doctrines* 129. These two terms gained acceptance as a result of the Trinitarian controversies of the fourth century and have continued through the Middle Ages down to the present. Cf Thomas Aquinas *Summa theologica* I q 29. Jerome *Dialogus contra Luciferianos* 9 PL 23 172C talks of 'tres personas, unam substantiam.'
303 See Rev 7:9–17.
304 Because they were martyrs they did not need miracles to attest their sanctity.
305 From here to the end of the paragraph is an addition to the text of the *editio princeps*.

I do not think that the argument Jerome brings forward when attacking Vigilantius is insignificant.[306] In their mortal lives the righteous are not at all free of sins and need the intercessory prayers of others. Nevertheless, they pray for their brethren and are heard by God.[307] We should all the more believe that these same persons, having cast off their mortality and free of the contagion of this life, can have some influence with God, especially when we must believe that they have not lost their love for their fellow humans or their devotion to us along with the loss of their lives.[308] We certainly cannot doubt that those who now live in heaven pray fervently for the salvation of all who profess the name of Christ. When they were among the living, they prayed even for those who were estranged from Christ and indeed for those by whom they were being afflicted and killed. How, then, is it consistent with this to believe that these same persons do not now pray for their brethren in danger and have no power before God, for whose love they surrendered themselves to death? If the man who said to Paul[309] while he was on earth, 'Pray for me to the Lord,'[310] was acting in a devout manner, will we regard as unrighteous a man who appeals to the same person when he is now in heaven?

If our opponents reply that in this life we can merit and that after this life we cannot, we can throw back at them their own dogma, since what they adduce is not stated in the Scriptures, namely, that after this life the righteous do not merit. Even if we were to grant that the saints do not merit after this life,[311] certainly those devout feelings with which through love of

* * * * *

306 Vigilantius (fl 400) protested against what he thought were superstitious practices of the church, including the veneration of relics and the sending of alms to Jerusalem as well as the invocation of saints. Jerome responded in his *Contra Vigilantium* (PL 23 354–68). With respect to the saints Jerome says, 'If the apostles and the martyrs can pray for all others when still in their earthly bodies, when they still ought to be troubled for themselves, how much more will they do so after their crowns, their victories, and their triumphs?' (*Contra Vigilantium* 7 PL 23 359). Erasmus expands upon this thought in the next three sentences.

307 The phrase 'by God' is not in the text but is supplied by the translator.

308 Cf Origen Περὶ εὐχῆς 11.2: 'The one supreme virtue is love for one's neighbour, which the departed saints must have for those who still struggle in this life' (Jay's translation).

309 A mistake for Peter, who was approached by Simon in Samaria; see Acts 8:18–24.

310 Acts 8:24

311 Cf Thomas Aquinas *Summa theologica* II-II q 83 art 11: 'The saints do not merit for themselves.'

Christ we worship the saints, in whom in fact we worship Christ himself, must be very pleasing to God.

We call upon their intercession for this reason: we judge ourselves unworthy of calling upon God himself and we believe that it has also pleased God, who in this life through his saints bestows many things that he could give by himself, to bestow many blessings on us through those whom he has deemed worthy of sharing in his kingdom. He wanted the living to pray for the living so that he might nourish mutual love among all. In the same way he wants the prayers of those whom he thought worthy of heaven to help us, so that we may be more eager to emulate their lives and hasten to fly to join those whose intercession we feel is effective for us.

As to what is adduced from the Epistle of Paul to Timothy, 'For there is one God, there is one mediator between God and men, the man Jesus Christ,'[312] if anyone presses this and takes only a literal meaning out of it, he will exclude even that prayer which one mortal makes for another. Indeed, if the Lord Jesus alone intercedes between God and mortals, why is an intercessor sought in this world to intercede with the intercessor? If, however, there is good cause for a mortal to importune God through a fellow mortal for what could be sought from him without any intercessor, then the reasons for us to importune the Lord through the saints, who are in heaven, would be validated. Some solve this problem by admitting that according to Paul's words it would not have been possible for anyone to invoke any of the saints other than Christ, had not the Scriptures clearly given an exception. The form of prayer prescribed by the Lord is such that whoever uses it prays not only for himself but also for others.[313] Moreover, in that very passage that we have recalled from Paul we are instructed 'that supplications, prayers, intercessions be made for all persons, but especially for kings and all who are in high positions,'[314] while the Lord instructs us to pray even for our enemies.[315] Since, however, there is no special provision in the Scriptures for invoking the saints who have passed from this life, it is thought to be impious to dare to do what has not been transmitted by that authority, and even much more impious to require it to be done.

In my opinion, it is in no way Paul's intention in that passage to exclude the intercession of the saints when he pronounces that the Lord Jesus is the sole intercessor. Rather, he wants to show that Christ died for

* * * * *

312 1 Tim 2:5
313 The Lord's Prayer
314 1 Tim 2:1
315 See Matt 5:44.

the whole world and that no one should place hope of salvation in anyone else. The Jews who denied Christ had faith in Moses and Abraham or were awaiting some messiah other than Christ, while most of the Jews who acknowledged Christ did not allow the gentiles to be received into a share of the grace of the gospel, because they declared that he had been sent to save the Jewish race alone. Paul, the apostle of the gentiles, refutes this view; for after telling us to pray for all persons he adds: 'This is good, and it is acceptable in the sight of God our Saviour, who desires all persons to be saved and to come to the knowledge of the truth. For there is one God, and there is one mediator between God and men, the man Jesus Christ, who gave himself as a ransom for all, confirming, at the fitting time, proof of this divine purpose. For this I was appointed as a preacher and apostle (I am telling the truth, I am not lying), a teacher of the gentiles in faith and truth.'[316] Each nation had its own gods; the Jews alone exulted in their God as if he were not the God of all the world. That is why Paul says that there is one God who is the saviour of all, and that there is one reconciler of God and mortals, he who died for all without exception. He is the one intercessor of all, and he also belongs to all. Thus there is one Son of God, and yet he is said to have many brothers, who are also themselves, of course, the sons of God.[317] Just as, then, the only Son does not exclude sons of God from sharing in the name, so one intercessor does not exclude other intercessors, since Jesus was the only one in whom the Father was present, when he was reconciling the world to himself,[318] and through whom all the other saints have whatever power they possess.

Finally, let us grant, just for the sake of argument and no more, that the saints enjoy Christ at leisure and cannot help us by their prayers. There is certainly no justification for disapproving of the devout sentiments of those who think themselves unworthy and do not dare raise their eyes to the throne of God's glory, but seek refuge in a saint who they think is pleasing to God and is always in God's presence. Sinners address a saint with all the more confidence because they know that he too was a sinner and won God's compassion. Christ did not condemn the feelings of the poor woman, sick for years with persistent bleeding, who, because she thought that she was unworthy of openly approaching Christ himself, touched the hem of his garment and was healed.[319]

* * * * *

316 1 Tim 2:3–7
317 Cf Rom 8:14.
318 Cf 2 Cor 5:18.
319 See Mark 5:25–34; Luke 8:43–8.

All the saints are members of the body of Christ. If he performs a good deed through his hem being touched, is it surprising if he does so through his members? Christ did not take any of his garments into heaven, but he has taken his members. In the Acts of the Apostles we read that the sick who were touched by the shadow of the apostles were cured,[320] and that those who were touched by the handkerchiefs and aprons that had touched the body of the apostle Paul were also freed of evil spirits.[321] All the glory of these happenings was owed to God. You will say, 'Why, then, did he give this glory to the disciples, and through them do what he could do by himself?'[322] Because that is how he wanted it to be, because that is how the Father himself wished to be glorified through his Son and how the Son wished to be glorified through his disciples. This was all to our advantage: we would recognize more clearly the fellowship of saints handed down to us by the apostles,[323] a fellowship embracing not only the living but also the holy souls of the dead and even the angels themselves.

Come now, surely you will not think it right to reprove those calling out frequently to a guardian angel[324] and entrusting him with carrying their prayers to Christ? I do not think so. Yet an angel is God's servant. If anyone were to respond, 'Why is it necessary to say these things to an angel when you can save time and say to Christ, "Hear my prayers"?' my riposte to this would be, 'Why was it necessary for us to be given angels to watch over us when we would be quite safe with Christ as our protector?' God wanted angels to be commended to us, he wanted his love for us to be shown through the angels' care for us. Why can what is said in devoutness to an angel not be said in devoutness to Peter and Paul?

The act itself has no appearance of impiety. First of all, it is devout to believe that the saints' souls have survived their bodies. It is Christian to believe that they now live with Christ, in accordance with the prayer of Paul, 'My desire is to depart and be with Christ.'[325] It is devout to believe that they are most pleasing to Christ, for whom they voluntarily lost their lives,

* * * * *

320 See Acts 5:15.
321 See Acts 19:12.
322 The last part of the sentence ('and through ... himself') is an addition to the text of the *editio princeps*.
323 A reference to the Apostles' Creed. The phrase *communionem sanctorum*, 'communion/fellowship of saints,' does not appear in versions of the creed until the fourth century at the earliest; see A.E. Burn *The Apostles' Creed* (London 1914) 40–4.
324 See n233 above.
325 Phil 1:23

and it is not impious to believe that Christ not only wanted their memory to be held in veneration by us but also wanted to be glorified by them when they had been granted immortality, just as he wished to be glorified by them when they were still mortals. It is devout, then, to believe that God wants to give us some things through them by whom he converted the world and by whom he will judge the world. If to call frequently upon the saints is at the same time to exercise our faith and to renew our love and to confirm our hope, what reason is there for thinking it worthy of reproof? If the merits of those doing battle here below benefit others (although there are some who declare that there are no merits),[326] will the merits of those reigning in heaven be of no advantage at all? No one will deny that the saints are gripped by an unceasing longing for our salvation. And yet this longing is itself a form of intercession. Whenever we call upon their help, we are praying that their longing will be fulfilled.

Now I think I hear, as I frequently do, those persons saying that the invocation of the saints should be curbed because it obscures the glory of Christ, to whom alone our whole trust should be transferred. Yet Christ himself did not have any fear about the loss of his glory when he dared to promise to his disciples that whoever believed in him would do not only what the Son had done, with his Father working in him, but also even greater things.[327] For this is how he decided to share his glory with those whom he thought worthy of it and whose servant[328] he did not deem it unworthy to become. Further, the worship of the saints consists in particular in three things – imitating their life, honouring them, and invoking them. Just as we do not deny that the most perfect example of holiness has been given us in the person of Christ, so we do not think that those who imitate Christ by imitating the saints, in whom his gifts shone, should be condemned. Similarly, we admit in all sincerity that supreme worship and all glory should be given to God. I do not think, however, that fault should be found with the practices of the church, which venerates the memory of the saints throughout the whole world by dedicating churches to them, by consecrating feast days to them, and by singing long-hallowed songs of praise. For in this way the church is worshipping Christ in his members, in whom he himself takes pleasure in being glorified and through whom his name has been glorified in human hearts. Finally, we admit in all sincerity that we should place the ultimate source for our salvation in Christ, through whom the Heavenly

* * * * *

326 A reference to the Protestant reformers
327 See John 14:12.
328 Cf Matt 20:28; Mark 10:45.

Father wished to bestow all his largesse upon us. I do not see, however, why there should be an outcry against those who, while respecting the great sublimity of the Lord, call in devout humility upon a saint as intercessor. They ask that the saint may favour and commend them before God, who perhaps is turned away from them. Indeed, in imitating the saints we do not detract from the most perfect example of holiness, Jesus Christ. Paul writes, 'Be imitators of me, as I am of Christ.'[329] Similarly, we do not detract from the glory of God in honouring the saints, but rather add to it, because in the saints we honour nothing but the gifts of God himself, 'from whom comes every good endowment and every perfect gift.'[330]

In calling upon the support of the saints, we do not thereby diminish the authority of Christ, the highest intercessor, any more than if someone, thinking himself unworthy and therefore fearful of appearing before his king, were to employ others who he knew were most pleasing to the king to plead on his behalf. First of all, the fellow's very shame, through which he not only recognizes his own unworthiness but also stands in awe of his king's greatness, commends him all the more to the king. Often a prince prefers to grant a request through others as intermediaries, especially if he wants in this way to win popularity and authority for them in the eyes of the people. Often[331] a prince will grant to a multitude of intercessors what he would refuse to one person because he is impressed with their consensus. What is more pleasing to God than to see the love and concord of the devout? A kindness given to one person does not produce an abundance of thanksgiving. God especially desires and asks that thanks be given by as many as possible for each single gift. Surely everyone confers a favour all the more gladly when he knows that more persons will be bound to him by it. The emperor does not reproach an intercessor, calling out: 'Why does he himself not ask these things of me? Does he believe that another will find me more merciful? Does he think I am unworthy of being addressed by him face to face?' Instead, the emperor likes the reverence of the man who, deterred by a ruler's majesty, is afraid to approach him.

Whoever call upon a saint as intercessor are also making a request of Christ, but in a different way. They address Christ, but through someone else. The emperor neither hears nor sees the actual pleader, Christ both sees and hears all things, and the farther petitioners withdraw from the sight of

* * * * *

329 1 Cor 11:1
330 James 1:17
331 The rest of this paragraph and the two following paragraphs ('... brethren') are an addition to the text of the *editio princeps*.

his majesty, the closer Christ thinks them to be. In the traditional litanies we first call upon the mercy of the Father, Son, and Holy Spirit, then the prayers of the saints. Someone may say, 'What is the point of all this, when God himself is the readiest of all to grant requests?' He loves the petitioners for their anxiousness and rejoices in bestowing some of his largesse on us through his friends. No one is more compassionate than God, I admit, and yet he wishes to be appeased through the instrumentality of a priest. Those who think themselves so completely worthless that they do not dare to call upon God are not at all judging the saint whom they use to be more responsive to them than God; rather they recognize the immense majesty of God and fear his justice.

Yet this 'fear is the beginning of wisdom.'[332] Let this be called feebleness, if you want; let it be called a mistake. This feebleness, however, is pleasing to God; God loves our mistake since it springs from piety. He was not offended by the fear of the woman who stealthily touched the hem of his garment; for he cured her when she touched it. He was pleased by the weakness of the publican who removed himself far from the high altar.[333] He loved these words of Peter: 'Depart from me, for I am a sinful man, O Lord.'[334] He was not displeased by the words of the centurion, 'I am not worthy of you that you come under my roof; but only say the word.'[335] The angels fear and tremble at the majesty of God. Do we, then, hurl insults at a mere mortal who does not dare to call to him? If it is a mistake, God prefers our error, which springs from humility, to the overconfidence of the Pharisees. He values this reverent feebleness more highly than arrogant wisdom.[336] Because of the greatness of their passion lovers address the bolts of the door of the betrothed whom they love, they kiss her ribbons, they converse with the violets that she sends. These actions, foolish in themselves, commend the lover to the girl, because they show the great depths of his love. How much less is God offended if out of love we greet and invoke the saints, even if they will not hear us. Moreover, how is it consistent for the dead Samuel to hear the words of a witch[337] and the saints not to hear the devout requests of their brethren?

* * * * *

332 Ps 111 (Vulg 110):10; Prov 9:10; Ecclus 1:16. Erasmus' text has *horror* for *timor* of the Vulgate.
333 See Luke 18:13–14.
334 Luke 5:8 (with a slight variation from the Vulgate text)
335 Matt 8:8; Luke 7:6–7
336 Cf 1 Cor 8:1.
337 See 1 Sam 28:7–19.

As it is, God himself has abundantly attested by his very actions that the devoutness of those who call upon the prayers of the saints is most pleasing to him. He performed many miracles at the tombs of the martyrs when the saints were called upon, he freed evil spirits, he healed the sick, he raised the dead. For I do not think that anyone will be so shameless as to claim that all the events that so many distinguished writers on the church have handed down to us in great agreement are mere stories, even if we admit that there are very many fabrications in such cases. Some[338] persons spurn these numerous accounts and demand clear scriptural evidence. It would be more justifiable for such persons to demand of these writers clear scriptural evidence about 'consubstantiality.' If they insist on such authority for everything, bishops will not be permitted to use staffs or mitres because nothing about such things has been transmitted by the apostles. There are countless examples such as these.

At this point someone, I think, will begin to talk of the great superstition of certain people in worshipping and invoking the saints, and we too in our writings have frequently warned against it. Many ask from the saints what they would not dare to ask from an upright person, and they do not think that the saints will hear them unless they are won over by certain rituals, almost magical in nature. What they ask for from one saint they do not ask from another, as if particular functions are assigned to each one, just as different cases are brought before the *centumviri*, the praetors, the senate, the Amphictionies, the Areopagus.[339] Some ask the saints for a healthy mind, as if they are not simply intercessors, but the source of such things. Given the way mortals are, however, such superstition should be tolerated if it does not result in impiety, or should be corrected as far as one can without causing disturbances; what is right in itself should not be condemned because of the foolishness of some, but the fault that is present should be corrected. For we do not prohibit the saints' being worshipped in a devout and moderate way just because some persons honour them improperly and

* * * * *

338 From here to the end of the paragraph is an addition to the text of the *editio princeps*.

339 The *centumviri*, the 'hundred men,' formed a panel of jurymen who heard inheritance cases in Rome. The praetors were Roman magistrates who presided over special courts that dealt with specific crimes such as extortion and bribery. In the early empire the Roman senate handled cases of treason and other criminal offences of senators and prominent equestrians. The Amphictionies were leagues of allied Greek states with special officers who tried offences against the Amphictionic laws. The Areopagus was an Athenian assembly whose main function by the second half of the fifth century was to hear cases of homicide.

intemperately; and we are not prohibited from imitating the lives of the saints just because some imitate what should be avoided. In the same way, the superstition of many who call upon the saints in an improper manner ought not to cause the invocation of the saints to be totally condemned. If this were our principle, we would have to avoid reading the Gospels because some people conceive the seeds of heresy from them, and we would have to forbid the invocation of Jesus because practitioners of magic also invoke that name. Error, however, must be exposed, ingenuousness admonished, and superstition corrected if, because of its nature, it should not be tolerated. In Flanders, for example, St Winnoc is venerated by the people there with some rites that are very unhealthy.[340]

Popular customs have developed to such an extent that neither bishops nor magistrates can suppress them. What superstition there is in many places when the relics of the saints are shown! In England the shoe of St Thomas, the former bishop of Canterbury, is offered to be kissed. This shoe perhaps belonged to a jester, and even if it is Thomas' what is sillier than to venerate a man's shoe? When they were showing the torn pieces of linen with which he is said to have wiped his nose and the little case that contained them was opened, I myself saw the abbot and all the others who were standing take up the posture of worship; they were filled with reverence, they fell to their knees and even raised their hands. John Colet, who was with me, thought this shameful.[341] I thought we should put up with it until the opportunity to correct it without causing civil uproar should present itself. Similarly, in public festivals and ecclesiastical processions we see a lot of superstition in some countries. Each guild of artisans carries round its own saints, and huge standards are borne by many sweating men, whom we are supposed to keep reviving by continually providing drinks. Some statues are carried on wagons, people dress up as famous individuals, and the deeds of saints, both male and female, are acted out, sometimes with

* * * * *

340 St Winnoc (sixth to seventh century) established a monastery at Wormhoudt in Flanders in northern France, where he was abbot. Perhaps Erasmus is referring to the custom of immersing 'his reliquary in the waters of the Colme in memory of a drowned child he was held to have brought back to life'; see NCE under 'Winnoc.'

341 For John Colet see CEBR I 324–8 and Ep 1211. This incident on Erasmus' and Colet's pilgrimage to Canterbury, sometime between the summer of 1512 and the summer of 1514, is described in the colloquy Peregrinatio religionis ergo. See Thompson Colloquies 285–312, especially 309–10 / CWE 40 619–74, especially 647–8.

much horseplay and jesting. Although the learned and the devout would want all this to be removed from Christian practice, nevertheless they tolerate it, since they see that it cannot be corrected without causing civil disturbances. They think that tolerating the practice is a lesser evil than applying a remedy.

Despite their nature, these practices are viewed with more tolerance by those who know and recall their origins. For the customs survive from the ancient pagans. In times past at sacred festivals Bacchus, Venus, Neptune, and Silenus and the satyrs were carried round. Since it was more difficult to change the religious belief of those who became Christians than their civic customs,[342] the holy Fathers thought that great progress had been made if instead of such gods the statues of devout persons were carried round, because their miracles showed that they reigned with Christ; if a pagan superstitious practice of running with torches in memory of the rape of Proserpine was turned into a religious custom so that Christians met in church with lit candles to honour the Virgin Mary; if those who previously called upon Apollo or Aesculapius in times of sickness now called upon St Roch or St Antony;[343] if women who had previously sought a pregnancy and an auspicious birth from Juno and Lucina made the same request to St Judocus[344] or any other of the saints; if those who had previously been in the habit of entrusting their possessions to Lar, Mercury, or Hercules for safekeeping and growth committed them to St Erasmus or St Nicholas;[345] if

* * * * *

342 The point is that, although it was desirable to bring about a change not only in beliefs but also in public festivals, success in the former, being the more difficult, satisfied the leaders of the church.

343 St Roch of Montpellier (1350–79) served those afflicted with the plague and was later invoked as a protector against pestilence. St Antony of Padua (1195–1231) was patron of the poor and was invoked for the return of lost property. Apollo, in his role as a god of medicine, could unleash plague against his victims, as at the beginning of the *Iliad*. Aesculapius, the son of Apollo by Coronis, was a skilled physician and was worshipped as god and hero.

344 St Judocus (also Josse or Joyce), a seventh-century saint from Brittany

345 St Erasmus, martyr of the persecutions under Diocletian, was patron of sailors. St Nicholas (d c 350), bishop of Myra in Lycia, was patron of sailors as well as of children. Both were among the Auxiliary Saints, the so-called Fourteen Helpers. The Lares were originally Roman divinities who protected the home, but they developed into guardian deities of travellers. Mercury, the Roman equivalent of Hermes, was the god of merchants. Hercules was also associated with trade in Rome and its environs, a tithe often being offered from commercial profits.

sailors called upon the Virgin Mary instead of Venus and the Twins[346] and sang to her the sailors' prayer *Salve, regina*[347] instead of irreligious hymns; if those who used to purify their harvest with foolish rituals or to appease Ceres with the singing of girls and boys carried round their fields a banner of the cross, chanting a hymn in praise of God and the saints; if the soldier who was about to go to war entrusted himself to St George or St Barbara instead of to Jupiter the Protector;[348] if each state adopted Bavo,[349] Mark, or another of Christ's disciples instead of their tutelary gods; if those who had been accustomed to ward off or obtain lightning by clucking noises[350] and other profane and superstitious remedies did the same with the sound of consecrated bells or with the smoke of consecrated leaves; if those who used to cure a pain in the heart with black magic cured it now by placing the Gospels against the chest, or if those who, as soon as the cuckoo was heard in May, were accustomed to destroy fleas and lice by scattering dust through their bedroom and removing it after drawing a circle around the mark of their right foot achieved the same result by bringing into the house the tunic of St Francis;[351] if those who used to try to cure impetigo on the head or the loss of hair by superstitious remedies did the same by applying the comb that was shared by Christ and Mary, which I hear is even now displayed at Trier; if those who were accustomed to arm themselves with

* * * * *

346 The Twins are the Dioscuri, Castor and Pollux, the twin sons of Leda, though, according to most accounts, by different fathers, Tyndareus and Zeus respectively. Like Venus (Aphrodite) they were often invoked by seafarers.

347 *Salve, regina*, a well-known hymn in honour of Mary, of uncertain authorship, originating at Le Puy in the eleventh century; see F.J.E. Raby *A History of Christian-Latin Poetry from the Beginnings to the End of the Middle Ages* 2nd ed (Oxford 1953) 226–7. It was recited or sung in Compline from the thirteenth century. Erasmus refers to its misuse, especially by sailors, in the colloquies *Naufragium* and Ἰχθυοφαγία; see Thompson *Colloquies* 141, 142, 355 / CWE 39–40 355, 356, 719. These references are owed to Germain Marc'hadour 'Erasmus as Priest: Holy Orders in His Vision and Practice' in Pabel *Erasmus' Vision* 129 n63.

348 St George, a martyr who died c 300 and whose deeds are shrouded in mystery, was patron of soldiers, particularly in the east. St Barbara was patron saint of soldiers and fortifications. She was thought to give protection from lightning and sudden death. The epithet 'Protector' was more commonly applied to the Roman goddess Juno than to Jupiter, though the latter was certainly associated with warfare as well.

349 St Bavo (c 589–654) was patron saint of Ghent.

350 See Pliny *Naturalis historia* 28.25.

351 See n13 above.

lucky swords and with garments over which a spell had been chanted now armed themselves with the wood of the cross. All these customs were tolerated by the Fathers, not because there was any Christian holiness in them but because they thought a considerable step in religious belief had been achieved in moving from those former customs that we have mentioned to the later ones.

For the same reason some of the early Fathers tolerated images that in their hatred of idolatry they vehemently abhorred.[352] They were glad that the people had progressed to worshipping images of Jesus the Saviour and of other saints instead of the likenesses of gods. Yet the use of these images has grown now to an immeasurable extent. Not for this reason, however, should all the images be driven from the churches; rather, the people should be taught the appropriate use of them. The faults in this practice ought to be corrected if this can be done without violent civil disturbance; what is good in it should be approved. It would be desirable that only what is worthy of Christ should be seen in churches. Nowadays we see depicted there so many silly and mythical stories, like the seven falls of the Lord Jesus,[353] the seven swords of the Virgin[354] or her three vows,[355] and other idle things of human invention, and also improper representations of the saints. For sometimes when a painter aims to represent the Virgin Mary or St Agatha[356] he takes as his model a wanton courtesan, and when he wants to depict Christ or Paul he models him on a drunkard or a wastrel. These are images that more readily incite one to wantonness than to holiness, but we tolerate them because we see more evil in removing than in enduring them. We

* * * * *

352 See *Explanatio symboli* 364–8 below.
353 None of the Gospels records that Jesus fell while bearing his cross, but three such falls came to be incorporated in the Stations of the Cross, devout meditations on Jesus' suffering and death promoted in the late Middle Ages by the Franciscans. In some works of art seven falls were depicted, as Erasmus indicates.
354 The Seven Sorrows: the prophecy of Simeon when the infant Jesus was brought into the temple, the flight to Egypt, the loss of the young Jesus in the temple, the carrying of the cross, the crucifixion, the taking down of Christ's body, and his burial. In art the Seven Sorrows are often depicted by swords in Mary's body. The image comes from Luke 2:35, 'and a sword will pierce through your own soul also,' spoken by Simeon to Mary. Erasmus seems to be criticizing a literal interpretation and extension of this metaphor.
355 Probably a reference to the three vows of purity, poverty, and obedience, not, however, actually made by the Virgin Mary. Cf Thomas Aquinas *Summa theologica* III q 28 art 4 (on whether Mary made a vow of chastity).
356 St Agatha (third century) was a virgin martyred at Catania.

see the exteriors and interiors of some churches packed with the insignia of noblemen, with shields, helmets, lions, dragons, vultures, hounds, bulls, gazelles, pelicans, standards plundered from the enemy; we see the place filled with the ostentatious monuments of the rich, we see the floor made unlevel and difficult to walk on,[357] as if the rich wish to oppress the people even when they are dead. If these things are tolerated in churches even though they are not praised, I think that it is right to put up with the images of the saints as well.

Now it is time for us to return to our subject. You have heard who is prayed to and who prays, although we shall touch again on the latter topic at the end. We must now turn our attention to what is to be prayed for. On this point a pagan gave advice that was not at all bad: 'You must pray for a healthy mind in a healthy body.'[358] For the common people often ask for what is harmful instead of what is beneficial. The orthodox Fathers rightly thought that nothing should be asked for from God except what the Lord prescribed for us in the Lord's Prayer or is in some way consonant with what it asks for.[359] There is no doubt that we should ask first for what is conducive to the glory of God and the eternal salvation of the human race, then for what pertains to the public weal rather than for what is for our own private advantage.

Yet it is not wrong to ask God to give us the temporal blessings without which life is hard or to keep away temporal evils, provided that the petitioner's intent is directed only at the goal of eternal salvation; for example, if someone asks God for good physical health so that he may not be a burden to his family or so that he may better serve the good interests of those closest to him, or if someone asks for long life for a bishop because he realizes that his learning and character are conducive to the glory of God and the interests of his flock. Accordingly, Paul tells us to pray for kings even if they are idolaters, not so that we may grow rich under them or that we may indulge the pleasures of the body, but, he says, 'so that we may lead a quiet and peaceable life, godly and respectful in every way.'[360] So it is right that we ask for our children to live, not so that we may take boastful pleasure in them, but so that they may be brought up in holiness and make progress in the Christian

* * * * *

357 Presumably, because of slabs and plaques commemorating the dead, set into the floor
358 Juvenal *Satires* 10.356
359 Cf Augustine *Sermones* 56.4 PL 38 379: 'you should not ask for anything other than what is written there [in the Lord's Prayer].'
360 1 Tim 2:2

religion. Therefore, since our unceasing prayer ought to be for eternal salvation, the conditions 'if the Lord wills'[361] and 'if it serves our salvation' must
underlie our requests for things of this life. Those who pray to be freed
from a horrible disease are not sinning, provided that they pray in this way:
'Lord, the salvation of all living things, remove this terrible disease from
me, if it can be done, but let your will be done, not mine. If you, who see all,
judge that this disease is necessary for my eternal salvation, treat me as your
holy will has decided; only give me power and strength so that I may bear
it and grant me the ability to endure your testing.' Whenever we pray for
peace, we pray that we do not experience war; whenever we ask for weather
conducive to health, we pray that there will not be pestilence; whenever we
pray for a rich harvest of grain, we pray that there will be no shortage;
whenever we pray for peace of mind, we pray that we will not be tested.

Even if what we pray for does not come to pass, let us not think that
our prayers have not been heard. Sometimes what we pray will not happen
is more conducive to that supreme goal than what we pray will happen;
nevertheless, our prayers are still heard. Frequently it is actually more profitable for us to be in want than to have excess, to be harassed by wars and
persecutions than to enjoy favourable circumstances, to be sick than to be
in good health, to die than to live, to be tempted than not to be assailed
by temptation. Paul hears the words 'My grace is sufficient for you,'[362] and
he glories in his own weakness. Following him, let us too give thanks to
God if ever he has preferred to give us what is salutary rather than what is
pleasurable.

Whoever asks for the good health of the body so as to please the
mistress whom he shamelessly loves, or for strength so that he may take
vengeance on a hated enemy, or for long life so that he may long enjoy this
world will not, I think, find any portion of the Lord's Prayer to which these
prayers may be referred. Anyone asking for intellectual powers does right,
and is following the advice of James, who says, 'If any of you lacks wisdom, let him ask God.'[363] The person, however, asking for wisdom so as to
be highly honoured among the teachers of this world forgets what is prescribed in the Lord's Prayer. David prays, 'Give me understanding, Lord,'[364]
but what does he add? 'So that I may learn your commandments.' We often
place the wrong value on what we may rightly ask for from God. Anyone

* * * * *

361 James 4:15
362 2 Cor 12:9
363 James 1:5
364 Ps 119 (Vulg 118):73

asking for wealth or good health more frequently or insistently than for
faith and love or knowledge of the Holy Scripture is making a mistake. Our
highest concern should be with the latter, and it is proper for us especially
to refer to these in our prayers. Nowadays, we see that the common people
reverse the worth of these two kinds of things, and some of them do not
even mention the only thing that we should ask for.

Those who actually ask God for what is unholy or for what will harm
their neighbours wander farther from the teaching of Christ. Take, for example, a mercenary's prayer, 'Grant that I may plunder churches and rob
harmless farmers and return home laden with sacrilegious booty,' or the
prayer of a wicked doctor, 'Let many fall victim to disease' or 'Let those
who are sick be sick for a long time so that I will make more money,' or
an heir's prayer, 'My relatives are too healthy. Let them die, so that my inheritance may come to me quickly.' The Spirit of God does not hear these
prayers since they come from the flesh, not from the spirit, or if he does
hear them, he does so at the cost of those who offer them; for they provoke
the anger of God. He heard the prayers of the people of Israel when they
demanded a king,[365] just as, in the *Fables*, Jupiter granted the demands of
the frogs when they asked for a king more energetic than the piece of wood
by giving them a stork.[366] More wicked are the prayers of those who are
goaded by spite and pray for misfortune for themselves so that someone
they hate may suffer more. In the *Fables* there is a story about two merchants
who envied each other. Mercury told them that, since Jupiter had granted
them access to him, one of them could ask for whatever he wanted; the other
would receive double this. Each refused to ask for anything. Finally, Mercury insisted, and one asked that he should lose one of his eyes, hoping that
the other would lose both.[367] In the *Fables* such stories are humorous, but
in all seriousness such actions are cause for tears when they occur in real
life and, even more so, when they are done by Christians, if in fact people
behaving in this way are worthy of the honour of this appellation. Among
such persons we find not only those who wish to have only one eye if their
enemy will thereby become blind, but even those who desire to purchase
the death of their enemy with their own death, who hasten to buy the disgrace of their enemy at the cost of losing their own good name. What, then,

* * * * *

365 See 1 Sam 8:4–22.
366 As told in Phaedrus 1.2. See B.E. Perry *Aesopica* (Urbana 1952) no 44.
367 As told in Avianus *Fabula* 22, B.E. Perry *Aesopica* (Urbana 1952) no 580; also in
Minor Latin Poets ed J. Wight Duff and Andrew Duff (Cambridge, Mass 1978).
But in Avianus' version Apollo, and not Mercury, is the god concerned.

is to be done with them? They should be advised to beseech God with copious tears to free them from such prayers, which make them more wretched than they would be if weighed down by the evils that they pray will befall others. For the soldier who plunders temples and the homes of the innocent is more unhappy because of his depraved cupidity than the victims are because of their calamity. The doctor who prays for death to befall others is much more unhappy through the vice of avarice than others are as a result of their disease. The envious man who prays for harm to befall his neighbours is much more unhappy because of his prayer than he would be if he suffered the misfortune that he prays will fall on them.

There is general agreement that we should ask God for nothing that is not in harmony with one of the seven parts of the Lord's Prayer. Any request that is directed at glorifying God's name relates to the first part: 'Hallowed be your name.' A prayer for the spreading and fulfilment of the gospel refers to the second: 'Your kingdom come.' Whatever is in keeping with the observance of God's precepts pertains to the third: 'Your will be done,' etc. A prayer to strengthen us in our earthly life refers to the fourth: 'Give us this day,' etc. Whatever pertains to harmony among us and to our being at peace with God looks to the fifth: 'Forgive us our trespasses,' etc. Being at peace with God depends on his compassion; he forgives without anger our daily failings. Harmony depends on neighbours' readiness to forgive the wrongs they do to each other. A prayer seeking the help of heavenly grace to fortify us against the assaults of demons, of the flesh, and of the world relates to the sixth: 'And lead us not,' etc. Whatever pertains to the end of all evils and to the complete fulfilment of our happiness (which in its perfect state does not befall us except after this life) is in harmony with the final part: 'But deliver us from evil.'

What we promised as the fourth topic, how one should pray, remains to be explained. One question discussed by the Fathers was whether it is right to pray in words different from those in the Lord's Prayer,[368] even though there is general agreement that we ought to ask for nothing that is not included in it.[369] The answer to this question is not difficult. It is clear from the Gospels that the Lord himself used different words when praying,

* * * * *

368 Cf Augustine *Epistolae* 130.22 PL 33 503: 'If we pray correctly and appropriately, we say nothing other than what is in the Lord's Prayer'; *Enarratio in psalmum 103* (*Sermones* 1.19) PL 37 1352: 'you will not be praying unless you say that prayer [the Lord's Prayer]; if you say a different one, he does not hear you.'
369 See n359 above.

as in John chapter 17: 'Father, the hour has come. Glorify your Son, that the Son may glorify you, since you have given him power over all flesh, to give eternal life to all whom you have given him,'[370] etc. This prayer expresses, in many words, exactly the same intent as the few words in the Lord's Prayer, 'Hallowed be your name.' Similarly, when Christ says in the garden, 'My Father, if it be possible,'[371] etc, he is simply praying that the Father's will be done in all things. In fact, the disciples too offer such prayers: 'Lord, who know the hearts of all men,'[372] and, in different words, in the fourth chapter of Acts, 'Lord, who made the heaven and the earth and the sea and everything in them,'[373] etc.

Most of the psalms are prayers to avert evils, but the church is not afraid to use them when offering its own prayers to the Lord. The church knows for certain that all their content reflects the sentiments expressed in the Lord's Prayer, even though the words are different.[374] Suppose we pray in the words of Ecclesiasticus: 'Pity us, Lord of all, look upon us, and show us the light of your compassion and send your terror upon peoples that have not sought you out so that they may realize that there is no God except you, so that they may tell of your great deeds. Raise your hand against the heathen so that they see your power. For as you have been sanctified in us in the sight of them, so may they learn of you as we have learned of you, that there is no God other than you. Renew your signs and transform your miracles; win glory for your hand and right arm.'[375] We are asking for, at great length, admittedly, and in different words, just what the apostles asked for in four[376] words, 'Hallowed be your name.' If, in the words of the psalmist, we said, 'All the nations you have made shall come and bow down before you, O Lord, and shall glorify your name. For you are great and do wondrous things. You alone are God,'[377] we would be making the same request. The same is true of anyone praying in these words: 'Be exalted, O God, above the heavens! Let your glory be over all the earth.'[378]

* * * * *

370 John 17:1–2
371 Matt 26:39
372 Acts 1:24
373 Acts 4:24
374 In *Epistolae* 130.22 PL 33 503 Augustine also illustrates how many of the prayers in the Psalms express the same idea as the parts of the Lord's Prayer and uses some of the same examples as Erasmus; see the immediately following notes.
375 Ecclus 36:1–7. Augustine cites the fourth verse.
376 The Latin text says 'three' (*sanctificetur nomen tuum*).
377 Ps 86 (Vulg 85):9–10
378 Ps 57:5 (Vulg 56:6)

Someone saying in a mystical sense that verse from the psalm, 'When you send forth your Spirit, they are created; and you renew the face of the ground,'[379] would be offering the same prayer, though in different words, that the apostles offered when they said, 'Your kingdom come.' Related to this is what the Psalms or the prophets say about conquering and crushing the enemies of the people of Israel, about establishing and building Jerusalem, about the eternal kingdom of David and Solomon. For it is agreed that by such types the kingdom of God and the church of Christ is meant.[380]

Those who pray in these words, 'Keep steady my steps according to your promise and let no iniquity get dominion over me,'[381] or in these, 'Teach me your way, O Lord, that I may walk in your truth. Unite my heart to fear your name,'[382] are not saying anything different from 'Your will be done, as it is in heaven and earth.' Prayers such as 'Give me neither poverty nor riches; feed me with the food that is needful for me,'[383] or 'Give me wisdom which sits beside your throne,'[384] or 'I am your servant,'[385] 'Give me the understanding that I may learn your commandments'[386] are asking for the same as 'Give us today our daily bread.' For just as whatever relates to the physical necessities of this life is embraced in the word 'bread,' so whatever strengthens the soul is bread, especially the words of the Lord.

The prayers 'Remember, O Lord, in David's favour, all his gentleness'[387] and 'O Lord, if I have done this, if there is wrong in my hands, if I have requited my friend with evil'[388] express the same meaning as 'and forgive us our trespasses.' Consider these prayers: 'Do not deliver the souls of those who believe in you to the beasts,'[389] 'Give me not up to the will of my adversaries, since they have arisen against me,'[390] 'Deliver me, O Lord, from evil men,'[391] 'Grant not, O Lord, the desires of the wicked. They have plotted

* * * * *

379 Ps 104 (Vulg 103):30
380 For 'types' see n96 above.
381 Ps 119 (Vulg 118):133, also cited by Augustine
382 Ps 86 (Vulg 85):11
383 Prov 30:8, also cited by Augustine
384 Wisd of Sol 9:4
385 Ps 143 (Vulg 142):12
386 Ps 119 (Vulg 118):73
387 Ps 132 (Vulg 131):1, also cited by Augustine. The Vulgate text differs from that reflected in RSV.
388 Ps 7:3–4 (Vulg 4–5)
389 Ps 74 (Vulg 73):19. The Vulgate text differs slightly from that reflected in RSV.
390 Ps 27 (Vulg 26):12. Erasmus omits *testes iniqui*, 'false witnesses,' in his quotation.
391 Ps 140:1 (Vulg 139:2)

against me; do not abandon me,'[392] 'Lord, Father, and God of my life, do not abandon me to evil thoughts, and do not allow me to fall into disgrace in accordance with their plans. Do not give me a supercilious eye, and turn away all evil desires from me. Remove from me gluttony and lust lest they overcome me, and do not give me an irreverent and unfit mind.'[393] Are these not asking for the same as 'Lead us not into temptation'? The prayer 'Deliver me, Lord, from my persecutors; for they are too strong for me! Bring me out of prison so that I may give thanks to your name. The righteous will surround me; for he will deal bountifully with me'[394] has different words but agrees in substance with the prayer 'Deliver us from evil.'

Accordingly, whoever goes through all of the Scriptures, which have different forms of prayer all through them, will find nothing that does not relate to some part of the Lord's Prayer. The sum of all things that are asked for should point to the same goal that the psalmist talks about: 'One thing have I asked of the Lord, that will I seek after, that I may dwell in the house of the Lord all the days of my life.'[395]

Of the countless forms of prayer, Christians have always given the highest authority to the one the Lord himself prescribed. We read that the apostles and their successors used this prayer at mass especially, because it was the most sacred of all. Since the Lord's Prayer suits all circumstances, it can scarcely be spoken on inappropriate occasions, except when foolish persons use it to call upon the saints, as when a merchant, about to set sail, entrusts his merchandise to St Christopher[396] and chants out three times to him the Lord's Prayer and even prays to the Virgin Mary. We used to laugh a little while ago at a fellow in Louvain, a man more simple than wicked; after mass he would walk to every single altar and hail the saints for whom he had a particular affection, saying the Lord's Prayer. When he had done this, he would bend his knees slightly and utter the name of the saint for whose favour he had prayed, saying, 'This is yours, St Barbara; receive this

* * * * *

392 Ps 140:8 (Vulg 139:9). For 'do not abandon me' the Vulgate text reads 'let them not be exalted' (*ne forte exaltentur*). Erasmus may have made a slip, but since the words 'do not abandon me' (*ne derelinquas me*) appear in the next quotation from Ecclesiasticus, the error may have been the printer's.

393 Ecclus 23:4–6

394 Ps 142:6–7 (Vulg 141:7–8). In the Vulgate text the subject of the last clause is the second person.

395 Ps 27 (Vulg 26):4

396 St Christopher, a legendary figure, supposedly martyred in the third century, was patron of travellers. He was one of the fourteen Auxiliary Saints (the Fourteen Helpers).

as yours, St Roch,'[397] so that none of the saints standing on the same altar might snatch for themselves what had been directed to another and thus there would be no cause of contention among them. We ought to suggest to such naïve persons that if they do not have anything to say in prayer, they may say this at least, 'St Peter, pray for me; St Barbara, pray for me.' For what is more absurd than to say to the Virgin, 'Our Father, who are in heaven', or to St Christopher, 'Hail Mary, full of grace,' or to St George, 'Forgive us our trespasses'? These persons can be taught, too, to remember in their prayers the virtue in which each of the saints excelled. They will say to the Virgin Mary, 'Grant me from your Son the gift of your chastity and modesty,' to Paul, 'Bravest herald of the gospel, entrust me to Christ so that helped by his grace I can do what he taught us through you,' to St Martin,[398] 'Help me by your prayers, so that I may imitate your gentleness while enduring wrongs.' The same goes for all the other saints. In this way the prayers of the uneducated will be less absurd and at the same time they will be reminded of what is to be imitated in each case.

Let us pursue, however, what we began. If we have to depart from the words of the Lord's Prayer, the next best thing will be to use words taken from the Scriptures, as our needs and situation demand. The book of Psalms will supply very many formulas of this kind, some of which Athanasius pointed out to us.[399] Yet on occasion everyone can take forms of prayer from all the other books of the Bible as well. Nothing should prevent us from interweaving into the same prayer parts taken from different places, as in a mosaic. Let those who seek help from God in avoiding the vice of disparaging others or of reviling them with foul language say from Psalm 119, 'Deliver me, O Lord, from lying lips, from a deceitful tongue,'[400] or, from the fourth chapter of Proverbs, 'Put away from me crooked speech, and put devious talk far from me'[401] and 'Place a guard on my mouth,'[402] or, from Paul, 'Let my speech always be gracious, seasoned with salt, so that I may know how I ought to answer to everyone.'[403] This is just by way of an example, since there are countless formulas in other places.

* * * * *

397 For St Barbara see n348 above; for St Roch see n343 above.
398 St Martin, bishop of Tours from 371 until his death in 397 and a strong promoter of monasticism
399 Athanasius (c 296–373), bishop of Alexandria and hostile to Arianism. Erasmus may be thinking here simply of his *Expositiones in psalmos* PG 27 59–546.
400 Ps 120 (Vulg 119):2
401 Prov 4:24. The Vulgate has 'you' for 'me' in this verse.
402 Ps 141 (Vulg 140):3
403 Col 4:6 (with change from the second person to the first)

Let nothing prevent us from adapting Scripture with a slight change of words to suit our purpose, as when we turn a precept or story or promise into a prayer. Here is an example. Solomon teaches us, 'Keep your heart with all vigilance; for from it flow the springs of life.'[404] You can change this into prayer in this way: 'Grant, O Lord, that I keep my heart with all vigilance under your care, so that eternal life may flow from it.' Hezekiah is said to have prayed in these words in the fourth chapter of the fourth book of Kings: 'Remember now, O Lord, I beseech you, how I have walked before you in faithfulness with a whole heart and have done what is good in your sight.'[405] Using this form any king or bishop will be able to pray in this way: 'I beseech you, O Lord, grant that I walk before you in faithfulness and with a whole heart, so that I may do before you what is good in your sight.' There is the promise 'If a man loves me, he will abide by my words and my Father will love him, and we will come to him and make our home with him.'[406] From this we will fashion the prayer 'Impart to me, Lord Jesus, your Spirit, that I may love you and abide by your words. May I be worthy of being loved by your Father and may you and your Father deem me worthy enough to make your home with me for eternity.' When we pray to avert evils we can make similar use of prayers in the Bible, but in this case those whose content is the opposite of what I have just been exemplifying, referring to sins instead of virtuous deeds, misfortunes instead of blessings, threats instead of promises. It is safest, however, and also more effective for the granting of your prayer if you do not depart from the words and thoughts of divinely inspired Scripture. For not only is there a particular forcefulness in the words themselves, but also God more gladly acknowledges his own words.

The third place of importance will be held by the prayers called 'Collects' that have been handed down to us by the ancients and that the church long ago began to use in divine worship and also at mass, before and after the consecration of the body of our Lord.[407] For not only do they contain much that reflects a sincere and apostolic spirit, but also most of them make their point with useful brevity and equal clarity. In these prayers the period consists generally of two members [membra] each of which can be divided

* * * * *

404 Prov 4:23
405 2 Kings 20:3. Erasmus cites this from the fourth book of Kings since in the Vulgate 1 and 2 Samuel are named 1 and 2 Kings.
406 John 14:23
407 Erasmus is referring to three prayers used at every mass, even in his own day. The 'Collect' was the opening prayer. Then came the 'Secret,' before the consecration, then the 'Post-Communion,' at the end of mass.

into two phrases [*commata*], and between the two members a phrase or solitary member may intervene.[408] Then there may follow the final flourish [*coronis*],[409] which generally consists of the same number of parts: *per Dominum
nostrum Iesum Christum*, 'through our Lord Jesus Christ.'[410] Even if the system or number of the phrases and members is not always the same as I
have said, nevertheless the periods always have their structure. I shall give
an example if you want one:[411] 'God whose providence' is a phrase; 'is not
deceived in its disposition' is a second phrase completing the first member. 'We suppliants beg you' is a third phrase, on its own and separating
the two members. 'That you remove all harmful things' is the first phrase
of the second member; 'and grant us all that will be to our advantage' is
the phrase completing it. Then follows the final flourish, generally with the
same number of words as there are members: *per Dominum nostrum*, 'through
our Lord.' There are some sentences consisting of two members that can be
divided into four phrases, after an initial phrase on its own. For example,
'Grant us, Lord, we beseech you, both that the course of the world may be
guided peacefully for us by your design and that your church may rejoice in
tranquil devotion.'[412] Some consist of more phrases, some of fewer. Rhetorical teaching does not require that these structures be followed too scrupulously. From the large number of prayers each will be able to choose for
himself fixed forms for most occasions of prayer, for example when praying for help against temptation, for forgiveness for committing a crime,
for an increase in love and faith, for civic peace, for the success of the
gospel.

Formerly priests used to pronounce these prayers in such a way that
the whole congregation heard and understood them and thereby, as it were,
prayed along with them (but with their feelings unexpressed), then finally

* * * * *

408 See Quintilian *Institutiones oratoriae* 9.4.122–5; Cicero *De oratore* 222–5; and
Isidore *Etymologiae* 2.18 for discussion and definition of these components of
sentences.
409 The *coronis* usually denotes the line or flourish used by scribes to mark the
end of a section or work.
410 The final five words may be divided into two members (*per Dominum* and
Iesum Christum) between which stands a solitary part (*nostrum*).
411 The following prayer is the Collect for the Seventh Sunday after Pentecost;
see *Missale Romanum* III 136.
412 Exactly how Erasmus would have divided this sentence is not clear. Perhaps
'Grant us' is to be taken as the introductory phrase, 'Lord, we beseech you' as
the first member consisting of two parts, and the rest as the second member,
again consisting of two larger parts. The prayer is the Collect for the Fourth
Sunday after Pentecost; see *Missale Romanum* III 100.

chanted in response in a clear voice, 'Amen.' This was a useful practice at that time since the priests performed the rites in the language that they shared with the people. Nowadays, although languages have changed, the old rite nevertheless remains. There is still not general agreement whether it is better to leave untouched or modernize what has become established over a very long time. I know that through their ignorance the common people are naturally inclined to revere more what they do not understand. All the same, they benefit less if only the sound of the priest's voice and not the meaning reaches them. I would not wish to propose modernizing the customary practice. Nevertheless, a remedy could be found for this disadvantage: the people could read privately to themselves the Collects of each day written in the vernacular. The same can be done for the Epistles and Gospels and the Lord's Prayer.

I have pointed out three formulas for prayer, although nothing forbids us from revealing our feelings to God in whatever words we wish, especially when we pray alone. We must, however, ask in the name of Jesus and seek what does not conflict with the goal of eternal salvation and is not at odds with the Lord's prescription for us in his prayer. It was not safe for the pagans to invoke Jupiter other than in the proper rites and words, and it is dangerous for someone not knowing the established formulas of speaking to speak before a king or a judge. Although God is above all others, he is not, however, fastidious in this kind of thing; he thinks well of everything he hears, he is not even offended by solecisms, provided the mind is pure. (There is a branch of rhetoric called 'petitory,' dealing with how one should make petitions. It is part of the rhetoric of persuasion. We have pointed out its nature elsewhere,[413] so that to repeat here what we have said would be superfluous. Moreover, the topic is also unsuitable when we are dealing with a sacred matter.) Paul said, 'We do not know what we ought to pray for or how, but the Spirit prays for us.'[414] Accordingly, to those who have the Spirit of Christ, the Spirit itself of its own accord suggests both what they ought to pray for and how.

Nothing, however, prevents me from demonstrating a mode of prayer that draws less on the precepts of the rhetoricians than on examples of prayers in the Scriptures. It is noticeable that these often begin with words

* * * * *

413 Erasmus may be referring to *De conscribendis epistolis* CWE 25 108–11, 172–80, where he discusses letters of persuasion and letters of request respectively. The latter is a sub-branch of the former, and thus also belongs to the deliberative branch of rhetoric; see Quintilian *Institutiones oratoriae* 3.8.

414 Rom 8:26 (quoted inexactly)

of praise or of complaint,[415] aimed at eliciting good will, and sometimes with the expression of thanks, which, as we have shown, is a form of praise.[416] Devices are used to make the listener attentive. In addition, use is made of narrative, which generally has a mixture of complaint, exaggeration of expression, and forcefulness,[417] which makes the listeners visualize the scene. You can see in Scripture the use of both argument and urgent entreaty – in brief, whatever one needs to use when speaking before a very important person whom you want to grant some request.

Praise sometimes lies in an honorific appellation alone. This ought to be suited to the particular situation; when you are praying for the members of Christ who are still in danger on earth, you say, 'Our Father, who are in heaven.' In Acts, the disciples themselves did not know what a person's true dispositions were, and so, when they asked the Lord to choose the man he thought more suitable, said, 'Lord, who know the hearts of all men.'[418] It will be right for anyone wishing to ask for wisdom to preface prayers with the words 'Eternal wisdom of the eternal Father, Jesus Christ.'[419]

We must take account of what is appropriate, not only in how we address our listener but in the whole prayer. For although it does not matter very much what you ask from which Person of the Trinity, it is more appropriate to ask for help from the omnipotent Father against enemies and demons, more suitable to ask the Son to reconcile his Father with us, more fitting to ask the Holy Spirit that divine grace be increased in us.

There is no need to recall examples of the use of complaint since we encounter these everywhere in the Scriptures. Sometimes complaints are added in the tone of a grievance; so Jeremiah says, 'O Lord, you have deceived me and I was deceived; you are stronger than I, and you have prevailed.'[420] Sometimes flattering words have the same effect; so Jeremiah prays, 'Be not a terror to me; you are my refuge in the day of evil.'[421] So also in the Psalms:

* * * * *

415 The term *conquestio*, here translated by 'complaint,' is a technical term in rhetoric, described at *Rhetorica ad Herennium* 3.24 as 'a speech which tries to elicit the sympathy of the listeners by exaggerating misfortunes'; cf Cicero *De inventione* 1.106.

416 153 above

417 The text reads *energeia*, 'forcefulness.' But the context makes *enargeia*, 'vividness,' possible.

418 Acts 1:24

419 Cf *Paean Virgini Matri* LB V 1230C: 'Son of God, wisdom of the eternal Father'; and 1 Cor 1:24, 30.

420 Jer 20:7

421 Jer 17:17

'Since my mother bore me you have been my God,'[422] and 'Lord, my hope from my youth.'[423]

When the poor give thanks, they are also petitioning. Those giving thanks to a very rich man for past kindnesses are silently asking for a new kindness. We judge those who acknowledge and remember a kindness worthy of having received it. We gain attention partly by making pressing requests (for example, 'Hear my prayer, O Lord; let my cry come to you,'[424] and 'Let my prayer come before you, incline your ear to my cry'),[425] partly if we show that our misfortune may harm the very person to whom we are praying: so in Psalm 113, 'Not to us, O Lord, not to us, but to your name give glory, for the sake of your steadfast love and your faithfulness, lest the nations ask, "Where is their God?"'[426] Similarly, in Psalm 78: 'Do not remember against us the iniquities of our forefathers; let your compassion come speedily to meet us, for we are brought very low. Help us, O God of our salvation, for the glory of your name; deliver us and forgive our sins, for your name's sake, lest the nations say, "Where is their God?"'[427] In this part of a prayer, however, it is more appropriate to use argumentation, about which I shall speak in a moment, but the greatest effect is achieved here when we declare that our merits and strength are of no help at all to us, that we have no hope in any other person, and that we depend completely on the help of him by whose compassion all are saved.

An example of narrative[428] is at Acts 4: 'For in this city there were gathered together against your child Jesus Christ,' etc.[429]

In using argument in prayer to persuade we especially make use of these aspects of God's nature: he is able, is willing, is accustomed, is obliged to grant our prayers. An example of invoking his power is 'Omnipotent God, who alone can do whatever you wish with a single nod of your head.' For his willingness, his very goodness and compassion are of course adduced. For his being accustomed to grant our prayers, either recall the examples of kindnesses to others or those that he has already often conferred on us, since it is to be expected that he who has always done kindnesses will

* * * * *

422 Ps 22 (Vulg 21):10
423 Ps 71 (Vulg 70):5
424 Ps 102:1 (Vulg 101:2)
425 Ps 88:2 (Vulg 87:3)
426 Ps 115:1–2 (Vulg 113:8–9)
427 Ps 79 (Vulg 78):8–10
428 The use of narrative in prayer, mentioned at 213 above, is treated here with only one example and with no explanation.
429 Acts 4:27. The unexpressed subjects are Herod and Pontius Pilate.

always be like himself. His obligation rests not on what we deserve, but on what he promised. For 'Remember, O Lord, David and all his gentleness,'[430] and 'Hear a just cause, O Lord,'[431] and psalms such as these are spoken, I believe, more in the person of Christ than of the human author. This is the 'trustworthiness' that is frequently linked with his compassion, as in Psalm 88: 'Compassion and trustworthiness will go before you.'[432] We say 'compassion' because we do not deserve what we ask for, 'trustworthiness' because in some way he has an obligation in accordance with his promise. He promised through the prophet forgiveness of all our sins.[433] He promised through his Son eternal life to whoever believed in the gospel, no matter at what hour sinners came to their senses and groaned in lamentation. Thus, in a way, we claim back from God what he promised.

The rhetoricians teach that promises should accompany petitions. We find this to be so in sacred prayers as well. David promises: 'I will teach transgressors your ways and sinners will return to you. And my mouth shall show forth your praise. Then will you delight in right sacrifices, in burnt offerings and whole burnt offerings.'[434] There is nothing else that we mortals can promise, and there is no other reward that we expect. Everything that is in prayer relates to us, not to God. For God is not assuaged by hearing his praises, as humans are; rather, by praising him we learn more and more and come to respect his greatness. When we tell of our misfortunes in great detail, it is not a question of his changing completely and of his becoming propitious instead of angry because of our prayers, but of our seeking more strenuously his compassion by better recognizing the greatness of our calamity. Similarly, when we say anything that attracts his attention, we are not rousing God from a former sleep, since nothing that lies hidden in the human heart escapes his notice; rather, we are asking more insistently and more zealously for what only those of us who importune him more passionately deserve to receive. Likewise, by stressing that we have faith in nothing else but in his promises and compassion, we learn to whose account we must credit whatever blessings we have. In promising that we will publicly proclaim his kindness to us, we are reminded not to be found unworthy of the grace of God by ascribing to ourselves what we have received, but to refer everything to his glory. In requiring from him

* * * * *

430 Ps 132 (Vulg 131):1. See n387 above.
431 Ps 17 (Vulg 16):1
432 Ps 89:14 (Vulg 88:15)
433 Cf Isa 43:25, 44:22.
434 Ps 51:13, 15, 19 (Vulg 50:15, 17, 21)

fidelity to his promises, our advantage is that we pray with certain faith not in our merits, but in those of him who has never abandoned anyone who believed in him. In arguing that it is also to the glory of his name that he should hear us, although otherwise unworthy, we learn that in good fortune and in bad we should direct everything only to his glory. The only point of our adjurations and supplications made in the name of his Son, in the name of his ineffable love for us, of his death, of his resurrection, and of all that he has done or suffered for our sake is that we completely understand from whom and through whom whatever pertains to eternal salvation comes to us. Whoever is well versed in the Scriptures will better compose any prayer.

A common question asked is whether we should pray aloud or whether the silent desires of a petitioning soul are sufficient. For my part, I think that in private prayers we have a free choice on whether we prefer to say aloud what we ask for in our soul or to beseech in silent prayers God's clemency, which places little value on our voices. Often more is granted to silent sighs and tears than to great cries. In fasting, however, we not only remove the mind from all the pleasures of this world, but also chastise our body by not eating since, if we are to enjoy in our whole being the reward of immortality, we must also serve God in our whole being. For the same reason, in the sacred duty of prayer it is right for us to sing with our voice as well as with spirit and soul. This habit is especially profitable for those who are not yet skilled in prayer. For by chanting the sacred prayers, they learn, as it were, how to pray, and the very exercising of the voice sometimes produces the appropriate disposition of the mind.

Religious ceremonies are useful in that through them we advance to the invisible through the visible, just as children are taught to read before they can understand what they are reading. In the same way we profit from the splendour and religious aura of the church as well as from the sacred vestments and the posture of the body, whether we prostrate ourselves on the ground or lower ourselves on bended knees or look up to heaven with upraised hands. All these can add strength to our prayers, even if God hears them no matter in what place or in what posture they are uttered, whether you pray while lying in bed or while washing in your bath or while toiling in the workshop. Nevertheless, while we are saying the traditional, established prayers we should not neglect the physical acts of worship out of consideration for the weak, since they profit from such rituals. We should participate in the ceremonies in such a way that others too are encouraged to pray. For it is not seemly to demand the mercy of God, shouting like a soldier or speaking in a lascivious tone of voice, and it is not appropriate for the voice to say, 'Pity me, O God, in accordance with your great mercy,'[435] while the face and eyes engage in lustful appraisal of young girls.

The whole act of divine worship, which consists of three elements in particular – hymns, lessons, and prayer – ought to be conducted in a language that all the people know, as was once the custom; everything should be enunciated clearly and distinctly so as to be understood by those who pay attention. In[436] this way many would participate together in the action at the same time, and the whole congregation would be part of the service. The priests would pray, the people, praying along with them, would respond, 'Amen.' The people would listen in silence to the Gospel and the Epistle, they would sing hymns together, not crudely shouting but singing in an angelic tone, full of modesty, full of reverence, as if they were in the sight of the supreme king, as if they were among the choirs of angels and of the souls of the devout. This would be more suitable, in my opinion, than what is done today in most places; while the priest performs his office with just a few attendants, the members of the congregation pray for, say, or think of different things, quite unrelated to what the priest is doing. They are of the church rather than the church itself. Yet even this is more tolerable than what we see happening in most areas. During the whole period of worship people either murmur some trifles into the ear of the person sitting next to them, or they stroll about, chatting in an unseemly way about worldly or silly affairs, sometimes so intemperately that the words of the priest cannot even be heard because of the din they make. This kind of behaviour ought to be completely eradicated from Christian conduct; fuller participation in the service in the way I have just suggested is one of those[437] features of human life that one can desire rather than believe will be accomplished.

Worship conducted publicly in churches and sacred places should not be too long (for nothing is worse than a surfeit of good things) and should be the same among all nations of the Christian faith. As things are now, what a difference there is from one church to another! In fact, some eagerly strive to resemble others in nothing. Some monks are burdened with very long-winded chants and prayers. After completing them somehow or other with great weariness, how joyfully they leave them for relaxation,

* * * * *

435 Ps 51:1 (Vulg 50:3)
436 An addition to the text of the *editio princeps* begins here (see the next note).
437 The addition ends here. Erasmus has also made a minor adjustment to the text of the *editio princeps* at this point, which actually says 'but there are many features ...'

conversation, and dinner parties. Yet if elegant dinner parties at which one rises from the table still with an appetite are praised more than long ones, that is all the more reason for divine worship to be completed quickly and without tedium so that we return to it with great eagerness. Certainly each individual should measure for himself his own prayers and limit the time spent in prayer either in accordance with the disposition of his mind, which is not always equally fervid, or in accordance with the pressing demands of business affairs. In communal prayers in which many participate at the same time everyone ought to begin and end at the same time to prevent noisy uproar in the church. A mean should be established for length so that those who are fervent and have leisure can to some extent be satisfied and those who are unenthusiastic and busy are not tortured by boredom. Nothing should prevent those praying by themselves or with a dear, close friend from lingering where they are for as long as they want if they feel moved more deeply while praying, or from interrupting their prayers to engage in a devout conversation. More suited for those who are busy are those prayers – very brief, but frequently unleashed, like arrows, so to speak – with which the monks in Egypt were wont at times to interrupt their manual work, perhaps to make the work itself more agreeable.[438] The human mind is scarcely able to concentrate its attention for long, but very soon it either becomes less focused as time goes on or is distracted with other thoughts. Someone may respond, 'Different life, different style of living.'[439] Formerly monks were generally members of the laity and spent their time in manual labours. Nowadays such labours are thought unsuitable for priests. Yet the apostle Paul did not think that it was unseemly to earn his keep by sewing skins together.[440] If the glory of Christian obedience and endurance rests in suffering through the tedium of excessively long prayers, tell me what praise the monks would have if they were compelled on order of the abbot to do at fixed times what Sisyphus is said to do in the underworld.[441] I think it is more suitable to use a rock for punishment than sacred hymns and prayers.

* * * * *

438 There is a reference to the Egyptian monks and to the image of their 'unleashing' their prayers in Augustine *Epistolae* 130.20 PL 33 502.
439 For the proverb, given in Greek in the text, see *Adagia* I ix 6 CWE 32 182. The proverb is applied to those who experience a change for the better in their fortunes and change their style of living.
440 See Acts 18:3.
441 The task of Sisyphus in the underworld was to roll a rock up a hill for eternity since it always rolled back once he reached the top.

Nothing should be included in prayers that is not taken from Holy Scripture or at least has not come down from those whose writings breathe of Christ. All the more, then, should all lasciviousness, mercenariness, flattery, and every other feeling that is unworthy of sacred worship be absent. When Christian is preparing to make war on Christian, a priest should not pray for a glorious victory for his side and destruction for the enemy – often both sides displease God in the prayers that their priests offer, in accordance with the teaching of Paul, for kings and those in positions of authority.[442] A more Christian prayer would be to ask that the prince be virtuous and worthy of God, that he have wisdom and holiness rather than triumphs, victories, and deeds of glory. Vainglorious titles such as 'most victorious,' 'most unconquerable,' 'most triumphant' are quite improper when spoken at the altar by the priest praying for his prince. That during holy rites some priests should venerate with clearly servile and abject flattery the prince for whose sake they have been hired to perform them is even more unseemly. In short, although we can approve of each priest's praying for his prince, a general reference in public prayers to all Christian princes would be fitting, without any mention of a particular person. In fact, it would be more proper to pray for the Turks or all the enemies of the Christian faith to receive the compassion of God than to pray for their destruction.

I wanted to give such advice in passing; now we return to what we were discussing. Brief prayers also suit those who hold public offices. For when kings are going into deliberations, they can silently pray in these words: 'O God, without whose spirit nothing can be done rightly, deign to be present in these considerations lest anything be decided that may offend your majesty.' A judge sitting at a tribunal can silently pray, 'O Lord, may your wisdom that controls all things be present so that while I am judge no one may suffer unjustly or be wronged.' While an envoy is riding on his mission, he can pray, 'Direct, Lord my God, my path in your sight,' or whatever else devout thoughts may suggest.

I see that now some monarchs have been persuaded to perform each day the office of those prayers that the order of clerics performs by hallowed tradition in the churches at fixed hours (whence the common appellation of these prayers as 'hours'). As often happens, the example of some rulers is daily spreading to more of them. I would in no way condemn such piety in princes, provided that they do not think that they have performed a wonderful act in what they have done, especially if they do not understand what

* * * * *

442 See 1 Tim 2:2.

they are saying (as is probably the case with many, at least with respect to the mystical meaning), or provided that they do not believe that it is a great achievement to have done no more than speak the words. I would prefer princes to devote whatever leisure time they have from the pressing demands of their affairs to learning by heart divine precepts, the Proverbs of Solomon or the *Sayings* of famous princes, a great number of which Plutarch collected,[443] or those books that learned men have left to us about running the state and our personal affairs. I am speaking of works such as Aristotle's *Politics, Economics,* and *Ethics,* Cicero's *On Duties,* Plato's *Laws* and *Republic,* Isocrates' *On Kingship,* Xenophon's *Education of Cyrus* and *Economics.* Some similar help will be given by our writings as well, *The Christian Prince,*[444] *War,*[445] *The Return of Philip,* the Spanish king.[446]

A prince has prayed enough if he has taken care that positions of authority are given to uncorrupted men of integrity, if he has avoided war through his prudent actions, if he has driven off the violence of the powerful from the shoulders of the weak, if he has put a stop to criminal activities with as little loss of blood as possible, if he has set public morals on a sound footing by holy laws and customs. For, if these things are neglected, to spend time saying prayers is by no means an act of piety; it is actually sinful hypocrisy. The people should be relieved of the oppression of robbers, and yet when they bring forward their complaints and ask for the help of their prince, they are told, 'Be off with you; the prince is praying.' The widow or ward is told, 'The prince is praying; he has no time to see you,' as if they are disturbing him. If, however, some girl or some fool or someone bringing a fine dog were to seek an audience, they perhaps would not hear the words 'The prince is praying.' When do we read that the Lord Jesus himself, King of Kings and Prince of Princes, kept at bay the despicable and wretched throng? When did he bid them be told, 'Be off with you; the Lord is dining'? He withdrew to a deserted place to pray, but he met again the thronging crowds.[447] How shameless, then, are those who are not afraid to reply to intruders, 'The prince is playing dice.' It would be more acceptable for bishops' attendants to reply, 'The bishop is praying,' if they used this

* * * * *

443 Plutarch *Regum et imperatorum apophthegmata* in *Moralia* 172A–208A: see Erasmus
      Apophthegmata LB IV 85–380.
444 *Institutio principis christiani* ASD IV-1 133–219
445 *Adagia* IV i 1 LB II 845–61: 'War is sweet to those who do not know it,' published
      under the title *Bellum* in 1517
446 *Panegyricus ad Philippum Austriae ducem* ASD IV-1 1–93
447 See Matt 17:1, 14; Luke 6:12–19.

excuse to visitors inviting him to engage in activities much more unholy than playing dice, but they do not do so! I think that St Gregory would have abandoned his private prayers for interruptions such as these.[448] We read that the emperor Hadrian had some virtues besides his many great vices.[449] When a woman, wishing to be heard by him, called to him as he made his way along a street, he replied, 'I don't have time,' since he was in a hurry to go elsewhere. Then she said, 'Don't be emperor, then.' The great emperor reacted with politeness to the woman's outspoken remark, he stopped and listened to her grievance.[450] A prince might more properly say, 'I don't have time,' to the priest calling him to prayer than to the wretched and the innocent who are in great difficulties. For a king not to have time for the latter is disgraceful (since this is precisely a king's duty) if he has time for longwinded prayers, hunting, games, dancing, court jesters, and gambling, not to mention even more wicked activities.

While Holy Scripture will provide those who engage frequently in prayer with an abundant amount of material, so will life itself, which is so varied with good fortune and bad; sad things, however, outnumber the good. If anything sad threatens or overwhelms you, you must pray. If good fortune befalls you, you must give thanks and pray that God may wish his gift to last forever. If you commit a sin, you must pray for forgiveness. If a virtuous act is performed, you must ask God to deign to increase his gifts in us. If you see someone endowed with outstanding qualities and, accordingly, very useful to the state, pray to God that he may wish many others to be like this. If you see someone who is extremely wicked and harmful, pray that he be given a better disposition and at the same time that God may preserve you from turning out like him. If you receive a public office, pray for the gift of wisdom, so that you can administer it in a proper manner. If it is taken away from you, pray that a better person succeed you. If you have an abundance of material things, ask that the one who gave it will also give you the disposition to use it well. In fact, customary expressions of good will are not actually very different from praying if they are spoken from a Christian heart and not just by habit: for example, when we say to someone undertaking a journey, 'May a kind angel take you and bring you back safe,' or to a husband, 'I pray that everything goes well when your wife gives birth,' or to a new magistrate, 'I pray that the office you have obtained will prove propitious

* * * * *

448 St Gregory (c 540–604), the fourth and last of the traditional Latin Doctors of the church, was elected pope in 590.
449 Hadrian was Roman emperor in 117–38 AD.
450 Cassius Dio 69.6

to you and the state,' or to a devout bishop, 'May Christ Almighty keep you long safe for his church.' There are countless other expressions of this kind.

The above is just what occurs to me when writing about prayer, distinguished and noble sir. Yet saying such things about prayer to a leading man of the royal court could seem somewhat out of place. If, however, the apostle Peter calls all Christians 'a royal priesthood,'[451] and if it is a particular sacred duty of Christians to pray, as we have said, it cannot be inappropriate to write to anyone about prayer unless he is not a Christian. In fact, probably none should pray more frequently and more fervently than important men; the greater the weight of affairs which they shoulder, the more they need divine help. Moses was not a priest but the leader of his people, and yet how often do we read that he prayed for them. David was a king, not a priest, and yet he spends a great deal of time praying. Solomon was a king, and yet at the dedication of the temple he prays for the whole people, like a priest.[452] A king who does not wish his people well should not pray for them, nor should a prince pray assiduously for himself if has no need of the supreme deity's help. Those words of James, 'Pray for one another, that you may be healed,'[453] were addressed to all, both the highest and the lowest. In his daily prayers the apostle Paul mentions before God those whom he had initiated into the gospel, but he asks them in turn to pray for him.[454] Those who are not gripped by longing for any blessing or by fear of any misfortune need not pray for themselves. Those who wish no one well except themselves need not pray for anyone else. In sum, those who think themselves estranged from the priesthood of Christians need not trouble to make this sacred offering to their God.

We do not deny that it is a particular duty of priests to pray for the people they have undertaken to guide; and they offer prayers not only for the living but also for the dead. James ordained that the elders of the church should be summoned to the sick to pray to God for their salvation and to anoint them in the name of the Lord. 'And the prayer of faith,' he says, 'will save the sick, and the Lord will raise him up, and if he has committed sins he will be forgiven.'[455] Abimelech is told to beg Abraham to pray for him because he was a prophet. For this is what you read in Genesis chapter 20: 'Now then restore the man's wife; for he is a prophet and he will

* * * * *

451 1 Pet 2:9
452 See 1 Kings 8:22–61.
453 James 5:16
454 See Rom 1:9, 16:30; Eph 1:16, 6:18–19.
455 James 5:14–15

pray for you, and you shall live.'[456] Prophets have knowledge because they
are accustomed to speak with God. For God speaks with them. Yet just as
all Christians are in some way priests after the Holy Spirit was poured into
all, so they are also prophets, since we all have access through Christ to
the throne of his glory.[457] We must not confound, however, the hierarchy in
the churches that has been established in a praiseworthy way and has been
handed down to us through our ancestors' hands. The priest standing at
the Lord's table has the authority to pray for the people. Similarly, when he
mounts the pulpit and speaks about the Holy Scripture he has the authority
to take on the role of prophet, while the people listen in silence. It would not
be right for just anyone to assume this responsibility. For where there is no
hierarchy, there is confusion. Can there be tranquillity where there is confusion? Peace, however, especially becomes the church of God, who deigns
to be present at an assembly gathered in his name. The priest, therefore,
prays for his brethren in accordance with the office that has been delegated
to him; the people pray in turn for their priest out of love for their brother.
Although the priest has the role of prophet in accordance with his ordination, all of us may teach our neighbours whatever holy learning we have
acquired when there is need to do so. Christian love shares its duties with
all in turn in such a way that the members of the body are healthily joined
to each other.

Someone may ask at what times in particular I think we ought to pray.
I see that the Holy Scriptures generally link three things together: wakefulness, sobriety, and prayers, because excessive drinking and sleep weigh
down the mind that wishes to speak with God. Therefore, we should become accustomed to address the Lord with a short prayer immediately we
awaken,[458] even in bed. You should do the same before you leave your bedroom and take yourself off to secular duties, and finally just before you re-
tire for the night. Nor should we despise the example of some who, after
leaving their bedroom, are concerned to be present for mass, if it is possible,
before they eat or before they put a hand to any of their ordinary tasks, provided that they do not do so out of superstition. For there are very many who

* * * * *

456 Gen 20:7
457 Cf Heb 4:16; Rom 5:2; Eph 2:18.
458 The context seems to demand this meaning of *a primo somno*, though the normal
    sense would be 'at the beginning of sleep,' in other words, just before falling
    asleep; see *Oxford Latin Dictionary* under *primus* 3b. Erasmus is describing in
    chronological order the times of day when we should pray, beginning with
    when we awaken and concluding with when we retire for the night.

believe that whatever they do will turn out as they wish if they have looked upon the bread and the chalice. Sometimes this is done by a pirate about to weigh anchor, by a Carian soldier[459] preparing to plunder the innocent, by a dishonest businessman when trying to make a profit anywhere at all.

Nor should we neglect that most praiseworthy of customs of many persons who begin a meal with prayers and conclude it with the giving of thanks. I wish, however, that these prayers were taken from the Holy Scriptures and that more suitable ones were spoken than those used by some. While I do not condemn 'May the hand of Christ bless us and what we are about to eat' and such chants, I would prefer that they gave way to better ones. Nor is it necessary to foist everything into such patchwork phrases. It is always right to say, 'Lord, have pity,' but some occasions are more suitable than others. It is holy to say, 'Blessed womb of the Virgin Mary,'[460] but the proper place for it is elsewhere. Perhaps praying on such occasions for those who have served us well is not unsuitable, if it can be done briefly. It seems more appropriate, however, to pray for a king, a bishop, for peace or war or other things by name at a different time. I approve of the practice among some of having a sacred reading added to the blessing at the table, so that even at a meal the first conversation should start from this.

Perhaps you will ask my views on those who perform in entirety the Liturgy of the Virgin Mary every day.[461] I would certainly prefer this to superstitious prayers that are very like spells. In this practice, however, I find it troublesome that what is said in the Holy Scripture about the church being the Bride of Christ and about the Lord Jesus being the wisdom of the Father[462] is distorted in its application to the Virgin Mary, and also that on these occasions the Virgin Mary is asked for what would be better asked of the Son: 'Protect us from the enemy, take us up at the hour of death.'[463] It

* * * * *

459 The Carians inhabited the southwestern area of Asia Minor and were renowned for their passion for fighting as well as for other barbarous traits. See *Adagia* I ii 30: 'You are Carizing with a Carian' and *Adagia* I vi 14: 'Risk it on a Carian.'

460 Recited or sung as the Communion Verse in the mass *Commune festorum Beatae Mariae Virginis*: 'I bless the womb of the Virgin Mary which bore the Son of the Eternal Father.' See Luke 11:27–8.

461 The *Officium parvum Beatae Mariae Virginis*, also known as the 'Book of Hours.' See Roger S. Wieck ed *Time Sanctified: The Book of Hours in Medieval Art and Life* (Baltimore and New York 1988).

462 Cf 1 Cor 1:24: 'Christ the power of God and the wisdom of God.' In the printed text *qui* is probably a slip for *quae*, made either by Erasmus or by the printer.

463 Two lines from the hymn *Memento salutis auctor* in the *Officium parvum Beatae Mariae Virginis*

is more proper to say to God, 'Free us from evil and take up my spirit.' Yet there is no impiety even in such words if you are willing to take into account without prejudice the sincerity of those who say them. With similar feelings some implore the help of the Virgin in their sermons,[464] calling on her as 'the fount of all grace.'[465] No one denies that great honour is owed to the most holy Virgin, but in those circumstances calling on the Spirit of Christ would be more appropriate. I approve more of those short prayers about the cross of our Lord that some say every day.[466] I would not at all condemn the numerous prayers offered by the laity in which, as they turn their rosaries, they repeat a fixed number of times the Lord's Prayer or 'Hail, Mary,' if some persons did not make unbelievable promises to those who do so. This would be the place to talk about how some common prayers often reflect different superstitions and are not dissimilar to magical incantations. If the best forms of prayer are laid out, it will not be difficult to reject whatever does not harmonize with these. For although the number of ways one can go wrong is infinite, the right kind of prayer is clear and simple to recognize.

Although[467] no time is unsuited for prayer, we should pray especially at night, in the morning, before and after eating, at nightfall, on feast days on which holy custom calls all to church for prayer. The apostles prayed at home whenever it pleased them, but nevertheless we read that they went to the temple for prayer at the ninth hour.[468] Sometimes also our actual circumstances prescribe the time of prayer. Whenever we are crushed by affliction or assailed by temptation, we must seek refuge in the help that prayer gives. No danger is so great that you cannot avoid or overcome it if you turn to fervent, earnest, and continual prayer.

We have touched to some extent on the place of prayer, although our views on this must be the same as about the time of prayer and other external features. When the Israelites were living outside their country, Moses instructed them to pray with their faces turned in the direction of the temple, since they could not go to it.[469] Our Lord prayed in the desert, but he also

* * * * *

464 The ASD text wrongly reads *condicionibus*, 'terms, conditions,' for *contionibus*.
465 Cf *Paean Virgini Matri* LB V 1227E.
466 For hymns to the cross see *Lateinische Hymnen des Mittelalters* ed F.J. Mone 3 vols (Freiburg im Breisgau 1853–5) I nos 102–14; cf also the hymn of Venantius Fortunatus *O crux, spes unice*, 'O cross, our sole hope.'
467 From here until the end of the essay, except for the final paragraph, is an addition to the text of the *editio princeps*.
468 See Acts 3:1.
469 Solomon, not Moses, prescribes facing in the direction of Jerusalem during prayer (1 Kings 8:35). Daniel is said to have prayed looking towards Jerusalem while in exile (Dan 6:10). Erasmus may have been mistakenly thinking of Exod

went to the temple on the appointed days.[470] When Paul was at Jerusalem, he entered the temple and showed his religious dedication by performing the solemn rites,[471] but he also prayed on bended knee on the seashore.[472] He prayed and sang hymns in prison,[473] not now on bended knee since his feet were bound fast in stocks; perhaps he could not even raise his hands on high to pray. We must not despise a place consecrated for prayer or the large congregations that gather to pray. God prefers to hear prayers uttered together by many of the same mind, especially if a priest, who is nearer to God, offers them. For Christians, however, everywhere we are is a temple: in a bedroom, kitchen, workshop, boat, carriage, on horseback, in the bath, even in the lavatory.

A Christian's heart is itself a temple of God, it carries round with it its own altar, it carries round with it the presence of God. The more you retreat into yourself, the holier the shrine you have entered, the nearer you have become to God. This is truly the house consecrated to prayer[474] that was turned into a den of robbers by the Pharisees and thus roused the Lord's anger.[475] The temple should certainly be pure, but all the same if the mind is defiled, it is cleansed through prayer. It is also fortified by prayer, so that it is not overcome again by foul thoughts. We should do this all the time since human nature inclines to evil, and that impure spirit that rejoices in contaminating with filth minds consecrated to the Holy Spirit is always abroad, waiting in ambush and trying to find a way where it can creep in. If it finds a mind that is pure but unguarded and unoccupied, it bursts in, not just on its own, but brings with it seven other spirits even more harmful.[476] Nothing fortifies and equips our mind more surely than prayer, which is ever on guard, which is always ready at the door to beat back Satan as he tries to burst in. Prayer also equips and fits out our home with a different array of virtues, since it always gains some new favour from our most generous God. He supplies what was missing, increases what was there, and preserves what he has increased. Continual prayer provides us with

* * * * *

33:7–11. See John J. Collins *Daniel: A Commentary on the Book of Daniel* (Minneapolis 1993) 268. Early Christian writers advocate facing east during prayer; see E.G. Jay *Origen's Treatise on Prayer* (London 1954) 42–3.
470 See John 5:1, 11:55–6.
471 See Acts 21:26.
472 See Acts 20:36.
473 See Acts 16:25.
474 Cf 1 Cor 3:16.
475 See Matt 21:13.
476 See Luke 11:26.

everything. The saying is true that our life on earth is like that of a soldier[477] who has a never-ending conflict with evil spirits, with the flesh, with
the world, with the many evils that life itself or human wickedness brings.
The safest armour against all these is prayer. Those who actually wage war
against their enemy use many arms, soldiers, and fortifications to ensure
their safety: ramparts, ditches, mounds, wagons, elephants, asses, mantlets,
shields, catapults, and spears. Yet often all these things fail, no matter that
they are in abundance and have been carefully made ready. Prayer alone,
however, is the safest defence against all craftiness or against any power
that wages war on our salvation. The Christian who is protected by the
shield of prayer[478] has sufficient arms, even if he must go into the bowels
of hell.[479]

Someone will bring as an objection what is said in the Gospel, 'Not
everyone who says to me, "Lord, Lord," shall enter the kingdom of heaven,
but only those who do the will of my Father who is in heaven.'[480] Far from
detracting anything from prayer, these words stimulate in us the desire to
live upright lives, without which prayer is not prayer, but mockery. Are not
they who say, 'Lord, Lord,' but are not afraid to ignore his commands in
their whole lives simply mocking him? It is not possible, however, for somebody who prays continually with all sincerity either to persevere long in sin
or to slip back easily into it. Those who have had the good fortune to meet
with the emperor become prouder because of having conversed with him
and think it is unworthy of them to have dealings with vile and unprinci-
pled persons. Once we have spoken with God, we will not become a friend
of Satan. Once persons have been forgiven by the emperor for a crime for
which they ought to have been flogged, they take extreme care not to offend by the same actions him whose clemency they have just received. Similarly, somebody who has received a splendid gift from him certainly takes
the utmost care not to alienate in some way the man whose generosity he
has just experienced. Will, then, those who have just been granted through
prayer remission of all their sins from our most merciful Lord immediately

* * * * *

477 Cf Job 7:1: 'Has not man a hard service [militia] upon earth?' and 2 Tim 2:3:
'Take your share of suffering as a good soldier of Christ Jesus.'
478 Cf Ambrose Enarratio in psalmum 38 PL 14 1094B: 'prayer is the good shield of
weakness.' More commonly the image of the shield is applied to the Lord; cf
Ps 33 (Vulg 32):20; Prov 30:5.
479 Hell must be used here in a metaphorical sense; cf De praeparatione ad mortem
409 and n138 below.
480 Matt 7:21

slide back into the same action? Will those who by their prayers have been granted so many gifts of the soul then leave the sight of God and show how ungrateful they are for such generosity? How will those who frequently so-licit God on behalf of their fellow beings be able to abuse their neighbours with the same tongue? How can those who sing the praises of God every day presume with the same tongue to hurl slander against those for whom the Son of God died? A base and abject mind is open to all the derision of evil spirits. Prayer makes the mind exalted, noble, and strong, impervious to all the blessings and evils of this world, even to life and death. Those who have daily intercourse with good persons are made better by their company. Can it be possible, then, for those who continually talk with God not to be made like him? There is nothing purer than God, nothing more sublime, nothing more untroubled or more tranquil.

If anyone casts up to me some monks and priests who pray and sing all day and all night and yet are not made the slightest bit better, I shall deny that they are praying. If they were really praying, they would certainly be transformed. 'God is spirit,'[481] and only those who speak in the spirit speak with him. We do not listen to a chatterbox reeling off what he himself does not understand. Will God listen to the noise coming from our lips when our hearts are far from God, perhaps set on our books or on the kitchen or on our bed?

Someone will object that many do not receive what they pray for, in-cluding even those who pray sincerely and from the bottom of their hearts. This results not through the weakness of prayer, but through our fault or by the will of God. When Paul prayed three times to be freed from Satan, who was assaulting him,[482] he was not heard, but this exposure to temp-tation was more useful to him. If God denies what is sought, he does so for our advantage. A father often denies what his especially beloved son asks for because he realizes that it will be harmful. He is not being a harsh parent, but acts out of love in looking after his son's interests better than he looks after them himself. If God delays granting our request, he delays for our good, so that we may receive what we ask for in more abundance. Therefore, those who immediately murmur against God if what they seek is not given act with impiety. What are you doing, thoughtless man? Your needy brother cries out to you, and you often pass him by with deaf ears. Yet he does not murmur against you. Moreover, if he did so, you would not

* * * * *

481 John 4:24
482 See 2 Cor 12:8.

tolerate it. And yet you accuse God unless he immediately gives what you ask for! Your refusal to listen to your neighbour as he calls out to you is a mark of inhumanity; that God does not hear you is a mark of his looking out for you with deep paternal love. It could even be seen as very justifiable retaliation if the ears of God were deaf to us, since we turn a deaf ear to our neighbour in need; for he made a compact with us on these terms and conditions: 'Give and it will be given, forgive and you will be forgiven.'[483] Anyone not acceding to his neighbour's request for forgiveness is foolish to ask God for forgiveness for his own sins.[484] Those who refuse to give their neighbours in need even a penny or worn clothing or food that cost little are shameless if they ask God for the precious gift of a holy mind. Therefore, whenever we do not receive what we ask for from God, let all wicked murmuring be absent. Rather, let us interpret the situation to mean either that God will give something better than what we ask for or that he postpones giving it so that he may give it in more abundance or that we have provided good cause that we should not be heard. We should worship his kindness in changing our prayer for the better; we should embrace his goodness in postponing what we request so that we receive it with interest; we should correct the fault that makes God stop his ears to us – our inhumanity to our neighbour.

What remains, then, but to close this long discourse with a brief epilogue? If we ask what is the importance of prayer, prayer is the particular responsibility of the angels, who for eternity stand beside God, speaking with him, singing hymns to him, interceding with him on our behalf, and carrying our prayers to him. If we ask what validates prayer, God himself showed it to us as a remedy. If we ask for an example, it is that of the patriarchs and prophets, of kings and priests, which Christ himself sanctioned and the apostles handed down to us. If we ask about the usefulness of prayer, without it God bestows nothing on us, and through it everything is bestowed. If we consider what makes us safe, it is by this weapon alone that we are safe against all that hostile powers can direct at us. What, then, should be embraced and assiduously practised by a Christian other than prayer, but prayer that is sincere, fervent, and continual, commended by deeds of compassion?

Noble Hieronim, this small gift was dedicated to you the moment of its conception and was undertaken for your sake so that you might have

* * * * *

483 Luke 6:38
484 Cf Matt 18:35.

something to remind you of me in my absence, as I remember you. If it meets with your approval, do not grudge sharing it with your fine brothers Jan and Stanisław. If you have better thoughts on this topic, follow them, but at least give me this recompense for my obvious warm affection for you – your wish to share with me what better thoughts you have.

AN EXPLANATION OF THE APOSTLES' CREED

Explanatio symboli apostolorum sive catechismus

translated by
LOUIS A. PERRAUD

annotated by
LAUREL CARRINGTON

The genre, special character, and reception of Erasmus' 'Explanation of the Apostles' Creed' are discussed in the general introduction to this volume (xx–xxvi), and theological points are elucidated in the notes to this translation. It would perhaps be useful to add a few observations about Erasmus' language and style.

Even within the fairly narrow limits that Erasmus has set for his subject here – a popular but systematic exposition of Christian belief – the master's supple Latin sounds a variety of tones. Erasmus strikes the strangest of these tones when he is fulfilling the demands of his chosen genre, the literary dialogue.[1] Perhaps to avoid further complicating his already complex theological material, he omits any literary element not required by his didactic purpose. The 'Explanation' lacks description of a specific setting; the two speakers of the dialogue, the 'Catechist' and the 'Catechumen,' far from being well-characterized individuals, are merely mouthpieces for Erasmus' theological arguments, and there is no attempt to create the illusion of conversation between them. Though Erasmus assigns the 'parts' necessary for maintaining the convention of a dialogue, therefore, the speakers express themselves in the same formal, highly stylized Latin that the author uses to treat theological subjects.

In the opening of the 'Explanation,' for example, the Catechumen expresses his desire to become a more committed member of the Christian community not in a simple declarative sentence, but rather in a stylized piece of rhetoric that ends with a little formal amplification of the word 'church': 'My soul has longed,' he says, 'to be enrolled in the society of the Catholic church, the house of God, outside of which there is no hope of eternal salvation' (236). Even the Catechumen's wishes and emotions as he learns the Christian doctrine are expressed in conventional, purely literary metaphors, such as 'Would that the Spirit might deign to write upon my heart ... with an imperishable seal,' (244) 'My soul takes fire,' (247) 'My thirst to hear the rest is even keener' (247).

In the sections of the 'Explanation' that expound the positive contents of the Apostles' Creed, Erasmus' tone is gravely measured and his diction conservative. He eschews, as his subject dictates, the humanist exuberance that led him in one work to use terms from pagan Roman religion to

* * * * *

1 For the theory and practice of Renaissance dialogue see K.J. Wilson *Incomplete Fictions: The Formation of English Renaissance Dialogue* (Washington 1985); Jon R. Snyder *Writing the Scene of Speaking: Theories of Dialogue in the Late Italian Renaissance* (Stanford 1989); *The Dialogue in Early Modern France* ed Colette Winn (Washington 1993).

describe Mary, Mother of God, as a 'divine power,' (*numen*), a 'goddess,' (*diva*), and even 'that famous threefold Diana' who has different manifestations in heaven, on earth, and in the underworld.[2] Instead, he confines himself to the traditional terminology of the Fathers, the great councils of the church, and the scholastic theologians.

Erasmus' usual scintillating style is, however, by no means totally absent from the 'Explanation.' Side by side with his explanation of orthodox dogmas Erasmus furnishes refutations of heresies that deviated from them, and to these he brings more varied rhetorical forms and stylistic relish than to his positive theological teaching. The refutation of false views of God's existence and nature (271–5), one of the longest sections on heresy, is given forceful, economical rhetorical structure by repetitions of a key introductory idea in the same or similar words – a rather broad form of the rhetorical device known as anaphora. The recurring formulas that Erasmus uses to bind his list of heresies together here emphasize the right-thinking Christian's horror of these errors. The sincere Christian 'condemns,' writes Erasmus, certain 'Cyclopean pagans' as well as polytheists and the Anthropomorphites. 'The believer condemns the Epicureans,' he continues, 'denounces the blasphemy of the Jews.' (271–2). He departs from the formula for a while in refuting Noetus and some other heretics, but then returns to it, making 'the believer' condemn in turn Seleucius, Menander, Saturnius, and Basilides (275). Erasmus uses the same rhetorical structure in his treatment of those who denied or distorted belief in the resurrection of the body. He 'takes leave' (appropriately, perhaps, since he is nearer the end of his doctrinal exposition) of the heretical sects one by one: 'Adieu ... to the ill-starred Sadducees,' he writes, and then bids adieu to two other groups without specific sect names, and, finally, to the Chiliasts (346).

To deal with denials that Christ died a true death for the sins of mankind, Erasmus uses a device that was beloved of early Christian writers and has its roots in Stoic and Cynic diatribe: reproachful direct address to a purely rhetorical straw man.[3] After quoting from the First Epistle of Peter the correct view that 'Christ died once for our sins' (1 Peter 3:18), Erasmus switches without warning to the second person singular. 'You,' he says accusingly to no one in particular, 'hear it stated clearly that he died once; you hear that he arose from the dead ... yet you deny that he died.' He then launches a similar attack in the second person singular against an

* * * * *

2 *Obsecratio ad Virginem Mariam* LB VI 1233F, 1236B
3 On diatribe see Eduard Norden *Die antike Kunstprosa* 2 vols (Leipzig 1923) I 129, II 556–8.

unidentified and purely hypothetical Jew, excoriating 'his' denial of the redemption (306). This pounding of imaginary opponents is as close as Erasmus' Latin gets to the techniques of street-corner preaching.

The attacks on heretics derive some of their literary vigour from being
so unsparingly ad hominem. Several times Erasmus uses his opponents' own
names to mock them. Noetus, whose name comes from the Greek word for
mind ($\nu o \hat{v}\varsigma$), is mindless or senseless ($\dot{\alpha}\nu\acute{o}\eta\tau o\varsigma$) (273); Eutyches, whose name
means 'good fortune' in Greek, is 'ill named' because of his unfortunate be-
liefs (297); Photinus, whose name comes from the Greek word for 'light,' is
doctrinally in the dark (293). Erasmus descends to downright sarcasm when
he mocks the 'compassion' of Basilides, who believed that Simon of Cyrene
was crucified instead of Christ (305). He gives a vivid picture of the deceptive lives that sometimes accompanied the heretics' deceptive beliefs (330).
The Pharisees crossing the stage of the Gospel in their dangling phylacteries, praying at the crossroads, but counting money and cheating others in
their rooms; the Manichees abstaining from animal meat but secretly gorg-
ing themselves with other expensive luxuries; the Euchites, praying superstitiously but living off others – these heretics and the rest of their tribe are
effectively singled out for satirical notice.

The translation which follows, based on the text in ASD, attempts to
catch all these varied aspects of Erasmus' style: the odd formality of literary
Latin conversation, the clarity of his theological exposition, and the sharp-
ness of his satire. I have benefited from a preliminary draft that the Reverend J.J. Sheridan completed before his death. However, in many places
I have differed with his interpretations of the Latin, and I have recast the
whole in a markedly different prose style. Any errors or infelicities are my
own responsibility.

LAP

ERASMUS OF ROTTERDAM TO THE MOST RENOWNED THOMAS A.
ROCHFORD, COUNT OF NORMANDY AND OF WILTSHIRE, GREETING.[1]
Illustrious Count, I saw that a charge of impropriety would be laid against
me by quite a number of people if I wrote something on the Apostles' Creed
in the wake of Doctors of the church who were so numerous and so distinguished. Among them, Cyprian[2] was the first of the Latin Fathers to treat
this theme; he did so in such a way that no one so far has been able to out-
strip him. Yet I would seem guilty of impropriety in my own eyes if I did
not comply with your wishes, especially when you ask for something so devout with an affection so devoted, and above all since you have so kindly
interpreted that former work of mine, in which I explained Psalm 22,[3] as a
compliance in love rather than a duty performed. Nor is it a secret to me that
you, who do not need me as a teacher, ask for this little work of mine for
others who are less well educated. Accordingly, I treated the subject with
the intention of accommodating the whole explanation to the grasp of less
experienced minds. I do not at all see what praise I shall gain from my endeavour, unless perhaps it is that some points are explained quite fully and
explicitly. Indeed, I have no regard for praise, but wish the recruits in the
Christian army may derive as much benefit from it as your notable piety,
renowned sir, leads you to desire, and as I have striven to impart, in keeping
with my small talent. Meanwhile, God must be asked in prayer to supply
from his goodness what is wanting in my strength; may he who inspired
you with this devout sentiment deign to crown it with happy success, not
only in this project, but also in everything which you undertake in your zeal
for godliness.
     Farewell.
     Freiburg im Breisgau, in the year of the Lord 1533

* * * * *

1 Sir Thomas Boleyn (1477–1539) was father of the famous Anne Boleyn, whose
   marriage in 1532 to King Henry VIII was instrumental in creating the con-
   stitutional crisis that led to the dissolution of the tie between the Church of
   England and Rome.
2 Cyprian: read Rufinus. Rufinus (b 345), a contemporary of Jerome, wrote the
   'Commentary on the Apostles' Creed' in about 404. It was believed during the
   Middle Ages to have been the work of Cyprian.
3 *In psalmum 22 enarratio triplex* LB V 311–46, which Erasmus wrote at Thomas
   Boleyn's request in 1530.

AN EXPLANATION OF THE APOSTLES' CREED

Personae: Catechumen and Catechist. The former is given the initials KA from the Greek, the latter the initials CA from the Latin.

Lesson 1

KA For a long time now, my soul has longed to be enrolled in the society[1] of the Catholic church, the house of God,[2] outside of which there is no hope of eternal salvation. I beg you to assist piously my childlike steps towards this goal.

CA If you have been validly baptized at the sacred font, you have also, by this very act, been enrolled in the family of the Catholic church.

KA This ceremony was carried out by my sponsors without my knowledge. Now, however, through God's kindness, I have reached this age, when I can as easily be corrupted by wickedness as taught goodness. Therefore I think it is right to free my sponsors from their pledge, to look after my own salvation and personally tend my own business. Accordingly, I ask that you treat me as completely ignorant, instruct me, and mould me.[3]

CA Dear son, the Lord himself, who has inspired you with this desire, will lead you on in his goodness to what you desire.[4]

KA Is there no need then for a catechist?

* * * * *

1 The term *consortium,* 'society,' denotes an association or fellowship. Compare with *familia,* 'family,' members of a household. Membership in the latter, achieved by baptism, is involuntary, while to belong to a *consortium* implies a mature commitment.
2 Cf 1 Tim 3:15.
3 The Catechumen simultaneously acknowledges that he is of an age to make such a commitment and shows a childlike trust as he places himself in the hands of the Catechist. Cf *Paraclesis* LB V 140A.
4 Cf Phil 1:6.

CA If there were no need, Christ's words to his apostles would have been meaningless: 'Go, teach all nations.'[5] Yet even if you employ six hundred catechists, it is still the Lord who really teaches this philosophy.[6] Such was the decision of God – that he should choose to bestow his gifts on humans through humans.

KA Why did he so decide?

CA First, to exclude all pride and arrogance, which that Spirit who loves meek and gentle minds loathes; further, in order that charity should be fostered, spread, and nourished by reciprocal acts of service among Christians. There is nothing here that the catechist can claim as his own if he performs his function, or the catechumen if he makes progress. All praise is due to the one who guides the teacher from within as his instrument and transforms[7] the mind of the learner. Let us then implore together the Lord's mercy, so that by his inspiration you may ask prudent questions and I give salutary answers.

KA I agree.

CA Now then, ask your questions.

KA As I have often said, the ineffable beauty of the house of God touches my soul and attracts it in a wonderful way, but where, I ask, does its entrance lie?

CA Those wishing to enter a house look for the door.

KA Show me the door.

CA That heavenly teacher, Paul, pointed it out. 'Anyone who would draw near to God,' he says, 'must believe,'[8] and in Romans 5: '... through whom we have access to that grace by faith.'[9] Again in Hebrews: 'Without faith it is impossible to please God.'[10] That door of faith is indeed

* * * * *

5 Matt 28:19

6 Cf 1 Cor 4:15 and *Paraclesis* LB V 139A: 'However, it is more desirable that Christ himself, whose business we are about, so guide the strings of our lyre that this song might deeply affect and move the minds of all ...' The term *philosophia*, 'philosophy,' refers to Erasmus' 'philosophy of Christ,' which he often encourages his readers to ponder, rather than to become engrossed in the thorny disputes of the philosophers and theologians of the schools; cf *Paraclesis* LB V 141E–F. For a discussion of this term see Georges Chantraine *'Mystère' et 'Philosophie du Christ' selon Erasme: étude de la lettre à P. Volz et de la 'Ratio verae theologiae'* (Namur 1971).

7 *Transformat:* cf *Ratio* LB V 77B: 'that you may be transformed into that which you learn'; and *Enchiridion* LB V 22A / CWE 66 56. See Marjorie O'Rourke Boyle *Erasmus on Language and Method in Theology* (Toronto 1977) 88.

8 Heb 11:6

9 Rom 5:2

10 Heb 11:6

lowly, but it shows a person who has passed through it the ineffable majesty of the divine power, wisdom, and goodness. Bow your head, then, that you may deserve to enter.[11]

KA What do you mean?

CA Lay aside the bodily senses and the cunning of human reason so that you may believe, simply and confidently, whatever divine authority has handed down for our salvation, even if it seems false, frivolous, absurd, or impossible to human understanding. Human reason deceives, these bodily senses deceive, God alone cannot deceive or be deceived, just as he cannot fail to be God.[12]

KA What is faith?

CA Since you are a beginner, let me explain it to you in relatively uncomplicated terms. There are two principal powers of the soul: intellect and will. By the former we decide what should be chosen, by the latter we seek what reason has indicated. The offence of the first human beings has impaired both these faculties. The contagion of this evil has spread abroad through their entire posterity.[13] Because of this, through reason as through an impaired eye, we think things exist that do not, or that they are not as they are; through our corrupted will we seek what is deadly rather than health-giving – something that usually happens to those who are diseased. Against this twin evil, the goodness of God has provided us with a twin remedy: faith, which purifies the heart, that is, the mind and reason or the source of the soul, and charity, which corrects the distorted will. Faith, shining forth, as it were, in the darkness,[14] drives out all delusion, at least in what pertains to salvation. Charity removes evil desire, so that we may be inclined only to what God has prescribed. Faith gives orders, charity carries them out as a servant of faith. The eye of faith, however, is above all directed towards God. Charity has, so to speak, two eyes: the right it directs to God, the left it turns aside to its neighbour, for it loves the former above

* * * * *

11 Cf *Enchiridion* LB V 8C / CWE 66 34: 'The doorway is low; make sure that you do not strike your head and be thrown backwards'; and *Ratio* LB V 76D.

12 Cf James 1:13; the Paraphrase on Romans 3:4 LB VII 785E; and Augustine *De symbolo ad catechumenos* 1.2 PL 40 627.

13 Erasmus' concept of original sin combines the view that we inherit the contamination from Adam and Eve with the view that we choose to sin in imitation of them. Cf the Paraphrase on Romans 5:12 LB VII 793B / CWE 42 34: 'And so it happened that the evil originated by the first of the race spread through all posterity, since no one fails to imitate the first parent.'

14 Cf John 1:5.

all things as the supreme good and the latter as a kinsman for God's sake.[15]

Faith, then, with which we are now dealing, is a gift divinely infused into our minds,[16] through which we believe without any hesitation that whatever God has handed down and promised to us in the books of both Testaments is the absolute truth. Faith extends to three periods of time – the past, the present, and the future; that is to say, it believes in the creation of the universe by God and in whatever Scripture relates happened in former ages; then, it believes that at present the world and the church are governed by God; finally, it believes that whatever Scripture promises to the good or threatens for the wicked will come to pass. By the gift of faith we believe all these things with far greater certitude than what we conclude by reason, or cling to because it is grasped by the individual senses.[17]

KA Given that the sacred volumes have come to us through human hands, what is the source of that firm and unshaken faith? No one is so sacrilegious as to suspect God of being untrustworthy, but it may be doubted whether all these books were written under divine inspiration.

CA This certainty arises from several factors, but one is most important, the concord of Scripture and intellect. For what is handed down in these books largely agrees with the innate judgment of reason, a certain spark of which remains even to this day in fallen mortals. Second, certainty comes from the astonishing miracles through which both the Old and the New Testaments came to be written. At no other time have such things happened, nor has anyone dared or been able to invent them. In addition, these things all fit together in a marvellously coherent way.

KA What things?

CA The figures and prophecies of the Old Testament; then too, faith and evidence agree in the fulfilment of types that the Old Testament has foreshadowed, and of promises it has made through the mouths of the prophets.[18] You know that in weighing testimony the agreement

* * * * *

15 Cf Mark 12:30–1.
16 Cf Eph 2:8. For another articulation of Erasmus' belief that faith is a gift of God, cf *Purgatio adversus epistolam Lutheri* LB X 1539A.
17 Cf Heb 11:1 and *Enchiridion* LB V 8C–D / CWE 66 34: 'Be convinced that of all the things you see with your eyes and touch with your hands nothing is so true as what you read therein.'
18 Cf Rufinus 9 PL 21 349 and the colloquy *Inquisitio de fide* ASD I-3 367:137–9 / Thompson *Inquisitio* 61–3 / CWE 39 425:24–7.

of witnesses is of the greatest consequence. Compare Christ as sketched in so many dark enigmas in the Mosaic law,[19] and as promised by so many prophets in diverse times and situations, with the Christ whom the gospel account places before our eyes, as if in a theatre.[20] You will see there is agreement down to the last detail. There is, moreover, miraculous agreement among prophets, while among worldly philosophers there is a great difference of opinion. Add too the unchanging consensus of all ages and nations, and the unbroken accord in regard to this philosophy.[21] Who was ever known to write something with such outstanding genius that the whole world embraced it in the same way, or held fast to it with a constancy so great that many thousands of men, boys, women, and virgins,[22] whose minds the light of faith had purified, could not be torn away from it by any type of death or by tortures more dreadful than death? Even more marvellous than that – this philosophy, like the sun, suddenly shone over the whole world and overcame it without the help of might, or wealth, or learning, or human ingenuity or, finally, through any forces of this world. Thus far in the face of royal power, in the face of worldly wisdom, in the face of heretics instructed in a thousand types of impiety, in short, in the face of all the machinations of the devil, it has stood unshaken, in keeping with the promise of Christ, 'And the gates of hell shall not prevail against it.'[23]

KA I feel some light illumining my eyes too, dimly though they see. But what is this one preliminary gift?[24]

CA What you have already grasped on your own.

KA What, without being aware of it?

* * * * *

19 Cf *Paean Virgini Matri* LB V 1230A.
20 Cf ibidem 1229A: 'the theatre in heaven has no marvel more admirable than you'; Tertullian *De spectaculis* 30 PL 1 735–8.
21 The importance of concord to Erasmus' philosophy of Christ is paramount; see McConica. Likewise, obscurity and disagreement among philosophers and theologians are signs of decadence and untruthfulness. Cf *Moria* LB IV 450–67 / CWE 27 125–9 and the annotation on Romans 1:5 LB VI 558D. For a classical articulation of a similar view cf Cicero *De oratore* 3.16.59–61.
22 Cf *Paraclesis* LB V 140B: 'It casts aside no age, no sex, no fortune or position in life. The sun itself is not as common and accessible to all as is Christ's teaching.'
23 Matt 16:18
24 *Praecipium*: the original meaning of this term denotes that which is received from an inheritance before the general distribution.

CA You feel, as you say, that some light has illumined the eyes of your heart. That, indeed, is the Spirit of Christ, who already has begun to exercise his power in your heart, and what he has begun, he will, I hope, bring to completion.[25] For this is the pledge of the divine Spirit thus strengthening our minds with his secret inspiration: that the power of neither devils nor angels nor any creature can separate them from the faith and hope which are in Christ Jesus.[26] No human persuasion produces this disposition in our souls, which is the surest proof that all these things are done by divine power. For nothing except this philosophy[27] calms our minds.

KA Happy are those to whom this gift falls!

CA Let us pray with confidence, and it will fall to our lot.

KA When you mention the two Testaments, you allude to a great, not to say measureless, sea. What do you set before me, still unschooled and not much more than an infant in Christ?

CA As you know, human disciplines have their rudiments. This heavenly philosophy also has its own.

KA Where am I to look for them?

CA In the creed that, partly because of its authority, partly to distinguish it from other creeds, is called the Apostles' Creed.[28] The ancients occasionally call it 'the rule of faith.'[29] It is a statement embracing in few words what must necessarily be believed by all to gain eternal salvation. In earlier times all catechumens who were being baptized as adults recited this creed publicly with their own lips before being bathed with the water of salvation.

KA Why is it called the rule of faith?

* * * * *

25 Cf Phil 1:6.
26 Cf Rom 8:38–9.
27 Philosophy: see 237 n6 above.
28 The legend that each apostle contributed an article to the creed was extant by the second century; Rufinus draws on this in Rufinus 2 PL 21 338. By Erasmus' time this legend had been severely tested by several scholars, notable among them being Lorenzo Valla; see Kelly *Creeds* 1–13. Erasmus' Parisian censors were concerned that he did not adequately attribute the creed to the apostles; see his reply in *Declarationes ad censuras Lutetiae vulgatas* LB IX 868C–870F. He states specifically in relation to Rufinus, 'Caeterum hoc symbolum fuisse natum ex collatione Apostolorum Cyprianus refert, sed refert ut humanam historiam' (870B).
29 Cf Augustine *De symbolo ad catechumenos* 1.1 PL 40 627: 'Hear, my sons, the rule of faith, which is called the creed.'

CA Because it is by this unvarying measure of truth that all human opinions are directed and corrected, as well as the errors of pagans, Jews, and heretics, which diverge from what is correct in a thousand ways. For divine truth is simple and unalterable, and says, 'Heaven and earth will pass away, my words will not pass away.'[30]

KA But what is the meaning of the word *symbolum* [creed]?

CA For the Greeks *symbolum* is derived from συμβάλλω. This in our language is *confero*, 'I commit, I devote.'[31] The Greeks use this word with a wide variety of meanings. Sometimes they give the name *symbolum* to the seal stamped on letters and vessels to prevent those who should not from opening them. At times those intending to hold a festive celebration gave a *symbolum* by common agreement, so that no one required for it might withdraw. At present a *symbolum* is exchanged by mutual consent between groom and bride so that they not be permitted to withdraw from the contract. Soldiers serving under the same standards were given a *symbolum*, at times certain words to be spoken aloud, at times a silent sign, which they called 'voiceless' (ἄφωνος). In this way, those serving under the same commander recognized one another, and if some enemy tried to disguise himself, they discovered him by this password or sign.[32]

KA I understand these things clearly, but I am waiting to hear about the relevance of these meanings.[33]

CA You see that in baptism the forehead of the one being born anew is marked with the sign of the cross. Blessed Paul, too, calls the Corinthians who had professed their faith in the gospel his 'epistle,'[34] not indeed written in ink on parchment but by the Spirit on hearts. The Spirit is called the finger of God.[35] When a soul is once signed over to God in this way, it is a sacrilege to undo the sign for Satan. The same Paul

* * * * *

30 Matt 24:35

31 This word: *symbolum*; it is derived from συμβάλλω, most literally, 'to bring or throw together.' Erasmus now proceeds to list its concrete applications.

32 Cf the colloquy *Inquisitio de fide* ASD I-3 365:57 / Thompson *Inquisitio* 57 / CWE 39 423:10–11: 'I note the military term, and I'm content to be regarded as an enemy of Christ if I deceive you on this subject.'

33 In other words, the Catechumen wishes to know the relevance of these meanings of *symbolum* to the idea of a rule of faith (see 241 above). Erasmus shows how each of the original applications of the term can be a metaphor for the relationship of the faithful to Christ.

34 2 Cor 3:2

35 Cf Exod 8:19; Luke 11:20.

says to the Corinthians: 'We have this treasure in earthen vessels.'[36] Our soul becomes a vessel of the Holy Spirit by baptism, and is sealed with the seal of faith – or rather, Christ has sealed it with his blood. In the Gospel the Lord compares the kingdom of heaven, that is, the grace of the gospel, to a magnificent feast to which all men and women of every nation are invited.[37] Anybody professing faith in Christ by baptism has made a commitment to this magnificent feast, so that it is no longer lawful to withdraw. Moreover, we frequently read that Christ is designated by the name of 'bridegroom,' just as the church is by the name of 'bride,' for instance, in the mystic Canticle and in John chapter 3.[38] In professing the faith, each and every soul is also united with Christ as its spouse.

Paul makes this clear when writing to the Galatians: 'For I betrothed you to one husband only, to present a chaste virgin to Christ.'[39] Therefore both parties are given a sign or symbol so that it may never be lawful to attempt a divorce. Christ bestows the pledge of his Spirit; man, 'believing in his heart unto justice and professing with his lips unto salvation,'[40] gives in turn a pledge to Christ. As the Apostle says, 'Great is the mystery of this union which joins Christ and the church by an indissoluble bond.'[41]

KA I used to think that only virgins who professed the monastic life are espoused to Christ.

CA These are in truth espoused anew rather than espoused, and they hold first place in the ranks of spouses, closer to him because they are more like him,[42] but in baptism the souls even of sailors, charioteers, and shoemakers become spouses of Christ. The same pledge is given to all equally, to the most despicable beggar and the most powerful king. Assuredly, that fact should give a certain pious pride to those who are

* * * * *

36 2 Cor 4:7
37 Cf Matt 22:1–14; Luke 14:16–24.
38 Song of Sol 4:9–12; John 3:29
39 2 Cor 11:2; Erasmus mistakenly attributes the passage to Galatians.
40 Rom 10:10
41 Eph 5:32
42 Erasmus' views on monastic life are the subject of much controversy and interest. Key texts are the colloquies *Virgo* μισόγαμος ASD I-3 289–97 / CWE 39 279–301 and *Virgo poenitens* ASD I-3 298–300 / CWE 39 302–5; see also Jean-Claude Margolin's introduction to *Encomium matrimonii* in ASD I-5 335–82. In the passage here Erasmus' treatment is comparatively even-handed, as his discussion addresses the theological basis for monastic life rather than the social reality.

castaways in the eyes of the world; in things that alone bring true happiness because they make people truly great, truly rich, truly powerful,
truly noble, they are on equal footing with monarchs, however rich.[43]

KA You are speaking of the Lord's unheard-of kindness.

CA Bah! Whom would that most mild lamb reject? Even as the thief on the
cross was professing his faith, Christ at once invited him to the nuptial
banquet, and from a criminal and blasphemer against himself he made
him a sharer in his kingdom.[44]

KA Indeed, so far everything is fitting together marvellously.

CA Finally,[45] those who are reborn by the sacred washing volunteer for the
army of the gospel and enlist under the immortal ruler, Jesus Christ,
and are bound by oaths of service to him. They receive the donative[46] of
the Spirit, so that to defect from this leader to Satan the tyrant would be
the utmost treachery and also ingratitude. However, not only those who
deny Christ and go over to the Turks or Jews defect, but also those who
with their whole heart are dedicated to the world and worldly comforts.
True, even just people fall as often as seven times a day,[47] but they soon
raise themselves up by the vigour of their faith, which, like a fire, strives
upwards towards the things of heaven.

KA Would that that Spirit might deign to write upon my heart, and seal
what he has written with an imperishable seal.[48]

CA Would that he might deign to entrust that priceless treasure to your
heart and mine[49] and protect with his seal what he has stored there.

KA But we should present him with an unstained parchment and a clean
vessel.

CA Yes, but he himself will supply us even with that, though not without
our cooperation.[50]

* * * * *

43 Cf 1 Cor 1:25–7.

44 Luke 23:42–3

45 Here Erasmus returns to his explanation of the meanings of *symbolum* in relation to faith, beginning his treatment of the fourth meaning following his
explanation of the monastic life.

46 The original meaning for *donativum* is largesse given by the emperor to his
soldiers on special occasions. Cf *Enchiridion* LB V 3A–B / CWE 66 26.

47 Cf Prov 24:16.

48 Seal: *symbolum*

49 Cf Matt 6:21; Luke 12:34.

50 Cf Augustine *Sermones* 169.11.13 PL 38 923: 'Qui ergo fecit te sine te, non te
justificat sine te' / 'Thus he who made you without your help, does not justify
you without your cooperation.'

KA How happy that feast! Here below it bestows the unending joy of a mind at peace with itself, and passes it on to the heavenly feast.

CA How happy is the union that makes us one with God. To cling to him is highest and unparalleled happiness.

KA But 'military service' implies toil.

CA Only someone who has competed according to the rules is crowned.[51] What is irksome here below is of brief duration. The crown is eternal and unfading.[52] The Spirit sweetens the toilsome part with so many consolations that the rest is borne not merely with patience, but with alacrity. Whether we like it or not, this life is a warfare;[53] we must do battle on the side of God or of Satan. Those who fight on the side of Satan, who is called the prince of this world, endure a harder lot than those who fight on the side of Christ. The soldiers of Christ have no less joy than those who hunt for pleasure by land and sea; on the contrary, they alone have real joy. As for remuneration, how enormous is the difference – to celebrate an eternal triumph with the leader Christ, or to be consigned to eternal fire with the tyrant Satan.

KA It is strange then that so many men lead a life under Satan's leadership.

CA The reason is that many recite the creed with their lips, but few believe with their hearts,[54] or if they do believe it, they believe without ardour.

KA I want to learn the rudiments of this heavenly philosophy at once.

CA Rudiments they are, but what is lowest here surpasses all the heights of worldly wisdom. Since, however, we understand better and sooner what we learn with eagerness, those who teach worldly disciplines make them more acceptable to their pupils by using various headings – especially author, matter, basis, and goal.[55]

KA I do not fully understand what you are saying.

CA For instance, medicine has Hippocrates[56] as its founder and, if we believe the poets, Apollo. It deals with what helps or hinders bodily health. This is its matter. It is based on knowledge of the things of nature and on experiments. Regard this as its basis. Its goal is the

* * * * *

51 Cf 2 Tim 2:5.
52 Cf Tertullian *De corona* 15.2 PL 2 122.
53 Cf 2 Cor 10:3–6, and the opening to the *Enchiridion* LB V 1A / CWE 66 24.
54 Cf Rom 10:10.
55 These are based on the four types of causes according to Aristotle's *Metaphysics* 4.2 1013b: material, formal, efficient, and final.
56 Hippocrates of Cos (c 460–380 BC), Greek physician, highly influential to the subsequent practice of medicine, although his works have been lost

good health of the body, in so far as it is granted to have good health
here.

KA No mention of financial gain?

CA That perhaps is the goal of some practitioners, but the goal of the art is
good health. To give another example: the Stoic philosophy has Zeno[57]
as its founder; its matter is questions of moral goodness and turpitude;
it makes deductions by logical reasoning; it promises peace of mind, but
only in this life, and false peace at that. For nothing gives true peace
to our souls except the grace of Christ, with which the Stoics have no
acquaintance, even in dreams.[58]

God, however, is the author of this philosophy for which you are now
a candidate; its matter is a holy life; its basis is inspiration by the eternal
Godhead; its goal is heavenly life. To put it better, God himself is all
these things. Zeno, however, deceives and is deceived in many matters,
and, since his mind is confused about the goal, he must of necessity
be blind about the means also. But here, where God is all things to all
people,[59] there can be no error, no darkness, no ambiguity. He himself
is the beginning, he is the movement forward, he is the consummation.
If people are found who are eager to learn human disciplines with the
greatest toil, great cost, and great expenditure of time, with how great
an ardour of heart is it fitting to learn thoroughly the philosophy[60] that,
originating with God, leads by the short path of an immaculate life to
that happy immortality!

KA You are assuredly giving an account of a precious pearl which can stand
comparison with every pearl ever sold.[61]

CA That pearl is a good bargain even at the cost of one's life – nay, rather,
it would be bought cheaply even at the cost of a thousand lives. Furthermore, I do not think that it is necessary to develop here the points
that would make you a well-disposed, attentive, and teachable student.
Love of the teacher is a great stimulus to progress. What, however, is
more lovable than God, or rather, what is at all lovable except him?
Who would be drowsy when listening to him promise eternal joys? If

* * * * *

57 Zeno of Citium (c 336–265 BC), Greek philosopher, founder of the Stoic school
of philosophy
58 Erasmus does not always show such contempt for pagan philosophy; cf the
colloquy *Convivium religiosum* ASD I-3 231–66 / CWE 39 171–243, or more specifically, *Enchiridion* LB V 13F / CWE 66 44, where Erasmus uses Stoic philosophy
as a support for his contention that reason must rule over the passions.
59 Cf 1 Cor 15:28.
60 See 237 n6 above.
61 Cf Matt 13:46.

someone loves God above everything else and without hesitation trusts in him alone in all things, he is willing and teachable.[62]

KA More and more my soul takes fire.

CA If you agree, let what we have discussed so far be the first lesson. When you have implored the aid of the Holy Spirit, turned the lesson over in your mind, and given some thought to it, come back to me to learn the rest.

KA It will be done.

Lesson 2

KA I have done what you ordered, and my thirst to hear the rest is even keener.

CA Thanks be to the most kind Spirit of Christ. What remains is that, first of all, you have the creed recited for you; you will more easily grasp it if you understand it in general and learn the order of its articles.

KA I am ready.

CA Listen.

KA I am listening.

CA 'I believe in God, the Father almighty, creator of heaven and earth, and in Jesus Christ, his only Son, our Lord, who was conceived of the Holy Spirit, born of the Virgin Mary, suffered under Pontius Pilate, was crucified, died, and was buried. He descended into hell, on the third day he arose again from the dead, ascended into heaven. He sits at the right hand of God, the Father almighty, thence he shall come to judge the living and the dead. I believe in the Holy Spirit, the holy Catholic church, the communion of saints, the forgiveness of sin, the resurrection of the body, and life everlasting. Amen.'

KA I am listening to what is clearly an abbreviated account.

CA And you see a grain of mustard seed.[1] You already hold, I believe, that there is one God, but that this name embraces three Persons, the Father who alone is from no one,[2] the Son begotten of the Father before time began, the Holy Spirit proceeding from both.

* * * * *

62 See 236 n3 above.

1 Matt 17:9; Luke 17:6

2 Cf the colloquy *Inquisitio de fide* ASD I-3 367:110 / CWE 39 424:33: 'The Father alone is from none'; and Thomas Aquinas *Summa theologica* I q 33 art 1, in which Aquinas concludes that the Father is a principle, 'as the Father is the one whence another proceeds,' being careful to note that a principle is not a cause.

KA Yes, I hold that.

CA Let not our minds imagine anything temporal or corporeal here; everything is eternal, ineffable, incomprehensible; things to which the human
mind is blind are perceived by faith alone. The three Persons are distinguished by properties, but in them is the same substance or nature or
(to use a word some think more fitting) essence,[3] the same omnipotence,
the same majesty, the same wisdom, the same goodness. Here we have
a threefold reality, but no inequality whatsoever. No Person is later in
time than another or inferior in dignity.[4] There is one divinity in the
three, and the three are one God. The major divisions in the creed arise
from this truth. The Father holds first place, the Son holds second, the
Holy Spirit, who is love and an ineffable bond between the other two,
holds the third. The Father creates the world, the Son restored it when
it had fallen, the Holy Spirit operates in concert with both.

KA I accept this.

CA In the Son the divine nature is in no way lessened or changed because
he alone assumed a human nature;[5] although he is one person, he has,
however, a threefold substance: the divine, in which he is identical with
the Father and the Holy Spirit, a human soul, and a human body. As
he is begotten of God the Father, he is true God. As born of a human
mother, he is true man. The church is attached to him as the human body
is attached to its head.[6] As that divine Spirit binds the Father and Son
closely together, so too he fastens the church to Christ by an invisible
and indissoluble bond. The mystical body of Christ occupies the fourth
part of the creed.[7] There are other divisions within it, but this basic one

* * * * *

3 Cf Augustine *De haeresibus* 49 PL 42 39: 'Father and Son and Holy Spirit are
of the same nature or substance or, to put it more clearly, essence, which is
called οὐσία by the Greeks.'

4 See the Paraphrase on John 1:2 LB VII 499C: 'He is always one, whole, and altogether in himself: and the Son is continually begotten of him ... eternal of him
that is eternal, almighty of him that is almighty, supreme good from supreme
good, in sum God from God, neither issuing later in time nor inferior.'

5 Human nature: Erasmus' debate with John Colet on Christ's agony in the garden of Gethsemane demonstrates Erasmus' concept of Christ's human nature
as fully human, capable of pain, grief, and fear of death. See *De taedio Iesu* 48–
50 above. In Ep 109, Erasmus writes, 'Surely at that moment he spoke as a
man, for men, to men, and in the words of men, expressing men's fears ...'
(lines 49–50).

6 Col 1:18

7 That is, the Holy Catholic church. The third part is 'I believe in the Holy
Spirit.'

will open a way of considerable light for the beginner. Now, then, you recite the creed.

KA I will. 'I believe in God, the Father almighty, creator of heaven and earth.'

CA You have the First Person.

KA 'And in Jesus Christ, his only Son, our Lord.'

CA You have now entered the second part of the creed, which deals with the divine nature of Christ about which we have spoken.

KA 'Who was conceived of the Holy Spirit,' and so forth.

CA You are now hearing about the true and perfect human nature of Christ, and are soon to hear about the redemption of the human race.

KA 'Suffered under Pontius Pilate, was crucified, died, and was buried.'

CA Besides hearing so many most trustworthy proofs that Christ was truly man, you are learning about the marvellous battle of Christ against Satan the tyrant.

KA 'He descended into hell.'

CA You are hearing what that most holy soul of Christ did during the time that his lifeless body rested in the tomb.

KA 'He arose the third day.'

CA You are being instructed about the victory of the head and the hope of the members.

KA 'He ascended into heaven.'

CA You are hearing of the victor's triumph.

KA 'He sits at the right hand of God, the Father almighty.'

CA You are hearing of the eternal and insuperable reign of Christ, 'to whom all power has been given in heaven as well as on earth.'[8]

KA 'Thence he shall come to judge the living and the dead.'

CA You are being told of the second coming. He first came in the humility of the flesh as saviour[9] of all; later he will come in the glory of the Father to judge both the devout and the impious and to give recompense to each and everyone according to his merits.[10]

KA 'I believe in the Holy Spirit.'

CA This is the third part of the creed.

KA 'The holy church,' and so forth.

* * * * *

8 Matt 28:18

9 Erasmus uses the classical Latin term *servator* for σωτήρ rather than *salvator*, the term preferred by most Christian writers; cf Rufinus 6 PL 21 345.

10 Cf Matt 16:27; Rom 2:6. The Vulgate uses the word *acta* rather than *meriti*, the term Erasmus uses here.

CA This is the fourth part of the creed, which describes the church, the mystical body of Christ. Now if you take it to be one with Christ, there are only three Persons. The holy church is also fittingly joined to the Holy Spirit, for by his favour true holiness exists in created things; that is why he is also called the 'Spirit of sanctification'[11] by Paul. He is the Spirit of the spouse who never withdraws from the embrace of the bride. Since the word 'church' [ecclesia] in Greek means 'assembly,' it is through him that whatever has been auspiciously brought together stays together. This is the indescribable circle that binds together in one the three Persons and with them holy human beings and holy angels.[12] The term 'church' can also include those blessed spirits, although the Lord did not come to redeem those who persevered in the state of happiness in which they were created. The human race, since it fell with our first parents, needed a redeemer. Go on reciting.

KA 'The communion of saints.'

CA Some interpret this small section as an explanation of the previous one, 'the holy church,' by apposition.[13] The word ecclesia [church] indicates a society, and among all the members of Christ there is a perpetual and inseparable union. Some interpreters prefer the opinion that the seven sacraments of the church are indicated by these words, some that the communion of all good works is indicated.[14]

KA 'The forgiveness of sin.'

CA Here you learn about the dealings of this society in this world, in which, just as perfect happiness does not exist, neither does perfect purity or fulfilment. There is thus often a need for a remedy for those who have fallen into serious faults, and a need for a way to strengthen the weak. The grace of God supplies both needs through various means, but especially through the sacraments of the church. When, therefore, you hear of the remission of sin, you are hearing of a twofold medicine[15] that has been prepared – one from the sacred washing in baptism, the other through the sacrament of penance.

KA 'The resurrection of the body.'

* * * * *

11 Rom 1:4
12 Cf Augustine *De civitate Dei* 10.7 PL 41 284: 'For with us [the angels] make one City of God.'
13 See Kelly *Creeds* 390.
14 See 337 n4 below.
15 This is a frequently used metaphor in Erasmus' work, notably in the dedicatory epistle to the Paraphrase on Luke LB VII 271–80.

CA Here is revealed the end of the warfare, the consummation of the church, and the eternal happiness or eternal misery of the entire person.

KA 'And life everlasting.'

CA You are hearing the incomparable reward that our general has prepared for his soldiers if, following the example of their leader, they fight faithfully under his standards and conduct themselves with zeal until the moment of their death. You now have the introduction, the body, and the conclusion[16] of this salvific drama; you have all the acts and the celestial scenes of this heavenly choragus[17] set forth in an arrangement beyond powers of description.

KA Are there some who would make more subtle divisions?

CA Some more recent interpreters have thirteen articles instead of twelve. Some have fourteen,[18] not following the arrangement of the text. Influenced by the fact that all the articles pertain either to the divine nature of all three Persons, or to the human nature of Christ, or to the mystical body of Christ, they accordingly introduce certain small sections and thus arrive at fourteen. This is, in truth, of little consequence for our purpose. Following that lead it would be possible to contrive further divisions because of different ways of conceptualizing and of different aspects of the same subject. But the source of all divisions is this: it says here that the world was created by God in his power and redeemed by the same God through his Son in his wisdom and mercy, and it describes the beginning and development of the church as the Holy Spirit guides it by inward inspirations, and the consummation of the church, when the Son hands over to the Father a kingdom that is pure and at peace.[19]

* * * * *

16 The *protasis*, or introduction, is the early part of a play, before the action has really begun. The *epitasis*, body, is the main part of the play, where the action takes place. The *catastrophe* or conclusion is the end of the play. Cf *Adagia* I II 36 LB II 83E–84A / CWE 31 177–8.

17 χορηγός in Greek originally meant the chorus-leader, a very important role in the drama. Both this term and its Latin counterpart *choragus* came to refer to the person who financed the play or banquet, and by extension, to one who supplies or provides.

18 There was a widespread use of fourteen articles in the Middle Ages; cf Thomas Aquinas *Summa theologica* II-II q 1 art 8. Erasmus in *Declarationes ad censuras Lutetiae vulgatas* LB IX 870C–D writes, 'non arbitror ad fidei causam pertinere, praesertim cum in partitione articulorum non consentiant Theologi, magisque placeat partitio, quae xiv. facit, quam quae xii' / 'I don't believe the matter is pertinent to the faith, especially since theologians disagree in dividing the articles, and more prefer dividing them into fourteen than into twelve.'

19 1 Cor 15:24

KA Some attribute each article to one of the apostles.[20]

CA If that is true, those who want fourteen articles are mistaken. But the attribution you mentioned, however, was devised for a practical purpose, that illiterate people might with the same effort fix in their memory, as if through images arranged in order, both the names of the apostles and the individual articles of the creed. It would in fact be eminently fitting that the halls of all Christians be decorated with panels of this kind.

KA Immortal God! What a wealth of philosophy this short creed embraces.

CA Yet it is probable that among the earliest Christians it was somewhat shorter, since they seem to have concluded the creed with this phrase: 'thence he will come to judge the living and the dead.' This can be deduced from the creed of Athanasius. When he is explaining it, he touches on none of the later articles; nor does the creed referred to in the canons as pre-Nicene go any further, except that it adds 'and in the Holy Spirit'; otherwise it differs in many words both from ours and from the one sung at mass, which seems to come from the Synod of Constantinople.[21] It can be deduced also from Tertullian, for example, from the book against Praxeas, and again from the opening section of the book 'On the Veiling of Virgins,' as well as from 'On Proscribing Heretics.'[22]

KA Then is what has been added redundant?

* * * * *

20 See 241 n28 above.

21 Bakhuizen van den Brink's introduction in ASD V-1 189–90 cites Albertus Magnus *Compendium* 5.21 from *Opera omnia* 34 ed A. Borgnet (Paris 1899) 170, who compares three creeds known in the church: the Apostles' Creed, the creed for the mass (which Albertus describes as the Nicene Creed but which actually was the creed affirmed by the 381 synod at Constantinople), and the Athanasian Creed. First appearing in its complete form in the ninth century, the Athanasian Creed, otherwise known as 'quicunque vult,' was during the Middle Ages attributed to the fourth-century anti-Arian bishop of Alexandria, but since the seventeenth century the association has been disproved. It is believed instead to have had its origin at a later date in southern Gaul.

22 Tertullian *Adversus Praxeam* 2 PL 2 156–7, in preparing to attack his opponent, includes a short, creedlike iteration of Christian belief which extends beyond the phrase mentioned by Erasmus to include the Holy Spirit. In *De praescriptionibus haereticorum* 13 PL 2 26–7 he announces and proclaims a rule of faith, more detailed than the former, including the resurrection of the body but not the sections pertaining to the Holy Spirit. *De virginibus velandis* 1 PL 2 937 includes a very brief formula, ending with the resurrection of the flesh but omitting any mention of the Holy Spirit, even in reference to Christ's nativity.

CA God forbid! No, those parts were added, however, to deal with contentious and stupid people, and to make the statement more explicit,
not longer. For when you hear 'who was conceived of the Holy Spirit,'
you hear a profession of faith in the Third Person. When you hear
that Christ suffered, you have at the same moment a knowledge of
the church for which he suffered, for the Lord did not suffer for angels,[23] who did not need it, or for demons, who have fallen irrepara-
bly, and much less for irrational animals. With the same expression
you hear of the source of universal forgiveness. Neither baptism nor
the sacrament of penance has its efficacy from any other source than
our Lord's most sacred death. Likewise when you hear 'he arose, ascended into heaven,' you witness a manifestation of the resurrection
of the body, which we all await with firm hope, for the head, reigning in heaven, will not suffer his members to be mutilated or incomplete. He arose whole and entire; we too will arise whole and entire.
Finally when you hear 'thence he shall come to judge the living and
the dead,' the word 'judge' designates the different recompenses for
the godly and the ungodly, which is then stated more clearly: 'and life
everlasting.'

KA Why is this called the Apostles' Creed?

CA So that it may be distinguished by its title from other creeds: the Nicene
Creed, the Constantinopolitan Creed, the Athanasian Creed, and several others.[24] It is probable, too, that this one was the first of all. Among
the men of old who were uncultivated, simple, unacquainted with de-
ceptions, men of good faith, contracts either were unwritten, even the
most important ones, or were as short as possible. It was sufficient to
note on paper, 'I freely give as a gift or bequeath so many acres of land
to such a church.' Thus, as long as sincerity and trust flourished in human hearts, either there was no need for a surety in one's own hand-
writing, or one in the fewest possible words was sufficient. The impious inquisitiveness of philosophers and the perversity of heretics gave
rise to a multitude of words and creeds, just as human cunning has
caused a need for so many and such wordy contracts.[25] In none of the
churches did the ardour of piety and sincerity of faith flourish longer
than in the Roman church; into none of them did heresy creep to a lesser

* * * * *

23 Cf Augustine *Enchiridion* 61.16 PL 40 260: 'It was not for the angels that Christ
died.'

24 See 252 n21 above.

25 Cf *Moria* ASD IV-3 110:724–111:739 / CWE 27 107.

degree or more slowly.[26] Would that the meretricious allurements of this world had not inundated it! Indeed the very creed which St Cyprian[27] proposed is somewhat shorter than the one we have.

KA Recite it, I beg you, if it is not too much trouble.

CA I believe in God, the Father almighty, and in Jesus Christ, his only Son, our Lord, who was born of the Holy Spirit from the Virgin Mary, was crucified under Pontius Pilate, and was buried; he arose on the third day, ascended into heaven, sits at the right hand of God; thence he shall come to judge the living and the dead; and in the Holy Spirit, the holy church, the forgiveness of sin, the resurrection of this body.

KA I see that much has been omitted and a little even added.

CA St Cyprian[28] does not conceal this fact. Right at the beginning of the first article, he points out that the eastern churches added, 'I believe in God, the Father almighty, invisible and incapable of suffering.'[29] Further, he denies that the addition 'he descended into hell' is found in the Roman Creed.[30] Concerning the phrase 'in the resurrection of *this* body' he acknowledges that the demonstrative pronoun was added in the church of Carthage.[31] Some things are missing – rather, not missing, but understood from context. Cyprian, it seems, does not add 'creator of heaven and earth,' but deduces it from the Greek word παντοκράτωρ,[32] which does not so much mean omnipotent as possessing all things and

* * * * *

26 Cf Rufinus 3 PL 21 339 / Kelly *Commentary* 31: 'Certain additions are to be found in this article in some churches. No such development, however, can be detected in the case of the church of the city of Rome. The reason, I suppose, is that no heresy has ever originated there.' Erasmus' statement is less positive, implying that some heresy has slowly managed to creep into even the Roman church.

27 Cyprian: read Rufinus.

28 Cyprian: read Rufinus here and below in this paragraph.

29 Rufinus 5 PL 21 344. He also points out that the eastern churches add 'I believe in *one* God, the Father Almighty' (ibidem 4 PL 21 340–1). According to Rufinus, the terms 'invisible' and 'impassible' were included in predecessors to the Roman Creed in order to thwart heretics. On the anti-heretical bias of creeds see Kelly *Creeds* 64–5, 97–9. Kelly sees the early creeds as written primarily to affirm faith, and only secondarily to thwart heresy, although a tendency towards the latter function became more pronounced in later creeds.

30 Rufinus 18 PL 21 356

31 Carthage: read Aquileia, which was the church in which Rufinus was baptized.

32 2 Cor 6:18; Rev 1:8, 4:8, 11:17, 21:22; see also Origen *De principibus* 1.2.10 PG 11 138–42. The Latin *omnipotens* appears to emphasize God's creative power, while παντοκράτωρ, literally, 'creator of all things,' emphasizes his having brought all things into being.

governing all things. This word not only indicates that the world was created by God, but is a reminder that it is governed by him also. God would not govern something created by another. Since, indeed, the pagans, instructed by the poets, believe that the world was created by God and the book of Genesis teaches it explicitly,[33] they decided that the truth of this phrase was too evident to need expression.

Also omitted are the words 'who was conceived,' because in the Gospel 'was born' is used for 'was conceived.' This is how the angel speaks to Joseph: 'For that which is born in her is of the Holy Spirit.'[34] This word, used to mean both conception and birth, seemed to the Fathers more suitable for indicating what was the work of the Holy Spirit, for there was no human concupiscence in the conception, or infringement of the Virgin's dignity and bodily integrity in the birth.[35] The word 'conception,' moreover, signifies something unformed and incomplete. The semen grows in the womb by degrees, and then is given life. We are loath to preach such things about the conception of the Lord.

Again, in the next article, Cyprian does not say,[36] 'He suffered,' as we do, but rather, 'He was crucified,' so as to indicate not only that he died, but even how he died. He did not then add 'He died,' but only 'He was buried.' For men are led to the cross that they may die there, and they are not buried unless it is certain that they are dead. Furthermore, when he adds 'He arose,' that is, he came to life again, Cyprian announces clearly enough that Christ died. Nor in this does Augustine differ from Cyprian for he says, 'Accordingly we believe in him who was crucified under Pontius and buried.'[37]

Cyprian does not say, 'He arose from the dead,' but only, 'He arose on the third day,' for no one comes back to life except from death. In the phrase 'He sits at the right hand of the Father' he does not add 'of God' or 'almighty'; these words seem to have been added from the creed of Athanasius.[38] What need was there for them? Shortly before he had called the Father of Jesus 'omnipotent God.'

* * * * *

33 Gen 1:1
34 Matt 1:20
35 See 294–5 below.
36 Cyprian: read Rufinus here and below in this paragraph, and in the next.
37 Augustine *De fide et symbolo* 5.11 PL 40 187
38 See Kelly *Creeds* 177–9, 375. Kelly attributes the first appearance of this addition to the creed of Priscillian (Spanish bishop and heretic, d 385), and ascribes little importance to it.

He does not have the reading 'I believe in the Holy Spirit,' lest he should seem to be starting a new creed. Rather, keeping in mind the opening words of the creed, he preferred to imply the expression 'I believe' for the Spirit, as he had implied it in the case of the Son: 'I believe in God the Father and in his only Son ... and in the Holy Spirit.'[39] It is the same faith by which we believe in three Persons with one essence.

Then, in the phrase 'in the holy church,' Cyprian omits the preposition 'in,' explaining at great length the reason why it should not be added,[40] and he does not add the word 'Catholic.' (Augustine does not add it in the creed either, although he indicates it in his interpretation: '... undoubtedly,' he says, 'Catholic.')[41] What need, however, was there to add the word? There is no holy church except the Catholic, which the epithet 'holy' separates from all the churches of heretics, Jews, and gentiles.[42] Furthermore, after Cyprian says, 'and in the Holy Spirit,' he immediately adds 'the holy church,' omitting even the preposition. It is clear that Cyprian[43] did not have the reading 'in the holy church.'

Finally the ending, 'and eternal life,' has been omitted.[44] It was sufficiently understood from the word 'resurrection,' in which are included the different recompenses of the devout and the impious; the concept of eternal life is implied as well as by the preceding phrase, 'to judge the living and the dead,' as has already been said. Furthermore, it is clear not only from Cyprian's commentary[45] but also from the epilogue he attached to it that Cyprian's text conforms to what I have read aloud, For he shows that the preposition 'in' is added only in the case of the Father, the Son, and the Holy Spirit, but not to any of the other articles, and he recites the creed accordingly.

* * * * *

39 Rufinus 35 PL 21 372 / Kelly *Commentary* 70
40 Cyprian: read Rufinus; Rufinus 36 PL 21 373 / Kelly *Commentary* 71–2.
41 Augustine *De fide et symbolo* 10.21 PL 40 193
42 See ibidem: 'Wherefore neither do the heretics belong to the Catholic church, which loves God, nor do the schismatics ...'; and *De symbolo ad catechumenos* 6.14 PL 40 635: 'This same is the holy church, the one church, the true church, the Catholic church, fighting against all heresies.'
43 Cyprian: read Rufinus; Rufinus 36 PL 21 373 / Kelly *Commentary* 71: '... in the clauses in which our faith in the Godhead is laid down, we use the form *in God the Father, in Jesus Christ his Son,* and *in the Holy Spirit*. In other clauses, where the theme is not the godhead but created things and saving mysteries, the preposition *in* is not interpolated.'
44 Rufinus 45 PL 21 383–4; see Kelly *Creeds* 386–7.
45 Cyprian: read Rufinus.

After these parts there follows 'the holy church, the remission of sins, the resurrection of this body.' He does not use the preposition 'in' with 'holy church' or 'remission of sins' or 'resurrection of the body.' (In his own explanation of the phrase 'resurrection of the body,' in the creed, however, he prefaces the word 'resurrection' with the preposition 'in.') The final article of the creed, which proclaims the resurrection, concludes that perfect summary concisely and briefly.[46] Does not Cyprian clearly call this clause the final one? Someone seems to have added two additional words, 'eternal life,' later, either from the Athanasian Creed or from the one that is sung at mass.[47]

Augustine's readings in his pamphlet *On the Creed* do not differ, except that for '... [conceived] of [*de*] the Holy Spirit' he reads '... [conceived] through [*per*] the Holy Spirit,'[48] and it is rather doubtful whether he added 'eternal life' at the end of the creed.[49] He probably agrees with Cyprian.[50] Certainly he does not mention the article 'he descended into hell,' nor does he add the demonstrative pronoun in the phrase '[resurrection] of *this* flesh.' Cyprian,[51] on the other hand, indicated discrepancies in some cases, and he would also have pointed it out in others if the Roman Creed differed from what he says himself.

KA Since there is so great a variation in a few words, how had some men the effrontery to assert that this creed was promulgated by common agreement among the apostles, or even written by them? Who indeed would dare to add or take away even one particle in the writing of any apostle?[52]

CA A certain king of Macedonia, in answer to the question as to why the ephors did not stand up to honour the king, said, 'Just because they are

* * * * *

46 Rufinus 41 PL 21 378; cf Jerome *Liber contra Ioannem Hierosolymitanum* 28 PL 23 380: 'In symbolo fidei et spei nostrae ... post confessionem Trinitatis et unitatem ecclesiae omne Christiani dogmatis sacramentum carnis resurrectione concluditur.'

47 Western creeds were slow in incorporating the reference to 'life everlasting' more characteristic of eastern creeds. See Kelly *Commentary* 149 n258.

48 See Augustine *De fide et symbolo* 4.8 PL 40 186: 'credentes in eum Dei Filium qui natus est per Spiritum sanctum ex virgine Maria.'

49 Augustine *De fide et symbolo* 10.24 PL 40 196 refers to eternal life, but the reference represents his interpretation of the resurrection of the body rather than another element of the creed.

50 Cyprian: read Rufinus here and in the rest of the paragraph.

51 See 254 above.

52 Cf *Declarationes ad censuras Lutetiae vulgatas* LB IX 869B–C.

ephors.'[53] I could now give you a similar answer: they assert that the apostles wrote the creed just because they are human. If they have read something in modern writers, they hold it tight between their jaws. If anything is cited from ancient writers, whom they do not read, they suspect that a scorpion is asleep under every rock, for they are very nervous in the matter of religion.

KA So this is not the creed of the apostles?

CA It most certainly is. The apostles learned from Christ whatever is handed down here, and what they have learned from him they have passed on to us in good faith. A few words do not change an unchangeable truth.[54] But passing over these matters, if you please, go over the material from beginning to end and, point by point, ask whatever questions the Spirit prompts.

KA You have taught me why the Father has been given first place, because he is the source of the whole godhead and of all created things. But why is the Father alone called 'God,' the Son merely 'Lord,'[55] and the Spirit nothing except 'Holy,' when they all partake of the same divinity?

CA This is the custom of the mystic Scripture. In references to the Persons, the Father is sometimes designated by the word 'God.' As, for example, when the Lord himself says in the Gospel, 'If you believe in God, believe also in me.'[56] And St Paul: 'God was in Christ, reconciling the world to himself.'[57] 'God did not spare his own Son.'[58] But it is clear from numerous scriptural passages that the three partake of the same divinity. When the Lord in the Gospel says, 'baptizing them in the name of the Father and the Son and the Holy Spirit,'[59] no Person is given the

* * * * *

53 Plutarch *Moralia* (*Apophthegmata Laconica*) 217C. Ephors were the highest officials in Sparta.

54 This reflects what is for Erasmus an important principle of interpretation; see eg his defence of his use of *sermo* in his annotation on John 1:1 LB VI 335 A–B.

55 *Inquisitio de fide* ASD I-3 366:106 / Thompson *Inquisitio* 61 / CWE 39 424:27–8: 'Quur igitur sacrae literae Filium magis apellant Dominum quam Deum?' / 'Why, then, does Sacred Scripture quite frequently call the Son "Lord" rather than "God"?' The Sorbonne censured this passage along with others from the *Colloquies* in 1526, claiming that both names are applied to Father and Son indifferently; see LB IX 943F–944A and Erasmus' defence, LB IX 944A–945B. See also ASD I-3 371:249 / Thompson *Inquisitio* 69 / CWE 39 428:27–8 for a parallel passage regarding the Holy Spirit, also censured by the Sorbonne.

56 John 14:1

57 2 Cor 5:19

58 Rom 8:32

59 Matt 28:19

epithet 'God,' so as to make us understand that the three are one God. For only God can remit sins through faith and baptism. Sometimes they also designate the Son by the word 'God' – for example, when we say that God became human for the salvation of the human race, that he was born of a virgin, that he died and came to life again. For neither the Father nor the Holy Spirit assumed flesh or died.

KA Can it be shown by any proof directed to the senses how they can be called three distinct Persons and yet one God?

CA There is nothing in creation which can properly be said to resemble the divine nature, nor are there any human words in which we might speak of it appropriately. Neither are there any human concepts which coincide by a measuring stick, as they say, with the divine essence. An injury too is done the majesty that demands adoration if it is rashly compared with things human. However, I will give an example similar in at least one respect, though very different in others. Consider the sun and the rays emanating from it, and then the heat that originates in both of them. As the sun is the source of light and heat, so the Father is the source of the Son, who is light from light.[60] And as heat emanates at the same time from both the sun and the rays, so too, the Holy Spirit proceeds from the Father and the Son. Now please imagine a sun that never had a beginning and will never cease to be. Would not eternal rays be born of this, and would not heat also proceed from both eternally?[61]

KA Certainly.

CA The following comparison finds favour with some: the same soul is mind, reason, and will. The mind is the source. Reason emanating from it makes judgments. The will, which proceeds from both, loves. In the same manner, the Father is the source; the Son is the word (λόγος), that is, reason; the Holy Spirit is love.[62] A third simile is favoured especially by the learned. It concerns the mind and the word conceived in the mind; if any mind were uncreated, without doubt its word would be uncreated. In order that we may include the Holy Spirit in this comparison, let us postulate a mind and a word born of the mind that fully expresses its thought to others. Let us also postulate breath, without which the mind

* * * * *

60 Cf Nicene Creed, 'lumen de lumine.'
61 Cf Tertullian *Adversus Praxeam* 8 PL 2 163: 'For God sent forth the Word, as the Paraclete also declares, just as the root puts forth the tree, and the fountain the river, and the sun the ray.'
62 Cf Augustine *De Trinitate* 9 PL 42 959–72, in which Augustine draws the analogy of the mind, its knowledge of itself, and its love for itself.

does not express the word. The mind is the Father, the word conceived in the mind is the Son, the utterance is the Holy Spirit.[63] The fountain-head too has some resemblance to the Father, as the stream rising from the fountain resembles the Son, and the fertility of the fields, which the fountain bestows on us through the stream, resembles the Holy Spirit.[64]

There are, however, countless discrepancies in these examples. A ray is not the same as the sun, since it is a substance in its own right. In so far as heat, on the other hand, is an accident, not a substance, it is that much further from being identical with the sun and its rays.[65] Our words are accidents and passing things, and so is the breath by which we exhale them; in fact, it is a movement of air.[66] Nor is fertility a substance, and it is not the same as the fountain and the river. Therefore let us dispense with these images. What human reason cannot reach, let faith hold fast;[67] what the sacred writings hand down, what Christ in the flesh taught, what has been confirmed by so many miracles, what the Spirit of Christ teaches through the church – these are to be held with far greater confidence than what is proved by a thousand demonstrations

* * * * *

63 Ibidem 9.7.12 PL 42 967: 'The true knowledge of things ... we bear with us as a word, and beget by speaking from within; nor does it depart from us by being born. But in conversing with others we add the service of our voice or of some bodily sign to the word that remains within, in order to produce in the mind of the listener, by a kind of sensible remembrance, something similar to that which does not depart from the mind of the speaker.' Augustine does not draw the analogy directly between these three elements and the three Persons of the Trinity as does Erasmus, but rather uses speech as a means to further his discussion of the relationship between knowledge and love.

64 Fountain: see 259 n61 above; see also Rufinus 4 PL 21 342; Bar 3:12.

65 Aristotle *Analytica posteriora* 1.22 83a23–7: 'Predicates which signify substance signify that the subject is identical with the predicate or with a species of the predicate. Predicates not signifying substance which are predicated of a subject not identical with themselves or with a species of themselves are accidental or coincidental ...' Erasmus' point, that nothing can be predicated accidentally of God, indicates that everything attributable to God is his by necessity, describing his essence.

66 Tertullian *Adversus Praxeam* 7 PL 2 162: 'For you will say, what is a word, but a voice and sound of the mouth, and ... air when struck against ... I, on the contrary, contend that nothing empty and void could have come forth from God; ... nor could that possibly be devoid of substance which has proceeded from so great a substance.' Cf also Augustine *Confessions* 11.7.

67 Cf Augustine *De symbolo ad catechumenos* 2.4 PL 40 629: 'First believe, then understand.'

or what you may perceive by six hundred senses, if you have that many senses.

KA Is it then a sin to inquire into things divine?

CA It is lawful, especially for those who have well-trained intellects, but it must be done with awe and seriousness[68] after the foundation of faith has been securely laid and, finally, only to the extent granted in this mortal life, where we see God by faith only dimly, as in a mirror.[69] In other respects, not even the minds of the seraphim comprehend the divine nature as it is, so that in their case too there is some room for faith, which believes what transcends all created intellect. It is, therefore, with the best right that the first word of this philosophy[70] is *credo,* 'I believe.'

KA Two syllables only?

CA Yes, but whoever pronounces them sincerely is blessed. For one does not truly believe in God unless he holds as completely authentic all that is recorded in the sacred volumes, hoping without doubt for what they promise, fearing what they threaten. In this life, the believer gives over his entire self, those connected with him, and all his possessions to the divine will, renouncing his own will in all things. Even if a thousand deaths should threaten, even if the demons in all their power should set ruin in motion, he is safest who fastens himself to this rock.[71] If this faith is lacking, neither baptism nor any other sacraments of the church are of use, and no good works bring eternal life.[72]

Further, Paul proclaims that whatever is without faith is also a sin.[73] Faith joins us to God the Father; faith joins us with Christ, the head; faith, through the Spirit of Christ, admits us to the number of the sons of God; faith introduces us to the eternal community of all the angels and saints;[74] faith shines in the darkness of this life, showing what is truly to be shunned, what is to be sought; faith arms us and makes us fearless and invincible in the face of all the devices of the world and

* * * * *

68 Cf Phil 2:12: 'You must work out your salvation with fear and trembling.'
69 1 Cor 13:12
70 *Philosophia Christi:* see 237 n6 above.
71 *Haec petra:* Matt 16:18
72 Cf the colloquy *Naufragium* ASD I-3 329:143–54 / Thompson *Colloquies* 143 / CWE 39 357:7–19 for a sense of Erasmus' attitude regarding the relationship between the sacraments and faith.
73 Rom 14:23
74 Cf Rufinus 41 PL 21 378–9: 'As a result, those who have been raised from the earth dwell no longer on the earth with brute beasts, but in heaven with angels'; and *Inquisitio de fide* ASD I-3 370:221–2 / CWE 39 427:39.

Satan; faith effectively consoles us with the hope of heavenly goods in times of sorrow, ever having on its lips the words 'If God is for us, who is against us?'[75] and 'The sufferings of this present time are not worth comparing with the glory that will be revealed in us.'[76] Faith truly calms the soul. Blessed Paul declares that anything ever done with fortitude, piety, and restraint by men renowned for holiness is attributable to faith. Through faith, we live as friends of God; through faith, we meet death eagerly and with strong confidence; through faith, we are carried to that blessed immortality. Again, for want of faith are born superstition, fortune-telling, idolatry and its brother avarice, ambition, blasphemy, moroseness, despair, pride, fear of death, desire for vengeance, and, finally, whatever evil prowls about the whole world.

KA I frequently hear many praying for good health, long life, and riches for themselves; I hear only a few seeking this great good from God.[77]

CA Clearly few know what ought to be prayed for and how. It was always appropriate to assail the divine ear with prayers that he grant us faith and day by day increase his gift in us.

KA Yet the common crowd call those who are none too wise 'credulous,' and a certain wise Hebrew gives the name 'light of heart' to those who believe easily.[78]

CA First of all, it is not a sign of levity or credulity to believe these things which, as so many arguments have made clear, originate not with human beings, but with God. Paul says that he would not listen to an angel if one should assert something different from the gospel of Christ.[79] Indeed, it is rather a mark of arrogant stupidity to doubt what has been handed down to us with such great authority, and for that reason Paul writes that the foolish heart of the philosopher was darkened, because the light of faith was missing.[80] Suppose some uneducated individual were to cry out against a philosopher such as Aristotle or Pythagoras,[81]

* * * * *

75 Rom 8:3
76 Rom 8:18
77 Cf the colloquy *Peregrinatio religionis ergo* ASD I-3 470–94 / CWE 40 619–74, mainly aimed at the cults of various saints. Erasmus gives examples of the types of petitions frequently offered.
78 Cf Eccl 19:4: 'To trust a man hastily shows a shallow mind.'
79 Cf Gal 1:8–9.
80 Cf Eph 4:18.
81 Pythagoras: Greek philosopher, born c 570 BC, whose followers were extremely devoted to an ascetic ideal of purity. The pursuit of wisdom through science and philosophy was for them the means of attaining salvation.

or one who was more learned than both, and discuss prime matter,[82] the origin of nature, the infinite, or the size, movement, and power of the celestial bodies, arguing about things, none of which he could comprehend. Would not such a person be regarded as arrogant and demented? Yet how much greater insanity it is not to trust in the philosophy of God, just because the human intellect cannot comprehend much of it! Between God and humans, however learned, there is an infinitely greater difference than between the wisest of men and the most uneducated swineherd.[83]

KA That is precisely how the matter stands.

CA Among philosophers one is regarded as shameless if he rejects the authority of a famous and approved teacher. For 'he himself said it' was sufficient proof among the Pythagoreans.[84] Does the Christian, then, equivocate when he hears, 'God said this; God did this'? No one has doubts about a document drawn up by a king once he has recognized the seal. What rashness, then, to wrangle about things divine, which, as we pointed out, have been sealed in so many ways!

KA While you discuss these things, I feel the seed of faith increase in me, too. But why does this form of speech, 'I believe in God,' find favour, a form which Latin speakers who use the language properly scarcely recognize?

CA Numerous philosophers also believe *that* God exists; demons also *believe God*,[85] for they know that he cannot lie. But only the devout believe *in* God – it makes no difference whether the accusative phrase *in Deum* or the ablative phrase *in Deo* is used for 'in God' – for they have fixed all their trust and all their hope in him. Thus Cyprian,[86] a person as learned as he was pious, does not think that the creed should read, 'I believe *in* the holy church,' but 'I believe *that* the holy church

* * * * *

82 Prime matter: a concept originating with the Pre-Socratics, c sixth century BC, based on the belief that there is an underlying substratum to all creation, that being limitless, undifferentiated matter. Aristotle develops from this principle the opposition between matter and form, form being that which gives matter its existence as individual entities: 'Matter is a medium insensible, and inseparable' (*De generatione et corruptione* 2.6 332a35–332b1).

83 Cf 1 Cor 1:25: 'For the foolishness of God is wiser than men, and the weakness of God is stronger than men.'

84 Quintilian *Institutiones oratoriae* 11.1.27

85 James 2:19: 'You believe that God is one; you do well. Even the demons believe – and shudder.'

86 Cyprian: read Rufinus.

exists.'[87] I too acknowledge the piety of his idea. The highest and sacred anchor of trust and hope, as the expression goes, must be fixed *in* God alone. The Latin figure of speech has its source in the Hebrew idiom, which frequently adds the preposition 'in' where the Latin language rejects it. Although the apostles wrote in Greek, nevertheless now and then they revert to the usage of their native Hebrew. A passage of this type is Luke 14: 'If he can attack *in* ten thousand men.'[88] But if it is completely wrong to add the preposition 'in' when we speak of human things, how can we excuse what the same evangelist, Luke, writes in chapter 12? He says, 'Whoever has professed *in* me before men, *in him* the Son of Man will profess before the angels of God.'[89] The preposition seems, at any rate, to add some vigour to the speech. I do not know whether 'I trust in you' [*confido in te*] is proper Latin, but 'I have trust in you' [*fiduciam habeo in te*] is; 'My hope is placed in you' [*in te spes mea sita est*] is correct, although those who are scrupulous about their Latin style would not dare to say, 'I hope in you' [*spero in te*]. Let us, however, dismiss quibbles over style, and embrace the meaning with our whole hearts, placing our entire hope not in angels, not in holy men, but in the one God.

KA Why does Cyprian not say, 'I believe in *one* God'?

CA Because by using the other phrase[90] he has, at this point, more effectively excluded a multitude of gods. No one says, 'I saw one sun,' 'One sun rose,' 'I saw one moon,' for the thought that there are or can be a plurality of suns and moons never even comes into anyone's mind. But someone who says, 'I saw one sun rising,' causes the hearers to wonder if he feels that there is a plurality of suns or moons; talking like this, he would be considered ridiculous. Nature does not exclude outright

* * * * *

87 See 256 n43 above.

88 Luke 14:31; Erasmus cites the passage here as *si potest in decem milibus occurrere*, although the Vulgate reads 'si possit cum decem milibus occurrere.' His annotation on this passage in the *Novum Testamentum* LB VI 293E gives the Greek as ἐν δέκα χιλιάσιν, and claims that 'the translator not unwisely changed *in*, the Greek preposition placed there from idiomatic Hebrew,' calling its use inelegant. Note that Erasmus has characteristically progressed from a discussion of the theological implications of the preposition's use to an examination of it as a problem of translation.

89 Luke 12:8; here Erasmus' Latin reads *qui in me confessus fuerit coram hominibus et Filius hominis confitebitur in illo coram angelis Dei*. The Vulgate's rendition includes the use of the preposition *in*, but Erasmus' Latin translation does not. Again, his annotation makes the point that the Greek rendition has its source in the Hebrew idiom (LB VI 283E).

90 That is, 'I believe in God' ('credo in Deum')

a plurality of suns, but it is absolutely impossible that there could be a plurality of gods. For what is absolutely the highest cannot be other than one.[91]

KA Why then in the creed that I have heard sung at mass, which some think comes from Nicaea and you think comes from Constantinople, does it say, 'I believe in *one* God'?[92]

CA This word 'one' was added later not so much against the pagans, who worshipped many gods, but against heretics, some of whom fantasized about two first principles, one of good, the other of evil.[93] Others divided the one God in two.[94] They maintained that the one, whom they called 'the just,' is the author of the Old Testament, and that the other, whom they professed to be good and denied to be just, was the author of the New Testament.[95] In truth, one God is the author of all created things[96] and therefore they are good, for God is not the author of evil things. 'He saw the things that he had made and they were very good.'[97] The same God is just and good, the same God is the author of the Old Law, the same God is the First Person of the New Testament and the unalterable ruler of all the ages.

When I deny that God is the author of evils, I am thinking of sins, not afflictions. An affliction which God sends is good, either because it is

* * * * *

91 Rufinus draws a similar analogy in Rufinus 5 PL 21 343, but to a different purpose, claiming that the use of 'one' in the eastern church does not imply God's *numerical* unity but rather his *absolute* unity.

92 The use of 'one' in the east and its omission in the west is a major difference between eastern and western creeds. See Kelly *Commentary* 105–6 n21.

93 Erasmus gives a not altogether accurate account of the origin of this variation. While the Nicene Creed is indeed later than the Roman Creed on which the Apostles' Creed under examination is based, and while the chief aim of those formulating it was to counter the Arian heresy, the use of 'one God' in the credal formulas in the east predates Nicaea and speaks not of a derivation or deviation from a western formula, but rather of a concurrent, related yet independent tradition. See Kelly *Creeds* 201–4.

94 The Arian heresy, chief target of the Council of Nicaea, did not teach a separate origin of evil. Its main teaching was that Christ, although indeed the Son of God, was not of one essence (οὐσία) with the Father, and thus he is not co-eternal with the Father. Those heretics who did preach separate origins of good and evil were the Gnostics, the most famous being the Manichees, to which group Augustine belonged in his youth. See 274 n152 below.

95 Erasmus may be thinking of the Marcionites here; see 273 n147 below.

96 See Augustine *De fide et symbolo* 4.5 PL 40 184 for a discussion of the term *condere* as being less ambiguous than *creare*.

97 Gen 1:31

justly inflicted for wrongs committed, or because it is a remedy to bring
one to his senses, or because it is a fruit and material of greater glory.
Nevertheless, that same race of evils would never exist among men if
sin had never come to exist. On the other hand, sin proceeded from the
devil and from the depraved concupiscence of humans.

KA Why did Cyprian add 'Father'?

CA To distinguish him from the other Persons. For the phrase 'and in Jesus
Christ, his only Son' is added next. He alone is called Father because
he alone begot a Son. Although the name of God is taken to signify
the entire Trinity and encompasses all the Persons equally, the Father is
rightly called God because he is the source of all created things. If you
understand the word 'father' in its general sense, as that from which
anything takes its origin, the First Person is unequivocally the Father of
all things. He did not 'beget' the Holy Spirit, nor did he 'beget' men or
angels of his own substance.[98] In a special way, however, he is called
the Father of those who fear him; for the same reason he is said to be
their God: Psalm 32:12, 'Blessed is the nation whose God is the Lord.'[99]
So too Psalm 143:15.[100] But to have begotten God the Son of his own
substance is a property of the First Person. He produced the world, but
not alone. He produces the blessed by the word of life, but through
the Son and the Holy Spirit. The Father alone begot the one and only
Word.

KA As human begets human?

CA In the same way, in so far as he begot from his own substance, begot a
son, begot God of God.[101] But as was said a little while ago,[102] in every
comparison that moves from created things to God there are numerous
discrepancies. The Father did not transfer part of his substance to the
Son, but communicated that same substance in its entirety to him. The
begetter and the begotten are not two gods, as a human father and a human son are two men. The begetter is not prior in time to the begotten,
but both share the same eternity. I pass over the other aspects of this
mystery, which are numberless.

* * * * *

98 The Holy Spirit proceeds from the Father, unlike the Son, who is begotten,
   and likewise unlike creation, which is made.
99 Ps 33 (Vulg 32):12
100 Ps 144 (Vulg 143):15
101 Cf Nicene Creed, 'Deum de Deo.'
102 Cf 260 above.

KA A man does not really procreate when he adopts a human being as his son;[103] when he has a son by his wife he is said to have procreated truly, because the birth is natural. But if the Father begets a Son in so many different ways, how is he really said to beget?

CA On the contrary, he more truly begets because he does so differently. Human generation compared with that unutterable one is merely a kind of shadow of generation. If among us generation is said to be true because it belongs to human nature, with much greater right is the generation that belongs to divine nature called true – unless, perhaps, you are going to deny that God really created the world because he created it in a different way than humans create a city or a home. It is not untrue to say that God is light,[104] life,[105] wisdom,[106] virtue,[107] or mind,[108] because these names are predicated of him differently than they are predicated of created things; rather they are less perfectly predicated of created things, because they are predicated of them differently than they are of God.[109]

KA Is it lawful to call God a substance?

CA If by substance you mean a subsisting person, it is not irreverent to profess one essence in three substances, although it is better, particularly because these terms are now out of the ordinary, to refrain from using them as in times past some pious people did.[110] If you understand substance as something in which accidents inhere, it is irreverent to use this word of God, who is completely simple, not composed of matter and form, or mingled with accidents; whatever is in him is one single

* * * * *

103 Adoptionism holds that Christ is God's Son not in substance, but by adoption. See 283 n38 below.

104 1 John 1:5

105 John 14:6

106 Cf Prov 8:22–31, which describes wisdom's role in the creation.

107 Virtue: see Thomas Aquinas *Summa theologica* 1 q 5 art 6, q 6 art 3.

108 Mind: see Rufinus 4 PL 21 341–2.

109 Cf Thomas Aquinas *Summa theologica* 1 q 13 art 5: 'no name is predicated univocally of God and creatures.' Neither is it predicated purely equivocally, but by analogy, for 'whatever is said of God and creatures, is said according to the relation of a creature to God as its principle and cause ...'

110 See ibidem 1 q 29 art 1, in which Aquinas cites Boethius as defining person as 'an individual substance of a rational nature.' In 1 q 29 art 3 he concludes that it is appropriate to apply this name as so defined to God, but in a more excellent way than when applied to creatures.

substance.[111] But if any words of this kind are used of God in the Sacred Scriptures, that is, to be angry,[112] to be pacified,[113] to regret,[114] to forget,[115] to remember,[116] be assured that the language of Scripture is accommodated to our senses, just as a mother lisps with her little child.[117] Furthermore, if you use the word substance of something fully subsisting of itself, there is nothing which that word fits more exactly than God. Whatever truly exists, exists through him, and the reality that gives being to everything else necessarily enjoys the most perfect existence.

KA In my opinion, you are explaining these subjects clearly and reverently. But to change the topic ... Seeing that many attributes come together in God, such as wisdom, goodness, eternity, changelessness, truth, justice, mercy, and innumerable others, why is 'omnipotent' the only one mentioned in the creed?[118]

CA You raise a good question. Whoever truly professes God likewise professes all the attributes belonging to the divine nature. But this identification 'omnipotent' is added to exclude any quibbling, for the creed is proposed to the uneducated for belief rather than discussion, and many things which seem impossible to human understanding exist not only in the created order, but also in the orders of redemption and consummation. Here is an example. Aristotle established with irrefutable proofs that the world existed from eternity, since nothing can be begotten of nothing.[119] To him the answer is given 'He who created the world, when it did not exist, is omnipotent.' Philosophers deny that privation allows any return of a characteristic, and therefore deny that Christ was born of a virgin or rose from the dead. The answer is given 'God, who performs these things, is omnipotent.' The Jews deny that a person is born

* * * * *

111 See Rufinus 4 PL 21 341 / Kelly *Commentary* 33–4: 'When "God" is uttered, you are to understand a substance without beginning or end, simple, uncompounded, invisible, incorporeal, ineffable, incomprehensible: a substance in which there is nothing accidental, nothing creaturely.' On substance and accident, see 260 n65 above.
112 Cf Ps 78 (Vulg 77):31.
113 Exod 32:14
114 Gen 6:7
115 Lam 5:10
116 Isa 43:25
117 Cf *Enchiridion* LB V 8F / CWE 66 35; *Paraclesis* LB V 140A; 1 Cor 3:2; Heb 5:12; and Rom 14:2.
118 See 254 n32 above.
119 Aristotle *Metaphysics* 10.6.291 262b24

of a person without the action of a male. The answer is given that it is God who willed this to be done, that it was God who was born, that it was God who prepared the Virgin's womb. Accordingly, the creed uses the description 'omnipotent' to strengthen the faith of the slow-witted. Since the power of God is infinite and incomprehensible, it is foolish to investigate how he did this or that, but with the faithful psalmist it must be said, 'Whatever the Lord pleases he does, in heaven and on earth, in the seas and all deeps.'[120]

KA 'Creator of heaven and earth.' Why is the creation of the world attributed to the Father alone?

CA The creation is indeed common to all the Persons, since the Father created all created things through the Son with the cooperation of the Holy Spirit[121] – in such a way, however, that you are to picture to yourself here neither an instrument nor an assistant. It was fitting that the opening of the profession of faith in the gospel should harmonize with the beginning of the Old Testament, in order that we may understand from the resemblance that there is one originator and author of both Laws. Genesis begins thus: 'In the beginning God created the heaven and the earth.'[122] However, the Son and the Holy Spirit were unknown to the Jews (I am speaking about ordinary people). They recognized only a Father, not because he had begotten God the Son, but because he was the creator and governor of the human race and the fount of all creation. The word 'father' designates origin, and it is evident that the most perfect concept of origin belongs to the Father for, as Cyprian[123] says, only the sole progenitor of everything else is himself without a progenitor.[124]

KA Why is it that what someone calls a 'founder,' another person calls 'creator,' and another 'maker'?

CA The Greeks have only one word, ποιήτης, and it is applicable indiscriminately to author, creator, and maker of any kind whatsoever, although the Latin language rejects the word *factor* [maker]. With a view to making

* * * * *

120 Ps 135 (Vulg 134):6
121 See Thomas Aquinas *Summa theologica* I q 45 art 6.
122 Gen 1:1
123 Cyprian: read Rufinus.
124 Rufinus 4 PL 21 341: 'For he who is the originator of all things is himself without origin. When "Father" is uttered, you are to understand the Father of the Son, the Son being the image of the above-mentioned substance'; cf the colloquy *Inquisitio de fide* ASD I-3 371:251–2 / CWE 39 428:30–1: 'Why is the Father alone called God?' 'Because . . . he is absolutely the author of all that are . . .' See also 247 n2 above.

a distinction, some have taught that someone who produces something from nothing 'creates,' and that this term applies to God alone; but someone who fashions something from some material, as nature produces the tree from a seed and the artisan makes a dish from silver, 'makes' it. A discussion then arises as to whether God created heaven and earth, since there seems to have been chaos before this, that is, matter without form, and God did not, therefore, create heaven and earth from nothing. None the less, as the one who created the very matter from which all other things were created, he is rightly said to have created from nothing. To dispose of this subtle objection, some have preferred to use the word 'establisher' [conditor].[125]

KA Why did that writer choose to call him 'creator of heaven and earth' rather than 'creator of all created things'?

CA Because, as I have just now said, he preferred to repeat the words of Genesis.[126] Heaven embraces all things, the other elements revolve around the earth; these two parts of the universe are most exposed to our senses. Scripture, as I have already reminded you, frequently accommodates its diction to the human senses. He who created heaven and earth certainly created all things that are contained in them.

KA On the other hand, the creed of Nicaea or Constantinople adds 'of all things visible and invisible.'[127]

CA It said the same thing but in greater detail, so that no one should think that angels or the souls of human beings were not created by God. What is said here cryptically is proclaimed more openly by the Apostle in Colossians 1:16: 'For through him all things were created in heaven and on earth, visible and invisible, whether thrones or dominations or principalities or powers – all things were created through him and in him.'[128] Whatever had no beginning is God, but the angels are the ministers of God, whom they glorify with unceasing awe, and adore as creator and lord.[129] On the other hand, whatever had a beginning drew its origin from one God, who alone knew no beginning

* * * * *

125 See 265 n96 above.
126 Gen 1:1
127 This is typical of eastern creeds; see Kelly *Creeds* 195; cf the colloquy *Inquisitio de fide* ASD I-3 365:68–9 / CWE 39 423:20–1: 'Quae nutu suo omnipotenti condidit, quicquid est rerum visibilium aut invisibilium' / 'Which by its omnipotent will created whatever exists, visible or invisible.'
128 Col 1:16
129 Cf Rev 7:11–12; Thomas Aquinas *Summa theologica* 1 q 107 art 3.

and knows no end, is not restricted by place, and is not altered by time.

KA What remains for us, except to pass on to the second article?

CA I rather think that we should dwell on this article a little longer.

KA I'll follow your lead.

CA The first step, then, towards salvation is to believe that God exists. The second is to trust in God, that is, to have faith in his words.[130] The third is to cast all our cares on him with complete trust.[131] Someone who does not believe in the existence of God is proclaiming that nothing ever exists, since whatever exists is from him. Someone who trusts in God proclaims that he is true in all things.[132] Someone who places all his trust in God professes that the universe is governed by him, and does not indeed believe that it is the first reality. Someone who imagines God as other than he is does not really believe in the existence of God. A more unseemly error is made by those who, though they profess faith in the existence of God, nevertheless deny that he is omnipotent or omniscient, or deny that the world was created by him, or admit that it was created by him but deny that it is governed by him. In the same way, you would be less angry, if I am not mistaken, with someone who thought you did not exist than with someone who believed that you did not have feelings, or a human mind and the other qualities without which a human being loses the name 'human.'

KA Yes, that is how the matter stands.

CA Someone who uses the name 'king' includes many outstanding characteristics in one word; someone who uses the name 'God' embraces the infinite total of all that is good. Very many say with their lips, 'I believe in God,' but someone who says with a Christian heart, 'I believe in God,'[133] condemns certain Cyclopean[134] pagans who do not believe that there is any God, as well as those who tick off for us many manifold gods, since by that very count they indicate that there is no God. For if there are many gods, there is a respect in which one differs from another: if that difference is a good, the one who lacks some good is not God; if it is an evil, God is subject to no evil.

* * * * *

130 Cf *Enchiridion* LB V 21D–22A / CWE 66 55–6.
131 Cf 1 Pet 5:7.
132 Rom 3:4
133 Cf Rom 10:9–10.
134 The Cyclops were a barbarous race of one-eyed giants living on an isolated island without government or religion. See Homer *Odyssey* 9.106–17.

Similar strictures also apply to those who believe that nothing at all exists beyond what they perceive with their bodily senses. The Anthropomorphites hold views that are not far removed from theirs.[135] Since they had read in the Scripture about the eyes, face, mouth, hands, heart, arm, womb, and breast of God, they thought that God was corporeal, made up of human shape and human limbs, although nothing is further removed from all sensible matter than God, and John writes, 'God is spirit.'[136]

The believer condemns the Epicureans,[137] who admit that there is a God, or gods, yet deny that they are concerned with the affairs of mortals. They make God powerless or stupid because he does not have the strength to rule what he created, or malevolent because he does not wish to do so, or silly and intoxicated because he neglects to do so. These statements, if made against a human monarch, are full of blasphemy; how much more so if they are used against God. Indeed, in the Gospel our Lord cried out that not even a little sparrow falls to the ground against the will of the Father,[138] and that the hairs on his disciples' heads were numbered by God, so that not a strand would be lost unless he willed it.[139] The disciple Peter also agrees with the master: '... casting all your anxieties on him, since he cares about you.'[140]

The believer also denounces the blasphemy of the Jews, who profess their belief in one God, but deny the existence of the Son and the Holy Spirit, although, in fact, the substance or essence of God is a unity, identical and, to speak in the manner of the logicians, numerically one in the Son begotten of the Father and in the Holy Spirit proceeding from both. The Father cries aloud from the clouds, 'This is my beloved Son,'[141] and the Jew says, 'He has no son.' The same Father proclaims through the mouth of Joel, 'I will pour out my Spirit on all flesh,'[142] and the Jew calls back, 'God has no Holy Spirit, but is alone.'

* * * * *

135 Anthropomorphites were, as Erasmus points out, influenced by the descriptions of God in human terms found in the Old Testament, eg Gen 3:8, 32:24–9; Exod 4:24. However, anthropomorphism predates Christianity. See Augustine *De haeresibus* 50 PL 42 39.
136 John 4:24
137 Epicurus (341–270 BC) denied that God was involved in the created order.
138 Matt 10:29
139 Matt 10:30
140 1 Pet 5:7
141 Matt 3:17; Mark 1:11
142 Joel 2:28

Both the senseless Noetus[143] and the impious Sabellius were nearly as mad.[144] From the latter sprang the heresy of Patripassianism,[145] which makes a distinction within the substance of God, not of three persons but of three names. The Father, they say, created the world. Under the name of Son, he also assumed flesh and suffered; with another change of name, he came to the disciples as the Holy Spirit. Deliberately and gladly I pass over here the doctrines of Basilides[146] and Marcion, which are more fantasy than blasphemy.[147] The Origenists[148] also approximate the ungodliness of the Jews. They make the Son of God a creature and the Holy Spirit the servant of a creature.

Arius is close to this last position.[149] He acknowledges the Son as son by will and resemblance, but not by nature. He takes this resemblance

* * * * *

143 Noetus of Smyrna (c 200 AD), condemned by city presbyters. What we know of him is mainly from the writings of Hippolytus. His doctrine is called modalistic monarchianism, and his teaching included a concept called Patripassianism; see n145 below.

144 Sabellius (third century AD) formulated a modalist concept of God as essentially one, the Father, of which the other two Persons are merely expressions.

145 Patripassianism: the belief that it was the Father himself, not the Person of the Son, who endured Christ's suffering on the cross.

146 Basilides: a Gnostic (fl 120–40) who lectured at Alexandria, believing in a descending order of spiritual beings, of which the supreme form was *nous*. It is this God who became incarnate in Jesus Christ to free humans from their imprisonment in the material order, which is the creation of the god of the Jews, a lesser deity to whom the supreme God is in opposition. See Irenaeus *Adversus haereses* 1.24 PG 7 673–6.

147 Marcion: from Sinope (second century AD); rejected the Old Testament on the basis of its legalism, which he saw as being in permanent opposition to the gospel message of love. His writings have been lost, but his beliefs have been reconstructed from Irenaeus, Tertullian, Clement of Alexandria, Augustine, and Origen; see eg Tertullian *Adversus Marcion* PL 2 239–524.

148 Origenists: although Origen was one of Erasmus' favourite interpreters, attacks had been made on Origenists in the fourth century for their Trinitarian doctrine, and in the sixth for a variety of reasons. Origen was condemned at the Second Council of Constantinople, 553. Origen's concept of Son and Holy Spirit combined the view that both were co-eternal with the Father with a strain of subordinationism; many followers emphasized this latter strain and referred to the Second and Third Persons as creatures.

149 Arius (fl c 318), founder of the widespread Arian heresy, taught that Christ was not of one substance with the Father, but rather, like all creatures, had been created out of nothing. In place of a human soul, Christ united the divine λόγος, itself a creation of God (according to Arius), with a human body. God foresaw that he would not sin, and bestowed special grace upon him, but

to be as imperfect as that between a shadow and a body, because he thinks that the similarity between creator and creature is slight and indistinct. Eunomius[150] outdoes this ungodliness when he teaches that the Son is different from the Father in all respects, since there is no affinity between creator and creature, just as there is none between the finite and the infinite. Macedonius[151] disagrees with Eunomius' assertion, but still does not assent to the teaching of the church. He states that the Son is like the Father in all things, but that the Holy Spirit has nothing in common with the Father and the Son.

We have already touched on the Manichees.[152] They fashion two principles contrary to each other. By one of these, visible things were created, as evil from evil; by the other, invisible things were created, as good from good. Hence they certainly made two gods from one God, a good God and an evil one, just as the Gnostics did. When Synerus[153] makes three principles, he makes as many gods. Again, those who separate the Son or the Holy Spirit from God, despite the fact that the other two Persons of the Trinity are united with the Father by nature, try to thrust a mutilated God upon us. So too, there are those who substitute nature for God. If nature is eternal and omnipotent, assumedly it is God; if it is not eternal and omnipotent, it is the servant of God and was created by God. (I think that one must make the same judgment in

* * * * *

Christ by nature was not incapable of sin. Many important writings were directed against his followers; see eg Ambrose *De fide* PL 16 545–726; Augustine *Contra sermonem Arianorum* PL 42 683–708 and *Collatio cum Maximino Arianorum episcopo* PL 42 709–42.

150 Eunomius (c 383), whose beliefs are a development of Arianism, taught that while the Son could not share the Father's divine essence, the Father could communicate his divine ἐνέργεια, or activity, to the Son, and thus the Son, while different from the Father, could share in his creative power.

151 Macedonius: bishop of Constantinople, deposed by Arians in 360. It is not clear that he had anything to do with a group known as Macedonians, who held that the Spirit was not fully divine.

152 Manichees: followers of the Babylonian prophet Mani (b c 216 AD), who preached a radical dualism between good and evil, or spirit and matter, each term of the opposition having a separate source. The process of redemption involves the releasing of oneself from the material world into the realm of pure spirit. Augustine writes about them extensively in his *Confessions,* eg 2.6–10.

153 Synerus: follower of Marcion. See Augustine *De haeresibus* 22 PL 42 29; Eusebius *Historia ecclesiastica* 5.13 PG 20 459–62.

regard to secondary causes – although, in my opinion, it is more reverent to assign whatever nature or secondary causes do to the operation of God alone. If his action ceased, the sun would no longer shine, the heavens would not revolve, and fire would not be hot; everything would suddenly collapse.)

The believer also condemns Seleucius,[154] who admits that the world was created by God, but says that matter existed from eternity, putting a formless and defective thing on a par with God. The believer also condemns Menander,[155] who, following in the footsteps of Plato, taught that the world was created not by God but by angels, giving the name 'angels' to what Plato called 'daimons, sons of select gods.' The believer also condemns Saturnius,[156] who, raving more disgracefully than these others, gibbered about the world having been founded by seven angels, and the most unseemly madman of all, Basilides,[157] who taught that the world was created from the three-hundred-and-sixty-fifth heaven. But heresies (and there is no end of them) are already becoming tiresome. To sum up, whoever has ideas about God other than what is true, or who does not believe in the God that the authority of divine Scripture portrays, does not believe in God, but puts his hope in an idol. You see how much philosophy so short an article has taught us, and from what great shadows and monsters of error it has freed us.

KA I certainly see that it is a great thing to say sincerely, 'I believe in God.'

CA You would say that belief was even greater, if you called to mind what a large crowd of people there is to whom the well-known dictum of St Paul applies: 'They avow that they know God but deny him by their works.'[158] Whatever a person prefers to God, that he makes his God.

KA How?

* * * * *

154 Seleucius: see Augustine *De haeresibus* 59 PL 42 41–2. He was a philosopher from Galatia who taught that matter is uncreated and eternal and that angels formed the soul from fire and spirit.

155 Menander of Samaria, second-century Gnostic, who claimed he was able to save people from supernatural doom through the transmission of his magical powers. Eusebius *Historia ecclesiastica* 3.26 PG 20 271–4 calls him the successor of Simon Magus, described in Acts 8:9–24.

156 Saturnius: a second-century Gnostic who taught that a Father unknown to all created a series of angels and other supernatural beings and that they in turn created man. See Eusebius *Historia ecclesiastica* 4.7 PG 20 315–18.

157 Basilides: see n146 above.

158 Cf 2 Cor 11:13–15.

CA God says, 'Thou shalt not commit adultery';[159] concupiscence says, 'Commit adultery.' Does not someone who ignores God and listens to concupiscence reject God and, to the same extent, put concupiscence in his place?

KA So it seems.

CA God says, 'You shall not swear falsely';[160] avarice says, 'Swear falsely.' Does not your avaricious person worship Mammon instead of the true God?[161] Scripture teaches us that God is present everywhere and nothing is hidden from his eyes.[162] Do people believe this who daily, under the eyes of God, commit crimes which they would not dare to commit if someone were to witness them?

KA It seems that they do not.

CA Those who, because of the death of children or the loss of their goods, take refuge in the noose surely do not believe that all human affairs are administered with wisdom and directed with compassion by God!

KA It would be strange if they really believed.

CA What about those who throughout their whole life are slaves to the world, rejoicing when they have done wrong and revelling in the most wicked things? Do they believe that God leaves no evil unpunished, and that those who have refused to do penance for their sins on earth are sent to eternal fire?

KA In my opinion at least, either they do not believe or their faith is lukewarm.[163]

CA Again, think of those who ponder the magnitude of their crimes and despair of obtaining pardon. Do they believe that God is infinitely merciful?

KA It is not likely that they do.

CA To know God, then, with a lively faith is of the greatest importance for a holy and happy life. How could someone who sincerely believes that God is the highest good and the highest excellence love anything more than him? Someone who believes that God is omnipotent will not try to resist him who cannot be overcome. Someone who believes that he is the highest wisdom will not murmur against him in adversity. For just as a person unskilled in medicine would be considered

* * * * *

159 Exod 20:14
160 Lev 19:12; Matt 5:33
161 Cf Matt 6:24.
162 Cf Heb 4:13.
163 Rev 3:16

irrational by all if he criticized a physician for prescribing different remedies for different people, so indeed the person who judges God in the same way, as if he did not know what is best for each person, would be stupid.[164] The physician puts a salve on one patient and washes him; cauterizes and operates on another; opens another's vein; gives another an enema and stops diarrhoea for another; prescribes fasting for one, but food for another; orders one to sleep, but forbids another to sleep. We say, he is a doctor, he knows what is best for the sick man. When God gives riches to this person, takes them away from another, gives children to one person, but denies them to another, gives this person sound health, but someone else a body prone to diseases, we ask, 'Why does God treat people in this fashion,' instead of saying, 'He is God, he knows what is best for each.'

A person who believes that God is supreme justice will never convince himself of impunity for his evil deeds. A person who believes that God is omniscient will not readily undertake in his sight what he would be ashamed to do in the presence of a good man. Someone who believes that God is the supreme truth will shudder at the punishments appointed for the wicked, and will yearn for the eternal happiness promised to the devout. A person who believes that this world was created for man's sake will, at every turn, be moved to adore so great a kindness on the part of the Godhead and will be afraid to use what has been granted by God in any way other than for his glory. But let this discourse end here. After you have prayed and chewed these reflections as an animal chews the cud, come back to me.

Lesson 3

KA I feel the grain of mustard seed[1] that you planted in my mind exercising its power more and more.

CA May the Lord help you grow into genuine maturity through my watering and planting![2]

KA But as I thought things over, this doubt disturbed my mind. In other courses of study it is customary to begin with the simplest things, those that are familiar and known to our senses. Why then has this branch

* * * * *

164 See 250 n15 above.
  1 Luke 17:6
  2 Cf 1 Cor 3:6–7.

of philosophy immediately taken its beginning from God? Nothing is
more difficult or further removed from the human senses than he is.

CA We begin from God because this is the philosophy of faith, not of reasoning,[3] which leads the mind through long digressions and tortuous
mazes, frequently deceiving it. Faith conducts the mind by a short route
to the heights and places our minds on a high lookout, so to speak, from
which they may discern and judge these things below more surely and
more thoroughly by relating everything to God, in whom is the beginning, growth, and perfection of all things. The process of knowledge
that originates in the senses is at times unreliable, since they quite often
lead us astray. For example, sight and hearing are the most powerful of
the external senses, yet the sun appears to us to be two feet in diam-
eter, although it is greater than the whole earth, and we see lightning
before we hear thunder.[4]

The process of learning derived from causes and the principles of
demonstration is not always reliable either, for we see that professors of
philosophy argue even about first principles. Furthermore, since faith
coming from God transcends the certitude of all the senses and of philosophical principles, there is no process of learning more reliable than
faith, and there also is none that is shorter and easier. Listen to a proof of
this. How many weavers, male and female, are there today who reason
about divine mysteries better than Plato and Aristotle, the foremost of
philosophers?[5] To what extent does Plato rave about selected gods and
spirits, the offspring of gods, about the creation of the world by spirits,
about souls descended from heaven?[6] As Aristotle tries to rise from the
lowest to the highest, through how many winding subjects does he lead
the mind, how long does he detain us in dialectics, in poetics, in rhetoric,
in physics, in meteorology, before he comes to ultramundane matters?
Nevertheless, he did not reach the knowledge of God for which so many
steps were laid – a knowledge to which youths are quite quickly and
easily led through faith, with no instruction in earthly disciplines.

The philosophy that is foremost and procures true happiness for humans is to know God and Jesus Christ sent by God. Since this philosophy is to a very great extent in accord with nature, every sex and every

* * * * *

3 *Philosophia:* see 237 n6 above.
4 See 239 n17 above.
5 Cf *Paraclesis* LB V 140C; see Marjorie O'Rourke Boyle 'Weavers, Farmers, Tailors
  . . . and Other Theologians' *Erasmus in English* 3 (1971) 1–7.
6 Plato *Timaeus* 41E–42A

age proves an apt pupil in this matter, but particularly the time of life that has not yet been corrupted by evil desires. Religion, indeed, is so much in keeping with nature that there is a belief that something of this sense is present in elephants and in other irrational animals.

KA But someone who simply believes what is stated about God will not be in a position to contend with philosophers and heretics.

CA No indeed. This philosophy is not learned for the rhetorical wrestling ground, but for a holy life. What is more arrogant than those who treat the divine nature in human terms? Not one of them is able to achieve full understanding of even a gnat or a little spider, although they see these daily. The searcher after majesty is overwhelmed by its glory,[7] just as those who look for some time at the sun with eyes intent and unmoved go away blind, so that now and again they even fall over a stake that lies in their way. The eye of faith is indeed simple and dove-like,[8] and reverently gazes on God as he has willed to become known to us. It does not examine too carefully what God has willed to be hidden from us for the time being, until we reach that heavenly vision[9] where he will present himself to the gaze of more purified eyes in a closer and clearer view. In this life, it is enough that you believe that God exists, and is one by nature in three distinct persons. You believe that the Son is born of the Father and that the Holy Spirit proceeds from both. You believe that God is not body but mind of infinite power, absolutely simple and eternal, since he existed before all time and is not changed by time. You believe that the entire universe was created by this omnipotent mind, and was created for the sake of human beings.

God needs neither the universe nor humankind nor, indeed, any creature as he is completely perfect in himself and of himself. However, since he is supremely good, he did not wish to be alone in his happiness, but extended it to angels and men and all creation in the measure that each thing is capable of sharing the divine bounty. He willed to become known to humanity by speaking in various ways.[10] In the beginning, he spoke to the human race in a particular manner when through the Son, who is the Word of the Father, he created the wonderful fabric of the universe, so that we might infer the nature of the maker from his

* * * * *

7 Cf Prov 25:27 (Vulg).
8 Matt 10:16; cf *Ratio* LB V 76D.
9 *Ad illud coeleste theatrum*: see 240 n20 above.
10 Cf Heb 1:1.

work.[11] Neither human nor angel could complete such a work. This was
the first step towards a knowledge of God. The Law came next: it was
a great help to the darkened human mind; but it was given to a single
race, and provided a sketch of God through allegories and figures,[12]
preparing the human mind for the light of the gospel which shone on
us through the Son. In their pride, philosophers have misused the natural light of reason; the Law was an occasion of even greater impiety for
many of the Jews.[13] The world was filled with idolatry; the Jews were
swollen with an empty conviction of righteousness; sin reigned unchal-
lenged in the world,[14] while the largest part of mankind imitated the
first parents of the human race.[15]

At this point the mercy of God, which is above all his works,[16] dis-
closed itself. Through this same Son, he graciously made himself known
to us more closely and more intimately, so that, challenged by favours
so numerous and so wonderful, we might, as a result, be swept into a
reciprocal love of him.[17] When we did not exist, he created us. He willed
to restore us when we were lost, for it would have been better not to
exist than to be lost. After the world was created in marvellous fashion, after the Law was given from heaven, after the prophets inspired
by the Spirit of God, he sent his only Son made human, so that we, being human, might at least love another of our kind. Moreover, he sent
him not as an avenger but as a saviour, through whose death he might

* * * * *

11 Here Erasmus recasts Gen 1:1 to interpret God's creative act as essentially an
   act of communication through the Word, which is the Son. Thus God's first
   means of communication with man was the creation itself, effected through
   the Son.
12 *Per typos et aenigmata ... deliniavit:* cf Rom 5:12; 1 Cor 13:12. On the tradition of the allegorical interpretation of Scripture, particularly of the Old Testament, see H. Lubac *Exégèse médiévale: les quatre sens de l'Ecriture* (Paris 1959–64).
   Thomas Aquinas *Summa theologica* I q 1 art 10 outlines the approach; for a discussion of Erasmus' use of it see Manfred Hoffmann 'Erasmus on Language
   and Interpretation' *Moreana* XXVIII 106–7 (1–20).
13 Cf Rom 5:13: 'For sin was already in the world before there was law, though in
   the absence of law no reckoning is kept of sin'; and Rom 5:20a: 'Law intruded
   into this process to multiply law-breaking.' Paul's emphasis is on the manner
   in which law makes sin explicit, while Erasmus seems more to emphasize the
   effect of the law in causing impiety through pride.
14 Rom 5:21
15 See 238 n13 above.
16 Cf Ps 145 (Vulg 144):9, and Erasmus' *De immensa Dei misericordia* 77–139 above.
17 Cf Augustine *De catechizandis rudibus* 4.7 PL 40 314.

recall us to life.[18] What more could the measureless love of God do?[19]
In a special way, he offered himself as a bodily presence; in so far as
he might, he gave himself up to death to restore us to true health. He
showed his omnipotence principally by the creation of the world, now
he showed his immense mercy and his inscrutable wisdom, his mercy
by redeeming us without recompense, his wisdom by redeeming us as
he did. What escape, therefore, now remains for humanity if it ignores
such overwhelming goodness on the part of God?

The Creed next teaches this part: 'and in Jesus Christ, his only Son,
our Lord.'

KA Why has he described the Person of the Redeemer by these names?

CA To make completely clear that the Second Person, who specifically assumed flesh, is true human of human and true God of God.[20]

KA How?

CA There are some who think that 'Jesus' is the word for the divine nature
and 'Christ' for the human nature. They seem to be drawn to this opinion by the fact that for the Hebrews 'Jesus' means 'saviour' and 'Christ'
means 'the anointed one.'[21] Moreover, no one can give eternal salvation
except God, and anointing signifies spiritual grace which belongs only
to man. In fact, however, both words refer to his human nature. 'Jesus'
is the name of an individual person, that is, of this man, who alone of all
men was born of a virgin, whom John pointed out with his finger to prevent them from clinging to someone else as the true Redeemer. 'Behold,'
he says, 'the Lamb of God.'[22] 'Christ' is a word pertaining to a kingdom or a priesthood. For among the Jews, both priests and kings were
anointed in a sacred anointing, and both titles, by way of honour, were
predicated of Christ.[23] Moreover, both titles are appropriate for Christ.
He was called 'a high priest after the order of Melchisedek,'[24] and as a
priest he offered himself on the altar of the cross as a truly immaculate
lamb for the salvation of the world, and as a king he appeared to his
disciples after his resurrection and in royal fashion said, 'All authority

* * * * *

18 John 3:17
19 John 15:13
20 True God from true God: from the Nicene Creed
21 See Rufinus 6 PL 21 345. The word Erasmus uses is *servator* (see 249 n9 above).
   Jesus is the Greek form of the Hebrew name Joshua, which means 'Jehovah is
   salvation.'
22 John 1:29
23 See Tertullian *Adversus Praxeam* 28 PL 2 192–3.
24 Heb 5:10

in heaven and on earth has been given to me.'[25] He did not spurn the words of the thief when he recognized him as king, 'Remember me when you come into your kingdom.'[26]

True, the Lord was never bodily anointed with chrism as Aaron was (Exodus 29)[27] or Saul (1 Kings 10).[28] He was the one, however, whom God in a unique way anointed with the plenitude of his Spirit.[29] The word 'Jesus,' in addition to designating an individual person, calls to mind a figure of the Old Testament. For that Jesus, the son of Nave, bore the image of Jesus, the Redeemer. Moses, who is a figure of sacred rites, could not lead the Israelite people to the promised land; but Jesus, the leader who succeeded him, led them there.[30] There is no access to true happiness except through faith and grace, which Jesus, the son of the Virgin, has brought to all. In the cognomen 'Christ,' which is frequently emphasized in the Gospels and the writings of the apostles, the Jews are upbraided for their stupid and tenacious unbelief, for even now they continue to hope for their messiah. (The Latin word for 'anointed one' is *unctus*, the Greek 'christus,' the Hebrew 'messiah.') They are, however, expecting a king abundantly equipped with riches, troops, and other worldly protection, who will restore to the Jewish nation, now rejected everywhere and in exile, freedom and their kingdom. That unfortunate race[31] finds consolation for its tragedy in this vain hope. Christian faith teaches, however, that he is in truth the one and only Messiah, promised by the prophet of old. Not by physical weapons but by his blood he would free not one nation from the tyranny of Satan, but true Jews in all quarters of the world, that is to say, those professing the name of Christ and circumcised in heart.[32] He would,

* * * * *

25 Matt 28:18
26 Luke 23:42
27 Exod 29:7
28 1 Sam 10:1
29 Cf John 3:34.
30 Joshua, son of Nun: see Deut 34:9; Josh 1:1. Reading the Old Testament figuratively, Erasmus interprets Moses as the law which must be transcended by grace: 'After the death of Moses the servant of the Lord, the Lord said to Joshua son of Nun, his assistant, "My servant Moses is dead; now it is for you to cross the Jordan, you and this whole people of Israel, to the land which I am giving them"' (Josh 1:1–2).
31 For a discussion of Erasmus' attitude towards the Jews, see Shimon Markish *Erasmus and the Jews* trans A. Olcott (Chicago and London 1986), and Manfred Hoffmann's review in ERSY 7 135–42.
32 Cf Rom 2:29.

when all their sins were forgiven, restore them to true liberty and finally admit them as co-heirs[33] and sharers[34] with him in the heavenly kingdom.

The name Jesus, then, is used to prevent an error in regard to the person. The cognomen Christ is added lest anyone, following the practice of the Jews, hope for another Messiah or another Redeemer. He came once, he consummated once that one and only wonderful sacrifice.[35] By mystic commemoration of it he willed that we should be nourished and sustained[36] until he comes a second time, no longer as a redeemer, but as judge and rewarder. First, then, the creed showed us that true and wonderful human being, destined from eternity for this task – that through him the world might be redeemed. Next, placed in the same article, the creed shows us the true God and his only Son, our Lord. Strictly speaking, nothing is born of God but God, just as in the course of nature nothing is born of humans but a human.

KA But the Scripture frequently calls pious men 'the sons of God.'[37]

CA And for that reason the creed adds 'one and only,' or 'only-begotten,' to set this Son of God by nature apart from the sons who are admitted to this honour by the favour of adoption.[38]

KA Is it impious to call Christ 'the son of adoption' in view of his assumed nature?[39]

CA It is more scrupulously exact to refrain from using such titles, lest we give any opening to the Arians.[40] Someone who was not beforehand a

* * * * *

33 *Cohaeredes:* Rom 8:17
34 *Consortes:* 2 Pet 1:4
35 Cf Rom 6:10; Heb 7:27.
36 He is speaking of the Holy Eucharist, which he interprets as the commemoration rather than the re-enactment of Christ's one sacrifice on the cross. Cf *Apologia adversus monachos* LB IX 1064F; see Payne 133–4.
37 Eg John 1:12; Wisd of Sol 5:5; Rom 8:14; John 3:1–2
38 Adoptionism: second-century heresy, also called dynamic monarchianism. This belief held that Christ was a human being of special virtue, but not possessing a divine nature. Such believers thought the attempt to portray Christ as true God from true God led to polytheism. See Eusebius *Historia ecclesiastica* 5.28 PG 20 511–18.
39 Assumed nature: his assumption of the flesh. The Catechumen is suggesting that while Christ in his divine nature is God's true son, in his human nature he might be regarded as an adopted son.
40 Arius: see 273 n149 above. According to Arius' Christology, Christ is able to be called Son of God only by a special grace, not by virtue of his having any special communion with the Father.

son is adopted just as we, who were born the sons of wrath,[41] became the sons of God through faith in Christ. However, there never was a time when Christ was not the Son of God; as he was conceived of the Holy Spirit, his blessed soul was created at the same time, filled with every heavenly grace. Although the Lord was born twice, of the Father beyond time and of a virgin at a time predetermined by God, there still are not two sons but one, not a second son, but the same one born in another manner. He was born of the substance of the Virgin, that we might recognize the reality of his human nature. To be conceived of the Holy Spirit without action on the part of a man and to be born without impairment to his mother's virginity was the exclusive right of his greatness.[42]

KA Why does it add 'our Lord'?

CA The Sacred Scriptures frequently honour him with this name, particularly in the New Testament. In so far as he was God of God, he was Lord of all, but not a Lord other than the Father, just as he is not another God either. For a special reason he is called the Lord of the Elect, whom he has freed from the domination of Satan and made the people of his own special possession.[43] Whoever commits sin makes himself its slave;[44] through sin Satan obtains his tyrannical sway. The creed then reminds us that dominion has been transferred from this most cruel tyrant to Jesus Christ, by far the kindest master of all, and it is by this title that the New Testament often designates the Son of God, pointing out the one to whom recipients of baptism dedicate their entire selves, and whose commands they must afterwards obey throughout their entire life without any objection, and under whose protection they can live a life free from trouble. For no one can wrest from him what he possesses.

KA How is the name of Lord appropriate to Christ? From his divine nature or his human nature or both?

CA From both, but not in the same way. In keeping with his higher nature, he was Lord of all things from the beginning of the world; in keeping with his assumed nature, by his death he deserved to enter into glory, 'and he was given a name which is above every name, so that at the

* * * * *

41 Eph 2:3
42 Cf the colloquy *Inquisitio de fide* ASD I-3 367:125–32 / Thompson *Inquisitio* 60 / CWE 39 425:11–19; *Ratio* LB V 94F.
43 1 Pet 2:9
44 Rom 6:17

name of Jesus every knee should bow in heaven and on earth and under the earth.'[45]

KA As man, then, is he lord of the angels?

CA Completely. He is also lord of the demons.

KA To what does the word 'only' [*unicum*][46] refer – to the word 'Son' which precedes it, or to the word 'Lord' which follows it?

CA That word, indeed, is ambiguous in the context, since it agrees with both 'Son' and 'Lord.' For, as the Son is unique by nature, he is likewise the unique Lord of all created things. However, the word is more correctly used of the Son, since this distinction clearly indicates the divine nature, which he has by generation from his Father, and in common with his Father.[47]

KA Why, then, has the creed not been made to read, 'in his only Son' [*in unico filio eius*]? Then there would have been no ambiguity.

CA The later position was more fitting for a word added to make a distinction. For indeed if the creed had said *unicum filium eius* it could be understood that the name 'Son of God' was not appropriate except for one man, Jesus. As it is, when he adds 'only' he does not divide the Son but points out his mode of generation,[48] so that we may understand that the same Word, born God from God the Father outside of time, is born human from human of the Virgin within time. Augustine in his book *On the Creed* puts two words instead of one: 'and in Jesus Christ, his only-begotten Son [*unigenitum*], our only [*unicum*]

* * * * *

45 Phil 2:10. They are discussing the ways in which Christ's assumed, or human, nature can appropriately be compared to his essential, or divine, nature, as Christ's personhood combines the two into perfect unity, and is at the same time in a relationship of perfect unity with the Father.

46 Cf Rufinus 8 PL 21 348. Only: Erasmus is referring to the placement of *unicum* between *filium eius* and *dominum* in the phrase 'Credit et in Iesu Christo filio eius unico, domino nostro.'

47 In other words, the purpose of the term's inclusion is to point to the unique nature of Christ's position as Son.

48 That is, between his divine and his human natures, as Erasmus will now explain. He is suggesting that the distinction could not have been highlighted in this way had the placement of *unicum* been earlier, for *unicum* in the later position modifies more emphatically Christ's nature in terms of his divine sonship, coming as it does directly after the pronoun *eius*, whose antecedent is of course God the Father. 'His Son, the one and only' is more emphatic than 'His only Son,' which could be perceived as one possibility among others (ie the Father could have had other sons but did not).

Lord.'⁴⁹ But it is not clear from his explanation that this was his own reading of the text; it is probable that 'only-begotten' [*unigenitum*] was added by someone who was trying to explain why the creed has 'only' [*unicum*]. For the Son of God in the Scriptures is at times called 'first-born' [*primogenitus*] in keeping with his assumed nature⁵⁰ and 'only-begotten' [*unigenitus*] in keeping with his divine birth: Romans 8, 'that he might be the first-born among many brethren';⁵¹ John 1, 'We have seen his glory, the glory as of the only-begotten Son of the Father';⁵² John 3, 'God so loved the world that he gave his only-begotten Son.'⁵³ According to the former generation, he is neither our brother nor the heir of God nor has he brothers or co-heirs; according to the latter, he has brothers and co-heirs.

KA Is there no difference between 'only' and 'only-begotten'?⁵⁴

CA 'Only' can be predicated of the one who is the sole survivor among the children; you could not correctly call him 'only-begotten.' Yet the interpreters of the sacred books translate the same word, μονογενής, at times as 'only,' at times as 'only-begotten.' For example, in Luke 7 the widow's son, whom the evangelist called μονογενής, is called 'only.'⁵⁵ Moreover, πρωτότοκος, that is, 'first-born,' is sometimes understood as 'only-begotten.' This is how Matthew speaks of the mother of Jesus: 'She gave birth to her first-born son.'⁵⁶ For 'first' is sometimes used not of what precedes others, but of what never was before. For example, when the statement is made 'I saw Caesar today for the first time,' the statement is correct, even if one were never to see him later. Thus 'first-born' can be said of one brought forth at a first birth, even if no other birth is

* * * * *

49 Augustine *De symbolo ad catechumenos* 2.3 PL 40 629: 'et in Iesum Christum Filium eius unigenitum, unicum Dominum nostrum'

50 Cf Col 1:15: 'Qui est imago Dei invisibilis primogenitus omnis creaturae' (Vulg) / 'He is the image of the invisible God, the first-born of all creation' (RSV). This phrase stresses Christ's assumed nature by placing him first in a continuum of all creation. N56 below gives another example that stresses the assumed nature.

51 Rom 8:29

52 John 1:14: 'gloriam quasi unigeniti a Patre' (Vulg), stressing the divine nature

53 John 3:16: 'sic enim dilexit Deus mundum ut Filium suum unigenitum daret' (Vulg), again stressing the divine nature

54 *Unicum* and *unigenitum*

55 Luke 7:12: 'filius unicus matri suae'

56 Matthew: read Luke 2:7.

to follow; otherwise, what the law orders to be done in the case of the first-born could not be put into effect unless there were two subsequent births.[57] For 'first' is used only in reference to one who holds the first of three places.[58]

KA But if Christ in accordance with his human nature is Lord of all, how is he said to have brothers?

CA Even if Christ were not Lord of all in accordance with his assumed nature, nevertheless, because of the substantial unity that embraces the three hypostases, he would be rightly called Lord of all, just as we piously say that God suffered and died. In this instance 'brother' is not a word indicating equality but similitude, association, and love. With the same regard, he calls his disciples 'friends rather than servants.'[59] Yet he does not renounce here the right that he recognizes elsewhere when he says, 'You call me master and Lord and you say well, for so I am,'[60] but rather reveals his extraordinary love, which refuses nothing, provided it is beneficial. What is strange, then, in his deigning to give the title of brothers to those for whom he did not disdain to act as a servant? The Jews used to give the title of brother to all of their own race and more especially to relatives. Moreover, the Lord was born a Jew from Jews, as Matthew and Luke clearly set forth in their genealogy.[61] In fact, every human is a brother or sister of every other human by reason of the same nature originating in the same ancestors and subject to like sufferings – provided that, in the case of Christ, I except sin and whatever turns towards it.

KA Original sin is not strictly speaking a sin.

CA But it is an obstacle to the fullness of grace that was in Christ, according to the testimony of John, and it inclines towards sin without forcing to it.[62] This is incompatible with the dignity of Christ. It was not fitting that the one who had come to cleanse the world from all sin would in any way be associated with sin.

* * * * *

57 Exod 22:29b
58 Thus Erasmus has two meanings for *primus*, one whereby the incidence of subsequent occurrences is irrelevant, and a second whereby, in recognition of the distinction between dual and plural, *primus* must be first in a series of at least three.
59 John 15:15
60 John 13:13
61 Matt 1:1–17; Luke 3:23–38
62 See 238 n13 above.

KA Hunger, thirst, fatigue, distress, weariness, death are the offshoots of original sin, and yet they are attributed to Christ in the Scriptures.[63]

CA There is a very great difference between created nature and fallen nature. Before Adam sinned he was a real human, and yet was free from these disadvantages by which all of us humans are afflicted to a greater or lesser extent. Sin in Scripture sometimes means the punishment due to sin, sometimes the victim by whom sin is expiated. Thus it was said to the priests of old, 'You will feed on the sins of my people.'[64] Paul, too, in 2 Corinthians 5, said, 'For our sake, he made the one who knew no sin a sin.'[65] The Lord took on himself not only the reality of our nature, but also the disadvantages that accompany fallen nature, except for those that are not in keeping with the dignity of the person who was both divine and human at the same time, or those that, as I just said, exclude the fullness of grace. For he did not take on himself the inclination to sin, or even the power to sin; nor did he take on himself error or ignorance. Moreover, those evils which he took on himself he accepted not by compulsion of nature but willingly for our sake, so that he might pay the debt which we had contracted.

KA Why did the creed make a change of preposition: 'of the Holy Spirit, from the Virgin Mary.'?

CA The Greeks have one and the same preposition, ἐξ, but it has different meanings. 'All things are from him and through him,'[66] as if originating from a progenitor. A dish is made from gold, that is its material; a tree is generated from a tree by propagation of the species; in this way human is born of human.

KA Why does the creed mention only the Spirit, since the whole Trinity together brought about this adorable mystery?

CA Because in the Gospel according to Luke the angel says to the Virgin, 'The Holy Spirit will come upon you.'[67] Not infrequently the Scripture assigns attributes to the individual Persons as though belonging to them, although they are common to all, as when it attributes eternity and omnipotence to the Father, wisdom to the Son, love and goodness to the

* * * * *

63 Hunger: Matt 4:2, Luke 4:2; thirst: John 4:7, 19:28; fatigue: John 4:6; distress: Mark 14:33; weariness: Mark 14:33; death: Mark 15:37, Luke 23:46, John 19:30. See 248 n5 above.

64 Hos 4:8

65 2 Cor 5:21

66 Rom 11:36; see the annotation on this passage in LB VI 628B.

67 Luke 1:35

Holy Spirit, or when the Father is said to have created the world through the Son[68] and to bestow charisms through the Spirit.[69] The creed, then, and Gabriel announcing this mystery, set forth the function of the three Persons. 'The Holy Spirit,' he says, 'will come upon you and the power of the Most High will overshadow you.'[70] When you hear 'Most High,' you understand that the Father is present as the source and origin, as the one from whom the Son is sent with the Holy Spirit; when you hear 'the power of the Most High' you understand that it is the Son who has exclusively assumed flesh. For neither the Father nor the Holy Spirit assumed a human form. It is fitting, then, that the Holy Spirit is said to 'come upon' Mary. This expression precludes all human thinking, which, when it hears the word 'conception' or 'birth,' has an image of male seed received into a female womb, or, when it is informed that a child has been born of a virgin, envisages something filthier than this, pondering what is spread abroad in human fables about some women who are said to have become pregnant from male seed floating in a bath, about mares pregnant by the wind, and about incubuses [71] – not to mention the fictions of the poets, by which the pagans were persuaded and believed that heroes are born from a union of gods and human beings. To prevent the spreading of any such extraordinary tales, the evangelist declares publicly that the heavenly Father was there instead of a husband and that he somehow begets his Son anew.[72] He declares publicly that the foetus did not originate from an incubus or from any prank of an impious spirit, but from the Holy Spirit. The whole course of the gospel narrative clearly declares that this is so; when the Virgin felt an uncertainty at the mention of conception and birth and asked, 'How will this come about?'[73] the angel, removing her doubt, answered, 'The Holy Spirit will come upon you.'[74]

KA Why does the creed set forth the Virgin's name?

CA To promote greater trust in the account. In the same way, the creed sets forth the name of Jesus Christ; in the same way, it sets forth the name

* * * * *

68 John 1:3
69 Acts 10:38; Rom 15:13
70 Luke 1:35
71 Incubuses: see Augustine *De civitate Dei* 15.23.1 PL 41 468.
72 Begets anew: the second begetting refers to Christ's appearance in human history; he has already been present with the Father since the beginning (John 1:1).
73 Luke 1:34
74 Luke 1:35

and surname of the governor: 'under Pontius Pilate.' For this purpose, Luke in the following passage carefully set forth all the names – of the month, of God who sent a deputy, of the angel sent as deputy, of the territory, of the city, of the spouse, of the house, and of the Virgin – when he says, 'In the sixth month the angel Gabriel was sent from God to a city of Galilee called Nazareth, to a virgin espoused to a man whose name was Joseph, of the house of David; the virgin's name was Mary.'[75] Those who are writing fiction and are afraid of being caught do not write their story in this way.

Long before, Isaiah, inspired by the Holy Spirit, prophesied, 'Behold, a virgin will conceive and bring forth a son, and he shall be called Emmanuel,'[76] which is interpreted 'God with us.' The evangelist, inspired by the same Spirit, points out the same Virgin with his finger, as it were. The angel, as though explaining the prophecy, says, 'And the child that will be born of you will be called holy, the Son of God.'[77] This is that Mary at whose name all pious souls are revivified. When we hear the name of Eve we groan, when we hear the name of Mary we are raised to high hope. Through Eve we are born the children of wrath,[78] through Mary we are born the children of grace.

KA Would someone be considered a heretic if he believed that the Virgin Mary bore other sons by her husband after the birth of Jesus?

CA Not only a heretic, but a blasphemer.

KA But people deny that this belief[79] is set forth in the Sacred Scriptures.

CA That is so, but it is an obvious inference from them, and the denial these people make is obviously at variance with the dignity of both the Son and the mother. Finally, from the beginning of the gospel to this very day, the Catholic church has believed, taught, and emphasized this with a unanimity so great that it should be no less persuasive than if it were set forth in the sacred writings.[80]

* * * * *

75 Luke 1:26–7
76 Isa 7:14
77 Luke 1:35
78 Eph 2:3
79 The doctrine of the perpetual virginity of Mary. The passage of Scripture that seems to refute this doctrine most clearly is Matt 13:55, referring to Jesus' brothers.
80 Erasmus is essentially correct in characterizing orthodox opinion as virtually unanimous. Cf Augustine *De catechizandis rudibus* 22.40 PL 40 339; Rufinus 9 PL 21 349. There was an indirect challenge from Tertullian, who claimed in *De carne Christi* 23 PL 2 790 that the Virgin's womb was opened when she

KA   I am looking forward to the account from the Scriptures.

CA   Ezekiel foreshadowed the perpetual chastity of the Virgin in a prophetic
allegory, when he turned back 'to the gate of the outer sanctuary, which
faced east,' and heard from the same Spirit who immortalized the purity
of Mary, 'This gate will be closed and it will not be opened and no man
shall pass through it, since the Lord God of Israel has entered by it, and
it will be closed to the prince.'[81] Has not the prophet portrayed aptly
enough the consecrated womb of the Virgin, from which there arose for
us that 'sun of justice'[82] which 'enlightens every man coming into this
world'?[83] Zacharias says of this sun in Luke, 'Rising from the deep he
has come to visit us, to give light to those who sit in darkness and the
shadow of death.'[84] This gate was closed before the birth, it was closed
too during the birth, it remained closed even after the birth. It lay open
for Christ the prince alone. By his entrance he sanctified it, and by his
emergence he sanctified it, since that gate faced only to the east, from
which there comes forth the purest sun, that sun that never sets, that
renews and enlivens all things. That gate faced the road leading to the
outer sanctuary, since that birth was set apart from the common birth of
men, and had nothing of human concupiscence mingled with it. Finally,
when Mary says to the angel, 'since I do not know man,'[85] she reveals
sufficiently her vow of perpetual virginity.

KA   But since marriage is of itself an honourable state, and conjugal union is
free from fault, what dishonour would there have been if the Lord had
been born in the same way as the other prophets and John, a person
more outstanding than all the prophets?

* * * * *

gave birth to Christ, thereby transforming her from a virgin into a woman
living according to the law of marriage, and thus no longer a virgin. Likewise in *Adversus Marcion* 4.19 PL 2 404–5 he claimed that Christ's brothers
were brothers in the flesh, although he did not explicitly state that Mary was
their mother (in which case the degree of kinship could have been less immediate). The most direct challenge came from Helvidius in 390, prompt-
ing Jerome's reply *De Mariae virginitate perpetua adversus Helvidium* PL 23
193–216.

81   Ezek 44:1–3; cf *Paean Virgini Matri* LB V 1230F–1231A. Erasmus selected this
text as a possible first reading in the liturgy he constructed for Our Lady of
Loreto, ASD V-1 97.

82   Mal 4:2

83   John 1:9

84   Luke 1:78–9

85   Luke 1:34

CA A marriage bond maintained with chastity is indeed honourable, but perpetual virginity is far more honourable, provided it is undertaken willingly and through love of piety.[86] The contagion of the original evil is passed on by concupiscence, without which humans are not conceived. But a more than angelic purity befitted that heavenly birth. Come, tell me, if someone were to turn a stone temple that was once consecrated to God by a bishop (despite his being merely human) into a cobbler's workshop, would not all exclaim that it was a most shameful deed?

KA By all means. They would stone the person.

CA Yet there is nothing disgraceful in the cobbler's art. And if one were to employ a vessel blessed for baptism, or holy oil, or other religious purposes, for everyday kitchen uses, would it not be considered an intolerable insult?

KA Certainly.

CA And yet there is no fault to be found with the art of cooking.

KA That is correct.

CA What, then, is to be said about the most sacred temple of the Virgin's body? No bishop consecrated it with oil perceived by the senses, but the Holy Spirit himself consecrated with a heavenly anointing the body in which that divine offspring rested for so many months as in a bedchamber, the body that served as a workshop where the entire Trinity completed that mystery to be adored by angelic minds.[87] Would it not appear entirely unbecoming if it had been opened, I will not say to a man, but even to an angel?

KA I see that clearly.

CA Now consider this: should one assent to the church, which is so unanimous, rather than to the Jews, who rave over other points as well, or to the obscure and unlearned Helvidius?[88] His error so clearly flows from an incorrect understanding of Scripture that he found scarcely any followers, and to the ancient Doctors of the church he seemed hardly worth refuting.

KA I see how perpetual virginity befitted that birth. But why did the Lord want to be born of a betrothed woman?

CA Care was taken that the young virgin have a protector, guardian, nurse, and attendant without evoking any sinister suspicion from the evil-

* * * * *

86 Erasmus makes the same point, but less emphatically, in *De vidua christiana* LB V 734D / CWE 66 201–2.

87 Cf *Paean Virgini Matri* LB V 1230D.

88 See 290 n80 above.

minded crowd, and also that she have a husband as the most important witness to her integrity. It was fitting that such a virgin should have the greatest tranquillity. Not only did it behoove the Mother of God to be entirely free from every stain, but it was also fitting that she should not be touched even by false tales; for that woman is indeed outstandingly chaste whom rumour blushes to detract. Therefore, this mystery was for long concealed. For it is probable that Mary and Joseph kept these mysteries in their hearts[89] until the Spirit was sent from heaven, and the gospel spread its light through every land.

See then how much we have learned, through this article, although it is compressed into a few words: that Jesus Christ is true God from God, and that he is also truly human, born of a human virgin, not through the action of a male, but by an act of the divine Spirit; that he came into this world not only to redeem the world, but also to instruct us with full authority and by various arguments to kindle the fires of love for the heavenly life.

Now, please consider how many spectral errors the light of this truth has scattered. I recount the detestable blasphemies and the unholy names of their authors reluctantly, but this subject will profitably result in our holding what we hold more firmly, and in our returning thanks to God more fully, because he has deigned to unveil so great a light to us. It is not too surprising that many have hallucinated about the divine birth from the Father; it is a mark of greater insanity that the human birth, presented with so many clear proofs, has been attacked by so many monstrous arguments. Carpocrates,[90] Cerinthus,[91] Ebion,[92] Paul of Samosata,[93] Photinus (whose name is light but whose doctrine is dark)[94]

* * * * *

89 Cf Luke 2:19.
90 Carpocrates: second-century Gnostic, refuted by Irenaeus in *Adversus haereses* 1.25 PG 7 680–6.
91 Cerinthus: Gnostic heretic; see Eusebius *Historia ecclesiastica* 3.28 PG 20 273–6, which attributes to him a vivid description of Christ's kingdom in terms of physical fulfilments; see also Irenaeus *Adversus haereses* 1.26.1 PG 7 686.
92 Ebion: derived from the Hebrew word for 'poor.' The Ebionites were a sect of Judaizing Christians who believed that Christ was the preordained Messiah, but not the Son of God by birth. See Irenaeus *Adversus haereses* 1.26.2 PG 7 686–7.
93 Paul of Samosata: adoptionist, condemned at Antioch in 268. He taught that Jesus was a man, conceived by the Holy Spirit, born of a virgin, who was inspired by the Holy Word, and gained full divine status progressively.
94 Photinus: see Rufinus 1 PL 21 336–7. A fourth-century bishop of Sirmium, eventually ejected in 351, he was a disciple of Marcellus of Ancyra (fl 335) and

acknowledge that Christ was truly human, but a mere human, born of a man and woman in the same way as other humans, although he did have a prophetic soul.[95] They cut away more than half of Christ's person.

The same writers say that Christ is called 'son' only by free adoption like other pious men, and that he did not exist at all before he was born of the Virgin.[96] John the Evangelist clearly refutes them when he proclaims that Christ is that Word that 'was with God in the beginning, and was God, and became flesh.'[97] In the work of the same evangelist, too, the Lord himself clearly says, 'Before Abraham came to be, I am.'[98] Again, in Romans 9 Paul says, 'From them, according to the flesh, is Christ, who is God over all things, blessed forever.'[99]

The Manichees are no less mad.[100] They attribute some part of the divine nature to Christ, maintaining, however, that he did not assume a real human body but a phantom one, in the same way that, as we read, angels and demons sometimes appeared to men. These people make Christ a trickster or a conjurer. But a spectre is not born of a human, nor does he do what Christ did year by year throughout his entire life – eating, drinking, sleeping, tiring, feeling hunger, feeling thirst, speaking, moving about in broad daylight, allowing himself to be touched and to be felt, to be crucified, and to be put to death. In the last chapter of Luke, when the disciples were terrified because they thought that they were seeing a spirit and a ghost, he himself said: 'Why are you disturbed, and why do questions rise in your hearts? See my hands and my feet, for it is I myself; feel and see, for a spirit does not have flesh and bones as you see that I have.'[101]

Valentinus,[102] the fabricator of Aeons, followed these heretics; he explained that Christ was not born of the substance of the Virgin, but

* * * * *

may have had an adoptionist Christology. The name Photinus is derived from τὸ φῶς, the Greek word for light.

95 This is not altogether accurate, although the heterodox teachings of these people centred on Christological issues.

96 Adoptionism: see 267 n103, 283 n38 above. Adoptionism is not inconsistent with a belief that the soul of Christ is the divine λόγος; where problems arise is in articulating the relation of the λόγος to the Father, or the unity of Christ's human and divine natures.

97 John 1:1, 14

98 John 8:58

99 Rom 9:5

100 Manichees: see 274 n152 above.

101 Luke 24:38–9

102 Valentinus: Gnostic teacher at Alexandria and Rome, mid-second century. According to his doctrine, Christ was one of a series of emanations (Aeons) from

brought a heavenly body down with him from heaven (or, as the demented Apelles[103] prefers, a body taken from elements in the air) and thus passed through the Virgin's body as water and light pass through a pipe or a crack. This is not birth in the true sense, but only a transition. It is not the crack that produces the ray, but the sun; it is not the water pipe that produces the water, but the spring. Moreover, when Paul, the Apostle, says to the Romans, 'who was born of the seed of David according to the flesh,'[104] and to the Galatians, 'God sent his Son born of woman,'[105] he clearly proclaims that Christ took the substance of his body from the Virgin.[106] Nor is whatever arises from humans in any way whatsoever automatically human. Otherwise, lice would be called human beings. But what is conceived in a womb of true human substance, is born at the proper time through natural channels, reproduces a man in all his distinguishing marks, and is called 'son' – this is certainly a man.

Arius,[107] with a madness that is the more wretched for its subtlety, attributes a human body to Christ, but takes away the human soul, and says that in its place there was a 'word.' Thus, in Christ there were only two natures, a human body and a 'word.' Arius maintains that this word is a creature – superior to all others, but still a creature. Yet how do they dare to acknowledge as human one from whom they take away the more important part of humanity? Who does not know that man is composed of two separable substances, a body as matter, a soul as form?[108] If some spirit moves the body of a dead person, no one will call

* * * * *

the supreme Father. His followers were denounced by Tertullian in *Adversus Valentinianos* PL 2 523–96.
103 Apelles: disciple of Marcion (see 273 n147 above), teacher at Alexandria and Rome. See Augustine *De haeresibus* 23 PL 42 29; Tertullian *De praescriptionibus haereticorum* 30 PL 2 42–3.
104 Rom 1:3
105 Gal 4:4
106 Regarding the theory that the mother provides the material substance of the infant's body, see Thomas Aquinas *Summa theologica* I q 118 art 1: 'In perfect animals, generated by coition, the active force is in the semen of the male, as the Philosopher says; but the foetal matter is provided by the female.' See also ibidem III q 31 art 5. On Christ's taking his flesh from a woman see ibidem III q 31 art 4.
107 Arius: see 273 n149 above.
108 See Thomas Aquinas *Summa theologica* I q 75 art 5. Erasmus is arguing as a dualist here, although he will proceed to divide the soul into two components, the sensible and the rational. Cf *Enchiridion* LB V 19A–20E / CWE 66 51–2, in which he argues as a trichotomist, dividing human nature into body, soul, and spirit.

what he sees a human, but a monster and a portent. Moreover, the Lord himself made mention of his soul and called himself the 'Son of Man,' in many passages, such as 'My soul is sorrowful even unto death';[109] 'Father, into your hands I commend my spirit';[110] 'No one takes away my soul from me but I lay it down';[111] 'You seek to kill me, a man who has told you the truth.'[112] Paul testifies that 'the human Jesus Christ is the mediator between God and humans.'[113]

If these heretics believe the Scriptures, how shameless to deny what the Scriptures so clearly proclaim! If they do not believe them, how shameless is their desire to be called Christian! If they wish to be considered philosophers ... whoever dreamt that what lacks human form could be called human? The presence of that form makes someone human, and its departure causes what was formerly human to lose the name. Those who are deranged in so strange a manner run the risk of seeming not to be human themselves.

The ravings of Apollinarius[114] are not much sounder. He allows a soul to be attributed to Christ, but he takes away his mind. In living plants there is something of soul; otherwise they would not grow, nor would they be said to die when they wither. There is also a soul in irrational animals; otherwise they would have no feelings; but mind, which the Greeks call νοῦς, is present only in humans among living things. This is the particular power of soul through which it judges individual things, by which it unites or divides them, and by which it deduces one thing from another through reasoning. But if they take away from Christ that which above all else distinguishes humans from the rest of living things, how do they have the effrontery to acknowledge him as human?

KA Did Christ then by reason deduce the unknown from the known?

CA Nothing was unknown to Christ, and yet, because it is the intrinsic condition of human nature, he had a rational soul. The angels do not understand by reasoning as we do, and we will not have the same kind of understanding after the resurrection. But when perfection is added

* * * * *

109 Matt 26:38
110 Luke 23:46 [Ps 31:5 (Vulg 30:6)]
111 John 10:18
112 John 8:40
113 1 Tim 2:5
114 Apollinarius of Laodicea (c 310–90): condemned by the Council of Constantinople in 381, he believed that in Christ the divine Word was substituted for the human mind, as well as the animating principle of the body. See Augustine *De haeresibus* 55 PL 42 40.

to nature it does not remove the reality of nature. Otherwise, glorified bodies would not be real bodies. Nor is it impious to say that the soul of Christ began to understand some things that it knew through the presence of divinity in a different and human way – not that he was ignorant of them before, but his way of learning was different. He had 'seen' Nathaniel when he was under the fig tree because he knew Nathaniel's whereabouts with greater certainty than we know what we see with our eyes. Later, when looking at him with his bodily eyes, he learned nothing new, but saw in a different way what he had seen before.[115]

Apollinarius adds another piece of madness to the effect that the Word did not assume flesh, but that part of the Word was changed into flesh. He misunderstood what John says, 'And the Word was made flesh.'[116] This means, as he wrongly interprets it, 'The Word was transmuted into flesh,' just as air when condensed turns into water, and water when vaporized into air. Humans are not made, however, of a plastic 'word' converted into a human body, but of a rational soul and a mortal body. If they interpret their 'word' as the Son of God, they err; for God, just as he consists of nothing but God, cannot be changed into anything else, nor can anything else be changed into him, strictly speaking. If philosophers deny that transmutation takes place between elements that have no mutual affinity – for instance, fire does not turn into water – how much more absurd it is to have an uncreated thing turn into a created one! They indeed make the Word a creature, but more excellent than all the angels. However, there is a greater difference between an angel and a human body than between fire and water. This error, arising from a fatuous interpretation of the words of the Evangelist, is clearly refuted by what follows immediately there: 'and he dwelt among us.'[117] For what is transformed into a body is not said to dwell in the body, but the body is rightly called the dwelling-place of the soul and man is rightly called the temple of God.[118]

The ravings of the ill-named Eutyches[119] were equally infelicitous. He placed just one nature composed of the divine and the human in Christ.

* * * * *

115 Cf John 1:47–50.
116 John 1:14
117 John 1:14
118 Cf 1 Cor 3:16, 6:19.
119 Eutyches: Erasmus calls him wrongly named because the name means 'good fortune.' Condemned in 451 at the Council of Chalcedon, he believed that Christ was of two natures before the Incarnation, but of one nature (φύσις)

If he had said that from two natures there was formed one person, singular and, as the dialecticians say, individual, he would have deserved a hearing. For it is agreed that there were two or even three natures, in Christ distinct from one another. Humans are composed of a soul and body, but the divine nature, since it is absolutely simple, rejects every designation of composition. It united itself into one hypostasis, or person, attaching itself to the body by means of the intervening soul, but it was not fused with the same human nature.

Nestorius, [120] intent on avoiding this lime-kiln, fell into the furnace when he maintained that there are two perfect natures in Christ, divine and human, but also postulated two persons, denying that the Word was united with the human in one person, and saying that the Word dwelt in the human person only by grace. From this he concludes that in the same Christ there is one human person and another divine person. Mary cannot rightly be called the Mother of God, but only the mother of the human person, since the angel in Luke says to the Virgin, 'Therefore what is born of you is holy, and will be called the Son of God.'[121] In truth, due to the unity of Christ's person, by a certain sharing of attributes, even these words which are appropriate only to his human nature are correctly predicated of him as God, provided they are used concretely.[122] God, but not the divinity, is born of the Virgin; God, but not the divinity, suffered; and God is a man, but the divinity is not human nature.

Although there is no end to error, I will make an end of this list. I fear that by mentioning so many things I have already bored you.

* * * * *

after. This, he believed, is because the humanity of Christ was completely absorbed by his divinity. The importance of the distinction Erasmus is making between *natura* or φύσις, 'nature,' and *persona* or πρόσωπον, 'person,' lies in the need for Christological doctrine ultimately to establish that Christ was at the same time fully human, fully divine, and simple and indivisible.

120 Nestorius: patriarch of Constantinople from 428 to 431. Nestorius' Christology was the centre of a major controversy. He argued for a rigorous separation between Christ's two natures, to the extent of denying Mary the title of Mother of God (θεοτόκος). Nestorius himself did not claim that Christ was two persons, as Erasmus suggests here, but others interpreted his teaching in that way.

121 Luke 1:35

122 *In vocibus concretis:* here Erasmus makes use of the scholastic logic he so often disparages, in distinguishing between abstract and concrete terms to establish a point of theology. Predication in the concrete form occurs when actions or qualities are predicated of individuals (such as 'God') rather than understood as attributes in abstraction from individuals (such as 'divinity').

KA Indeed, I pity those fellows. Yet I have benefited from their insanity, since through them I been made to see the truth more clearly and believe more firmly.

CA We owe the heretics no thanks, but we owe the greatest thanks to God. His goodness turns the evil of others into a growth of piety in his own people.

KA Why does the creed issued by the Synod of Constantinople not consider it sufficient to say, 'born of the Virgin Mary,' adding 'and he was made human'?

CA Because those who wished to expound more subtly about Christ, although held fast by different errors, agree in this – they deny that he is human, taking from him something whose absence would prevent any one of us from being truly called human. Accordingly, it is clearly explained, 'and he was made human,' to prevent anyone infected by the poison of those persons from coming forward to be baptized. In any case, who is so devoid of common sense that, when he hears that the Gracchi were sons of Cornelia, he would ask if the Gracchi[123] were men?

KA Why such strange human blindness?

CA Because they have preferred to investigate divine matters rather than simply believe in them. Scripture says that we will not understand unless we believe.[124] They, however, decided to seek understanding through the turgid philosophy of the world[125] before believing. Let this conversation end here, so that, having turned these subjects over in your mind and given thanks to the divine Spirit, you may be more eager to understand the rest when you return.

Lesson 4

KA The creed continues, 'suffered under Pontius Pilate, was crucified, died, and was buried.'

CA The same people who attribute an imaginary body to Christ say, 'Everything he is alleged to have suffered in the flesh, he endured not in reality,

* * * * *

123 Gracchi: Tiberius (d 134 BC) and Gaius (d 121 BC) Gracchus, tribunes in the Roman republic, whose attempts at sweeping land reform resulted in their violent deaths, thus setting the stage for a century of political unrest and, ultimately, revolution.

124 Isa 7:9; cf Augustine *De fide et symbolo* 1.1 PL 40 181.

125 Philosophy of the world: Erasmus poses this in direct opposition to the philosophy of Christ; see 237 n6 above.

but in appearance.' We who, instructed by heaven, believe that he was truly human, likewise believe that he really suffered in both soul and body, that he was really crucified, that he died and was buried. The natural death of a human being is the separation of the soul from the body. We all know what a person's corpse is like when this takes place; the soul, however, since it is immortal, remains alive with Christ after the body has collapsed, if it has departed in faith and with the expectation that its own body will rise again.

KA What is the difference between an angel and a soul separated from its body?

CA They differ in this – the soul is indeed a mind, as the angels are, but when it is being infused into the body, it is created from nothing in such a way that it is naturally suited to give life to, rule, and move not any body whatsoever, but that one for which it was especially designed by God. The difference between the death of Christ and our death lies in the fact that our soul is driven out by the force of disease or a lack of humours, while the Lord willingly laid down his life, just as he willingly approached the cross.[1] The proof of this is that he died on the cross immediately after uttering a loud cry. Indeed, he himself says in John, 'No one takes my life from me, but I lay it down of my own accord.'[2]

KA But where, meanwhile, was the Word of God, which, you kept saying, was so closely united to the human that it formed the same person? In the separated soul or in the dead body?

CA St Augustine piously believed that the Word was not separated from either the body or the soul.[3] But it is better not to enter a labyrinth of questions of this kind. We are dealing with the basics, not with the high points, and we are laying the foundation, not applying the finishing touches, since we are instructing a catechumen, not a theologian; in sum, we are training a recruit for the faith, not a veteran for battle.

KA Why do we add 'he suffered,' since these words are not added by people of former times? Does not whoever is crucified suffer?

CA It appears that this small part was added to combat certain persons who explained that the Word took on and absorbed, as it were, a body, and somehow rendered it transformed in himself, so that it could not be touched by any feeling of pain. They say that Galanus[4] was the author

* * * * *

1 Cf Augustine *De Trinitate* 4.13.16 PL 42 898–9.
2 John 10:18
3 See Augustine *Sermones* 242.4.6 PL 38 1140–1.
4 Galanus: Gaianus, head of a monophysite sect originating in the fifth century; see DTC VI 999–1023. See also Aquinas *In articulos fidei et sacramenta ecclesiae,*

of this tenet. But the Scripture refutes this on every side. First Isaiah says, 'Surely he has borne our griefs and carried our sorrows.'[5] Lest anyone could quibble about this, objecting that the prophecy is obscure, and that it might possibly refer to someone other than Christ, St Luke relates in Acts chapter 8 how Philip, urged by the Holy Spirit, entered the chariot of the eunuch and by the same Spirit explained for him this whole passage about the suffering of Christ.[6] Pious men too have applied the contents of Jeremiah's Lamentations to the sufferings of Christ: 'O, all of you who pass by, look and see if there is any sorrow like my sorrow.'[7] In the Gospel according to Luke also the Lord says, 'Was it not necessary that Christ should suffer and so enter into his glory?'[8] Likewise in 1 Peter 2: '... who, when he suffered, did not make threats.'[9] Again in the same place: 'Christ suffered for us, leaving you an example that you should follow in his steps.'[10] How, then, can we follow him by bearing sufferings, if he endured no pain? Also in Paul's Epistle to the Romans chapter 8: '... if only we suffer with him, in order that we may be glorified with him.'[11] Paul uses the word for 'to suffer with' not with the meaning 'to feel pain at' the sufferings of another, but to follow his example and bear persecution by the wicked patiently. Christ himself also testifies to what he suffered in his soul as well, when he says, 'My soul is sorrowful even unto death.'[12] Add to these testimonies that he suffered for us throughout his entire life when he was thirsty, hungry, weary, insulted, cast out, bound, spat upon, beaten with fists.[13] The word 'suffer' can be applied to these things and others like them.

KA   Why does the creed describe so carefully the manner of his death?

* * * * *

Expositio in Aquinas Opuscula 118: 'Secundus est error Galani, qui in Christo unam naturam posuit, sed incorporalem et immortalem.'

5 Isa 53:4

6 Acts 8:26–35

7 Lam 1:12

8 Luke 24:26

9 1 Pet 2:23

10 1 Pet 2:21

11 Rom 8:17

12 Matt 26:38; Erasmus' De taedio Iesu 13–67 above is a commentary on this verse.

13 Thirsty: John 4:7, 19:28; hungry: Matt 4:2, Luke 4:2; weary: Mark 14:33; met with insults: Matt 27:39–44; cast out: Matt 21:39, Mark 12:8, Luke 20:15; bound: Mark 15:1; spat upon: Matt 26:67, Mark 15:19; beaten with fists: Matt 26:67, Mark 14:65

CA For the same reason that it mentions the name and surname of Pilate,[14] that is, to increase the credibility of the account.

KA But why did God will to redeem the world by the death of his Son, and by such a death?

CA You tell me this first. Suppose that a physician, by far the most skilled in his art, should take charge of a patient suffering from a fatal disease and someone, totally unskilled in the art, should rudely ask him, 'Why are you curing the person by that procedure?' Would not the questioner rightly seem shameless? How much more impudent it is to demand from God the reason why he willed to redeem the world in this way! We must believe with unshaken faith that only what is best pleases God, whether it seems so to us or not.[15]

KA The foundation of faith stands unshaken.[16] Nevertheless, it is, I think, lawful to ask questions about these things in a reverent manner.

CA And for us to answer them, but with the same reverence. These problems call for special treatment, but I will touch on a few points in passing, as it were. Through an earthly being death invaded the world, and it was fitting that it should be removed through a heavenly being.[17] Through unlawful pleasure the ruin of the human race crept in; through pain salvation was restored. Through a virgin deceived by the breath of the serpent, misfortune came; through a virgin pregnant by the breath of the Holy Spirit, happiness returned. Furthermore, the law of Moses created the conviction that when God has been offended he is propitiated by the blood and slaughter of cattle,[18] and Abel, right at the very beginning of the world, made an offering from his first-born sheep. Thus even peoples who did not know the true God became convinced that the sins of men are wiped out by death and blood.[19]

Among certain peoples it was a public custom to support diligently for a whole year a man who had offered himself voluntarily for death; in the meantime, they venerated him as a sacred victim dedicated to God. When the year was over, they threw him into the sea, thinking that by the death of one whatever evils threatened the city could be averted.

* * * * *

14 Cf Rufinus 18 PL 21 356.
15 See 250 n15 above.
16 Cf 2 Tim 2:19.
17 Cf 1 Cor 15:47.
18 Exod 30:10
19 Gen 4:4

Codrus,[20] Quintus Curtius,[21] and the Decii,[22] who devoted themselves to the infernal deities for the safety of the state, are honoured with great enthusiasm. When the salvation not of one city or people but of the whole world was in question, it was fitting that a true and efficacious victim be sacrificed, who would invalidate all other sacrificial victims as superstitious or ineffective. So great was Christ's love, so great was his purity, that when he had been sacrificed once, he was able to wipe out all the crimes of the human race, even if there had been more than one world.[23] Certainly this was the true burnt offering that was totally consumed through his love for the human race; this was that most pure blood of the immaculate Lamb that, rubbed on door-posts, kept the destroying angel at a distance.[24]

Moreover, the type of death, in addition to being most painful, brought with it the deepest disgrace, especially among the Jews, in whose eyes 'everyone hanging on a cross was accursed.'[25] Great should be the suffering which washes away eternal punishment for all, and fortunate was the ignominy which had opened the road to eternal glory for all. Nothing is more accursed in the eyes of God than sin. This ignominy and curse he transferred to himself for a time to gain for us his blessing. It also enhanced the credibility of the account that he was publicly condemned by judicial sentence, and was raised on high when he breathed his last, lest anyone suspect that his was not a true death, or that someone else was substituted for Christ. Finally, it was fitting that he should die with his arms stretched aloft, since in his ineffable love

* * * * *

20 Codrus: legendary king of Athens, eleventh century BC. The Dorians invaded Attica during his reign. When he discovered that the Delphic oracle had claimed their invasion would be successful if his life were spared, he sacrificed his life to save his country.

21 Quintus Curtius: most likely Erasmus is referring to Marcus Curtius, another legendary example of bravery and self-sacrifice. He is said to have leapt while on horseback into a chasm which opened in the Forum, in fulfilment of an oracle's prophecy, to save his country.

22 Decii: father, son, and grandson, all named Publius, all consuls of Rome (in 340, intermittently between 312 and 295, and in 279 BC respectively), and all believed to have shown extreme devotion to their country.

23 Cf Thomas Aquinas *In symbolum apostolorum scilicet 'Credo in Deum,' Expositio* art 4 in Aquinas *Opuscula* 142: 'For the passion of Christ was of such virtue that it is sufficient to expiate all the sins of the entire world, even if there were one hundred thousand [worlds].'

24 Exod 12:12–13

25 Deut 21:23

he desired to embrace all men and women and to save all, as he himself says to his disciples, when indicating the manner of his death: 'When I have been raised up from the earth, I will draw all things to myself.'[26]

Furthermore, I have reminded you above[27] that the Lord came to earth not only to cleanse us from sin, but to show the road by which one must reach eternal glory, and to strengthen the weakness that inclines us to fall into sin again, we who are equally weak in the face of joy and sorrow, corrupted by the one, broken and cast down by the other. Whoever fixes his eyes with full faith on the crucified Christ is afraid to crucify him again somehow, whenever he commits those sins which Christ died to wash away. So too, scarcely anyone is so foolish that he would not bear the afflictions of this world with calmer mind when he reflects on how much the one who was free from every contact with evil suffered for us. Who could be found so inhuman and ungrateful that he would not love in return the one who so loved him first, and invited him to a mutual love by such great favours? In a word all philosophy, all consolation, all strength for the Christian mind are in the cross of Christ. But contemplation of these things does not belong to the task that we have taken in hand.

KA Why did he choose to hang between two thieves?[28]

CA To show that even for criminals at the very moment of execution there is hope of salvation if they implore the mercy of Christ.

KA Why did he choose not to have his legs broken?

CA Because it was mysteriously prophesied, 'You shall break no bone of his.'[29]

KA Yet these actions were not accomplished in this way because prophecies had said they would be; rather, the prophecies announced the manner of fulfilment that God had ordained for them from eternity.

CA You are entirely right in feeling that nothing was done without forethought or by chance in Christ's life; everything was accomplished by decree of the eternal Godhead. Granted, the Scriptures at times use the words 'that the Scriptures might be fulfilled.'[30] In this type of expression, however, the conjunction 'that' signifies the result, not the purpose. The Scripture came first, the result later. Moreover, it was fitting that

* * * * *

26 John 12:32
27 See 293 above.
28 Matt 27:38; Mark 15:27; Luke 23:32–3
29 John 19:36; see Exod 12:46; Num 9:12.
30 Eg Matt 1:22, 2:15, 12:17, 21:4; John 19:28, et al

that most sacred body should have no defect (I mean a maimed, lame, or twisted limb), just as we believe that our bodies will not have them in the resurrection. For proof of the resurrection, the marks of the five wounds sufficed – they did not disgrace his body, but adorned it like special jewels.[31] For the same reason, he did not want his body to decompose in the tomb. He died before they came to break his legs;[32] he arose before his dead body could decay. These things emphasize his greatness without posing the slightest obstacle to the reality of his human nature.

KA Why did he want to be laid in a new tomb where no one had yet been buried,[33] one, moreover, cut from living and solid rock?

CA He did that partly for the dignity of the Christ, and partly for the credibility of the account. Great mysteries are concealed in each of these events, and you will learn more when you put aside your infancy; we are now offering milk to an infant.[34]

KA Given that this narrative is supported by so many proofs, were there still some who disputed its truth?

CA The Jews say that Christ was really crucified, but not for the salvation of the world. Then there were Christians who acknowledged that he truly suffered in the flesh, and for the salvation of the world, but asserted (or rather conjectured) that his soul suffered among the dead for the souls detained there,[35] just as he had suffered in the body on earth for living men; that he was crucified again in the air, or was to be after his resurrection, for the spirits who dwell there. Basilides,[36] a compassionate man, says that Christ himself was not crucified, but that Simon of Cyrene,[37] who was compelled to carry the Lord's cross in his place, was substituted for him. But if another person was crucified in Christ's place, he himself did not die, did not rise from the dead or redeem us by his death.

These are, forsooth, the dreams of a human brain. Scripture teaches us in the clearest terms that Christ suffered only once[38] and died on the

* * * * *

31 Cf John 20:24–9.
32 John 19:33
33 John 19:41
34 Cf 1 Cor 3:1–2.
35 Cf the colloquy *Inquisitio de fide* ASD I-3 369:182–3 / Thompson *Inquisitio* 65 / CWE 39 426:34–5: 'But, as I believe he descended to hell, so I do *not* believe he suffered anything there.'
36 Cf 273 n146 above.
37 Matt 27:32; Mark 15:21
38 Cf Heb 7:27.

cross under Pontius Pilate to redeem humans, and humans only. Paul cries out, 'Christ, rising from the dead, now dies no more; death no longer has dominion over him.'[39] And: 'The death he died he died to sin, once for all, but the life he lives he lives to God.'[40] Peter exclaims, 'Christ died once for our sins.'[41]

You hear it stated clearly that he died once; you hear that he arose from the dead, that he will die no more. Yet you deny that he died, and say that someone else's death was substituted for his, just as in the myths a white hind was substituted for Iphigenia in Aulis.[42] You crucify his soul again among the dead; in addition, you crucify the whole Christ again in the air. And you, O Jew, do you hear the Prince of the Apostles crying aloud, 'Christ suffered for us,'[43] and refuse to have his death benefit every human being? Let us go on to other things.

KA Next in the creed comes 'He descended into hell.'

CA This is the article which, as I mentioned, Cyprian says is not found in the Roman Creed, and is not even added in the churches of the east.[44] There is nothing in the creeds of Nicaea or Constantinople that corresponds to this short sentence, although they are intended precisely to amplify the Roman Creed.[45] Finally, the very inelegance of the language proves that this is an addition interpolated by someone else. The words 'he was buried' refer to his body, which, put to sleep by death, rises again or awakes, so to speak. But the expression 'to descend to hell' refers to his soul, which neither was buried nor arose again, but, separated for a time, soon returned to his dead

* * * * *

39 Rom 6:9

40 Rom 6:10

41 1 Pet 3:18

42 Iphigenia: oldest daughter of King Agamemnon of Argos, she was to be sacrificed by her father to the goddess Artemis before the expedition set off for Troy, in order to ensure a favourable outcome. In the *Agamemnon* Aeschylus implies that she was killed, but in the *Cypria* it is claimed that she was rescued by the goddess when a white hind was substituted as the sacrifice.

43 1 Pet 2:21

44 Cyprian: read Rufinus; see Rufinus 18 PL 21 356. This article's first official credal appearance was in 359 in the Fourth Formula of Sirmium. Cf also the colloquy *Inquisitio de fide* ASD I-3 369:175–7 / Thompson *Inquisitio* 65 / CWE 39 426:26–8. There is evidence for its inclusion in older Syrian credal material as well; see Kelly *Creeds* 378–9.

45 This is no longer thought to be the case. While the Roman Creed is an important source for subsequent creeds in the west, it is not a source for either the Nicene Creed or the Constantinopolitan Creed.

body.[46] I cannot decide whether or not Thomas Aquinas accepted this
addition. There is some suspicion that this short sentence was added by
another hand,[47] particularly on the ground that it is out of place, for
Thomas makes the resurrection his third article of faith, and the descent
into hell his fourth – unless, perhaps, he believed that Christ returned
to life in soul and body, and then descended into hell. Another little
work which is being circulated under Thomas' name gives a different
interpretation of the creed and uses a different order. There, the descent
into hell precedes the resurrection. However, this short work, though
learned and pious, does not seem to be by Thomas Aquinas.[48]

KA Why was this clause not added?

CA Because the earliest Fathers took scrupulous care not to assert anything,
at least in the creed, which had not been clearly taught in the sacred
books of the Old or the New Testament. All the articles of the creed,
with this one exception, are of this kind.

KA On what grounds did later writers add it?

CA Because they thought they had deduced this clearly enough from a
rather careful examination of Sacred Scripture. To scriptural evidence
they added quite a few arguments which, though not certain, did not
lack some value as proof. They cite from the Psalms, 'And thou hast
led me into the dust of death.'[49] Likewise this: 'What value is there in
my death while I go down into corruption?'[50] And again: 'I went down
into the deep mire and there is no foothold.'[51] Again this: 'O Lord, you
have led my soul from the underworld, you have saved me from among

* * * * *

46 In this Erasmus disagrees with Rufinus, who in Rufinus 18 PL 21 356 claims
that the meaning of the statement that Christ descended into hell is no different from that of the statement that Christ was buried. Tertullian in *De anima*
55 PL 2 742–5 explains that Christ's soul, as the souls of all men, descended
into Hades. See also the colloquy *Inquisitio de fide* ASD I-3 369:177 / Thompson *Inquisitio* 65 / CWE 39 426:27–8, in which Erasmus suggests Tertullian did
not include this passage in his statements of the creed. While this is so, Tertullian's argument in *De anima* shows that he did in fact believe in the descent,
as does Erasmus in the *Inquisitio*.

47 In Aquinas *In articulos fidei et sacramenta ecclesiae, Expositio* in Aquinas *Opuscula*
119 the article pertaining to *decensus* follows that of the resurrection.

48 Aquinas *Expositio in symbolum* art 5 in Aquinas *Opuscula* 142–4 puts the descent before the resurrection, as does Erasmus here. The reason for Erasmus'
doubting of the authenticity of this work is unclear.

49 Ps 22:15 (Vulg 21:16)

50 Ps 30:9 (Vulg 29:10)

51 Ps 69:2 (Vulg 68:3)

those going down to the pit.'[52] Likewise this: 'You will not abandon my soul to the underworld.'[53] Peter in Acts teaches that this declaration was made beforehand about Christ, not about David as the Jews interpreted it.[54] They also cite the following: 'You have delivered my soul from the depths of the underworld.'[55] And again this: 'I am reckoned among those who go down into the pit; I have become like a man without support, forsaken among the dead.'[56] There is likewise this statement of Osee: 'O death, I shall be your death; hell, I shall be your sting.'[57]

From the Gospel according to Matthew they cite the words of the Baptist: 'Are you he who is to come, or are we to look for another?'[58] Some interpret these words as referring to the descent of Christ to the underworld. From the Epistle of Peter they cite, '... Christ, put to death in the flesh but made alive in the spirit, in which he came and preached to spirits who were in prison.'[59] From chapter 24 of Ecclesiasticus they cite what is said in the person of wisdom: 'I shall make my way through the lower parts of earth, and I shall look upon all who are sleeping, and I shall enlighten all who hope in the Lord.'[60] They also quote several other things of the same kind.

None of these passages would compel a determined critic to believe that the soul of Christ of itself descended to Tartarus or, as they say, to limbo; for the Scripture often calls death and burial the underworld, as in Genesis 44, 'He will die and your servants will bring down his grey hairs with sorrow to the underworld.'[61] It called an aged body 'grey hairs' and 'burial' the underworld. (Cyprian[62] briefly alludes to this objection when he adds in his preface that this clause is not found in either the western or the eastern church.) The word 'to go down' [descendere][63] seems to refer to burial also, because when the one buried

* * * * *

52 Ps 30:3 (Vulg 29:4)
53 Ps 16 (Vulg 15):10
54 Acts 2:30–1
55 Ps 86 (Vulg 85):13
56 Ps 88:4–5 (Vulg 87:5–6)
57 Hos 13:14
58 Matt 11:3
59 1 Pet 3:18–19
60 Eccles 24:45
61 Gen 44:31
62 Cyprian: read Rufinus.
63 Erasmus means that it can pertain either to physical burial or to the descent of the soul to hell.

is said 'to go down,' this can only mean to be buried in a tomb. The Lord, speaking of his own burial, said that his tomb was in the heart of the earth.[64] Among these citations there are some that carry practically no weight. Every one of them either is beclouded by allegory or admits various interpretations. The arguments which they advance are not of much more importance. One of them is entirely rejected.

KA Which one is that?

CA Because original sin brought spiritual torment as well as physical death, and because through it the vision of the divine countenance was lost to men, they think it is fitting that Christ should take away the torment of souls by spiritual suffering, just as he wiped out the body's debt of punishment by his physical death.

KA Is one free to accept or reject that clause?

CA If the universal church has already accepted it, one may not reject it.[65] It suffices for you to profess your belief in Christ's descent to the underworld as the Scriptures and the church perceive it. It is the mark of a prudent Christian, however, not to accept too readily as certain what has not been revealed in the Holy Scriptures, and likewise of a modest Christian not to reject petulantly what devout persons have brought forth from devout contemplation for the consolation or the instruction of the faithful. The following beliefs also belong to this category: the Holy Spirit took a most pure drop of blood from the heart of the Virgin and placed it in the Virgin's womb,[66] and from it the complete body of a man was formed, as tiny as a little spider; he then burst out of the egg, his body parts finished; at the same moment a soul was infused, equally perfect in all its faculties; it is now in heaven.[67] Similarly, they teach that, because of the nature of Christ's human body, which in their opinion was made of extraordinarily fine matter and therefore was unusually sensitive, he suffered more painful torture than any human being could bear, except for the tortures of the damned in hell.[68] Let these and similar opinions gain a hearing as pious human reflections on Christ, not as articles of faith.

Certain persons have also offered many such explanations of this short added clause, recounting whom Christ took with him from hell,

* * * * *

64 Matt 12:40
65 See 329 n200 and 335 n239 below.
66 Thomas Aquinas *Summa theologica* III q 31 art 5
67 Cf ibidem III q 33 art 2; *Ratio* LB V 90E.
68 Cf Thomas Aquinas *Summa theologica* III q 46 art 6.

whom he left there, what he said to whom at different meetings. It is enough for us that he was born a human once in the flesh, that he really suffered, that he really died and was buried, that he came to life again when the same soul returned to his natural body.

Next in the creed comes 'He arose on the third day.' If Christ had not risen, all hope of immortality would have been taken from us. He arose, the creed in the mass adds, 'according to the Scriptures.' As the blessed Apostle says, 'I have delivered to you as of first importance what I have received, that Christ died for our sins according to the Scriptures, and that he was buried, and that he arose the third day according to the Scriptures.'[69]

The resurrection of the Lord was foreshadowed in many figures. The Lord himself explained the one about Jonah, who was in the whale's belly for three days and three nights.[70] The resurrection was promised in the pronouncements of many prophets, and foretold quite often by Christ himself in clear words unobscured by clouds of trope or allegory. Finally, it was confirmed by the clear testimonies of many apostles. Yet those could be found who, as the adage goes, in the midst of sunlight were truly left in darkness.[71] For Cerinthus[72] said that Christ had not yet arisen, but would arise at a future time. Others taught that Christ indeed had arisen, but our bodies would never come to life again. Paul openly refuted them, arguing as strict implications that if Christ did not arise from the dead, neither will we, and that if we are to rise from the dead, Christ had to do so first.[73] For, as he suffered for us that through him we might be freed from eternal death, so too he rose for us that through him we might attain eternal life. He arose as 'the first-fruits of those who have fallen asleep,'[74] but he who is first cannot be the only one, and the head will not desert his members.

Some, on the authority of Valentinus,[75] admit the resurrection of spirit and soul, but deny the resurrection of bodies, although the model of our resurrection is revealed in Christ. He arose in his entirety. But it is impossible to fight against those who deny the clear, consistent teaching of

* * * * *

69 1 Cor 15:3–4
70 Matt 12:40
71 Quintilian *Institutiones oratoriae* 1.2.19
72 See 293 n91 above.
73 1 Cor 15:12–17
74 1 Cor 15:20
75 Valentinus: see 294 n102 above.

Scripture. Nothing has been transmitted by the evangelists with greater care than the proofs of the resurrection. St Paul, too, not only corroborates everywhere the fact of the resurrection, but also describes the manner of the resurrection to the Corinthians and Thessalonians.[76]

The Chiliasts fantasize[77] that for a thousand years after the resurrection of the body we will fully enjoy every kind of pleasure that titillates the bodily senses. This is not dogma but outlandish absurdity. The human mind begets quibbles over how the same body, changed from one thing to another in so many ways, can be restored to its exact identity. They are shattered by our faith that God who does these things exists and is omnipotent, and that he who created nature is not subject to the laws of nature. What wonder if he, who created the first heaven and earth and the angels from nothing, restores the body from its elements? Again, since we perceive so many miracles in natural things – a massive tree grows from the minutest seed; a young cricket flies out of an old one when it discards its skin; a moist, winged butterfly springs from a dying caterpillar – why should anything that the Almighty does beyond the laws of nature seem incredible?

Next in the creed comes 'He ascended into heaven, sits at the right hand of God the Father.' 'No one,' says John, 'has ascended into heaven but he who descended from heaven the Son of Man, who is in heaven.'[78] The Word descended from heaven without leaving the Father or changing place, since the divine nature, which is everywhere, is not bounded by any place. The same Word that by a dispensation entered the Virgin's womb really returned, when the mystery of redemption had been accomplished, still incarnate, to heaven. In this way, he withdrew the sight of his body from his disciples and raised their minds to heavenly things, so that they might be receptive to the Spirit that was to come.[79] He did not shed the body he had assumed and lay it in the earth, as the ill-starred Seleucius[80] fondly imagined. Thus the one who, in keeping with his divine nature, was ever in the same glory as the Father, now

* * * * *

76 See 1 Cor 15:35–57; 1 Thess 4:13–17.
77 Chiliasts: believed that Christ's second coming would be followed by a thousand-year reign on earth. Cerinthus elaborated on the physical delights awaiting the righteous during this period, for which he was rebuked by Eusebius in the *Historia ecclesiastica* 3.28 PG 20 274–6.
78 John 3:13
79 See Acts 1:9.
80 Seleucius: see 275 n154 above.

too in his human nature sits in the Father's glory as well, being Lord of all things that are in heaven and on earth.

KA It does not seem absurd to attribute a right or left side to Christ, but to imagine any such thing of the Father seems to verge on the error of the Anthropomorphites.[81]

CA 'To sit on the right' is said here only by way of metaphor, to help you understand that there is equality of dignity and community of authority.

KA Why indeed is belief not expressed in the simple and suitable words 'He ascended into heaven, where he reigns equal to the Father'?

CA I have already reminded you[82] that Scripture often accommodates its language to our feelings. The creed, in turn, repeats the mystic terminology of Scripture. In the Psalms the Holy Spirit speaks of God the Father and the glorified Christ in this way: The Lord said to my Lord, 'Sit at my right hand.'[83] The Lord himself in the Gospel also says: 'Nevertheless I say to you: Hereafter you will see the Son of Man sitting at the right hand of God.'[84] Likewise, the apostle Peter, speaking of Christ, says, '... who is at the right hand of God,'[85] sitting in heaven. Similarly, Paul writes to the Ephesians, '... according to the working of his great might, which he accomplished in Christ Jesus, setting him at his right hand in heaven above every principality and power and virtue and domination and every name that is named not only in this age, but in the age that is to come.'[86] Stephen in Acts saw the heavens open and Jesus standing at the right hand of God.[87]

KA How did Jesus appear to him to be standing? Elsewhere he is said to be sitting.

CA Consider this a trope also. Sitting is a mark of someone at rest, a ruler and a judge; standing of someone giving assistance. Anyone who rules all things without anxiety is seated. Anyone who is ready to help all who call on him stands. As a judge he is seated, as an advocate he stands. 'We have,' says Paul, 'an advocate in heaven.'[88]

KA But Christ in his human nature is not equal to the Father.

*****

81 Anthropomorphites: see 272 n135 above.
82 See 268, 270 above.
83 Ps 110 (Vulg 109):1
84 Matt 26:64
85 1 Pet 3:22
86 Eph 19–21
87 Cf Acts 7:55–6
88 Paul: read John; 1 John 2:1.

CA   What creature could be equal to the creator?[89] However, because of the unity of Christ's person, everything that belongs to his human nature is rightly attributed to him, provided we use the terminology of person or, as others say, hypostasis [*suppositum*].[90]

KA   Given that Christ declares that he will remain with us 'until the end of the age,'[91] why was his body taken up to heaven in 'sight of all his disciples'?[92]

CA   The Apostle answers that question in Colossians 3: 'Seek what is above, where Christ is sitting at the right hand of God; set your mind on what is above.'[93] This vision is placed before our bodily eyes to lure our minds away from earthly cares to a longing for heavenly life. Accordingly, God's sending his Son to earth for the sake of our salvation and handing him over to death on the cross give us certainty that through him we are freed from the dominion of Satan. Through his resurrection, we are given further reassurance that on that day (which God willed should be unknown to us) we shall live again with the same bodies that we have now. By his ascension into heaven, he taught us by a clear proof that we are not to seek true happiness here below, but are to use this world in passing, as it were, as though not using it,[94] and that all our concerns are to be redirected towards that heavenly and eternal life. By sitting at the right hand of the Father, he creates for us a great sense of security in the face of all the terrors of the world, since we have such a caring and powerful advocate.

Lest the great goodness of God should lure us to sin more freely, the creed adds 'Thence he will come to judge the living and the dead.' In this way, we may understand that those who have ignored God's benevolence in this world must anticipate the judge's inexorable severity in the next. The more that is given to us, the more will be demanded from us. For he will come no longer in the dress of a slave, but in the majesty of the Father, as he himself clearly says in Matthew: 'When the Son of

* * * * *

89   Note that it is only specifically in terms of his *human* nature that Christ is a creature and thereby unequal to the creator.

90   Erasmus' Latin term *suppositum* is synonymous with the Greek term ὑποστά-σεως, meaning the underlying substance or essence, 'that which is placed under.' In Christ's essence are fully united his human and divine natures (*naturae*).

91   Matt 28:20

92   Acts 1:9

93   Col 3:1–2

94   Cf 1 Cor 7:31.

Man comes in his majesty, and all the angels with him, then he will sit
on his majestic throne, and there will be gathered before him all the nations,' etc.[95] There the separation of the just and the unjust will be made
clear and eternal, when the net is drawn to the shore.[96] Peter in Acts 10
makes the same declaration: he 'is the one ordained by God to be the
judge of the living and the dead.'[97] The one who endured judgment and
condemnation for us in this world, then will judge the whole world, to
render each his due according to his works.[98]

KA Why did God will that no one know that day?

CA For the same reason that he willed the last day of life to be absolutely
certain for everyone and yet uncertain. No one doubts that he will die
sometime; but no one knows for certain when he will die, so that in
every hour we may be prepared to depart, if God calls us hence.

KA Why does he add 'living and dead'? How can dead bodies be judged?

CA Since the entire creed is taken from Scripture, it fittingly repeats the
terminology of Scripture. Some interpret 'living' as 'just,' 'dead' as unjust'; this is somewhat forced. Simplicity befits Scripture, since it was
prepared for simple people.[99] It is quite probable that the word 'dead'
refers to those who died before the Day of Judgment, for as soon as
they come to life again, they will be judged, and that the word 'living'
refers to those whom that day will come upon while they are still living
in the body. Some believe that they will die from the violent transition
and immediately come to life again. Others think that they will not die,
but will be transformed to life eternal. The judgment of the church does
not reject either opinion; yet the suggestion that those who are found
still living will not die but will be transformed to life eternal better fits
Paul's words in 1 Corinthians 15 and 1 Thessalonians 4.[100] However,
God-fearing reverence finds no pleasure in a dispute.

KA What need is there for a judgment? Souls are judged at once, as soon
as they depart from the body. They pass on to a heavenly life if they

* * * * *

95 Matt 25:31–2
96 Cf Matt 13:47–8.
97 Acts 10:42
98 Matt 16:27; Rom 2:6
99 Simplicity: this represents Erasmus' standard for understanding Scripture in
his *Annotationes*, his prefaces, and his controversy with Luther; eg *Paraclesis* LB
V 140A. Augustine advances both interpretations in *De symbolo ad catechumenos*
4.12 PL 40 634.
100 1 Cor 15:51; 1 Thess 4:15–17. Erasmus comments extensively on this passage
in the *Annotationes* LB VI 740F–743F.

go hence undefiled, or are dragged down to hell if they are liable to condemnation. If they are stained with slighter blemishes, they are conducted to the fire of purgatory – whatever or of whatsoever kind that is.

CA There were some who taught that neither unjust spirits nor unjust souls are to be handed over to eternal punishments before that last day of the world, and that just souls will not enjoy heavenly life before the aforesaid day.[101] But the authority of the church sets aside the opinion of these people. The following is believed to be probable: After that judgment, the torments of impious spirits will increase, for impious men will then pay their full penalty in body as well as soul. The happiness of the pious will then also be complete, when they receive their own bodies back – now glorified – so that they may have their old assistant in good works and companion in suffering as the sharer of their rewards and joy.

KA If all the people who existed during the many thousands of years since the creation of the world are to be placed before the tribunal of Christ, what space will be capable of holding the infinite multitude? Or what time will suffice for an examination of so many human deeds?

CA Scripture, as I have reminded you, adjusts its language to our human disposition, accommodating[102] itself to our dullness, when it says that all human beings must be placed before the tribunal of Christ. Similarly, it says that some will be liable to the judgment, others to the council, others to hell;[103] that on the Day of Judgment an account must be given of every idle word.[104] Again, the style is the same when it tells what the judge will say to those standing at his right hand, and what those who are standing at his left will hear or answer in turn.[105]

The judgment of God is conducted far differently from the judgment of man. However, it does not fail to be accomplished truly because it is

* * * * *

101 Erasmus is probably referring to the opinion of Pope John XXII (1316–34), rejected by Pope Benedict XII in the constitution *Benedictus Deus*, 29 January 1336. See DTC II 657–96.

102 *Attemperat:* the principle of accommodation, a prominent theme in all of Erasmus' work; eg his dedicatory epistle to the Paraphrase on Romans, Allen Ep 710:40–8 / CWE Ep 710:45–53, in which he describes himself as *temperantes* in taking the needs of his various readers into account. See also McConica, and Marjorie O'Rourke Boyle *Rhetoric and Reform: Erasmus' Civil Dispute with Luther* (Cambridge, Mass 1983).

103 Cf Matt 5:22.

104 Cf Matt 12:36.

105 Cf Matt 25:34–5.

not accomplished in human fashion. It is absolutely true that Christ will appear to all in his glorified body. To the just, he will bring consolation, to the unjust, terror. The angels in Acts, who appeared right after the Lord was lifted up to heaven, state this explicitly: 'This Jesus who was taken up from you into heaven, will come in the same way as you saw him go.'[106] The same Christ will come, and he will be seen in human form, but now shining with the glory of immortality. This whole business will be accomplished in a moment and instant of time.[107] There will be no need for lengthy discussion when all the secrets of hearts lie open, when each one's own conscience will condemn him.

Indeed, bodies transformed by immortality will not occupy the three-fold spatial dimension of length, breadth, and depth; it will be possible for countless bodies to be enclosed in a minimum of space. Otherwise, the human mind would be at a loss to understand how Tartarus, which they plausibly place in the depths of earth, could hold so many bodies.

KA Why does the chorus of the church here chant, 'of whose kingdom there will be no end?'

CA This clause is added from the words of the angel in St Luke, who spoke as follows to the Virgin: 'And the Lord God will give to him the throne of his Father, and he will reign over the house of Jacob for ever; and of his kingdom there will be no end.'[108] It has been added because of some who have foolishly uttered certain outlandish blasphemies about the Platonic cycles.[109] It was from this source that Origen drew his erroneous teaching (if indeed he really believed what he reported rather than asserted in his writings) that after many thousands of years the demons would become angels and the angels would become demons; that those condemned to hell would sometime or other be freed from suffering and return purified to a state of happiness; that, finally, Christ would be crucified again, and in this way the kingdom that Christ prepared for himself by his death would sometime come to an end.[110]

This blasphemy is too senseless to be refuted. Since there were some Greeks, however, who paid considerable attention to this nonsense, the

* * * * *

106 Acts 1:11
107 Cf 1 Cor 15:32.
108 Luke 1:32-3
109 See Plato *Phaedrus* 246-9 for the doctrine of the transmigration of souls.
110 See Origen *De principibus* 1.4.1 PG 11 155-6, 1.6.2 PG 11 166-7, and 4.3.13 PG 11 398-9; cf Jerome's letter to Avitus, *Epistolae* 124.3 PL 22 1061-2 and 124.13 PL 22 1071.

eastern churches added 'And of his kingdom there will be no end.' The kingdom of the devil hid itself for a time; now it wages war against the kingdom of Christ. So also the rule of the Antichrist will be temporary. But when the kingdom of Christ is cleansed from all the revolts of the evil ones, it will abide forever, as Daniel 7 clearly predicted. After Daniel has described that figure's arrival in majesty and with many thousands of angels and then the dread judgment, he adds 'And to him was given dominion and glory and kingdom, that all peoples, nations, and languages should serve him.'[111] His dominion is an everlasting dominion, which shall not pass away, and his kingdom one that shall not be destroyed.

The creed thus far would suffice if the world had clung in simple faith to what had been handed on. But since perverse heretics have introduced certain impious opinions about the Third Person, the Holy Spirit, and since the character of the church in this world seemed to be treated rather obscurely, this next part was added. It attributes to the Holy Spirit more explicitly the divine nature that he has in common with the Son and the Father, and lucidly explains how the Holy Spirit directs the body of Christ. Accordingly, it refers again to the Third Person: 'I *believe in* the Holy Spirit,' so that by acknowledging him in the third place with the same words,[112] it may clarify the Persons' distinction of properties and equality of nature.[113] No one believes with Christian faith (that is to say, places his highest trust) in a creature, but in the one and only God. So too, one who professes his belief in the Holy Spirit certainly professes his belief that he is God, not another God but the same one.

Some have said that the 'holy spirit' is not a substance, but the movement of a pious mind. That movement of our mind certainly proceeds from the Spirit, but, however, is not itself the Spirit, just as imagination proceeds from the mind, but is not the mind itself. That movement in us is an accident;[114] but the divine nature is neither an accident nor mingled with any accident. Others have said that the Holy Spirit is a creature assigned to the service of the Son, whom they also represent as

* * * * *

111 Dan 7:14
112 'I believe in' applied only to the Persons of the Trinity, as opposed to 'I believe,' which applied to the other articles of the creed. See 256 n43 above.
113 The coexistence of distinction in properties and equality in nature reflects the fact that the three Persons are of one essential substance.
114 Accident: see 260 n65 above.

a creature.[115] They openly deny that the Holy Spirit is God. However, when the Lord links the Father, Son, and Holy Spirit in the formula of baptism, he does not intermingle creature with creator or accident with substance; he represented the three Persons as of one essence.[116]

Since errors concerning the Holy Spirit raged especially among the Greeks, although they did not shake the Roman church so violently, the creed of Constantinople added some sentences concerning the Holy Spirit, calling him 'Lord and Giver of Life.'[117] By calling him Lord, they make him equal to the Son and exclude the name of servant, for there is only one Lord. The Son is not called Lord Holy Spirit, but Lord of all created things, and lordship is common to the three Persons. Nevertheless, the word κύριος does not always denote dominion for the Greeks, but sometimes authorship. The Spirit is the author of all the sacred books; the church regards them as inspired, and their authority is inviolable.

In the Gospel, the Father gives testimony to the Son, 'This is my beloved Son, hear him,'[118] thus giving him supreme authority. The Greeks therefore added to the creed 'the Spirit, Lord ...' to preclude anyone's thinking that the authority of the Spirit is less than that of the Son. By calling him 'Giver of Life,' it again makes him equal to the Son and Father. The Lord says in St John, 'As the Father raises the dead, so also the Son gives life to whom he will.'[119] Lest anyone should believe that the Spirit was excluded here, the Greeks added 'Giver of Life.' The Son spoke openly in the flesh, the Spirit spoke through prophets and today speaks in a hidden manner through the church; so too, the Son raised dead bodies to life as the author and first-fruits of the resurrection, the Holy Spirit, by forgiving sin, brings back spiritual life. Sin is

* * * * *

115 Others: a group called the Macedonians, named after Macedonius, fourth-century patriarch of Constantinople. According to Kelly *Doctrines* the association of this group with Macedonius is incorrect, and a more appropriate name for them would be 'Pneumatomachians.' See also Aquinas *Expositio in symbolum apostolorum* art 8 in Aquinas *Opuscula* 146: 'Fuerunt autem aliqui qui male sentientes de Spiritu sancto, dixerunt, quod erat creatura, et quod erat minor Patre et Filio, et quod erat servus et minister Dei.' The belief was condemned by the Second Ecumenical Council, Constantinople, 381.

116 Cf Matt 28:18.

117 He is referring to the council of 381, with which the Constantinopolitan Creed is associated. The new language used also plainly asserts that the Spirit is worshipped and glorified together with the Father and the Son.

118 Luke 9:35

119 John 5:21

the death of the soul,[120] and to reverse it is a greater work than to raise Lazarus from the tomb when he was four days dead, except that for God all things are equally easy.

    With us physical breath [*spiritus*] is something inconstant, changeable, and mutable. To prevent us imagining that the Holy Spirit is similar, they called him κύριος, that is, 'of solid and inviolable truth.'[121] In John, the Lord himself calls him 'the Spirit of truth.'[122] This will distinguish air from the Holy Spirit. Since we live according to the flesh by inhaling and exhaling air, he is aptly called the Spirit who gives life, who grants us the life of our higher selves. Since this physical air seems, on the other hand, to be something cruel when it stirs up the seas, when it shakes the earth, when it smashes trees, they attribute goodness to the Holy Spirit.

KA   Why is he called Holy?

CA   To distinguish him from other spirits. We read in Scripture that Saul had an evil spirit from the Lord,[123] and that there was a 'lying spirit in the mouths of prophets,'[124] 'a spirit of confusion,'[125] 'the spirit of a serpent,[126] 'the spirit of envy,'[127] 'a most evil spirit,'[128] 'the spirit of fornication,'[129] 'the evil spirit,'[130] 'an unclean spirit,'[131] 'the spirit of this world,'[132] 'the spirit of Satan,'[133] and 'human spirits, swollen with conceit and puffed up.'[134] (Compare Proverbs 16:18, 'A haughty spirit will go before a fall.')[135] Apart from all these is the Holy Spirit, who makes the savage gentle, who removes every association with Satan, who inspires a real contempt for this world, who purifies the heart through

* * * * *

120 Cf Rom 6:23.
121 As a noun the Greek word κύριος means 'lord,' but as an adjective it can mean 'valid,' 'appointed,' 'legitimate.'
122 John 15:26, 16:13
123 1 Sam 16:14
124 1 Kings 22:22–3
125 Isa 19:14
126 Isa 29:4
127 Num 5:14, 30
128 Judg 9:23
129 Hos 4:12, 5:4
130 1 Sam 16:14; Acts 19:12
131 Mark 1:23, 3:30, 5:2–13, 7:25; Luke 9:42
132 1 Cor 2:12
133 Cf Luke 22:3.
134 2 Tim 3:2–4
135 Prov 16:18

faith, who drives away all malice, who bestows true charity, who is not
suspicious and thinks no evil, who reveals the secrets of the Scriptures,
who leads to all truth.

KA Are not angels called spirits and, for that matter, holy?

CA Yes, they are. The human spirit is rightly called holy in the same sense,
but there is only one Spirit who is holy by nature and of himself sanctifies all things that are really holy. In ordinary language, anything incorporeal is called a spirit. Thus, in the Gospel God is called a spirit,[136] and
all three Persons are so by their divine nature; but when we name the
Third Person specifically we call him the Holy Spirit, the Spirit of God,
the Spirit of Christ, the Spirit who is the Paraclete,[137] that is, the Consoler
or Advocate,[138] and the Spirit of truth. Some had said that the prophets
had not announced their predictions under the inspiration of the divine Spirit, but with the aid of a visible one. Against them, the Synod
of Nicaea or Constantinople added the phrase 'who spoke through the
prophets.' From this we were to understand that both Testaments were
produced by the same Spirit, and that no other spirit spoke through the
mouths of the holy prophets[139] but the one who descended in the shape
of a dove on the Lord,[140] came upon the disciples in the form of fire,[141]
and today rests between the breasts of his spouse, the church.

KA Did the Spirit take to himself a body in which he appeared, as Christ
did?

CA Absolutely not. Christ took up a body into union with his person. The
Spirit took to himself a body in the way that angels frequently appear in
human shape.[142] These bodies are 'put on,' not natural. The synod also
added 'who, together with the Father and the Son, is adored and glorified,'[143] to exclude further the blasphemy of those who make the Spirit
inferior to the Son. Creatures are glorified and adored, but nothing is
adored together with the Father and the Son except God. Holy men are

* * * * *

136 John 4:24
137 John 14:16, 15:26, 16:7
138 The Greek παράκλητος is often translated 'consoler' or, better, 'advocate.'
139 Cf 2 Pet 1:21. See Kelly *Creeds* 341; with reference to the Constantinopolitan
    Creed, Kelly speaks of 'the words "who spoke through the prophets," which
    of course had a long history in creeds and went back to the primitive kerygma
    of Christendom . . .'
140 Matt 3:16; John 1:32
141 Acts 2:3
142 Cf Gen 18:1–2, 19:1, 32:24–30; Judg 13:3, 6, 9–20; Acts 12:7–10.
143 He is referring to the council in Constantinople, 381.

honoured under God and on account of God; what is one with God is glorified with him. For the same reason they add 'who proceeds from the Father and the Son.' As the Son is shown to be of the same substance as the Father because he is born of him, so the Holy Spirit is shown to have the same nature as both, because he proceeds from both.[144] It seems, however, that the words 'and the son' [filioque] were added by the Latin church and also in the Athanasian Creed, since they are not found in the Greek creed that we have prefixed to the second edition of the New Testament,[145] or in any creed which is included in the volume of Canons. For the procession of the Holy Spirit from both Father and Son was not accepted at that time, I think, particularly among the eastern churches, and Christians were not required to believe it.[146] It was sufficient to profess belief in a Spirit proceeding from the Father and abiding in the Son, as described in the Life of St Andrew.[147] They would not deny that the Spirit proceeded from the Son also, but they did not dare to declare it positively until the Lord should reveal it. For what is sent by another does not automatically proceed from his substance. A sending in time is one thing, eternal procession another.

KA Since the Fathers tried with so many words to exclude inequality, why did they not proclaim briefly and clearly that the Spirit proceeded as God from God, when they had emphatically set this forth in regard to the Son: 'God from God, light from light, true God from true God'?[148] In this way all subterfuge would have been excluded.

CA Here I have no answer to give, except that it was a matter of the early Christians' admirable discretion in speaking of divine matters, and of certain persons' impious prating. They preferred to imply the name 'God' of the Spirit rather than mention it explicitly, so that pious minds

* * * * *

144 The theologian who articulated this position most clearly was Augustine; see De Trinitate 4.20.29 PL 42 908: 'Neither can we affirm that the Holy Spirit does not proceed from the Son, for it is not without reason that the one and the same Spirit is called the Spirit of the Father and Son.' See also ibidem 15.17.29 PL 42 1081 and 15.26.47 PL 42 1094–5.

145 Erasmus here indicates his own edition, published by Froben in Basel, 1519.

146 The filioque clause was a source of bitter disagreement between the eastern and western churches for centuries. Rome held back from fully endorsing it in order to avoid conflict with the eastern church, which rejected it, but under pressure from the Carolingians and, later, Emperor Henry II, the popes eventually gave way.

147 Cf Eusebius Historia ecclesiastica 3.25 PG 20 269–72.

148 From the Nicene Creed

might understand the mystery and impious ones might not be pro-
voked to blasphemy. However, that synod expressed indirectly the truth
Athanasius clearly proclaimed: 'God the Father; God the Son; God the
Holy Spirit; and yet there are not three Gods but one God.'[149]

KA Why do they attribute goodness and love to the Holy Spirit?

CA Two actions belong to goodness or kindness, forgiveness of sin and bestowing of gifts; the union of the two is charity. As our body parts are
united in an integral whole thanks to breath, so too the body of the
mystic Christ is united through the Holy Spirit. Christ cast out devils in the Spirit of God. Moreover, he calls the Holy Spirit the 'finger
of God.'[150] Through sin, evil spirits reign in man, as the Lord clearly
taught in the parable of the spirit who was cast out, and returned to the
empty house with seven others more evil than himself.[151] Accordingly,
the good spirit is properly said to cast out evil spirits when sins have
been abolished. After this has been done, he does not allow the house to
remain empty, but furnishes it with various gifts to prevent a return of
the vices that were cast out. Thus the sin of blasphemy, which is committed against the Holy Spirit, is said in the Gospel to be unforgivable.[152]
What hope of forgiveness does someone who offends the author of forgiveness have left? 'Charity,' as blessed Peter says, 'covers a multitude
of sins.'[153] To the woman in the Gospel are forgiven 'many sins, because
she has loved much.'[154] In addition, when the Lord gave the apostles the
power to forgive sin, he breathed on them, saying, 'Receive the Holy
Spirit,'[155] etc.

Goodness is shown in the description of the many and varied gifts
that St Paul mentions[156] as 'the favours of one Spirit.' He, by his own
decision, allots them to each person by the measure of his faith. It is the
mark of the triumphant to scatter gifts among the people from on high.
Thus Christ, after his triumphant ascent into heaven, according to the
prophecy of the psalmist,[157] 'led captivity captive,' when he led away in

* * * * *

149 From the Athanasian Creed; see 252 n21 above.
150 Luke 11:20. On the Holy Spirit as the finger of God, see Augustine *Ennarationes
in psalmos* 8.7 PL 36 111.
151 Matt 12:43–5
152 Mark 3:29
153 1 Pet 4:8
154 Luke 7:47
155 John 20:22
156 1 Cor 12:4
157 Cf Ps 68:18 (Vulg 67:19); Eph 4:8.

his company those whom he had snatched from hell. Not content with this, he gave gifts to the persons left on earth: prophecy,[158] tongues,[159] knowledge,[160] healing,[161] repelling poisons and evil spirits,[162] in a word, the whole choir of virtues. Christ bestowed all of these on his followers, and bestows them today through the Holy Spirit.

The word 'good' to Latin-speakers sometimes means mild and gentle, sometimes bounteous and liberal. Thus Paul, challenging the Galatians to leave vengefulness for kindness, emphasizes the name of the Spirit, saying: 'If we live by the Spirit, let us also walk by the Spirit. Brethren, if a man is overtaken in any trespass, you who are spiritual should correct him in a spirit of gentleness.'[163] David says, 'Your good spirit will lead me on a level path.'[164] And Paul: 'God's love has been poured into our hearts through the Holy Spirit, who has been given to us.'[165] Again, when writing to the Romans, he calls him 'the Spirit of sonship, through whom we cry, "Abba, Father."'[166] He writes in a similar vein to the Galatians: 'Because you are sons, God has sent the Spirit of his Son into our hearts, crying, "Abba! Father."'[167] 'Son' and 'Father' are words of love which no one can truly utter except by the help of the Holy Spirit. So too, according to the testimony of John, no one calls Jesus Lord except by the Holy Spirit.[168] Those who have the spirit of this world falsely cry out, 'Abba, Father'; they falsely say to Christ, 'Lord, Lord,' since they lack his Spirit.[169] A person who does not have the Spirit of Christ does not belong to him.[170] As the Holy Spirit is the ineffable bond by which the three Persons are inseparably joined to one another in eternal harmony, so too the same Spirit joins the spouse of Christ to her spouse by an indissoluble bond, uniting all the members of the mystical body in an eternal compact.

* * * * *

158 1 Cor 12:10; Rom 12:6
159 1 Cor 12:10, 28, 30; Mark 16:17
160 1 Cor 12:8
161 1 Cor 12:9, 28, 30
162 Mark 16:17–18
163 Gal 5:25–6:1
164 Ps 143 (Vulg 142):10
165 Rom 5:5
166 Rom 8:15
167 Gal 4:6
168 John: read Paul; 1 Cor 12:3.
169 Cf Matt 7:21.
170 Rom 8:9

KA If the Holy Spirit proceeds from the substance of God the Father and God the Son, what is to prevent him from also being called 'son'?

CA Cyprian,[171] Hilary, and Augustine found a satisfactory answer to this question in Scripture, which calls the Second Person 'the Son' and states that he is born of the Father. It nowhere says that the Holy Spirit 'is born' or 'is the Son.'[172] What satisfied such men should satisfy you too. If one stream came forth from two fountains, it would rightly be said to proceed or be sent from both; however, it would not be called the son of either.

KA Is it enough then to believe what you have stated about the Holy Spirit?

CA No. One must believe that this Spirit, foretold by the prophets and promised by Christ, descended on the disciples on the day of Pentecost, as St Luke relates.[173] This truth must be stressed because of the impious arrogance of some who do not fear to say, 'I am that Paraclete promised by Christ to lead you to all truth,' whether it was Manicheus,[174] or Basilides,[175] or Montanus[176] – accursed names!

KA Consider how he descended on the disciples, and that he was given to those baptized by laying on of the apostles' hands. Was the very substance of the Spirit or some gift and energy of the Spirit bestowed?

CA It is more probable that the Spirit, who fulfils all things according to his nature but remains incomprehensible, was present on this occasion in some unusual manner, under a visible sign appropriate to his property as a Person. But to deal with these matters now is, as the saying goes, getting out of bounds.[177] You have learned about the Spirit that sanctifies all things; hear now of the church that is sanctified by him.

KA From the beginning of the world there was an association of all the saints, and the Holy Spirit was present in all good people. Why then was there no name prior to the Law for this secret company? After the Law was promulgated, it was called the synagogue; after the gospel was

* * * * *

171 Cyprian: read Rufinus; see Rufinus 35 PL 21 372–3.
172 See Hilary *De Trinitate* 12.55 PL 10 468–9; Augustine *De Trinitate* 15.27 PL 42 1095–7 and *De fide et symbolo* 9.16 PL 40 189.
173 Cf Acts 2:4.
174 Manicheus: see 274 n152 above.
175 Basilides: see 273 n146 above.
176 Montanus: founder of a Phrygian ecstatic movement c 156, believing themselves to be the recipients of new revelations from the Holy Spirit. Tertullian compromised his orthodoxy by defending their practice of ecstatic prophecy; see eg *Adversus Marcion* 4.22 PL 2 413–16 and 5.8 PL 2 489–90.
177 Cf *Adagia* I x 93 LB II 394F–395B / CWE 32 277–8: *Ultra septa transilire.*

revealed, the name was changed, and it was called the church.

CA We have no clear indication of what the name was before the Old Law. However, it is probable that there was a name of some kind, since the reality was the same. Christ always recognized his spouse, and the Spirit of Christ never failed her. At the beginning, the distinction of persons was known to few, but they professed belief in one God, a formula that tacitly includes the three Persons; few knew the Person of the Son, fewer still the Holy Spirit. Similarly, this association was also comprised of a few people, and was confined within narrow limits until the light of the gospel came. After Christ had assumed a body and dwelt among men, after he clearly united with himself his spouse, who had been redeemed by his death and cleansed by his blood, after he clearly and copiously poured forth his Spirit, and after the grace of the gospel had spread not over one race but over the whole world, the apostles changed the name 'synagogue' to 'church.'[178] It cannot be doubted that this was done under the inspiration of the Spirit.

KA I am eager to learn the reason.

CA Although there is no difference in the meanings, the change of names added to the glory of the gospel. The word 'synagogue' had been accepted by all to mean the assembly of Jews who acknowledged the law of Moses. Just as that Law was hated by other nations, so too, the word 'synagogue' was displeasing to gentile ears. The apostles had been instructed by the Lord to preach the gospel to every creature,[179] not just within the boundaries of Judaea and Samaria, but even unto the ends of the earth. Taught by the Spirit, they knew that Jews would come forward who would try to obscure the grace of the gospel and faith in the Lord Jesus by teaching that there is no hope of salvation for anyone unless he was circumcised and by this sign acknowledged the entire law of Moses.[180] They then decided that the ceremonies of the Law were to be abolished, and the novelty of grace be manifested by a change of terms. 'The Law' was to be called 'the gospel,' that is, joyous tidings, and 'the synagogue' 'the church.' For the Law, in its demand for obedience to its precepts, threatened punishment; the gospel promises eternal life through the grace of the Spirit and faith in Christ without the works of the Law. The obstinacy of the Jews was so great that the apostles could get rid of their superstition only with difficulty; it would have been all

* * * * *

178 Cf *Annotationes in Mattheum* 11:17 LB VI 55D.
179 Cf Mark 13:10; Col 1:23.
180 Acts 15:1

the harder if the word 'synagogue' had been used in their preaching instead of the word 'church.' When people heard the old name, they would have thought that in reality nothing had been changed.

KA Is there not then some difference between the words?

CA Both are from Greek. 'Synagogue' is derived from συνάγειν, which means 'to collect,' that is, 'to bring together.' (This is how Maro speaks: 'Tityrus, collect the flock.')[181] 'Church' [ecclesia] is derived from ἐκκαλεῖν, which means 'to summon forth.' The former word is more in keeping with the gross, hard, and rebellious race of the Jews, who through fear of punishment or hope for mundane advantages used to be kept corralled, so to speak, by the Law, to keep them from decaying into every form of ungodliness.[182] The latter word, however, is more appropriate to gentiles, who readily obeyed the gospel, attracted by what they heard (that is a mark of humans) and not drawn by their noses like wild oxen. A herd is rounded up; men are summoned to a meeting, not to perform rites according to the ceremonies of the Law but to listen. 'Faith,' as Paul says, 'comes from what is heard.'[183] They were called away from dead idols to the living God, from the darkness of ignorance to the light of gospel truth, and they obeyed. So too, the Jews were summoned away from ceremonies to true piety, from shadows to the light, from the letter to the Spirit,[184] and they refused to come. Consequently, the name of God is invoked among Goths and Vandals; on the other hand, to this very day the Jews in their synagogue treat the adorable name of Jesus with insults; they still are slaves to the letter, and resist the Holy Spirit. 'Where the Spirit really is, there is freedom.'[185] To be compelled is a mark of slaves, to be summoned is a mark of children.[186] For this reason, Paul is wont to describe those who acknowledge the grace of the gospel as ἅγιοι, 'called saints.'[187]

KA What in particular does this word 'holy' mean for Latin-speakers?

CA Strictly speaking, whatever it is a crime to violate is holy. For example, the laws and walls and gates of a city are holy because they are public property. Some things are holy, that is, inviolate, because they have been consecrated to a divinity; thus what is sacred to the Lord is said to

* * * * *

181 Maro: Virgil; *Eclogues* 3.20
182 See 282 n31 above.
183 Rom 10:17
184 2 Cor 3:6
185 2 Cor 3:17
186 Cf Gal 4:7.
187 Cf Rom 1:7; 1 Cor 1:2.

be 'holy' to him. The word is also used metaphorically to signify both cleanliness and purity. The holy church is so inviolable that, according to the words of the Lord, 'the gates of hell cannot prevail against it,'[188] for the sole reason that it is dedicated to Christ, from whom no one can snatch what the Father gave him.[189] It is pure because Christ purified it with his own blood, so that he might 'present to himself a spouse without spot or wrinkle.'[190] The word 'spot' applies particularly to heretics who endeavour to disfigure pure truth with sprinklings of errors; the word 'wrinkle' describes those who have the right belief, but live a life soiled with the dirt of sins. Wrinkles bespeak old age. Such is that old man whom we have inherited from Adam. Paul tells us to shake off him and his practices altogether, so that we may put on the new man[191] and, with spiritual powers renewed, follow the footsteps of Christ and walk in newness of life. Christ is a fastidious lover. He cannot love a synagogue that is wrinkled by its ancient ceremonies and its zeal for the Old Law; nor does he tolerate the churches of the heretics, disfigured by leprosy and various marks of false doctrine.

KA If it is truly said that no one lives free from sin, where is that spouse who was praised in the Canticle as totally beautiful and free from every stain?[192]

CA It is given to very few to live their life free from the venial sins that steal over human nature through carelessness. But these are small spots rather than stains. As they appear daily, so too are they washed away daily by a short prayer, or by alms-giving, or by atonement with some good work, but especially by reception of the Lord's body. However, those who have acknowledged Christ should and can, with God's help, refrain from sinning seriously.

KA Are we to conclude, therefore, that people who are stained by sin do not belong to the holy church?

CA They do and they do not. In so far as their faith remains unimpaired, they belong to the church, and they are not prevented from sharing in the sacraments unless they are cut off from membership in the church by public decree, owing to clearly established and enormous crimes. The church strictly so called is a hidden society directed to the eternal life of the predestined; the greater part of it already lives with Christ, and

* * * * *

188 Matt 16:18
189 Cf John 10:28–9.
190 Eph 5:27
191 Col 3:9–10
192 Song of Sol 4:7

the remnant has been called to work its way to the highest purity. One rightly denies, therefore, that the church has stain or wrinkle, a negation justified either by synecdoche[193] or by the church's goal and purpose, from which even logicians admit that the name of an entity is taken. Sometimes the meaning of the word 'church' is extended, however, to include all those who have been washed in baptism, whether they live a holy life or not.[194] Sometimes the ministers or judges of the church are called the church. They are to be obeyed even if they openly live an evil life, provided they do not command or teach what is impious, especially if there would be a greater loss of public peace in removing them than in tolerating them.[195] Corrupt clergy are among those who wish evil to the church, and the Bridegroom hates them.

Anyone who acknowledges the holy church curses and abjures every schismatic conspiracy against the peace of its hierarchy and also all covens of heretics, whatever the pretexts they use to recommend themselves. They are countless, while the dove is one.[196]

KA Once upon a time heretics had churches. In that state of affairs when individuals shout, 'Christ is not there but he is here,'[197] by what sign do we identify that one and only dove of Christ?

CA Anything that strays from the Sacred Scriptures is not of Christ.

KA But the heretics attack the church with these very same weapons.

* * * * *

193 'Synecdoche' is the rhetorical figure that describes a whole by one of its parts; eg 'under my roof' for 'in my house.'

194 Cf Augustine *De catechizandis rudibus* 19.31 PL 40 333; Erasmus *Declarationes ad censuras Lutetiae vulgatas* LB IX 947C: 'But the church militant strictly speaking consists of those who are the predestined ones, whom God alone knows.' Erasmus was censured by the Sorbonne for having suggested in the colloquy *Inquisitio de fide* that the church consists of none but the righteous, although they were still fallible men (ASD I-3 372:263–5 / Thompson *Inquisitio* 69 / CWE 39 429:11–13). In the passage here he allows for two understandings of the term *ecclesia*, one strict and another more inclusive, a solution that he reaches also in the *Ecclesiastes*, written in 1535. See LB V 1071 D–E: 'Again, it is taken in two senses, that the name includes either only those who are true and living members of Christ, destined for blessed immortality, who are known only by God; or the entire congregation under the communion of those living with the sacraments of the church, which includes and tolerates the mixing of the bad with the good.'

195 For a discussion of Erasmus' concern for peace and the church's role in promoting it, see McConica.

196 Song of Sol 6:8

197 Cf Matt 24:23.

CA That is not surprising, for they follow in the steps of that false spirit who tempted the Lord to wrongdoing by distorted proofs from the Scriptures.[198] The false interpretation of the Scriptures must be rebutted by a true interpretation.

KA That was easy for Christ to do, but for us mere mortals it is a slippery business.

CA Not everybody is meant to contend with heretics, but only those who are equipped with the suit of armour that St Paul mentions several times.[199] For you and people like you it is enough to hold with unshaken faith what the church has clearly and expressly handed down as necessary.[200]

KA If someone has received baptism and religious instruction in a heretical sect, what should he do?

CA Let him not repeat a baptism he has received in the name of the Father and Son and Holy Spirit; let him purify what he has been taught, withdraw from unclean assemblies, and be reconciled with the holy church.

KA But that was just what I was asking – by what mark can the holy church be identified?

CA By combining many inferences into one argument, it is easy to discover where the dove is. First, there is the authority of the ancient councils, especially when they are confirmed by the constant consent of so many ages and so many nations. Next comes the authority of interpreters whose holiness the church has recognized and whose books it has approved. Disagreement with them is not completely excluded, since on occasion they argue among themselves and differ in their conclusions, but they must be read with reverence and their teachings must not be rashly rejected.[201] I think that we must hold the same opinion of approved colleges of theologians who strive tirelessly to unearth for us the truth hidden in the Sacred Scriptures. In the third place, one must consider how widely a belief is held. No heresy has ever spread as far as Catholic teaching. Finally, the believer's way of life must be observed quite closely.

KA But those others too have Christ on their lips, and there is an account of the marvellous fasting of the Manichees[202] as well as of their continence;

* * * * *

198 He is referring to the temptation in the desert; see Matt 4:1–11; Luke 4:1–13.
199 Cf Rom 13:12; Eph 6:13; 1 Thess 5:8.
200 An important aspect of Erasmus' thought, especially in his debate with Luther, is the role of authority in the church; eg *De libero arbitrio* LB IX 1215D. See 335 n239 below.
201 Cf ibidem LB IX 1215A–B.
202 Manichees: see 274 n152 above.

the Ebionites[203] despise riches; the Psalliani[204] pray continually; the Anthropomorphites[205] used to live in deserts, take shelter in huts, torture their flesh with fasting, physical labour, and sleeping on the ground. When such men, assembled in crowds, cry out, 'Here is Christ,'[206] would not one placed, as it were, at a crossroads rightly hesitate over what direction he should take?

CA Crossing the very stage of the Gospel[207] you see Pharisees venerable for their dangling phylacteries,[208] made thin by fasting,[209] praying copiously,[210] bestowing their riches on the poor.[211] These external things, although they have the appearance of piety, are nevertheless very often pretences for some temporary gain, especially profit or glory; therefore I added that their practitioners should be observed quite closely. If anyone does so, he will discover that the same things indeed are done by good people and bad, but in a different way. In their fasts and abstinence the devout are cheerful, the others gloomy and sour;[212] the devout do not boast of these things, but rather conceal them, nor do they proclaim their greatness, but consider them unimportant and make light of them. They do not disdain others who do not follow the same practices, but interpret the difference kindly – that they would do greater things if their bodily weakness permitted it, or that they have a less rebellious body so that they have no need to subdue it by such methods, or that by other good deeds they offer a more pleasing sacrifice to God. The religion of the devout is simple and without deceit.

John's disciples fasted, but they disparaged the disciples of Christ because they fasted rather infrequently.[213] The Manichees abstained from all animal meat, but they condemned what God created, and secretly

* * * * *

203 Ebionites: see 293 n92 above; cf *Amabili ecclesiae concordia* LB V 485E: 'Magna divitiarum contentio in Ebionitis, prodigiosa orandi assiduitas in Euchitis, magna abstinentia ac vitae severitas in Manichaeis.'
204 Psalliani: see Augustine *De haeresibus* 57 PL 42 40–1 (where they are called Messaliens); *Modus orandi Deum* 179 above.
205 Anthropomorphites: see 272 n135 above.
206 Matt 24:23
207 Stage of the Gospel: see 240 n20 above.
208 Phylactery: a small case containing passages of Scripture. Cf Deut 6:8–9; Matt 23:5.
209 Matt 6:16
210 Matt 6:7; Luke 20:47
211 Matt 6:2–4
212 Matt 6:16
213 Matt 9:14; Mark 2:18; Luke 5:33

gorged themselves with luxuries that were more sumptuous and more expensive. The Pharisees prayed but it was at the crossroads;[214] in their chambers they cheated people or counted their money. The Euchites[215] prayed, but superstitiously. Under the pretext of praying, they lived off others and did not work with their hands in order to supply themselves with a livelihood and share something with the poor, as Paul had taught.[216] The Ebionites[217] and the incorrectly styled Apostolics[218] possessed no private property, but condemned others who owned anything, and attributed piety to themselves, although true piety is rooted not in land or money, but in the right disposition.

The apostles poured themselves out to attract as many as possible to Christ, and they could not be forced by any unjust harshness to abandon this attitude towards any person. They devised revenge against no one, but when they were thrown into prison they sang psalms and returned thanks to God;[219] when they were beaten with rods and crushed by stones[220] they rejoiced, praying for those at whose hands they suffered these evils. When they were raising the dead,[221] casting out devils,[222] or healing the sick by their shadow,[223] a word of pride never fell from their lips, but openly professing that they were only men,[224] they returned all the praise to God. A person who eagerly manifests this charity, this endurance at all times bears fruit by which the good tree can be identified.[225]

KA I hear that there is scarcely an ancient writer who does not deviate in some points from the rule of Catholic faith. Why has the church accepted their books?

CA It has received them not as canonical scriptures, that is, of irrefutable authority, but as the explanations of good and learned men. Not every

* * * * *

214 Matt 6:5
215 Euchites: another name for the Psalliani or Messaliens; see 330 n204 above.
216 See Acts 20:34; 1 Cor 4:12; 1 Thess 4:11.
217 Ebionites: see 293 n92 and 330 n203 above.
218 Apostolics: ascetical sect, followers of Tatian, a second-century Christian apologist who wrote a gospel narrative harmonizing the four Gospels. He later turned to Gnosticism. See Augustine *De haeresibus* 40 PL 42 32.
219 Acts 16:25
220 Cf Acts 16:22.
221 Acts 9:36–42
222 Mark 3:15
223 Acts 5:15
224 Acts 14:15
225 Cf Matt 7:17.

error makes a man a heretic. In times past, allowance was made for expositors of Scripture if they were undecided about certain beliefs that it would be wrong to question now that the church's teaching has been promulgated, or if their interpretation of something in obscure writings differed from the church's present authoritative teaching. Not all Greeks who asserted the belief that the Holy Spirit proceeds from the Father alone were heretics. Perhaps Origen was not a heretic either simply because, in his zeal for investigating truth, he questioned whether the Son and the Holy Spirit have the same divine essence as the Father, or are created beings superior to all others.[226] Even three hundred years after the birth of Christ, it was permitted to debate whether there was any fire in purgatory; some interpreted fire to mean charity. But it is heretical to rebel insolently against a doctrine that is clear and proclaimed by public authority.

KA How many books does the title 'canonical Scripture' embrace?

CA It is easy to answer that: St Cyprian[227] has given the information. First, all of Scripture is divided into the Old Testament and the New Testament. The Old Testament includes the Pentateuch, that is the five books of Moses: Genesis, Exodus, Leviticus, Numbers, Deuteronomy. To these are added the two books[228] of Joshua, Judges and Ruth. After these come the four books of Kings, which the Hebrews compress into two.[229] Next is the book of Paralipomenon, that is, 'of things passed over,' which is called the 'book of Days' by the Hebrews.[230] Then follow the first two books of Esdras, which the Hebrews reckon as one, since Third and Fourth Esdras are regarded as apocryphal.[231] Next come the four major

* * * * *

226 See Origen *De principibus* 1.3.3, 1.3.5 PG 11 147–51, and Jerome *Epistolae* 124.2 PL 22 1060–1.
227 Cyprian: read Rufinus; see Rufinus 37–8 PL 21 373–5.
228 Cf ibidem 37. Rufinus puts Ruth together with Judges, in agreement with the arrangement of contemporary Jews and in accordance with the Greek Scriptures.
229 He is referring to 1 and 2 Samuel and 1 and 2 Kings; cf Rufinus 37.
230 1 and 2 Chronicles. The title Paralipomenon comes from the Septuagint. These books fill in material that is missing from 1 and 2 Kings.
231 Erasmus is following the enumeration of the Vulgate here. Esdras is the Greek form of the Hebrew Ezra. The Hebrew canon includes the books called Ezra and Nehemiah, written to describe the history of the Jews' return to Jerusalem. In addition to this rendering, two books of the Apocrypha, 1 and 2 Esdras, are part of the Greek Scripture. The first of these contains material from 2 Chronicles, the book of Ezra, and some verses from Nehemiah, with additional material all rearranged in a new sequence. 2 Esdras contains new material of

prophets: Isaiah, Jeremiah, Ezekiel, and Daniel.[232] To these is joined a single book containing the twelve minor prophets. In addition to these, there are the single books Job and Psalms, three books of Solomon – Proverbs, Ecclesiastes, and the Canticle of Canticles. The authority of the ancients has limited the books of the Old Testament to this number; it is sinful to doubt their reliability. The book of Wisdom, which some suspect to be a work of Philo Judaeus, and another called Ecclesiasticus, attributed to Jesus, son of Sirach, have been accepted for use in the church, as well as Tobit, Judith, Esther, and two books of Maccabees. Two stories which the Hebrews did not have, one about Susanna, the other about Bel and the Dragon, are appended to the book of Daniel and are also accepted.[233] (Jerome asserts that he translated them from the edition of Theodotion.)[234] Only the Spirit of the church knows whether or not the church has accepted these books as of equal authority with the others. Under the title New Testament, the four Gospels – Matthew, Mark, Luke, John – and with them the Acts of the Apostles hold first place. Next come the letters of the apostles: fourteen of Paul, two of Peter, one of the apostle James, one of Jude, three of John. The Apocalypse of John holds last place.

The Hebrews make a threefold division of all Scripture. They give the name 'canonical'[235] to Scripture that has unquestionably been prompted

* * * * *

an apocalyptic nature. In the Vulgate, the books are enumerated as follows: 1 Esdras (based on the Septuagint translation of Ezra), 2 Esdras (Nehemiah), 3 Esdras (called 1 Esdras in the Apocrypha), and 4 Esdras (called 2 Esdras in the Apocrypha). Erasmus rightly asserts that the Hebrew canon accepts books 1 and 2, but not 3 and 4. See 334 n237 below on the Apocrypha.

232 Erasmus omits the book of Esther, which is included in Rufinus' list of the canon. It is also affirmed by Origen, Cyril, Jerome, and Augustine. Erasmus includes it instead in the list of books that are not strictly canonical but are accepted 'for use in the church.'

233 Rufinus omits these.

234 Cf *Incipit: Prologus Hieronymi in Danihele propheta*: 'Danihelem prophetam iuxta Septuaginta interpres Domini Salvatoris ecclesiae non legunt, utentes Theodotionis editione, et hoc cur acciderit nescio.' Theodotion was a second-century Greek translator whose version of the book of Daniel was the source for almost all extant manuscripts.

235 Erasmus seems to be using this term in a sense that is at variance with its use several lines earlier. 'Canonical' Scripture consists of those books of the Old Testament which Erasmus has listed, with the exception of the Apocrypha. The Hebrews divided these sacred books into three categories: the Law or Torah, encoded in the Pentateuch; the prophets, consisting of Joshua, Judges, Samuel,

by the inspiration of the Holy Spirit; if anything occurs in it that seems absurd on the surface, it is unlawful to judge adversely what has been written. Rather, a scrupulous search must be made for the hidden meaning, and the dullness of our intellect must be blamed, not the Scripture. They give the name Hagiographa[236] to books written by holy men on holy subjects. They allowed them to be reverently read in assemblies, but did not allow their authority to be used to argue in serious matters. They gave the name Apocrypha[237] to Scripture that each person was permitted to read at home as he wished. Beyond that, these works were not to be read at liturgical assemblies, nor was anyone to be burdened by their authority. Not everything sung in a sacred place is automatically Sacred Scripture, and I wish that all observed the decree of the Council of Carthage [238] to read only canonical Scripture in churches, which in times past was orally interpreted by bishops and priests.

KA At present we are steered away from reading the sacred volumes.

CA Reading them was once the very pinnacle of religion, but the rashness of readers required a display of the rod. If a man reads with reverence, honouring what he cannot comprehend there, if he is all the more ready to be instructed by a learned man because he is somehow prepared by

* * * * *

Kings, Isaiah, Jeremiah, Ezekiel, and the twelve minor prophets; and the Hagiographa or Writings, which include the Psalms, Proverbs, Job, Song of Songs, Ruth, Lamentations, Ecclesiastes, Esther, Daniel, Ezra-Nehemiah, and Chronicles. See Jerome's preface to Samuel and Kings, called the *Prologus galeatus,* 'helmeted preface,' in the Vulgate. Jerome, incidentally, lists Ruth as part of the book of Judges. See also Augustine *De doctrina christiana* 2.8 PL 34 40–1, which divides the books into a historical narrative beginning with Genesis and ending with Chronicles, a disunited collection of books that are chiefly historical (Job, Tobias, Esther, Judith, Maccabees, and Esdras), and the prophets, in which category he includes the Psalms, Proverbs, Song of Songs, and Ecclesiastes in addition to the prophetic works.

236 The Hagiographa or Writings are none the less part of the canon, as indicated in the preceding note.

237 The Apocrypha, sometimes called the Deuterocanonical writings and not included by the Hebrews in the canon, are included in the Septuagint and were translated by Jerome as part of the Vulgate. Jerome's prefaces establish their secondary status; see eg the *Prologus galeatus* and the Preface to the Wisdom of Jesus son of Sirach. Cf Rufinus 38 PL 21 374–5. Augustine in *De doctrina christiana* 2.8 PL 34 40–1 makes no distinction in status between the Apocrypha and other writings.

238 Council of Carthage: he is referring to the synod that met in 397; however, it like the earlier Synod of Hippo took an inclusive attitude to the Apocrypha.

reading, if he does not read to be equipped for a dispute, but always draws from the Scriptures help for living a holy life,[239] that rule is not aimed at him; it is opposed to rashness, not the desire for holiness.

KA Since the same God the Father, the same Christ, the same Holy Spirit are present in both Testaments, why is the one called 'New,' the other 'Old'? Things divine know no old age.

CA The divine nature, as you say, knows neither old age nor youth, but it was to our advantage that certain exterior observances be reformed. Christ used the name 'New Testament' when consecrating the bread and wine.[240] If you ask me what has been renewed, I could give a long list. First, clear truth has taken the place of shadowy regulations; and what that Law darkly promised has been opened to the human senses. The word that kills has been locked up again, and the Spirit who gives life has made his appearance.[241] Some external ceremonies have been entirely abolished, others changed into something more fitting. Jewish laws regulating the choice of foods have been totally abrogated; we are permitted to wear clothing woven from wool and linen;[242] it is permitted to plough with an ox and an ass[243] – not to mention countless other examples. In place of so many different kinds of sacrifices, we have one spiritual victim and one only; in place of just the one temple in Jerusalem (for it was not permitted to offer sacrifice elsewhere),[244] we have a church that is spread throughout the entire world, in which a clean oblation is now offered, and pure hands are raised to heaven in every place; a gentle washing has been substituted for the wound of circumcision. The Sabbath has been changed to Sunday; Christ, the Son, has taken the place of Moses the servant; the grace of the Spirit, which formerly was distributed sparingly to a few, is openly and abundantly poured forth on all nations beneath the sky.[245] Finally, heaven,

* * * * *

239 Here Erasmus strikes a balance between the lack of emphasis given to personal study of Scripture in the Roman church, and the strong advocacy of such reading by the Evangelical reform. In particular, Erasmus wishes personal interpretations of Scripture always to be guided by the authority of the church. Cf Ep 1334, the preface to Erasmus' edition of the works of Hilary (lines 245–74).
240 Matt 26:28
241 2 Cor 3:6
242 Cf Deut 22:11.
243 Cf Deut 22:10.
244 Cf Deut 12:11.
245 Cf Acts 2:17.

which was formerly closed even to good people, has been opened by the gospel. Owing to these and many other changes, this is rightly called the New Testament – not because it is in any way a different testament, but because it has been revealed differently. Those Jews who lived in hope of heavenly life in the ardour of the Spirit were under the New Testament. On the other hand, those who measure holiness today by external ceremonies, who gaze with eagerness at worldly goods but are cold in charity and hot in revenge, still cling to the Old Testament, since they have not yet put off the old man.[246]

KA You have explained all these points clearly.

CA We are coming to the holy church, in which we adore the Father, Creator of all things, the Son, Redeemer of the world, the Holy Spirit, Sanctifier of all men. Let us remain in this church. Let us walk in it according to the Spirit, not according to the flesh.[247] Let us, with hearts united, fight the good fight[248] in it, so that we may reach the reward of eternal life. But, if you don't mind, let this lesson end.

Lesson 5

KA What is the significance of the church's adding the phrase 'communion of saints' to the creed?

CA This phrase is not added in Cyprian[1] or Augustine, and they do not even mention the words in passing. On this evidence, it is probable that the phrase was added by someone who was anxious to explain what was meant by 'holy church.' The church is a society and association[2] not of just anyone, but of saints, just as the word *contio* for Latin-speakers means a formal meeting not of just anybody but of citizens of the same republic assembled to take thought for their common interests. Some more recent theologians, however, interpret the holy church as a society of earthly soldiers under the leadership of Christ, and the communion of saints as a society of saints triumphant in heaven. Others, again, explain the communion of saints as the church's intercessory prayer,[3] useful to

* * * * *

246 Cf Eph 4:24; Col 3:9.
247 Cf Rom 8:4; Gal 5:16.
248 Cf 1 Tim 6:12; 2 Tim 4:7.
  1 Cyprian: read Rufinus.
  2 *Contubernium*: literally, a tent-companion in a military campaign
  3 *Suffragia*: prayers of intercession; see Thomas Aquinas *Summa theologica* II-II q 83 art 7.

all who belong to the body of the holy church. Still others explain it as the sacraments of the church, which are of no value to anyone except those who attach themselves to the church. Yet another group thinks that the word 'communion' designates the Eucharist, which the Greeks sometimes call σύναξις, union, because this sacrament signifies and strengthens the very close connection between the mystical body and the head. The term also signifies a mystical association among professed Christians of the kind that is natural among all parts of the same living being.[4]

Those, I say, who have devised these explanations indeed proclaim the truth, but they do not, in my opinion at least, explain the explicit content of these words, except to the extent that all these ideas are implicitly included in the phrase 'holy church.' This fact is beyond dispute – there is no gift in the Catholic church that does not flow down to it from Christ, its head, although different members have different functions.[5]

KA Nowhere on the globe is there any good that does not flow from Christ.

CA That is a fact, but we are speaking of those good things that, through faith in Christ and the sacraments of the church, bestow true holiness. In other respects, God grants many advantages to the wicked, to asses, and to oxen.

KA If those who live impiously are not in the fellowship of the church, and if we do not know whether most people are good or evil, what can that society of human beings who do not know each other be?

* * * * *

4 *Communio sanctorum*: Erasmus' enumeration reveals that this article has been the source of considerable controversy. One issue at stake involves the meaning of *sanctorum*: is it the genitive plural of *sanctus*, 'holy person,' or of *sanctum*, 'holy object'? Most believe the former, but even this meaning is open to further interpretation: are the *sancti* an elite group of martyrs and saints, or is the term a more inclusive one indicative of all Christians? The former interpretation, implied by Erasmus' first example, would tend to support the elaborate cults honouring saints and martyrs, of which Erasmus himself was so critical (see eg the colloquy *Peregrinatio religionis ergo* ASD I-3 470–94 / CWE 40 619–74 or *Naufragium* ASD I-3 325–32 / CWE 39 349–67). The third interpretation proposed by Erasmus holds that the root of *sanctorum* is *sancta*, sacred things, ie the sacraments. Thomas Aquinas adopts this position in his *In symbolum apostolorum, Expositio* art 10 in Aquinas *Opuscula* I 213–15; however, he also includes the understanding that the benefits of the church's holiest members, in other words, its saints, accrue to all who are one with them in the church. Finally, the last possibility ties the meaning of the Latin term to its Greek equivalent.

5 Cf 1 Cor 12:4–6.

CA We do not know any of the angels, although they serve us. You do not
know your own soul, yet you owe your life, your mobility, and your
reason to it. No one has to know whether this man or that is a living
member of the church. It suffices to believe that there is on earth a special society for the life of the predestined[6] and that Christ has welded
it together by his Spirit, whether it be among the Indians, the Phoeni-
cians, the Hyperboreans,[7] or the Africans. There may possibly be some
land, some islands, or some continents in the universe that have not yet
been discovered by sailors or geographers, but in which Christian faith
may flourish.[8] To look into the depths of hearts belongs to God alone;
thus human judgments frequently happen to be uncertain.

KA Why, then, are some people expelled from the church?

CA There are some public crimes which, as St Paul says,[9] proceed to judgment. Mortals pass sentence on them when they can, in order to maintain
public order. And yet it sometimes happens that a thief who is being led

* * * * *

6 One might find such a view surprising, in the light of Erasmus' debate with
Luther on freedom of the will. In the *Inquisitio de fide*, written at about the
same time as *De libero arbitrio*, Erasmus claims that the holy church consists
only of good men, although even these could fall away (ASD I-3 372:263–5 /
Thompson *Inquisitio* 69 / CWE 39 429:11–13). In response to the Sorbonne's
censure of this passage, Erasmus replies, 'Sed Ecclesia militans propria dicta
constat ex praedestinatis, quos solus Deus novit' (*Declarationes ad censuras Lutetiae vulgatas*, 1532, LB IX 947C). See Thompson *Inquisitio* 100. Thompson's view
is that Erasmus believed his difference with Luther had more to do with the
reformer's destructive approach than with doctrine, although the doctrinal
dispute went deeper than he recognized; however, these later references to
predestination suggest more of an underlying congruence with Luther than
Thompson's interpretation assumes.

7 Hyperboreans: in Greek mythology, a race of people allegedly living north of
the river Oceanus, in a land where the temperature was always mild, the soil
fertile, and the people fabulously long-lived.

8 This is one of the few occasions on which Erasmus shows an awareness of
the activity of explorers during his time. Bakhuizen van den Brink calls this
comment a 'ludic fantasy' (ASD V-1 283:261n); however, it does accord in spirit
with certain passages from the *Paraclesis*; see LB V 140C. Cf ASD I-3 371:256–
60 / Thompson *Inquisitio* 69 / CWE 39 429:4–7, in which Erasmus describes
the faithful as those throughout the world who agree in the gospel, worship
God the Father, believe in the Son, and are guided by the Spirit. This formu-
lation does not claim explicitly that those to whom the faith is unknown can
be Christians through Christ's spirit, although it contains the possibility for
such an interpretation to be developed.

9 1 Tim 5:24

to the cross[10] is free from guilt, while the judge who condemned him deserves to be hanged. It can happen, too, that a person who has been excommunicated is in communion with the church, and the excommunicator is cut off from the church. So too, someone dragged to the fire as a heretic may be a victim most pleasing to God, but those who dragged him deserve to be burned.

KA Can this occur even when someone is expelled from the church for confessed and indisputable murder or sacrilege?

CA Certainly. For it can happen that, before the bishop hurls his thunderbolt at the guilty man, he has, by his heartfelt contrition, already returned to God's favour. Since that situation escapes people's notice, it offers no protection against his being barred from the church door.

KA Why does God will that it should be unknown in the meantime who are truly good and predestined[11] for eternal life?

CA So that evil persons may not lose hope and fall into more dreadful sins, and so that good ones may act more cautiously and moderately. Consider the great dissensions that exist now; what kind of war would there be if the division were plain to see? The Lord refused to make his betrayer known to the rest of the disciples.[12] Because it is now unknown whom God has chosen[13] for blessed immortality, those who stand are careful not to fall, and those who have fallen try to rise. Finally, those who are afire with charity are anxious to deserve well of the bad and the good equally – of those whose wickedness is obvious, that they may come to their senses; of those whose goodness is doubtful, that they may become better if they are good. Though charity here may be wasting its service, it does not lose its reward.

KA What are these sacraments of the church that you mentioned a short while ago? And what does the word 'sacrament' mean?

CA Those who have spoken more precisely give the name of sacrament to an oath or obligation that is confirmed by the intervention of divine power and religion. Our ancestors, however, adjusted the word to mean what the Greeks call a mystery, and what you might a secret religious rite.[14]

* * * * *

10 Cf Luke 23:39–43.

11 Cf Augustine *De corruptione et gratia* 13.40 PL 44 940–1; see 338 n6 above.

12 The gospel accounts appear to be somewhat at variance with Erasmus' statement. Cf Matt 26:20–5; Mark 14:17–21; Luke 22:21; and John 13:21–30.

13 *Eligo*: to choose or elect; Matt 24:22; Mark 13:20; Rom 8:33; 2 Tim 2:10

14 *Sacramentum:* in ancient Rome, the term had both legal and military connotations, meaning the bond posted by parties to a civil suit (and thereby coming

KA Why is it called secret?

CA Because ordinary persons were excluded from performing these rites, although today many of them take place in public, such as the blessing of baptismal water. These ceremonies and even the words in which they are carried out used to be hidden from the people, and one bishop personally passed them on to another, so that there might be greater veneration for the sacraments. As soon as the bishop appeared to consecrate the bread and wine, it became unlawful for a layman to remain within the sanctuary. After a certain pope had answered a number of questions for a bishop (English, if I am not mistaken) who was asking about sacramental rites, he did not dare to write down the formula for consecrating the oil, lest, as often happens, the letter be intercepted and the secret made public.[15]

This account of the sacraments is not without foundation. However, the more accurate and widespread explanation is that the sacraments, through certain sensible signs, infuse invisible grace in harmony with those outward signs.[16]

KA How many sacraments of that kind are there?

CA Seven have been handed down to us by the ancients: matrimony, through which we are born into this world;[17] baptism, through which we are born again in Christ. To baptism is closely allied penance, a kind of second baptism by which we are reconciled to God, although in this case the wounds are not healed without cost, or without scars. Next comes confirmation, by which the beginner is strengthened against the temptations of Satan; people of an age when sin becomes a danger for the first time, that is, after their seventh year, are usually fortified by this sacrament. Soon afterwards the Eucharist strengthens them, like young men growing up to face righteous battles. Through it, a lively faith is

* * * * *

to signify the suit itself), or an oath sworn to a military commander. The term appears in the Vulgate indicating 'secret' (Tob 12:7) and 'mystery' (1 Tim 3:16; Eph 5:32; Rev 1:20), the equivalent of the Greek μυστήριον. Kelly *Doctrines* 193 claims we have no evidence that either term came into use to indicate the external rites of the church before the Alexandrian Fathers and Tertullian.

15 It has been impossible to find a source for this strange story.

16 Cf Augustine *De catechizandis rudibus* 26.50 PL 40 314–15; Ambrose *De mysteriis* 3.8 PL 16 408; Aquinas *In articulos fidei et sacramenta ecclesiae* part 2 in Aquinas *Opuscula* 147–51.

17 Bakhuizen van den Brink (ASD V-1 285:305n) remarks with astonishment on Erasmus' choice of matrimony as the sacrament with which to begin. This is indeed a departure from tradition, which tends to place baptism first.

stirred up in us, and we are enriched with abundant grace by mystical commemoration of the sacred death, and we renew for ourselves, so far as is permitted, that unique sacrifice to which we owe our salvation.[18] Since there is also a struggle at the end of life, aid is sought from extreme unction, so that by it a sick person may regain his strength, if such is the will of God, or may fall asleep in the Lord in faith and good hope. In donatives[19] like these, the kindness of Jesus the captain is poured out for this time below, consoling and enlivening his soldiers until they may be drawn on to receive the pay[20] of eternal life when the battle is over. There is one sacrament left, ordination, which confers the authority to perform sacred ministry. This sacrament contributes to the dignity and peace of the church's hierarchy, for it is fitting that in a Christian community ecclesiastical functions should not be assigned to just anyone, but that the suitable persons should be chosen. There cannot be harmony where no one obeys any one else, but each claims for himself the right to do whatever he wishes. In fact, Paul includes the gift of governing among the gifts of the Holy Spirit.[21]

KA What grace does each sacrament confer?

CA They are all conferred on the condition that one receives them properly. Through the sacrament of matrimony, with the accessory prayer of the priest, the gift of the Spirit by which a man may love his wife with chaste love as Christ loved the church is granted; the wife in turn may, for Christ's sake, love and revere her husband as her lord; and both may, with the greatest care, direct the children, if any are granted them, to Christian piety.[22] It is not necessary to speak of baptism. Everyone knows that in it the old man dies with all his sins wiped out, whether you refer to original sin or personal sin, and a new one, whom Paul calls 'the new creation,' arises cleansed from every stain through faith in Christ.[23]

It was not proper that a person who had been once reborn and cleansed by Christ's blood should return to a cesspool of filth. Yet since

* * * * *

18 See 283 n36 above.

19 Donatives: the Latin word *donativum* that Erasmus here uses was the technical term for a monetary gift from a general to his troops. See 244 n46 above.

20 *Stipendium:* the full remuneration for military service; cf Rom 6:23. Erasmus is continuing the military metaphor with which he has been working throughout, not suggesting that eternal life can be bought.

21 1 Cor 12:28

22 Eph 5:21–33

23 2 Cor 5:17

charity has grown cold in many and faith grows listless, divine goodness has granted the remedy of penance, which we will soon be discussing.[24] Those of tender age are more inclined to wantonness than to
piety, but sacred confirmation diminishes this tendency, and increases
their receptiveness to holiness, in order to prevent them from being corrupted by vice before they know what vice is. Furthermore, since after
the sixteenth year the devil moves all his engines of war against the
soldier of Christ, first the engines of lust, gluttony, and other low desires, a little later those of ambition and anger, from then on he is rein-
vigorated by real food and drink from heaven. In this way, carrying
Christ himself and his Spirit in his breast, he may withstand all the assaults of Satan with brave heart. In times past, the body and blood of the
Lord was given to little infants immediately after baptism. This custom
was changed, and perhaps it would also be better to change a custom
that prevails in certain regions, administering confirmation to infants.
These sacraments are not absolutely necessary, as baptism is. For that
reason, mothers rightly prepare in haste for the latter; the former are
more suitably administered at their own time, and are conferred with
greater profit if a short admonition is added to the sacrament.

In those who are chosen to administer the sacraments, the gift of the
Spirit is increased by the sacrament of orders to help them carry out the
office assigned them in worthy fashion. For instance, we read that hands
were imposed on Paul and Barnabas so that they might set out to spread
the gospel.[25] Paul writing to Timothy bears witness to the imposition of
hands on Timothy too.[26]

That suffices for a cursory treatment of the sacraments! Next in the
creed comes 'the forgiveness of sins.' No one dares to enter the king's
hall in rags and bespattered with mud; it is much more unseemly to
enter a holy church defiled by sin. For this reason, the means of washing
is supplied right at the threshold, so that one may be pure on entry. This
cleansing was formerly performed in a religious ceremony outside the
church. A porter at the church door sprinkled those entering with holy
water.

Ancient authorities, however, related this article to the grace of baptism, by which all sins are forgiven without penalty.[27] In the creed that

*****

24 See 343–5 below.
25 Acts 13:3
26 1 Tim 4:14
27 Kelly *Creeds* 161 writes, 'We are therefore justified in concluding that in practice, at the time it obtained entrance to the Old Roman Creed, *the remission of*

is sung in the mass, there is a also a mention of baptism, but none of penance: 'I believe in one baptism for the forgiveness of sin.' In the Athanasian Creed, no mention is made of either baptism or penance, since, as I pointed out before,[28] it does not expound this part of the Apostles' Creed. More recent authors correctly understand penance as included under the name of baptism. Penance would scarcely have found a place in the church had not Paul given orders that a man who had married his father's wife be handed over to Satan, and then commanded that the same man be received again into the grace and fellowship of the saints.[29]

In Africa, the right to return to the church was granted only once, so as to prevent church discipline from losing its rigour; further, in some ages, persons who had lapsed into grave crime were kept from entering the church building and were not received back except through public confession and severe, lengthy penance. Later, on account of the impudence of the rich, who preferred stirring up schisms to submitting to the church, remedial penance was moderated by the bishops, so that from then on an individual priest would hear what the whole people used to hear, and so that he might heal the wounds with far milder remedies. This gentle approach is granted not only because of human weakness, but also for the protection of the simple and the innocent, for whom it is better not to know the names of many vices.

KA Have there been no errors in connection with this article?

CA Pelagius and Jovinian taught that infant baptism is superfluous, since infants have no stain that could be washed away.[30] They say that original sin existed in no one but Adam and Eve. Others are born free from every sin, and for them, therefore, baptism is nothing more than a token of honour by which the baptized are received into the adoption of children and commended to the good will of Christians. The church rejected their teaching, and followed the statement of Christ (John 3), 'Unless one is born again of water and the Holy Spirit, he cannot enter the

* * * * *

sins must have conveyed the idea of the washing away of past offences and the opening up of a new life through the instrumentality of baptism.' Augustine concurs with this evaluation in Sermones 213.8.8 PL 38 1064–5, with the additional admonition that 'since we are destined to live in this world where no one lives without sin, on that account the remission of sins depends not solely on the washing in holy baptism, but also on the Lord's daily prayer ...'

28 See 252 above.
29 1 Cor 5:1–5
30 Augustine De haeresibus 88 PL 42 48

kingdom of God';[31] and Romans 3, 'All have sinned and will need the glory of God.'[32] Among the Africans, some rose up who did not receive those baptized by heretics into communion with the church, unless they received baptism anew from orthodox persons. The church rejected this doctrine also and taught, following Paul, that there is but one baptism,[33] and that anyone can be its minister, however impious and evil he may be, provided that, in keeping with the mind of the church, he baptizes by calling on the holy Trinity. Nevertheless, when there is no question of necessity, it is fitting that baptism be administered by a priest or deacons. It is safer to rebaptize those baptized by pagans or Jews, adding this condition, 'If you are not validly baptized,' etc.

In the same Africa that, according to the Greek proverb, is ever producing some new portent,[34] the Donatists arose.[35] They boasted that the grace of baptism had departed from every church except their own, and for this reason they preached that the sacrament was of no avail to anyone unless it was received again from them. The church taught that a mortal is nothing but the minister of baptism, and that Christ is its true author, in keeping with the testimony of John the Baptist: 'The one on whom you see the Holy Spirit descending, he it is who baptizes.'[36] The power conferred by baptism is a capacity coming from the blood of Christ through faith. What God bestows through faith cannot be invalidated by a defect in the minister. Its grace cannot be exhausted, since it is infinite and more than sufficient to wipe out all the crimes in the world, even if there were ten worlds far more iniquitous than this one.

Before the Donatists came the Seleucians,[37] who did not receive the baptism of water, but only of the Spirit. There were not wanting, furthermore, people who adopted a baptism of fire because the Baptist says (Matthew 3), 'He will baptize you in the Spirit and fire,'[38] although he

* * * * *

31 John 3:5
32 Rom 3:23
33 Eph 4:5
34 *Adagia* III vii 9; cf *Adagia* III vii 8, *Adagia* III vii 10.
35 Donatists: fourth-century sect believing that the sacraments were invalid if administered by unworthy or sinful clergy. They broke away from the Catholic church on the grounds that it tolerated unholy people in its ranks and was thereby invalidated.
36 John 1:33
37 Seleucians: see 275 n154 above.
38 Matt 3:11

understood by 'Spirit' the hidden grace of faith, which only the Holy Spirit bestows, and by 'fire' charity, without which faith is dead.

The Jews were the first to teach falsely that baptism and faith are not sufficient for attaining salvation unless circumcision is added. Their error was repudiated by the apostles themselves, especially Paul,[39] so that now there is no need for further refutation. Novatus[40] and Montanus[41] did not admit into the fellowship of the church a baptized person who after baptism had dishonoured and afflicted the church by an enormous and public crime. In my opinion, they did not want to wrest all hope of salvation from such people, but they would deprive them of the honour of fellowship to strike terror into others. This is the clear teaching of St Augustine about those who had been reconciled once with the church through penance, but fell into the same or a similar crime.[42] Mortal can close the doors of the church to mortal; no one but God can close heaven. Thus, in former times, deacons or priests who had committed a public crime were erased from the register of clerics with no hope of reinstatement. The same was done to bishops. This severity too, however, was mitigated by succeeding generations.

Once there was a great controversy too about confession and penance, and it has now been renewed. I think the safest path and the one most conducive to preserving public harmony is to follow in simple obedience what the authority of the church has handed down to us, that is, in keeping with the Greek proverb, to favour the luckier side and avoid matters about which you have doubts.[43]

The last part of the creed remains to be discussed: 'the resurrection of the body.' In this phrase you learn about the end of the world, when the good shall be separated from the evil, so that the evil have no hope of their suffering ending, and the good have no pain of any kind or fear of harm, since that very part of nature which groans within us will

* * * * *

39 Rom 3:25–9
40 Novatus: Eusebius *Historia ecclesiastica* 6.43 PG 20 615–30 describes Novatus, a third-century heretic, as part of a sect whose members saw themselves as puritans.
41 Montanus: see 324 n176 above.
42 Augustine *Epistolae* 265.6–7 PL 33 1088–9 distinguishes his teaching from that of Novatus, whose errors his letter is explicitly refuting, particularly Novatus' claim that the apostle Peter did penance but had not been baptized. The purpose of penance according to Augustine is to reconcile to the church already baptized members who have subsequently sinned.
43 See 329 n200 above.

be freed from every trouble. All things will be new,[44] changed not in substance but in quality.[45] The creed gives the name 'flesh' to the human body and 'resurrection' to renewal of life.

All articles are indeed to be held with unshaken faith, but this one in particular, for it brings special consolation to good people who are afflicted in this world, but terror to evil ones who would fall into every crime without restraint, if, after this life, recompenses were not made for good and evil. This is the basis of our whole faith, and it must be fixed as firmly as possible. If it wavers, belief in the rest is practically in vain. Adieu then to the ill-starred Sadducees.[46] They do not believe in the resurrection of bodies or in the existence of either angels or spirits, as if there were nothing in nature except what is obvious to the bodily senses, despite the fact that these things furthest removed from the senses are the greatest realities – and nothing is further removed from them than the Godhead itself. Adieu to those[47] who maintain that souls will rise again but not bodies, on the ground the soul cannot die or come to life again because it is immortal. They call it 'the resurrection of souls' when, according to their idle fancies, souls will be called forth to happiness from the hidden recesses in which they have been concealed for a certain time.

Adieu to those[48] who maintain that the body that we have will not live again, but that another one far superior is to be bestowed on each person. We will not be the same persons if we do not receive the same bodies. What need is there to create new ones? God by his omnipotent will can restore our old bodies to the highest splendour and happy immortality, not by changing their substance but by changing their qualities for the better. Adieu to the Chiliasts.[49] From misunderstanding the

* * * * *

44 Rev 21:5

45 Substance and quality: see 260 n65 above regarding substance and accident. Quality is the principle of differentiation that inheres in substance; in *Categories* 8 8b25 Aristotle writes, 'By quality, I mean that according to which certain things are said to be what they are, ie such and such.'

46 Sadducees: Jewish sect in the time of Christ, which believed in a strict adherence to the law and rejected the belief in resurrection (Mark 12:18; Luke 20:27). See Tertullian *De resurrectione carnis* 2 PL 2 796.

47 Tertullian mentions certain heretics who believe this in *De resurrectione carnis* 2 PL 2 796 and 4 PL 2 799–800, and in *De haereticorum praescriptionibus* 61 PL 2 70–1 he specifies Cerdo, Marcion, Lucan, and Apelles as holding this view.

48 Cf Tertullian *De resurrectione carnis* 51–3, 55–60 PL 2 868–83, who discusses this issue at length.

49 Chiliasts: see 311 n77 above; cf Rev 20:1–6.

Apocalypse of John, they idly imagine that all of us will one day come to life again, and for a thousand years enjoy all the pleasures of the world to our hearts' content. We heed the words of blessed Job when he says, 'And again I shall be covered with my skin, and in my flesh I shall see my God whom I am to see myself, and my eyes shall gaze upon him and not someone else';[50] we listen to Paul who wrote, 'He who raised Jesus from the dead will raise us too with Jesus,'[51] fully persuaded that at the end of the world all men and women will come to life again with the same bodies which they have on earth, and will rise exactly as Christ rose. He will bring our bodies into conformity with his glorified body.[52]

Physical immortality will be common to the good and the evil. To the latter, immortality will bring eternal torment, to the good, eternal happiness. Yet, in the case of the evil, 'eternal death' is a more correct description than immortality. Therefore the phrase 'life everlasting,' which some have added from the creed of the mass,[53] refers only to the good, while the word 'resurrection' refers equally to the good and the evil. (The word 'resurrection,' however, is also used at times to refer only to the good. For example, the Lord says in John, 'I am the resurrection and the life.'[54] Paul too scarcely uses this word anywhere without a good connotation. None the less, the Lord does make a distinction in John 5: 'And those who have done good will rise to the resurrection of life, but those who have done evil will rise to the resurrection of judgment.'[55] He uses the word 'judgment' for condemnation.)

This is expressed more clearly in the Athanasian Creed: '. . . at whose coming all men can rise again with their own bodies and will render an account of their individual doings, and those who have done good will go to eternal life, but those who have done evil will go to eternal fire.'[56] St Paul too speaks in this vein in Romans 8: 'The wages of sin is death; the grace of God, however, is eternal life in Christ Jesus, our Lord.'[57] He added the word 'eternal' because, just as there is no hope of alleviation for the damned, so there is no fear for the good that their happiness

* * * * *

50 Job 19:26–7
51 2 Cor 4:14
52 Cf Phil 3:21.
53 See 257 n47 above.
54 John 11:25
55 John 5:29
56 Athanasian Creed: see 252 n21 above.
57 Rom 6:23

will ever end or lessen, and that illustrious communion of all the saints will add to it greatly. The 'charity' that 'does not pass away'[58] will burn most brightly. Charity rejoices no less in the blessings of others than it does in its own. There is no reason here for our imagining bodily pleasures which consist in food, drink, or recourse to sex. Then there will be no use for these things, but bodies will be spiritual, and we will live in them as the angels of God do, for the happiness of angels is to see the face of the Father who is in heaven.[59] The Lord made the same statement in John: 'For this is eternal life, that they should know thee the only true God and Jesus Christ whom you sent.'[60] That knowledge begins on earth through faith. There it will be perfected, when we shall see his glory with face revealed.

KA Are these things sufficient for attaining salvation?

CA To obtain baptism, it is enough for a lay person to believe in these things. The learned and those who are more advanced must believe in everything that is revealed in Holy Writ and can clearly be deduced from it, and, in addition, whatever the Catholic church has approved by universal and uninterrupted consent. Whatever it has decreed on this basis was probably handed down by word of mouth from the apostles personally, or drawn from the Scriptures as secret nourishment for us, or inspired by the Holy Spirit as the times required. However, in the case of contentious and obscure doctrines, like the ones you are dealing with, let it suffice to profess your faith in these with this safeguard: 'I believe as the church believes.'[61] This is safer than to make a strong assertion about what you are unsure of or what you do not understand.

KA In the last analysis, is it enough to have the faith in one's heart, or must it also be professed orally?

CA Paul will answer you in my place: 'With the heart one believes unto righteousness; and with the mouth confession is made unto salvation.'[62] Also, the Lord threatens not to recognize before God as his soldier the man who is afraid or blushes to profess him before men.[63] But it is one thing not to profess the faith, and it is another to deny it. When there is

* * * * *

58 1 Cor 13:8
59 Cf Matt 18:10.
60 John 17:3
61 See 329 n200 above.
62 Rom 10:10
63 Matt 10:33: 'but whoever denies me before men, I also will deny before my Father who is in heaven.'

no hope of a favourable outcome, when there is grave danger, it is not necessary to make yourself known, as we read that some did, rushing into the forum of their own accord to be put to death with other Christians, or attacking the pagans' solemn orations – not with the intention of drawing anyone to Christ, but of being killed by them and enrolled in the catalogue of martyrs. Christ did not allow his apostles any violent defence against the impious, but only flight.[64] Peter fled from prison;[65] Paul was let down from the walls in a basket and escaped from Damascus.[66] However, whenever a situation has reached the point where the name of the Lord Jesus must be glorified before the pious and impious equally, what the church has taught must be professed eagerly and frankly with contempt for all allurements or terrors.

The doctrine of the Elcesaites is rejected.[67] They taught that in time of persecution it is lawful for people to deny Christ verbally, provided they maintain sincere faith in their hearts. If this is true, vain were the many tears that Peter shed because, terrified by the fear of death, he three times denied the Lord,[68] when he did not yet have even as much spiritual knowledge of him as the light of the gospel has revealed to us. Tertullian, who is unduly inclined to the opposite opinion, does not consent even to flight in time of persecution, maintaining that at that time it was a species of denial.[69] What he says could in certain circumstances be true. Certainly those commit a less grievous sin who, stricken with human fear, deny Christ in words only, than those who, with their eye on temporal advantages, defect in heart and speech from the commander under whom they have enlisted.

KA When there is a threat of tortures more grievous than any death, what will human frailty do?

CA The Lord himself has laid down the procedure for us. When that fear, weariness, and agony invade us, we will recognize the weakness of our powers, and, completely distrusting our own resources, we will prostrate ourselves on the ground and with deep trust implore the aid of the divine power, scarcely considering at all how horrible are the cruelties

* * * * *

64 See Matt 10:23, 24:16; Mark 13:14.
65 Acts 12:7–11
66 Acts 9:25
67 Elcesaites: an Arabic sect, second century; see Eusebius *Historia ecclesiastica* 6.37–8 PG 20 597–600.
68 Matt 26:75; Mark 14:72
69 Tertullian *Ad uxorem* 1.3 PL 1 1278–9 and *De fuga in persecutione* 5 PL 2 108

that threaten us, or the frailty of our nature, but rather the power and mercy of the Lord under whose auspices we battle. He is not deaf whenever he is invoked with faith, but either frees us from evil or gives additional strength so that we may endure to the end.[70] For faith is truly a thing unconquered in any type of battle – and battles even among Christians are not wanting for those who are eager to live a holy life in Christ Jesus.[71] Those who have daily practice in what one might call these lighter skirmishes are found undaunted in the face of that supreme conflict. Therefore it is right that the Christian soldier be especially zealous to stir up and increase the vigour of his faith daily.[72]

KA What are the right means to achieve this?

CA First is the one that the Lord pointed out: 'Ask and you shall receive.'[73] But lest prayer prove unprofitable, let alms-giving come to its aid, not only acting from without to restore the body, but also acting spiritually, giving a loving warning to someone who is on the wrong path, gently teaching someone who is untaught, mercifully pardoning someone who has committed an injury. To prayer and alms-giving should be added regular hearing of sermons and, in turn, the reading of the sacred text, frequent recollection of the Lord's death, especially after receiving his body and blood, and, finally, frequent commemoration of the men and women who fought the good fight for Christ. The spark of faith is nourished, fanned, and increased by this kindling.

KA Good sir, I am grateful to the Spirit of Christ, who has graciously used your powers of speech to teach me such marvellous wisdom . . . or does some other topic remain to be discussed?

CA There is not much left for me to teach, but perhaps there is still some advice that I can give – that is, if you haven't had your fill of advice, despite my giving you some before in passing.

KA As I learn, I get thirstier for learning.

CA Then we shall add in the next discussion what further needs to be said.

Lesson 6

KA Here I am, waiting for the last course of this most delectable banquet.

CA Our remaining task was to confirm the individual articles of the creed by various proofs from the Old and New Testaments. Nothing is taught

* * * * *

70 Cf Matt 10:19–20.
71 Cf 2 Tim 3:12.
72 Cf *Enchiridion* LB V 22B / CWE 66 56.
73 Matt 7:7; Luke 11:9; John 16:24

here that was not foreshadowed in various ways many thousand years before in the figures of the Mosaic law and foretold in the declarations of the prophets:[1] some matters were even revealed in plain language. Belonging to this class are the statements that there is not a plurality of gods and that this world was created by one God. Whoever led a holy life, even before the enactment of the Law, worshipped one God, creator of the whole world. Then John the Baptist's prophetic gift took its place on the border between the two laws, so to speak. It was his good fortune to see face to face and point out directly the one whose coming others showed, as it were, through a cloud from afar.[2]

Out of all of them, however, the Lord himself was his own most reliable prophet, showing by his deeds and explaining, under the guise of parables in public, among his disciples sometimes symbolically and sometimes plainly, what had been suggested in outline through the riddles of the Old Law. He showed his divine nature by his actions to a greater extent than he expressed it in words. Who would understand that the bronze serpent hung on a tree typified Christ crucified, if the Lord himself had not deigned to explain it?[3] His statement 'Destroy this temple and within three days I will raise it up'[4] was understood even by the disciples only after the resurrection. Furthermore, who would suspect that Jonah, swallowed by a whale and brought back alive on the third day, had prefigured the burial and resurrection of Christ?[5] When the time of his death was pressing closer upon him, however, he plainly forewarned his disciples that he would be handed over to the gentiles to be mocked and crucified, but he consoled them with the promise that he would rise again on the third day.[6] Thus before death he foretold his ascension into heaven rather obscurely, after his resurrection unmistakably.[7]

Similarly, he predicted the spread of the grain of mustard seed,[8] that is, faith in the gospel, through the entire world from very small beginnings. He also predicted what would befall the preachers of the gospel. Nor did he pass over in silence the abolition of the Jewish religion

* * * * *

1 See 239–40 above.
2 See 281 above; cf Matt 3:11–12; Luke 1:7–8, 3:16–17; John 1:26–7.
3 Num 21:8–9; John 3:14–15. Cf the colloquy *Inquisitio de fide* ASD I-3 368:163–6 / Thompson *Inquisitio* 63 / CWE 39 426:12–16.
4 John 2:19
5 Jonah 1:17–2:10; Matt 12:39–40
6 Matt 17:22–3; Mark 9:31; Luke 9:22
7 John 20:17
8 Matt 13:31–2; Luke 13:19

and the transmission of the gospel's sacred teaching to the gentiles;[9] the Jews would cling to their realm of darkness, until in due time, according to the prediction of St Paul,[10] from Jews and gentiles there should be made one fold under one shepherd, Christ.[11] He did not fail to mention that the church would be assailed by diverse heresies, but not overthrown.[12]

What need to say more? Since all things turned out just as they were predicted, to have any doubts about the last judgment and the rewards of the pious and impious seems to indicate the utmost blindness. We believe a godly person if he has made a true prediction three or four times; on the last remaining point will we not believe him who spoke the truth in so many matters that were so incredible from a human point of view? But just now we will pass over this part of the creed, since it concerns Jews and pagans more than it does Christians and has been carefully treated by Tertullian[13] and Cyprian,[14] most learned men. We are content that we pointed out the sources that you can draw on, if you wish, in these matters.

I must still admonish you that we are to live rightly, in keeping with the true faith. Wherever faith is, it is a thing afire, not a thing at rest. Just as in a lamp the oil feeds the flame to prevent it from being extinguished, so works of charity nourish faith to prevent it from failing. Faith begets good works, but these in turn nourish their parent; the light failed in the foolish virgins' lamps because the oil of good works was lacking.[15] The right way of living is customarily sought out in every book of Scripture, yet this creed, brief as it is, contains the entire philosophy of a holy life; there is no virtue for which it does not prepare us, nor any vice against which it does not arm our souls. For that perverter of law wanders around the fold of the church, 'like a roaring lion seeking whom he may devour.' St Peter orders us to resist him, strong not in confidence in works or our strength, but in faith.[16]

* * * * *

9 Matt 21:43
10 Cf Rom 11:25–7.
11 Cf John 10:16.
12 Cf Matt 7:15–16; Mark 13:22–3.
13 Tertullian *Apologeticus* 18.5 PL 1 377–81: '[Deus iudicaturus] profanos in ignem aeque perpetem et iugem.'
14 Cyprian *De zelo et livore* 5 PL 4 642: 'Iudaei none inde perierunt, dum Christo malunt invidere quam credere?'
15 Matt 25:1–12
16 1 Peter 5:8–9

KA You have armed me with faith; now you are performing a pious work by teaching this beginner how to use its weapons.

CA The Lord himself has taught us that all the precepts of the Law are contained in one command: 'You will love the Lord your God with your whole heart, with your whole mind, and with your whole strength and your neighbour as yourself.'[17] No one can love God above all things unless he believes that nothing is fairer, better, more truthful, or more lovable than God. For if someone believes that anything apart from God is more outstanding than he or equal to him, he does not believe that there is a God. Accordingly, someone who casts himself totally onto God can love nothing except what he loves on account of God, can fear nothing except what he fears on account of God.

By this beginning, 'I believe in God,' all the passions of the flesh are checked or at any rate weakened. If you submit to any of them and neglect the precepts of God, you are certainly fashioning another god for yourself out of whatever you prefer to him. When the Lord calls God and mammon two lords,[18] he compares the opponents as if they were two gods, and Paul calls avarice, that is, greed for money, idolatry.[19] The same writer brands those given over to the gain and benefit of the body with a disgraceful tag: '. . . whose god,' he says, 'is their belly.'[20] Again, writing to the Corinthians, he calls the Tempter the 'god of this world,'[21] not because he is really god or lord, but because for those who ignore the Lord God and commit themselves to slavery he is in some way both.

What has been said about eagerness for money must be applied to all the vices, particularly the capital ones. Apostasy, that is, defection, is a word of ill repute among Christians, and justly so. If the name 'deserter' is detestable where mere men are concerned, how much more disgraceful it is to desert of one's own accord from such a leader, to whom we are bound by so many sacraments, so many offerings, so many contracts – to desert not to a better or equal leader, but from the best of all to the worst of all. Christians practically shudder at the sound of the word 'apostate,' but I wish their minds abhorred the actuality in the same way.

* * * * *

17 Mark 12:30; Luke 10:27
18 Matt 6:24; Luke 16:13
19 Col 3:5
20 Phil 3:19
21 2 Cor 4:4

Satan almost always attacks us with three snares, ignorance, hope of advantages, and fear of reverses. Now faith, as has been said, dispels all darkness of mind; thus false hope with its blandishments does not deceive a person, nor fear with its terrors dislodge him from his post, if he has placed his entire trust in God. How wretched does passionate longing to know the future make many! One person wishes for a long life, shudders with fear of death, and consults horoscope readers. But a true believer in God, free from care, says with Paul, 'For me to live is Christ, and to die is gain.'[22] Another person has a ship at sea loaded with precious merchandise, and he consults the astrologers. The pious person, however, says, 'May the Lord prosper the business venture if he judges that it is advantageous; if he does not, what he will give in return for this loss is greater than all merchandise.' Another person is beset by disease and sends for the sorcerer; the pious person says, 'He is Lord, he is the Father; let him scourge me as he wills, provided that he acknowledges me among his children and the heirs to eternal happiness.' In sum, if a person fears the one who, when offended, can send soul and body to hell, he has little fear of all that this life regards as dreadful.[23] Someone who realizes that God promises eternal life after this momentary one places little trust in its advantages.

Who is so foolish as to disdain anyone, if he considers that he himself, compared to that ineffable majesty, is less than a fly compared with an elephant?[24] Or how can he regard as worthless one whom Christ, by no means a foolish trader, did not hesitate to buy back with his own blood? If it is a splendid thing to have a well-disposed prince, here is the prince of all princes; if it is dangerous to incur the anger of a king, here is 'the King of kings and the Lord of lords.'[25] Humble ancestry saddens many, but faith raises their spirits when it reminds them that the truly noble are those whom God recognizes as sons, daughters, and heirs,[26] and from whose lips he rejoices to hear 'Father.' The renown of their ancestors puffs up others,[27] but faith points out to them the common Father of all, for whom there is no distinction between prince and

* * * * *

22 Phil 1:21
23 Matt 10:28
24 Cf *Adagia* I ix 69 LB II 359A–B / CWE 32 219: *Elephantum ex musca facis.*
25 1 Tim 6:15
26 Cf James 2:5
27 Cf *Moria* ASD IV-3 126:29–128:36 / CWE 27 116.

plebeian, poor and rich, slave and free.[28] The more someone pleases God by piety, the more he is noble, powerful, and rich. Christ shows us this one and only Lord that we may rightly fear him. He shows us this Father that we may love him, that we may obey him without argument, that we may, as worthy sons and daughters, imitate him. 'Be perfect,' he says, 'as your heavenly Father is perfect, who makes his sun rise on the good and the bad and his rain fall on the just and the unjust.'[29]

Those who have an abundance of worldly advantages – riches, honours, renown, power, beauty, and whatever else there is that puffs up the mind – find their huffing turned to trembling if they consider to what Lord they owe all these things. It is in his power, whenever he wills, to take away without recompense what he gave without recompense. They know an account must be rendered to him of each and every thing. From him they hear constantly, 'Earth and ashes, of what are you proud?'[30] Why are you selling yourself in borrowed feathers?[31] Why do you dare to despise your neighbour as lowly, when you both have the same Father and the same Lord? Why do you despise your neighbour as a slave, although he was redeemed at the same price as you? Why do you scorn him as a pauper, when the Father and Lord of all cares for him? Were they poor to whom the Apostle writes, 'All things belong to you, and you to Christ'?[32] Why do you hold him of no account, like a fellow without property, when he is equally entitled to inherit eternal life, and on that score will perhaps be considered more important than you? Why was it said of the poor in the Gospel, to the disadvantage of the rich, '. . . that they may receive you into their eternal dwellings'?[33] The one whom you oppress as a slave is your fellow servant. The one whom you look down on as common is your brother. The one whom you disregard because he is poor and destitute has angels ministering to him. Proudly dwelling in your palace, you deride the shack of a pauper who has no hearth. But for this pauper our common Father has constructed the palace of the world: for him as much as for you the stars are shining, the globes are turning, and the earth bears fruit.

* * * * *

28 Cf Col 3:11.
29 Cf Matt 5:45, 48.
30 Cf Gen 18:27.
31 Cf *Moria* ASD IV-3 72:41–74:42 / CWE 27 87; Horace *Epistles* 1.3.19.
32 Cf 1 Cor 3:22–3.
33 Luke 16:9

In this way, the very same faith prevents worldly prosperity from engendering insolence, and adverse circumstances from engendering desperation. Whoever believes that God governs everything also believes that he is more intensely present to each one of us than any person is to himself, that he sees the recesses of our heart[34] more accurately than we see a body before our eyes in full light. How does it happen then that people do not regulate their actions with deep dread and profound reverence, whether they are at work in darkness or in the light, alone or with a crowd, so that there may not be anything that would offend the eyes of their Father and Lord, who is also their judge? This entire world is the temple of God in which he himself presides; if we would be ashamed to commit any unseemly act in a temple built of stone, with how much greater reverence does it befit us to conduct ourselves in this temple!

Manifold are the darts with which that tyrant attacks us, but one shield is sufficient against all of them: 'I believe in God.' If he attacks you with the dart of pride, interpose the shield, 'I believe in God,' who has shown clearly in the case of Lucifer[35] how he hates haughty minds. If anger goads you to revenge, answer, 'I believe in God,' who reserved to himself the right of taking vengeance when he cried out, 'Vengeance is mine and I will repay.'[36] If envy sets your mind aflame, say, 'I believe in God,' who allots his blessings to each person according to his own judgment. Why do I begrudge the kindness of a common Father and Lord to a brother and fellow servant? How much more equitable it is to thank God for two reasons, because he has bestowed so much on me beyond my deserts, and also because he bestowed these gifts through a brother. For whatever is given to one member is both a gain and an embellishment for the whole body.[37]

Avarice may incite you to cheating and robbery, saying, 'Unless you make haste to amass possessions by lawful or unlawful means, poverty will crush you in your old age, and your children will be beggars.' Then answer, 'I will not commit the crime, because I believe in God, who clothes the sparrow, who nourishes the lilies of the field.[38] He will

* * * * *

34 Cf Ps 44:21 (Vulg 43:22); Jer 20:12.
35 Isa 14:12
36 Heb 10:30
37 Cf 1 Cor 12:26.
38 Cf Matt 6:25–30; Luke 12:22–8. Erasmus reverses the order here; both Gospels speak in terms of feeding the birds and clothing the lilies.

not allow his servant to die from hunger.' If concupiscence incites you to self-indulgence, say, 'Far be it from me to do this, since I believe in God, who in his munificence bestowed these things on me not to abuse but to use in moderation.' Whatever is spent beyond moderation on concupiscence is theft, is robbery, nay, is sacrilege and idolatry; what is over and above necessary expenses used to belong to the poor and was owed to the members of Christ.[39] What is spent on drunkenness and intoxication is sacrificed to demons in contempt of God. If lust incites to lewdness and adultery, spit it out, saying: 'I believe in God the Father, to whose eyes these things are displeasing. I will not, for so tiny a pleasure, commit a crime by which I will cut myself off from inheriting heavenly joys and from the serenity of a good conscience.' Someone who agrees to such an exchange is a foolish trader. If he would be ashamed to commit such a crime with his earthly father as witness and judge, how much more should he fear the eyes of his heavenly Father?

Let us now turn to Christ, who has given us a more personal example of a holy life – what part of Christian philosophy cannot be fully learned from this source? Who would not be fired with a zeal for virginity and chastity when he hears that Christ was born of a virgin, and in his own body commended virginity to each of us? Who would not be ashamed to defile his marriage by adulteries, or be a slave to lust in his marriage, when he meditates on the union of Mary and Joseph, which was more chaste than any virginity? Would not someone be afraid to throw himself away on the pleasures of the stomach and genitals, worthy of cattle, when he has considered that human nature is held in such great honour that it has been united with the divine person in Christ and is seated at the right hand of the Father? The angels recognize and venerate this mystery, as Peter testifies in the opening chapter of his First Epistle.[40] For the same reason, in Apocalypse 19, the angel stopped John from prostrating himself and adoring him, saying, 'Take care not to do that, I am the fellow servant with you and your brothers who have testimony of Jesus.'[41] However, before the incarnation of Christ, Abraham or Daniel, when he was adoring the angel, did not hear the same message.[42] Accordingly, since angels recognize the dignity of human nature, how shameful it is for us to pollute it with the most degraded and filthy

* * * * *

39 See Gratian *Concordia discordantium canonum* D 42 C 1.
40 1 Pet 1:12
41 Rev 19:10
42 See Gen 18:2; Dan 14:38 (Vulg).

vices! Surely, we listen rather to St Peter exhorting us by these blessings 'great and precious which he has granted us, that through them
we may be made sharers of the divine nature, fleeing the corruption
of worldly concupiscence.'[43] Further, how will someone who in sincere
faith professes allegiance to this Lord shamelessly dare to steal something belonging to him and bestow it on Satan? He himself is entirely
the property of the one to whom he dedicated his entire self in baptism. Why does someone who proclaims that he belongs to Jesus hunt
for salvation elsewhere? If someone proclaims that Christ is king and
high priest, how does he have the effrontery to neglect his laws? How
does he have the shamelessness to allow the sacrifice of that adorable
victim, which the Lord wished to bring salvation to all, to be useless
in his case? The Son of God was made human for love of you, so that
he might change you from a human to a god. Do you, in contempt
of him, change yourself from a human to an animal lower than any
cattle?

Further, what are Christ's whole life, death, and resurrection, if not a
very clear mirror of the philosophy[44] of the gospel? Not without cause
is obedience highly praised. It is owed without exception in the first
place to God. Christ obeyed the Father 'unto death, even the death of
the cross.'[45] Next he made himself obedient to his parents when he was
not understood by them (Luke 2).[46] Obedience is due, and to no small
extent, to those holding public office, even if they are evil. He did not
withdraw from his trial, but, adjured by Caiaphas,[47] he answered. He
made some replies even to Pilate;[48] Herod he ignored because he held
no public office there, but was trying to procure a miracle to amuse
himself.[49] Jesus rejected completely Satan the tempter,[50] and did not
allow himself even to be addressed by unclean spirits. Contempt for
human glory is a great virtue. Although he was God, he carried out
the role of a servant on earth,[51] he turned aside from the kingdom offered him,[52] and consecrated the glory from his teaching and miracles to

* * * * *

43 2 Pet 1:4
44 See 237 n6 above.
45 Phil 2:8
46 Luke 2:50–1
47 Matt 26:64; John 18:20–1
48 Matt 27:11; Mark 15:2; Luke 23:3; John 18:33–7, 19:10–11
49 Luke 23:8–9
50 Matt 4:1–11
51 Phil 2:6–7
52 Matt 4:10

the Father.[53] The essence of charity is to injure no one, to benefit all. His entire teaching, every miracle he performed, and, finally, his whole life was nothing other than a blessing to all. He never sought what belonged to him but gave himself entirely to the service of others; here was that great sacrifice, unique and most pleasing to God.

How glowing is the voice of his charity when he says: 'I have come to send fire on earth, and what do I choose but that it be kindled? I am to be baptized with the baptism, and how distressed I am until it is accomplished!'[54] 'No one,' he says, 'has greater charity than this, that he should lay down his life for his friends.'[55] He not only gave up his life but also bore the ignominy of the cross, and that too while praying in his last words for his enemies,[56] for those through whom he had been brought to the cross, and by whose blasphemous words he was assailed in the very moment of his torment. Yet the Lord was not speaking falsely, for when he said 'No one,' he was speaking of human charity. Certain examples of outstanding friendship between humans are told more truthfully than people believe. In these examples, a friend has cast himself into mortal danger for a friend. Christ's charity surpasses all human charity. It was a heavenly fire not an earthly one, which the Holy Spirit kindled, not a mere natural feeling – and are we not ashamed to be called Christians? We not only fail to give up our life to save our friends, but for a small gain deceive our neighbour by pretences, lies, and perjuries, rob him by violence, drag him into mortal danger by false accusations. Love of riches is a common disease, just as contempt of them is an extraordinary virtue. What in this world is more destitute than he who had not even a place to lay his head?[57] He did not acknowledge the coin of Caesar (I am speaking of Christ as human);[58] his clothes, which were the only spoils remaining, were divided among the soldiers.[59]

* * * * *

53 John 5:19
54 Luke 12:49–50
55 John 15:13
56 Luke 23:34
57 Cf Matt 8:20; Luke 9:58.
58 Cf Matt 22:20, where Jesus asks the Pharisees whose likeness and inscription are on the coin. Most readers understand this as a rhetorical question, leading to Christ's admonition to 'render therefore to Caesar the things that are Caesar's.' Erasmus interprets the question as a request for information, indicating that Jesus never carried money, in order to make his point about Jesus' poverty. As a man Christ may have been ignorant, but as God incarnate he would not of course need the Pharisees' help.
59 Cf John 19:23–4.

I do not make these statements because one ought to seek out dire want, but because it is disgraceful for a professed Christian to bear his personal poverty with so little restraint that he cries out that he is thrice and four times miserable. Why should you be ashamed of a poverty that you have in common with Christ, Lord of all things? Why does someone think less of his neighbour because of his poverty rather than honour the image of Christ in him?

Lust for revenge is an emotion of tyrants. It is difficult to be well disposed to someone who has depleted your possessions or attacked your life or reputation. It will, however, prove easier if you turn your gaze on that lamb free from every stain who was assailed by so many reproaches, beset by so many plots, and then bound, spat upon, beaten by so many slaps, harassed by every type of mockery, and hung on the cross between thieves. He gave no indication of an angry spirit in speech or gesture, and uttered nothing but words of the most glowing charity and mercy. Likewise, after his resurrection he appeared only to his disciples and friends, to take away their grief and strengthen their faith.[60] He did not show himself to any other people, to taunt them with the uselessness of their wicked plots and say: 'This is he whom you unjustly condemned, whom you reviled, whom you wished to be so completely destroyed that there would not remain any trace of honourable remembrance. I am alive in spite of you.' What did he do instead? He instructed the apostles to teach to these same people by whom he had been most undeservedly mistreated the forgiveness of the gospel,[61] that is, unearned pardon of all sins and eternal life in the world to come.

This life brings with it numerous troubles. If we bear these patiently with our eyes on the Lord, we are suffering along with him; but we suffer with him even more if we are undeservedly abused for the sake of justice and an upright life. If we make our daily goal that the desires of the flesh submit to the Spirit without revolt, we are learning what it means to die with Christ. If we are separated from this world, not so much in body as in desire, and have reached that state of perfection where we find rest in the hope of resurrection, we are buried together with Christ. If through baptism 'we are once cleansed from dead works and every stain, we then walk in the newness of life'[62] (to use the words of St Paul), not only do we escape returning to the filth from which we

* * * * *

60 See Matt 28:9–10; Mark 16:9–14; Luke 24:31; John 20:16–19, 21:1.
61 See Matt 28:19–20; Mark 16:15; John 20:21.
62 Cf Rom 6:4.

have been purified, but we in fact hasten through the stages of all the virtues to perfection. We are already rising with Christ, who, risen from the dead, dies no more.[63] When, by these means, contempt for earthly things grows daily in us and the desire for the heavenly life increases, we ascend to heaven with him, treading the earth with our bodily feet but abiding in heaven by our hearts' desires. Thus we arrange all our thoughts and regulate all our actions as if we were acting in the presence of God and in the assembly of all the saints, as in truth we are.

We now come to the Holy Spirit, who, according to the teaching of Paul, is the guest of holy souls, whom he consecrated to himself as temples. How could it happen that someone would believe this and not be afraid to profane the temple of God?[64] In fact, the temple is profaned even by impure thoughts when no impure actions have occurred, and the loving guest is expelled from it to make out of God's temple a stable for Satan. Harmony among Christians is praised; without it there is no religion, no happiness.[65] You have the highest example of this in the harmony among the Father, Son, and Holy Spirit. You have another example right at hand in the word 'church,' which is united by so many bonds, for it has one God, one faith, one collection of laws, one baptism, the same sacraments, the same Spirit, expectation of the same inheritance. If anyone perseveres in this church, even if he has fallen in some respect, he has many by whom he can be raised up; he cannot easily perish when there are so many thousands of intercessors praying for him. For those who keep themselves within the enclosures of the sheepfold there is less danger from wolves. Since, however, we have here below a perpetual struggle with an adversary,[66] we should walk cautiously according to the laws laid down by our commander and Lord. Since, in our weakness, we are inadequate to keep those laws, we must by continuous prayer seek heavenly help, which is at hand if asked for ardently, if asked for continuously, if asked for with trust mingled with fear.

We shall be better fitted for both these tasks if, first of all, we attribute everything we have to God as its source and origin, and if we then accustom ourselves to have regard not for individuals, but for the whole society of humankind. If we have first acted this way in all matters, we shall thank God for whatever happens that is to our liking, and if

* * * * *

63 Cf Rom 6:9.
64 Cf 1 Cor 3:16–17.
65 See 240 n21 above.
66 Cf *Enchiridion* LB V 1A / CWE 66 24.

anything irksome befalls us, the external misfortune will be turned to our true benefit, provided that we bear it in patience as sent by God, either to improve us or to try us. I will give you a clear example: the crop flourishes in the fields. In this case the pagan[67] will praise his own diligence, he will praise the perfect weather that summer. But the Christian, as if he has received all these things from God's hand, gives thanks to the kind Father who provides for his sons and daughters and for his servants with such abundance.

If anything good comes our way through human beings, we will recognize the goodness of God, who granted such mortals the desire and the power to do this. Suppose, however, that something irksome befalls us. This train of thought may come to mind as we contemplate vengeance: 'It is better to put up with this injury, lest we provoke our enemy and he wound us more seriously; as a friend, he will be in a position to compensate for this damage with substantial interest.' If such are our thoughts, we might perhaps gain some praise for worldly wisdom, but none for piety. Suppose, on the other hand, we reflect as follows: 'The Lord scourges me through the malice of this person. For love of him I will bear whatever evil is in this situation.' With this attitude we will be less angry with a neighbour, and will be more inclined to correct our lives than to avenge an injury. In a word, human greed, which in its violence is wont to drag us away from the observance of divine law to the practice of evil deeds, will lose its tyrannical grip on us. Accordingly, the soul must become accustomed to direct its eyes immediately to God in all things, both joyous and sad. Next, in our thoughts we must look on the universal church as one body under one head, Christ. In this way, we will bear our own troubles more easily, if we consider that we are bearing them for many and with many. We will boast of others' prosperity more than our own, and will envy no one, if we keep in mind that whatever advantages belong to the companionship of the church belong to us.

Finally, God will hear our prayers more willingly if we are not carrying on our business strictly for ourselves, but are seeking the common good for his glory. (The love of God is most gracious and 'seeks not what is its own'[68] but what is Jesus Christ's. The church, moreover, is the body of Christ.) In that way, God, pleased by your charity, will

* * * * *

67 Here Erasmus plays on the classical sense of the word 'pagan' (a person from the countryside) and its Christian meaning of 'non-believer.'
68 Phil 2:4

grant just this very favour that you were about to ask only for yourself, and more generously than if you had sought it for yourself alone. If this type of reflection passes into a habit, it will broaden our minds so that one neither is offended at every turn, nor rears up at petty insults, nor, when about to perform a service, takes trifles into account[69] – not saying 'This person is French, I am German; he is unknown, I am renowned; he said this about me long ago,' but bestowing the favour cheerfully as for a member of Christ, a Christian, and a fellow human being.

KA If it would not be too much trouble, I would also like to get from you the answers to these questions: What are the principal laws that a person should have as a standard to direct his actions? What is the best formula of prayer?

CA The precepts of the Decalogue[70] are known to everybody, and no one can hand down any better than these – God himself hands them down. Nor can any form of prayer be prescribed better than what God himself deigned to prescribe;[71] the Son knows what form of prayer especially pleases the Father.

KA But these commandments were handed down by Moses; the Lord has freed us from that Law.

CA Careful, dearest son! The whole of the Law agrees with our gospel, except that we acknowledge as fulfilled what they looked forward to as to come, and what was set before them in allegory because they were beginners is proclaimed to us more clearly.[72] The only difference is that certain external ceremonies have been partly abolished, partly changed, and brought into accord with gospel piety. However, the gospel frees us from the obligation of the commandments only in that, because love has increased in us, we gladly do of our own free will what the Jewish people did through fear of punishment. Otherwise, in the last analysis, what kind of freedom would that be, if we were allowed to commit perjury, to commit adultery, or to steal? Christ did not come into the world so that we might sin with impunity, but so that we might not sin at all, being reborn in him who knew no sin.[73]

We worship the same God as the Jews, although with a different sacrificial rite. Moreover, the source of all the commandments is the first

* * * * *

69 To take into account trifling matters: μικρολογεῖν
70 Exod 20:1–17
71 Matt 6:9–13
72 See 280 n12 above.
73 Cf 2 Cor 5:21.

and greatest: Love God with your whole heart and your neighbour as yourselves.[74] This statement summarizes all the commandments for living our lives. Someone who is deficient in love of God and neighbour does not observe the Law, even if he performs what the words of the Law prescribe and avoids what it forbids. So too, someone who refrains from killing an enemy not because he lacks ill will towards him, but because he fears the threats of the Law, is a murderer in God's eyes. Conversely, someone has indeed observed the precept of the Law if love of God and neighbour diverts him from a crime when he is afire with anger. These will be his thoughts: 'Far be it from me to fall from God's love because of an enemy, and injure a neighbour. Even if he is evil, I nevertheless owe him good will for the love of God, to whom it is most pleasing if we repay an injury with an act of kindness. It does not concern me either if a person repays favours with ill will. I have an unshakeably trustworthy debtor, to whom I make this loan at interest. He will repay it with inestimable profit.' The person who reasons in this way has indeed observed the precept of the Law.

KA I am now waiting to hear about those Ten Commandments written by the finger of God.[75]

CA They are recorded in chapter 20 of Exodus, and they need no interpretation. For the words of a law should be clear, and if anything in these laws calls for an interpreter, there are many who have fully performed this task. We will remind you in just a few words that each and every commandment has a wider application, especially among Christians, than the great mass of mortals think. Thus the first commandment is 'You shall have no other gods before me. You shall not make for yourself a graven image, or any likeness of anything that is in heaven above, or that is in the earth beneath, or that is in the water under the earth.'[76]

This commandment is in accord with the first article of the creed, so that there is no need to say much here, and I have already warned that it is violated not only by those who worship the sun, the moon, and stars, or a human being, a serpent, an ox or dog, or images of these beings or of demons. All the prying arts – divination, feats of legerdemain, magic cures – incline towards idolatry, for even if they imply no manifest conspiracy with demons, they do, none the less, contain some secret communication with them and, to that extent, silent denial of God. If you

* * * * *

74 Cf Matt 22:37–40; Mark 12:29–31; Luke 10:25–8.
75 Finger of God: see 322 above; cf Exod 31:18.
76 Exod 20:3–4

ask for proof, one is ready. When a sorcerer is preparing to take a lance tip from your body, say in good faith to yourself, 'If this is being done in keeping with the will of God, may it succeed; if not, I prefer a bodily wound to ungodliness of soul.' You will see that the enchanter accomplishes nothing. Moreover, I am well aware of the false arguments that those who attribute much to natural magic and the prophecies of astrology[77] are wont to make. It is a mark of Christian piety to flee from things which carry the danger or appearance of impiety. Whoever has professed his faith in one true God truly has rejected all these superstitions and has abjured all false gods. No human favour whatsoever that involves an offence against God should be accepted.

In sum, every crime is connected with idolatry. The man who offends God to please his wife has denied God and worshipped his wife in place of God.[78] Someone who robs innocent orphans to please his king or commits some similar crime worships his prince in place of God. Let them flatter themselves as much as they wish, let them repeat this commandment a thousand times a day and profess God aloud; Paul cries out against them, 'By their deeds, they deny him.'[79]

KA Why then are they not punished as idolaters?

CA Partly because human frailty furnishes an excuse, partly because of the large number of sinners, principally because it is very difficult for us to judge the human soul. In any case, as to those who with an obstinate mind pursue wealth by means fair or foul throughout their lives, hunt for pleasure, rejecting equally both the fear and the love of God – let them know that they are no better than those who burn incense in honour of Jupiter or sacrifice a lamb to Venus or a he-goat to Bacchus.

KA Since in the same commandment the making of likenesses is forbidden with so much earnestness, how has it come to pass that today the Christian churches are filled with images?

CA The Jewish people were very stupid and strangely inclined to gentile superstition, so that they had difficulty in believing in the existence of anything that they could not see with their eyes.[80] Therefore the Law explicitly deters and moves them farther away from a most dangerous pitfall. Now that all paganism has been extinguished by the light of the gospel there is not the same danger, and if any superstition remains in

* * * * *

77 Cf Augustine *De doctrina christiana* 2.21–2 PL 34 51–3.
78 Cf 1 Cor 7:32–4.
79 Titus 1:16
80 See 282 n31 above.

the minds of some ignorant people, it can easily be driven out by admonition and devout teaching. Until the time of Jerome, there were men of approved faith who, because of the Anthropomorphites, tolerated no images in churches, whether painted, sculptured, or woven – not even, I think, of Christ.[81] Gradually, however, the use of images crept into churches. Perhaps it would not be unseemly if, in these places where God is solemnly adored, no images were set up except that of Christ on the cross. None the less, if a picture is fittingly employed, it will, in addition to the proper pleasure it brings, contribute to the memory and understanding of sacred history. Thus it was cleverly said by someone that a picture is for the illiterate what books are for the learned.[82] Indeed, even a learned person sometimes sees more in a painting than in a written document and is more deeply stirred, just as we would be more moved if we saw Christ hanging on the cross than if we read that he was crucified. The picture sets the reality before our eyes in so far as it is permissible, and provides the clarity that rhetoricians aim at. The life of Christ and the apostles, as they are set forth in the canonical writings, may be rightly placed in porticoes, vestibules, and peristyles. Images of this sort suggest a number of pious reflections even if we are engaged in some other activity. However, just as Christians of former times rightly enacted a law that nothing should be recited in the churches except canonical Scripture, so it would be fitting that subjects that do not appear in the sacred books not be painted or sculpted.

Finally, Moses, on the instructions of God, placed two cherubim of gold in the tabernacle at the ends of the mercy seat (Exodus 25 and 3 Kings 7).[83] In the vessels belonging to the temple that Solomon built, there were sculptured images of cows, lions, and cherubim.[84] There were cherubim sculptured on the walls (2 Paralipomenon 3).[85] There was an image of the moon on the priest's mitre; there were images of pomegranates on his garment. It is unlikely, therefore, that the Jews

* * * * *

81 Anthropomorphites: see 272 n135 above.
82 For a discussion of the controversy between Iconoclasts and the supporters of images in the early church see L.W. Barnard *The Graeco-Roman and Oriental Background of the Iconoclastic Controversy* (Leiden 1974) especially 89–103.
83 Exod 25:18; 1 Kings 6:23. Erasmus enumerates 1 and 2 Samuel and 1 and 2 Kings as the books of Kings. See 332 n229 above.
84 1 Kings 7:29
85 2 Chron 3:10

were forbidden every kind of image without exception; they probably were not permitted to have ones that were set out for adoration after the fashion of the gentiles. As if to make this point, when the book of Deuteronomy refers to this commandment, it adds 'You shall not bow down to them or serve them.'[86] For the same reason, it further adds 'in my sight.'[87] An image placed before God and put on an equality with God is envisioned.

Nothing that lacks reason can be adored, that is, externally venerated, or worshipped, that is, internally venerated. If a Christian bows his head to the image of the crucified, he knows that no honour is due to the wood, but he uses the image as a chance to venerate what it represents. Someone, because he loves Christ, may cherish a precious image of him, kiss it at times, and put it back in a clean place. I do not think that this sentiment displeases God, so long as no superstition is involved. Moreover, when we kiss the Gospel book in churches, we do not adore the parchment or the gold or ivory, but venerate the teaching of Christ. Perhaps it would be useful for each bishop to set regulations for his own church in this matter in keeping with the current needs of his flock, if he could do so without causing uproar and violence. Certainly, not even human regulations prescribe that there should be images in churches. It is both easier and safer to remove all images from churches than to assure that their use is kept within limits and free of superstition.

Even if the soul is free of superstition, a person may not be free of its semblance, falling down in prayer before a wooden figure, keeping the eyes riveted on it, addressing it in words, planting kisses on it, not praying at all except before the image. I will say more – whenever humans fashion for themselves a God different from what he is, they worship a sculptured idol in violation of this commandment. The Jews do not have images in their temples, but they have the most unseemly idols in their souls when they represent the Father as childless although he has a Son, when they represent him as alone although he has the Son and Holy Spirit in union with him. Thus, they do not worship God, as they boast, but in his place they worship an idol that they have fabricated in their minds for themselves. It is enough to have mentioned this perversion by way of example; you will find others on your own.

The dignity of God's supreme majesty does not solely demand that you think of him with adoration in your own mind and refrain from

* * * * *

86 Exod 20:5
87 'In my sight': *coram me;* Exod 20:3: 'non habebis deos alieno coram me.'

worshipping images; you must also avoid dishonouring him in human company by irreverent speech. For this reason, the commandment is added 'You shall not take the name of God in vain.'[88] The habit of using trifling words gradually diminishes in speakers and hearers the reverence due to the divinity. In former times there was a custom among the pagans of dragging into conversations certain expressions, however foolish or even obscene: 'by Zeus, by Pollux, by Castor,[89] 'a god is my witness.' Would that there were no Christians today who from bad habit add to every third word 'by God,' 'by the death of God,' especially when they are playing dice or are drunk and sacrificing to Bacchus.[90] We read that certain Roman emperors, although pagans, gave orders that those who had sworn by the *genius* of the emperor should be punished with the scourge. So great was the Jews' reverence for the divine name, that they wrote that mystic word which they call *tetragrammaton* in letters not to be pronounced.[91] Be assured that the tetragrammaton was revealed by God to the dense minds of the Jews, for God is as unnameable as he is unimaginable and invisible.

It is a mark of gospel piety never to use the name of God or Christ or the Holy Spirit rashly or irreverently, lest the words pass into feelings and the feelings into actions. You must consider that God did not say, 'You shall not name God,' but 'You shall not *take* the name of God.' What is taken is put to some use; what is taken for a profane and common use is taken 'in vain,' or to no purpose, or rashly, as when someone swears by God in a matter of little importance. Those who swear in order to deceive more easily, or in drunkenness or anger, or to ease their minds, are very near to blasphemy. Let us at least give to God, the ruler of all, what the French give to their king; they do not use his name without adding words of good omen and touching their hats.[92] For that reason, when we use the name God or Christ, let us genuflect or uncover our heads, or, if neither is possible, let us display our reverence by a slight bow of the head and by the expression on our faces.

* * * * *

88 Exod 20:7
89 Castor and Pollux: twin sons of Leda, the first by her mortal husband Tyndareus and the second by the god Zeus. After their deaths they became the constellation Gemini.
90 Bacchus: the god presiding over wine, whose cult involved riotous festivals
91 *Tetragrammaton*: the four-letter name for God, YHWH, introduced to Moses from the burning bush (Exod 3:14–15), where it is rendered as a form of the verb 'to be'
92 Cf *Enarratio psalmi 33* LB V 404C.

KA From what you say, four difficulties trouble my mind. The first is that this commandment seems to refer to love of neighbour, since we are forbidden to deceive him by use of this name. The second is that what was forbidden by the first commandment seems to be allowed by the second, for the name of God is a created thing and similar to an image. The third is that this commandment seems to make the same prohibition as the first one. No one commits perjury in the name of God if he knows God aright; for he thinks that God does not know what we are thinking, or else that he is not offended by evil. The fourth is that those who take oaths today seem, for the most part, to violate this commandment if indeed, according to the sermon of Ecclesiastes, human affairs are 'vanity of vanities and all is vanity.'[93] In earthly matters, then, it would never be lawful to swear.

CA To answer each objection in a few words: the first three commandments are in a certain way one. They refer especially to *latria*,[94] which is the highest veneration due to God alone, because he is the best of all and his sublimity does not admit of partnership with any creature. In so far as contempt for God results in a neighbour's misfortune, this commandment extends also to love of neighbour; in the same way, every injury to a neighbour is also classified as an insult to God. Someone who disdains God's commandment and injures his neighbour offends God who is in his neighbour; but a person who swears by the name of God to deceive his neighbour is closer to blasphemy than someone who deceives in ordinary words. The person who swears falsely to satisfy his own greed abuses both the honour of God's name and the religious sensibilities of his neighbour, who, although he would not believe what has been sworn without the oath, believes it because it has been sworn in God's name.

My answer to the second difficulty is as follows: the name of God uttered by humans is a created thing, and they do not bend their knees to honour this word, but to honour the person whom the word indicates. Images are a different case. There is no danger that a human voice would be adored, but in images there is a danger, pointed to by certain philosophers,[95] of demons entering a skilfully made statue, just as a soul

* * * * *

93 Eccles 1:2
94 *Latria* (Gr λατρεία): worship due to God alone, sometimes contrasted with *dulia*, veneration accorded the saints
95 Certain philosophers: cf Augustine *De civitate Dei* 8.26.2 PL 41 253–4, in which he refers to the legendary Hermes Trismegistus.

enters a body aptly fashioned by nature. Yet it is necessary that God be manifested by some sign; human speech has been provided principally for this purpose.[96]

In my opinion, at least, you can consider this an answer to the third difficulty: those who swear in drunkenness or anger, or knowingly commit perjury from a desire to deceive or injure, violate the first commandment rather than the second. For such people, as you admit, either do not believe that God exists, or believe that he is so stupid as to be ignorant of human actions, or so sleepy that he does not care, or so evil that he promotes wrongdoing, or so unjust that he does not punish it. However, those who swear on the spot, without a serious reason, either from habit or without a serious reason, also sin against this commandment.[97]

To make some answer to the fourth difficulty: among the exhortations to perfection, the Lord includes this one: we are to refrain entirely from any swearing. This command was ratified by certain approved Doctors of the church.[98] Let others find an excuse for the habit of those people nowadays who swear constantly in practically every transaction. In my opinion, uttering an oath can scarcely be excused except when required by necessity or the seriousness of the matter in hand. By frequent swearing we learn to perjure ourselves. I do not know if anyone swears rightly when he swears as Paul did, deliberately, but for the glory of the gospel rather than vengeance or money.[99] I would not say that all habitual or rash swearing is a mortal sin, but it certainly comes close to sin, and is not a good river bank to disembark on. It is safer, therefore, to follow the advice of the Lord and James.[100]

The third commandment has several aspects, for it looks to the worship of God, setting apart every seventh day so that the whole person may be free for acts of *latria*, that is, for hymns, prayers, sacred doctrine, sacrifices, alms-giving, and other exercises which stir up our faith and love of God. Thus no one will be able to offer the excuse that, because of

* * * * *

96 That God is represented to humans in the language of the Gospel is an idea well represented in Erasmus' thinking; that speech was given to man principally to make God manifest is an unusual pronouncement, yet not inconsistent with his thinking elsewhere. See *Lingua* ASD IV-1 296–301 / CWE 29 326–31, in which the relationship between truth and falsehood in speaking is construed in terms of right worship or idolatry.

97 Cf *Lingua* ASD IV-1 300-1 / CWE 29 331–2.

98 See eg Augustine *Enarrationes in psalmos* 89.4 PL 37 1142.

99 Cf 1 Tim 5:21; 2 Tim 4:1, in which Paul charges Timothy *coram Deo*.

100 James 5:12

necessary business, he does not have free time to concentrate on pious pursuits. The third commandment also concerns kindness towards one's neighbour. Once upon a time such harshness and greed existed among the Jews (as, alas, today among some Christians) that they gave their servants, maids, and foreign mercenaries no time for relaxation. The Law does not leave this situation unnoticed when it adds in Deuteronomy 5 'Remember that you too were a slave in Egypt and the Lord your God led you thence.'[101] The memory of divine kindness should set an example of charity towards a neighbour. The Jubilee, that is, the year of freedom every seventh year, was instituted for a similar reason.[102] Moreover, what is added in Deuteronomy 5 about the ox and the ass[103] is directed against the insatiable greed of some, who, although they are not allowed to perform servile work themselves, hire out their beasts of burden to others for gain on the Sabbath, or else the passage adds hyperbole, so that we may be farther removed from unkindness towards men when we are ordered to spare beasts of burden. At the least, cruelty towards animals is a step towards cruelty to people who are subject to us, since beasts of burden serve us too. Further, when Paul asks, 'Is it for oxen that God is concerned?'[104] he does not imply that God has no concern for oxen, since, on the testimony of the Lord in the Gospel, not even a little sparrow falls to earth without his will.[105] Rather, Paul says that they are not God's sole and principal care. Just as he created beasts of burden on account of humans, so he takes care of them as a favour to humans.

KA What is servile work?

CA Any physical work that is generally engaged in for gain, such as ploughing, building, trading.

KA Why is something holy forbidden?

CA It is not forbidden because it is wicked, but in order that what is good in itself may give way to what is best, to what humans were especially created for, namely to know, honour, adore, and love God above all things.

* * * * *

101 Deut 5:15

102 Cf Lev 25:1–24. The jubilee year occurred every fifty years, not every seven, which is the sabbath year. The sabbath is 'a year of solemn rest for the land' (Lev 25:5) during which no farming is to take place. During the jubilee year people are authorized to return from whatever leaseholds they are farming to their ancestral lands (Lev 25:13).

103 Deut 5:14

104 1 Cor 9:9

105 Matt 10:29

KA Does the body have to be at rest for God to be adored?

CA He both can and should be adored even in the midst of work. But a person can hardly raise his mind to God as he should unless he is free from these tasks that take time, lay claim to a great part of his mind, and call it away from the quiet decorum of public worship. This law has been enacted especially for men who are weak-minded and stupid, so that by physical repose they might learn how to keep their minds free from such turbulent passions as hatred, anger, ambition, lust, and the other desires of the flesh. Thus, those who rested on the Sabbath so that they might give over those days to sleep or storytelling or laziness by no means kept this commandment, since they did not fulfil the purpose for which it was given. Therefore the Law speaks as follows: 'Remember to keep holy the Sabbath day.'[106] To keep this day holy is to pass it in pious works and not profane it by any actions unworthy of God.

KA Why was the seventh day chosen for this?

CA The Law itself mentioned the reason: 'The seventh day is the Lord your God's Sabbath.'[107] 'Sabbath' means 'rest' in Hebrew. This is set forth more plainly in Exodus 31: 'In six days the Lord made heaven and earth, and on the seventh day he rested from all work.'[108] Do not imagine my point here to be that the construction of the earth was completed by six days' work, and that the architect, grown weary on the sixth day, refreshed his weary body by resting on the seventh. The whole of Genesis, that mystical scripture, was intended to remind the Jews that this world was created by God, not for us to find peace in what belongs to it, but to recognize the creator from his creation. Following his example, we must take our rest undistracted by the love of visible things and through faith and innocence of life, which confers true peace of mind, hasten towards that great eternal rest.

You are learning, really, about three sabbaths. The first belonged to God alone, without us. The second is ours through his kindness, but is imperfect in this life. The third is the perfect one in the world to come. God wished a thankless and forgetful people to remember the divine mercy through which they had been freed from the very harsh yoke of Pharaoh. This foreshadowing warns us, too, to keep in mind that, through the blood of the immaculate Lamb, we were redeemed from

* * * * *

106 Exod 20:8
107 Exod 20:10
108 Exod 31:17

the foul tyranny of Satan. This memory will prevent our slipping back, through ungratefulness, into a greater servitude.

KA You repeatedly said that the Mosaic law was abrogated where it concerned ceremonies. However, this commandment seems, for the most part, to refer to the domain of ceremonies.

CA I said that some ceremonies were abrogated, not all of them. Praying on bended knees has not been abrogated, and neither has fasting or sermons. Other ceremonies have been changed and adapted to gospel piety. One of these is the observation of the Sabbath.

KA Why then has the seventh day been changed to the eighth for us?

CA Indeed, it seems plausible that this was done by the authority of the apostles.[109] The day was changed lest we, because we agreed with the Jews in this one matter, might seem to agree with them in the rest as well. So too Chrysostom[110] (and also others) with wonderful zeal urges Christians not to fast on the days that the Jews held their solemn fast.

KA Therefore the seventh day was not changed to the eighth, rather than to the tenth or twelfth, without serious deliberation.

CA Right. In a way, God created the world twice, and with it humanity. First he created what did not exist, of course through the Son;[111] later through the same Son incarnate he restored what had been lost.[112] On the first occasion he is said to have rested from the work of creation.[113] But now Christ, resting from the work of redemption while his body reposes in the tomb, abrogates, as it were, the Jews' observance of the seventh day. When he arose again immortal at dawn on the eighth day, he commended to us the Sabbath of the gospel. Thus that day is called the day of the Lord,[114] and on Sunday the church choir sings, 'This is the day which the Lord has made.'[115] It is called the day of the Passover, reminding us by this name of its ancient foreshadowing. The Jews, restored by the lamb, crossed the Red Sea;[116] we, restored by the blood of Christ, direct our course to the heavenly land. The blood of a lamb

* * * * *

109 Cf Matt 28:1; Acts 20:7; 1 Cor 16:2.
110 Chrysostom *In libros octo contra Judaeos* 4.1–3 PG 48 871–6; Erasmus' translation of this homily appears in LB VIII 7A–15A.
111 Cf John 1:3: 'all things were made through him.'
112 Cf John 1:14.
113 Cf Gen 2:2.
114 Rev 1:10
115 Ps 118 (Vulg 117):24
116 Exod 14:22

smeared on the door-post saved them from the destroying angel;[117] the blood of Christ has freed us from the tyranny of sin.

KA This all makes sense. Does it suffice to worship God on Sundays?

CA Truly for a holy person every day is a Sunday, not because he always refrains from external works, but because every day he continually raises his mind to God whenever he has a chance, stirring up his faith, exciting his charity, whetting his hope, singing hymns of praise, seeking something that leads to salvation, returning thanks for all things. But just as it is an act of piety to meditate daily, so it is a sin, that can scarcely be atoned for, not to do this on Sundays, since the teaching of Christ and the apostles summons us to do so,[118] as do the Christian people's solemn assembly, sacred Scripture, sacred preaching, and the religious rites instituted of old.

KA Do those, therefore, who perform some task on feast days commit a mortal sin?

CA They do, unless they are excused by a great necessity or great advantage; this is what the Lord himself clearly taught us. He excused the disciples for plucking ears of grain on the Sabbath,[119] using the example of the Levites,[120] who used to work in the temple on Sabbath days. He countered the Pharisees' misrepresentation of his healing on the Sabbath with their leading their ox to the water on the Sabbath and pulling out their ass that had fallen into a pit on the Sabbath.[121] Finally, he stated publicly that man was not made for the Sabbath, but the Sabbath made for man.[122] Thus you can understand that this commandment is not one that must never yield to charity.

KA How is it appropriate that Sunday is called the day of rest, since we sometimes read, 'On it you shall afflict your souls'?[123]

CA That song is sung for the Jews, whose lot it is to weep, since they do not know the Spouse. Far different is the song of the Christians as they exhort one another, 'Let us rejoice and be glad on this day.'[124] However, among Christians of former times there was a fast on Sabbath days so

* * * * *

117 Exod 12:13
118 Heb 10:24–5
119 Matt 12:1–8; Mark 2:23–6; Luke 6:1–5
120 Matt 12:5
121 Luke 13:15; cf Matt 12:11–12; Luke 14:5.
122 Mark 2:27
123 Lev 16:29
124 Ps 118 (Vulg 117):24

that they might come to the celebration of the Lord's day with purer minds. If anyone shares Jewish feelings, let him chastise his soul by confession and penance so that, reconciled with God, he may, with his mind at peace, enjoy the delights of the day. Sunday is called *Soendach* in the German vernacular,[125] not from the word 'sun ' [*sonne*], as some infer, but from the word 'reconciliation' [cf *Versöhnung*]. Thus if, during other days of the week, some stain rubs off from dealing in human affairs, one may, on either Saturday evening or Sunday morning, return to favour with God. Then if he has any conflict with someone else, let him cast it from his soul so that, free from hatred and from every offence, he may enter the Lord's temple in peace.

Some, following the words of the Lord 'Learn from me; for I am gentle and lowly in heart, and you will find rest for your souls like newborn babies,'[126] have laid aside all malice. Transcending human affairs, they are transported with their whole hearts to the contemplation of that great eternal peace. They at length perceive what happiness it is, how joyful, how peaceful it is to celebrate the gospel Sabbath, that is, after imitating the burial of the Lord, to experience his resurrection.[127] This is truly the Sabbath of God. The world outside has its peace on the surface, but within it has tasks far more servile than the Hebrews bore when they were slaves to the Egyptians amid mortar and brick.[128]

KA Your explanation has certainly been clear enough for me to follow.

CA The greatest blasphemy is one which directly attacks God, next is the one which offends God through human beings. God is honoured and loved for his own sake, humans for the sake of God. After God, the highest honour is to be paid to parents, through whom he has given us this gift of life, whose care has raised us when we were otherwise doomed to

* * * * *

125 See Bakhuizen van den Brink's note on ASD V-1 311:150. *Soen* in Dutch is 'reconciliation,' which accounts for Erasmus' peculiar etymology. Bakhuizen van den Brink points out that this fanciful explanation was popularized in the fourteenth century by a Jan Matthijsz of Brille, but that the ancient Christian writers adopted the legitimate equivalence of Sunday with 'sun' (eg Tertullian *Apologeticus* 16 PL 1 369–71). In the light of Erasmus' scrupulous concern for correct etymologies, and of his otherwise invariable preference for writers of the early church over more recent scholars, it is peculiar to find him supporting this account of the meaning of Sunday, except perhaps for the sake of the lesson embedded in it.
126 Cf Matt 11:29.
127 Cf Rom 6:4.
128 Cf Exod 1:14.

perish, through whom he has educated us with a knowledge of God, the supreme parent, and elevated us to a love of him. He says, therefore, 'Honour your father and your mother, that your days may be long in the land which the Lord your God will give you.'[129] Among those who speak Latin, 'honour' frequently means 'recompense'; hence that remark in comedy,[130] 'He considers this an honour to you,' and 'Honour nourishes the arts.' Thus, duty to parents is a type of recompense for the expense, annoyances, and labours borne for us in childhood, the time when a mother submits to the pain of gestation and birth, the duty of nursing and nourishing; duty to parents is likewise a recompense for the long-standing troubles which a father endures when he bears the expenses and takes every care to have the children educated in holiness.

Now it happens very frequently that parents worn out by age, or dispirited by some other misfortune, may need the help of their children. In this case, our first obligation is to our parents. The Greeks call this ἀντιπελάργεον, 'to make a stork's recompense,' because storks are said to take their turn nourishing and cherishing their parents when they are worn out by old age.[131] Among the pagans also, Aeneas is praised because he hoisted his father Anchises onto his shoulders and carried him from the burning city.[132] Among the same people, the girl who secretly nourished her mother at her own breasts did not go without her reward.[133] Hence the common noun 'piety' is added to the Latin language. Piety, strictly speaking, is an attitude towards God, parents, and our fatherland, which is the common father of many, just as God is the Father of all. To return thanks to those through whom we have received life or recovered it pertains to piety. To return thanks to those who have first deserved well of us pertains to gratitude. We owe a special gratitude to teachers, because just as we have received life through our parents, so too, we have been given a good life through our teachers; as we carry about the physical life received from the former, so too, we owe our spiritual and intellectual life to the latter – for what else are we born but irrational brutes? By instruction we are made human beings.

* * * * *

129 Exod 20:12
130 *Adagia* I viii 92 LB II 330F–331B / CWE 32 174
131 See Aelianus *De animalium natura* 3.23
132 Virgil *Aeneid* 2.707–9.
133 See Valerius Maximus 5.4.7.

The greatest honour, then, is due those parents who have provided all these things concurrently.[134]

KA What if the mother were to shun even the annoyance of nursing[135] and neither parent were to give instruction in good morals, regarding the children as slaves and demanding their service in disgraceful actions?

CA The less of their duty they fulfil, the less honour is due them. Yet for God's sake they too must be treated with the customary respect (as the remark from tragedy suggests, 'If you were not a father . . .'),[136] unless they give orders displeasing to God. In that case, it is only right that they should hear the reply, 'We must obey God rather than men.'[137]

Furthermore, what has been said about parents applies to all who are related to us by blood or who have taken upon themselves the obligations which devoted parents are wont to fulfil for their children; for to have given birth to a body is the least part of parents' duties. It behooves us to be generous to all, but in these matters there is a gradation. After parents, the closer the relative, the higher his claim on our support; otherwise, when your liberality had been bestowed on others, you would have nothing left to assist the members of your own household. Paul proclaimed that the woman who does not take care of her family 'is worse than an unbeliever.'[138] He does not mean that it is a more serious sin to neglect relatives than to reject the gospel. He means that, despite the fact that gospel piety perfects rather than erases natural affections, such a woman does not give the care to her own family that even pagans manifestly give to their relatives.

The Lord also condemns in the Gospel those who neglect their parents and put their riches in the treasury.[139] I will add that this commandment refers not only to parents, but also to bishops, teachers, and public functionaries, who, in some way, fulfil the office of parents. When people are enjoined to perform duties that merit the greatest thanks, we, in turn, are commanded to reward them with honour. On that account the

* * * * *

134 Cf the colloquy *Puerpera* ASD I-3 468:555–7 / CWE 39 606:14–17.
135 See ibidem, in which Erasmus' character Eutrapelus delivers a long reproach to the new mother Fabulla for turning her child over to a wet-nurse rather than breast-feeding him herself.
136 Sophocles *Antigone* 755
137 Acts 5:29
138 Cf 1 Tim 5:8, which does not specify women and children but anyone (*quis*) who does not take care of his or her family.
139 Cf Mark 7:11.

blessed Paul, when returning to this commandment in Ephesians 6 and other places, reminds both parties of their obligation. 'Fathers,' he says, 'do not provoke your children to anger, but bring them up in the discipline and instruction of the Lord.'[140] Since he forbids angering the children, he excludes domineering; when he adds 'in the instruction of the Lord,' he recommends a gentle training in piety, to ensure that our attitude towards those subject to us may be the same as God's attitude towards us. How do they have the effrontery to complain about their children's extravagance when they themselves have instructed them in extravagance and wantonness?

KA Well then, are all who piously honour their parents long-lived?

CA St Paul noted that this was the first commandment that carried a reward even in this life.[141] The obtuse Jews had to be addressed in this way. Like infants, they had to be enticed to perform their duties to parents by the hope of temporal advantages. Having been cruelly treated in Egypt and worn out by long journeys over the deserts, they longed with intense desire for the land flowing with milk and honey. Consequently, the words were added to the commandment 'that it may be well with you, and that you may live long upon the earth which the Lord will give you.'[142] However, it is likely that many of the people to whom the Law was given did not reach the promised land, yet showed respect for their parents. Indeed, those who judge spiritual things in a spiritual manner[143] do not look for the reward of their piety on earth, but in that land of the living.[144] For someone who lives an evil life cannot be well off. Even if this life is dragged out to a decrepit old age, it is by no means long. No, it is rather an instant of time compared with eternity. Anyone who has merited eternal life by good deeds has lived long and, perfected, has completed many years in a short time.[145]

Still, even in this life, God often reserves a reward for reverence towards parents. Part of the reward is an honourable reputation. For even the pagan rabble curses those who slight their parents and grieve them. It frequently happens that the way a person has treated his parents is the way his children will treat him, and there is no other more serious

* * * * *

140 Eph 6:4
141 Eph 6:2
142 Eph 6:3
143 1 Cor 2:13
144 Ps 27 (Vulg 26):13
145 Wisd of Sol 4:13

misfortune for a man or woman than having undutiful children. Moreover, the wages of ingratitude are that the ingrate loses unwillingly what
he has gained undeservedly. We owe our lives to our forebears, and if
we have shown gratitude towards them, it is right that we should long
enjoy what we have received. Yet those who do not happen to live long
lives on earth are not cheated of the promise. For if what was literally
promised is not bestowed, then something far superior to it is. Someone
who promises glass and gives a gem is not cheating.

We are warned by these four commandments to be thankful to those
who have deserved well of us, and to deserve well of those for whom
we somehow fulfil the role of God. Next, to check the gross ill will of the
Jews,[146] the commandments expressly forbid actions by which human
injures human. Of all crimes the most hideous is homicide.[147] Under the
term homicide are included all feelings that tend to it. The first stage
is anger, begotten in the mind, and hatred.[148] Anger is pain demanding
revenge, hatred is inveterate anger, a feeling that is ready to injure on
every occasion. The former is more violent, like a raw wound, the latter
is incurable. Worse than both is envy, through which someone interprets
another's success as an injury to himself. The next stage is anger that
bursts forth into the contemptuous term that Christ calls 'raca.'[149] The
third is pain breaking forth into open reproach, as when we say, 'You
idiot.'[150] Among humans, a person who has taken his neighbour's life is
indicted for homicide; in God's eyes, anyone who hates his neighbour,
that is, who wishes him evil, is guilty of homicide. We become angry
also with those whom we wish well, not to hurt them but to correct
them, and in the person we hate not what God has made, but what the
individual himself has done.

The slanderer and the flatterer use their tongues for a sword, a dart,
and poison.[151] The miser, when he refuses to help a needy person, kills
him with hunger, for a person who does not save a life when he can is
a murderer.[152] Perhaps his neighbour does not die, but as far as the one
who did not help the endangered person is concerned, that person is

* * * * *

146 See 282 n31 above.
147 See Exod 20:13; Deut 5:17.
148 Cf Matt 5:21–2.
149 Matt 5:22
150 Ibidem
151 Cf *Lingua* ASD IV-1 319 / CWE 29 352.
152 See 357 n39 above.

already dead. Witches destroy by incantations.[153] The slanderer drives one to death. It does not matter by what means someone takes life; whenever the perverse will to injure is present, there is homicide. Women who procure abortion by drugs commit infanticide. People who assault someone with defamatory pamphlets kill him with reed pens.[154]

KA   If killing is absolutely unlawful, what shall we say about wars and public judicial sentences?[155]

CA   In legitimate sentences, the law itself puts to death, not the judge. The law is from God, who orders that one limb be removed for the safety of the whole body, although doctors do not proceed to amputate as long as there is hope of regaining health in some other way. It is the duty of a Christian judge and prince to have recourse to capital punishment only after every other means has been tried and his hand is forced. Someone who gives a corrupt judgment or misuses the laws to satisfy his private hatred or to gain an advantage, even if the guilty party deserves death, is still guilty of judicial murder.

What shall I say about war? Would that all people abhorred war, as if killing in war were parricide, since all Christians are brothers and sisters! In a war justly undertaken and lawfully conducted, however, it is the law that kills, not the person.[156] On the other hand, a prince who begins a war not through necessity or zeal for the state but through personal desires commits as many homicides as there are men who perish in that conflict or are reduced to starvation. Add this to your instances

* * * * *

153 The famous charge against allowing witches to live is found in Exod 22:18 and repeated in further detail in Deut 18:10–11. While persons believed to be witches were subjected to persecution throughout the Middle Ages, the widespread hunting down and killing of witches did not begin until after Erasmus' death and continued for about a century.

154 Defamatory writing was a particular sore point for Erasmus, who feared persecution by those who he felt were deliberately misreading his works as heretical. In the inflamed environment of the period, this was a reasonable fear. Note that while he condemns abortion as murder he does not describe it as being any worse than defamation of character. The concept of homicide, as with all crimes, is for Erasmus grounded in intent.

155 For a thorough discussion of just war theory in canon law, see F.H. Russell *The Just War in the Middle Ages* (Cambridge 1975).

156 Here Erasmus appears to take a somewhat more moderate opinion than in *Dulce bellum inexpertis* (*Adagia* IV 1 i LB II 957) or 'Complaint of Peace' (ASD IV-2 61–100 / CWE 27 293–322), both of which concentrate on the evil of virtually all wars. The thrust of this passage is to place the responsibility for waging war on princes, and to focus on the intent of all who participate.

of murder: whoever rushes into war through hatred or hope for booty is a homicide, even if he does not kill anyone. For the intention of killing was not absent, but the power or the opportunity was not added to the intention.

KA What if some private individual were to kill an attacker?

CA If certain death is in the offing and there is no means of escape, I would exhort the perfect person to call for God's assistance. It is often nearer than we think, as we read that a dragon roused by the cry of a man who had cared for him as a nursling ran to him and freed him from robbers.[157] If the person threatened chooses to be killed rather than to kill, I would think he has done the duty of a Christian. Many special circumstances are required to remove a mortal danger lawfully by killing a potential murderer; this special case is not germane to our purpose here.

KA What of those who lay violent hands on themselves?

CA If they are not functioning in a human way, they do not kill a human. Thus I make an exception in the case of a disease that deprives a person of all power of judgment.[158]

KA What of those who put an end to their life or cut it short by fasting, vigils, nakedness, and other bodily afflictions?

CA If it is a matter of hypocrisy, they are murderers; if their motive is pure, their sin is lighter, especially if they exceed due measure through a desire to help a neighbour. Charity excuses many things.[159]

Murder is the most wicked way to inflict injury on your neighbour. Adultery ranks second. There is in fact nothing closer to a man, nothing dearer, than his lawful wife, and so too, there is no affront more intolerable than a wife debauched by adultery. *Adulterare* in Latin, like μοιχεύειν in Greek, is a generic word referring to every kind of corruption. Someone who counterfeits money adulterates it, and those who bring an evil disposition to explaining the word of God adulterate it. In its more common use, however, the term 'adultery' is applied to a marriage defiled by illicit intercourse. Those who think every kind of abominable coitus is also forbidden by this commandment are correct. To this class belong incest in deed or in thought, homosexual acts, coitus with incubuses or irrational animals,

* * * * *

157 Cf *Ecclesiastes* II LB V 866A–B; Pliny *Naturalis historia* 8.22.61.
158 Erasmus recognizes that mental disorders can lead to spiritual disorders as well; cf *Encomium medicinae* ASD I-4 168:119–172:165 / CWE 29 39–41.
159 Cf Luke 7:47.

all uncleanness.[160] Finally comes simple fornication, which, although it is the lightest sin in this class, can become more serious than adultery under special circumstances. The sin of adultery is committed even in lawful wedlock if lust is gratified immoderately, or if intercourse is carried out so as to frustrate the possibility of offspring.[161] At this point, some authorities add spiritual adultery, which indeed is committed in every crime, but more especially in apostasy, when someone leaves the worship of the true God for the worship of demons. I give an account of this sin under the first commandment.

Now, please, consider how fitting the following order is. The first three commandments refer to God, than whom there is nothing better or dearer. The fourth refers to parents, to whom, next after God, honour is due. The fifth refers to life and body, the possessions most dear to everybody. The sixth refers to wives, who are one flesh with their husbands. The seventh refers to external goods, without which life is impossible.[162] For this reason, if someone robs a poor person of what he needs to live, that robber does his best to murder the person. In this regard, a certain pagan poet said that wealth is the breath of life for wretched mortals.[163] Indeed, 'robber' is the generic name for embezzlers who pilfer from the public treasury, for the sacrilegious who carry off consecrated things, for cattle thieves who take away another's beasts or herds, for kidnappers who carry off another's slaves or children, for pirates and plunderers who rob men by force and the pretence of war, and for those who secretly snatch another's goods. These types of theft are very well known to everybody. Other types are more hidden but equally vicious, if not more so.

KA What are they?

CA Someone who cheats a hired hand of the wage owed him is not actually called a thief, but he is one. Someone who accepts a loan, service, or deposit and keeps it with the intention of avoiding repayment, if possible, is no less a thief than someone who smashes money boxes and

* * * * *

160 For a discussion of patristic and canon law views of homosexuality and various other types of intercourse deemed unclean, see James A. Brundage *Law, Sex, and Christian Society in Medieval Europe* (Chicago 1987) 73–4, 212–14, 313–14, and 398–401.

161 See ibidem regarding excessive or inappropriate sexual intercourse within marriage, 89–93, 154–64, and 239–42.

162 Exod 20:15

163 Cf Hesiod *Works and Days* 686.

carries off what belongs to another. So too, a worker who does not perform what he promised, or takes ten days to finish what he could do in five, is a thief if he accepts full pay. Need I mention those who by trickery devaluate state currency? What of frauds who sell artificial jewels as real, or impoverish a neighbour by a similar ruse? What of merchants who sell their wares not for as much as they should, but for as much as they can?[164] They call it profit, but in reality it is robbery. The same must be said about monopolies. Wine merchants and drivers are not excused for selling sulphured water or lye for wine, because it is customary. Nor may millers, bakers, and drapers escape the name of thief when they either secretly appropriate another's goods, or damage them with the excuse that everybody does it. Some add to this clerics and priests who receive ecclesiastical income and do not try to perform the duties for which they were ordained, or those who receive ecclesiastical ordination although they abhor sacred rites. In short, 'theft' applies to whatever you will be compelled to make restitution for, if the opportunity offers. Someone who robs a person of his good name is also a thief, as is a man who craftily corrupts the innocent mind of a maiden.

Three commandments remain.[165] The first of them restrains the tongue and the other two spiritual concupiscence. They are explanations of certain of the preceding commandments rather than new ones. If someone who injures his neighbour by false testimony does so through love of gain, the offence falls under the commandment about theft; if he does it through hatred, it falls under murder. So great was the stupidity of that notorious people, however, that they believed only what was inflicted by sword or club to be murder, although the tongue is more injurious than any sword. It makes good sense that, just as the name 'murder' includes every physical injury, the term 'false witness' covers every verbal injury we do to our neighbour.

Moses provided a notable example, including perjury under false witness.[166] In former times two judges used to hear cases under oath, and witnesses gave their answers under oath. Someone who crushes

* * * * *

164 See Gratian *Concordia discordantium canonum* D 42 C 3.
165 Exod 20:16–17, against false witnesses, coveting. As Erasmus discusses below, he has broken up the latter commandment into two precepts, one against concupiscence and the other against greed. This of course would add up to eleven commandments altogether, but Erasmus is less concerned with enumeration than with showing the common threads of intent running through them.
166 Cf Exod 23:1–2.

an innocent person by false witness slays him no less than someone
who kills him with a sword. A person who despoils his neighbour of
his income by a corrupt decision or false testimony is no less a plun-
derer than the person who despoils by open robbery. There is the same
disposition of mind, the same desire; only the means are different.[167]
Everyone who injures a neighbour, whether by detraction, or flattery,
or deceitful advice, or corrupt doctrine, stumbles against this rock. The
more they oppose Christian charity, the closer they come to mortal sin.

The remaining two are laid down in Exodus thus: 'You shall not covet
your neighbour's house; you shall not covet your neighbour's wife, or
his manservant, or his maidservant, or his ox, or his ass, or anything
that is your neighbour's.'[168] In Deuteronomy they go as follows: 'Neither
shall you covet your neighbour's wife, his field, or his manservant, or his
maidservant, his ox, or his ass, or anything that is your neighbour's.'[169]
If you separate desire for the wife from desire for other possessions,
there will be two commandments, the first referring to adultery, the
second to theft.

KA   What need was there for these two commandments? Does not the prohibition of an evil deed also forbid an evil intention?

CA   This was a concession to the ignorance of that people. The Law laid
down no penalty for evil intentions, and they were disposed to believe
that what carried no human punishment was sinless in God's eyes –
although evil intentions were free of judicial penalty because the human mind is changeable, not because they are not crimes; a deed can be
proved, but intention is known to God alone.

KA   Why is covetousness not mentioned in the commandment forbidding
perjury and murder?

CA   Some would reply that desire for sex or for ownership is more deeply
ingrained in human nature than the desire to commit perjury or homicide. We are rather inclined to shrink from the latter, unless violent passion overwhelms our natural good sense. However, the Jewish nation
was more inclined to vengeance than to lust, and for this reason they
were permitted to give a certificate of divorce.[170] It seems to me (I speak
with respect for all interpretations) that in the Decalogue 'covetousness'

* * * * *

167 Cf Erasmus' long passage on slander in *Lingua* ASD IV-1 309–32 / CWE 29 340–
67.
168 Exod 20:17
169 Deut 5:21
170 Certificate of divorce: Matt 5:31; Deut 24:1–4

does not mean any desire for another's wife or property, so much as an inclination to evil. For example, we are said to 'assault' someone not because we have injured him, but because we tried to do so by contriving an ambush. That stupid nation, however, would have judged that attempted adultery or robbery is not a crime unless it succeeds. (In fact, it is not automatically a sin to desire what belongs to someone else. One might wish to marry a woman if her husband should die, or to acquire another's property by gift or purchase.) Not every theft is punished by execution, nor is every attempt at adultery, for the guilty parties suffer no penalty unless they are caught in copulation. A murder that has been carried out is punished by death, and an attempted murder subjects the would-be killer to judicial condemnation. For this reason, covetousness is expressly forbidden in circumstances in which the attempted offence is not punished by law.

Here I see that some have worked hard to reduce all commandments, both those that order actions and those that prohibit them, to these ten, relating the seven deadly sins to one or another of them. Their work, though assiduous, is hardly to be taken seriously. With that approach, all the commandments become confused. At one time they all are included in one category, and at another the same ones are placed in different categories. These laws were enacted for a rustic and uncultivated people, and a law should be straightforward and clear. Which of the Jews, therefore, could suspect that under the term 'adultery' every act of unchastity, even simple fornication, was forbidden? Or that all ill will was forbidden under murder? Accordingly, in my opinion at least, it is simpler to say that these ten commandments were enacted as first principles for an intractable people, to prevent them from falling into every type of crime. Then from these beginnings they were to proceed to the countless other precepts in the Law, in the prophets, and in the proverbs of Solomon. Finally they approach the perfection of the Gospel, some examples and prescripts of which are contained in the books of the Old Testament. Thus the Lord, the best interpreter of the Law, made the following answer to the young man: 'If you would enter life, keep the commandments,'[171] indicating that the Decalogue is the threshold and entrance to holiness, though not the fullness of religion. Since in this dialogue, however, you are playing the part of an immature child,[172] it is reasonable that you be satisfied with these basics for the time being.

* * * * *

171 Matt 19:17
172 Cf 236 n3 above.

There remains the matter of prayer. The best formula is the one that the Lord himself prescribed for us.[173] When Peter professed that Christ was the Son of the living God,[174] he spoke for all the apostles, and someone who recites the creed does so with the voice of the entire church, for the faith of all Christians is the same. By analogy, someone who prays with the Lord's words also prays with the voice of the whole church. The pronouns 'us,' 'we,' and 'our' indicate this union. Prayer, indeed, is worthless unless it is accompanied by faith and charity. Faith adds trust, charity adds ardour. Someone who hesitates does not believe him who said, 'Whatever you ask the Father in my name, he will give you.'[175] Someone who lacks charity prays without fervour and for himself more than others.

There is one Spirit common to all the children of God, and with one voice all of them pray for each one, and each one prays for all of them to the heavenly Father, in whom we are reborn through Christ. They entreat him that his name may be glorified throughout the entire world. Thus, all will exult together in a common Father and no one in himself, in order that the Father's Spirit may reign in the souls of all, when the tyranny of sin has been driven out. Just as there is no rebellion against God in that heavenly city, so too in his earthly city, which is struggling towards his image and destined for his inheritance, every action will be brought into conformity with the will of the most high Father and Prince.

In this short statement, the reward and the example are indicated together. Whoever renounces his own will on earth and obeys the will of God directs his course straight to life in heaven, where there is no strife and no rebellion. Meanwhile, in this life of warfare, his children seek no salary or supplies other than what they receive from their commander, the food of mind and body to enable them to discharge their duties energetically. They do not ask for honours, wealth, or the delights of this world or treasures; they seek only what is necessary for the health of their souls and life of their bodies. This is what the words 'daily bread' mean.

Moreover, that there may be complete harmony between children and parents, and also among brothers and sisters, they pray that God may deign to forgive the trespasses without which this earthly life cannot

* * * * *

173 Matt 6:9–13; Luke 11:2–4
174 Matt 16:16
175 John 16:23

be lived. They are in no position to ask for this, unless they themselves have laid claim to the mercy of God by mutually forgiving each other's faults.[176] It is unfair to demand that God, when offended, should forgive humans, if humans, suffering much lighter offences, refuse to forgive. Finally, when they consider how kind a Lord they have, how loving a Father, who gave his only Son over to death to redeem them from the tyranny of Satan, they pray that they may not be returned to the powers of that Evil One by his permission, that they may not be led into temptation and deserve to be disinherited by a Good Father.

KA Why do they not ask for eternal life?

CA Because it is a sign of good soldiers simply to perform the tasks which the commander prescribes, and be confident of their pay. It is a sign of good children to strive for this alone, that their Father be at peace with them and graciously disposed, and that they be totally unconcerned about their inheritance, especially when they have such a Father, one who is wiser, kinder, and more truthful than all others. I will not discuss the Lord's Prayer at greater length. There are at hand commentaries on this prayer, by pious and learned men, particularly St Cyprian's.[177] If it is not a burden for you to read the paraphrase on it that I once wrote,[178] you will pray and learn how to pray at the same time. At least, if I am not mistaken, you will reach this goal – that you will come some time or other to read, with a mind more prepared, the authors whom I have mentioned.

* * * * *

176 Cf Matt 6:15.
177 Erasmus is referring to Cyprian's *De domini oratione* CSEL 3 part 1 265–94.
178 *Precatio dominica* LB V 1217–29

PREPARING FOR DEATH

De praeparatione ad mortem

translated and annotated by
JOHN N. GRANT

On 19 June 1533 Thomas Boleyn, earl of Wiltshire and Ormond, and father of Anne Boleyn, the second wife of Henry VIII, wrote to Erasmus, asking him to write, as quickly as possible, a short work on the subject of preparing for death (*libellus . . . de praeparatione ad moriendum*).[1] The dedicatory letter of the work, addressed to Boleyn, is dated 1 December of the same year, and the work itself appeared in print in early 1534 from the Froben press in Basel, entitled *Liber . . . de praeparatione ad mortem*, 'A Book about Preparing for Death,' with a subtitle *Liber quomodo se quisque debeat praeparare ad mortem*, 'A Book on How All Ought to Prepare Themselves for Death.' Erasmus says in this letter that he had been occupied with such a work even before he received Boleyn's request. Erasmus' anticipation of Lord Thomas' wish may account for his completing the work very soon after receiving the request.

Erasmus' essay stands in the tradition of tracts which deal with the 'art of dying' (*ars moriendi*), one of the earliest of which is part of Jean Gerson's *Opus tripartitum*, composed circa 1408. The main focus of the fifteenth-century *Artes moriendi* was on the importance of the time of death for deciding the dying person's fate for eternity. What should be done by and for the dying when death is imminent occupies part of *De praeparatione ad mortem*, but, as the title indicates, Erasmus, like others before him, stresses too the need for an upright and righteous life as necessary preparation for our inevitable end. As Carlos Eire points out, 'The *Ars Moriendi* . . . is transformed into an *Ars Vivendi* and it becomes a manual to be read not just at the moment of death, but throughout the course of one's life.'[2] The topic involved some of the important differences between Protestant and Catholic beliefs (for example, on purgatory, the power of the sacraments, and the invocation of the saints). It is not surprising, therefore, that this 'genre' was very popular in the sixteenth century and beyond. The significance of Erasmus' essay within this tradition is treated at greater length in the introduction to this volume (xxvi–xxix above).

Although an autograph manuscript of Erasmus' work survives (Copenhagen, Royal Library GKS 95 fol), it does not reflect Erasmus' final conception of the work, as is shown by A. van Heck, the editor of *De praeparatione ad mortem* in the Amsterdam edition (see ASD V-1 328–9). The *editio princeps* carries more authority and is the basis for the translation that follows, as it is also for the text of van Heck's edition.

* * * * *

1 For further information on Thomas Boleyn see CEBR I 161–2.
2 See Carlos M.N. Eire 'Ars moriendi' in *The Westminster Dictionary of Christian Spirituality* ed Gordon S. Wakefield (Philadelphia 1983) 21–2, with bibliography.

The notes that accompany the translation are heavily indebted to van Heck, though in keeping with the nature of CWE they are briefer and more limited in scope than his annotation. Some notes, however, are new, and thanks are owed to Brian E. Daley of Weston Jesuit School of Theology for the identification of some patristic sources.

JNG

DESIDERIUS ERASMUS OF ROTTERDAM SENDS GREETINGS TO THE
MOST NOBLE LORD THOMAS, EARL OF WILTSHIRE AND ORMOND.[1]
You call me to the very keystone[2] of Christian philosophy, my noble lord –
and your nobility springs more from your devoutness than from the adorn-
ments of fortune – in urging me to add to my earlier works[3] a fairly short
essay on 'how all ought to prepare themselves for death.' For death is the
last act of human life, like the final act of a play,[4] on which depends whether
we shall either enjoy everlasting happiness or suffer everlasting damnation.
This is the final conflict with the enemy from which the 'soldier of Christ'[5]
expects eternal triumph if he conquers, eternal shame if he is defeated. I
had actually been wholly engrossed in this task for some time when your
exhortation came to me as a spur to a running horse.[6] But you in your devoutness desire that the fruit of this work may also through us be shared
by many. May the Lord in his kindness bestow a succesful result on your
most holy requests and on my endeavour. I shall certainly not resist the will
of him who, I think, inspired you to ask me to oblige you in this matter.
     Farewell.
     Freiburg im Breisgau, 1 December 1533

* * * * *

1 The prefatory letter is Ep 2884, to Thomas Boleyn, the father of Anne Boleyn,
  the second wife of Henry VIII.
2 Literally, 'the finishing touch' (*colophon*). Cf *Adagia* II iii 45 CWE 33 158: 'He
  added the colophon.'
3 Erasmus had already written *In psalmum 22 enarratio triplex* and *Explanatio symboli* at the request of Lord Thomas (see Allen Epp 2232, 2266, 2772).
4 For the common comparison of life with a play and the theatre cf Seneca
  Epistulae morales 77.20; *De conscribendis epistolis* CWE 25 164.
5 2 Tim 2:3
6 Cf *Adagia* I ii 47 CWE 31 189: 'To spur on the running horse'; Pliny *Epistulae*
  1.8.1.

PREPARING FOR DEATH

'Of all terrifying things the most terrifying is death': so says a philosopher of great repute,[1] but he had not heard that heavenly philosopher,[2] who taught us as much by clear example as by his words that we do not perish when the body dies but that our parts are separated: the soul is drawn out as if from the most oppressive of prisons into blessed rest; the body likewise will live again at some time and join the soul in glory. He had not heard that adage of the Spirit, 'Blessed are the dead who die in the Lord.'[3] He had not heard Paul lamenting with a deep sigh, 'I wish to be released and to be with Christ,'[4] and 'To me to live is Christ, to die is gain.'[5] Yet it is not surprising if those who believe that every part of us perishes in death and do not have the hope that faith alone in Christ offers us bewail the death of others and even shudder at the thought of their own death and curse it. What is more surprising is that there are so many people like me; although they have learned and profess the complete Christian philosophy, they are nevertheless terrified of death. Either they believe nothing survives after they have breathed their last, or they do not trust in the promises of Christ, or they are in complete despair about their fate. The first of these attitudes is characteristic of Sardanapalians,[6] the second of unbelievers, the third of those who do not know the compassion of God. This last group seems to be

* * * * *

1 Aristotle *Nicomachean Ethics* 1115a26
2 Christ, referred to as 'the father of philosophy' in *Antibarbari* CWE 23 102 and frequently in the *Paraclesis*
3 Rev 14:13
4 Phil 1:23 (with slight deviation from the text of the Vulgate)
5 Phil 1:21
6 Men of a luxurious style of living, after Sardanapalus, an Assyrian king with a reputation for luxury, slothfulness, and effeminacy. Cf *De conscribendis epistolis* CWE 25 84, where Sardanapalus is cited as an example of 'a man more corrupt than any women'; see also *Adagia* III vii 27: 'Sardanapalus.'

like 'the pagans who do not know God';[7] for those who do not know that God has infinite compassion do not know God. It is beyond dispute that the great terror felt by the mass of people at the thought of death springs partly from the weakness of their faith, partly from their love of worldly things. Fear is unknown to those who say in complete confidence with the Apostle, 'If we live, we live for the Lord; if we die, we die for the Lord; and so, whether we live or die, we are the Lord's.'[8]

What the Lord has once received into his protection cannot perish. Hence come those words of the prophet that are witness to a mind free of all fear, 'If I walk in the shadow of death, I shall fear no evil, since thou art with me.'[9] For the Lord keeps faith[10] and never deserts those who have entrusted themselves completely into his care, but 'guards them as if they were the apple of his eye.'[11] For he is the Lord of both life and death; to him no one is dead, all who cling to him in faith live.[12]

The love of temporal comforts springs from weakness of faith. For if we believed with all our heart what God promised us through his Son Jesus, all the things of this life that give delight would readily become worthless, and death, which transports us to these promises in a crossing that, though troublesome, is brief, would be less fearful. That wise Hebrew cries out, 'O death, how bitter is the thought of you.'[13] But what does he add? 'To a man who finds peace in his material things.' He does not say, 'To a man who has riches' – for many devout men have possessed riches – but 'to him who finds peace in these things.'

What has been said about possessions is valid for our feelings about honours and pleasures, about our wives, children, relatives, and friends, about beauty, youth, and good health – in short, every kind of blessing that death snatches from the righteous and wicked alike. The more extravagantly we are attached to something, the more grudgingly we are separated from it. 'You will be unwilling to cast aside whatever you look upon with wonder,'[14] says a certain wise man, pagan though he is. It is admiration for these temporal things that is shown by whoever finds peace in them – as if they

* * * * *

7 Tob 8:5; 1 Thess 4:5
8 Rom 14:8
9 Ps 23 (Vulg 22):4
10 Cf Ps 145 (Vulg 144):13.
11 Deut 32:10. Cf Ps 17 (Vulg 16):8.
12 Cf Luke 20:38.
13 Ecclus 41:1
14 Horace *Epistles* 1.10.31–2

are possessions that belong to him and will last for ever when they are only on loan and transitory.[15] Yet they must be put aside not only with complete equanimity but even 'with the giving of thanks'[16] when he who bestowed them claims them back.[17] I say this, for to find one's peace in the blessings of this world is to enjoy what one ought to have used – but to have done so incidentally and as if we are just passing through. As the Apostle advises the Corinthians: 'From now on, let those who have wives live as though they had none, and those who mourn as though they were not mourning, and those who rejoice as though they were not rejoicing, and those who deal with the world as though they had no dealings with it. For the form of this world passes away.'[18] We are travellers in this world, not permanent residents; we are not living in our homeland, but are visitors in a foreign land, lodging at inns or, to express the idea more clearly, living away from home in nothing more permanent than tents.[19] Our whole life here is nothing but a journey towards death[20] and a very short journey at that, but death is the gateway to eternal life.[21] In Jewish law leases could not extend beyond a fixed date; the shorter the time of the contract, the cheaper the price of property.[22] How much more worthless, then, ought we to think all these transitory things are, subject as they are to so many mischances. Even if no misfortune snatches them away, death certainly removes everything from every one of us.

Consider too how 'those who run in the race'[23] can see how much ground they have covered and how much is left to the winning post; and in times past those who observed the year of the Jubilee knew how long they could have use of the property they had bought.[24] Yet there is no mortal who knows for certain that he will be alive the next day. We are running,

* * * * *

15 Cf *De conscribendis epistolis* CWE 25 161–2; Terence *Andria* 716; Lucilius 551 Marx; Horace *Satires* 2.2.129–35.
16 Phil 4:6
17 Cf Job 1:21.
18 1 Cor 7:29–32
19 Cf Cicero *Cato* 84; *Adagia* IV x 74: 'Human life is a journey away from home.'
20 Cf *De conscribendis epistolis* CWE 25 160: 'For what is life itself other than a continuing course towards death.'
21 Cf St Bernard PL 183 484B: 'Death is, so to speak, the gateway to life.'
22 In Jewish thought the freehold of land belonged to Jehovah. Leases expired at the end of every fiftieth year, called the year of the Jubilee, and the 'purchase' price of land was calculated with respect to the number of years that the land would be held before the next jubilee year. See Lev 25:15–16.
23 1 Cor 9:24
24 Cf n22.

but with death in our feet – in fact we carry it around with us in every part of our body. We accepted life from our Lord without any cost to us, but on this condition, that we return it at any moment if he asks for it back. Even though we may reach old age, everyone is aware of how few do so. In the name of immortal God, is not the whole life of man nothing but a very short race in which, whether we wish it or not, we are continuously running – 'whether we are sleeping or awake,'[25] whether we are enjoying pleasures or being tortured? Like a torrent, the ever-moving passage of time is carrying us off, even if we and others think that we are resting. If, therefore, we were to estimate the value of worldly things by the shortness of time, we ought to think of them as worthless since there is no certainty that they will last beyond even an hour. We are easily parted from what we do not value highly. Similarly, those who are not at home but are travelling abroad do not at all place great importance on any happy circumstances they encounter in their lodging-houses or on the road, since they will soon leave behind what pleases them. In the same way, they readily endure discomfort. Their thoughts are 'Lunch here, dinner elsewhere.'[26] 'The things that are seen are transient, but the things that are unseen are eternal,' says Paul.[27] And this is the important part of Christian philosophy: it prepares us for death so that through contemplating eternal and heavenly things we learn to think little of the temporary and earthly.

Plato thought that the whole of philosophy was nothing other than the 'meditation upon death.'[28] By meditation, however, he meant preparation and training for death, just as the raw recruit who is to fight to the end against an enemy trains with a dummy.[29] Nothing more useful than this has been said, if, that is, we Christians take in a Christian way what was said by a philosopher in a philosophical sense. For neither the contemplation of abstract mathematical forms nor the picturing in our minds of Platonic Forms equips us to die in the way that we should. We are equipped by looking continually with the eyes of faith upon those things that pass beyond the grasp of human senses – the blessings that God promised, through

* * * * *

25 1 Thess 5:10
26 Cf Valerius Maximus 3.2.3 *externa*: 'Lunch now, fellow soldiers, as if you will dine with the shades below' (the words of Leonidas to his fellow Spartans).
27 2 Cor 4:18
28 Plato *Phaedo* 67E4–5, also referred to in *De conscribendis epistolis* CWE 25 32. Cf Cicero *Tusculan Disputations* 1.74; Seneca *Epistulae morales* 70.18.
29 With a dummy: literally, 'at the stake' or 'at the pole.' Cf Seneca *Epistulae morales* 18.8.

his Son Jesus, to those who believed in him and the evils that he threatened on the unbelievers and the disobedient.[30] The latter will deter us from sinning, the former will stimulate us to virtuous acts. There is indeed eternal truth in some branches of human learning, but it wins true blessedness for no one. Eternal is he who gave us his promise, eternal is he in whose name he gave us his promise, eternal are his promises. They bring eternal happiness to those who embrace them in faith, eternal unhappiness to those who ignore them. This meditation upon death is the meditation upon the true life. Not only does it achieve what the philosopher promises – the mind leaves less grudgingly its bodily abode – but it even brings it to pass that, as if eagerly longing to leave a dark and troublesome prison,[31] the spirit rushes with alacrity into blessed freedom and into that life that is desirable and that does not know darkness. For 'the perishable body weighs down the soul, and its frame of earth burdens the mind so full of thoughts.'[32] That is why that divine psalmist cries out, 'Lead out my soul from its prison so that it may confess your name, O Lord.'[33] It is the sum of human good fortune to contemplate and praise our Creator, our Redeemer, and our Guide. For it was to this end that mankind was created.

This good fortune is often diminished by the weakness of this poor body of ours that we carry around, exposed as we are to so many exigencies, so many evils, so many dangers. So too, blessed Paul, 'weighed down in the tabernacle of flesh and groaning in sorrow,'[34] called out, 'Wretched man that I am, who will deliver me from this body of death?'[35] For he saw that 'those who lived in the house of the Lord, praising him for age after age, were supremely happy.'[36] This is how the truly pious feel; although physically they live on earth, nevertheless their treasure, their heart,[37] their 'citizenship is in heaven.'[38] Few, however, have such fortitude; it has not been granted to all to say with Paul, 'To me life is Christ and death is gain,' and 'I wish to be removed from this life and be with Christ.'[39] I, in my weakness, am

* * * * *

30 Cf John 3:36.
31 Cf Plato *Phaedo* 67D1–2.
32 Wisd of Sol 9:15
33 Ps 142:7 (Vulg 141:8)
34 2 Cor 5:4
35 Rom 7:24
36 Ps 84:4 (Vulg 83:5)
37 Cf Matt 6:21: 'For where your treasure is, there will your heart be also.'
38 Phil 3:20
39 Phil 1:21, 23

providing this as consolation for those who share my weakness. For them, however, those having the strength of righteousness are the examples that spur them on to acquire spiritual fortitude.

This preparation for death must be practised through our whole life, and the spark of faith must be continually fanned so that it grows and gains strength. Love, joined to it, will attract hope, which gives no cause for shame.[40] None of these things, however, comes from us; rather they are gifts of God to be sought by continuous prayers and petitions if we lack them; if they should be present, they must be strengthened so that they grow. The stronger is our faith, accompanied by love and hope, the more diminished is our fear, since the reason that many of us shrink in the way that we do from the mention of death is for the most part, as has been said,[41] weakness of faith. Yet our confidence in the promises of God ought to be by far the most certain of all; for he is the only one who is truthful in nature and 'cannot deny himself.'[42] The wonderful psalmist sings, 'Your word lasts forever, Lord; your faithfulness is in heaven and lasts for eternity.'[43] The Lord also proclaims about himself in the Gospels, 'Heaven and earth will pass away, but my words will not.'[44] What did he promise? He promised victory over death, victory over flesh, the world, and Satan; he promised remission of sins; he promised 'a hundredfold in this age and eternal life in the future.'[45] On what basis did he make this promise? On the basis of our righteousness? Not at all, but through the grace of 'faith which is in Jesus Christ,'[46] and so that we would be less fearful, he first made void that contract[47] which the first man, Adam,[48] unfortunately wrote out for us, and then 'wiped it out, fixing it to the cross,'[49] and gave us a contract of grace that he sealed with his own blood and confirmed by the countless testimony of prophets, apostles, martyrs, and virgins who signed it with their own blood as well. 'The whole church of saints'[50] also signed it. Meanwhile he

* * * * *

40 Cf Rom 5:5.
41 394 above
42 2 Tim 2:13
43 Ps 119 (Vulg 118):89–90 (with some deviation from the Vulgate text in verse 90)
44 Mark 13:31; Matt 24:35
45 Cf Matt 19:29.
46 1 Tim 3:13; 2 Tim 3:15
47 Cf Col 2:14.
48 Cf 1 Cor 15:45.
49 Col 2:14
50 Cf Ecclus 31:11.

added too the pledge of the Spirit[51] so that our confidence could in no way weaken.

Not content with this, God in his goodness deigned to display to all a clear and prominent example in his only-begotten Son. For what he conquered he conquered especially for his members, giving his whole self for us, since what could we, mere worms,[52] do from our own resources? Christ is our righteousness,[53] Christ is our victory, Christ is our hope and security, Christ is our triumph and our crown. He was born a child, but, as Isaiah did not overlook, 'he was born for us, to us he was given.'[54] In the same way, it was for us that he taught, that he cured diseases,[55] that he drove out demons.[56] It was for us that he suffered hunger and thirst,[57] that he endured insults, that at the moment of death he was stricken with anguish and distress. It was for us that he sweated blood,[58] for us that he was bound and whipped, for us that he died and lived again. In short, it is for us that 'he sits at the right hand of his Father.'[59]

In taking onto himself all the evils that were owed to us, he handed them over to be overcome by us, having clearly already diminished their strength and having given us the extra strength of the spirit to match the measure of our afflictions. He pointed out the way to victory, he gives us in addition the desire to struggle, as we struggle he supplies us with help. In this way he prevails through us if only we are steadfast in him.[60] We stand firm through faith and love.

If anyone should ask, 'Where, tell me, is this contract which is to free us from all fear?' it is in the canonical Scriptures, in which we read the words of God, not the words of man. You must have no less belief in these than if God had spoken them to you from his own lips. I shall dare to say even more on this. For if God spoke to you through some created form, perhaps you would follow the example of some devout persons and be uncertain as to whether some deceit lay hidden in the image. The unceasing

* * * * *

51 Cf 2 Cor 1:22, 5:5.
52 Cf Ps 22:6 (Vulg 21:7).
53 Cf 1 Cor 1:30.
54 Isa 9:6
55 See Luke 6:19.
56 See Matt 9:32–3.
57 See Matt 4:2, 25:35.
58 See Luke 22:44.
59 Cf 'You who sit at the right hand of your Father,' in the Gloria in the *Ordo missae*; see *Missale Romanum* 1 738. Cf Ps 110 (Vulg 109):1.
60 Cf John 15:4–10.

consensus in faith of the Catholic church, however, has completely removed all that uncertainty of ours. Therefore to think deeply about this contract through our whole lives is the best preparation for death; as the Apostle says, 'so that by steadfastness and the encouragement of the Scriptures we may have hope.'[61] Again, if anyone should ask how and when did Christ conquer these things, he conquered the flesh and showed the way to victory when in accordance with his assumed nature he shrank from death and said to his Father, 'Yet not as I will, but as you will.'[62] Elsewhere he attests about himself that he did not come to do his own will, but 'to do the will of him who sent me.'[63] There is no part of human experience that is so terrifying that it cannot be overcome through the help of Christ if we entrust and submit our whole selves to the divine will and if, when we are battered by the most severe of afflictions, we keep in mind those words of that noble old man and most glorious king, 'It is the Lord; let him do what seems good in his eyes.'[64] These are not words of magic, but are more powerful than any incantation. Whoever says these words in all sincerity and stands firm in his reliance upon them has no cause to despair of anything, even if the whole army of evils accompanied by the very powers of hell rush upon him, standing alone.

Omnipotent is he who fights for us and says in the psalm, 'I am with him in trouble, I will rescue and glorify him.'[65] When you hear, 'with him,' do not calculate *your* strength, but consider the power of your helper. When you hear, 'I will rescue him,' do not lose courage if the affliction presses upon you for any length of time. Without doubt he will do what he has promised, and knows when it is best for you to be relieved from your misfortunes. When you hear, 'I will glorify him,' be certain that just as you shared the cross with Christ you will share in future glory.[66] Remember, however, what preceded these words: 'He called to me.'[67] It is your task to call out, and to call upon the Lord, not upon the forces of the world, not

* * * * *

61 Rom 15:4
62 Matt 26:39. For Erasmus' views about Christ's fear of death, see *De taedio Iesu* 13–67 above.
63 John 4:34
64 1 Sam 3:18. The words as cited are those spoken by Eli to Samuel. Erasmus is also thinking of a similar sentiment expressed by David at 2 Sam 15:26. Cf also 2 Sam 10:12 (spoken by Joab).
65 Ps 91 (Vulg 90):15
66 Cf 2 Cor 1:7.
67 Ps 91 (Vulg 90):15. Erasmus quotes this part of the verse with the perfect tense, not the future tense of the Vulgate.

upon your own strength and good deeds, but upon the Lord, who alone can save you from these misfortunes.

There is nothing more fragile than human nature, and yet no one would be able to match in his words the number and nature of the dreadful misfortunes to which we are exposed. For, to say nothing of thunderbolts, earthquakes, tidal waves, gaping chasms opening up on land, wars, brigandage, murders, witchcraft, who could list all the forms of disease? Among their great number are some so terrifying and painful that we tremble at just their mention, as, for example, epilepsy, paralysis, suppurating boils,[68] dementia. I say nothing of the frequent attacks of plagues that constantly change their form for the worse in the face of doctors' remedies. 'Poor wretches we, we die but once, but death can come a thousand ways':[69] that is a very true saying. How can it be possible for us to be strong enough to withstand such powerful assaults when both our bodies and our minds are so weak? It would have been all over for us, even if we were free of all sin, had not 'the right hand of the Lord'[70] supported us in our feebleness.

There remains, however, the world, which brings no little struggle for believers. By the world I mean 'the old nature of mankind with all its practices,'[71] and 'covetous desires.'[72] It is not inappropriate to understand as the world those who are devoted to this world, those who have never ceased and will never cease to fight with all their might against Christ and his disciples. Christ, however, gives us courage for this struggle, saying, 'Be of good cheer, I have overcome the world.'[73] He shows how estranged from the covetousness of worldly things he was when he says, 'The Son of Man has nowhere to lay his head.'[74] For each of us lays his head where his mind finds repose and, so to speak, falls asleep there. Those who earnestly try 'to live a godly life in Christ Jesus'[75] know how violent and wicked this world is. Christ took on himself our covetous desires, but in the same way that he took our sin upon himself he paid on our behalf the punishment that was owed to our passions and acts. Yet this world unleashed against our Lord all the deceitful tricks that it has: abuse, infamy, treachery, coercion, crucifixion, death.

* * * * *

68 Cf Exod 9:10; Ep 1347:177–81.
69 Statius *Thebaid* 9.280
70 Ps 118 (Vulg 117):16
71 Col 3:9
72 Gal 5:24
73 John 16:33
74 Matt 8:20; Luke 9:58
75 2 Tim 3:12

What did the world not do to try to extinguish completely the name of Christ? And yet, look! He lives and flourishes in heaven as well as on earth. The Lord prevailed, however, not so that we might lie back in ease, but so that we might not despair. The enemy that he handed over to us was not completely dead, only broken and vulnerable, so that we might have to struggle to win 'the crown of glory.'[76] If you should ask how the world is conquered, John, the disciple closest to Christ, teaches us. He says that your 'faith is the victory that conquers the world.'[77] Fight, therefore, with faith, placing all confidence in your Lord, and do not doubt that you will come off the victor under his auspices and protection.

There remains the sin in which, unhappily, we were born[78] and to which, more unhappily, we return after baptism, a great weight that pushes our body and mind down into hell. The Lord deigned to take upon himself this burden too, one that we cannot carry, as Isaiah prophesied: 'The chastisement that brings us peace is upon him and with his stripes we are healed.'[79] Similarly the Apostle says, 'For our sake he made him who committed no sin to be sin so that we might be made the righteousness of God in him.'[80] Sin is the one thing that creates enmity between God and the human race, as Isaiah attests.[81] Since no animal sacrifice powerful enough to abolish the crimes of the human race could be found, 'our merciful Father'[82] 'sent his own Son,'[83] a lamb free of all stain,[84] thus 'reconciling the world with him'[85] through this truly pure victim.

Someone may say at this point, 'If sin has been removed by Christ, how is it that the *whole* life of mortals is completely suffused with sins?' (I say 'whole,' for I am speaking now of good persons as well.) Christ did not remove sin completely, but he broke its strength, not so that there would be no sin in us, but 'so that it would not hold sway over us'[86] as it holds sway in those who have not fixed the anchor of their hope[87] in the Lord Jesus and

* * * * *

76 1 Thess 2:19
77 1 John 5:4
78 Cf Ps 51:5 (Vulg 50:7).
79 Isa 53:5
80 2 Cor 5:21
81 See Isa 59:2.
82 Luke 6:36
83 Gal 4:4; 1 John 4:14
84 Cf Exod 12:5; 1 Pet 1:19.
85 2 Cor 5:19
86 Cf Rom 6:12.
87 Cf Heb 6:19; *Adagia* I i 24 CWE 31 72: 'To let go the sheet-anchor.'

who are slaves to their desires. That is why Paul urges us not to allow 'sin to hold sway over our mortal body.'[88] We still have within us the source of our struggle, but we have been offered the weapons to strengthen us and to allow us to be victorious. In this way we achieve the righteousness of God, not as a result of our own works but from the grace of God.[89] By whose agency? By the agency of him whom God 'made to be sin for our sake,'[90] and 'from whose sharing in our sin God condemned sin.'[91]

There remains Satan, the begetter of both sin and death and the 'prince of this darkness';[92] from his power and never-ceasing evil arts 'the sons of light'[93] shrink and in their fear they call to their Father, 'Lead us not into temptation, but deliver us from evil.'[94] This is that tempter and 'accuser of our brothers'[95] who, according to the words of St Peter, 'prowls around like a roaring lion, seeking someone to devour.'[96] Not only did the Lord himself overcome his assaults, he also taught us how to overcome them. Satan frequently attacked the Lord; for Luke implies this when he says, 'And he departed from him for the time being.'[97] Yet he always departed conquered. How was he conquered? He was repulsed by the shield of the Scriptures, pierced by the sword of the Word of God.[98] Therefore, whenever Satan suggests to us that he fights with the divine will that is expressed in the Scriptures, let him be pierced with the sword of the divine word. As in the example of David, let him be cast down 'by five smooth stones gathered from the stream'[99] of the Scriptures. When we are about to face this Goliath, let us first throw away the armour of Saul, which is the panoply of arrogance;[100] this is to put confidence in worldly wisdom and to place trust in our own strength and merits, but so far from fortifying us these weigh us down.

* * * * *

88 Rom 6:12
89 Cf Titus 3:5, 7.
90 2 Cor 5:21
91 Rom 8:3
92 Cf Eph 6:12.
93 Luke 16:8; Eph 5:8; 1 Thess 5:5
94 Matt 6:13; Luke 11:4
95 Rev 12:10
96 1 Pet 5:8
97 Luke 4:13
98 Cf Eph 6:17.
99 1 Sam 17:40. Erasmus used this and the following example (of putting aside the armour of Saul) in *Enchiridion* CWE 66 37, in the same context – a confrontation with Satan.
100 David was fitted out with Saul's armour for his contest with Goliath, but this encumbered David and he cast it off. See 1 Sam 17:38–9.

Let the staff of faith,[101] which consoles and supports us in this pilgrimage, suffice and the five commands that the blessed Paul gives for the ministry of the church.[102] If Satan should assail you more fiercely, let him hear, 'Get behind me, Satan.'[103] It is more just for you to obey God who calls you to eternal happiness than to obey one who allures you to eternal death. In this situation faith plays the leading part. This is why Peter says, 'Resist him, firm in your faith.'[104] Believe in the Scriptures and place all your confidence in Christ; then victory is in your grasp. Moreover, there is a kind of demon 'that is cast out only by prayer and fasting'[105] – see, you have two further weapons.

Even though Satan had so often assailed our Lord without success, we may assume that he employed every weapon in his arsenal when Christ was on the cross and Satan saw that death was near. For this is the final conflict, and its outcome determines whether we hope for eternal triumph or expect the mark of eternal shame. Christ says, 'The prince of this world comes to me and yet finds nothing of the world in me,'[106] and there is no doubt that what Satan dared to do against our Lord he will dare also against us, who are the members of his body.[107] Yet just as he was conquered by Christ himself, so will he be conquered in us by the help of Christ. For when he attacks those in whom 'Christ lives through faith'[108] and love, he is waging war with Christ himself. As long as we stand firm in Christ, we shall defeat him, and this will cause him more shame than to have been overcome by Christ himself. 'I can do all things in him who strengthens me,' says the Apostle.[109] Satan, with whom we are in conflict, is called 'prince of this world'[110] not because he has any jurisdiction over any part of creation, but because in a certain

* * * * *

101 Cf 1 Sam 17:43.
102 See 2 Tim 4:5. Erasmus is referring to the five imperatives in this verse in the Vulgate text. The RSV translation of the verse reflects the Greek text, in which there are four commands.
103 Mark 8:33
104 1 Pet 5:9
105 This verse, Matt 17:20 in the Vulgate text, is omitted (as Matt 17:21) in the RSV and other translations.
106 John 14:30. Erasmus quotes the verse with *invenit*, 'finds,' for *habet*, 'holds,' of the Vulgate. With the latter reading the sense is 'and yet holds no power over me.'
107 Cf 1 Cor 6:15.
108 Eph 3:17
109 Phil 4:13
110 John 14:30

way he rules in the minds of those who love the world.[111] He who guards us, however, is Lord of heaven and earth, and by simply nodding his head is more powerful than the whole throngs of demons with their armament. He alone could enter the house of that strong man, bind him, and steal his goods.[112]

What temptations are still left? Death, death I say, at the mention of which all things are saddened. It cannot be driven off by force, avoided by flight, or eluded by skill. The prime natural instinct of every creature is for self-preservation.[113] Death, however, contrary to this natural disposition, threatens destruction, and is all the more detestable in that it separates things very closely joined, and body and soul are bound together most tightly of all.[114]

Yet the Lord in his clemency has assuaged this fear of ours. First, because for our sake he himself ungrudgingly faced the horror of death and ungrudgingly accepted death itself – and, what is more, a death both shameful and painful. He did not wish any of the devout to be free from this, however outstanding they might be: not the faithful Abraham,[115] not his beloved Moses,[116] not David, 'a man of his own heart,'[117] none of the prophets, not John the Baptist, on whose merits the Lord himself gives wonderful testimony,[118] not his uniquely beloved mother, not even the disciple that he loved more dearly than all the others.[119] From the time of the first human being 'right down to the end of the world,'[120] 'it has been laid down that all must die at one time or another.'[121] The Greek word for 'death' is μόρος, from μείρω, 'apportion by fate,'[122] because it is shared by all equally[123] – kings, priests, satraps, as well as peasants and beggars. How refractory it would be, then, to be unwilling to endure a misfortune that we share in

* * * * *

111 Cf 1 John 2:15.
112 Cf Matt 12:29.
113 Cf Cicero *De officiis* 1.11.
114 Cf *De pueris instituendis* CWE 26 314; *Encomium medicinae* CWE 29 39.
115 Cf Ecclus 44:21 (Vulg 20): 'and when Abraham was tested, he was found faithful'; cf also 1 Macc 2:52.
116 Cf Ecclus 45:1: 'Moses, beloved by God.'
117 Acts 13:22
118 See Matt 11:7–11.
119 See John 21:20.
120 Matt 28:20
121 Heb 9:27
122 The Greek in the text is drawn from *Etymologicum magnum* 591, 4.
123 *Adagia* III ix 12: 'Death is common to all.'

common with such persons and with so many! Do you shrink from pay-ing with all the saints what must be paid to nature, whether you wish it or not? He who was immortal by nature was made mortal for your sake. Do you want alone to be thought immortal, although you were born to die and have so often deserved death? If you think over, then, how many and what kind of persons share your lot, you will bear your condition with more equanimity.

Yet if we are angry because we are destined to die, there is no more cause for shame than if we were to be angry because we have been born[124] or because we have been created as human beings instead of as angels. Awareness of this is a first step to soothing our fear of death and is in no way insignificant. That remedy will be more effective if we take true ac-count of the nature of what we leave behind here. For many are tortured by the thought of death because they look only at the good things they leave. This is when they think how pleasing is the sight of the sun, how beautiful is the firmament, how delightful nature is in spring; they think of their games, their banquets, their wives, their children, their homes, their gardens.[125] You must open the other eye, however, so that you may per-ceive that you are leaving behind many more bad things than good, and that those very things that are thought of as good involve some adversity and bitterness. Cast your mind over all the stages of life and recall the sordidness of conception, the dangers of being carried in the womb, the wretchedness of birth, the exposure to many misfortunes in infancy, the wrongs suffered in adolescence, the vices by which we are defiled in our early maturity, the anxieties and troubles when we are in our prime, the suf-ferings of old age. Suppose God were to grant us the chance to go through once again in exactly the same way all that had happened in our lives in the past from conception itself to old age. I do not think you would find anyone who had enjoyed such good fortune that the offer would be ac-cepted. How unbelievably foolish it is, then, to be so distraught when we have to give up what we would not accept if we had the opportunity to re-peat it afresh. I pass over now the misfortunes with which this life is so beset that some pagan writers have judged that the most generous gift of the gods (to speak in their terms) was that they gave the ability to human beings to end their lives whenever they so wished.[126] That famous poet did not hesitate to say that 'no animal is more prone to misfortune than the

* * * * *

124 Cf *De conscribendis epistolis* CWE 25 156.
125 Cf Horace *Odes* 2.14.21–4.
126 The Stoics in particular allowed suicide. See eg Seneca *Epistulae morales* 70.14.

human species.'[127] If the authority of a pagan poet carries little weight, the holy Preacher was not afraid to write that 'the day of death is better than the day of birth.'[128]

So much for the bad things. Now for the blessings. Calculate how much trouble and anxiety your material resources have brought you, resources from which you cannot now be parted; your wife has, by far, brought 'more aloes than honey,'[129] and yet it is because of love of her that you now shrink from death; the rearing of your children has caused you much worry, their behaviour much vexation and shame. In addition, one's mind is ever turning to evil. For though it is not true in every case, what Augustine says is true in most: 'The older we are, the more wicked we are.'[130] In short, put the blessings of life on the right side, the unpleasantness on the left and calculate how short is the whole life that we are to live here. We pass through infancy without awareness of what is happening, our youth flies past as we are engaged in many different activities, our maturity is taken up with worries of all kinds, old age creeps upon us unawares. What is the sum of all this but a moment of time compared with that eternity to which we willingly go if we have lived an upright life here, to which we are dragged if we have lived a wicked one? Serious contemplation of these things is no worthless remedy against our horror of death.

There is another remedy, even more effective: our Lord died for us and brought it about that death, previously the passage to hell, is now the gateway to heaven, and what was previously the beginning of eternal torments is now the entrance to heavenly joys. The result is that death, so far from inflicting losses, now brings the highest profits to those who believe in Christ. So that we would not long for any part of ourselves, he himself rose again with many saints and gave us the certain hope that our bodies would live again on the last day[131] and, now glorified, each body would receive its own soul to reside within it; our bodies would be a solace for us from then on, not a burden.

The place for speaking about death will come soon. To complete what we are now discussing, besides all these evils heaped up in one pile there is

* * * * *

127 Homer *Iliad* 17.446–7
128 Eccles 7:2
129 Juvenal *Satires* 6.181 (also of a wife). Cf *Adagia* I viii 66 CWE 32 162: 'More aloes than honey in it.'
130 *Confessions* 7.1.1 (an inexact adaptation of 'quanto aetate maior, tanto vanitate turpior' / 'the older in years, the more disgraceful in vanity')
131 Cf John 6:39–40.

a more terrible one: hell, 'whence they say no one returns,'[132] which sucks up all things and never gives back what it has devoured. This is the abyss of despair and, as Revelation says, 'a second death.'[133] Let each of us consider what kind of life is that where the greatest of evils is immortality, where a great part of torture is to associate with demons and wicked humans, where there is inextinguishable fire compared with which the fire that we know is mere ice. Moreover, in that place being burned is the least of sufferings, although these sufferings are so severe that they cannot be grasped by the human intellect, just as the happiness of the devout is beyond our comprehension. Even in our most painful and long-lasting sufferings, hope, like a star that casts its light from afar, piercing even the densest mist, brings us some alleviation. Hell, however, with its extreme sufferings brings extreme despair.

Fear of hell surpasses all fear, but our most compassionate Redeemer deigned to subject himself to it so that he might lessen it for us. When he felt fear in the garden and was so seized by extreme anguish that he sweated blood,[134] this was the infirmity of our nature, but when he was fixed to the cross and called out, 'My God, my God, why have you forsaken me and far from my salvation are the words of my sins,'[135] he seems to have felt the horror of hell in his mind. For what is left for those abandoned by God except extreme despair? It ought not to seem strange that he showed this most distressing state of mind when he had taken upon himself the sins of all[136] so that each evil that could not be overcome by the strength in us could be overcome by his compassion. Nor do these things diminish the dignity of the Redeemer, but prove his ineffable love towards the human race. As in a foreshadowing of Christ, David says in the Psalms, 'The pains of death surrounded me and the torrents of iniquity have cast me down,' and 'The snares of death have seized me.'[137] We had deserved hell, he in his innocence feels dread on our behalf so that, if a similar emotion invades our mind either from awareness of our crimes or from the weakness of our nature, we shall not abandon all hope, but with our eyes set on Christ shall have hope even in despair.

* * * * *

132 Catullus 3.12
133 Rev 21:8
134 See Luke 22:44. See also n62 above.
135 Ps 22:1 (Vulg 21:2); cf Matt 27:46. The second part of this quotation is not, *pace* Erasmus, spoken by Christ in Matthew's account. I have used the Douai-Rheims translation for the difficult Vulgate version of that part.
136 Cf Isa 53:12.
137 Ps 18:4–5 (Vulg 17:5–6)

Although the flesh despairs, although reason despairs, nevertheless let faith call to the Lord even from hell itself,[138] just as Jonah, already given up as lost, 'called from the belly of the whale and was heard.'[139] For the psalmist demonstrates this too when he immediately goes on to say, 'In my distress I called upon the Lord, to my God I cried for help, and from his holy temple he heard my voice.'[140] The church is 'God's temple';[141] this is the citadel of faith, 'Sion is a city of strength.'[142] If anyone directs a call here even from the depths of hell and a spark of faith is still flickering in him, he is heard. Therefore, even though the whole strength of an individual has been sunk into hell, let faith call out with most blessed Job, 'Even if he should kill me, I shall place my hope in him.'[143] For this is 'to have hope against hope,'[144] like Abraham,[145] the teacher of faith.

Not only has the goodness of our Lord, then, weakened and broken these great evils for us so that they do not have the strength to destroy us even if they assail and terrify us; but also he transformed our greatest losses into the richest profit. For what harm does sin do to those who cling to Christ? None; for when sin is there in abundance, grace too is present in abundance,[146] and he loves more those in whom more has been forgiven.[147]

What does Satan achieve when he ceaselessly attacks the members of Christ? Nothing, except that he increases their rewards and lights up their crowns. In fact, even those misfortunes that along with our mortality we share with the righteous and the wicked alike have been turned to our profit by the clemency of our Redeemer, or they can help to cure us, which is also to our profit. These misfortunes become profit if, free of sins, we bear them with endurance, 'giving thanks to the Lord for all';[148] they become medicine

* * * * *

138 In this paragraph Erasmus appears to suggest that even in hell faith can save the dead. This not only poses theological problems but contradicts what Erasmus says later in the essay ('For after the death of the body there is no "place for repentance"' [411]; 'there is hope of forgiveness for as long as we breathe' [413]). He must be using the term 'hell' metaphorically, of the state of sinners in their earthly life; cf what he says later (413), 'Assuredly, the sinner is already in hell.'
139 Jon 2:2 (a close paraphrase)
140 Ps 18:6 (Vulg 17:7)
141 1 Cor 3:16
142 Isa 26:1
143 Job 13:15
144 Rom 4:18
145 See Rom 4:16 and n115 above.
146 Cf Rom 5:20.
147 Cf Luke 7:47.
148 Eph 5:20

if anything resides in us that has to be purged either by surgery or cautery or by bitter drugs. Such misfortunes are disease, poverty, old age, loss of our loved ones, and the other countless troubles by which all human lives are beset on all sides. If these things induce in us grumbling complaints, despair, or blasphemy, they become the tools of Satan, and instead of remedies they become poisons. If they are endured only because they cannot be avoided (which was the attitude of those who, not knowing Christ, bore without relief torture and death), they are afflictions of nature. If, however, we accept these misfortunes with compliance and even 'with an expression of thanks'[149] – as if they come from the hand of a kindly disposed parent – and consider that we have deserved much more grievous things and that Christ, though innocent, suffered horribly for our sins, these are no longer afflictions but either health-giving remedies or the means of increasing our heavenly rewards. If they are the former, we should give thanks to a most indulgent parent who 'scourges every son he acknowledges,'[150] while healing our sores by quick and gentle remedies, so that he may spare us 'in the life that is to come.'[151] If they are the latter, we ought to praise the kindness of our general,[152] who provides his soldiers with the opportunity to show their bravery so that he may crown them more magnificently. In either case there is great profit, unless perhaps it seems only a modest profit either for a man who is labouring with a terminal disease to swallow down bitter-tasting pills, with only slight and short-lasting discomfort, and thus to escape the danger of death and to enjoy the everlasting sweetness of good health,[153] or for a soldier to acquire the highest honours and great wealth for the rest of his life in return for fighting for one brief hour.

In this way too our most compassionate Lord draws all things to himself,[154] if only we direct our eyes to that sign displayed in the heavens.[155] He takes all our evils on himself and turns them to our profit and to his glory, glory that he shares with us who are engrafted to him by faith. What

* * * * *

149 Phil 4:6
150 Heb 12:6
151 Mark 10:30
152 For Christ as *imperator*, 'general,' see *Explanatio symboli* 387 above; *Enchiridion* CWE 66 26; *De conscribendis epistolis* CWE 25 160. See n220 below.
153 The everlasting sweetness of good health: perhaps an echo of part of the Collect of the *Commune festorum Beatae Mariae Virginis*, 'everlasting good health of mind and body'; see *Missale Romanum* I 940.
154 Cf John 12:32.
155 This may be a reference to the sign of the cross in the sky seen by Constantine at the battle of the Mulvian Bridge in 312 AD.

profit do they enjoy who in adversity turn away their eyes from Christ and murmur against God? They make what must by necessity be endured twice as vexatious, or, to speak more truthfully, they make it ten times worse; by not accepting the medication in the way that they should they transform it into a poison that will destroy them. This assuredly is the sublime and effective philosophy of and meditation upon death, and if a strong and healthy man has been carefully trained in it death will not come upon him unprepared.

From what has been said one can infer that death is fourfold: the spiritual, the natural, the transformative, and the eternal. The natural death is the separation of the soul from the body;[156] the spiritual is the separation of God from the soul. For just as the soul is life to the body, so God is life to the soul. Spiritual death must inevitably produce natural death; so, at any rate, is the devout opinion of the older theologians.[157] The union of the spiritual death and of the natural death results in the death that is hell. For after the death of the body there is no 'place for repentance.'[158]

There remains the death by which we are transformed from the image of the old Adam into the image of the new Adam,[159] who is Christ the Lord. This is the separation of the flesh from the spirit. Here the struggle is great, and there is not even any hope of victory unless the Spirit of Christ helps the weakness of our flesh.[160] His grace, however, destroys our old nature;[161] the result is that we are led not by our spirit, but by the Spirit of God,[162] and we ourselves do not live, but Christ lives in us.[163] I do not know whether anyone has fully experienced this happiest of deaths in this life. Nevertheless, the Lord in his generosity deigns to supply from his own resources what we lack in our weakness. This is the death that we must seek out and must contemplate with all our devotion through the whole of our lives. As St Paul writes to the Corinthians, 'We always carry around in our body the death of Jesus Christ so that the life of Jesus may be revealed in our body.'[164] In the same way he urges the Colossians, 'Put to death those parts of you that

* * * * *

156 Cf Thompson *Colloquies* 89 / CWE 39 259 (*Proci et puellae*).
157 Cf Augustine *Sermones* 231.2 PL 38 1104; *De civitate Dei* 13.2, 21.3 PL 41 377, 711; *Enarrationes in psalmos* PL 36 556, on Ps 49:14 (Vulg 48:15).
158 An echo of the Vulgate text of Job 24:23
159 Cf 1 Cor 15:45.
160 Cf Matt 26:41.
161 Cf Col 3:9.
162 Cf Rom 8:14.
163 Cf Gal 2:20.
164 2 Cor 4:10

are of this earth.'[165] He does not order our eyes to be torn out or our hands to be amputated or our genitals to be cut off. But what parts, then, does he mean? He adds 'fornication, indecency, lust, evil cravings, and greed.'[166] The common herd of humans mourns the dead, but blessed Paul congratulates the Colossians on this kind of death. 'You are dead,' he says, 'and your life is hidden with Christ in God.'[167] This death is the mother of spiritual life, just as sin is the father of spiritual death and even of hell.

To those kinds of death most mortals react in quite the opposite way. How we shrink in fear at the thought of physical death! The ancients regarded the cypress and parsley as hateful since the former is a customary presence at funerals and because they garlanded their tombs with the latter.[168] Even today some people utter dreadful curses when they smell incense. The reason, I think, is that incense is used for purification at a funeral. Spiritual death, however, is more horrible than six hundred deaths of the body, and yet it is to this that we hasten voluntarily and eagerly, taking pride in our evil actions and exulting in the most wicked things. We are terrified when we are exposed to the risk of our soul abandoning this wretched body, although it will live more happily when freed from its prison. How much more virtuously ought we to be terrified whenever we run the risk that God, our eternal life, may desert our soul.

We call the house in which someone has died a house of mourning and pass by with our nostrils covered; and yet the Wise Man judges that it is far 'better to go to the house of mourning than to the house of feasting.'[169] In bereavement we are naturally saddened, but this 'sadness, because it is borne in God's way, produces lasting salvation in us';[170] it reminds us of what awaits us at the very end, it calls upon us to repent and does not allow us to sin for eternity. Lucky are those who experience grief and mourn someone else's physical death in such a way that they begin to mourn for themselves through terror at a worse kind of death.

Which is better, then, to swallow a bitter pill so that at the cost of one hour's discomfort you may acquire everlasting health or to drink at a party

* * * * *

165 Col 3:5
166 Ibidem
167 Col 3:3
168 For the cypress cf Horace *Odes* 2.14.22–4 and for the parsley (more accurately, celery) see Erasmus *Adagia* II x 85 CWE 34 161: 'It's celery he needs.' For the adorning of tombs with wreaths of parsley, see Plutarch *Timoleon* 26.
169 Eccles 7:3
170 2 Cor 7:10

sweet poison that will bring you death after brief pleasure? Many, however, take absolutely no account of these things; drunken, they sing in brothels; they applaud themselves because they have increased their property by deceit; because they have attained honours by wicked means they are exultant. Does not the common herd describe wallowing in the delights and pleasures of the flesh as 'really living'? Yet those who live in this way are twice dead, first because they do not have the spirit of God, second because they are already the sons of hell. For, just as the lives of the devout who are dead in the flesh 'are hidden in God'[171] and will appear along with Christ,[172] so in those who have surrendered themselves to the flesh there is hidden death in hell, which they carry around with them and which will appear at the final judgment.

Hope alone separates the sinner in this life from hell, since there is hope of forgiveness for as long as we breathe.[173] We must, however, take care constantly that we are not deceived by a hope that does not spring from faith and love. Someone deludes himself by thinking in this way: 'I am young, I shall enjoy the pleasures of the world now, I shall cultivate goodness when I reach old age.' But, my dear fellow, who has promised you that you will reach old age? Another says: 'I shall indulge myself[174] while I am in my prime. I shall be virtuous when I marry.' Yet you are deceiving yourself.[175] How do you know whether you will be alive the day after next? Perhaps someone else thinks: 'Someday I shall become a monk. Then I will bewail my misspent life; meanwhile I will enjoy the world.' Even though you may live long enough to do so, who has promised you that you will have the frame of mind that desires penitence instead of pleasures? Is there anyone who can have this intention of his own accord? Only the grace of Christ brings it about that the sinner returns to his senses.[176] Moreover, Christ gives it freely to whom he wishes and when he wishes.

Assuredly, the sinner is already in hell. Is it not the mark of astounding blindness for those in such a horrible situation to fix ahead of time the day when they wish to recover their senses? If a man fell into a well or were

* * * * *

171 Col 3:3
172 Cf Col 3:4.
173 A particular application of the proverb *Dum spiro, spero,* 'While there's breath, there's hope.' See A. Otto *Die Sprichwörter ... der Römer* (Leipzig 1890) under *sperare.*
174 Literally, 'I shall indulge my genius.' Cf Persius 5.151 and *Adagia* II iv 74 CWE 33 228: 'To indulge one's genius.'
175 Cf *Moria* CWE 27 123.
176 Cf Isa 46:8.

thrown into prison, he would think that his rescuers were acting too slowly even if they were hurrying as fast as they could to bring him out. If a man were in a well, he would immediately call from it for the help of a fellow human being. Surely if he were spending his life in evil ways, he should immediately call upon the help of God, who alone rouses the dead? Whoever, then, has carefully thought about transformative death during his life and has been in terrible fear of spiritual death and hell will dread much less the imminent death of the body. For the death of the body does not separate us from God but joins us more closely to him. This puts an end once and for all to all the afflictions that batter us on all sides in this life, this leads to eternal rest. 'You say, "leads to rest," but you are referring only to the souls of the good.' Yes; for 'the death of sinners is most terrible.'[177]

While you live and are strong, therefore, see to it that you are one of the righteous. For those too[178] are righteous who sincerely recognize and condemn their unrighteousness and, terrified by hell, seek refuge at the sanctuary of divine mercy and in the saving remedy of repentance. As for those who indulge their desires all their lives as if they are immortal, who are, as the saying goes, deafer than the shore at Torone[179] to the words of God when he calls them so often and so lovingly to repentance, is it in any way surprising that they are distraught when the final necessity of death presses upon them? Then they have to deal with physically incapacitating disease, with doctors, heirs, legatees and those seeking legacies, with creditors and debtors, with wives and children, with stewards and servants, with friends and enemies, with funeral rites and burial, with confessions, dispensations, and censures, with acts of restitution and propitiation, with various scruples of conscience, finally even with the tenets of faith. In addition to this they must deal with the world; since they loved it too much, they leave it against their will. Moreover, they must deal with the actual death of the body, for which they are not prepared. Finally, they must deal with Satan and with hell; for it is at this time that Satan presses hard with every trick at his disposal; it is at this time that hell heaps upon us all its ghostly terrors. And yet that short period of time when we are dying is not sufficient for such a host of activities; rather, we should strive with all our might to

* * * * *

177 Ps 34:21 (Vulg 33:22)
178 That is, as well as those who have died and are righteous with God
179 This is a variant of *Adagia* II ix 8 CWE 34 94: 'As deaf as the harbour at Torone'. Erasmus ad loc refers to the variant 'shore' for 'harbour.' The meaning is that it is impossible to hear anything on this shore other than the sound of breaking waves.

come to that final conflict, the most serious of all, like a soldier who could not be more ready for action.

Someone may ask, 'How can this be achieved?' Let us listen to the good advice of the Preacher: 'Remember your Creator in the days of your youth, before the time of affliction comes.'[180] Let us listen also to the son of Sirach: 'Before judgment comes, acquire goodness, before illness take medication, and before judgment examine yourself and you will find forgiveness in the sight of God. Before illness humble yourself, and show your penitence at the moment of your weakness.'[181] This is good advice, even if we knew the day of our death. As it is, we should follow it all the more, seeing that we all ought to regard each day as our last, since we do not know whether another day will follow it. As long as we have life and good health, let us disentangle the complexities of business matters as far as we can, and 'let us set our house in order'[182] before illness confines us to our bed. The most important thing is 'to remember our Creator' so that by sincere confession and repentance we may return with him into grace. Let us examine our consciences, cutting out whatever we find there that is hateful to God, so that when disease brings us before his judgment seat[183] 'we may find forgiveness.'[184] Surely we see how those who stand arrogantly and without fear before God when things are prosperous abase themselves if a serious illness threatens death. How much more pleasing it is to God if we do at the proper time and of our own accord what sickness drives us to do at the last minute. 'If we prostrate ourselves in the sight of God'[185] along with the publican and the sinful woman in the Gospel,[186] appeasing the wrath of God by tears, alms, prayers, and other acts of piety, in the time of our last sickness we shall be the same as we have been in our life.

Some shrink from writing their will, thinking that it is an omen of death to do so. Such thoughts come from the weakness of our flesh. And yet, sir, you will not die more quickly because you have made your will; you will die more peacefully. In this respect those who live in a respectable monastery are more fortunate because they are free of all worries about a will. Let those, however, who have children or brothers or other legitimate

* * * * *

180 Eccles 12:1
181 Ecclus 18:19–21
182 Isa 38:1
183 Cf Rom 14:10; 2 Cor 5:10.
184 Ecclus 18:20
185 Dan 9:20
186 See Luke 18:10–13 for the publican; Luke 3:37 for the woman.

heirs see to it that no dispute in dividing up their possessions should arise among blood relatives and relatives by marriage. Those who do not have such heirs should not leave behind to the next generation cause for lawsuits or opportunity of theft. In short, they should set in order and arrange these affairs when they are in good health, so that there is no need to be tortured by such inappropriate worries when they are ill.[187] Moreover, any persons involved in complicated business affairs, relating to marriage, for example, or ecclesiastical censures, or solemn promises, or acts of restitution and reconciliation, should settle these when they are healthy and strong and should not put off any difficult cases until the day of death. Some wait until they are dying to entrust their heirs with the restitution of things they have fraudulently acquired; this is a virtuous act. Others, however, act with more foresight; when they are healthy they themselves do what is often not done by those they instruct to do it. Some wait until the point of death to forgive the offences of all who have done them harm, and in turn to beg forgiveness for their wrongdoings against others, and these too are virtuous acts. It is far more pleasing to God, however, and much better for an untroubled conscience if they were to do these things when they are in good health, not out of fear of death but out of love of Christ. Some on their deathbed assign part of their wealth for the help of the poor – again a virtuous act, but the sacrifice will be much more pleasing to Christ if you yourself, during your lifetime, lessen the poverty of your neighbours as your resources allow. For the needy do not always receive what a dying man has marked out for them in his will. Even if they do receive it, the money that is being expended is no longer yours, but comes from someone else.

Are there not many diseases of such a kind that they do not allow us time to make such provisions – quite apart from the sudden and unexpected accidents that, though they do not take all of us by surprise, all of us must expect, since they can befall us all? So it happened to that foolish man in the Gospel who promised himself a long and easy life and then heard the words 'This night your soul is required of you.'[188] All pray that they will not meet a sudden and unforeseen death,[189] since everywhere we hear these

* * * * *

187 Cf the colloquy *Funus*, where one of the dying (Cornelius) has made his will when he was healthy, the other makes arrangements on his deathbed; see Thompson *Colloquies* 364–6, 370 / CWE 40 771–2, 776.
188 Luke 12:20
189 Cf Ep 1347:72–5 (a letter of consolation to Joost Vroye on the sudden death of a common friend).

words: 'Free us from a sudden and unforeseen death, Lord.'[190] What is it that they are praying for? Is every unexpected death to be abhorred? Not at all. 'For the good man will be at rest no matter what untimely death he meets.'[191] However sudden a death will be, it cannot be bad if it has been preceded by a good life.[192] Why do we not pray, then, in these words: 'Free us from an evil life, O Lord.'

What effrontery we have to call death unforeseen when every day it presents itself to all our senses. From our childhood what else do we hear but the groans of the dying? What else do we see but the dead being carried out for burial, the procession of mourners, and the monuments and epitaphs of the dead? If the deaths of strangers touch us but lightly, how often does death come nearer to us and pluck us by the ear[193] at the funerals of in-laws and relatives who are connected to us by the close tie of blood and at the funerals of friends bound more tightly to us by mutual love than any relative joined to us by the bonds of nature![194] And if even this is not sufficient, how often are we ourselves reminded of our fragility! For who of us has not at different times been in danger of losing his life – in a storm or in a robbery or in war or when a building has collapsed or by pestilence or by sickness? Wherever you turn, death lies in wait. For each of us our home is a safe refuge. Yet how many are crushed by collapsing roofs? Does not the earth, the solid element, sometimes subside and suck in whole cities? The very air by which we breathe and live is often the cause of death, just as food and drink are. Finally, do not hunger and thirst threaten death every day if we do not assuage them?

Are we not reminded of death whenever the term 'human' is applied to us?[195] For 'human' and 'mortal' mean the same thing to us. Are not, then, those who pray that a sudden death may not strike them simply accusing themselves of improvidence? For those who are unprepared every kind of death is sudden, even if it comes when they are a hundred years old. Do you call death unforeseen just because you do not see it, though it presents itself to and impinges on all our senses? In the same way the flood was unforeseen

* * * * *

190 An invocation in the Litany of the Saints; see the *Rituale Romanum.*
191 Wisd of Sol 4:7
192 Cf Ep 1347:106–7: 'No one can die badly who has lived well.'
193 Cf Virgil *Copa* 38: 'Death plucks at our ear and says, "Live life to the full, for I am coming"'; *Adagia* I vii 40 CWE 32 90: 'To pluck by the ear.'
194 Cf Prov 18:24.
195 Erasmus seems to be thinking of the etymological links between *homo,* 'a human being,' and *humus,* 'the earth.'

by the wicked who laughed at Noah, the herald of justice, while he was building the ark, and who 'ate, drank, and took spouses,'[196] as if what God was threatening was not going to come to pass. In the same way the people of Sodom, who laughed at Lot as he left the town, did not foresee their destruction.[197] The same would have happened to the people of Nineveh had they not paid heed to the proclamation of Jonah and repented.[198] Let whoever knows that he has an angry God expect punishment at any moment, but rather let him avoid it, following the example of David[199] and of the people of Nineveh.

Terrible is the wrath of God, but if we humble ourselves and repent, he will 'think of mercy in his wrath.'[200] The people of Nineveh turned to repentance at the news brought by the stranger Jonah. We are deaf, however, to the many intimations that come from our Lord, and pray that we may escape sudden death. So that we may be prepared for death at every moment he assails us in our forgetfulness and tardiness with many examples and parables: Noah, Lot, and the people who were crushed by the tower at Siloam when it collapsed unexpectedly.[201] He gives us too the examples of the thief who comes in the night, the faithful servant, the ten virgins,[202] and so often calls out, 'Keep awake; for you do not know the day and the hour.'[203] Does any death come to us unforeseen? Yes, but it is because we are improvident, or (to express it better) because we are deaf, blind, and witless. We do not listen to the calls of the Lord, we do not see what presents itself before our eyes, we do not feel what stings us on all sides.

It does not matter that the Lord's words seem to relate to the final day of the world. For the last day of our lives is the last day of the world for each of us. 'At the end of the world'[204] the universal judgment will take place publicly, but in the meantime the souls of all persons are judged as soon as they leave the body, although we do not know the outcome of the

* * * * *

196 Luke 17:27; Matt 24:37. For the building of the ark see Gen 6:13–22.
197 Cf Luke 17:28–9. For the departure of Lot from Sodom see Gen 19:15–23.
198 See Jon 3:4–10.
199 After arranging the death of Uriah and marrying his wife, David was threatened with death by the Lord, but because of his repentance he was saved. See 2 Sam 12:1–13.
200 Hab 3:2
201 See Luke 13:4.
202 Thief in the night: Matt 24:42–4; faithful servant: Matt 25:14–30; ten virgins: Matt 25:1–13
203 Matt 25:13
204 Matt 28:20

judgment of each individual. The Lord, however, wished that both days be equally unknown to us, in this way too showing his most generous love for us. For, when we see their intolerable violence at the present time, what would the rich and criminal do if they knew that they were going to live longer? Similarly, if the weak, as most mortals are, knew for certain that they were going to reach old age, they would put off till then the desire for a more virtuous way of living. If, however, the weak were sure that only a few days of life were left to them, they would live in sorrow and anxiety and would be more dilatory in performing many actions that would help the common weal. As things are, the providence of the supreme power has employed this mode of restraint: death is so certain for all human beings that they all know that they will die as certainly as they know that they were born, and neither the highest nor the lowest can flatter themselves with vain hope; yet the day of death is so uncertain that the Lord did not wish it to be known even to those most dear to him. The result is that the wicked do not hurt the good as much as they might and that the good refrain from evil actions, thinking that they may die the next day. Let them apply themselves to good deeds on the assumption that they will live for a long time![205]

What, then, do those want for themselves who rush to palm-readers, astrologers, physiognomists, horoscope-casters, ventriloquists, astronomers, and magicians so that they may know the length of their life? The Preacher proclaims: 'None of us knows when our end will be. Like fish caught on the hook and birds in a snare, so we mortals are taken when bad times come upon us suddenly.'[206] Do we want to know from people like these when our end will be when they themselves do not know theirs? Will we learn from foolish men what Christ, the eternal truth, wished to be left unknown, because it was not to our advantage to know? Do Christians approve of the example of ungodly Saul?[207] What good to him, however, was the sorceress, except that he died twice?

Some people (and they are certainly not evil) ask God to know for certain how they will die and pray that they may lie on a bed of sickness

* * * * *

205 This sentence is marked off from what precedes by a colon in LB. In ASD it is printed as part of the preceding sentence. The translation would be 'and apply themselves to good deeds on the assumption that they will live for a long time.' This punctuation, however, does not fit the argument unless a negative is added ('that they will *not* live for a long time').

206 Eccles 9:12

207 See 1 Sam 28:6–14. In his fear of the Philistines Saul made use of a witch or medium, to whom Samuel appeared from the dead.

for a known number of months so that they may devote this time at least to repentance and confession.[208] More holy (for it springs from love) is the prayer of those who ask to die in such a way that they will be of least trouble to their family. It is the mark of stronger faith, however, to entrust the nature of one's death and the length of one's sickness to God. He knows what is to our advantage, and he will give what is best for us. There are countless forms of death, some of them horrible: those that kill suddenly, as happens to some who die even as they are at the banquet table; those that involve severe and lengthy pain, like paralysis and sciatica; those that cause a frightful appearance, as in the case of those who turn black because they are strangled by phlegm that cannot be dislodged; those that take away the power of speech and sanity, like a stroke or madness and some fevers; and other peculiar illnesses that drive us to throw ourselves from a great height or to leap into a well or to hang ourselves or to thrust a sword into our body. For there are diseases that infect the workings of the mind – these the masses call possession by an evil spirit. Yet not even in such cases should we judge people, since Chrysostom consoles in a most loving manner the monk who is possessed by an evil spirit.[209] Nevertheless, it is characteristic of Christian devoutness to abominate and pray for escape from those kinds of diseases that seem to present in their appearance clear evidence of ungodliness. We do, in contrast, see some people dying in such tranquillity that they seem to be falling asleep instead of dying.

No matter what kind of death befalls us, we should never be judged by it. We should not make rash judgments even about those who because of their crimes pay the penalty required by the laws, although the kind of death that has fallen to their lot is a shameful one. A man whose body is quartered because he has incited sedition may pass into the company of the angels,[210] while a man who dies in the Franciscan habit and is buried with proper religious rites may go to hell.[211] It is the Lord who judges them. God makes trial of and cleanses his followers in different ways, but, as I have said,[212] no death ought to be thought of as bad if it has been preceded by a good life. Sometimes those who expire in the most peaceful manner

* * * * *

208 Cf Ep 1347:99–100.
209 Chrysostom *Ad Stagirium* PG 47 423–48
210 Cf *Enarratio psalmi* 33 LB V 414C–D.
211 There was a belief that the dead would escape the pains of purgatory if they were buried in the Franciscan habit. See Thompson *Colloquies* 369 / CWE 40 774 (*Funus*); Thompson *Colloquies* 501, 504 / CWE 40 1000, 1006 (*Exequiae seraphicae*).
212 417 above

move on to eternal torture, while those who suffer a most torturous death sometimes escape into peace.

Some people desire to make full confession, to have the final anointing, and to partake of communion before they die – apparently sharing the same view as those who at one time postponed baptism to the very last day of life, and the baptizer was not summoned until the doctor admitted that his skill was not sufficient to save the patient. Why do we desire to receive only once what we ought to and can receive every day? For the best plan is that we should all carefully examine our consciences before we surrender ourselves to sleep, and, if we suddenly think about a sin that we have committed that day, we should beat our breast and ask in tears for forgiveness from the Lord; having called upon divine help, we should make it our firm goal to lead a more upright life. There is no reason for anyone to say: 'I am preoccupied with various business matters. I do not have time.' A quarter of an hour is sufficient to do something that is so necessary. It does not take long to say, 'I have sinned; pity me.' This is all that needs to be said, if indeed it is said sincerely.

No one can be certain that he will awake when he surrenders him to sleep. What a great risk there is in falling asleep in that state in w we shall perish for eternity if death, the sister of sleep,[213] should follow brother and come upon us unexpectedly! We can escape that great d by a very brief period of contemplation. This we can do every day God. Yet to purge your conscience three or four times or more in a sincere confession before a priest, the representative of God, will b the greatest peace of mind, with the result that anxiety about confe not torture you at all when you are dying.

Moreover, since the greatest solace at the moment of death templation of the death of our Lord and of the communion o church, which is the body of Christ, it will be to your advan yourself diligently during your life to contemplate both; an a ally repeated will become a habit, the habit will become a stat become part of your nature. This will happen if our conscie un- all desire to sin and if we take frequently the sacred bread ip of the sacred cup, since this sacrament commends two thing ist, the matched love of the head for its members and the very c the members themselves. All that is good in the body flow the same head; all that is good in the body is shared by all mem

ath are children

* * * * *

213 Homer *Iliad* 14.231, 16.672. According to Hesiod, Sleep
   of Night (*Theogony* 212).

as in the body of a living thing; for, although the members of such a body are quite different from each other, meant to perform different functions, nevertheless the same source of life that starts from the head is diffused through all the members in such an indivisible union that (as the blessed Paul teaches) 'if one member suffers, all suffer; if one rejoices, all rejoice with it.'[214] To be sure, this is what is meant in the Apostles' Creed: 'The holy [sancta] church, the communion of saints [sancti].' For the grace of Christ is no more confined to a small space in his mystic body than is the life-giving force in the body of an animal.

When death is very near, those who send to a monastery of the Carthusians or of the Franciscans and beg them to pray for the dying person act with devotion. It is a much more effective solace, however, if the sick person considers that the whole church is concerned for its member. When I say church, what a blessed and populous society I mean, one that includes the prophets, the apostles, the throngs of many martyrs and virgins, and many souls dear to God! This whole fellowship prays unceasingly for any members of Christ who are in danger and relieves their suffering by its merits and prayers. It does not matter that the church cannot be seen. You do not see your soul either, though it is by the good offices of the soul that all the parts of your body live and move. The church that is joined to such a rich head cannot be poor, for 'in him dwells the whole fullness of godhead in bodily form.'[215] No member that is helped by so many thousands of saints can be abandoned. The cross taken up to redeem us especially shows the love and kindness of the head towards us. We renew the memory and power of all this whenever we eat the Lord's flesh and drink his blood in faith and with the proper reverence.[216] At the same time we are reminded that all who eat the same bread and drink from the same cup are one body.[217] Let one, then, be despondent if a member is weak and worn out, since the d is omnipotent. Let no one who is helped by the merits and prayers of hole church think himself abandoned.

hese beliefs will bring more consolation in death to whoever has dili- pplied himself to their contemplation in life. For then by their own ey will present themselves as if they are intimate friends of the rdingly, in my opinion, those who divided up the story of the

2
215
216 C6–7
217 Cf
24–5.
7.

death of our Lord hour by hour so that the children might be accustomed to recall with gratitude a portion of it each day devised a devout practice. Although those who have substituted for this the Liturgy of the Virgin[218] have not created something that is unholy, they have (if it is permitted for me to say the truth) turned wine into water.

These are the best ways to ensure that we are best prepared and that 'sudden and unforeseen death'[219] will not strike us down. We must leave behind our sweet children, our dear wife, our beloved friends, our cultivated fields, our magnificent buildings, our great wealth. The 'soldier of Christ'[220] has trained himself to think lightly of all these things; his soul is on guard in the fortress of the body, awaiting at every moment the trumpet call of his general[221] ordering him to enter the fray, and always alert for these words: 'Set your house in order; for you will die and not live.'[222] He regards his body not as a permanent home but as a tent; he does not store away his treasure there, but carries in his belt enough for a daily ration; he is always awake and on guard, and always has his weapons at the ready against sudden attacks of the enemy, refusing no hardship provided he please the general in whose army he enlisted. 'The life of man on this earth is like that of a soldier,' says the blessed Job.[223]

The wise Sirach exhorts the recruit to this army in these words: 'My son, if you wish to come forward to serve God, stand in righteousness and in fear, and prepare your soul for testing.'[224] To serve God is to be a Christian soldier. The soldier's duty is to stand in the battle line, ready to fight. 'Stand in righteousness' – not in pride, which puffs itself up against God,[225] but 'in righteousness.' Soldiers fighting for this world are prostrate and asleep. The soldier of Christ, however, is always on his feet, prepared to perform any

* * * * *

218 This is probably a reference to the 'Book of Hours,' that is, the *Officium parvum Beatae Mariae Virginis*. See *Time Sanctified: The Book of Hours in Medieval Art and Life* ed Roger S. Wieck (Baltimore and New York 1988).

219 See n189 above.

220 2 Tim 2:3. The Pauline image of the Christian as the soldier of Christ had been elaborated more than thirty years earlier in Erasmus' *Enchiridion militis christiani*; see CWE 66 275 n18. In the following paragraphs he applies the metaphor to the Christian's confrontation with death.

221 See n152 above.

222 Isa 38:1

223 Job 7:1

224 Ecclus 2:1

225 Cf 2 Chron 25:19.

good action. The best action of all is to die in the Lord in righteousness. For a life lived free of sin gives one most confidence to face Satan. Faith does not know how to yield ground to the enemy, hope does not know how to submit to him, love nourishes the soldier as he stands.

If a pure life produces confidence, however, why was the phrase 'in fear' added? If you are righteous, what do you fear? If you are not righteous, how do you 'stand'? This kind of fear is not the one that is the father of despair (of which Solomon says, 'Fear casts down the idle,'[226] – though fear 'is cast out by love'),[227] but the one that is the finest guardian of innocence. 'The fear' sons have 'is pure and lasts for ever.'[228] 'Let him who is standing take care he does not fall,' says the Apostle.[229] And again, 'You stand your ground through faith; do not be too arrogant, but have fear.'[230] There is 'the pure fear of the Lord'[231] goading us on to good deeds and driving us away from evil, and there is the fear of the 'worthless slave'[232] that constrains us to cowardice. 'I was afraid,' he said, 'and I went and hid your talent in the earth.'[233] Fear, however, that is the companion of righteousness makes us have less confidence in our own strength, work more keenly with the help of the Spirit, and preserve more carefully the gifts of God.

Moreover, every kind of human righteousness, however perfect it may be, trembles whenever it is called to the tribunal of divine righteousness, 'in whose sight not even the stars are pure'[234] 'and iniquity is found in the angels.'[235] Why should not we, who are weak and 'living in houses of clay,'[236] fear this judgment, when Job, tested and not found wanting by God, says: 'I feared all my actions, knowing that you would not spare my sins. If I wash in waters of melted snow and if my hands gleam and are as clean as they

* * * * *

226 Prov 18:8 (Vulg)
227 1 John 4:18
228 Ps 19:9 (Vulg 18:10)
229 1 Cor 10:12
230 Rom 11:20. On the danger of arrogance cf *Antibarbari* CWE 23 85–6 and *Adagia* I ii 15 CWE 31 158–61: *Suum cuique pulchrum*, 'What is one's own is beautiful.'
231 Ps 19:9 (Vulg 18:10)
232 The expression, referring to the slave who did not forgive a fellow slave's debt, is from Matt 18:32, though Erasmus seems to be thinking of the slave who hid his talent in the ground in the parable of the ten talents. See the following note.
233 Matt 25:25
234 Job 25:5
235 Job 4:18
236 Job 4:19

can be, you will nevertheless thrust me in the mire';[237] and Paul, a more practised soldier than Job, says, 'I have no evil on my conscience, but this does not acquit me.'[238]

After 'in fear' we read 'prepare your soul for testing.'[239] There are different forms of tests by which God appraises his soldiers, but the most demanding of all is death. For in death we are truly in hand-to-hand combat, and it is not a mere skirmish but a fight to the finish with everything at stake, and with both parties using all their might. We must always, then, be preparing our souls for this conflict. For in these circumstances what will the soldier do who is inexperienced in battle, who has never fought against the enemy, who has never experienced the enemy's strength, his trickery, his skill and treachery, and has never tested his own bravery? It is important for victory to know the enemy with whom one is waging war. Blessed Paul, that bravest of soldiers or rather the bravest of generals, said this: 'Let us see to it that we are not deceived by Satan. For we are not unaware of his wiles.'[240] It is not surprising that he knows the tricks of him whom he had so often faced in combat; for he was experienced in every kind of danger. Facing Satan is the time of testing that shows what each person has achieved and the base on which it has been constructed.

Sometimes in this situation we see the same thing occurring as happens with those engaged in military service of this world. Those who seemed more fearful in camp and who turned pale at the sound of the trumpet turn out to be the bravest of all in the actual conflict, while those who seemed very bold when danger was not near at hand are the most frightened. Similar to the latter are those who, when in good health, boast that their consciences are at rest and untroubled, that they not only are prepared for the final day but actually desire to flee from this life fraught with calamities. They rely on some kind of faith, in that Christ promised us life and paid the penalty for our sins, and say it does not matter what kind of deeds we have performed, whether they are good or evil; to believe that we shall be saved is alone sufficient.[241] I am afraid, however, that

* * * * *

237 Job 9:28, 30–1
238 1 Cor 4:4
239 Erasmus now expands upon the last part of the citation from Ecclus 2:1 that he has quoted above (see n224).
240 2 Cor 2:11
241 This looks like a distortion of Luther's belief in 'justification by faith alone.' In fact it resembles one of the theses criticized by Luther in his *Theses Articulated among the Brethren*, published in 1537, where Luther attacks the views of John Agricola and his followers. To them he imputes the sentiment that 'if you are

many of those who boast of this carefreeness when their health is unimpaired are extremely frightened when the final critical moment presses more closely upon them and when that day is at hand on which the issue is not one of empty words but of the truth. They put much stress on how blasphemous it is to have doubts about the promises of God, but none are more frightened than those who have no doubts about the promises of God.[242] Indeed, death is feared less by the person who does not believe that hell is prepared for those who live wicked lives but believes that death brings the end of all bad things along with the destruction of the whole person.

Faith, therefore, begets in the wicked 'the fear of God, which is the beginning of wisdom,'[243] as Job attests when he says, 'The fear of God is wisdom itself, and to abandon evil is understanding.'[244] Similarly Isaiah says it is from fear of you, Lord, 'that we have conceived, we have been in labour and have brought forth the breath'[245] of salvation. In the third chapter of the Gospel according to Luke the people were terrified by the preaching of John the Baptist, who was inviting them to repent, saying, 'Now the axe is laid into the root of the tree.' They ask, 'What shall we do?'[246] But if they had not believed John, they would not have said, 'What shall we do?' Similarly in the Acts of the Apostles the crowd, in terror at the preaching of Peter, 'are cut to the heart and say to Peter and the rest of the apostles, "What, brothers, shall we do?"'[247] Their terror arose from their faith, since they would in no way have said this if they had not had faith and had not faith goaded their consciences with fear of hell. This fear, even in a man who lives a devout life, does not, however, spring from a lack of confidence in God's promises or threats or from disbelief in the articles of faith or from doubts about the efficacy of the sacraments – efficacy which they have because of the death of Christ.[248] Rather, it arises from the awareness of our own feebleness, which is too great to be fully understood by us.

* * * * *

a whore, a rascal, an adulterer, or otherwise a sinner, as long as you believe, you are on the road to salvation'; taken from Mark U. Edwards, Jr, *Luther and the False Brethren* (Stanford 1975) 163.

242 This again looks like a criticism of Luther, here of his self-confident certitude on matters of dogma, which contrasted strongly with Erasmus' more cautious and balanced approach to theological issues.

243 Ps 111 (Vulg 110):10

244 Job 28:28

245 Isa 26:18

246 Luke 3:9–10

247 Acts 2:37

248 The threats and promises of God are recurring themes in Luther's writings.

About particular individuals[249] we are not constrained to be free of doubts, although we must not give up hope completely about anybody. Consider, by way of example, that, while it is necessary to believe that whoever receives the sacrament of baptism in faith receives freely remission of all his misdeeds, it is not necessary, however, to believe that a particular person who has been baptized is free of all sins. For there may be something peculiar to this person that impedes the general power of the sacrament. The same is true for the sacrament of confession. It is wicked to doubt whether a person who has properly received this sacrament has been absolved from his sins. It is not heretical, however, to doubt whether a particular individual has been absolved; for we have no sure knowledge whether or not there are impediments peculiar to this person. (I make an exception of some special and clear revelation or of irrefutable authority when neither Scripture nor the church expresses itself on this matter in such a way that we are driven to the opposite view.) These doubts are not a mark of our lack of faith but reflect a temperate and balanced religious concern; in our doubts we submit wholeheartedly to divine will and judgment even when we might wish to condemn a man. We will not be condemned for such doubts, but will earn absolution by the very act of submission if with our religious concerns we fuse the trust that comes from the compassion of Christ. The same is true of the Eucharist. We are compelled to believe in general that when the priest performs his office in proper fashion he consecrates the body and blood of Christ. It is not irreligious, however, to have some doubts about whether a specific priest has done so. For this is not to have doubts about the sacrament but about peculiar circumstances that impede the power and purpose of the sacrament. Similarly, we must believe that we attain eternal salvation through our faith in and our love of the Lord Jesus. It is right, however, to have doubts about whether a particular person is in that state. Yet we ought not rashly to judge badly of others, and hope for others ought to grow in us as our faith and love grow. We should think the same about the promises and threats of the Scriptures. For the cause of our doubts does not spring from God, who cannot lie,[250] but from us.

No one is unaware of the outstanding blessings that God has promised, but these are promised to those who fear and love him. Nevertheless, how many of us are there who have shown the fear owed to such a Master and the love owed to such a parent? We are not doubting, therefore, whether

* * * * *

249 About particular individuals: a translation of *de singularibus*, which has also been taken to refer to particular points of doctrine (so Pierre Sage in his French translation, Montreal 1976) rather than to persons
250 Cf Titus 1:2.

God's promises are true but whether we ourselves are worthy of them. Faith, hope, love, fear: these are the gifts of the Spirit. Who of us knows, therefore, whether the faith and love that we have are among those gifts that make us pleasing to God and whether they are sufficient to win eternal salvation? Similarly, God promised forgiveness for all sins through his Son, but once and for all through baptism if it were undertaken properly. Yet how few of us are there who have not defiled in many ways the white vestment that we were given freely in baptism![251]

The cure of repentance is there at hand for us, but only for those who have turned with all their heart to the Lord. At this point let every one of us examine closely whether we have turned with all our hearts to the Lord, whether we have a heart that is truly 'contrite and humble,'[252] and if so, whether to a sufficient degree. John the Baptist calls out, 'Make the fruits of repentance worthy of it.'[253] Who would dare to be proud of themselves for hating and detesting their sins in the way that they ought to? God threatens wrath and hell on those who violate his precepts. How often have we cast aside our fear of him and violated them? How few can one find who are more afraid of the wrath of our living God than the wrath of a mortal prince or judge? Again, how often does it happen that some persons love a fellow human more than God and endure for a mortal friend what they would refuse to suffer to win the grace of God?

For my part, I am of the opinion that the faith of the devout is always joined with religious fear. (I make an exception of a few whom God wished to have as exceptional, obviously as an example to stimulate all, but to be matched by few.) Those who tremble at God's justice have a more certain hope of his mercy. Those who say, therefore, 'Believe that you will be saved and you will be,' err twice. If they are speaking about a trivial kind of faith, their words are false; but if they are talking about living faith, it is foolish to say, 'Believe,' as if it is in anyone's power to believe when he wishes to, given the fact that I do not know if we can be certain whether the gift of faith[254] is in us.

We frequently have as little knowledge of ourselves as others have of us, but nothing, however concealed, can escape the eyes of God. 'The heart

* * * * *

251 Cf the *Ordo baptismi* in the *Rituale Romanum*, where after the baptism and anointing the priest says, 'Accept a white vestment for you to keep undefiled ...'
252 Ps 51:17 (Vulg 50:19)
253 Luke 3:8
254 Cf Eph 2:8.

of man is inscrutable'[255] to us, but no part of our heart is hidden from him 'who fashioned our heart.'[256] Often what is wicked in the eyes of God seems righteous to us, what is impure seems pure. It happens, then, that a man believes himself free of sin even when he has a wounded conscience without knowing it. Why should not this happen to us? For the palmist says: 'Who understands his sins? Lord, cleanse me from my secret faults.'[257] The safest refuge is with reverent fear to flee from God's justice to his mercy and to say with the writer of the Psalms, 'Do not enter into judgment with your servant, because in your sight no living man will be found righteous.'[258] No one, therefore, will be able to withstand such a judgment if our merits are weighed in the divine scale unless 'mercy triumphs over judgment.'[259] That is why the same psalm begins, 'Hear me in your truthfulness, in your righteousness.'[260] Whoever wishes to be heard gives up struggling, and those who wish to be heard in the truthfulness of God do not have confidence in their own truthfulness, knowing that only 'God is truthful, while every mortal is a liar.'[261]

Those who ask to be heard in the righteousness of God do not have trust in their own righteousness. Christ is the truthfulness and righteousness of God; he is the giver of evangelical grace. For 'through Moses was given the law' that made known our wickedness, but 'grace came through Jesus Christ,'[262] who shared his righteousness with us. We lie to God whenever we violate his laws, to which we swore obedience at the fount of regeneration,[263] and we are wicked whenever we do not repay in kind our Creator and Redeemer. More than that, we deny him whenever we abandon what has been agreed upon. Although we deny him like traitors, 'he is ever faithful and cannot deny himself,'[264] ever true to his promises, so that 'he is shown to be just in what he says and proved right in his judgment.'[265]

The Father, therefore, listens to us in his truthfulness, by which through his Son he promised absolution of our sins. He listens, however, not

* * * * *

255 Jer 17:9
256 Ps 33 (Vulg 32):15
257 Ps 19:12 (Vulg 18:13)
258 Ps 143 (Vulg 142):2
259 James 2:13
260 Ps 143 (Vulg 142):1
261 Rom 3:4
262 John 1:17
263 A reference to the vows sworn at baptism; cf Titus 3:5.
264 2 Tim 2:13
265 Ps 51:4 (Vulg 50:6). In this paragraph Erasmus' position is the same as Luther's.

in our righteousness, but in his, because through his Son he makes righteous all who believe, 'purifying our hearts through faith.'[266] Blessed are those, therefore, who 'serve the Lord in fear and exult in him with trembling.'[267] Why should not mortals, who are addicted to sin, tremble before him when the host of angels so tremble? It is good to be in fear before judgment, so that in judgment we may find mercy.

We learn from history with what joy the blessed Andrew went to the cross.[268] We hear, by contrast, that not a few men, famous for their reputation for devoutness, were in great fear and trembling at the time of death, as they were terrified of the judgment of God and condemned the whole life that they had lived. For it is told about one man, who was distraught at the time of death, that when his brothers, who were present, said, 'Why is it that you are so afraid, seeing that you have striven for piety all your life?' he replied in this way: 'O my brothers, the judgments of mortals and the judgments of God are quite different.' Benedict, Bernard, and Augustine are said to have uttered similar words.[269]

The same faith, then, not only causes us to tremble but is strong enough to make us stop trembling. It causes us to tremble when it shows how great is he whom 'we have offended in many things.'[270] It overcomes our trembling by showing us Christ, whose love purges our sins and whose grace fills out our imperfect form. Just as it is not necessarily a sign of bravery or faith not to be terrified of death (for sometimes it is the mark of stupidity and madness, sometimes of the savage nature of the Scythians),[271] so it is not always a sign of the absence of faith or of a guilty conscience to be terrified when death is imminent. Sometimes it is a matter of our quite natural disposition; just as our bodies are different, so in some of us our feelings are more restrained, while in others they are stronger. Hezekiah shrank from death, a man who with 'a perfect heart'[272] was close to God, but he shrank from it, not murmuring against God, but praying tearfully

* * * * *

266 Acts 15:9
267 Ps 2:11
268 Cf the sixth lesson in Matins for 30 November, the feast of St Andrew, in the *Breviarium Romanum*.
269 The allusion is too generic to be traced with any exactitude. No such expression is found, for instance, in the Rule of St Benedict. See ASD V-1 375:854n for suggestions.
270 James 3:2
271 The Scythians were associated with barbarity by the Greeks; cf *Adagia* II iii 35 CWE 33 148: 'Scythian language.'
272 2 Kings 20:3

that it would not come, and his words were heard by God. I know some women who trembled at just the mention of death, but they showed more courage or constancy than anyone when death was near. That dread did not come from a bad conscience but from a peculiar weakness of their sex or nature. Natural dispositions, if they are overcome by virtue, bring added glory; of themselves they do not prove a lack of faith.

Similarly, you may see some people who are by nature so in love with themselves that they readily feel self-satisfaction in any situation. There are, in contrast, tedious people who are never satisfied with their actions even if they have done something right. Although you give them every kind of solace, they nevertheless feel mental anguish tempting them to discount what they have done; and they infer from this that their God is not yet appeased because they never experience tranquillity of conscience. If, however, we were to distinguish nature from virtue, those who are pleased with themselves all the time will not have any confidence at all in their tranquillity, and those who think their mind is always sinking to worse things will not immediately give up hope. The latter disposition is a flaw of a particular nature, not of the will, and it must be ignored if it cannot be overcome; what the spirit says should be regarded as valid, however much the flesh protests. I think that the former disposition too is a part of nature; when the day of death is at hand men are generally so changed that they do not approve of any of their pursuits during their lives, not because these are wicked but because they are human activities and are far from perfect. Yet we must fight with the strength of the spirit against these natural feelings, although it is not proper to judge other persons or ourselves on the basis of them.

Let us return, therefore, to what we had begun and show how human beings can be helped when they are dismayed by the proximity of death; for most of them are weak, and their lives are marked by much indifference, neglect, and inertia in spiritual matters. Their evil deeds far outnumber good deeds, and the good deeds, such as they are, have been corroded by rust so that to bring them forth into the sight of God will simply anger him. The soul is either not at all prepared for death or only slightly equipped for it.

What are we to do for such a person at this critical moment? While there is breath, no one must be despaired of. The final struggle presses close upon us. Time is short, and we need a well-prepared plan. What, I say, shall we advise this man, who, with every justification, is distraught? First, if he has legitimate heirs, he should have made provision for assigning all the duties of executing his will to them. This first point really amounts to saving some time and energy. If this has not been done, however, let him finish the business as quickly as possible by means of codicils or in whatever way will be more convenient. When that has been completed, let him dismiss from his presence those who are clamouring about wordly things. Many persons behave badly in these circumstances: they cast up doubts about his will in a dying man's mind and compel him to sign papers relating to material matters even as he is dying, although sometimes he resists and does not wish to do so and begs them to give up harassing him, since they are not allowing him to die in peace. Can anyone be less a friend than friends like these? Second, if his condition allows it, let him strive to care for the soul rather than the body through a short confession, but one that is sincere and free of all deceit, and let him receive from the priest the remedy for repentance with complete faith and the highest reverence; let him beg for the mercy of God from deep within his heart, and let him resolve to lead a purer life if he should happen to recover. If, however, the services of a priest are by chance not at hand, let him not immediately be fearful and despondent, as some superstitious people are wont to be, but let him confess from his heart his unrighteousness to God himself. In his clemency God will deign to accept his thoughts as equivalent to actual confession and will supply from his own grace what is missing from the external signs of the sacraments. It is through him that all sacraments have their power, for they are in some way small signs of his divine kindness to us. Yet he also takes thought for our salvation without these signs when there is need, provided that there is no neglect of and contempt for the sacraments and provided that faith and a clearly expressed desire for them are present.[273]

It seemed profitable to give this advice since we frequently see that some persons are very perturbed if they think that they are going to die without sacramental confession, without communion, and without the last anointing. In fact we hear many people say something like this: 'He died in a Christian manner, he confessed three times before death, and he received all the sacraments.' If, however, we hear that someone has died without these rites, we make the sign of the cross. Certainly the duty of the Christian is to pray that he will not lack any of these sacraments. They provide great solace to our minds and strengthen our faith, and it is a mark of Christian purity 'to fulfil all righteousness,'[274] when one can. To wish for faith and love, however, is more Christian; without these the sacraments profit us nothing.

* * * * *

273 Erasmus emphasized the need for contrition and inner confession (the *votum confessionis*) without denying the efficacy of the formal administering of the sacraments. See Payne 193–4.

274 Matt 3:15. Just as Christ 'followed all righteousness' by submitting to the rite of baptism by John, so must the Christian observe the rites of the church.

We should not judge anyone because these visible rites have not been performed, unless we are sure that they have been passed over out of contempt or out of neglect, which is tantamount to contempt. I for my part think that many who have not been absolved by a priest, who have not received communion, who have not been anointed, or who have not been buried in accordance with the rites of the church pass over into rest, while others are snatched away to hell, although all the ceremonies have been solemnly conducted for them and even though they have been buried in church next to the high altar.[275] Let examples of the former be persons who have died through shipwreck or by execution or, for instance, through a sudden illness or accident. Such persons, then, must be given confidence to believe for sure that they are no less absolved than if they had confessed to a priest and that they do not receive less spiritual grace than if they had received communion and the last anointing. The only proviso is that they should have a burning faith and an obvious desire for these rites, as I was just saying. If a priest is at hand but the extreme nature of the illness does not not allow complete confession – which requires speaking at some length – let the dying person confess with deep submission in his heart that he is a sinner in all things, and let him seek with devout sentiments absolution from the priest and let him believe in full confidence that he has been absolved.

Whenever necessity excludes us from what we desire, God in his goodness embraces what our thoughts aspire to. Accordingly, those who in such a situation torture a man with a general confession or with repetition of the confession, with anxious discussion of the circumstances of every sin[276] and with listing each misdeed, should consider whether they are acting devoutly. In my opinion, they are certainly acting inappropriately. At such a time let one confession of the chief misdeeds that come to mind suffice – and let the confession be a short one at that, though sincere. Or if even that is not possible, let the zealous desire for confession suffice.

An additional point: if a person has been injured by someone, let him dismiss from his mind the thought of retribution. If the offender is unworthy of having his guilt forgiven, Christ is worthy of having the desire of vengeance being commended to his care. Accordingly, let no one reflect upon how badly he has been injured by this person or that, but rather how

* * * * *

275 In the colloquy *Funus* George, the recipient of an ostentatious funeral, is buried near the high altar in a marble tomb, four feet high; see Thompson *Colloquies* 366 / CWE 40 772.
276 A reference to the common teaching that the mitigating or aggravating circumstances of sins needed to be confessed.

many things he asks God to forgive in himself. If he himself has injured someone, let him strive to be reconciled with that person as far as is possible. If that person does not wish to return to friendly terms, let him pray that the other will receive a better disposition. He himself is excused before God since he has done all that he could.

If good deeds are looked for, no deed is more efficacious for obtaining the Lord's mercy than to consign sincerely and freely whatever sins others have committed against us to the grace of Jesus Christ. We would be following his example; for, when Christ was hanging on the cross, he prayed[277] for those by whom he had been driven to endure the cross and for those who assailed him with abuse – abuse that was heavier to bear than the cross. Probably no deed is more difficult to do, and, therefore, this favour should especially be sought from the Lord. Illness itself, however, helps us attain this goal, for it tames the fierceness of the human spirit and makes it milder, disposing it towards forgiveness.

In such circumstances those attending the dying person have some part to play in making the patient shake off a common view, the belief of many that death is brought on more quickly by confession, communion, and the last anointing. Rather, they should persuade him (which is the truth) that these sacraments increase the hope of recovering good health, either because spiritual sickness makes an illness much worse or because frequently the poor health of the body flows from the soul or, finally, because God hears more quickly the prayers of those who are interceding for someone who has been reconciled with him than for someone who has not. Then they should summon a learned and articulate priest, who knows how to support a wearied soul with his words, and who can speak to the ill person in such a way that he does not deceive him by excessive flattery or throw him into despair by inappropriate severity and does not 'break a bruised reed' or 'quench smoking flax.'[278] For many err in both ways.

Nor should you readily admit just anyone to the patient, but only those whose conversation will help him. Keep away those persons whose appearance can evoke again in him the desire to sin, for example, those who gambled or enjoyed immoral pleasures with him, or his bitter enemies.[279] Let him not spurn the help of doctors, but let him not regard it with worshipful awe. Let the highest hopes be fixed on God; for just as he alone infuses

* * * * *

277 See Luke 23:34.
278 Erasmus literally says 'staff' and not 'reed,' as is found in the Vulgate at Isa 42–3 and Matt 12:20.
279 Cf Ep 1347:141–3.

the soul into the body, so he alone, when he wishes, removes it. Sometimes, however, a doctor must be summoned, lest we seem to be tempting God, especially in sudden illnesses that the doctors call critical. Keep away a large number of doctors. For, just as too many generals destroyed Caria in the Greek proverb,[280] so a host of doctors in attendance frequently kills many patients. They are presumptuous and never give up. They offer conflicting advice, and each (to the patient's peril) wants to seem to be the wisest. Sometimes drug after drug is administered. The result is that the patient has no time to devote the appropriate care to the affairs of the soul.[281]

When death presses more closely, the most effective kind of solace must be given. At such a time some people try to deceive the patient who is on the very point of death with crude and quite ineffective remedies – and many people actually delude themselves by applying these to themselves! Someone, for instance, advises the sick man to give orders that he be buried in some monastic habit or other, or to proclaim a promise to God that he will enter the Carthusian order if he should recover. Rather, the sick should be advised to refrain from such promises while they are ill. It is enough if they decide to change their lives for the better. Let them postpone thinking about the way of life that they will undertake until they are in good health and free from fear and mental anxiety. 'For a foolish promise displeases God,'[282] and a promise extorted from a troubled mind by fear is a foolish one.

Somebody else says, 'Die free of worry; I shall go to Jerusalem on your behalf within a year, or I shall crawl over the threshold of the blessed Peter[283] on bare knees, or I shall enter the cave of Patrick in Ireland.'[284] I know a noble woman of good sense who left a generous sum of money

* * * * *

280 *Adagia* II vii 7 CWE 34 6: 'Excess of generals ruined Caria'; cf *Corpus paroemiographorum Graecorum* 1.298, 2.618, where the proverb is explained – 'of those who cannot agree.'

281 Cf the description of the doctors attending George in the colloquy *Funus*. They were numerous, avaricious, and quarrelsome. See Thompson *Colloquies* 360–1 / CWE 40 767.

282 Eccles 5:3. Cf the colloquy *Exequiae seraphicae*, where a dying man promises to enter the Franciscan order if he lives; see Thompson *Colloquies* 504 / CWE 40 1000–1.

283 A pilgrimage to St Peter's basilica in Rome. In the colloquy *Funus* a similar pilgrimage is imposed by a father on his son; see Thompson *Colloquies* 365 / CWE 40 771.

284 The cave of St Patrick, on an island in Lough Dearg in County Donegal, attracted pilgrims right through the Middle Ages. Erasmus refers to it at *Adagia* I vii 77 CWE 32 115.

to a priest that he should offer the sacrifice of the mass every day for a year at Rome, as if Roman masses are more holy than British ones! And yet this money would have been better invested if she had used it to bind that sacrificer to a promise never to go to Rome. For I knew him quite well, and I think he sacrificed more to the wife of Vulcan[285] than to God.

Some advise the sick to buy all the prayers and spiritual benefits of some excellent monastery or order.[286] I do not deny that there is great solace in the communion of saints, but I am certainly doubtful whether God regards transactions like this as valid. In my opinion a more powerful remedy against despair is to place the communion of the whole church before the eyes of the ill person. This assembly stretches out as far as can be imagined, and includes all the righteous people 'who have pleased God from the beginning of the world.'[287] In this society are also the angels. This whole group helps the sick with promises and petitions and awaits a splendid victory. Why, then, should someone who has such a huge force helping him throw away his shield? If the prayers of one monastery provide hope against death, then so too do the prayers of all the monasteries of the church. I do not say this because it is unprofitable to beg for the prayers of particular individuals or because I think such prayers are not useful, especially prayers that spring from unstinting Christian love, but because contemplation of the universal fellowship is more useful for raising the hopes of the sick. For in this way the soul is gladdened.[288]

The most effective solace of all, however, is never to move the eyes of faith from Christ, who gave himself completely for us, whom 'we have as our advocate before God,'[289] who always cries out, 'Come to me all who labour and are burdened, and I shall refresh you.'[290] Let the sick man conceal himself in the caverns of *this* rock,[291] let him hide in the wounds of Christ[292] and he will be safe from Satan. No matter to where that cunning serpent diverts him, let him ever keep his eyes on the brazen serpent that is

* * * * *

285 Venus, the goddess of love and sexuality
286 In return for a financial donation the monks will direct the benefit of all their prayers to the dying man's well-being.
287 Wisd of Sol 9:19 (Vulg)
288 Literally, 'expanded.' Cf Pss 4:2, 119 (Vulg 118):32.
289 1 John 2:1
290 Matt 11:28
291 Cf Song of Sol 2:14.
292 Possibly an allusion to a verse from the well-known prayer 'Anima Christi,' from the fourteenth century: 'Within your wounds hide me.' See *Dictionnaire de spiritualité* 1 670–2.

fixed on a high tree,[293] to whose contemplation Paul calls the Galatians, who had begun to weaken because they had turned their eyes from him who had been crucified.[294] The poisoned bites of winged spirits will not destroy you if faith looks with unwavering eyes at that sign of eternal salvation. Christ hanging on the cross is a sign of triumph, a sign of victory, a sign of everlasting glory. It was for us he fought, it was for us he conquered, it was for us that he obtained the triumph, provided that we keep the eyes of our faith watchful and fixed on him.

In struggles with our fellow humans never to close one's eyes, a characteristic of Socrates praised by Alcibiades,[295] contributes much to victory. In this conflict of ours with the spiritual enemy, however, hope of victory lies wholly in the eyes. Yet there is a great difference between the two. In the former we must watch on all sides with keen eyes what the enemy is doing; in the latter we must not listen to or look at Satan's tricks. We must have our eyes fixed only on the sign of grace, and our ears must be attentive so as to hear the words of the Redeemer. Satan places in our mind thoughts that magnify God's wrath; Christ hanging on the cross shows the proof of his compassion. Satan rails against us, and his abuse sinks us into despair; Christ speaks words that raise our spirits and give us hope. For faith has ears as well as eyes.

The Holy Spirit requires both senses from the soul, as Psalm 44 says: 'Listen, daughter, and see and incline your ear.'[296] 'Listen' to what your betrothed teaches you, and 'see' what he promises. If it seems absurd that such happiness is procured for those who place their faith in Jesus Christ, 'incline your ear' so that you may believe what surpasses human comprehension for this very reason, that it is the Lord who has promised, whose mercy is no less incomprehensible than his omnipotence. Psalm 84 mentions those ears: 'Let me hear what the Lord says to me.'[297] Do not listen to what the flesh or Satan or human reasoning says to you, for they speak nothing but despair. Listen to 'what the Lord says, for he speaks peace to his people.'[298]

* * * * *

293 Moses made a bronze statue of a snake for any of the Israelites who had been bitten by snakes to look upon so that they would be cured (see Num 21:6–9). Here the statue is a metaphor for Christ raised on the cross; cf John 3:14–15.
294 Cf Gal 3.1.
295 Plato *Symposium* 215A–225A. Alcibiades does not allude explicitly to Socrates' never closing his eyes. Erasmus may be thinking of the behaviour of Socrates described at 220C–D, where he stands the whole day in concentrated thought.
296 Ps 45:10 (Vulg 44:11)
297 Ps 85:8 (Vulg 84:9)
298 Ibidem

The church is the people of the Lord, a special race and 'a people claimed by God as his own.'[299] Belong to this group and you will hear the Lord saying words of peace. Then there follow in the psalm the words 'and to his saints.'[300] At this we collapse in our human frailty and cry out: 'I am ruined. I am weighed down with sins. What fellowship can I have with the saints?' He does not say, however, 'to the saints of the law or of Moses,' but 'to *his* saints.' His saints are those whom he has sanctified through his Son. If our minds are still not at ease, listen to what follows: 'and to those who turn to him in their hearts.'[301] Do not weigh up the magnitude of your sins, only come to your senses and you will hear 'the Lord speaking peace'[302] within. The words that the well-known woman sinner heard were words of peace: 'Your faith has saved you; go in peace.'[303] Say with David, but from the heart, 'I have sinned against the Lord.'[304] By these few words you will turn the punishment clearly prepared for you into mercy. The ears of him who said, 'You did not demand burnt offering for my sin. You have opened my ears,'[305] were receptive.

Psalm 12 speaks about eyes: 'Give light to my eyes, so that I may never sleep in death and so that my enemy may never say, "I have prevailed over him."'[306] You see that in these circumstances victory lies in your eyes rather than in your hands. Death covers in darkness the eyes of the body, but there is no reason that our enemy should exult over us as long as faith shines in our heart and never turns its eyes from Christ crucified. In fact, the purpose of this whole psalm is to lift up, through the contemplation of divine mercy, someone who is locked in a struggle and is in danger of perishing in despair. For this reason there follow the words, 'Those who trouble me will exult when I am overthrown,' that is, if I weaken in my faith. You hear the great danger; accept, however, the powerful help that is present: 'I have placed my hope in your mercy.' Where does the hope of mercy come from? 'My heart will rejoice in your salvation. I will sing to the Lord, who is bountiful to me.' 'The salvation of God'[307] is Christ, and there is 'no other name whereby we

* * * * *

299 1 Pet 2:9
300 Ps 85:8 (Vulg 84:9)
301 Ibidem
302 Ibidem
303 Luke 7:50
304 2 Sam 12:13
305 Ps 40:6 (Vulg 39:7)
306 Ps 13:3–4 (Vulg 12:4–5). The immediately following quotations are from the rest of the psalm.
307 Luke 3:6

may be saved.'[308] The contemplation of Christ crucified for us has such great force that despair is turned into hope, hope into exultation. Because of this anyone who was previously near despair used to say, 'Those who trouble me will exult when I am overthrown,' now says, 'My heart will rejoice in your salvation.'[309] You hear the victory; now hear the song of triumph. 'I will sing to the Lord who is bountiful to me.'

Some do not have their own blessings to sing of; let those sing of the blessings that God bestows freely through his Son. If we place our confidence in our good actions, our adversary will rejoice. But if we fix the sacred anchor of hope[310] in the Lord Jesus, our enemy will fall, just as the Apostle says in exultation: 'If God is for us, who can be against us? He did not spare even his own Son, but gave him up for us all. How will he not give all things to us along with his Son? Who will accuse God's chosen ones? It is God who acquits. Who, then, is to condemn?'[311] The result is that everything is suddenly reversed and the person we thought was given up as lost will carry off the victory through the protection of Christ; the enemy who had already begun to exult in his victory will leave the field broken and repulsed. This assuredly is the victory of faith of which blessed John said in the fifth chapter of his Epistle: 'All that is born of God conquers the world. And the victory that conquers the world is our faith. Who is there who conquers the world unless he believes that Jesus,' whom his Father wished to be a sacrifice for the sins of the human race, 'is the Son of God?'[312] As long as the 'soldier of Christ'[313] stands on this step, he will not be overcome, no matter how vigorously the enemy besieges and assaults him.

In this final battle the enemy contrives with all his might to lead the sick into despair, which is the gravest of all sins. Therefore, we must strive all the more against it at this time. We must provide the sick with all that will give them hope and strengthen their resolve. For this it will be helpful if the image of the crucified Christ is displayed directly in the view of the dying to refresh continually their weak memory. Helpful too are pictures of the saints, in whom the Lord wished there to be a reminder of his goodness and compassion: the sinful woman of the Gospels;[314] Peter weeping after he had

* * * * *

308 Acts 4:12
309 Erasmus now repeats the quotations from Ps 13 (Vulg 12).
310 Cf Heb 6:19.
311 Rom 8:31–4
312 1 John 5:4–5
313 2 Tim 2:3
314 See Luke 7:50.

denied Christ;[315] others like these. We should also read aloud passages from the Holy Scripture which commend to us the measureless mercy of God[316] and of the love he showed to the human race, but especially we should read what the Lord Jesus deigned both to do and to suffer for the salvation of the world.

There are countless passages of this kind that can give great and effective solace to the soul as it wavers – for it is at this time that Satan showers on us all that can extinguish the spark of faith and hope. He exaggerates how often the majesty and justice of God have been spurned and violated; he goes on at length about how God's gentleness and generosity to us have been neglected and rejected through all our lives, twisting what actually ought to have nourished hope for forgiveness into a proof for hopelessness. He assails the dying with thoughts of the many years that they have spent in wickedness and of the many lost opportunities that beckoned them to do good deeds; whatever good actions they have done are distorted by him so that they think them faults. He puts to the test also our faith, so that we have doubts about the authority of the Scriptures and about the doctrines that the church has handed down; he makes us think about the arguments of philosophers and heretics and about difficult questions such as the creation and redemption of the world, the immortality of the soul, the resurrection of the body, whether Christ was really God and man, the efficacy of the sacraments of the church, God's foreknowledge, and predestination. He distorts everything so that we lose faith and hope, perverting to this end even the testimony of the Scriptures, as he dared to do also to the Lord himself, the author of the Scriptures.[317] Our adversary is helped to achieve this result by favourable circumstances: the distress of illness, the fear of death, the horror of hell, and the natural weakness of the mind and sadness of spirit that a serious disease brings. The enemy is quick, therefore, to take advantage of the change in us that these circumstances cause, using every kind of weapon so that, as we falter, he may dislodge us from our position and cast us headlong into ruin.

Instead of wrestling with thoughts of our sins we should turn our mind from them to the grace of Christ. Similarly, instead of engaging in a disputation with Satan, we should say to him when he suggests evil thoughts, 'Get behind me, Satan.'[318] It is not right for me to entertain doubts about

* * * * *

315 See Matt 26:75.
316 Cf *De immensa Dei misericordia* 98 above.
317 See Matt 4:5–6; Luke 4:9–12.
318 Mark 8:33

what the church, taught by the Holy Spirit, has handed down to us, and it is enough to accept in faith what I cannot grasp with my intellect. Some tell a story, admittedly not taken from the Scriptures but all the same quite appropriate to what we are now discussing. It is about two men whose faith the devil made trial of as death approached. One was skilled in philosophy, the other was an ordinary, uneducated Christian. To the former the devil brought up the question of what he believed. Was Christ both God and man? Was he born from a virgin? Will the dead rise again? The devil began to demonstrate by philosophical arguments that opposites – for example, the finite and the infinite and the created and the uncreated – cannot be joined together. Then he argued that it was contrary to nature that a virgin should give birth without sexual union with a man and that, according to Aristotle, the prince of philosophers, 'there is no return to a state once the essential nature of that state has been lost.'[319] Enough said! The fellow staggered and was thrown to the ground; the enemy went off the victor.

When the other man, the unsophisticated one, was asked what he believed about this or that, he replied briefly, 'I believe what the church believes.' When the devil asked what the church believed, he said, 'What I believe.'

'What do you believe, then?'

'The same as the church.'

'What does the church believe?'

'The same as I do.'[320]

From this fellow, unequipped for disputation but steadfast in a simple faith, the tempter went off the vanquished.

This reply is quite sufficient to drive away that treacherous enemy. It is most effective, however, in obscure and difficult matters. For example, if the enemy or if some nuisance of a fellow should bring up the question of how three persons can have precisely the same essence and of how they are distinguished from each other, let the answer be, 'In the way that the church believes.'

* * * * *

319 Aristotle *Categories* 13a31–6. The devil is adducing Aristotle to refute the resurrection of the dead. Once a 'living' being dies, and thus loses life, he cannot return to the state of being a living being. Van Heck relates the Aristotelian passage to the question of Mary's virginity (ASD V-1 385:122n), but an argument against Mary's virginity has already been brought forward.

320 This latter part of the imaginary interchange with the devil also appears in Allen Ep 2878:9–12, written on 18 November 1533, while Erasmus was composing *De praeparatione ad mortem*.

'How can the same body be in different places at the same time, and how in the Eucharist can the true body of a man be confined in a very small area?'[321]

'In the way that the church believes.'

And again, if he should ask what the fire in hell is like and how fire, a corporeal thing, acts upon incorporeal substance, let the reply be, 'In the way that the church believes.'[322] Or if a specific reply has to be given, let it be brief, either from the Apostles' Creed, which ought to be recited to the sick every day,[323] or from divine Scripture or from the inspiration that faith provides.

If Satan should keep bringing up to someone how great his sins were, let that person turn to God and say, 'Avert your gaze from my sins,'[324] and 'Look at the face of your anointed Prince,'[325] Christ Jesus.

'Your crimes exceed in number the grains of "sand that is on the seashore."'[326]

'More plentiful is the compassion of the Lord.'

'How do you hope for the reward of righteousness, when you are wholly unrighteous?'

'Christ is my righteousness.'[327]

'Will you pass into rest in the company of Peter and Paul, when you are covered with sins?'

'No, but in the company of the thief who on the cross heard, "Today you will be with me in paradise."'[328]

'Where do you find that confidence when you have done nothing good?'

'Because I have a good Lord, a judge who is easily moved and an advocate who looks kindly upon us.'[329]

'You will be dragged down to hell.'

* * * * *

321 These are two problems about the Eucharist debated by medieval theologians: if Jesus is bodily present in the Eucharistic bread, this means, first, that his body is in many places at the same time, and second, that his body is reduced to the size of a Eucharistic wafer. Cf Thomas Aquinas *Summa Theologica* III q 76.
322 Cf Thomas Aquinas *Summa theologica* III supp 97.5.
323 Or 'which the sick ought to recite every day'
324 Ps 51:9 (Vulg 50:11)
325 Ps 84:9 (Vulg 83:10)
326 Gen 22:17. Cf *Adagia* I iv 44 CWE 31 354: 'You are measuring the sands.'
327 Cf 1 Cor 1:30.
328 Luke 23:43
329 Cf 1 John 2:1.

'My leader is in heaven.'

'You will be damned.'

'You are a false accuser, not the judge. You are damned, and you cannot damn others.'

'Many legions of demons await your soul.'

'I would have no hope, if I did not have a protector who has crushed your tyranny.'

'God is unjust if he gives eternal life in return for evil deeds.'

'He who keeps his promises is just, and because of his justice I have long since called upon his mercy.'

'You delude yourself with vain hope.'

'Truth cannot lie; it is your way to deceive by false promises.'

'You can see what you leave behind, you cannot see what you are going to have.'

'"The things that are seen pass away, the things that are not seen are eternal,"[330] and those who have strong belief see more.'

'You leave here weighed down by evil deeds, naked and unadorned with any good works.'

'I shall ask the Lord to unburden me of my wickedness and clothe me with his goodness.'

'"But God does not listen to sinners."[331]

'But he listens to the repentant, and he died for sinners.'

'Your repentance is too late.'

'It was not too late for the thief.'[332]

'His faith was strong, yours wavers.'

'I shall ask the Lord to increase my faith.'[333]

'You are mistaken in believing that you have a merciful Lord, when he tortures you with so many evils.'

'He heals like a compassionate doctor.'

'Why did he wish death to be so painful?'

'He is the Lord; he can wish only what is good. Why should I, his useless servant, shrink from suffering what the Lord of glory endured?'

'Death is a wretched thing.'

'"Blessed are those who die in the Lord."[334]

* * * * *

330 2 Cor 4:18
331 John 9:31
332 The thief on the cross referred to above. Cf Luke 23:43.
333 Cf Luke 17:5.
334 Rev 14:13

'But "the death of sinners is worst of all." '[335]

'Those who recognize that they are sinners but that they have hope of mercy have ceased to be sinners.'

'You are leaving behind this world.'

'I am leaving a sad place of exile to return to my true homeland.'

'You leave behind here so many good things.'

'But far more bad things.'

'You are abandoning your wealth.'

'What I leave does not belong to me; I take what is mine with me.'

'What do you take when there is nothing that is good in you?'

'What the Lord gives me freely, this is truly mine.'

'You are abandoning your wife and children.'

'They belong to the Lord; I entrust them to him.'

'It is hard to be torn from those who are dearest to you.'

'They will follow me soon.'

'You are parted from pleasant friends.'

'I hurry to meet more pleasant ones.'

This very clever enemy tempts those whom he cannot drive to despair to pledge themselves to him so that those whom he is not strong enough to push into the abyss are crushed by him when they are raised aloft. The sick must be fortified against this danger too, no insignificant one. We are protected against the Charybdis[336] of despair if, the more Satan makes the awareness of our crimes weigh heavily upon us, the more we take strength in our confidence in divine mercy and mystical union with Christ. There will be a powerful remedy against the Scylla[337] of arrogance if consideration of our own weakness makes us abase ourselves. For whoever is brave and raised high in Christ but humble and abject in himself cannot be cast down by Satan or crushed by him. Such is what we read in the records of the ancients about the monk St Antony, whom Satan assailed in a thousand ways but was never able to overcome. Finally, when he had used in vain every weapon in his armament and had had no success, he admitted that he was defeated in these words: 'I strive in vain; if I cast you down, you

* * * * *

335 Ps 34:21 (Vulg 33:22)

336 Charybdis, the daughter of Poseidon and Ge, lived in a cave in the Straits of Messina and threatened passing sailors by sucking in the waters of the sea and spewing them out again.

337 Scylla, a sea nymph, was changed by Amphitrite into a frightening monster with a ring of dogs' heads. She attempted to devour sailors as they passed through the Straits of Messina.

raise yourself up; if I raise you up, you actually cast yourself down.'[338] If Satan says in keeping with this image, 'You are worthy to sit among the angels,' let the sick man reply, 'My worthiness rests only in recognizing my unworthiness.'

'You have prayed much, you have fasted much, you have led an austere life, you have given out very much to the needy.'

'All that you say can be said also of Pharisees, who are damned. If any good work has sprung from me, it belongs to the Lord, it is not mine.'

'But you are unblemished by the vices that weigh down others.'

'That is a reason, then, for me to give thanks to the Lord; it is not a reason for me to feel self-satisfied. For had not the mercy of the Lord protected me and had a similar temptation assailed me, I would have done these same deeds or even more wicked ones.'

The dying man must be fortified with responses like these, brief and readily available against the wicked insinuations of Satan. The examples of the saints must be recalled to his mind, but those in whom the mercy of the Lord shone most brightly: David, for example, who added murder to his adultery and yet escaped punishment in two words;[339] the people of Nineveh,[340] Ahab,[341] the prodigal son;[342] the publican, whose sense of right the Lord prefers to the hypocrisy of the Pharisees;[343] the woman sinner who heard the Lord say, 'Your sins are forgiven';[344] the adulterous woman who heard him say, 'Go and sin no more';[345] Peter, who denied the Lord three times;[346] Paul, who 'persecuted the Church of God,'[347] binding and killing those who bore witness to the name of the Lord Jesus;[348] Cyprian, a sorcerer

* * * * *

338 St Antony of Egypt (251–356) lived as a hermit in the desert of Egypt for twenty years, where 'he underwent a series of temptations usually associated with the hermit life'; *The Oxford Dictionary of Saints* ed D.H. Farmer (Oxford 1978) ad loc. The words ascribed to him here are not found in the *Vita Antonii* of Athanasius (PG 26 835–976), but cf Jerome PL 23 17–328 and PL 73 125–70.

339 Adultery: 2 Sam 11.2–4; murder: 2 Sam 11:14–17. For the two words, *peccavi Domino*, 'I have sinned against the Lord,' see 2 Sam 12:13.

340 See Jon 3:1–10.

341 See 1 Kings 21:27–9.

342 See Luke 15:11–32.

343 See Luke 18:10–14.

344 Luke 7:48

345 John 8:11

346 See Matt 26:69–75.

347 1 Cor 15:9

348 See Acts 9:1–2, 21.

who became a martyr;[349] and many others who, though guilty of idolatry, blasphemy, and horrible crimes, won, through faith in Christ, mercy and the crown of glory.

The words of the New Testament are more suited than those of the Old to drive away despair and to raise our hopes. It is not surprising: Moses terrified the Jews with the Commandments, Christ gave consolation to all peoples through faith and grace.[350] The sacred books have an abundance of examples and words that can cause terror or console the terrified. All that the prophets say unfolds generally in this way: they exaggerate how God punishes those who have turned away from him, but also emphasize the mercy of God to those who have turned to penitence. Each is a remedy bringing salvation if applied judiciously and in the appropriate circumstances. Words that evoke terror should be applied to those who are physically healthy but who are weak in resolve, and to those who are recklessly intoxicated by the prosperity of this life or who are drugged by the pleasures of the world as if they have consumed mandrake.[351] In this way they will come to their senses as if they have been given hellebore,[352] or they will regain sobriety as if they have taken cabbage,[353] or they will rouse themselves by being more vehemently reviled and railed at. Words offering hope of forgiveness should be spoken to those who are agitated and fearful, especially if they are at the critical moment of death. Yet we should not inject terror in the former without instilling at the same time the hope of forgiveness, and we should not speak soothing words to the latter in such a way that they are misled. To reform is one thing, to cast down is another; it is one thing to console, another to flatter. What kind of persons attend the sick, therefore, is of great importance. They should have at hand different passages of the Scriptures with which they can give support to the sick as they waver, either by reading them aloud or by interpreting them. The same end will be served by short prayers that are suitably phrased. I say 'suitably,' for some prayers are used that have been composed by ignorant men, and these are cast upon the sick by the equally ignorant.

* * * * *

349 Erasmus is referring to Cyprian of Antioch, martyred c 300, who was allegedly a sorcerer, and not the much better known Cyprian, bishop of Carthage.
350 Cf John 1:16–17.
351 The mandrake was a soporific. See *Adagia* IV v 64: 'To drink mandrake.'
352 Hellebore was considered a remedy for madness. See *Adagia* I viii 51 CWE 32 152: 'Drink hellebore.'
353 According to Cato *De agricultura* 156–7 cabbage surpassed all other vegetables in medicinal value. Moreover, the consumption of raw cabbage seasoned with vinegar allowed one to drink as much as one wanted.

When hope has been stirred up in this way, the fear of purgatory still remains; even this some people try to assuage and remove by remedies that in my opinion are not at all sound. Some promise freedom from the fire of purgatory by buying letters of indulgences,[354] but I fear that this may not relieve the sick, and indeed may deceive the dying. Those who advise that the tortures of purgatory must be diminished by celebrations of mass and prayers of good people and by alms act more properly. Most effective of all is to advise the sick to rouse to the best of their ability their faith and their love for God and their neighbour, to forgive in all sincerity all who have done them harm, and to bear the pains of disease and their imminent death with endurance through the love of Christ. They should submit themselves completely through all that happens to the divine will, reflecting that God does not give judgment twice[355] against them and that Christ paid the penalty on the cross for our sins. From these fountains, so to speak, and especially from his blood let them seek to cool the fires of purgatory. Thus, not trusting in themselves but relying on the measureless mercy of God, the merits of Christ, and the prayers of all the saints, let them say 'with contrite heart'[356] and with deeply felt conviction, 'Into your hands, Lord, I commend my spirit.'[357] We should not be resentful if the sinner and the weak use the Lord's words; for the head of our church expressed these words in his own situation so that we, 'who are members of his body,'[358] might imitate him. Let those who wish to draw an example from other saints as well say with the blessed Stephen, 'Lord Jesus, accept my spirit.'[359]

Examples have great power to stir our resolve, since they show, as in a mirror, what is proper and what is not. In non-spiritual matters we are more powerfully affected by what we see than by what we hear; similarly, we shall profit greatly by being frequently at the bed of the dying. We will then avoid what we have seen to be detestable in them and will imitate what is

* * * * *

354 So in the colloquy *Funus* a plenary indulgence 'was read, promising forgiveness of all sins and banishing fear of purgatory entirely' (Thompson *Colloquies* 367 / cwe 40 773). For Erasmus' attitude to indulgences cf also *Moria* cwe 27 114 and the colloquy *De votis temere susceptis* Thompson *Colloquies* 7 / cwe 39 39.

355 A basic principle of Roman law was that a person could not be charged a second time if a judgment had been given the first time.

356 Ps 51:17 (Vulg 50:19)

357 Luke 23:46, but with 'Father' for 'Lord'; cf Ps 31 (Vulg 30):6.

358 Eph 5:30

359 Acts 7:59

righteous and holy; for at the moment of death the nature of each person's faith and conscience is clear to see.

We shall find, however, no more perfect example than the model that our Lord created for us in his own situation. When that last night was hanging over him, he fortified his disciples against the approaching storm of temptation by providing the nourishment of his holy body and his blood,[360] thus indicating to us that whenever we fall into misfortune or become ill with a disease that threatens death we should immediately purge our consciences by confession, just as the Lord 'washed the feet of his disciples.'[361] Then we should reverently receive the body of Christ; this food will make us strong and unconquerable in the face of the spiritual enemy. The Lord made no final testament, but all his ardent words that John reports with great exactness[362] and the institution of the sacrament of the Eucharist for the remembrance of his death take the place of one. The words from the cross, 'Woman, behold your son,' and the words to his disciple, 'Behold your mother,'[363] also resembled a final will.

About non-spiritual things, therefore, we need say little; much needs to be said about what is conducive to faith and love. For the words of the dying are usually listened to more eagerly and usually settle more deeply in the minds of the listeners, partly because we do not believe that anyone lies at such a time, partly because, while the soul begins to be separated from the body, which weighs it down, it often gives intimation of the freedom and knowledge attained at the end of the journey just begun.

Let us return to the example of the Redeemer. After the sacramental supper he left the house for the garden, where, after telling the rest of the disciples to remain behind, he took only three farther into the garden, Peter and the sons of Zebedee, John and James.[364] He wished those whom he had chosen to witness his glory on the mountain[365] to be also the witnesses of his human weakness. He admitted to them his extreme sadness, which is often more oppressive than death itself. He told them to 'keep awake and pray,'[366] and then went off to pray, as he had done before. (There is a great mystery in the physical withdrawal of the Lord. Those preparing themselves

* * * * *

360 See 1 Cor 11:23–6.
361 John 13:5
362 See John 17:1–26.
363 John 19:26, 27
364 See Matt 26:36–7.
365 The transfiguration of Christ. See Matt 17:1–9; Mark 9:2–8; Luke 9:28–36.
366 Matt 26:41; Mark 14:38

for death should withdraw from all emotional involvement with business or household affairs, cast away all thought of the state, strip themselves completely of worry about possessions, entrust their wives and children to the Lord, remove themselves from dependence on friends and relatives, and admit not even the closest of friends into the cares of the soul. Those who wish to talk with the Heavenly Father when the final temptation assails them ought to be alone in the open, under the sky.) Three times he found them sleeping and admonished them to 'keep awake and pray that they enter not into temptation.'[367] Anyone surrendering himself into the power of the tempter 'enters into temptation.' Temptation does indeed touch those who are 'awake and praying,' but it soon passes by. What the Lord advised the three disciples he told us all. They slept and therefore succumbed to temptation. Peter, the strongest of them all, denied that he knew the Lord,[368] while all the others scattered in fear, and would have denied him all the more if they had been exposed to terror similar to Peter's. In this way at the critical moment of death human beings are overcome in their weakness unless they call upon the help of him who alone 'raises the dead to life,'[369] and do so with urgency, with pure desires, and with unshakeable confidence.

Moreover, the Redeemer thought it right to show by his own example how we should pray in these circumstances. He got to his knees. This was not enough: 'he fell prostrate.'[370] He called to his Father from earth, so loudly that his plea was heard by the three disciples even though they were in a deep sleep about a stone's throw away from him. Twice he returned to make the same prayer; three times he said the same words, 'Not as I will, but as you will.'[371] Those who subject themselves totally to the divine will fall to their knees. Those who are completely dissatisfied with themselves, who have no trust at all in their strength and good deeds, and who expect solace only from from the mercy of the Lord 'fall prostrate.' We must not immediately despair if consolation does not come at once. Again and again we must return to call out, not with our voice, but with our heart. To be sure, if we imitate spiritually what the Lord did openly, a good angel will be with us to wipe away the sweat of blood from our mind. He either will snatch us away from death or will add strength to our spirit so that we may endure death bravely.

* * * * *

367 Matt 26:38, 41
368 See Matt 26:69–75; Mark 14:66–72; Luke 22:54–62.
369 John 5:21; Rom 4:17
370 Matt 26:39
371 Ibidem

Finally, we must ascend the cross naked with the Lord, far from all earthly desires, our spirits raised to the love of the heavenly life, so that we may say with the blessed Paul, 'The world is crucified unto me, and I unto the world.'[372] Fixed there by three nails – faith, love, and hope – let us persevere unshakeably, fighting Satan to the end with all our strength until he is conquered and we pass over into eternal rest through the protection and grace of our Lord Jesus Christ, to whom with the Father and the Holy Spirit may praise and glory be given forever. Amen.

* * * * *

372 Gal 6:14

WORKS FREQUENTLY CITED

SHORT-TITLE FORMS FOR ERASMUS' WORKS

INDEX

WORKS FREQUENTLY CITED

This list provides bibliographical information for publications referred to in short-title form in introductions and notes. Erasmus' letters are cited by number and line in the CWE translation unless Allen or another edition is indicated. For Erasmus' other writings see the short-title list following.

Allen *Opus epistolarum Des. Erasmi Roterodami* ed P.S. Allen, H.M. Allen, and H.W. Garrod (Oxford 1906–58) 11 vols, plus index

Aquinas *Opuscula* *Sancti Aquinatis opuscula theologica* ed Raymond Verardo OP (Marietti 1954) 2 vols

ASD *Opera omnia Desiderii Erasmi Roterodami* (Amsterdam 1969–)

Bataillon *Erasme et* Marcel Bataillon *Erasme et l'Espagne* new ed, ed Daniel
l'Espagne Devoto and Charles Amiel (Geneva 1991) 3 vols

CCL *Corpus christianorum, series Latina* (Turnhout 1954–)

CEBR *Contemporaries of Erasmus: A Biographical Register of the Renaissance and Reformation* ed Peter G. Bietenholz and Thomas B. Deutscher (Toronto 1985–7) 3 vols

CSEL *Corpus scriptorum ecclesiasticorum Latinorum* (Vienna and Leipzig 1866–)

CWE *Collected Works of Erasmus* (Toronto 1974–)

Denzinger H. Denzinger and A. Schönmetzer *Enchiridion symbolorum definitionum et declarationum de rebus fidei et morum* 33rd ed (Barcelona 1965)

DTC *Dictionnaire de théologie catholique* ed A. Vacant, E. Mangenot, and E. Amman (Paris 1899–1950) 15 vols

ERSY Erasmus of Rotterdam Society Yearbook

Fokke G.J. Fokke 'An Aspect of the Christology of Erasmus of Rotterdam' *Ephemerides theologicae Lovanienses* 54 (1978) 161–87

Godin *Erasme lecteur* A. Godin *Erasme, lecteur d'Origène* (Geneva 1982)

Kasper W. Kasper *Jesus the Christ* trans V. Green (London and New York 1976)

Kelly *Commentary*   *Rufinus: A Commentary on the Apostles' Creed* trans and annotated by J.N.D. Kelly, Ancient Christian Writers 20 (Westminster, Md and London 1955)

Kelly *Creeds*   J.N.D. Kelly *Early Christian Creeds* (London and New York 1950; 3rd ed 1972)

Kelly *Doctrines*   J.N.D. Kelly *Early Christian Doctrines* (London and New York 1958)

LB   *Desiderii Erasmi Roterodami opera omnia* ed J. Leclerc (Leiden 1703–6; repr 1961–2) 10 vols

McConica   James K. McConica 'Erasmus and the Grammar of Consent' in *Scrinium Erasmianum* ed J. Coppens 2 vols (Leiden 1969) II 77–99

Missale Romanum   *Missale Romanum cum lectionibus* (Vatican City 1977) 4 vols

NCE   *New Catholic Encyclopedia* prepared by an editorial staff at the Catholic University of America (New York 1967–79) 17 vols

NK   W. Nijhoff and M.E. Kronenberg *Nederlandsche bibliographie van 1500 tot 1540* (The Hague 1923–71)

Pabel *Erasmus' Vision*   *Erasmus' Vision of the Church* ed Hilmar M. Pabel, Sixteenth Century Essays and Studies 33 (Kirksville 1995)

Payne   John B. Payne *Erasmus: His Theology of the Sacraments* (Richmond 1970)

PG   *Patrologiae cursus completus ... series Graeca* ed J.P. Migne (Paris 1857–1912) 162 vols

PL   *Patrologiae cursus completus ... series Latina* ed J.P. Migne (Paris 1844–1902) 221 vols

Rufinus   Rufinus *Commentarius in symbolum apostolorum* PL 21 335B–386D

Santinello   Giovanni Santinello 'Tre meditazioni umanistiche sulla passione' in *Studi sull'umanesimo europeo: Cusano e Petrarca, Lefèvre, Erasmo, Colet, Moro* (Padua 1969) 77–128

Screech   M.A. Screech *Ecstasy and the Praise of Folly* (London 1980)

Tentler

Thomas N. Tentler *Sin and Confession on the Eve of the Renaissance* (Princeton 1977)

Thompson *Colloquies*

The Colloquies of Erasmus ed and trans Craig R. Thompson (Chicago and London 1965)

Thompson *Inquisitio*

Inquisitio de fide ed Craig R. Thompson, Yale Studies in Religion 15 (New Haven 1950)

Tracy

James D. Tracy 'Humanists among the Scholastics: Erasmus, More, and Lefèvre d'Etaples on the Humanity of Christ' ERSY 5 (1985) 30-51

WA

D. Martin Luthers Werke, Kritische Gesamtausgabe (Weimar 1883–)

WA *Briefwechsel*

D. Martin Luthers Werke, Briefwechsel (Weimar 1930–78) 15 vols

Titles following colons are longer versions of the same, or are alternative titles. Items entirely enclosed in square brackets are of doubtful authorship. For abbreviations, see Works Frequently Cited.

Acta: Acta Academiae Lovaniensis contra Lutherum *Opuscula* / CWE 71

Adagia: Adagiorum chiliades 1508, etc (Adagiorum collectanea for the primitive form, when required) LB II / ASD II-1, 4, 5, 6 / CWE 30–6

Admonitio adversus mendacium: Admonitio adversus mendacium et obtrectationem LB X

Annotationes in Novum Testamentum LB VI / CWE 51–60

Antibarbari LB X / ASD I-1 / CWE 23

Apologia ad Caranzam: Apologia ad Sanctium Caranzam, or Apologia de tribus locis, or Responsio ad annotationem Stunicae . . . a Sanctio Caranza defensam LB IX

Apologia ad Fabrum: Apologia ad Iacobum Fabrum Stapulensem LB IX / ASD IX-3 / CWE 83

Apologia adversus monachos: Apologia adversus monachos quosdam Hispanos LB IX

Apologia adversus Petrum Sutorem: Apologia adversus debacchationes Petri Sutoris LB IX

Apologia adversus rhapsodias Alberti Pii: Apologia ad viginti et quattuor libros A. Pii LB IX

Apologia contra Latomi dialogum: Apologia contra Iacobi Latomi dialogum de tribus linguis LB IX / CWE 71

Apologia de 'In principio erat sermo' LB IX

Apologia de laude matrimonii: Apologia pro declamatione de laude matrimonii LB IX / CWE 71

Apologia de loco 'Omnes quidem': Apologia de loco 'Omnes quidem resurgemus' LB IX

Apologiae contra Stunicam: Apologiae contra Lopidem Stunicam LB IX / ASD IX-2

Apologia qua respondet invectivis Lei: Apologia qua respondet duabus invectivis Eduardi Lei *Opuscula*

Apophthegmata LB IV

Appendix de scriptis Clithovei LB IX / CWE 83

Appendix respondens ad Sutorem LB IX

Argumenta: Argumenta in omnes epistolas apostolicas nova (with Paraphrases)

Axiomata pro causa Lutheri: Axiomata pro causa Martini Lutheri *Opuscula* / CWE 71

Carmina LB I, IV, V, VIII / ASD I-7 / CWE 85–6

Catalogus lucubrationum LB I

Ciceronianus: Dialogus Ciceronianus LB I / ASD I-2 / CWE 28

Colloquia LB I / ASD I-3 / CWE 39–40

Compendium vitae Allen I / CWE 4

Concionalis interpretatio (in Psalmi)

Conflictus: Conflictus Thaliae et Barbariei LB I

[Consilium: Consilium cuiusdam ex animo cupientis esse consultum] *Opuscula* / CWE 71

De bello Turcico: Consultatio de bello Turcico (in Psalmi)

De civilitate: De civilitate morum puerilium LB I / CWE 25

Declamatio de morte LB IV

Declamatiuncula LB IV

Declarationes ad censuras Lutetiae vulgatas: Declarationes ad censuras Lutetiae vulgatas sub nomine facultatis theologiae Parisiensis LB IX

De concordia: De sarcienda ecclesiae concordia, or De amabili ecclesiae concordia (in Psalmi)

De conscribendis epistolis LB I / ASD I-2 / CWE 25

De constructione: De constructione octo partium orationis, or Syntaxis LB I / ASD I-4

De contemptu mundi: Epistola de contemptu mundi LB V / ASD V-1 / CWE 66

De copia: De duplici copia verborum ac rerum LB I / ASD I-6 / CWE 24

De esu carnium: Epistola apologetica ad Christophorum episcopum Basiliensem de interdicto esu carnium LB IX / ASD IX-1

De immensa Dei misericordia: Concio de immensa Dei misericordia LB V / CWE 70

De libero arbitrio: De libero arbitrio diatribe LB IX / CWE 76

De praeparatione: De praeparatione ad mortem LB V / ASD V-1 / CWE 70

De pueris instituendis: De pueris statim ac liberaliter instituendis LB I / ASD I-2 / CWE 26

De puero Iesu: Concio de puero Iesu LB V / CWE 29

De puritate tabernaculi: De puritate tabernaculi sive ecclesiae christianae (in Psalmi)

De ratione studii LB I / ASD I-2 / CWE 24

De recta pronuntiatione: De recta latini graecique sermonis pronuntiatione LB I / ASD I-4 / CWE 26

De taedio Iesu: Disputatiuncula de taedio, pavore, tristicia Iesu LB V / CWE 70

Detectio praestigiarum: Detectio praestigiarum cuiusdam libelli germanice scripti LB X / ASD IX-1

De vidua christiana LB V / CWE 66

De virtute amplectenda: Oratio de virtute amplectenda LB V / CWE 29

[Dialogus bilinguium ac trilinguium: Chonradi Nastadiensis dialogus bilinguium ac trilinguium] *Opuscula* / CWE 7

Dilutio: Dilutio eorum quae Iodocus Clithoveus scripsit adversus declamationem suasoriam matrimonii CWE 83

Divinationes ad notata Bedae LB IX

Ecclesiastes: Ecclesiastes sive de ratione concionandi LB V / ASD V-4, 5

Elenchus in N. Bedae censuras LB IX

Enchiridion: Enchiridion militis christiani LB V / CWE 66

Encomium matrimonii (in De conscribendis epistolis)

Encomium medicinae: Declamatio in laudem artis medicae LB I / ASD I-4 / CWE 29

Epistola ad Dorpium LB IX / CWE 3 / CWE 71

Epistola ad fratres Inferioris Germaniae: Responsio ad fratres Germaniae Inferioris ad epistolam apologeticam incerto autore proditam LB X / ASD IX-1

Epistola ad graculos: Epistola ad quosdam imprudentissimos graculos LB X

Epistola apologetica de Termino LB X

Epistola consolatoria: Epistola consolatoria virginibus sacris, or Epistola consolatoria in adversis LB V / CWE 69

Epistola contra pseudevangelicos: Epistola contra quosdam qui se falso iactant
    evangelicos LB X / ASD IX-1
Euripidis Hecuba LB I / ASD I-1
Euripidis Iphigenia in Aulide LB I / ASD I-1
Exomologesis: Exomologesis sive modus confitendi LB V
Explanatio symboli: Explanatio symboli apostolorum sive catechismus LB V /
    ASD V-1 / CWE 70
Ex Plutarcho versa LB IV / ASD IV-2

Formula: Conficiendarum epistolarum formula (see De conscribendis epistolis)

Hyperaspistes LB X / CWE 76–7

In Nucem Ovidii commentarius LB I / ASD I-1 / CWE 29
In Prudentium: Commentarius in duos hymnos Prudentii LB V / CWE 29
Institutio christiani matrimonii LB V / CWE 69
Institutio principis christiani LB IV / ASD IV-1 / CWE 27

[Julius exclusus: Dialogus Julius exclusus e coelis] *Opuscula* / CWE 27

Lingua LB IV / ASD IV-1A / CWE 29
Liturgia Virginis Matris: Virginis Matris apud Lauretum cultae liturgia LB V /
    ASD V-1 / CWE 69
Luciani dialogi LB I / ASD I-1

Manifesta mendacia CWE 71
Methodus (see Ratio)
Modus orandi Deum LB V / ASD V-1 / CWE 70
Moria: Moriae encomium LB IV / ASD IV-3 / CWE 27

Novum Testamentum: Novum Testamentum 1519 and later (Novum instrumentum
    for the first edition, 1516, when required) LB VI

Obsecratio ad Virginem Mariam: Obsecratio sive oratio ad Virginem Mariam in
    rebus adversis LB V / CWE 69
Oratio de pace: Oratio de pace et discordia LB VIII
Oratio funebris: Oratio funebris in funere Bertae de Heyen LB VIII / CWE 29

Paean Virgini Matri: Paean Virgini Matri dicendus LB V / CWE 69
Panegyricus: Panegyricus ad Philippum Austriae ducem LB IV / ASD IV-1 / CWE 27
Parabolae: Parabolae sive similia LB I / ASD I-5 / CWE 23
Paraclesis LB V, VI
Paraphrasis in Elegantias Vallae: Paraphrasis in Elegantias Laurentii Vallae LB I /
    ASD I-4
Paraphrasis in Matthaeum, etc (in Paraphrasis in Novum Testamentum)
Paraphrasis in Novum Testamentum LB VII / CWE 42–50
Peregrinatio apostolorum: Peregrinatio apostolorum Petri et Pauli LB VI, VII
Precatio ad Virginis filium Iesum LB V / CWE 69

Precatio dominica LB V / CWE 69

Precationes: Precationes aliquot novae LB V / CWE 69

Precatio pro pace ecclesiae: Precatio ad Dominum Iesum pro pace ecclesiae LB IV, V / CWE 69

Psalmi: Psalmi, or Enarrationes sive commentarii in psalmos LB V / ASD V-2, 3 / CWE 63–5

Purgatio adversus epistolam Lutheri: Purgatio adversus epistolam non sobriam Lutheri LB X / ASD IX-1

Querela pacis LB IV / ASD IV-2 / CWE 27

Ratio: Ratio seu Methodus compendio perveniendi ad veram theologiam (Methodus for the shorter version originally published in the Novum instrumentum of 1516) LB V, VI

Responsio ad annotationes Lei: Liber quo respondet annotationibus Lei LB IX

Responsio ad collationes: Responsio ad collationes cuiusdam iuvenis gerontodidascali LB IX

Responsio ad disputationem de divortio: Responsio ad disputationem cuiusdam Phimostomi de divortio LB IX / CWE 83

Responsio ad epistolam Pii: Responsio ad epistolam paraeneticam Alberti Pii, or Responsio ad exhortationem Pii LB IX

Responsio ad notulas Bedaicas LB X

Responsio ad Petri Cursii defensionem: Epistola de apologia Cursii LB X / Allen Ep 3032

Responsio adversus febricitantis libellum: Apologia monasticae religionis LB X

Spongia: Spongia adversus aspergines Hutteni LB X / ASD IX-1

Supputatio: Supputatio calumniarum Natalis Bedae LB IX

Tyrannicida: Tyrannicida, declamatio Lucianicae respondens LB I / ASD I-1 / CWE 29

Virginis et martyris comparatio LB V / CWE 69

Vita Hieronymi: Vita divi Hieronymi Stridonensis Opuscula / CWE 61

Index

Aaron 170, 282
Abel 169, 302
Abimelech 169, 222
abortion 380
Abraham 94, 120, 135, 169, 175, 222, 405, 409
Adam 100, 130, 151, 411
adoptionism. *See* Arius, Arianism
adultery 276, 357
Aeneas, Peter's disciple 164
Aeneas, Virgil's hero 28, 376
Aeschinus, character in Terence's *Adelphi* 108
Aesculapius 199
Aesop *Fables* 204
Agatha, St 45
Ahab 128, 445
Alexander the Great 79
alms-giving. *See* mercy, works of
Amalek 170
Ambrose, St 3, 17, 19, 21, 31, 37, 47, 51, 156
Amsdorf, Nikolaus von xxi
anadiplosis, rhetorical figure 88
Ananias 98, 164
Anchises 376
Andrew, St 45–6, 49, 430
angels 175–6, 193; different from soul 300
Anthropomorphites 272, 312, 330
Antinous, Hadrian's favourite 79
Antony of Egypt, St 444
Antony of Padua, St 199
Apelles, heretic 295
Apollinarius, heretic 296–7
Apollo 199

apostasy, sin of 353
Aristippus 29
Aristotle 33, 123, 220, 278
Arius, Arianism 185, 273–4, 283–4, 295–6
Ars moriendi xxvii–xxix, 390
astrologers, astrology 354, 365
Athanasius, St 52, 209
Augustine of Hippo, St 3, 20–1, 32, 59, 61, 324, 336, 345, 407; *De fide et symbolo* 257, 285–6; *Enarratio in psalmum* 21 19; *Epistola 130* 143
avarice 353, 356–7

Bakhuizen van den Brink, J.N. xxi, xxiv
baptism, sacrament of 123–5, 236, 340, 341, 343–5, 427–8; infant 343; valid among heretics 344
Barbara, St 200, 208
Basilides 273, 275, 305, 324
Bathsheba 86
battologia 178–9
Bavo, St 200
Bede the Venerable, St 3, 52
belief, beliefs. *See* faith
Bernard, St 56
bestiality 381
blasphemy 81–2, 322
body: resurrection of the 345–8; transformed 316
Boleyn, Anne xx, 390
Boleyn, Sir Thomas xx, xxvi, 235, 390, 392
Bonaventure, St xii, 3, 23, 24
bravery, especially in the face of death 27–35

This book

was designed by

VAL COOKE

based on the series design by

ALLAN FLEMING

and was printed by

University

of Toronto

Press